The Discipline of Organizing

The Discipline of Organizing

Edited by *Robert J. Glushko*

Principal Authors: Robert J. Glushko, Jess Hemerly, Murray Maloney, Kimra McPherson, Vivien Petras, Ryan Shaw, and Erik Wilde

Contributing Authors: Rachelle Annechino, J.J.M. Ekaterin, Ryan Greenberg, Michael Manoochehri, Sean Marimpietri, Matthew Mayernik, Karen Joy Nomorosa, Hyunwoo Park, Alberto Pepe, Daniel D. Turner, and Longhao Wang

THE MIT PRESS • CAMBRIDGE, MASSACHUSETTS • LONDON, ENGLAND

The Discipline of Organizing

Editor: Robert J. Glushko
Principal Authors: Robert J. Glushko,
Jess Hemerly, Murray Maloney,
Kimra McPherson, Vivien Petras, Ryan Shaw,
and Erik Wilde
Contributing Authors: Rachelle Annechino,
J.J.M. Ekaterin, Ryan Greenberg,
Michael Manoochehri, Sean Marimpietri,
Matthew Mayernik, Karen Joy Nomorosa,
Hyunwoo Park, Alberto Pepe,
Daniel D. Turner, and Longhao Wang

Acquisitions Editor: Marguerite B. Avery
Copy and Markup Editor: Murray Maloney
Cover Design: Jen Wang
Interior Design: Nellie McKesson
Illustrators: Divya Anand, Ajeeta Dhole,
Christina Pham, and Raymon Sutedjo-The
Bibliography Editors: Lisa Jervis, Shohei
 Narron, and Anne Wootton
Glossary and Index Editor: Murray Maloney
CSS Print Consultant: Adam Witwer
DocBook Consultant: Bob Stayton

Printed and bound in the United States of America.

Library of Congress Cataloging-in-Publication Data

The discipline of organizing / edited by Robert J. Glushko.
 p. cm
Includes bibliographical references and index.
ISBN 978-0-262-51850-5 (hardcover : alk. paper)
1. Information organization. 2. Information resources management. 3. Metadata.
I. Glushko, Robert J., editor of compilation.
Z666.5.D57 2013
025—dc23   2012038046

10 9 8 7 6 5 4 3 2

To Aristotle, Plato, Linnaeus, Condorcet, Wittgenstein...

Panizzi, Cutter, Ragananthan, Svenonius...

Gibson, Norman, Rosch, Barsalou...

Adam Smith, Coase, Williamson...

Simon, Salton, Miller, Dumais...

Bush, Engelbart, Nelson, Berners-Lee...

...and the countless others whose diverse perspectives we have synthesized in the discipline of organizing.

Table of Contents

Foreword

This wonderful book arrives at the right time. It is more than a textbook—it defines and creates the field for which it is a text. Befitting a book that lays out a discipline of organization that spans print and digital media, this volume is carefully organized, with a focus on future print and digital editions.

The Discipline of Organizing has a broad scope. Even more valuable is its depth, the result of years of examining and thinking through related concepts—often overlapping but not identical—from the fields of library science, information science, business, and computer science. The rare combination of breadth and depth empowers readers by providing a new perspective and framework for organizing subsequent experiences. The organization is comprehensive and systematic, but it is not simple. A lot of concepts must be assimilated. Yet thanks to the authors' thoroughness, you can proceed confident that investing the time to master novel concepts will pay off, that a coherent structure is being assembled, without inconsistencies or confusions. Into this framework you can fit your own examples, alongside the many provided by the authors. You can identify extensions and form new associations, building on a strong foundation.

The authors ask us to step back and adopt a general, multidisciplinary perspective. This is unusual for a textbook. For good reason, the world is marked by increasing specialization, the division of labor on which complex civilization depends. First we master a discipline; then we are encouraged to be multidisciplinary, interdisciplinary, and transdisciplinary—to balance our specialized pursuits. But scholars thrive within single disciplines, and even in fields created as multidisciplinary efforts, such as the neurosciences or cognitive science, most researchers soon become highly specialized. So why should a student of information undertake to master this broad perspective?

By growing from insignificance to centrality in the century-old field of information management in a few decades, digital technology has forced a disciplinary merger. Library science, information science, computer science or informatics, and information systems have developed different terminologies and sets of abstractions. Rather than asking each camp to learn the others' languages, the authors ask each of us to engage with a new terminology and set of abstractions.

The analogy of the artificial language Esperanto may come to mind, but we are in a better position. Esperanto is only useful if you are in a community of Esperantists. The abstractions in this book will be useful if others share them, but any reader will benefit by understanding the correspondences across the approaches to information organization that we encounter today. Unlike Esperanto, which is just another language, the concepts in this book reveal linkages and dependencies that we would not otherwise appreciate. The book provides a deep foundation for understanding changes that affect our lives and will do so more in the years ahead, a foundation that you will carry even if much of the time you converse in the language of one or another professional tribe.

Why do I say the timing is perfect, that this effort is worthwhile today? Haven't people gotten by without it until now? The answer has two parts. One, which is important even if you have heard it before, is that this is a time of extraordinary change in our uses of information. The other is that people have not always "gotten by" very well; years have been wasted and careers damaged by not understanding the principles in this book. The likelihood of such wreckage is growing, as the waves of change are larger and come at us faster. On the positive side, the waves offer tremendous opportunity for accomplishment. The coming era of monster waves may be risky if we surf with a narrow focus, but thrilling for those whose view extends up and down the shoreline. I believe that if you read this book, you will see this point and be glad you read it. Let me know.

We are used to hearing about Moore's law and related legislation, but familiarity lowers our guard. Human beings do not reason well about exponential growth, our experience is linear, not exponential. What we overlook is that exponential growth can proceed for a long time under the radar—one grain of rice, two grains, four grains, etc., not adding up to much, but when it reaches the point of having an impact, the impact comes so fast that we are unprepared for it. Decades passed before accessible digital technology could support high-quality photography, but when the time came, film photography disappeared so quickly that most major companies went bankrupt. Digital audio and video were a long time coming, then panicked and shuttered major industries. The expanding capacity and diminishing cost of information storage alter the balances described in this book. Bandwidth, increasing more slowly, is also reaching disruptive levels. This book provides the best tools available for understanding the disruptions of today and tomorrow in information management.

This perspective is invaluable now. It would have been useful earlier, but it was not considered imperative for the disciplines of library science, information science, informatics, and information systems. Historically they prospered despite interacting less than one might have expected. Library and information science, rooted in the humanities, focused technology efforts primarily on administrators and specialized users. Delivering services to the public was secondary. In contrast, academic computer science and human-computer interaction focused on widespread applications.

This book consciously connects fields that have focused on aspects of information organization and management such as archiving, records management, and curation, to information retrieval and related aspects of informatics. It explores how related issues play out in different contexts. The authors are admirably positive. They do not drag us through the myriad disasters that resulted when library and information science did not understand the potential contributions of digital technology and the equally unfortunate disasters that resulted when technologists ignored a century of work on information organization.

However, I will sound a cautionary note about what might go wrong if you do not understand the principles laid out in this book. First, for computer scientists and engineers: Major system-building efforts foundered due to a lack of insight into the principles of information organization. I will describe an early one, whose protagonists, good or bad, right or wrong, are all equal now.

Although not a computer scientist or computer engineer, Vannevar Bush had as much influence on the field as anyone through his work on shaping government support for research after the Second World War and through his 1945 *Atlantic* essay "As We May Think". Discussed in Chapter 2, this essay describes a hypothetical machine called the Memex that would enable information retrieval through a complex "associative memory" that supports links much like those found in the World Wide Web today. Although Bush's design was based on microfilm and optical scanning rather than silicon, his vision has inspired countless researchers to this day.

Less well known are Bush's classified efforts from the 1930s through early 1950s to build machines for the military and information agencies with Memex capabilities. Meticulously detailed by historian Colin Burke in the book *Information and Secrecy: Vannevar Bush, Ultra, and the other Memex*, these projects consumed massive funding, occupied many brilliant MIT scientists for years, and produced nothing useful. A working machine was finally produced, but Bush never consulted with library science scholars who understood information organization from decades of work and made naïve assumptions about how information could be organized for retrieval—the extraordinarily expensive machine was not usable in the real world.

Computer scientists interested in information should adopt a broad perspective, and this book is a place to begin. Several fields of computer science garner attention today, such as machine learning, data mining, information visualization, and design. Those centered on information, which is most directly affected by Moore's law, are likely to have the greatest impact.

The library and information science side of the bridge was also severely disrupted. Pride in a century of disciplinary accomplishment led to complacency and inertia. When silicon could no longer be avoided, there was not enough time to react gracefully. Major library schools closed. Today there are schools of information and a range of "library and information science" schools, some more forward-looking than others. Curriculum change has been relatively ad hoc, shaped by local personnel and context. Consider Information to be a large new volcanic cone pushing up in the midst of other peaks. No consistent approach has emerged to navigate the range. This book provides bridges where before there were slippery trails.

What can you do by virtue of reading and studying this book? Most importantly, perhaps, you can avoid confusion—when reading something or talking with someone from a different discipline, when asked a question in a job interview or by a colleague with a different background. Knowing that differences in terminology and abstractions are possible, you can ask questions and home quickly in on understanding. I have written elsewhere that through my career, such confusions frequently arose when I interacted with people in diverse disciplines, such as management information systems, software engineering, human factors, and so on. Because there was no book like this to clarify, it took me years to comprehend the source of many communication problems.

Beyond that, this book provides a foundation and framework for organizing and thinking about your experiences. This is a textbook, pointing to areas for research, providing ways of looking at new developments, and revealing to the perceptive reader yet unexplored territory in the spaces between disciplines. This is a book to read and put on the bookshelf—or in a folder in your digital reader—to reread in a few years' time.

Jonathan Grudin, 17 December 2012

Preface

In our daily lives organizing is a common personal and group activity that we often do without thinking much about it. Organizing is also a fundamental issue in library and information science, computer science, systems analysis, informatics, law, economics, and business. But even though researchers and practitioners in these disciplines think about organizing all the time, they have only limited agreement in how they approach problems of organizing and in what they seek as their solutions.

This book analyzes these different contexts and disciplines to propose a discipline of organizing that applies to all of them. Whether you are organizing physical resources like printed books or museum paintings, or digital resources like web pages, MP3s, or computational services implemented in software, you are creating an **Organizing System—an intentionally arranged collection of resources and the interactions they support.**

The transdisciplinary concept of Organizing System lets us see that resource selection, organizing, interaction design, and maintenance take place in every one of them. We can also identify many design principles and methods that apply broadly when we describe resources, create resource categories, and classify resources by assigning them to categories. A vocabulary for discussing common organizing challenges and issues that might be otherwise obscured by narrow disciplinary perspectives helps us understand existing organizing systems better while also suggesting how to invent new ones by making different design choices.

Motivation

This book began as the lecture notes from a graduate course on Information Organization and Retrieval I have taught since 2005 at the University of California, Berkeley. My goal was to teach these traditionally distinct subjects in a more integrated way. The former is the focus of library and information science, while the latter is core to computer science and informatics, and their conventional textbooks and topics are widely divergent. But while these academic disciplines are divided, in the "real world" information organization and retrieval are increasingly intermixed and converging.

With the World Wide Web and ubiquitous digital information, along with effectively unlimited processing, storage and communication capability driven by Moore's Law, millions of people create and browse websites, blog, tag, tweet, and upload and download content of all media types without thinking "I'm organizing now" or "I'm retrieving now." When people use their smart phones to search the web or run applications, location information transmitted from their phone is used to filter and reorganize the information they retrieve. Arranging results to make them fit the user's location is a kind of computational curation, but because it takes place quickly and automatically we hardly notice it. Likewise, almost every application that once seemed predominantly about information retrieval is now increasingly combined with activities and functions that most would consider to be information organization.

We needed a book that could bridge—or better yet, synthesize—the two disciplines of library science and computer science. We believe that their intellectual intersection is the study of organizing, and in particular, the analysis and design of Organizing Systems.

Collaboration

A book motivated by the prospect of multidisciplinary synthesis implies a multidisciplinary collaboration to create it. The principal authors of this book are mostly professors or former professors at different universities whose backgrounds include computer science and software engineering, library science, digital humanities, and cognitive science. Many of the other authors are former graduate students currently working in major web firms, web start-ups, consulting organizations, academic and government research labs, and law firms. This diverse set of authors with different backgrounds and aspirations gives this book a broad and contemporary perspective that would be impossible for a single author to achieve.

Customization

Multidisciplinary collaboration poses its own challenges. How can a book satisfy the need for breadth, to represent all the disciplines that contribute to it, without compromising the need for depth, to treat each contributing discipline in a substantive way? Our design solution was to write a core text and to move disciplinary and domain-specific content into nearly six hundred supplemental endnotes tagged by discipline. This book design allows the book to emphasize the concepts that bridge the different organizing disciplines while enabling it to satisfy the additional topical needs of different academic programs.

There are ten types of endnotes:

- LIS — Library and Information Science; these aren't the same, but this is a conventional disciplinary category. Endnotes that discuss issues that apply broadly to libraries, museums, and archives are also categorized here.

- Museums — Endnotes that discuss issues that apply more narrowly to museums and cultural collections are categorized here.

- Archives — Endnotes that discuss issues that apply more narrowly to archives are categorized here.

- Computing — includes Computer Science, Software Engineering, Data and Document Modeling, and Computing Technology.

- Web — includes endnotes that discuss Web Architecture, Web Standards, and particular web sites and web services.

- CogSci — Cognitive Science as a discipline can be defined as the intersection of psychology, linguistics, philosophy, anthropology, and computer science. This category of endnotes includes those that broadly discuss human perception, decision making, problem solving and other activities that affect organizing systems and actions, especially personal ones.

- Linguistics — Endnotes that discuss issues that apply more narrowly to language construction and use are categorized here.

- Philosophy — Endnotes that discuss issues that apply more narrowly to philosophy are categorized here.

- Law — Copyright law, license or contract agreements, "cultural property," terms of use and so on.

- Business — Intellectual Capital, HR, access control, branding, decision support and strategic planning, economics.

We do not claim that this set of endnote categories is complete, and indeed we encourage instructors whose perspectives on organizing complement those of the book's authors to propose new categories for endnotes, BD (Big Data), Bioi

(Bioinformatics), GIS (Geographic Information Systems), and Hum (Digital Humanties) have been mentioned. We look forward to notes from these fields that will extend the disciplinary customization of the book.

In the print version of this book readers can customize their experience by turning to the endnotes section of each chapter. In the initial ebook versions, readers can follow hypertext links to the associated endnotes.

ebooks

We have thought since the beginning of this project that this book should not just be a conventional printed text. A printed book is an intellectual snapshot that is already dated in many respects the day it is published. In addition, the pedagogical goal of this book is made more difficult by the relentless pace of technology innovation in our information-intensive economy and culture.

The emergence of ebook publishing opens up innovative possibilities for this book. We are already working on a next-generation ebook application that can create a vastly more engaging and integrated reader experience with the tagged endnotes. Instead of requiring the reader to follow a hypertext link, our ebook application will present selectable icons that dynamically transclude the endnote text into the core text. Furthermore, we are making the set of endnote types completely extensible. In addition to the six types that occur in the book as first published (ten in the 2nd Printing), any instructor or institution will be able to create other endnote types to meet new requirements for customization. New annotations and content suggestions can be incorporated as additional endnotes without jeopardizing the overall integrity of the text.

DisciplineOfOrganizing.org Website

These additional endnotes will join a living repository of resources to enhance the use of the book among the instructors and students using it in university courses. "A living repository for collaboration" is not just a cliché here. We have been experimenting with this idea for over a year with a companion website, *http://DisciplineOfOrganizing.org*.

The multi-disciplinary multi-campus collaboration needed to create this book has grown broader over time to include discussion and sharing of lecture notes, course assignments, and exam questions. In addition, student created-content such as course-related blog posts and commentary has also been shared between schools using the book. The site also contains a blog by the book's authors and instructors. New versions of ebooks will be distributed through the site as they become available.

Robert J. Glushko, 1 September 2013

Chapter 1
Foundations for Organizing Systems

Robert J. Glushko

1.1 The Discipline of Organizing

To *organize* is **to create capabilities by intentionally imposing order and structure.** Organizing is such a common activity that we often do it without thinking much about it. We organize the shoes in our closet, the books on our book shelves, the spices in our kitchen, and the folders into which we file information for tax and other purposes. Quite a few of us have jobs that involve specific types of organizing tasks. We might even have been explicitly trained to perform them by following specialized disciplinary practices. We might learn to do these tasks very well, but even then we often do not reflect on the similarity of the organizing tasks we do and those done by others, or on the similarity of those we do at work and those we do at home. We take for granted and as givens the concepts and methods used in the Organizing System we work with most often.

The goal of this book is to help readers become more self-conscious about what it means to organize things—whether they are physical resources like printed books and shoes or digital resources like web pages and MP3 files—and about the principles by which the resources are organized. In particular, this book introduces the concept of an *Organizing System*: **an intentionally arranged**

collection of resources and the interactions they support. The book analyzes the design decisions that go into any systematic organization of resources and the design patterns for the interactions that make use of the resources.

This book evolved from a master's level university course on "Information Organization & Retrieval" I taught for several years at the *University of California, Berkeley's School of Information*. My goal was to synthesize insights from library science, information science, cognitive science, systems analysis, and computer science to provide my students with a richer understanding about information organization than any discipline alone could provide. I came to realize that information was just one of the many types of resources to organize and that it would be beneficial to think about the art and science of organizing in a more abstract way. This book is the product of countless discussions with students and faculty colleagues at Berkeley and other schools, and we are collaboratively developing a new discipline that unifies four types of organizing, as follows:

We organize physical things. Each of us organizes many kinds of things in our lives—our books on bookshelves; printed financial records in folders and filing cabinets; clothes in dressers and closets; cooking and eating utensils in kitchen drawers and cabinets. Public libraries organize printed books, periodicals, maps, CDs, DVDs, and maybe some old record albums. Research libraries also organize rare manuscripts, pamphlets, musical scores, and many other kinds of printed information. Museums organize paintings, sculptures, and other artifacts of cultural, historical, or scientific value. Stores and suppliers organize their goods for sale to consumers and to each other.

We organize information about physical things. Each of us organizes information about things, when we inventory the contents of our house for insurance purposes, when we sell our unwanted stuff on eBay, or when we rate a restaurant on Yelp. Library card catalogs, and their online replacements, tell us what books a library's collection contains and where to find them. Sensors and RFID tags track the movement of goods—even library books—through supply chains, and the movement (or lack of movement) of cars on highways.

We organize digital things. Each of us organizes personal digital information —email, documents, e-books, MP3 and video files, appointments, and contacts— on our computers, smart phone, e-book readers or in "the cloud," through information services that use Internet protocols. Large research libraries organize digital journals and books, computer programs, government and scientific datasets, databases, and many other kinds of digital information. Companies organize their digital business records and customer information in enterprise applications, content repositories, and databases. Hospitals and medical clinics maintain and exchange electronic health records and digital X-rays and scans.

We organize information about digital things. Digital library catalogs, web portals and aggregation websites organize links to other digital resources. Web search engines use content and link analysis along with relevance ratings to organize the billions of web pages competing for our attention. Web-based services, data feeds and other information resources can be combined as "mashups" or choreographed to carry out information-intensive business models.

Let's take a closer look at these four different types or contexts of organizing. Are there clear, systematic and useful distinctions between them? We contrasted "organizing things" with "organizing information." At first glance it might seem that organizing physical things like books, compact discs, machine parts, or cooking utensils has an entirely different character than organizing intangible digital things. We often arrange physical things according to their shapes, sizes, material of manufacture, or other visible properties; for example, we might arrange our shirts in the clothes closet by style and color, and we might organize our music collection by separating the old vinyl albums from the CDs. We might arrange books on bookshelves by their sizes, putting all the big heavy picture books on the bottom shelf. Organization for clothes and information artifacts in tangible formats that is based on visible properties does not seem much like how you store and organize digital books on your Kindle or arrange digital music on your music player. Arranging, storing, and accessing X-rays printed on film might appear to have little in common with these activities when the X-rays are in digital form.

It is hardly surprising that organizing things and organizing information sometimes do not differ much when information is represented in a tangible way. The era of ubiquitous digital information of the last decade or two is just a blip in time compared with the more than ten thousand years of human experience with information carved in stone, etched in clay, or printed with ink on papyrus, parchment or paper. These tangible information artifacts have deeply embedded the notion of information as a physical thing in culture, language, and methods of information design and organization. This perspective toward tangible information artifacts is especially prominent in rare book collections where books are revered as physical objects with a focus on their distinctive binding, calligraphy, and typesetting.

Nevertheless, at other times there are substantial differences in how we organize things and how we organize information, even when the latter is in physical form. We more often organize our "information things" according to what they are about rather than on the basis of their visible properties. At home we sort our CDs by artist or genre; we keep cookbooks separate from travel books, and fiction books apart from reference books. Libraries employ subject-based classification schemes that have a few hundred thousand distinct categories.

Likewise, there are times when we pay little attention to the visible properties of tangible things when we organize them and instead arrange them according to functional or task properties. We keep screwdrivers, pliers, a hammer, a saw, a drill, and a level in a tool box or together on a work bench, even though they have few visual properties in common. We are not organizing them because of what we see about them, but because of what we know about to use them, The task-based organization of the tools has some similarity to the subject-based organization of the library.

We also contrasted "organizing things" with "organizing information about things." This difference seems clear if we consider the traditional library card catalog, whose printed cards describe and specify the location of books on library shelves. When the things and the information about them are both in physical format, it is easy to see that the former is a primary resource and the latter a surrogate or associated resource that describes or relates to it.

What Is Information?

Geoff Nunberg has eloquently explained in *Farewell to the Information Age* that "Information" is "a collection of notions, rather than a single coherent concept." Most of its hundreds of definitions treat it as an idea that swirls around equally hard-to-define terms like "data," "knowledge," and "communication." Moreover, these intellectual and ideological perspectives on information coexist with more mundane uses of the term, as when we ask a station agent: "Can you give me some information about the train schedule?"

An abstract view of information as an intangible thing is the intellectual foundation for both modern information science and the information economy and society. Nevertheless, the abstract view of information often conflicts with the much older idea that information is a tangible thing that naturally arose when information was inextricably encoded in material formats. We often blur the sense of "information as content" with the sense of "information as container," and we too easily treat the number of stored bits on a computer or in "the cloud" as a measure of information content or value.

Michael Buckland's oft-cited essay *Information as Thing* rebuts the notion that information is inherently intangible and instead defines it more broadly and provocatively based on function. This makes the objects in museum or personal collections into information-as-thing resources because they can be learned from and serve as evidence.[1]

When it comes to "organizing information about digital things" the contrast is much less clear, When you search for a book using a search engine, first you get the catalog description of the book, and if you're lucky the book itself is just a click away. When the things and the information about them are both digital, the contrast we posed is not as sharp as when one or both of them is in a physical format. And while we used X-rays—on film or in digital format—as examples of things we might organize, when a physician studies an X-ray, is it not being used as information about the subject of the X-ray, namely the patient?

These differences and relationships between "**physical things**" and "**digital things**" have long been discussed and debated by philosophers, linguists, psychologists and others (See the Sidebar, "What Is Information?" (page 4)).

The distinctions among organizing physical things, organizing digital things, or organizing information about physical things or digital things are challenging to describe because many of the words we might use are as overloaded with multiple meanings as information itself. For example, some people use the term "document" to refer only to traditional physical forms, while others use it more abstractly to refer to any self-contained unit of information independent of its instantiation in physical or digital form. The most abstract definition, presented in *What is a Document?* is when Buckland provocatively asserts that an antelope is both "information as thing" and also a "document" when it is in a zoo, even though it is just an animal when it is running wild on the plains of Africa. Similar definitional variation occurs with "author" or "creator."[2]

If we allow the concept of information to be anything we can study—to be "anything that informs"—the concept becomes unbounded. Our goal in this book is to bridge the intellectual gulf that separates the many disciplines that share the goal of organizing but that differ in what they organize. This requires us to focus on situations where information exists because of intentional acts to create or organize.

Many of the foundational topics for a discipline of organizing have traditionally been presented from the perspective of the public sector library and taught as "library and information science." These include bibliographic description, classification, naming, authority control, and information standards. We need to update and extend the coverage of these topics to include more private sector and non-bibliographic contexts, multi- and social-media, and new information-intensive applications and service systems enabled by mobile, pervasive, and scientific computing. In so doing we can reframe the foundational concepts to make them equally compatible with the disciplinary perspectives of informatics, data and process modeling, and document engineering.

We also need to take a transdisciplinary view that lets us emphasize what the different disciplines have in common rather than what distinguishes them. Resource selection, organizing, interaction design, and maintenance are taught in every discipline, but these concepts go by different names. A vocabulary for discussing common organizing challenges and issues that might be otherwise obscured by narrow disciplinary perspectives helps us understand existing systems of organizing better while also suggesting how to invent new ones by making different design choices.

> ## The Discipline of Organizing
>
> A *discipline* is an integrated field of study in which there is some level of agreement about the issues and problems that deserve study, how they are interrelated, how they should be studied, and how findings or theories about the issues and problems should be evaluated.
>
> *Organizing* is a fundamental issue in many disciplines, most notably library and information science, computer science, systems analysis, informatics, law, economics, and business. However, these disciplines have only limited agreement in how they approach problems of organizing and in what they seek as their solutions. For example, library and information science has traditionally studied organizing from a public sector bibliographic perspective, paying careful attention to user requirements for access and preservation, and offering prescriptive methods and solutions.[3] In contrast, computer science and informatics tend to study organizing in the context of information-intensive business applications with a focus on process efficiency, system architecture and implementation.
>
> This book presents a more abstract framework for issues and problems of organizing that emphasizes the common concepts and goals of the disciplines that study them. A *framework* is a set of concepts that provide the basic structure for understanding a domain, enabling a common vocabulary for different explanatory theories. Our framework proposes that every system of organization involves a collection of resources, and we can treat physical things, digital things, and information about such things as resources. Every system of organization involves a choice of properties or principles used to describe and arrange the resources, and ways of supporting interactions with the resources. By comparing and contrasting how these activities take place in different contexts and domains, we can identify patterns of organizing and see that Organizing Systems often follow a common life cycle. We can create a discipline of organizing in a disciplined way.

1.2 The "Organizing System" Concept

We propose to unify many perspectives about organizing and information with the concept of an *Organizing System*, **an intentionally arranged collection of resources and the interactions they support.** This definition brings together several essential ideas that we will briefly introduce in this chapter and then de-

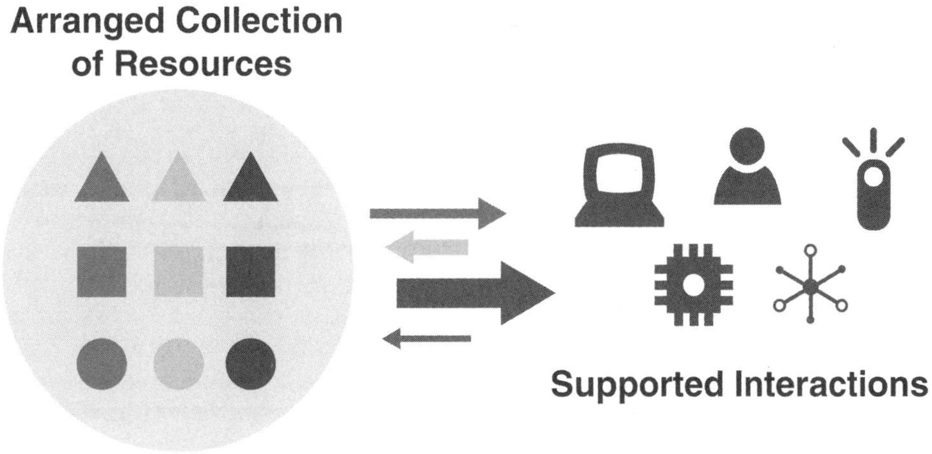

**Arranged Collection
of Resources**

Supported Interactions

Figure 1.1. An Organizing System.

velop in detail in subsequent chapters. Figure 1.1 depicts a conceptual model of an Organizing System that shows intentionally arranged resources, interactions (distinguished by different types of arrows), and the human and computational agents interacting with the resources in different contexts.

An Organizing System is an abstract characterization of how some collection of resources is described and arranged to enable human or computational agents to interact with the resources. The Organizing System is an architectural and conceptual view that is distinct from the physical arrangement of resources that might embody it, and also distinct from the person, enterprise, or institution that implements and operates it. These distinctions are sometimes hard to maintain in ordinary language; for example, we might describe some set of resource descriptions, organizing principles, and supported interactions as a "library" Organizing System. However, we also need at times to refer to a "library" as the institution in which this Organizing System operates, and of course the idea of a "library" as a physical facility is deeply engrained in language and culture.

Our concept of the Organizing System was in part inspired by and generalizes to physical and web-based resource domains the concepts proposed in 2000 for bibliographic domains by Elaine Svenonius in *The Intellectual Foundation of Information Organization*. She recognized that the traditional information organization activities of bibliographic description and cataloging were complemented, and partly compensated for, by automated text processing and indexing that were usually treated as part of a separate discipline of information retrieval. She proposed that decisions about organizing information and decisions about retrieving information were inherently linked by a tradeoff principle and thus needed to be viewed as an interconnected system: *"The effectiveness of a system for accessing information is a direct function of the intelligence put into organizing it" (p.ix).* We celebrate and build upon her insights by beginning each of the sub-parts of §1.3 with a quote from her book.[4]

A systems view of information organization and information retrieval captures and provides structure for the inherent tradeoffs obscured by the silos of traditional disciplinary and category perspectives: the more effort put into organizing information, the more effectively it can be retrieved, and the more effort put into retrieving information, the less it needs to be organized first. A systems view no longer contrasts information organization as a human activity and information retrieval as a machine activity, or information organization as a topic for library and information science and information retrieval as one for computer science. Instead, we readily see that computers now assist people in organizing and that people contribute much of the information used by computers to enable retrieval.

1.2.1 The Concept of "Resource"

Resource has an ordinary sense of "anything of value that can support goal-oriented activity." This definition means that a resource can be a physical thing, a non-physical thing, information about physical things, information about non-physical things, or anything you want to organize. Other words that aim for this broad scope are **entity**, **object**, **item**, and **instance**. **Document** is often used for an information resource in either digital or physical format; **artifact** refers to resources created by people, and **asset** for resources with economic value.

Resource has specialized meaning in Internet architecture. It is conventional to describe web pages, images, videos, product catalogs, and so on as resources and the protocol for accessing them, *Hypertext Transfer Protocol (HTTP)*, uses the *Uniform Resource Identifier (URI)*.[5]

Treating as a **primary resource** anything that can be identified is an important generalization of the concept because it enables web-based services, data feeds, objects with RFID tags, sensors or other "smart devices" or computational agents to be part of Organizing Systems.

Instead of emphasizing the differences between tangible and intangible resources, we consider it essential to determine whether the tangible resource has information content—whether it needs to be treated as being "about" or "representing" some other resource rather than being treated as a thing in itself. Whether a book is printed or digital, we focus on its information content, what it is about; its tangible properties become secondary. In contrast, the hangars in our closet and the measuring cups in our kitchen are not about anything more than their obvious utilitarian features, which makes their tangible properties most important. (Of course, there is no sharp boundary here; you can buy "fashion hangers" that make a style statement, and the old measuring cup could be a family memento because it belonged to Grandma).

Many of the resources in Organizing Systems are *description resources* or *surrogate resources* that describe the *primary resources*; library catalog entries or the list of results in web search engines are familiar examples. In museums, information about the production, discovery, or history of ownership of a resource can be more important than the resource; a few shards of pottery are of little value without these **associated** information resources. Similarly, business or scientific data often cannot be understood or analyzed without additional information about the manner in which they were collected.

Resources that describe, or are associated with other resources are sometimes called **metadata**. However, when we look more broadly at Organizing Systems, it is often difficult to distinguish between the resource being described and any description of it or associated with it. One challenge is that when descriptions are embedded in resources, as metadata often is in the title page of a book, in the masthead of a newspaper, or in the source of web pages, deciding which resources are primary is often arbitrary. A second challenge is that what serves as a metadata for one person or process can function as a primary resource or data for another one. Rather than being an inherent distinction, the difference between primary and associated resources is often just a decision about which resource we are focusing on in some situation. An animal specimen in a natural history museum might be a *primary resource* for museum visitors and scientists interested in anatomy, but information about where the specimen was collected is the *primary resource* for scientists interested in ecology or migration.

Organizing Systems can refer to people as resources, and we often use that term to avoid specifying the gender or specific role of an employee or worker, as in the management concept of the "human resources" or HR department in a firm. The shift from a manufacturing to an information and services economy in the last few decades has resulted in greater emphasis on intellectual resources represented in skills and knowledge rather than on the natural resources of production materials and physical goods.[6] It is important to consider the capabilities and motivations of the people who create and participate in Organizing Systems. We might discuss how human resources are selected, organized, and managed over time just as we might discuss these activities with respect to library resources. Nevertheless, these topics are much more appropriate for texts on human resources management and industrial organization so we will not consider them much further in this book.

1.2.2 The Concept of "Collection"

A **collection** is a group of resources that have been selected for some purpose. Similar terms are set (mathematics), aggregation (data modeling), dataset (science and business), and corpus (linguistics and literary analysis).

We prefer "collection" because it has fewer specialized meanings. *Collection* is typically used to describe personal sets of physical resources (my stamp or record album collection) as well as digital ones (my collection of digital music). A collection can contain identifiers for resources along with or instead of the resources themselves, which enables a resource to be part of more than one collection, like songs in playlists.

A *collection* itself is also a *resource*. Like other resources, a collection can have description resources associated with it. An **index** is a *description resource* that contains information about the locations and frequencies of terms in a document *collection* to enable it to be searched efficiently.

Because *collection*s are an important and frequently used kind of *resource* it is important to distinguish them as a separate concept. In particular, the concept of *collection* has deep roots in libraries, museums and other institutions that select, assemble, arrange, and maintain resources. Organizing Systems in these domains can often be described as collections of collections that are variously organized according to resource type, author, creator, or collector of the resources in the collection, or any number of other principles or properties.

1.2.3 The Concept of "Intentional Arrangement"

Intentional arrangement emphasizes explicit or implicit acts of organization by people, or by computational processes acting as proxies for, or as implementations of, human intentionality. Intentional arrangement excludes naturally-occurring patterns created by physical, geological, biological or genetic processes. There is information in the piles of debris left after a tornado or tsunami and the strata of the Grand Canyon. But they are not Organizing Systems because the patterns of arrangement were created by deterministic natural forces rather than by an identifiable agent following one or more organizing principles selected by a human agent.

Self-organizing systems can change their internal structure or their function in response to feedback or changed circumstances. Requiring arrangement to be intentional also excludes those systems from our definition of Organizing System. These self-organizing systems have been used in physics, chemistry, and mathematics to explain phase transitions and equilibrium states. Self-organizing is also used to describe numerous natural and man-made phenomena like climate, communication networks, business and biological ecosystems, traffic and habitation patterns, neural networks, and online communities. All of these systems involve collections of resources that are very large and open, with complex interactions among the resources. The resource arrangements that emerge cannot always be interpreted as the result of intentional or deterministic principles and instead are more often described in probabilistic or statistical terms. Adam Smith's "invisible hand" in economic markets and Charles Darwin's "natural selection" in evolutionary biology are classic examples of self-organizing mechanisms. The web as a whole with its more than a trillion unique pages is in many ways self-organizing, but at its core it follows clear organizing principles (See the Sidebar, "The Web as an Organizing System").[7]

The Web as an Organizing System

Today's web barely resembles the system for distributing scientific and technical reports it was designed to be when physicist and computer scientist Tim Berners-Lee devised it in 1990 at the European Organization for Nuclear Research (CERN) lab near Geneva. However, as an *Organizing System* the web still follows the principles that Berners-Lee defined at its creation. These include standard data formats and interaction protocols; no need for centralized control of page creation or linking; remote access over the network from anywhere; and the ability to run on a large variety of computers and operating systems. This architecture makes the web open and extensible, but gives it no built-in mechanisms for authority or trust.[8]

Because the web works without any central authority or authorship control, any person or organization can add to it. As a result, even though the web as a whole does not exhibit the centralized intentional arrangement of resources that characterizes many Organizing Systems, we can view it as consisting of millions of organizing systems that each embody a separate intentional arrangement of web pages. In addition, we most often interact with the web indirectly by using a search engine, which meets the definition of *Organizing System* because its indexing and retrieval algorithms are principled.

A great many Organizing Systems are implemented as collections of web pages. Some of these collections are created on the web as new pages, some are created by transforming existing collections of resources, and some combine new and existing resources.

Taken together, the intentional arrangements of resources in an Organizing System are the result of decisions about what is organized, why it is organized, how much it is organized, when it is organized, and how or by whom it is organized (each of these will be discussed in greater detail in §1.3, "Design Decisions in Organizing Systems" (page 18)). An Organizing System is defined by the composite impact of the choices made on these design dimensions. Because these questions are interrelated their answers come together in an integrated way to define an Organizing System.

1.2.3.1 The Concept of "Organizing Principle"

The arrangements of resources in an Organizing System follow or embody one or more organizing principles that enable the Organizing System to achieve its purposes. ***Organizing principles*** are directives for the design or arrangement of a collection of resources that are ideally expressed in a way that does not assume any particular implementation or realization.

When we organize a bookshelf, home office, kitchen, or the MP3 files on our music player, the resources themselves might be new and modern but many of the principles that govern their organization are those that have influenced the design of Organizing Systems for thousands of years. For example, we organize resources using easily perceived properties to make them easy to locate, we group together resources that we often use together, and we make resources that we use often more accessible than those we use infrequently. Very general and abstract organizing principles are sometimes called design heuristics (for example, "make things easier to find"). More specific and commonly used organizing principles include *alphabetical ordering* (arranging resources according to their names) and *chronological ordering* (arranging resources according to the date of their creation or other important event in the lifetime of the resource). Some organizing principles sort resources into pre-defined categories and other organizing principles rely on novel combinations of resource properties to create new categories.

Expressing organizing principles in a way that separates design and implementation aligns well with the three-tier architecture familiar to software architects and designers: user interface (implementation of interactions), business logic (intentional arrangement), and data (resources). (See the Sidebar, "The Three Tiers of Organizing Systems" (page 13)).

The logical separation between organizing principles and their implementation is easy to see with digital resources. In a digital library it does not matter to a user if the resources are stored locally or retrieved over a network. The essence of a library Organizing System emerges from the resources that it organizes and the interactions with the resources that it enables. Users typically care a lot about the interactions they can perform, like the kinds of searching and sorting allowed by the online library catalog. How the resources and interactions are implemented are typically of little concern. Similarly, many email applications have migrated to the web and the system of filters and folders that manage email messages is no longer implemented in a local network or on personal computers, but most people neither notice nor care.

The separation of organizing principles and their implementation is harder to recognize in an Organizing System that only contains physical resources, such as your kitchen or clothes closet, where you appear to have unmediated interactions with resources rather than accessing them through some kind of user interface or "presentation tier" that supports the principles specified in the "middle tier" and realized in the "storage tier." Nevertheless, you can see these different tiers in the organization of spices in a kitchen. Different kitchens might all embody an *alphabetic order* organizing principle for arranging a collection of spices, but the exact locations and arrangement of the spices in any particular kitchen depends on the configuration of shelves and drawers, whether a spice rack or rotating tray is used, and other storage-tier considerations. Similarly, spices could be logically organized by cuisine, with Indian spices separated from Mexican spices, but this organizing principle does not imply anything about where they can be found in the kitchen.

The Three Tiers of Organizing Systems

Software architects and designers agree that it is desirable to build applications that separate the storage of data, the business logic or functions that use the data, and the user interface or presentation components through which users or other applications interact with the data. This modular architecture allows each of the three tiers to be upgraded or reimplemented independently to satisfy changed requirements or to take advantage of new technologies. An analogous distinction is that between an algorithm as a logical description of a method for solving a computational problem and its implementation in a particular programming language like Java or Python.

These architectural distinctions are equally important to librarians and information scientists. Our new way of looking at Organizing Systems emphasizes the importance of identifying the desired interactions with resources, determining which organizing principles can enable the interactions, and then deciding how to store and manage the resources according to those principles. Applying architectural thinking to Organizing Systems makes it easier to compare and contrast existing ones and design new ones. Separating the organizing principles in the "middle tier" from their implications in the "data" and "presentation" tiers often makes it possible to implement the same logical Organizing System in different environments that support the same or equivalent interactions with the resources. For example, a new requirement to support searching through a library catalog on a smart phone would only affect the presentation tier.

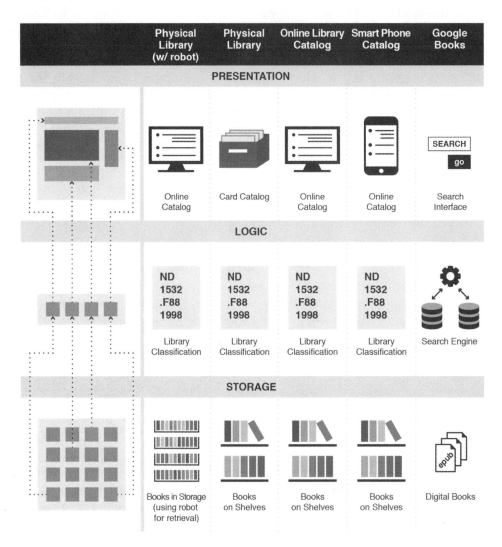

	Physical Library (w/ robot)	Physical Library	Online Library Catalog	Smart Phone Catalog	Google Books
PRESENTATION					
	Online Catalog	Card Catalog	Online Catalog	Online Catalog	Search Interface
LOGIC					
	ND 1532 .F88 1998	ND 1532 .F88 1998	ND 1532 .F88 1998	ND 1532 .F88 1998	
	Library Classification	Library Classification	Library Classification	Library Classification	Search Engine
STORAGE					
	Books in Storage (using robot for retrieval)	Books on Shelves	Books on Shelves	Books on Shelves	Digital Books

Figure 1.2. Presentation, Logic and Storage Tiers.

Figure 1.2, "Presentation, Logic and Storage Tiers." illustrates the separation of the presentation, logic, and storage tiers for four different types of library Organizing Systems and for Google Books. No two of them are the same in every tier. Note how a library that uses inventory robots to manage the storage of books does not reveal this in its higher tiers.

Because tangible things can only be in one place at a time, many Organizing Systems—like that in the modern library with online catalogs and physical collections—resolve this constraint by creating digital proxies or surrogates to organize their tangible resources, or create parallel digital resources like digitized books.[9] The implications for arranging, finding, using and reusing resources in any Organizing System directly reflect the mix of these two embodiments of information; in this way we can think of the modern library as a digital Organizing System that primarily relies on digital resources to organize a mixture of physical and digital ones.

The Organizing System for a small collection can sometimes use only the minimal or default organizing principle of *collocation*—putting all the resources in the same container, on the same shelf, or in the same email in-box. If you do not cook much and have only a small number of spices in your kitchen, you do not need to alphabetize them because it is easy to find the one you want.[10]

Some organization emerges implicitly through a *frequency of use* principle. In your kitchen or clothes closet, the resources you use most often migrate to the front because that is the easiest place to return them after using them. But as a collection grows in size, the time to arrange, locate, and retrieve a particular resource becomes more important. The collection must be explicitly organized to make these interactions efficient, and the organization must be preserved after the interaction takes place; i.e., resources are put back in the place they were found. As a result, most Organizing Systems employ organizing principles that make use of properties of the resources being organized (for example, name, color, shape, date of creation, semantic or biological category), and multiple properties are often used simultaneously. For example, in your kitchen you might arrange your cooking pots and pans by size and shape so you can nest them and store them compactly, but you might also arrange things by cuisine or style and separate your grilling equipment from the wok and other items you use for making Chinese food.

Unlike those for physical resources, the most useful organizing properties for information resources are those based on their content and meaning, and these are not directly apparent when you look at a book or document. Significant intellectual effort or computation is necessary to reveal these properties when assigning subject terms or creating an index. The most effective organizing systems for information resources often are based on properties that emerge from analyzing the collection as a whole. For example, the relevance of documents to a search query is higher when they contain a higher than average frequency of the query terms compared to other documents in the collection, or when they are linked to relevant documents. Likewise, algorithms for classifying email messages continuously recalculate the probability that words like "beneficiary" or "Viagra" indicate whether a message is "spam" or "not spam" in the collection of messages processed.

1.2.3.2 The Concept of "Agent"

Many disciplines have specialized job titles to distinguish among the people who organize resources (for example: cataloger, archivist, indexer, curator, collections manager...).[11] We use the more general word, **agent**, for any entity capable of autonomous and intentional organizing effort, because it treats organizing work done by people and organizing work done by computers as having common goals, despite obvious differences in methods.

We can analyze *agents* in Organizing Systems to understand how human and computational efforts to arrange resources complement and substitute for each other. We can determine the economic, social, and technological contexts in which each type of agent can best be employed. We can determine how the Organizing System allocates effort and costs among its creators, users, maintainers and other stakeholders.

A group of people can be an organizing *agent*, as when a group of people come together in a service club or standards body technical committee in which the members of the group subordinate their own individual agency to achieve a collective good.

We also use the term *agent* when we discuss interactions with Organizing Systems. The entities that most typically access the contents of libraries, museums, or other collections of physical resources are human agents—that is, people. In other Organizing Systems like business information systems or data repositories interactions with resources are carried out by computational processes, robotic devices, or other entities that act autonomously on behalf of a person or group.

In some Organizing Systems the resources themselves are capable of initiating interactions with other resources or with external *agents*. This is most obvious with human or other living resources and is also the case with resources augmented with computational or communication capabilities. We are all familiar with RFID tags, which enable the precise identification and location of physical resources as they move through supply chains and stores.

1.2.4 The Concept of "Interactions"

An *interaction* is an action, function, service, or capability that makes use of the resources in a collection or the collection as a whole. The interaction of **access** is fundamental in any collection of resources, but many Organizing Systems provide additional functions to make access more efficient and to support additional interactions with the accessed resources. For example, libraries and similar Organizing Systems implement catalogs to enable interactions for **finding** a known resource, **identifying** any resource in the collection, and discriminating or **selecting** among similar resources.[12]

> ## The Digital Zoo
>
> Consider the Organizing System of a zoo, which typically organizes the physical resources that we usually call animals according to principles of biological taxonomy or common habitat. The most important interaction supported by a modern zoo is enabling visitors to observe the behavior of animals in environments resembling their natural environments.
>
> If all the animals are "stored" in a single location and we prefer unmediated interaction with them, the physical requirements for housing and showcasing the animals and our own mobility limits how big a zoo can be. However, this is simply a conventional manner of storing the animals and supporting interactions with them.
>
> We can imagine a "digital zoo" in which all of the world's zoos are treated as a single digital collection. Instead of physical co-presence to enable viewing of the animals, "telepresence" quality video camera connections to zoo exhibits would enable us to view animals in the San Diego, Berlin, Singapore, Toronto and other great zoos from our living rooms almost as if we were there. Instead of a walk from exhibit to exhibit, a tour of a digital zoo would be implemented as a list of video connections, and different tours implemented as different sequences of cameras. Sensors in each animal habitat could detect activity and image recognition software could classify the behavior, enabling us to search the combined zoo for particular combinations of active animals to view (e.g., a mother and infant chimpanzee). No zoo would need to change how it "stores" the animals to enable these new principles of organization and our new kinds of interactions with them.

Some of the interactions with resources in an Organizing System are inherently determined by the characteristics of the resource. Because many museum resources are unique or extremely valuable, visitors are allowed to view them but cannot borrow them, in contrast with most of the resources in libraries. A library might have multiple printed copies of *Moby Dick* but can never lend more of them than it possesses. After a printed book is checked out from the library, there are many types of interactions that might take place—reading, translating, summarizing, annotating, and so on—but these are not directly supported by the library Organizing System and are invisible to it. For works not in the public domain, copyright law gives the copyright holder the right to prevent some uses, but at the same time "fair use" and similar copyright doctrines enable certain limited uses even for copyrighted works.[13]

Digital resources enable a greater range of interactions than physical ones. Any number of people or processes can request a weather forecast from a web-based weather service because the forecast is not used up by the request and the marginal cost of allowing another access is nearly zero. Furthermore, with digital resources many new kinds of interactions can be enabled through application software, web services, or *application program interfaces (APIs)* in the Organizing System. In particular, translation, summarization, annotation, and keyword suggestion are highly useful services that are commonly supported by web search engines and other web applications. Similarly, an Organizing System with digital resources can implement a "keep everything up to date" interaction that automatically pushes current content to your browser or computing device.

But just as technology can enable interactions, it can prevent or constrain them. If your collection of digital resources (ebooks or music, for example) is not stored on your own computer or device, a continuous Internet connection is a requirement for access. In addition, access control policies and digital rights management (DRM) technology can limit the devices that can access the collection and prevent copying, annotation and other actions that might otherwise be enabled by the fair use doctrine.

Just as with organizing principles, it is useful to think of interactions in an abstract or logical way that does not assume an implementation because it can encourage innovative designs for Organizing Systems. (See the Sidebar, "The Digital Zoo" (page 17)).

1.3 Design Decisions in Organizing Systems

A set of resources is transformed by an Organizing System when the resources are described or arranged to enable interactions with them. Explicitly or by default, this requires many interdependent decisions about the identities of resources; their names, descriptions and other properties; the classes, relations, structures and collections in which they participate; and the people or technologies who interact with them.

One important contribution of the idea of the Organizing System is that it moves beyond the debate about the definitions of things, documents, and information with the unifying concept of resource while acknowledging that "what is being organized" is just one of the questions or dimensions that need to be considered.

These decisions are deeply intertwined, but it is easier to introduce them as if they were independent. We introduce five groups of design decisions, itemizing the most important dimensions in each group:

- **What is being organized?** What is the scope and scale of the domain? What is the mixture of physical things, digital things, and information about things in the Organizing System? Is the Organizing System being designed to enable a resource collection to be created, for an existing and closed resource collection, or for a collection in which resources are continually added or deleted? Are the resources unique, or are they interchangeable members of a class? Do they follow a predictable "life cycle" with a "useful life"?

- **Why it is being organized?** What interactions or services will be supported, and for whom? Are the uses and users known or unknown? Are the users primarily people or computational processes? Does the Organizing System need to satisfy personal, social, or institutional goals?

- **How much is it being organized?** What is the extent, granularity, or explicitness of description, classification, or relational structure being imposed? Is this description and structure imposed in a centralized or top-down manner or in a distributed or bottom-up manner? What organizing principles guide the organization? Are all resources organized to the same degree, or is the organization sparse and non-uniform?

- **When is it being organized?** Is the organization imposed on resources when they are created, when they become part of the collection, when interactions occur with them, just in case, just in time, all the time? Is any of this organizing mandated by law or shaped by industry practices or cultural tradition?

- **How or by whom, or by what computational processes, is it being organized?** Is the organization being performed by individuals, by informal groups, by formal groups, by professionals, by automated methods? Are the organizers also the users? Are there rules or roles that govern the organizing activities of different individuals or groups?

How well these decisions coalesce in an Organizing System depends on the requirements and goals of its human and computational users, and on understanding the constraints and tradeoffs that any set of requirements and goals impose. How and when these constraints and tradeoffs are handled can depend on the legal, business and technological contexts in which the Organizing System is designed and deployed; on the relationship between the designers and users of the Organizing System (who may be the same people or different ones); on the economic or emotional or societal purpose of the Organizing System; and on numerous other design, deployment, and use factors.

1.3.1 Organizing Systems in a "Design Space"

Classifying Organizing Systems according to the kind of resources they contain is the most obvious and traditional approach. We can also classify Organizing Systems by their dominant purposes, by their intended user community, or other ways. No single fixed set of categories is sufficient by itself to capture the commonalities and contrasts between Organizing Systems.

We can augment the categorical view of Organizing Systems by thinking of them as existing in a multi-faceted or multi-dimensional design space in which we can consider many types of collections are at the same time.

1.3.1.1 Conventional Ways to Classify Organizing Systems

We distinguish law libraries from software libraries, knowledge management systems from data warehouses, and personal stamp collections from coin collections primarily because they contain different kinds of resources. Similarly, we distinguish document collections by resource type, contrasting narrative document types like novels and biographies with transactional ones like catalogs and invoices, with hybrid forms like textbooks and encyclopedias in between.

But there are three other conventional ways to classify Organizing Systems. A second way to distinguish Organizing Systems is by their dominant purposes or the priority of their common purposes. For example, libraries, museums, and archives are often classified as "memory institutions" to emphasize their primary emphasis on resource preservation. In contrast, "management information systems" or "business systems" are categories that include the great variety of software applications that implement the Organizing Systems needed to carry out day-to-day business operations.

A third conventional approach for classifying Organizing Systems is according to the nature or size of the intended user community. This size or scope can range from personal Organizing Systems created and used by a single person; to "community-based" Organizing Systems used by informal social groups; to those used by the employees, customers or stakeholders of an enterprise; to those used by an entire community or nation; to global ones potentially used by anyone in the world.

A fourth way to distinguish Organizing Systems is according to the technology used to implement them. Large businesses use different software applications for inventory management, records management, content management, knowledge management, customer relationship management, data warehousing and business intelligence, e-mail archiving, and other subcategories of collections.[14]

We can become overwhelmed by this proliferation of ways to classify collections of resources, especially when the classification is not clearly based on just one of these many approaches. For example, the list of "library types" used by the International Federation of Library Associations to organize its activities includes resource-based distinctions (e.g. art libraries, law libraries, social science libraries), purpose-based ones (e.g., academic and research libraries), and user-based distinctions (e.g., public libraries, school libraries, libraries serving persons with print disabilities).[15]

1.3.1.2 A Multifaceted or Multidimensional View

A type of resource and its conventional Organizing System are often the focal point of a discipline. Category labels like library, museum, zoo, and data repository have core meanings and many associated experiences and practices. Specialized concepts and vocabularies often evolve to describe these. The richness that follows from this complex social and cultural construction makes it difficult to define category boundaries precisely. Consider Borgman's commonly accepted definition of libraries as institutions that "select, collect, organize, conserve, preserve, and provide access to information on behalf of a community of users." Many Organizing Systems are described as libraries, although they differ from traditional libraries in important respects. See "What Is a Library?"

What Is a Library?

Most birds fly, but not all of them do. What characteristics are most important to us when we classify something as a bird? What characteristics are most important when we think of something as a library?

We might treat *circulation*, borrowing and returning the same item, as one of the interactions with resources that defines a library. In that case, an institution that lends items in its collection with the hope that the borrowers return something else that is better hardly seems like a library. But if the resources are the seeds of heirloom plants and the borrowers are expected to return seeds from the plants they grew from the borrowed seeds, perhaps "Seed Library" is an apt name for this novel Organizing System. Similarly, even though the resources in its collection are encyclopedia articles rather than living species, the Wikipedia open-source encyclopedia resembles the Seed Library by encouraging its users to "return" articles that are improvements of the current ones.

The photo-sharing website Flickr functions for most of its users as a personal photo archiving site. Flickr's billions of user-uploaded photos and the choice of many users to share them publicly transform it into a searchable shared collection, and many people also think of Flickr as a photo library. But Flickr lacks the authoritative description and standard classification that typify a library.

A similar categorization challenge arises with the Google Books digitization project. Google co-founder Sergei Brin characterized its ambitious project to put tens of millions of books from research libraries online as "a library to last forever." But the Google Books project was widely criticized as not being true to library principles.[16]

We can always create new categories by stretching the conventional definitions of "library" or other familiar Organizing Systems and adding modifiers, as when Flickr is described as a web-based photo-sharing library. But whenever we define an Organizing System with respect to a familiar category, the typical or mainstream instances and characteristics of that category that are deeply embedded in language and culture are reinforced, and those that are atypical are marginalized. In the Flickr case this means we suggest features that are not there (like authoritative classification) or omit the features that are distinctive (like tagging by users).

More generally, a categorical view of Organizing Systems makes it matter greatly which category is used to anchor definitions or comparisons. The Google Books project makes out-of-print and scholarly works vastly more accessible, but framing it in library terms to suggest it is a public good upsets many people with a more traditional sense of what the library category implies. We can readily identify design choices in Google Books that are more characteristic of the Organizing Systems in business domains, and the project might have been perceived more favorably had it been described as an online bookstore that offered many beneficial services for free.

A complementary perspective on Organizing Systems is that they exist in a multi-faceted or multi-dimensional design space. This *framework* for describing and comparing Organizing Systems overcomes some of the biases and conservatism built into familiar categories like libraries, museums, and archives, while enabling us to describe them as design patterns that embody characteristic configurations of design choices. We can then use these patterns to support multi-disciplinary work that cuts across categories and applies knowledge about familiar domains to unfamiliar ones. A dimensional perspective makes it easier to translate between category and discipline-specific vocabularies so that people from different disciplines can have mutually intelligible discussions about their organizing activities. They might realize that they have much in common, and they might be working on similar or even the same problems.

A faceted or dimensional perspective acknowledges the diversity of instances of collection types and provides a generative, forward-looking framework for describing hybrid types that do not cleanly fit into the familiar categories. Even though it might differ from the conventional categories on some dimensions, an Organizing System can be designed and understood by its "family resemblance" on the basis of its similarities on other dimensions to a familiar type of resource collection.

Thinking of Organizing Systems as points or regions in a design space makes it easier to invent new or more specialized types of collections and their associated interactions. If we think metaphorically of this design space as a map of Organizing Systems, the empty regions or "white space" between the densely-populated centers of the traditional categories represent Organizing Systems that do not yet exist. We can consider the properties of an Organizing System that could occupy that white space and analyze the technology, process, or policy innovations that might be required to let us build it there. Try this analogy test: Google Books is to Library as ? is to Natural History Museum.[17]

But even though digital technology is radically subdividing the traditional categories of collections by supporting new kinds of specialized information-intensive applications, an opposite and somewhat paradoxical trend has emerged. Jennifer Trant argues that the common challenges of "going digital," and the architectural and functional constraints imposed by web implementations, are causing some convergence in the operation of libraries, museums, and archives. Similarly, Anne Gilliland suggests that giving every physical resource in a collection a digital surrogate or proxy that is searchable and viewable in a web browser is "erasing the distinctions between custodians of information and custodians of things."[18]

Taken together, these two trends have one profound implication. If the traditional categories for thinking about collections are splintering in some respects and converging in others, they are less useful in describing innovative collections and their associated interactions. Thus, we need a new concept—the Organizing System—that:

- Applies comprehensively and consistently to collections of resources of any type;
- Reuses familiar categories where they are appropriate, but does not impose them on new types of collections and services where they do not fit well;
- Makes it easier to trace the connections between specific requirements or constraints and particular functions or implementation choices.

1.3.2 What Is Being Organized?

"What is difficult to identify is difficult to describe and therefore difficult to organize."

—(Svenonius 2000, p. 13)

Before we can begin to organize any resource we often need to identify it. It might seem straightforward to devise an Organizing System around tangible resources, but we must be careful not to assume what a resource is. In different situations, the same thing can be treated as a unique item, as one of many equivalent members of a broad category, or as component of an item rather than as an item on its own. For example, in a museum collection, a handmade carved chess piece might be a separately identified item, identified as part of a set of carved chess pieces, or treated as one of the 33 unidentified components of an item identified as a chess set (including the board). When merchants assign a stock-keeping unit (SKU) to identify the things they sell, an SKU can be associated with a unique item, to sets of items treated as equivalent for inventory or billing purposes, or to intangible things like warranties.

You probably do not have explicit labels on the cabinets and drawers in your kitchen or clothes closet, but department stores and warehouses have signs in the aisles and on the shelves because of the larger number of things a store needs to organize. As a collection of resources grows, it often becomes necessary to identify each one explicitly; to create surrogates like bibliographic records or descriptions that distinguish one resource from another; and to create additional organizational mechanisms like shelf labels, store directories, library card catalogs and indexes that facilitate understanding the collection and locating the resources it contains. These organizational mechanisms often suggest or parallel the organizing principles used to organize the collection itself.

Organization mechanisms like aisle signs, store directories and library card catalogs are embedded in the same physical environment as the resources being organized. But when these mechanisms or surrogates are digitized, the new capabilities that they enable create design challenges. This is because a digital Organizing System can be designed and operated according to more abstract and less constraining principles than an Organizing System that only contains physical resources. A single physical resource can only be in one place at a time, and interactions with it are constrained by its size, location, and other properties. In contrast, digital copies and surrogates can exist in many places at once and enable searching, sorting, and other interactions with an efficiency and scale impossible for tangible things.

When the resources being organized consist of information content, deciding on the unit of organization is challenging because it might be necessary to look beyond physical properties and consider conceptual or intellectual equivalence. A high school student told to study Shakespeare's play *Macbeth* might treat any printed copy or web version as equivalent, and might even try to outwit the teacher by watching a film adaptation of the play. To the student, all versions of *Macbeth* seem to be the same resource, but librarians and scholars make much finer distinctions.[19]

Archival Organizing Systems implement a distinctive answer to the question of what is being organized. Archives are a type of collection that focuses on resources created by a particular person, organization, or institution, often during a particular time period. This means that archives have themselves been previously organized as a result of the processes that created and used them. The "original order" of the resources in an archive embodies the implicit or explicit Organizing System of the person or entity that created the documents and it is treated as an essential part of the meaning of the collection. As a result, the unit of organization for archival collections is t~~he~~ *fonds*—~~the original arrangement~~ ~~or grouping, preserving any hierarchy of boxes,~~ folders, envelopes, and individu~~al documents~~—and thus they are ~~not re-organized according to other~~ (perhaps more systematic) ~~classifications~~.[20]

Some Organizing Systems contain legal, business or scientific documents or data that are the digital descendants of paper reports or records of transactions or observations. These Organizing Systems might need to deal with legacy information that still exists in paper form or in electronic formats like image scans that are different from the structural digital format in which more recent information is likely to be preserved. When legacy conversions from printed information artifacts are complete or unnecessary, an Organizing System no longer deals with any of the traditional tangible artifacts. Digital libraries dispense with these artifacts, replacing them with the capability to print copies if needed. This enables libraries of digital documents or data collections to be vastly larger and more accessible across space and time than any library that stores tangible, physical items could ever be.

An increasing number of Organizing Systems handle resources that are born digital. Ideally, digital texts can be encoded with explicit markup that captures structural boundaries and content distinctions, which can be used to facilitate organization, retrieval, or both. ~~In practice the digital representations of texts~~ ~~are often just image scans that do not support much processing or interaction.~~ A similar situation exists for the digital representations of music, photographs, videos, and other non-text content like sensor data, where the digital formats are structurally and semantically opaque.

1.3.3 Why Is It Being Organized?

"The central purpose of systems for organizing information [is] bringing like things together and differentiating among them."

—(Svenonius 2000 p. xi)

Almost by definition, ~~the essential purpose of any Organizing System is to de-~~ ~~scribe or arrange resources so they can be located and accessed later.~~ The organizing principles needed to achieve this goal depend on the types of resources or domains being organized, and in the personal, social, or institutional setting in which organization takes place. "Bringing like things together" is an informal organizing principle for many Organizing Systems. But there will likely be a number of more precise requirements or constraints to satisfy.

Organizing Systems involving physical resources are more likely to emphasize aesthetic or emotional goals than those for information resources, which more often are dominated by functional goals like efficiency of storage and access. This contrast is often magnified by the tendency for major library and museum collections to be housed in buildings designed as architectural monuments that over time become symbols of national or cultural identity.

The fine distinctions between Organizing Systems that have many characteristics in common reflect subtle differences in the priority of their shared goals. For example, many Organizing Systems create collections and enable interactions with the goals of supporting scientific research, public education, and entertainment. We can contrast zoos, animal theme parks, and wild animal preserves in terms of the absolute and relative importance of these three goals with respect to animal resources.[21]

When individuals manage their papers, books, documents, record albums, compact discs, DVDs, and other information resources, their Organizing Systems vary greatly. This is in part because the content of the resources being organized becomes a consideration. Furthermore, many of the Organizing Systems used by individuals are implemented by web applications, and this makes them more accessible because their resources can be accessed from anywhere with a web browser.[22]

Put another way, an information resource inherently has more potential uses than resources like forks or frying pans, so it is not surprising that the Organizing Systems in offices are even more diverse than those in kitchens.

When the scale of the collection or the number of intended users increases, not everyone is likely to share the same goals and design preferences for the Organizing System. If you share a kitchen with housemates, you might have to negotiate and compromise on some of the decisions about how the kitchen is organized so you can all get along. In more formal or institutional Organizing Systems conflicts between stakeholders can be much more severe, and the organizing principles might even be specified in commercial contracts or governed by law. For example, Bowker and Star note that physicians view the creation of patient records as central to diagnosis and treatment, insurance companies think of them as evidence needed for payment and reimbursement, and researchers think of them as primary data. Not surprisingly, policymaking and regulations about patient records are highly contentious.[23]

Almost as soon as libraries were invented over two thousand years ago, the earliest librarians saw the need to develop systematic methods for arranging and inventorying their collections.[24] The invention of mechanized printing in the fifteenth century, which radically increased the number of books and periodicals, forced libraries to begin progressively more refined efforts to state the functional requirements for their Organizing Systems and to be explicit about how they met those requirements.

Today, the Organizing Systems in a large academic research library must also support many functions and services other than those that directly support search and location of resources in their collections. In these respects, the Organizing Systems in non-profit libraries have much in common with those in corporate information repositories and business applications. (See the Sidebar, "Library {and, or, vs.} Business Organizing Systems" (page 27)).

Library {and, or, vs.} Business Organizing Systems

Any information-driven enterprise must have processes and technologies in place that govern information creation or capture and then manage its entire life cycle. In addition to the Organizing Systems that manage and provide access to their collections, large libraries also need business Organizing Systems to support acquisition, billing, interlibrary loan record routing and systems, licenses of digital resources from publishers, course material websites, and the library's own web presence. Commercial firms need processes for transacting with customers or other firms to carry out business operations, to support research and innovation, and to develop business strategy and tactics in compliance with laws and regulations for accounting, taxes, human resources, data retention, and so on. In large firms these functions are so highly specialized and complex that the different types of Organizing Systems have distinct names: Enterprise Resource Planning (ERP), Enterprise Content Management (ECM), Supply Chain Management (SCM), Records Management, Customer Relationship Management (CRM), Business Intelligence (BI), Knowledge Management (KM), and so on. And even though the most important functions in the Organizing Systems of large enterprises are those that manage the information resources needed for its business operation, these firms might also need to maintain corporate libraries and archives.

Preserving documents in their physical or original form is the primary purpose of archives and similar Organizing Systems that contain culturally, historically, or economically significant documents that have value as long-term evidence. Preservation is also an important motivation for the Organizing Systems of information- and knowledge-intensive firms. Businesses and governmental agencies are usually required by law to keep records of financial transactions, decision-making, personnel matters, and other information essential to business continuity, compliance with regulations and legal procedures, and transparency. As with archives, it is sometimes critical that these business knowledge or records management systems can retrieve the original documents, although digital copies that can be authenticated are increasingly being accepted as legally equivalent.

Chapter 7, *"Classification: Assigning Resources to Categories"* more fully explains the different purposes for Organizing Systems, the organizing principles they embody, and the methods for assigning resources to categories.

1.3.4 How Much Is It Being Organized?

"It is a general bibliographic truth that not all documents should be accorded the same degree of organization."

—(Svenonius 2000 p. 24)

Not all resources should be accorded the same degree of organization. In this section we will briefly unpack this notion of degree of organization into three important and related dimensions: the amount of description or organization applied to each resource, the amount of organization of resources into classes or categories, and the overall extent to which interactions in and between organizing systems are shaped by resource description and arrangement. Chapter 4 and Chapter 6, more thoroughly address these questions about the nature and extent of description in Organizing Systems.

Not all resources in a collection require the same degree of description for the simple reason we discussed in §1.3.3, "Why Is It Being Organized?" (page 25): Organizing Systems exist for different purposes and to support different kinds of interactions or functions. Let's contrast two ends of the "degree of description" continuum. Many people use "current events awareness" or "news feed" applications that select news stories whose titles or abstracts contain one or more keywords. This exact match algorithm is easy to implement, but its all-or-none and one-item-at-a-time comparison misses any stories that use synonyms of the keyword, that are written in languages different from that of the keyword, or that are otherwise relevant but do not contain the exact keyword in the limited part of the document that is scanned. However, users with current events awareness goals do not need to see every news story about some event, and this limited amount of description for each story and the simple method of comparing descriptions are sufficient.

On the other hand, this simple Organizing System is inadequate for the purpose of comprehensive retrieval of all documents that relate to some concept, event, or problem. This is a critical task for scholars, scientists, inventors, physicians, attorneys and similar professionals who might need to discover every relevant document in some domain. Instead, this type of Organizing System needs rich bibliographic and semantic description of each document, most likely assigned by professional catalogers, and probably using terms from a *controlled vocabulary* to enforce consistency in what descriptions mean.

Similarly, different merchants or firms might make different decisions about the extent or granularity of description when they assign SKUs because of differences in suppliers, targeted customers, or other business strategies. If you take your car to the repair shop because windshield wiper fluid is leaking, you might be dismayed to find that the broken rubber seal that is causing the leak cannot be ordered separately and you have to pay to replace the "wiper fluid reservoir" for which the seal is a minor but vital part. Likewise, when two business applications try to exchange and merge customer information, integration problems will arise if one describes a customer as a single "NAME" component while the other separates the customer's name into "TITLE," "FIRSTNAME," and "LAST-NAME."

Even when faced with the same collection of resources, people differ in how much organization they prefer or how much disorganization they can tolerate. A classic study by Tom Malone of how people organize their office workspaces and desks contrasted the strategies and methods of "filers" and "pilers." Filers maintain clean desktops and systematically organize their papers into categories, while pilers have messy work areas and make few attempts at organization. This contrast has analogues in other Organizing Systems and we can easily imagine what happens if a "neat freak" and "slob" become roommates.[25]

Different preferences and disagreements between stakeholders in an Organizing System about how much organization is necessary often result because of the implications for who does the work and who gets the benefits, especially the economic ones. Physicians prefer narrative descriptions and broad classification systems because they make it easier to create patient notes. In contrast, insurance companies and researchers want fine-grained "form-filling" descriptions and detailed classifications that would make the physician's work more onerous.[26]

The cost-effectiveness of creating systematic and comprehensive descriptions of the resources in an information collection has been debated for nearly two centuries and in the last half century the scope of the debate grew to consider the role of computer-generated resource descriptions.[27]

An alternative and complement to man-made descriptions for each resource are computer-generated indexes of their textual contents. These indexes typically assign weights to the terms according to calculations that consider the frequency and distribution of the terms in both individual documents and in the collection as a whole to create a description of what the documents are about. These descriptions of the documents in the collection are more consistent than those created by human organizers. They allow for more complex query processing and comparison operations by the retrieval functions in the Organizing System. For example, query expansion mechanisms or thesauri can automatically add synonyms and related terms to the search. Additionally, retrieved documents can be arranged by relevance, while "citing" and "cited-by" links can be analyzed to find related relevant documents.

A second constraint on the degree of organization comes from the size of the collection within the scope of the Organizing System. Organizing more resources requires more descriptions to distinguish any particular resource from the rest, and more constraining organizing principles. Similar resources need to be grouped or classified to emphasize the most important distinctions among the complete set of resources in the collection. A small neighborhood restaurant might have a short wine list with just ten wines, arranged in two categories for "red" and "white" and described only by the wine's name and price. In contrast, a gourmet restaurant might have hundreds of wines in its wine list, which would subdivide its "red" and "white" high-level categories into subcategories for country, region of origin, and grape varietal. The description for each wine might in addition include a specific vineyard from which the grapes were sourced, the vintage year, ratings of the wine, and tasting notes.

At some point a collection grows so large that it is not economically feasible for people to create bibliographic descriptions or to classify each separate resource, unless there are so many users of the collection that their aggregated effort is comparably large; this is organizing by "crowdsourcing." (See the Sidebar on "Web 2.0" in §1.3.6). This leaves two approaches that can be done separately or in tandem. The simpler approach is to describe sets of resources or documents as a set or group, which is especially sensible for archives with its emphasis on the *fonds* (see §1.3.2, "What Is Being Organized?" (page 23)). The second approach is to rely on automated and more general-purpose organizing technologies that organize resources through computational means. Search engines are familiar examples of computational organizing technology, and §7.6, "Computational Classification" (page 305) describes other common techniques in machine learning, clustering, and discriminant analysis that can be used to create a system of categories and to assign resources to them.

Finally, we must acknowledge the ways in which information processing and telecommunications technologies have transformed and will continue to transform Organizing Systems in every sphere of economic and intellectual activity. A century ago, when the telegraph and telephone enabled rapid communication and business coordination across large distances, these new technologies enabled the creation of massive vertically integrated industrial firms. In the 1920s the Ford Motor Company owned coal and iron mines, rubber plantations, railroads, and steel mills so it could manage every resource needed in automobile production and reduce the costs and uncertainties of finding suppliers, negotiating with them, and ensuring their contractual compliance. Adam's Smith's invisible hand of the market as an organizing mechanism had been replaced by the visible hand of hierarchical management to control what Ronald Coase in 1937 termed "transaction costs" in *The Nature of the Firm*.

But in recent decades a new set of information and computing technologies enabled by Moore's Law—unlimited computer power, effectively free bandwidth, and the Internet—have turned Coase upside down, leading to entirely new forms of industrial organization made possible as transaction costs plummet. When computation and coordination costs drop dramatically, it becomes possible for small firms and networks of services (provided by people or by computational processes) to out-compete large corporations through more efficient use of information resources and services, and through more effective information exchange with suppliers and customers, much of it automated. Herbert Simon, a pioneer in artificial intelligence, decision making, and human-computer interaction, recognized the similarities between the design of computing systems and human organizations and developed principles and mechanisms that could apply to both.[28]

Chapter 8, *"The Forms of Resource Descriptions"*, focuses on the representation of resource descriptions, taking a more technological or implementation perspective. Chapter 9, *"Interactions with Resources"*, discusses how the nature and extent of descriptions determines the capabilities of the interactions that locate, compare, combine, or otherwise use resources in information-intensive domains.

1.3.5 When Is It Being Organized?

"Because bibliographic description, when manually performed, is expensive, it seems likely that the 'pre' organizing of information will continue to shift incrementally toward 'post' organizing."

—(Svenonius 2000, p. 194-195)

The Organizing System framework recasts the traditional tradeoff between information organization and information retrieval as the decision about *when* the organization is imposed. We can contrast organization imposed on resources "on the way in" when they are created or made part of a collection with "on the way out" organization imposed when an interaction with resources takes place.

When an author writes a document, he or she gives it some internal organization via title, section headings, typographic conventions, page numbers, and other mechanisms that identify its parts and their significance or relationship to each other. The document could also have some external organization implied by the context of its publication, like the name of its author and publisher, its web address if it is online or has a website, and citations or links to other documents or web pages.

Digital photos, videos, and documents are generally organized to some minimal degree when they are created because some descriptions like time and location are assigned automatically to these types of resources by the technology used to create them.[29]

Digital resources created by automated processes generally exhibit a high degree of organization and structure because they are generated automatically in conformance with data or document schemas. These schemas implement the business rules and information models for the orders, invoices, payments, and the numerous other types of document resources that are created and managed in business Organizing Systems.

Before a resource becomes part of a library collection, its author-created organization is often supplemented by additional information supplied by the publisher or other human intermediaries, such as an *International Standard Book Number (ISBN)* or *Library of Congress Call Number (LOC-CN)* or *Library of Congress Subject Headings (LOC-SH)*.

In contrast, Google and other search engines apply massive computational power to analyze the contents and associated structures (like links between web pages) to impose organization on resources that have already been published or made available so that they can be retrieved in response to a user's query "on the way out." Google makes use of existing organization within and between information resources when it can, but its unparalleled technological capabilities and scale yield competitive advantage in imposing organization on information that was not previously organized digitally. Indeed, Geoff Nunberg criticized Google for ignoring or undervaluing the descriptive metadata and classifications previously assigned by people and replacing them with algorithmically assigned descriptors, many of which are incorrect or inappropriate.[30] One reaction to the poor quality of some computational description has been the call for libraries to put their authoritative bibliographic resources on the open web, which would enable reuse of reliable information about books, authors, publishers, places, and subject classifications. This "linked data" movement is slowly gathering momentum.[31]

Google makes almost all of its money through personalized ad placement, so much of the selection and ranking of search results is determined "on the way out" in the fraction of a second after the user submits a query by using information about the user's search history and current context. Of course, this "on the way out" organization is only possible because of the more generic organization that Google's algorithms have imposed, but that only reminds us of how much the traditional distinction between "information organization" and "information retrieval" is no longer defensible.

In many Organizing Systems the nature and extent of organization changes over time as the resources governed by the Organizing System are used. The arrangement of resources in a kitchen or in an office changes incrementally as frequently used things end up in the front of the pantry, drawer, shelf or filing cabinet or on the top of a pile of papers. Printed books or documents acquire margin notes, underlining, turned down pages or coffee cup stains that differentiate the most important or most frequently used parts. Digital documents do not take on coffee cup stains, but when they are edited, their new revision dates put them at the top of directory listings.

The scale of emergent organization of websites, photos on Flickr, blog posts, and other resources that can be accessed and used online dwarfs the incremental evolution of individual Organizing Systems. This organization is clearly visible in the pattern of links, tags, or ratings that are explicitly associated with these resources, but search engines and advertisers also exploit the less visible organization created over time by information about which resources were viewed and which links were followed.

The sort of organic or emergent change in Organizing Systems that takes place over time contrasts with the planned and systematic maintenance of Organizing Systems described as *curation* or *governance*, two related but distinct activities. **Curation** usually refers to the methods or systems that add value to and preserve resources, while the concept of **governance** more often emphasizes the institutions or organizations that carry out those activities. The former is most often used for libraries, museums, or archives and the latter for enterprise or inter-enterprise contexts. (See §2.5.4, "Governance" (page 77) for more discussion).

The Organizing Systems for businesses and industries often change because of the development of *de facto* or *de jure* standards, or because of regulations, court decisions, or other events or mandates from entities with the authority to impose them.

1.3.6 How (or by Whom) Is It Organized?

"The rise of the Internet is affecting the actual work of organizing information by shifting it from a relatively few professional indexers and catalogers to the populace at large. ... An important question today is whether the bibliographic universe can be organized both intelligently (that is, to meet the traditional bibliographic objectives) and automatically."

—(Svenonius 2000 p. 26)

In the preceding quote, Svenonius identifies three different ways for the "work of organizing information" to be performed: by professional indexers and catalogers, by the populace at large, and by automated (computerized) processes. Our notion of the Organizing System is broader than her "bibliographic universe," making it necessary to extend her taxonomy. Authors are increasingly organizing the content they create, and it is important to distinguish users in informal and formal or institutional contexts. We have also introduced the concept of an organizing *agent* (§1.2.3.1) to unify organizing done by people and by computer algorithms.

Professional indexers and catalogers undergo extensive training to learn the concepts, controlled descriptive vocabularies, and standard classifications in the particular domains in which they work. Their goal is not only to describe individual resources, but to position them in the larger collection in which they reside.[32] They can create and maintain Organizing Systems with consistent high quality, but their work often requires additional research, which is costly.

The class of professional organizers also includes the employees of commercial information services like Westlaw and LexisNexis, who add controlled and, often, proprietary metadata to legal and government documents and other news sources. Scientists and scholars with deep expertise in a domain often function as the professional organizers for data collections, scholarly publications and proceedings, and other specialized information resources in their respective disciplines. The National Association of Professional Organizers (NAPO) claims several thousand members who will organize your media collection, kitchen, closet, garage or entire house or help you downsize to a smaller living space.[33]

Many of today's content creators are unlikely to be professional organizers, but presumably the author best understands why something was created and the purposes for which it can be used. To the extent that authors want to help others find a resource, they will assign descriptions or classifications that they expect will be useful to those users. But unlike professional organizers, most authors are unfamiliar with controlled vocabularies and standard classifications, and as a result their descriptions will be more subjective and less consistent.

Similarly, most of us do not hire professionals to organize the resources we collect and use in our personal lives, and thus our Organizing Systems reflect our individual preferences and idiosyncrasies.

Non-author users in the "populace at large" are most often creating organization for their own benefit. These ordinary users are unlikely to use standard descriptors and classifications, and the organization they impose sometimes so closely reflects their own perspective and goals that it is not useful or others. Fortunately most users of "Web 2.0" or "community content" applications at least partly recognize that the organization of resources emerges from the aggregated contributions of all users, which provides incentive to use less egocentric descriptors and classifications. The staggering number of users and resources on the most popular applications inevitably leads to "tag convergence" simply because of the statistics of large sample sizes.

Web 2.0, Enterprise 2.0, Library 2.0, Museum 2.0, Science 2.0, Gov 2.0, ...

The World Wide Web was invented as a publishing and document distribution medium, and later became a platform for business transactions. But after the bursting of the "dot com bubble" in 2000-2001 it was clear that moving a transactional business model to the web was not enough. In 2005 Tim O'Reilly and Dale Dougherty proposed the concept of "Web 2.0" for firms whose applications literally get better the more people use them because they "harness the collective intelligence" of their users.

Google, Amazon.com, eBay, Wikipedia, Facebook, Twitter, and YouTube are familiar web-based examples where value is based on aggregating, interpreting, and responding to enormous amounts of user-generated data and content. Websites and resources that attract many visitors collect user interactions implicitly and also allow users to annotate, "tag," and evaluate them explicitly. These bottom-up and distributed activities have been called "folksonomies" and "crowdsourcing."

Tagging, bookmarking, and rating mechanisms are rapidly being adapted for use inside companies as techniques for knowledge management, a trend named "Enterprise 2.0" by Andrew McAfee to emphasize its similarity with "Web 2.0" while pointing out how it differs. Because every user is authenticated to their real identities, and organizational norms and incentives shape the purposes and nature of user contributions, Enterprise 2.0 applications have been successful at capturing expertise and institutional knowledge.

The core Web 2.0 design principle of empowering users to contribute information to help organize some collection of resources is rapidly being generalized to many other domains of Organizing Systems. Some "Library 2.0" discussions contemplate personalized catalogs and information services and enabling patrons to interact online in affinity groups. Similarly, some museums, scientific repositories, and governments are conducting "open access" or "citizen participation" experiments by allowing users access to identify and annotate items, analyze raw data, or create "mashups" or applications that reuse and transform information formerly available only in summary form or finished documents.[34]

Finally, the vast size of the web and the even greater size of the deep or invisible web composed of the information stores of business and proprietary information services makes it impossible to imagine today that it could be organized by anything other than the massive computational power of search engine providers like Google and Microsoft.[35] Nevertheless, in the earliest days of the web, significant human effort was applied to organize it. Most notable is Yahoo!, founded by Jerry Yang and David Filo in 1994 as a directory of favorite websites. For many years the Yahoo! homepage was the best way to find relevant websites by browsing the extensive system of classification. Today's Yahoo! homepage emphasizes a search engine that makes it appear more like Google or Microsoft Bing, but the Yahoo! directory can still be found if you search for it.

1.4 Organizing This Book

Devising concepts, methods, and technologies for describing and organizing resources have been essential human activities for millennia, evolving both in response to human needs and to enable new ones. Organizing Systems enabled the development of civilization, from agriculture and commerce to government and warfare. Today Organizing Systems are embedded in every domain of purposeful activity, including research, education, law, medicine, business, science, institutional memory, sociocultural memory, governance, public accountability, as well as in the ordinary acts of daily living.

With the World Wide Web and ubiquitous digital information, along with effectively unlimited processing, storage and communication capability, millions of people create and browse websites, blog, tag, tweet, and upload and download content of all media types without thinking "I'm organizing now" or "I'm retrieving now." Writing a book used to mean a long period of isolated work by an author followed by the publishing of a completed artifact, but today some books are continuously and iteratively written and published through the online interactions of authors and readers. When people use their smart phones to search the web or run applications, location information transmitted from their phone is used to filter and reorganize the information they retrieve. Arranging results to make them fit the user's location is a kind of computational curation, but because it takes place quickly and automatically we hardly notice it.

Likewise, almost every application that once seemed predominantly about information retrieval is now increasingly combined with activities and functions that most would consider to be information organization. Google, Microsoft, and other search engine operators have deployed millions of computers to analyze billions of web pages and millions of books and documents to enable the almost instantaneous retrieval of published or archival information. However, these firms increasingly augment this retrieval capability with information services that organize information in close to real-time. Further, the selection and presentation of search results, advertisements, and other information can be tailored for the person searching for information using his implicit or explicit preferences, location, or other *contextual information*.

Taken together, these innovations in technology and its application mean that the distinction between "information organization" and "information retrieval" that is often manifested in academic disciplines and curricula is much less important than it once was. This book has few sharp divisions between "information organization" (IO) and "information retrieval" (IR) topics. Instead, it explains the key concepts and challenges in the design and deployment of Organizing Systems in a way that continuously emphasizes the relationships and tradeoffs between IO and IR. The concept of the Organizing System highlights the design dimensions and decisions that collectively determine the extent and nature of resource organization and the capabilities of the processes that compare, combine, transform and interact with the organized resources.

Chapter 2, *"Activities in Organizing Systems"*. Developing a view that brings together how we organize as individuals with how libraries, museums, governments, research institutions, and businesses create Organizing Systems requires that we generalize the organizing concepts and methods from these different domains. Chapter 2 surveys a wide variety of Organizing Systems and describes four activities or functions shared by all of them: selecting resources, organizing resources, designing resource-based interactions and services, and maintaining resources over time.

Chapter 3, *"Resources in Organizing Systems"*. The design of an Organizing System is strongly shaped by what is being organized, the first of the five design decisions we introduced earlier in §1.3.2, "What Is Being Organized?" (page 23). To enable a broad perspective on this fundamental issue we use *resource* to refer to anything being organized, an abstraction that we can apply to physical things, digital things, information about either of them, or web-based services or objects. Chapter 3 discusses the challenges and methods for identifying the resources in an Organizing System in great detail and emphasizes how these decisions reflect the goals and interactions that must be supported—the "why" design decisions introduced in §1.3.3, "Why Is It Being Organized?" (page 25).

Chapter 4, *"Resource Description and Metadata"*. The principles by which resources are organized and the kinds of services and interactions that can be supported for them largely depend on the nature and explicitness of the resource descriptions. This "how much description" design question was introduced in §1.3.4, "How Much Is It Being Organized?" (page 28); Chapter 4 presents a systematic process for creating effective descriptions and analyzes how this general approach can be adapted for different types of Organizing Systems.

Chapter 5, *"Describing Relationships and Structures"*. An important aspect of organizing a collection of resources is describing the relationships between them. Chapter 5 introduces the specialized vocabulary used to describe semantic relationships between resources and between the concepts and words used in resource descriptions. It also discusses the structural relationships within multipart resources and between resources, like those expressed as citations or hypertext links.

Chapter 6, *"Categorization: Describing Resource Classes and Types"*. Groups or sets of resources with similar or identical descriptions can be treated as equivalent, making them members of an *equivalence class* or category. Identifying and using categories are essential human activities that take place automatically for perceptual categories like "red things" or "round things." Categorization is deeply ingrained in language and culture, and we use linguistic and cultural categories without realizing it, but categorization can also be a deeply analytic and cognitive process. Chapter 6 reviews theories of categorization from the point of view of how categories are created and used in Organizing Systems.

Chapter 7, *"Classification: Assigning Resources to Categories"*. The terms *categorization* and *classification* are often used interchangeably but they are not the same. *Classification* is applied categorization—the assignment of resources to a system of categories, called classes, using a predetermined set of principles. Chapter 7 discusses the broad range of how classifications are used in Organizing Systems. These include enumerative classification, faceted classification, activity-based classification, and computational classification. Because classification and standardization are closely related, the chapter also analyzes standards and standards-making as they apply to Organizing Systems.

Chapter 8, *"The Forms of Resource Descriptions"*. Chapter 8 complements the conceptual and methodological perspective on the creation of resource descriptions with an implementation perspective. Chapter 8 reviews a range of metamodels for structuring descriptions, with particular emphasis on XML, JSON, and RDF. It concludes by comparing and contrasting three "worlds of description" —document processing, the web, and the *Semantic Web*—where each of these three metamodels is most appropriate.

Chapter 9, *"Interactions with Resources"*. When Organizing Systems overlap, intersect, or are combined (temporarily or permanently), differences in resource descriptions can make it difficult or impossible to locate resources, access them, or otherwise impair their use. Chapter 9 reviews some of the great variety of concepts and techniques that different domains use when interacting with resources in Organizing Systems—integration, interoperability, data mapping, crosswalks, mashups, and so on. Similarly, processes for information retrieval are often characterized as comparing the description of a user's needs with descriptions of the resources that might satisfy them. Chapter 9 extends and more broadly applies this core idea to describe IR and related applications of natural language processing (NLP) in terms of locating, comparing, and ranking descriptions.

Chapter 10, *"The Organizing System Roadmap"*. Chapter 10 complements the descriptive perspective of Chapter 2—Chapter 9 with a more prescriptive one that analyzes the design choices and tradeoffs that must be made in different phases in an Organizing System's life cycle. System life cycle models exhibit great variety, but we use a generic four-phase model that distinguishes a domain identification and scoping phase, a requirements phase, a design and implementation phase, and an operational phase. This model is then used to guide the analysis of four case studies that span the range of Organizing Systems.

Notes

1. [LIS] (Nunberg 1996, 2011). (Buckland 1991). See also (Bates 2005).

2. [LIS] (Buckland 1997); (Glushko and McGrath 2005) and others with an informatics or computer science perspective take an abstract view of "document" that separates its content from its presentation or container (see §3.3.3, "Identity and Information Components" (page 111)). In contrast, the library science perspective often uses presentation or implementation properties in definitions of "document." On authorship: when we say that "Herman Melville is the author of *Moby Dick*" the meaning of "author" does not depend on whether we have a printed copy or a e-book in mind, but what counts as authorship varies a great deal across academic disciplines. Furthermore, different standards for describing resources disagree in the precision with which they identify the person(s) or organization(s) primarily responsible for creating the intellectual content of the resource, which creates interoperability problems (see Chapter 9).

3. [LIS] We can continue the debate in the previous paragraphs and the Sidebar, "What Is Information?" (page 4) by pointing out that in both common and professional usage, "bibliographic" activities involve describing and organizing information resources of the kinds that might be found in a library. But noted information scientist Patrick Wilson argued for a much broader expanse of the bibliographic universe, suggesting that "it includes manuscripts as well as printed books, bills of lading and street signs as well as personal letters, inscriptions on stone as well as phonograph recordings of speeches, and most notably, memorized texts in human heads and texts stored up in the memories of machines" (Wilson 1968, p. 12).

4. [LIS] (Svenonius 2000).

5. [Web] The URI identifies a resource as an abstract entity that can have "multiple representations," which are the "things" that are actually exposed through applications or user interfaces. The HTTP protocol can transfer the representa-

tion that best satisfies the content properties specified by a web client, most often a browser. This means that interactions with web resources are always with their representations rather than directly with the resource *per se*. The representation of the resource might seem to be implied by the URI (as when it ends in *.htm* or *.html* to suggest text in Hypertext Markup Language (HTML) format), but the URI is not required to indicate anything about the "representation." A web resource can be a static web page, but it can also be dynamic content generated at the time of access by a program or service associated with the URI. Some resources like geolocations have "no representations at all;" the resource is simply some point or space and the interaction is "show me how to get there." The browser and web server can engage in "content negotiation" to determine which "representation" to retrieve, and this is particularly important when that format further requires an external application or "plug-in" in order for it to be rendered properly, as it does when the server returns a PowerPoint file or an other file format that is not built into the browser.

Internet architecture's definition of *resource* as a conceptual entity that is never directly interacted with is difficult for most people to apply when those resources are physical or tangible objects, because then it surely seems like we are interacting with something real. So we will most often talk about interactions with resources, and will mention "resource representations" only when it is necessary to align precisely with the narrower Internet architecture sense.

6. [Business] The intellectual resources of a firm are embodied in a firm's people, systems, management techniques, history of strategy and design decisions, customer relationships, and intellectual property like patents, copyrights, trademarks, and brands. Some of this knowledge is explicit, tangible, and traceable in the form of documents, databases, organization charts, and policy and procedure manuals. But much of it is tacit: informal and not systematized in tangible form because it is held in the minds and experiences of people; a synonym is "know-how." A more modern term is *Intellectual Capital*, a concept originated in a 1997 book with that title (Stewart 1997).

7. [Web] (Banzhaf 2009).

8. [Web] The "plain web" (Wilde 2008a), whose evolution is managed by the *World Wide Web Consortium (W3C)*, is rigorously standardized, but unfortunately the larger ecosystem of technologies and formats in which the web exists is becoming less so. Web-based Organizing Systems often contain proprietary media formats and players (like Flash) or are implemented as closed environments that are intentionally isolated from the rest of the web (like Facebook or Apple's iTunes and other smart phone "app stores").

9. [Web] Instead of thinking of a digital book as a "parallel resource" to a printed book, we could consider both of them as alternate representations of the same abstract resource that are linked together by an "alternative" relationship,

just as we can use the HTML ALT tag to associate text with an image so its content and function can be understood by text-only readers.

10. [Computing] For collections of non-trivial size the choice of searching or sorting algorithm in computer programs is a critical design decision because they differ greatly in the time they take to complete and the storage space they require. For example, if the collection is arranged in an unorganized or random manner (as a "pile") and every resource must be examined, the time to find a particular item increases linearly with the collection size. If the collection is maintained in an ordered manner, a binary search algorithm can locate any item in a time proportional to the logarithm of the number of items. Analysis of algorithms is a fundamental topic in computer science; a popular textbook is *Introduction to Algorithms* by (Cormen et al. 2009).

11. [LIS] For precise distinctions, see the US Department of Labor, Bureau of Labor Statistics occupational outlook handbooks at *http://www.bls.gov/oco/ocos065.htm* and *http://www.bls.gov/oco/ocos068.htm* and *http://www.michellemach.com/jobtitles/realjobs.html*.

12. [LIS] The four objectives listed in this paragraph as those proposed in 1997 by the *International Federation of Library Associations and Institutions (IFLA)*. The first statement of the objectives for a bibliographic system was made by (Cutter 1876), which (Svenonius 2000) says it is likely the most cited text in the bibliographic literature. Cutter called his three objectives "finding," "co-locating," and "choice."

13. [Law] Copyright law, license or contract agreements, terms of use and so on that shape interactions with resources are part of the Organizing System, but compliance with them might not be directly implemented as part of the system. With digital resources, digital rights management (DRM), passwords, and other security mechanisms can be built into the Organizing System to enforce compliance.

14. [Computing] Sometimes many of these Organizing Systems and their associated applications are implemented using a unified storage foundation provided by an enterprise content management (ECM) or enterprise data management (EDM) system. An integrated storage tier can improve the integrity and quality of the information but is invisible to users of the applications.

15. [LIS] IFLA Library Types (*http://www.ifla.org/library-types*).

16. [Law] In 2004, Google began digitizing millions of books from several major research libraries with the goal of making them available through its search engine (Brin 2009). But many millions of these books are still in copyright, and in 2005 Google was sued for copyright infringement by several publishers and an author's organization. In 2011 a US District Court judge rejected the proposed settlement the parties had negotiated in 2008 because many others objected to

it, including the US Justice Department, several foreign governments, and numerous individuals (Samuelson 2011).

The major reason for the rejection was that the settlement was a "bridge too far" that went beyond the claims made against Google to address issues that were not in litigation. In particular, the judge objected to the treatment of the so-called "orphan works" that were still under copyright but out of print because money they generated went to the parties in the settlement and not to the rights holders who could not be located (why the books are "orphans") or to defray the costs of subscriptions to the digital book collection. The judge also was concerned that the settlement did not adequately address the concerns of academic authors—who wrote most of the books scanned from research libraries—who might prefer to make their books freely available rather than seek to maximize profits from them. Other concerns were that the settlement would have entrenched Google's monopoly in the search market and that there were inadequate controls for protecting the privacy of readers.

Google's plan would have dramatically increased access to out of print books, and the rejection of the proposed settlement has heightened calls for an open public digital library (Darnton 2011). A good start toward such a library was the digital copies that the research libraries received in return for giving Google books to scan, which were collected and organized by the Hathi Trust (See the Sidebar, "The Hathi Trust Digital Library" (page 71)). In 2010 the Alfred P. Sloan Foundation provided funding to launch the Digital Public Library of America (DPLA): *http://dp.la/*. This non-proprietary goal might induce the US Congress and other governments to pass legislation that fixes the copyright problems for orphan works.

17. [LIS] Depending on which characteristics of Google Books and libraries you think about, you might complete this analogy with an animal theme park like Sea World (*http://www.seaworld.com/*) or a private hunting reserve that creates personalized "big game" hunts. Or maybe you can invent something completely new.

18. [LIS] (Trant 2009a), (Gilliland-Swetland 2000).

19. [LIS] Organizing Systems that follow the rules set forth in the Functional Requirements for Bibliographic Records (FRBR) (Tillett 2005) treat all instances of *Macbeth* as the same "work." However, they also enforce a hierarchical set of distinctions for finer-grained organization. FRBR views books and movies as different "expressions," different print editions as "manifestations," and each distinct physical thing in a collection as an "item." This Organizing System thus encodes the degree of intellectual equivalence while enabling separate identities where the physical form is important, which is often the case for scholars.

20. [Archives] Typical examples of archives might be national or government document collections or the specialized Julia Morgan archive at the University of California, Berkeley (*http://www.oac.cdlib.org/findaid/ark:/13030/tf7b69n9k9/*), which houses documents by the famous architect who designed many of the university's most notable buildings as well as the famous Hearst Castle along the central California coast. The "original order" organizing principle of archival Organizing Systems was first defined by 19th century French archivists and is often described as *"respect pour les fonds."*

21. [CogSci] Seeking absolute boundaries between types of Organizing Systems is an impossible quest because how we define them varies with context or point of view. Zoos, animal theme parks, and wild animal parks all contain live animals, so we might conclude that they are more similar to each other than to a natural history musuem in which the animals are all dead. Colonial Williamsburg (*http://www.colonialwilliamsburg.com*) has people re-enacting 18th century Virginia and describes itself as a "living history museum," but could it not be considered an animal theme park that has human animals? Is a cemetery in some ways a natural history museum?

22. [Web] For example, many people manage their digital photos with Flickr, their home libraries with Library Thing, and their preferences for dining and shopping with Yelp. It is possible to use these "tagging" sites solely in support of individual goals, as tags like "my family," "toread," or "buythis" clearly demonstrate. But maintaining a personal Organizing System with these web applications potentially augments the individual's purpose with social goals like conveying information to others, developing a community, or promoting a reputation. Furthermore, because these community or collaborative applications aggregate and share the tags applied by individuals, they shape the individual Organizing Systems embedded within them when they suggest the most frequent tags for a particular resource.

23. [LIS] (Bowker and Star 2000).

24. [LIS] (Casson 2002).

25. [CogSci] (Malone 1983) is the seminal research study, but individual differences in organizing preferences were the basis of Neil Simon's Broadway play *The Odd Couple* in 1965, which then spawned numerous films and TV series.

26. [Computing] See Grudin's classic work on non-technological barriers to the successful adoption of collaboration technology (Grudin 1994).

27. [LIS] Sir Anthony Panizzi is most often associated with the origins of modern library cataloging. In 1841 (Panizzi 1841) published 91 cataloging rules for the British Library that defined authoritative forms for titles and author names, but the complexity of the rules and the resulting resource descriptions were widely criticized. For example, the famous author and historian Thomas Carlyle argued

that a library catalog should be nothing more than a list of the names of the books in it. Standards for bibliographic description are essential if resources are to be shared between libraries. See (Denton 2007), (Anderson and Perez-Carballo 2001a, 2001b).

28. [Business] Coase won the 1991 Nobel Prize in economics for his work on transaction costs, which he first published as a graduate student (Coase 1937). Berkeley business professor Oliver Williamson received the prize in 2009 for work that extended Coase's framework to explain the shift from the hierarchical firm to the network firm (Williamson 1975, 1998). The notion of the "visible hand" comes from (Chandler 1977). Simon won the Nobel Prize in economics in 1978, but if there were Nobel Prizes in computer science or management theory he surely would have won them as well. Simon was the author or co-author of four books that have each been cited over 10,000 times, including (Simon 1997, 1996) and (Newell and Simon 1972).

29. [Computing] At a minimum, these descriptions include the creation time and storage format for the resource, or chronologically by the auto-assigned file-name (*IMG00001.JPG*, *IMG00002.JPG*, etc.), but often are much more detailed. Most digital cameras annotate each photo with detailed information about the camera and its settings in the *Exchangeable Image File Format (EXIF)*, and many mobile phones can associate their location along with any digital object they create. Nevertheless, these descriptions are not always correct. For example, Microsoft Office applications extract the author name from any template associated with a document, presentation, or spreadsheet and then embed it in the new documents. And if you have not set the time correctly in your digital camera any timestamp it associates with a photo will be wrong.

30. [Computing] (Nunberg 2009) calls Google's Book Search a "disaster for scholars" and a "metadata train wreck." He lists scores of errors in titles, publication dates, and classifications. For example, he reports that a search on "Internet" in books published before 1950 yields 527 results. The first 10 hits for Whitman's *Leaves of Grass* are variously classified as Poetry, Juvenile Nonfiction, Fiction, Literary Criticism, Biography & Autobiography, and Counterfeits and Counterfeiting.

31. [Web] (Byrne and Goddard 2010).

32. [LIS] This is an important distinction in library science education and library practice. Individual resources are described ("formal" cataloging) using "bibliographic languages" and their classification in the larger collection is done using "subject languages" (Svenonius 2000, Ch. 4 and Ch. 8, respectively). These two practices are generally taught in different library school courses because they use different languages, methods and rules and are generally carried out by different people in the library. In other organizations, the resource description (both formal and subject) is created in the same step and by the same person.

33. [Business] NAPO: *http://www.napo.net*.

34. [Web] The "manifesto" for Web 2.0 is Tim O'Reilly's *What is Web 2.0?* (*http://oreilly.com/web2/archive/what-is-web-20.html*).

"Folksonomy" was coined by Thomas Van der Wal at about the same time in 2004; see *http://vanderwal.net/folksonomy.html* and (Trant 2009b).

The term "Crowdsourcing" was invented by Jeff Howe in a June 2006 article in Wired magazine, *http://www.wired.com/wired/archive/14.06/crowds.html*, and the concept was developed further in a book published two years later (Howe 2008).

(Millen et al. 2005) describe an enterprise application of social bookmarking at *IBM* called Dogear. The Library 2.0 idea is presented in (Maness 2006) and several more recent surveys of Web 2.0 features in university library websites have been reported by (Xu et al. 2009) and (Harinarayana and Raju 2010).

Nina Simon's book, *The Participatory Museum*, is itself an example of Web 2.0 concepts, available online with reader comments (*http://www.participatory museum.org/read/*). For Science 2.0., see (Shneiderman 2008). For Government 2.0, see (Robinson et al. 2008) and (Drapeau 2010).

35. [Web] (He et al. 2007) estimate that there are hundreds of thousands of websites and databases whose content is accessible only through query forms and web services, and there are over a million of those. The amount of content in this hidden web is many hundreds of times larger than that accessible in the surface or visible web.

Chapter 2
Activities in Organizing Systems

Robert J. Glushko
Erik Wilde
Jess Hemerly

2.1 Introduction

There are four activities that occur naturally in every *organizing system*; how explicit they are depend on the scope, the breadth or variety of the resources, and the scale, the number of resources that the organizing system encompasses. Consider the routine, everyday task of managing your wardrobe. When you organize your clothes closet, you are unlikely to write a formal *selection* policy that specifies what things go in the closet. You do not consciously itemize and prioritize the ways you expect to search for and locate things, and you are unlikely to consider explicitly the organizing principles that you use to arrange them. From time to time to you will put things back in order and discard things you no longer wear, but you probably will not schedule this as a regular activity on your calendar.

Your clothes closet is an organizing system; defined in Chapter 1 as "an intentionally arranged collection of resources and the interactions they support." As such, it exposes these four highly interrelated and iterative activities:

Selecting

Determining the scope of the organizing system by specifying which resources should be included. (*Should I hang up my sweaters in the clothes closet or put them in a dresser drawer in the bedroom?*)

Organizing

Specifying the principles or rules that will be followed to arrange the resources. (*Should I sort my shirts by color, sleeve type, or season?*)

Designing resource-based interactions

Designing and implementing the actions, functions or services that make use of the resources. (*Do I need storage places for clothes to be laundered? Should I have separate baskets for white and colors? Dry cleaning?*)

Maintaining

Managing and adapting the resources and the organization imposed on them as needed to support the interactions. (*When is it time to straighten up the closet? What about mending? Should I toss out clothes based on wear and tear, how long I have owned them, or whether I am tired of them? What about excess hangers?*)

Figure 2.1, "Four Activities in all Organizing Systems." illustrates these four activities in all organizing systems, framing the depiction of the organizing and interaction design activities shown in Figure 1.1, "An Organizing System." with the *selection* and *maintenance* activities that necessarily precede and follow them.

These activities are not entirely separable or sequential, and they can be informal for your clothes closet because its scope and scale are limited. In institutional organizing systems the activities and the interdependencies and iterations among them are more carefully managed and often highly formal. In addition, these activities are deeply ingrained in academic curricula and professional practices, with domain-specific terms for their methods and results.

Libraries and museums usually make their *selection* principles explicit in **collection development** policies. Adding a resource to a library collection is called **acquisition**, but adding to a museum collection is called **accessioning**. Documenting the contents of library and museum collections to organize them is called **cataloging**. **Circulation** is a central interaction in libraries, but because museum resources don't circulate the primary interactions for museum users are **viewing** or **visiting** the collection. *Maintenance* activities are usually described as **preservation** or *curation*.

In business information systems, *selection* of resources can involve **data generation** or **capture** or **extraction**. Adding resources could involve **loading, integration** or **insertion**. **Schema development** and **data transformation** are important organizing activities. Supported interactions could include **querying**,

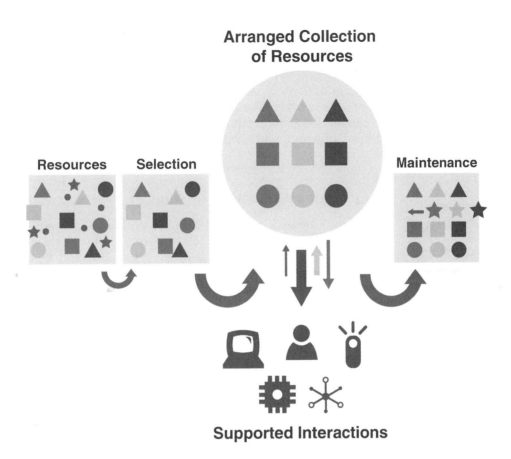

Figure 2.1. Four Activities in all Organizing Systems.

reporting, **analysis**, or **visualization**. *Maintenance* activities are often described as **deletion**, **purging**, **data cleansing**, **governance**, or **compliance**.

These domain-specific methods and vocabularies evolve over time to capture the complex and distinctive sets of experiences and practices of their respective disciplines. We can identify correspondences and overlapping meanings, but they are not synonyms or substitutes for each other. We propose more general terms like *selection* and maintenance, not as lowest common denominator replacements for these more specialized ones, but to facilitate communication and cooperation across the numerous disciplines that are concerned with organizing.

It might sound odd to describe the animals in a zoo as resources, to think of viewing a painting in a museum as an interaction, or to say that destroying information to comply with privacy regulations is maintenance. Taking a broader perspective on the activities in organizing systems so that we can identify best practices and patterns enables people with different backgrounds and working in different domains to understand and learn from each other.

Part of what a database administrator can learn from a museum curator follows from the rich associations the curator has accumulated around the concept of curation that are not available around the more general concept of maintenance. Without the shared concept of *maintenance* to bridge their disciplines, this learning could not take place.

What about "Creating" Resources?

Our definition of organizing system as an intentionally arranged collection of resources might seem to imply that resources must exist before they are organized. This is often the case when we organize physical resources because the need for principled organization only arises when the collection gets too big for us to see everything in the collection at once.

However, organizing systems for digital resources are often put in place as a prerequisite for creating them. This is always necessary when the resources are created by automated processes or data entry in business systems, and usually the case with professional writers in a technical publications context. We can think of database or document schemas (at the implementation tier) or data entry forms or word processor templates (in the user interface tier) as embodiments of the organizing principles in the data records or documents that are then created in conformance with them.

In §1.2.1, "The Concept of "Resource"" (page 8) and §1.3.2, "What Is Being Organized?" (page 23) we briefly discussed the fundamental concept of a *resource*. In this chapter, we describe the four primary *activities* with resources, using examples from many different kinds of organizing systems. We emphasize the activities of organizing and of designing resource-based interactions that make use of the organization imposed on the resources. We discuss *selection* and *maintenance* to create the context for the organizing *activities* and to highlight the interdependencies of *organizing* and these other *activities*. This broad survey enables us to compare and contrast the activities in different resource domains, setting the stage for a more thorough discussion of resources and *resource description* in Chapter 3 and Chapter 4.

2.2 Selecting Resources

When we talk about organizing systems, we often do so in terms of the contents of their collections. This implies that the most fundamental decision for an organizing system is determining its resource domain, the group or type of resources that are being organized. This decision is usually a constraint, not a choice; we acquire or encounter some resources that we need to interact with over time, and we need to organize them so we can do that effectively.

Selecting is the process by which resources are identified, evaluated, and then added to a collection in an organizing system. *Selection* is first shaped by the domain and then by the scope of the organizing system, which can be analyzed through six interrelated aspects:

1. the number and nature of users

2. the time span or lifetime over which the organizing system is expected to operate

3. the size of the collection

4. the expected changes to the collection

5. the physical or technological environment in which the organizing system is situated or implemented

6. the relationship of the organizing system to other ones that overlap with it in domain or scope.

In Chapter 10, *"The Organizing System Roadmap"*, we discuss these six aspects in more detail.

2.2.1 Selecting {and, or, vs.} Organizing

Many types of resources are inevitably evaluated one-at-a-time. It is impossible to specify in advance every property or criterion that might be considered in making a selection decision, especially for unique or rare resources like those being considered by a museum or private collector. As a result, organizing activities typically occur after selection takes place, as in the closet organizing system with which we began this chapter.

When the resources being considered for a collection are more homogeneous and predictable, it is possible to specify selection criteria and organizing principles in advance. This makes selection and organizing into concurrent activities. You expect your email in-box will receive spam messages, so you might as well create a spam folder where the spam filter can deposit the messages it classifies as spam.

Some organizing systems acquire all resources of a particular type or from a particular source. Resources are then automatically added to the collection according to an organizing decision that need be made only for the first resource, with subsequent resources further organized according to properties that minimally distinguish them from each other, like their creation or acquisition dates. Syndicated or subscription resources like news feeds or serial publications are most often organized in this manner, where the organization imposed on the first resource acquired is replicated for each subsequent one. If you subscribe to a printed magazine, the magazines undoubtedly end up in a stack or pile with the most recent issue on the top.

Finally, as we pointed out in the Sidebar, "What about "Creating" Resources?" (page 50) selection can sometimes follow organizing. An order management system cannot add new orders until it has a defined schema for creating them.

2.2.2 Selection Principles

Selection must be an intentional process because, by definition, an organizing system contains resources whose selection and arrangement was determined by human or computational agents, not by natural processes. Selection methods and criteria vary across resource domains. Resource selection policies are often shaped by laws, regulations or policies that require or prohibit the collection of certain kinds of objects or types of information.[36]

Libraries typically select resources on the basis of their utility and relevance to their user populations, and try to choose resources that add the most value to their existing collections. Museums often emphasize intrinsic value, scarcity, or uniqueness as selection criteria, even if the resources lack any contemporary use. Both libraries and museums typically formalize their selection principles in *collection development* policies that establish priorities for acquiring resources that reflect the people they serve and the services they provide to them. Precise and formal *selection* principles enable users of a collection to be confident that it contains the most important and useful resources.

Adding a resource to a museum implies an obligation to preserve it forever, so many museums follow rigorous *accessioning* procedures before accepting it. Likewise, archives usually perform an additional appraisal step to determine the quality and value of materials offered to them.[37]

In the for-profit sector, well-run firms are similarly systematic in selecting the resources that must be managed and the information needed to manage them. "Selecting the right resource for the job" is a clichéd way of saying this, but this slogan nonetheless applies broadly to human resources, functional equipment, or information that drives business processes.[38]

The organizing systems for managing sales, orders, customers, inventory, personnel, and finance information are tailored to the specific information needed to run that part of the company's operations. Identifying this information is the job of business analysts and data modelers. Much of this operational data is combined in huge "data warehouses" to support the "business analytics" function in which novel combinations and relationships among data items are explored by selecting subsets of the data.[39]

Selection is an essential activity in creating organizing systems whose purpose is to combine separate web services or resources to create a composite service or application according to the business design philosophy of "Service Oriented Architecture" (SOA).[40] When an information-intensive enterprise combines its internal services with outsourced ones provided by other firms, the resources are selected to create a combined collection of services according to the "core competency" principle: resources are selected and combined to exploit the enterprise's internal capabilities and those of its service partners better than any other combination of services could.[41]

Even when the selection principles behind a collection are clear and consistent, they can be unconventional, idiosyncratic, or otherwise biased by the perspective and experience of the collector. This is sometimes the case in museum or library collections that began or grew opportunistically through the acquisition of private collections that reflect a highly individual point of view.

It is especially easy to see the collector's point of view in personal collections. Most of the clothes and shoes you own have a reason for being in your closet, but could anyone else explain the contents of your closet and its organizing system, and why you bought that crazy-looking dress or shirt?

2.2.3 Selection of Digital and Web-Based Resources

Digitization is substantially changing how libraries select resources. Digital content can be delivered anywhere quickly and cheaply, making it easier for a group of cooperating libraries to share resources. For example, while each campus of the University of California system has its own libraries and library catalogs, system-wide catalogs and digital content delivery reduce the need for every campus to have any particular resource in its own collection.[42]

Digitization has had extremely important impacts on the manner in which collections of information resources are created in information-intensive domains such as transportation, retailing, supply chain management, healthcare, energy management, and "big science" where a torrent of low-level information is captured from GPS devices, RFID tags, sensors and science labs. Businesses that once had to rely on limited historical data analysis and printed reports now have to deal with a constant stream of real-time information.

An analogous situation has evolved with personal collections of photographs. Less than two decades ago, before the digital camera became a consumer product, the time and expense of developing photographs induced people to take photos carefully and cautiously. Today the proliferation of digital cameras and photo-capable phones has made it so easy to take digital photos and videos that people are less selective and take many photos or videos of the same scene or event.

The nature and scale of the web changes how we collect resources and fundamentally challenges how we think of resources in the first place. Web-based resources cannot be selected for a collection by consulting a centralized authoritative directory, catalog, or index because one does not exist. And although your favorite web search engine consults an index or directory of web resources when you enter a search query, you do not know where that index or directory came from or how it was assembled.[43]

The contents of a collection and how it is organized always reflect its intended users and uses. But the web has universal scope and global reach, making most of the web irrelevant to most people most of the time. Researchers have attacked this problem by treating the web as a combination of a very large number of topic-based or domain-specific collections of resources, and then developing techniques for extracting these collections as digital libraries targeted for particular users and uses.[44]

2.3 Organizing Resources

Organizing systems arrange their resources according to many different principles. In libraries, museums, businesses, government agencies and other long-lived institutions, organizing principles are typically documented as cataloging rules, information management policies, or other explicit and systematic procedures so that different people can apply them consistently over time. In contrast, the principles for arranging resources in personal or small-scale organizing systems are not usually stated in any formal way and might even be inconsistent or conflicting.

For most types of resources, any number of principles could be used as the basis for their organization depending on the answers to the "why?" (§1.3.3), "how much?" (§1.3.4), and "how?" (§1.3.6) questions posed in Chapter 1.

A simple principle for organizing resources is *collocation* — putting them in the same place. However, most organizing systems use principles that are based on specific resource properties or properties derived from the collection as a whole. What properties are significant and how to think about them depends on the number of resources being organized, the purposes for which they are being organized, and on the experiences and implicit or explicit biases of the intended users of the organizing system. The implementation of the organizing system also shapes the need for, and the nature of, the resource properties.[45]

Many resource collections—even very large ones—acquire resources one at a time or in sets of related resources that can initially be treated in the same way. Therefore, it is natural to arrange resources based on properties of individual resources that can be assessed and interpreted when the resource is selected and becomes part of the collection. Decisions about which resource properties will be used in organizing must often precede the creation or collection of the resources. This is especially critical for archaeologists, naturalists, and scientists of every type. Without information about the context of creation or discovery, what might otherwise be important resources could be just a handful of pottery shards, a dead animal, or some random set of bits on a computer.

"Subject matter" organization involves the use of a classification system that provides categories and descriptive terms for indicating what a resource is about. Because they use properties like ***aboutness*** that are not directly perceived, methods for assigning subject classifications are intellectually-intensive and require rigorous training to be performed consistently and appropriately for the intended users.[46] Nevertheless, the cost and time required for this human effort motivates many organizing systems for information resources to use computational approaches for arranging them. As computing power steadily increases the bias toward computational organization gets even stronger.

2.3.1 Organizing Physical Resources

When the resources being arranged are physical or tangible things—such as books, paintings, animals, or cooking pots—any resource can be in only one place at a time in libraries, museums, zoos, or kitchens. Similarly, when organizing involves recording information in a physical medium—carving in stone, imprinting in clay, applying ink to paper by hand or with a printing press—how this information can be organized is subject to the intrinsic properties and constraints of physical things.

The inescapable tangibility of physical resources means that their organizing systems are often strongly influenced by the material or medium in which the resources are presented or represented. For example, museums generally collect original artifacts and their collections are commonly organized according to the type of thing being collected. There are art museums, sculpture museums, craft museums, toy museums, science museums, and so on.

Similarly, because they have different material manifestations, we usually organize our printed books in a different location than our record albums, which might be near but remain separate from our CDs and DVDs. This is partly because the storage environments for physical resources (shelves, cabinets, closets, and so on) have co-evolved with the physical resources they store.[47]

The resource collections of organizing systems in physical environments often grow to fit the size of the environment or place in which they are maintained—the bookshelf, closet, warehouse, library or museum building. Their scale can be large: the Smithsonian Institute in Washington, D.C., the world's largest museum and research complex, consists of 19 museums, 9 research facilities, a zoo and a library with 1.5 million books. However, at some point, any physical space gets too crowded, and it is difficult and expensive to add new floors or galleries to an existing library or museum.

2.3.1.1 Organizing with Properties of Physical Resources

Physical resources are often organized according to intrinsic physical properties like their size, color or shape, or intrinsically associated properties such as the place and time they were created or discovered. The shirts in your clothes closet might be arranged by color, by fabric, or style. We can view dress shirts, T-shirts, Hawaiian shirts and other styles as configurations of shirt properties that are so frequent and familiar that they have become linguistic and cultural categories. Other people might think about these same properties or categories differently, using a greater or lesser number of colors or ordering them differently, sorting the shirts by style first and then by color, or vice versa.

In addition to, or instead of, physical properties of your shirts, you might employ behavioral or usage-based properties to arrange them. You might separate your party and Hawaiian shirts from those you wear to the office. You might put the shirts you wear most often in the front of the closet so they are easy to locate. Unlike intrinsic properties of resources, which do not change, behavioral or usage-based properties are dynamic. You might move to Hawaii, where you can wear Hawaiian shirts to the office, or you could get tired of what were once your favorite shirts and stop wearing them as often as you used to.

Some arrangements of physical resources are constrained or precluded by resource properties that might cause problems for other resources or for their users. Hazardous or flammable materials should not be stored where they might spill or ignite; lions and antelopes should not share the same zoo habitat or the former will eat the latter; and adult books and movies should not be kept in a library where children might accidentally find them. For almost any resource, it seems possible to imagine a combination with another resource that might have unfortunate consequences. We have no shortage of professional certifications, building codes, MPAA movie ratings, and other types of laws and regulations designed to keep us safe from potentially dangerous resources.

2.3.1.2 Organizing with Descriptions of Physical Resources

To overcome the inherent constraints with organizing physical resources, organizing systems often use additional physical resources that describe the primary physical ones, with the library card catalog being the classic example. A specific physical resource might be in a particular place, but multiple description resources for it can be in many different places at the same time.

When the description resources are themselves digital, as when the printed library card catalog is put online, the additional layer of abstraction created enables additional organizing possibilities that can ignore physical properties of resources and many of the details about how they are stored.

In organizing systems that use additional resources to identify or describe primary ones "adding to a collection" is a logical act that need not require any actual movement, copying, or reorganization of the primary resources. This virtual addition allows the same resources to be part of many collections at the same time; the same book can be listed in many bibliographies, the same web page can be in many lists of web bookmarks and have incoming links from many different pages, and a publisher's digital article repository can be licensed to any number of libraries.

2.3.2 Organizing Digital Resources

Organizing systems that arrange digital resources like digital documents or information services have some important differences from those that organize physical resources. Because digital resources can be easily copied or interlinked, they are free from the "one place at a time" limitation.[48] The actual storage locations for digital resources are no longer visible or very important. It hardly matters if a digital document or video resides on a computer in Berkeley or Bangalore if it can be located and accessed efficiently.[49]

Moreover, because the functions and capabilities of digital resources are not directly manifested as physical properties, the constraints imposed on all *material* objects do not matter to digital content in many circumstances.[50] [51]

An organizing system for digital resources can also use digital description resources that are associated with them. Since the incremental costs of adding processing and storage capacity to digital organizing systems are small, collections of both primary digital resources and description resources can be arbitrarily large. Digital organizing systems can support collections and interactions at a scale that is impossible in organizing systems that are entirely physical, and they can implement services and functions that exploit the exponentially growing processing, storage and communication capabilities available today.[52]

There are inherently more choices in the arrangement of digital resources than there are for physical ones, but this difference emerges because of multiple implementation platforms for the organizing system as much as in the nature of the resources. Nevertheless, the organizing systems for digital books, music and video collections often maintain the distinctions embodied in the organizing system for physical resources because it enables their co-existence or simply because of legacy inertia. As a result, the organizing systems for collections of digital resources tend to be coarsely distinguished by media type (e.g., document management, digital music collection, digital video collection, digital photo collection, etc.).

Information resources in either physical or digital form are typically organized using intrinsic properties like author names, creation dates, publisher, or the set of words that they contain. Information resources can also be organized using extrinsic or behavioral properties like subject classifications, assigned names or identifiers, or even access frequency.[53]

Complex organization and interactions are possible when organizing systems with digital resources are based on the data type or data model of the digital content (e.g., text, numeric, multimedia, statistical, geospatial, logical, scientific, or personnel data). These distinctions are often strongly identifiable with business functions: operational, transactional and process control activities require the most fine-grained data, while strategic functions might rely on more qualitative analyses represented in narrative text formats. Managerial and decision support functions might require a mixture of digital content types.

Accordingly, just as there are many laws and regulations that restrict the organization of physical resources, there are laws and regulations that constrain the arrangements of digital ones. Many information systems that generate or collect transactional data are prohibited from sharing any records that identify specific people. Banking, accounting, and legal organizing systems are made more homogeneous by compliance and reporting standards and rules.

2.3.2.1 Organizing Web-Based Resources

The *Domain Name System (DNS)* is the most inherent scheme for organizing web resources. Top-level domains for countries (.us, .jp, .cn, etc) and generic resource categories (.com, .edu. .org, gov, etc.) provide some clues about the resources organized by a website. These clues are most reliable for large established enterprises and publishers; we know what to expect at `ibm.com`, `Berkeley.edu`, and `jstor.org`.[54]

The network of hyperlinks among web resources challenges the notion of a collection, because it makes it impractical to define a precise boundary around any collection smaller than the complete web.[55] Furthermore, authors are increasingly using "web-native" publication models, creating networks of articles that blur the notions of articles and journals. For example, scientific authors are interconnecting scientific findings with their underlying research data, to discipline-specific data repositories, or to software for analyzing, visualizing, simulation, or otherwise interacting with the information.[56]

The conventional library is both a collection of books and the physical space in which the collection is managed. On the web, rich hyper linking and the fact that the actual storage location of web resources is unimportant to the end users fundamentally undermine the idea that organizing systems must collect resources and then arrange them under some kind of local control to be effective. The spectacular rise and fall of the AOL "walled garden," created on the assumption that the open web was unreliable, insecure, and pernicious, was for a time a striking historical reminder and warning to designers of closed resource collections.[57] But Facebook so far is succeeding by following a walled garden strategy.

2.3.2.2 "Information Architecture" and Organizing Systems

The discipline known as ***"information architecture"*** can be viewed as a specialized approach for designing the organizing systems and their associated interactions for information-intensive products and services, especially those implemented as websites, intranets, and online communities.[58] Abstract patterns of information content or organization are sometimes called architectures, so it is straightforward from the perspective of the discipline of organizing to define the activity of ***Information Architecture*** as **designing an abstract and effective organization of information and then exposing that organization to facilitate navigation and information use**.

Our definition of information architecture implies a methodology for the design of user interfaces and interactions that puts conceptual modeling at the foundation, considering presentation or physical design issues afterwards. Best practices in information architecture emphasize logical design patterns for organizing the resources, tasks, subject categories, and tools in user interfaces. The logical design is then translated into physical arrangements using windows, panes, menus, and other user interface components.[59] Separating content and structure from presentation, as we discussed in §1.2.3.1, "The Concept of "Organizing Principle"" (page 12), gives organizing systems more implementation alternatives and makes them more robust in the face of technology changes.

A model-based foundation is essential in information visualization applications, where users interact to explore the structure and meaning of large collections of data by taking multiple points of view at different levels of abstraction.[60]

Unfortunately, some practitioners of information architecture put less emphasis on conceptual modeling as an "inside-out" foundation for interaction design and more emphasis on an "outside-in" approach that highlights graphical and other presentation-tier considerations. Not beginning with explicit organizing principles implies more heuristic and design methods and less predictable results.

2.3.3 Organizing with Multiple Resource Properties

Multiple properties of the resources, the person organizing or intending to use them, and the social and technological environment in which they are being organized can collectively shape their organization. For example, the way you organize your home kitchen is influenced by the physical layout of counters, cabinets, and drawers; the dishes you cook most often; your skills as a cook, which may influence the number of cookbooks, specialized appliances and tools you own and how you use them; the sizes and shapes of the packages in the pantry and refrigerator; and even your height.

If multiple resource properties are considered in a fixed order, the resulting arrangement forms a **logical hierarchy**. The top level categories of resources are created based on the values of the property evaluated first, and then each category is further subdivided using other properties until each resource is classified in only a single category. A typical example of hierarchical arrangement for digital resources is the system of directories or folders used by a professor to arrange his personal document collection in a computer file system; the first level distinguishes personal documents from work-related documents; work is then subdivided into teaching and research, teaching is subdivided by year, and year divided by course. For physical resources, an additional step of mapping categories to physical locations is required; for example, resources in the category "kitchen utensils" might all be arranged in drawers near a workspace, with "silverware" arranged more precisely to separate knives, forks, and spoons.

An alternative to hierarchical organization that is often used in digital organizing systems is **faceted classification**, in which the different properties for the resources can be evaluated in any order. For example, you can select wines from the **wine.com** store catalog by type of grape, cost, or region and consider these property facets in any order. Three people might each end up choosing the same moderately-priced Kendall Jackson California Chardonnay, but one of them might have started the search based on price, one based on the grape varietal, and the third with the region. This kind of interaction in effect generates a different logical hierarchy for every different combination of property values, and each user made his final selection from a different set of wines.

Another way to understand *faceted classification* is that it allows a collection of description resources to be dynamically re-organized into as many categories as there are combinations of values on the descriptive facets, depending on the priority or point of view the user applies to the facets. Of course this only works because the physical resources are not themselves being rearranged, only their digital descriptions.

Chapter 7, *"Classification: Assigning Resources to Categories"* explains principles and methods for hierarchical and faceted classification in more detail.

2.4 Designing Resource-Based Interactions

There would be no point in selecting and organizing resources if they could not be accessed or interacted with in some way. Organizing systems vary a great deal in the types of resource-based interactions they enable and in the nature and extent of access they allow.

It is essential to distinguish the interactions that are designed into and directly supported by an organizing system from those that can take place with resources after they have been accessed. For example, when a book is checked out of a library it might be read, translated, summarized, criticized, or otherwise used —but none of these interactions are directly designed into the library. We need to focus on the interactions that are enabled because of the intentional acts of description or arrangement that transform a collection of resources into an organizing system. Note that some of these "designed interactions" might be explicitly supported in an organizing system containing digital books, as in Google's search engine where language translation is a supported service.

Users have direct access to original resources in a collection when they browse through library stacks or wander in museum galleries.[61] They have mediated or indirect access when they use catalogs or search engines, and sometimes they can only interact with copies or descriptions of the resources.

2.4.1 Affordance and Capability

The concept of **affordance**, introduced by J. J. Gibson and then extended and popularized by Donald Norman, captures the idea that physical resources and their environments have inherent actionable properties that determine, in conjunction with an actor's capabilities and cognition, what can be done with the resource.[62]

When organizing resources involves arranging physical resources using boxes, bins, cabinets, or shelves, the affordances and the implications for access and use can be easily perceived. Resources of a certain size and weight can be picked up and carried away. Books on the lower shelves of bookcases are easy to reach, but those stored ten feet from the ground cannot be easily accessed. Overhead and end-of-aisle signs support navigation and orientation in libraries and stores, and the information on book spines or product packages help us select a specific resource.

We can analyze the organizing systems with physical resources to identify the affordances and the possible interactions they imply. We can compare the affordances or overall interaction *capability* enabled by different organizing systems for some type of physical resources, and we often do this without thinking about it. The tradeoffs between the amount of work that goes into organizing a collection of resources and the amount of work required to find and use them are inescapable when the resources are physical objects or information resources are in physical form. We can immediately see that storing information on scrolls does not enable the random access capability that is possible with books. When you implement the organizing system for your clothes closet, you can see the number and arrangement of the shelves and consider the tradeoff between extensive and minimal organization and the implications for the amount of interaction effort required to put away and find clothes in each case.

What and how to count to compare the capabilities of organizing systems becomes more challenging the further we get from collections of static physical resources, like books or shoes, where it is usually easy to perceive and understand the possible interactions. With computers, information systems, and digital resources in general, considerations about affordances and capabilities are not as straightforward. First, the affordances we can perceive might not be tied to any useful interaction. Donald Norman joked that every computer screen within reaching distance affords touching, but unless the display is touch-sensitive, this affordance only benefits companies that sell screen-cleaning materials.[63]

Second, most of the interactions that are supported by digital resources are not apparent when you encounter them. You cannot tell from their names, but you probably know from past experience what interactions are possible with files of types ".doc" and ".pdf." You probably don't know what interactions take place with".xpi" and ".mobi" files.[64]

Once you have discovered it, the *capability* of digital resources and information systems can be assessed by counting the number of functions, services, or application program interfaces. However, this very coarse measure does not take into account differences in the capability or generality of a particular interaction. For example, two organizing systems might both have a search function, but differences in the operators they allow, the sophistication of pre-processing of the content to create index terms, or their usability can make them vastly differ in power, precision, and effectiveness.[65]

An analogous measure of functional capability for a system with dynamic or living resources is the behavioral repertoire, the number of different activities, or range of actions, that can be initiated.

We should not assume that supporting more types of interactions necessarily makes a system better or more capable; what matters is how much value is created or invoked in each interaction. Doors that open automatically when their sensors detect an approaching person do not need handles. Organizing systems can use stored or computed information about user preferences or past interactions to anticipate user needs or personalize recommendations. This has the effect of substituting information for interaction to make interactions unnecessary or simpler.

For example, a current awareness service that automatically informs you about relevant news from many sources makes it unnecessary to search any of them separately. Similarly, a "smart travel agent" service can use a user's appointment calendar, past travel history, and information sources like airline and hotel reservation services to transform a minimal interaction like "book a business trip to New York for next week's meeting" into numerous hidden queries that would have otherwise required separate interactions.[66]

2.4.2 Interaction and Value Creation

A useful way to distinguish types of interactions with resources is according to the way in which they create value, using a classification proposed by Apte and Mason. They noted that interactions differ not just in their overall intensity but in the absolute and relative amounts of physical manipulation, interpersonal or empathetic contact, and symbolic manipulation or information exchange involved in the interaction. Furthermore, Apte and Mason recognized that the proportions of these three types of value creating activities can be treated as design parameters, especially where the value created by retrieving or computing information could be completely separated or disaggregated from the value created by physical actions and person-to-person encounters.[67]

2.4.2.1 Value Creation with Physical Resources

Physical manipulation is often the intrinsic type of interaction with collections of physical resources. The resource might have to be handled or directly perceived in order to interact with it, and often the experience of interacting with the resource is satisfying or entertaining, making it a goal in its own right. People often visit museums, galleries, zoos, animal theme parks or other institutions that contain physical resources because they value the direct, perceptual, or otherwise unmediated interaction that these organizing systems support.

Physical manipulation and interpersonal contact might be required to interact with information resources in physical form like the printed books in libraries. A large university library contains millions of books and academic journals, and access to those resources can require a long walk deep into the library stacks after a consultation with a reference librarian. For decades library users searched through description resources—first printed library cards, and then online catalogs and databases of bibliographic citations—to locate the primary resources they wanted to access. The surrogate descriptions of the resources needed to be detailed so that users could assess the relevance of the resource without expending the significant effort of examining the primary resource.[68]

However, for most people the primary purpose of interacting with a library is to access the information contained in its resources. For most people access in a digital library to copies of printed documents or books is equivalent to or even better than access to the original physical resource because the incidental physical and interpersonal interactions have been eliminated.[69]

In some organizing systems robotic devices, computational processes, or other entities that can act autonomously with no need for a human agent carry out interactions with physical resources. Robots have profoundly increased efficiency in materials management, "picking and packing" in warehouse fulfillment, office mail delivery, and in many other domains where human agents once located, retrieved, and delivered physical resources. A "librarian robot" that can locate books and grasp them from the shelves shows promise.[70]

Interactions with physical resources often have highly tangible results; in the preceding examples of fulfillment and delivery interactions, resources move from one location to another. However, if we take an abstract or architectural perspective on interaction design and value creation, this often creates more flexibility in carrying out the interactions while still producing the value that the user of the organizing system expects. For example, the user of the organizing system that implements an Internet-based retail business model need not know and probably doesn't care which delivery service carries out a request to deliver a package from a warehouse. Presenting the interaction to the user as the "delivery service" rather than as a "FedEx" or "UPS" service allows the retailer to choose the best service provider for each delivery. Going even further, if you need printed documents at a conference, sales meeting, or somewhere else other than your current location, the interaction you desire is "provide me with documents at this location" and not "deliver my documents." It does not matter that FedEx will print your documents at their destination rather than shipping them there. In general, more abstract descriptions of interactions and services allow for transparent substitution of the implementation, potentially enabling a computational process to be a substitute for one carried out by a person, or vice versa.

2.4.2.2 Value Creation with Digital Resources

With digital resources, neither physical manipulation nor interpersonal contact is required for interactions, and the essence of the interaction is information exchange or symbolic manipulation of the information contained in the resource.[71] Put another way, by replacing interactions that involve people and physical resources with symbolic ones, organizing systems can lower their costs without reducing user satisfaction. This is why so many businesses have automated their information-intensive processes with self-service technology like ATMs, websites, or smart phone apps.

Similarly, web search engines eliminate the physical effort required to visit a library and enable users to consult more readily accessible digital resources. A search engine returns a list of the page titles of resources that can be directly accessed with just another click, so it takes little effort to go from the query results to the primary resource. This reduces the need for the rich surrogate descriptions that libraries have always been known for because it enables rapid evaluation and iterative query refinement based on inspection of the primary resources.[72]

The ease of use and speed of search engines in finding web resources creates the expectation that any resource worth looking at can be found on the web. This is certainly false, or Google would never have begun its ambitious and audacious project to digitize millions of books from research libraries. While research libraries strive to provide access to authoritative and specialized resources, the web is undeniably good enough for answering most of the questions ordinary users put to search engines, which largely deal with everyday life, popular culture, personalities, and news of the day.

Libraries recognize that they need to do a better job integrating their collections into the "web spaces" and web-based activities of their users if they hope to change the provably suboptimal strategies of "information foraging" most people have adopted that rely too much on the web and too little on the library.[73] Some libraries are experimenting with *Semantic Web* and "Linked Data" technologies that would integrate their extensive bibliographic resources with resources on the open web. But whether and how libraries should expose their collections is somewhat controversial.[74]

In contrast, museums have aggressively embraced the web to provide access to their collections. While few museum visitors would prefer viewing a digital image over experiencing an original painting, sculpture, or other physical artifact, the alternative is often no access at all. Most museum collections are far larger than the space available to display them, so the web makes it possible to provide access to otherwise hidden resources.[75]

The variety and functions of interactions with digital resources are determined by the amount of structure and semantics represented in their digital encoding, in the descriptions associated with the resources, or by the intelligence of the computational processes applied to them. Digital resources can support enhanced interactions of searching, copying, zooming, and other transformations. Digital or "e-books" demonstrate how access to content can be enhanced once it is no longer tied to the container of the printed book, but ebook readers vary substantially in their interaction repertoires; the baseline they all share is "page turning," resizing, and full-text search.[76]

Richer interactions with digital text resources are possible when they are encoded in an application or presentation-independent format. Automated content reuse and "single-source publishing" is most efficiently accomplished when text is encoded in Extensible Markup Language (XML), but much of this XML is produced by transforming text originally created in word processing formats. Once it is in XML, digital information can be distributed, processed, reused, transformed, mixed, remixed, and recombined into different formats for different purposes, applications, devices, or users in ways that are almost impossible to imagine when it is represented in a tangible (and therefore static) medium like a book on a shelf or a box full of paper files.[77]

Businesses that create or own their information resources can readily take advantage of the enhanced interactions that digital formats enable. For libraries, however, copyright is often a barrier to digitization, both as a matter of law and because digitization enables copyright enforcement to a degree not possible with physical resources. As a result, digital books are somewhat controversial and problematic for libraries, whose access models were created based on the economics of print publication and the social contract of the copyright first sale doctrine that allowed libraries to lend printed books.[78]

Software-based agents do analogous work to robots in "moving information around" after accessing digital resources such as web services or sensors that produce digital information. Agents can control or choreograph a set of interactions with digital resources to carry out complex business processes.

2.4.3 Access Policies

Different levels of interactions or access can apply to different resources in a collection or to different categories of users. For example, library collections can range from completely open and public, to allowing limited access, to wholly private and restricted.

The library stacks might be open to anyone, but the rare documents in a special collection might be accessible only to authorized researchers. The same is true of museums, which typically have only a fraction of their collections on public display.

Because of their commercial and competitive purposes, organizing systems in business domains are more likely to enforce a granular level of access control that distinguishes people according to their roles and that further distinguishes them according to the nature of their interactions with resources. For example, administrative assistants in a company's Human Resources department are not allowed to see employee salaries; HR employees in a benefits administration role can see the salaries but not change them; management-level employees in HR can change the salaries. Some firms limit access to specific times from authorized computers or IP addresses.[79]

A noteworthy situation arises when the person accessing the organizing system is the one who designed and implemented it. In this case, the person will have qualitatively better knowledge of the resources and the supported interactions. This situation most often arises in the organizing systems in kitchens, home closets, and other highly personal domains but can also occur in knowledge-intensive business and professional domains like consulting, customer relationship management, and scientific research.

Many of the organizing systems used by individuals are embedded in physical contexts where the access controls are applied in a coarse manner. We need a key to get into the house, but we do not need additional permissions or passwords to enter our closets or kitchens or to take a book from a bookshelf. In our online lives, however, we readily accept and impose more granular access controls on our personal computers and in the applications we use. For example, we might allow or block individual "friend" requests on Facebook or mark photos on Flickr as public, private, or viewable only by named groups or individuals.

We can further contrast access policies based on their origins or motivations.

Designed resource access policies are established by the designer or operator of an organizing system to satisfy internally generated requirements. Examples of designed access policies are: (1) giving more access to "inside" users (e.g., residents of a community, students or faculty members at a university, or employees of a company) than to anonymous or "outside" users; (2) giving more access to paying users than to users who don't pay; (3) giving more access to users with capabilities or competencies that can add value to the organizing system (e.g., material culture researchers like archaeologists or anthropologists, who often work with resources in museum collections that are not on display).

Imposed Policies are mandated by an external entity and the organizing system must comply with them. For example, an organizing system might have to follow information privacy or security regulations that restrict access to resources or the interactions that can be made with them. University libraries typically complement or replace parts of their print collections with networked access to digital content licensed from publishers. Typical licensing terms then require them to restrict access to users that are associated with the university, either by being on campus or by using virtual private network (VPN) software that controls remote access to the library network.[80] Copyright law limits the uses of a substantial majority of the books in the collections of major libraries, prohibiting them from being made fully available in digital formats. Museums often prohibit photography because they do not own the rights to modern works they display.

Whether an access policy is designed or imposed is not always clear. Policies that were originally designed for a particular organizing system may over time become best practices or industry standards, which regulators or industry groups not satisfied with "self-regulation" later impose. Museums might aggressively enforce a ban on photography not just to comply with copyright law, but also to enhance the revenue they get from selling posters and reproductions.

2.5 Maintaining Resources

Maintaining resources is an important activity in every organizing system regardless of the nature of its collection because resources or surrogates for them must be available at the time they are needed. Beyond these basic shared motivations are substantial differences in *maintenance* goals and methods depending on the domain of the organizing system.

Different domains sometimes use the same terms to describe different *maintenance* activities and different terms for similar activities. The most common terms are *storage*, *preservation*, *curation*, and *governance*. Storage is most often used when referring to physical or technological aspects of maintaining resources; backup (for short-term storage), archiving (for long-term storage), and migration (moving stored resources from one storage device to another) are similar in this respect. The other three terms generally refer to activities or methods and more closely overlap in meaning; we will distinguish them in §2.5.2 through §2.5.4.

Ideally, *maintenance* requirements for resources should be anticipated when organizing principles are defined and implemented. In particular, resource descriptions to support long-term preservation of digital resources are important.[81]

2.5.1 Motivations for Maintaining Resources

The concept of "memory institution" broadly applies to a great many organizing systems that share the goal of preserving knowledge and cultural heritage.[82] The primary resources in libraries, museums, data archives or other "memory institutions" are fixed cultural, historic, or scientific artifacts that are maintained because they are unique and original items with future value. This is why the Louvre preserves the portrait of the *Mona Lisa* and the United States National Archives preserves the *Declaration of Independence*.[83]

In contrast, in the organizing systems used by businesses many of the resources that are collected and managed have limited intrinsic value. The motivation for preservation and maintenance is economic; resources are maintained because they are essential in running the business. For example, businesses collect and preserve information about employees, inventory, orders, invoices, etc., because it ensures internal goals of efficiency, revenue generation and competitive advantage. The same resources (such as information about a customer) are often used by more than one part of the business.[84] Maintaining the accuracy and consistency of changing resources is a major challenge in business organizing systems.[85]

Many business organizing systems preserve information needed to satisfy externally imposed regulatory or compliance policies and serve largely to avoid possible catastrophic costs from penalties and lawsuits. In all these cases, resources are maintained as one of the means employed to preserve the business as an ongoing enterprise, not as an end in itself.

Unlike library, archives, and museums, indefinite preservation is not the central goal of most business organizing systems. These organizing systems mostly manage information needed to carry out day-to-day operations or relatively recent historical information used in decision support and strategic planning. In addition to these internal mandates, businesses have to conform to securities, taxation, and compliance regulations that impose requirements for long-term information preservation.[86]

Of course, libraries, museums, and archives also confront economic issues as they seek to preserve and maintain their collections and themselves as memory institutions.[87] They view their collections as intrinsically valuable in ways that firms generally do not. Art galleries are an interesting hybrid because they organize and preserve collections that are valuable, but if they do not manage to sell some things, they will not stay in business.

In between these contrasting purposes of preservation and maintenance are the motives in personal collections, which occasionally are created because of the inherent value of the items but more typically because of their value in supporting personal activities. Some people treasure old photos or collectibles that belonged to their parents or grandparents and imagine their own children or grandchildren enjoying them, but many old collections seem to end up as offerings on eBay. In addition, many personal organizing systems are task-oriented, so their contents need not be preserved after the task is completed.[88]

2.5.2 Preservation

At the most basic level, **preservation** of resources means maintaining them in conditions that protect them from physical damage or deterioration. Libraries, museums, and archives aim for stable temperatures and low humidity. Permanently or temporarily out-of-service aircraft are parked in deserts where dry conditions reduce corrosion. Risk-aware businesses create continuity plans that involve off-site storage of the data and documents needed to stay in business in the event of a natural disaster or other disruption.

When the goal is indefinite preservation, other *maintenance* issues arise if resources deteriorate or are damaged. How much of an artifact's worth is locked in with the medium used to express it? How much restoration should be attempted? How much of the essence of an artifact is retained if it is converted to a digital format?

2.5.2.1 Digitization and Preserving Resources

Preservation is often a key motive for **digitization**, but digitization alone is not preservation. Digitization creates preservation challenges because technological obsolescence of computer software and hardware require ongoing efforts to ensure the digitized resources can be accessed.

Technological obsolescence is the major challenge in maintaining digital resources. The most visible one is a result of the relentless evolution of the physical media and environments used to store digital information in both institutional or business and personal organizing systems. Computer data began to be stored on magnetic tape and hard disk drives six decades ago, on floppy disks four decades ago, on CDs three decades ago, on DVDs two decades ago, on solid-state drives half a decade ago, and in "cloud-based" or "virtual" storage environments in the last decade. As the capacity of storage technologies grows from kilobytes to megabytes to gigabytes to terabytes to petabytes, economic and efficiency considerations often make the case to adopt new technology to store newly acquired digital resources and raise questions about what to do with the existing ones.[89]

The second challenge might seem paradoxical. Even as the capacities of digital storage technologies increase at a staggering pace, the expected useful lifetimes of the physical storage media are measured in years or at best in decades. Colloquial terms for this problem are "data rot" or "bit rot." In contrast, books printed on acid-free paper can last for centuries. The contrast between printed and digital resources is striking; books on library shelves don't disappear if no one uses them, but digital data can be lost just because no one wants access to it within a year or two after its creation.[90]

However, limits to the physical lifetime of digital storage media are much less significant than the third challenge, the fact that the software and its associated computing environment used to parse and interpret the resource at the time of preservation might no longer be available when the resource needs to be accessed. Twenty-five years ago most digital documents were created using the Word Perfect word processor, but today the vast majority is created using Microsoft Word and few people use Word Perfect today. Software and services that convert documents from old formats to new ones are widely available, but they are only useful if the old file can be read from its legacy storage medium.[91]

Because almost every digital device has storage associated with it, problems posed by multiple storage environments can arise at all scales of organizing systems. Only a few years ago people often struggled with migrating files from their old computer, music player or phone when they got new ones. Web-based email and applications and web-based storage services like Dropbox, Amazon Cloud Drive, and Apple iCloud eliminate some data storage and migration problems by making them someone else's responsibility, but in doing so introduce privacy and reliability concerns.

It is easy to say that the solutions to the problems of digital preservation are regular recopying of the digital resources onto new storage media and then migrating them to new formats when significantly better ones come along. In practice, however, how libraries, businesses, government agencies or other enterprises deal with these problems depends on their budgets and on their technical sophistication. In addition, not every resource should or can always be migrated, and the co-existence of multiple storage technologies makes an organizing system more complex because different storage formats and devices can be collectively incompatible. Dealing with interoperability and integration problems will be discussed further in Chapter 9, *"Interactions with Resources"*.

The Hathi Trust Digital Library

The Hathi Trust (*http://www.hathitrust.org/*) is a worldwide partnership of several dozen major research institutions and libraries dedicated to "collecting, organizing, preserving, communicating, and sharing the record of human knowledge." The Hathi Trust was established in 2008 to coordinate the efforts of libraries in managing the digital copies of the books they received in return for providing books to Google for its book digitization projects. Since then the Hathi Trust has broadened its scope to include the public domain books collected by the Internet Archive and numerous other digital collections, and today its digital library has over ten million volumes. The costs of running the Hathi Trust and its digital library are shared in a transparent manner by the institutions that contributed digital collections or that want access to them, which reduces the costs for everyone compared to a "go it alone" strategy. The Hathi Trust Digital Library has separate modes for catalog search and full-text search of the library contents, unlike commercial search engines that do not distinguish them. A second important difference between the Hathi Trust Digital Library and commercial search engines is the absence of display advertising and "sponsored search" results.

2.5.2.2 Preserving the Web

Preservation of web resources is inherently problematic. Unlike libraries, museums, archives, and many other kinds of organizing systems that contain collections of unchanging resources, organizing systems on the web often contain resources that are highly dynamic. Some websites change by adding content, and others change by editing or removing it.[92]

Longitudinal studies have shown that hundreds of millions of web pages change at least once a week, even though most web pages never change or change infrequently.[93] Nevertheless, the continued existence of a particular web page is hardly sufficient to preserve it if it not popular and relevant enough to show up in the first few pages of search results. Persistent access requires preservation, but preservation isn't meaningful if there is no realistic probability of future access.

Comprehensive web search engines like Google and Bing use crawlers to continually update their indexed collections of web pages and their search results link to the current version, so preservation of older versions is explicitly not a goal. Furthermore, search engines don't reveal any details about how frequently they update their collections of indexed pages.[94]

> ### The Internet Archive and the "Wayback Machine"
>
> The Internet Archive (**Archive.org**), founded by Brewster Kahle, makes preservation of the web its first and foremost activity, and when you enter a URI into its "Wayback Machine" you can see what a site looked like at different moments in time. For example, `www.berkeley.edu` was archived about 2500 times between October 1996 and January 2013, including about twice a week on average during all of 2012. Even so, since a large site like berkeley.edu often changes many times a day, the Wayback Machine's preservation of berkeley.edu is incomplete, and it only preserves a fraction of the web's sites. The Internet Archive has recently launched the "Archive-It" service to enable schools, libraries and other public institutions to archive collections of digital resources.[95]

2.5.2.3 Preserving Resource Instances

A focus on preserving particular resource instances is most clear in museums and archives, where collections typically consist of unique and original items. There are many copies and derivative works of the *Mona Lisa*, but if the original *Mona Lisa* were destroyed none of them would be acceptable as a replacement.[96]

Archivists and historians argue that it is essential to preserve original documents because they convey more information than just their textual content. Paul Duguid recounts how a medical historian used faint smells of vinegar in eighteenth century letters to investigate a cholera epidemic because disinfecting letters with vinegar was thought to prevent the spread of the disease. Obviously, the vinegar smell would not have been part of a digitized letter.[97]

Zoos often give a distinctive or attractive animal a name and then market it as a special or unique instance. For example, the Berlin Zoo successfully marketed a polar bear named Knut to become a world famous celebrity, and the zoo made millions of dollars a year through increased visits and sales of branded merchandise. Merchandise sales have continued even though Knut died unexpectedly in March 2011, which suggests that the zoo was less interested in preserving that particular polar bear than in preserving the revenue stream based on that resource.[98]

Most business organizing systems, especially those that "run the business" by supporting day-to-day operations, are designed to preserve instances. These include systems for order management, customer relationship management, inventory management, digital asset management, record management, email archiving, and more general-purpose document management. In all of these domains, it is often necessary to retrieve specific information resources to serve customers or to meet compliance or traceability goals.

2.5.2.4 Preserving Resource Types

Some business organizing systems are designed to preserve types or classes of resources rather than resource instances. In particular, systems for content management typically organize a repository of reusable or "source" information resources from which specific "product" resources are then generated. For example, content management systems might contain modular information about a company's products that are assembled and delivered in sales or product catalogs, installation guides, operating guides, or repair manuals.[99]

Businesses strive to preserve the collective knowledge embodied in the company's people, systems, management techniques, past decisions, customer relationships, and intellectual property. Much of this knowledge is "know how"—knowing how to get things done or knowing how things work—that is tacit or informal. **Knowledge management systems** (KMS) are a type of business organizing system whose goal is to capture and systematize these information resources.[100] As with content management, the focus of knowledge management is the reuse of "knowledge as type," putting the focus on the knowledge rather than the specifics of how it found its way into the organizing system.

Libraries have a similar emphasis on preserving resource types rather than instances. The bulk of most library collections, especially public libraries, is made up of books that have many equivalent copies in other collections. When a library has a copy of *Moby Dick* it is preserving the abstract "work" rather than the particular physical "instance"—unless the copy of *Moby Dick* is a rare first edition signed by Melville.

Even when zoos give their popular animals individual names, it seems logical that the zoo's goal is to preserve animal species rather than instances because any particular animal has a finite lifespan and cannot be preserved forever.[101]

2.5.2.5 Preserving Resource Collections

In some organizing systems any specific resource might be of little interest or importance in its own right but is valuable because of its membership in a collection of essentially identical items. This is the situation in the data warehouses used by businesses to identify trends in customer or transaction data or in the huge data collections created by scientists. These collections are typically analyzed as complete sets. A scientist does not borrow a single data point when she accesses a data collection; she borrows the complete data set consisting of millions or billions of data points. This requirement raises difficult questions about what additional software or equipment need to be preserved in an organizing system along with the data to ensure that it can be reanalyzed.[102]

Sometimes, specific items in a collection might have some value or interest on their own, but they acquire even greater significance and enhanced meaning because of the context created by other items in the collection that are related in some essential way. The odd collection of "things people swallow that they should not" at the Mütter Museum is a perfect example.[103]

2.5.3 Curation

For almost a century **curation** has been used to describe the processes by which a resource in a collection is maintained over time, which may include actions to improve access or to restore or transform its representation or presentation.[104] Furthermore, especially in cultural heritage collections, curation also includes research to identify, describe, and authenticate resources in a collection. Resource descriptions are often updated to reflect new knowledge or interpretations about the primary resources.[105]

Curation takes place in all organizing systems—at a personal scale when we rearrange a bookshelf to accommodate new books or create new file folders for this year's health insurance claims, at an institutional scale when a museum designs a new exhibit or a zoo creates a new habitat, and at web scale when people select photos to upload to Flickr or Facebook and then tag or "Like" those uploaded by others.

An individual, company, or any other creator of a website can make decisions and employ technology that maintains the contents, quality and character of the site over time. In that respect website curation and governance practices are little different than those for the organizing systems in memory institutions or business enterprises. The key to curation is having clear policies for collecting resources and maintaining them over time that enable people and automated processes to ensure that resource descriptions or data are authoritative, accurate, complete, consistent, and non-redundant.

2.5.3.1 Institutional Curation

Curation is most necessary and explicit in institutional organizing systems where the large number of resources or their heterogeneity requires choices to be made about which ones should be most accessible, how they should be organized to ensure this access, and which ones need most to be preserved to ensure continued accessibility over time. Curation might be thought of as an ongoing or deferred selection activity because curation decisions must often be made on an item-by-item basis.

Curation in these institutional contexts requires extensive professional training. The institutional authority empowers individuals or groups to make curation decisions. No one questions whether a museum curator or a compliance manager should be doing what they do.[106]

Resource descriptions are more important in company Intranets than in the open web because the contents of the former lack the links that are critical in the latter.

2.5.3.2 Individual Curation

Curation by individuals has been studied a great deal in the research discipline of Personal Information Management (PIM).[107] Much of this work has been influenced for decades by a seminal article written by Vannevar Bush titled "As We May Think." Bush envisioned the Memex, "a device in which an individual stores all his books, records, and communications, and which is mechanized so that it may be consulted with exceeding speed and flexibility." Bush's most influential idea was his proposal for organizing sets of related resources as "trails" connected by associative links, the ancestor of the *hypertext links* that define today's web.[108]

2.5.3.3 Social and Web Curation

Many individuals spend a great amount of time curating their own websites, but when a site can attract large numbers of users, it often allows users to annotate, "tag," "like," "+1," and otherwise evaluate its resources. The concept of curation has recently been adapted to refer to these volunteer efforts of individuals to create, maintain, and evaluate web resources.[109] The massive scale of these bottom-up and distributed activities is curation by "crowdsourcing," the continuously aggregated actions and contributions of users.[110]

The informal and organic "folksonomies" that result from their aggregated effort create organization and authority through network effects.[111] This undermines traditional centralized mechanisms of organization and governance and threatens any business model in publishing, education, and entertainment that has relied on top-down control and professional curation.[112] Professional curators are not pleased to have the *ad hoc* work of untrained people working on websites described as curation.

Most websites are not curated in a systematic way, and the decentralized nature of the web and its easy extensibility means that the web as a whole defies curation. It is easy to find many copies of the same document, image, music file, or video and not easy to determine which is the original, authoritative or authorized version. Broken links return "Error 404 Not Found" messages.[113]

Problems that result from lazy or careless webmastering are minor compared to those that result from deliberate misclassification, falsification, or malice. An entirely new vocabulary has emerged to describe these web resources with bad intent: "spam," "phishing," "malware," "fakeware," "spyware," "keyword stuffing," "spamdexing," "META tag abuse," "link farms," "cybersquatters," "phantom sites," and many more.[114] Internet service providers, security software firms, email services, and search engines are engaged in a constant war against these kinds of malicious resources and techniques.[115]

Since we cannot prevent these deceptions by controlling what web resources are created in the first place, we have to defend ourselves from them after the fact. "Defensive curation" techniques include filters and firewalls that block access to particular sites or resource types, but whether this is curation or censorship is often debated, and from the perspective of the government or organization doing the censorship it is certainly curation. Nevertheless, the decentralized nature of the web and its open protocols can sometimes enable these controls to be bypassed.

2.5.3.4 Computational Curation

Search engines continuously curate the web because the algorithms they use for determining relevance and ranking determine what resources people are likely to access. At a smaller scale, there are many kinds of tools for managing the quality of a website, such as ensuring that HTML content is valid, that links work, and that the site is being crawled completely. Another familiar example is the spam and content filtering that takes place in our email systems that automatically classifies incoming messages and sorts them into appropriate folders.

In organizing systems that contain data, there are numerous tools for "name matching," the task of determining when two different text strings denote the same person, object, or other named entity. This problem of eliminating duplicates and establishing a controlled or authoritative version of the data item arises in numerous application areas but familiar ones include law-enforcement and counter-terrorism. Done incorrectly, it might mean that you end up on a "watch list" and are hassled every time you want to fly on a commercial plane.

One might think that computational curation is always more reliable than any curation carried out by people. Certainly, it seems that we should always be able to trust any assertion created by context-aware resources like a sensor that reports the temperature or reports current location. But can we trust the accuracy of web content? Search engines use the popularity of web pages and the structure of links between them to compute relevance in response to a query. But popularity and relevance don't always ensure accuracy. We can easily find popular pages that prove the existence of UFOs or claim to validate wacky conspiracy theories.

Furthermore, search engines have long been accused of bias built into their algorithms. For example, Google's search engine has been criticized for giving too much credibility to websites with .edu domain names, to sites that have been around for a long time, or that are owned by or that partner with the company, like Google Maps or YouTube.[116]

2.5.4 Governance

"Governance" overlaps with "curation" in meaning but typically has more of policy focus (what should be done) rather than a process focus (how to do it). Governance is also more frequently used to describe the curation of the resources in business and scientific organizing systems rather than in libraries, archives, and museums. Governance has a broader scope than curation because it extends beyond the resources in a collection and also applies to the software, computing, and networking environments needed to use them. This broader scope also means that governance must specify the rights and responsibilities for the different types of people who might interact with the resources, the circumstances under which that might take place, and the methods they would be allowed to use.

"Corporate governance" is a common term applied to the ongoing maintenance and management of the relationship between operating practices and long-term strategic goals. Libraries and museums must also deal with long-term strategy, but the lesser visibility of "library governance" and "museum governance" might simply reflect the greater concerns about fraud and malfeasance in for-profit business contexts than in non-profit contexts and the greater number of standards or "best practices" for corporate governance.[117]

"Data governance" policies are often shaped by laws, regulations or policies that prohibit the collection of certain kinds of objects or types of information. Privacy laws prohibit the collection or misuse of personally identifiable information about healthcare, education, telecommunications, video rental, and might soon restrict the information collected during web browsing.[118]

2.5.4.1 Governance in Business Organizing Systems

Governance is essential to deal with the frequent changes in business organizing systems and the associated activities of data quality management, access control to ensure security and privacy, compliance, deletion, and archiving. For many of these activities, effective governance involves the design and implementation of standard services to ensure that the activities are performed in an effective and consistent manner.[119]

Today's information-intensive businesses capture and create large amounts of digital data. The concept of "business intelligence" emphasizes the value of data in identifying strategic directions and the tactics to implement them in marketing, customer relationship management, supply chain management and other information-intensive parts of the business.[120] A management aspect of governance in this domain is determining which resources and information will potentially provide economic or competitive advantages and determining which will not. A conceptual and technological aspect of governance is determining how best to organize the useful resources and information in business operations and information systems to secure the potential advantages.

Business intelligence is only as good as the data it is based on, which makes business data governance a critical concern that has rapidly developed its own specialized techniques and vocabulary. The most fundamental governance activity in information-driven businesses is identifying the "master data" about customers, employees, materials, products, suppliers, etc. that is reused by different business functions and is thus central to business operations.[121]

Because digital data can be easily copied, data governance policies might require that all sensitive data be anonymized or encrypted to reduce the risk of privacy breaches. To identify the source of a data breach or to facilitate the assertion of a copyright infringement claim a digital watermark can be embedded in digital resources.[122]

2.5.4.2 Governance in Scientific Organizing Systems

Scientific data poses special *governance* problems because of its enormous scale, which dwarfs the data sets managed in most business organizing systems. A scientific data collection might contain tens of millions of files and petabytes of data. Furthermore, because scientific data is often created using specialized equipment or computers and undergoes complex workflows, it can be necessary to curate the technology and processing context along with data in order to preserve it. An additional barrier to effective scientific data curation is the lack of incentives in scientific culture and publication norms to invest in data retention for reuse by others.[123]

2.6 Key Points in Chapter Two

- Selection, organizing, interaction design, and maintenance activities occur in every organizing system.

- These activities are not identical in every domain, but the general terms enable communication and learning about domain-specific methods and vocabularies.

- The most fundamental decision for an organizing system is determining its resource domain, the group or type of resources that are being organized.

- Even when the selection principles behind a collection are clear and consistent, they can be unconventional, idiosyncratic, or otherwise biased.

- Most organizing systems use principles that are based on specific resource properties or properties derived from the collection as a whole.

- Some arrangements of physical resources are constrained or precluded by resource properties that might cause problems for other resources or for their users.

- Digital organizing systems can support collections and interactions at a scale that is impossible in organizing systems that are entirely physical.

- Multiple properties of the resources, the person organizing or intending to use them, and the social and technological environment in which they are being organized can collectively shape their organization.

- We focus on the interactions that are designed into and directly supported by an organizing system because of intentional acts of description or arrangement.

- The tradeoffs between the amount of work that goes into organizing a collection of resources and the amount of work required to find and use them are inescapable when the resources are physical objects or information resources are in physical form.

- We should not assume that supporting more types of interactions necessarily makes a system better or more capable; what matters is how much value is created or invoked in each interaction.

- With digital resources, the essence of the interaction is information exchange or symbolic manipulation of the information contained in the resource.

- The variety and functions of interactions with digital resources are determined by the amount of structure and semantics represented in their digital encoding, in the descriptions associated with the resources, or by the intelligence of the computational processes applied to them.

- Preservation of resources means maintaining them in conditions that protect them from physical damage or deterioration.

- Preservation is often a key motive for digitization, but digitization alone is not preservation.

- Comprehensive web search engines use crawlers to continually update their indexed collections of web pages and their search results link to the current version, so preservation of older versions is explicitly not a goal.

- The essence of curation and governance is having clear policies for collecting resources and maintaining them over time that enable people and automated processes to ensure that resource descriptions or data are authoritative, accurate, complete, consistent, and non-redundant.

- Personal Information Management has been influenced for decades by a seminal article written by Vannevar Bush titled "As We May Think".

- Governance is essential to deal with the frequent changes in business organizing systems and the associated activities of data quality management, access control to ensure security and privacy, compliance, deletion, and archiving.

- Scientific data poses special governance problems because of its enormous scale.

Notes

36. [Law] Some governments attempt to preserve and prevent misappropriation of "cultural property" by enforcing import or export controls on antiquities that might be stolen from archaeological sites (Merryman 2006). For digital resources, privacy laws prohibit the collection or misuse of personally identifiable information about healthcare, education, telecommunications, video rental, and might soon restrict the information collected during web browsing.

37. [LIS] Large research libraries have historically viewed their *collections* as their intellectual capital and have policies that specify the subjects and sources that they intend to emphasize as they build their collections. See (Evans 2000). Museums are often wary of accepting items that might not have been legally acquired or that have claims on them from donor heirs or descendant groups; in the USA, much controversy exists because museums contain many human skeletal remains and artifacts that Native American groups want to be "repatriated." In archives, common appraisal criteria include uniqueness, the credibility of the source, the extent of documentation, and the rights and potential for reuse. To

oversimplify: libraries decide what to keep, museums decide what to accept, and archives decide what to throw away.

38. [Business] *Selection* of a person involves assessing the match between competencies and capabilities (expressed verbally or in a resume, or demonstrated in some qualification test) and what is needed to do the required activities. Selection of athletes for sports teams can involve psychological, behavioral, and performance criteria and has become highly data-intensive, as the *Moneyball* book (Lewis 2003) and 2011 movie starring Brad Pitt demonstrate.

39. [Computing] On data modeling: see (Kent 2012), (Silverston 2000), (Glushko and McGrath 2005). For data warehouses see (Turban et al. 2010).

40. [Computing] See (Cherbakov et al. 2005), (Erl 2005a). The essence of SOA is to treat business services or functions as components that can be combined as needed. An SOA enables a business to quickly and cost-effectively change how it does business and whom it does business with (suppliers, business partners, or customers). SOA is generally implemented using web services that exchange XML documents in real-time information flows to interconnect the business service components. If the business service components are described abstractly it can be possible for one service provider to be transparently substituted for another—a kind of real-time resource selection—to maintain the desired quality of service. For example, a web retailer might send a Shipping Request to many delivery services, one of which is selected to provide the service. It probably does not matter to the customer which delivery service handles his package, and it might not even matter to the retailer.

41. [Business] The idea that a firm's long term success can depend on just a handful of critical capabilities that cut across current technologies and organizational boundaries makes a firm's core competency a very abstract conceptual model of how it is organized. This concept was first proposed by (Pralahad and Hamel 1990), and since then there have been literally hundreds of business books that all say essentially the same thing: you cannot be good at everything; choose what you need to be good at and focus on getting better at them; let someone else do things that you do not need to be good at doing.

42. [LIS] See (Borgman 2000) on digitization and libraries. But while shared collections benefit users and reduce acquisition costs, if a library has defined itself as a physical place and emphasizes its **holdings**—the resources it directly controls—it might resist anything that reduces the importance of its physical reification, the size of its holdings or the control it has over resources (Sandler 2006). A challenge facing conventional libraries today is to make the transition from a perspective that emphasizes creation and preservation of physical collections to facilitating the use and creation of knowledge regardless of the medium of its representation and the physical or virtual location from which it is accessed.

43. [Web] (Arasu et al. 2001), (Manning et al. 2008). The web is a graph, so all web crawlers use graph traversal algorithms to find URIs of web resources and then add any hyperlink they find to the list of URIs they visit. The sheer size of the web makes crawling its pages a bandwidth- and computation intensive process, and since some pages change frequently and others not at all, an effective crawler must be smart at how it prioritizes the pages it collects and how it re-crawls pages. A web crawler for a search engine can determine the most relevant, popular, and credible pages from query logs and visit them more often. For other sites, a crawler adjusts its "revisit frequency" based on the "change frequency" (Cho and Garcia-Molina 2000).

44. [Web] Web resources are typically discovered by computerized "web crawlers" that find them by following links in a methodical automated manner. Web crawlers can be used to create topic-based or domain-specific collections of web resources by changing the "breadth-first" policy of generic crawlers to a "best-first" approach. Such "focused crawlers" only visit pages that have a high probability of being relevant to the topic or domain, which can be estimated by analyzing the similarity of the text of the linking and linked pages, terms in the linked page's URI, or locating explicit semantic annotation that describes their content or their interfaces if they are invokable services (Bergmark et al. 2002), (Ding et al. 2004).

45. [CogSci] In this book we use "property" in a generic and ordinary sense as a synonym for "feature" or "characteristic." Many cognitive and computer scientists are more precise in defining these terms and reserve "property" for binary predicates (e.g., something is red or not, round or not, and so on). If multiple values are possible, the "property" is called an "attribute," "dimension," or "variable." See (Barsalou and Hale 1983) for a rigorous contrast between feature lists and other representational formalisms in models of human categories.

46. [LIS] Libraries and bookstores use different classification systems. The kitchen in a restaurant is not organized like a home kitchen because professional cooks think of cooking differently than ordinary people do. Scientists use the Latin or binomial (genus + species) scheme for identifying and classifying living things to avoid the ambiguities and inconsistencies of common names, which differ across languages and often within different regions in a single language community.

47. [LIS] Many of the ancient libraries in Greece and Rome have been identified by archaeologists by characteristic architectural features (Casson 2002). See also (Battles 2003).

48. [Law] In principle, it is easy to make perfect copies of digital resources. In practice, however, many industries employ a wide range of technologies including digital rights management, watermarking, and license servers to prevent copying of documents, music or video files, and other digital resources. The de-

gree of copying allowed in digital organizing systems is a design choice that is shaped by law.

49. [Web] Web-based or "cloud" services are invoked through URIs, and good design practice makes them permanent even if the implementation or location of the resource they identify changes (Berners-Lee 1998). Digital resources are often replicated in content delivery networks to improve performance, reliability, scalability, and security (Pathan et al. 2008); the web pages served by a busy site might actually be delivered from different parts of the world, depending on where the accessing user is located.

50. [Computing] Whether a digital resource seems intangible or tangible depends on the scale of the digital collection and whether we focus on individual resources or the entire collection. An email message is an identified digital resource in a standard format, RFC 2822 (Resnick 2001). We can compare different email systems according to the kinds of interactions they support and how easy it is to carry them out, but how email resources are represented does not matter to us and they surely seem intangible. Similarly, the organizing system we use to manage email might employ a complex hierarchy of folders or just a single searchable in-box, but whether that organization is implemented in the computer or smart phone we use for email or exists somewhere "in the cloud" for web-based email does not much matter to us either. An email message is tangible when we print it on paper, but all that matters then is that there is well-defined mapping between the different representations of the abstract email resource.

On the other hand, at the scale at which Google and Microsoft handle billions of email messages in their Gmail and HotmaiL services the implementation of the email organizing system is extremely relevant and involves many tangible considerations. The location and design of data centers, the configuration of processors and storage devices, the network capacity for delivering messages, whether messages and folder structures are server or client based, and numerous other considerations contribute to the quality of service that we experience when we interact with the email organizing system.

51. [Archives] An emerging issue in the field of digital humanities (Schreibman, Siemens, and Unsworth 2005) is the requirement to recognize the *materiality* of the environment that enables people to create and interact with digital resources (Leonardi 2010). Even if the resources themselves are intangible, it can be necessary to study and preserve the technological and social context in which they exist to fully understand them. For example, a "Born-Digital Archives" program at Emory University is preserving a collection of the author Salman Rushdie's work that includes his four personal computers and an external hard drive (Kirschenbaum 2008), (Kirschenbaum et al. 2009).

52. [Web] For example, a car dealer might be able to keep track of a few dozen new and used cars on his lot even without a computerized inventory system, but web-based AutoTrader.com offered more than 2,000,000 cars in 2012. The cars are physical resources where they are located in the world, but they are represented in the AutoTrader.com organizing system as digital resources, and cars can be searched for using any combination of the many resource properties in the car listings: price, body style, make, model, year, mileage, color, location, and even specific car features like sunroofs or heated seats.

53. [Computing] Even when organizing principles such as *alphabetical, chronological,* or numerical ordering do not explicitly consider physical properties, how the resources are arranged in the "storage tier" of the organizing system can still be constrained by their physical properties and by the physical characteristics of the environments in which they are arranged. Books can only be stacked so high whether they are arranged alphabetically or by frequency of use, and large picture books often end up on the taller bottom shelf of bookcases because that is the only shelf they fit. Nevertheless, it is important to treat these idiosyncratic outcomes in physical storage as exceptions and not let them distort the choice of the organizing principles in the "logic tier."

54. [Web] The Domain Name System (DNS) (Mockapetris 1987) is the hierarchical naming system that enables the assignment of meaningful domain names to groups of Internet resources. The responsibility for assigning names is delegated in a distributed way by the Internet Corporation for Assigned Names and Numbers (ICANN) (*http://www.icann.org*). DNS is an essential part of the Web's organizing system but predates it by almost twenty years.

55. [Web] HTML5 defines a "manifest" mechanism for making the boundary around a collection of web resources explicit even if somewhat arbitrary to support an "offline" mode of interaction in which all needed resources are continually downloaded (*http://www.w3.org/TR/html5/browsers.html#offline*), but many people consider it unreliable and subject to strange side effects.

56. [Web] (Aalbersberg and Kahler 2011).

57. [Web] (Munk 2004).

58. [Computing] This definition of "information architecture" combines those in a Wikipedia article (*http://en.wikipedia.org/wiki/Information_architecture*) and in a popular book with the words in its title (Morville and Rosenfield 2006). Nevertheless, given the abstract elegance of "information" and "architecture" any definition of "information architecture" seems a little feeble.

59. [Computing] See (Tidwell 2008) for a repertoire of design patterns. (Morville and Rosenfield 2006) classify design patterns as "organization schemes" and "organization structures," reinforcing the idea that information architecture is a sub-specialty of the discipline of organizing.

60. [CogSci] The classic text about information visualization is *The Visual Display of Quantitative Information* (Tufte 1983). More recent texts include (Few 2012) and (Yau 2011).

61. [Museums] Except when the resources on display are replicas of the originals, which is more common than you might suspect. Many nineteenth century museums in the United States largely contained copies of pieces from European museums. Today, museums sometimes display replicas when the originals are too fragile or valuable to risk damage (Wallach 1998). Whether the "resource-based interaction" is identical for the replica and original is subjective and depends on how well the replica is implemented.

62. [CogSci] (Gibson 1977), (Norman 1988). See also (Norman 1999) for a short and simple explanation of Norman's (re-)interpretation of Gibson.

63. [CogSci] (Norman 1999, p. 39).

64. [Computing] The ".xpi" file type is used for Mozilla/Firefox browser extensions, small computer programs that can be installed in the browser to provide some additional user interface functionality or interaction. The ".mobi" file type was originally developed to enable better document display and interactions on devices with small screens. Today its primary use is as the base ebook format for the Amazon Kindle, except that the Kindle version is more highly compressed and locked down with digital rights management.

65. [Computing] See (Hearst 2009), (Buettcher et al. 2010).

66. [Computing] (Glushko and Nomorosa 2013). These queries are interconnected by logical or causal dependencies that are represented by information that overlaps between them. For example, all travel-related services (airlines, hotels, ground transportation) need the traveler's identity and the time and location of his travel. A New York trip might involve all of these services, and they need to fit together in time and location for the trip to make sense. The hotel reservation needs to begin the day the flight arrives in the destination city, the limousine service needs to meet the traveler shortly after the plane lands, and the restaurant reservation should be convenient in time and location to the hotel.

67. [Business] (Apte and Mason 1995) introduced this framework to analyze services rather than interactions *per se*. They paid special attention to services where the value created by symbolic manipulation or information exchange could be completely separated or disaggregated from the value created by person-to-person interactions. This configuration of value creation enables automated self-service, in which the human service provider can be replaced by technology, and outsourcing, in which the human provider is separated in space or time from the customer.

68. [LIS] Furthermore, many of the resources might not be available in the user's own library and could only be obtained through inter-library loan, which could take days or weeks.

69. [Museums] In addition, many of the interactions in libraries are searches for known items, and this function is easily supported by digital search. In contrast, far fewer interactions in museum collections are searches for known items, and serendipitous interactions with previously unknown resources are often the goal of museum visitors. As a result, few museum visitors would prefer an online visit to experiencing an original painting, sculpture, or other physical artifact. However, it is precisely because of the unique character of museum resources that museums allow access to them but do not allow visitors to borrow them, in clear contrast to libraries.

70. [LIS] (Viswanadham 2002), (Madrigal 2009), (Prats et al. 2008). A video of a robot librarian in action at the University of Missouri, Kansas City is at *http://www.youtube.com/watch?v=8wJJLlTq7ts*.

71. [LIS] Providing access to knowledge is a core mission of libraries, and it is worth pointing out that library users obtain knowledge both from the primary resources in the library collection and from the organizing system that manages the collection.

72. [Web] It also erodes the authority and privilege that apply to resources because they are inside the library when a web search engine can search the "holdings" of the web faster and more comprehensively than you can search a library's collection through its online catalog.

73. [Web] (Pirolli 2007).

74. [Web] (Byrne and Goddard 2010).

75. [Museums] See (Simon 2010). An exemplary project to enhance museum access is Delphi (Schmitz and Black 2008), the collections browser for the Phoebe A. Hearst Museum of Anthropology at University of California, Berkeley. Delphi very cleverly uses natural language processing techniques to build an easy-to-use faceted browsing user interface that lets users view over 600,000 items stored in museum warehouses.Delphi is being integrated into Collection Space (*http://www.collectionspace.org/*), an open source web collections management system for museum collections, collaboratively being developed by University of California, Berkeley, Cambridge University, Ontario Academy of Art and Design (OCAD) , and numerous museums.

76. [Computing] To augment digital resources with text structures, multimedia, animation, interactive 3-D graphics, mathematical functions, and other richer content types requires much more sophisticated representation formats that tend to require a great deal of "hand-crafting."

An alternative to hand-crafted resource description is sophisticated computer processing guided by human inputs. For example, Facebook and many web-based photo organizing systems implement face recognition analysis that detects faces in photos, compares features of detected faces to features of previously identified faces, and encourages people to tag photos to make the recognition more accurate. Some online services use similar image classification techniques to bring together shoes, jewelry, or other items that look alike.

77. [Computing] Even sophisticated text representation formats such as XML have inherent limitations: one important problem that arises in complex management scenarios, humanities scholarship, and bioinformatics is that XML markup cannot easily represent overlapping substructures in the same resource (Schmidt 2009).

78. [Law] Digital books change the economics and first sale is not as well-established for digital works, which are licensed rather than sold (Aufderheide and Jaszi 2011). To protect their business models, many publishers are limiting the number of times e-books can be lent before they "self-destruct." Some librarians have called for boycotts of publishers in response (*http://boycotthar percollins.com*).

In contrast to these new access restrictions imposed by publishers on digital works, many governments as well as some progressive information providers and scientific researchers have begun to encourage the reuse and reorganization of their content by making geospatial, demographic, environmental, economic, and other datasets available in open formats, as web services, or as data feeds rather than as "fixed" publications (Bizer 2009a), (Robinson et al. 2008). And we have made this book available as an open content repository so that it can be collaboratively maintained and customized.

79. [Business] These access controls to the organizing system or its host computer are enforced using passwords and more sophisticated software and hardware techniques. Some access control policies are mandated by regulations to ensure privacy of personal data, and policies differ from industry to industry and from country to country. Access controls can improve the credibility of information by identifying who created or changed it, especially important when traceability is required (e.g. financial accounting).

80. [Law] In response to this trend, however, many libraries are supporting "open access" initiatives that strive to make scholarly publications available without restriction (Bailey 2007). Libraries and e-book vendors are engaged in a tussle about the extent to which the "first sale" rule that allows libraries to lend physical books without restrictions also applies to e-books (Howard 2011).

81. [Archives] (Guenther and Wolfe 2009).

82. [LIS] This is the historical and dominant conception of the research library, but libraries are now fighting to prove that they are much more than just repositories because many of their users place greater value "on-the-fly access" of current materials. See (Teper 2005) for a sobering analysis of this dilemma.

83. [Archives] Today the United States National Archives displays the *Declaration of Independence*, *Bill of Rights*, and the *U.S. Constitution* in sealed titanium cases filled with inert argon gas. Unfortunately, for over a century these documents were barely preserved at all; the Declaration hung on the wall at the United States Patent Office in direct sunlight for about 40 years.

84. [Business] Customer information drives day-to-day operations, but is also used in decision support and strategic planning.

85. [Web] For businesses "in the world," a "customer" is usually an actual person whose identity was learned in a transaction, but for many web-based businesses and search engines a customer is a computational model extracted from browser access and click logs that is a kind of "theoretical customer" whose actual identity is often unknown. These computational customers are the targets of the computational advertising in search engines.

86. [Law] The *Sarbanes-Oxley Act* in the United States and similar legislation in other countries require firms to preserve transactional and accounting records and any document that relates to "internal controls," which arguably includes any information in any format created by any employee (Langevoort 2006). Civil procedure rules that permit discovery of evidence in lawsuits have long required firms to retain documents, and the proliferation of digital document types like email, voice mail, shared calendars and instant messages imposes new storage requirements and challenges (Levy and Casey 2006). However, if a company has a data retention policy that includes the systematic deletion of documents when they are no longer needed, courts have noted that this is not willful destruction of evidence.

87. [LIS] Libraries are increasingly faced with the choice of providing access to digital resources through renewable licensing agreements, "pay per view" arrangements, or not at all. To some librarians, however, the failure to obtain permanent access rights "offends the traditional ideal of libraries" as memory institutions (Carr 2010).

88. [CogSci] For example, students writing a term paper usually organize the printed and digital resources they rely on; the former are probably kept in folders or in piles on the desk, and the latter in a computer file system. This organizing system is not likely to be preserved after the term paper is finished. An exception that proves the rule is the task of paying income taxes for which (in the USA) taxpayers are legally required to keep evidence for up to seven years after

filing a tax return (*http://www.irs.gov/Businesses/Small-Businesses-&-Self-Employed/How-long-should-I-keep-records%3F*).

89. [Computing] (Rothenberg 1999).

90. [Computing] (Pogue 2009).

91. [Archives] Many of those Word Perfect documents were stored on floppy disks because floppy disk drives were built into almost every personal computer for decades, but it would be hard to find such disk drives today. And even if someone with a collection of word processor documents stored of floppy disks in 1995 had copied those files to newer storage technologies, it is unlikely that the current version of the word processor would be able to read them. Software application vendors usually preserve "backwards compatibility" for a few years with earlier versions to give users time to update their software, but few would support older versions indefinitely because to do so can make it difficult to implement new features.

Digital resources can be encoded using non-proprietary and standardized data formats to ensure "forward compatibility" in any software application that implements the version of the standard. However, if the e-book reader, web browser, or other software used to access the resource has capabilities that rely on later versions of the standards the "old data" will not have taken advantage of them.

92. [Web] This is tautologically true for sites that publish news, weather, product catalogs with inventory information, stock prices, and similar continually updated content because many of their pages are automatically revised when events happen or as information arrives from other sources. It is also true for blogs, wikis, Facebook, Flickr, YouTube, Yelp and the great many other "Web 2.0" sites whose content changes as they incorporate a steady stream of user-generated content. In some cases the changes are attempts to rewrite history and prevent preservation by removing all traces of information that later turned out to be embarrassing, contradictory, or politically incorrect.

93. [Web] (Fetterly et al. 2003).

94. [Web] However, when a website disappears its first page can often be found in the search engine's index "cache" rather than by following what would be a broken link.

95. [Archives] Brewster Kahle has been described as a computer engineer, Internet entrepreneur, internet activist, advocate of universal access to knowledge, and digital librarian (*http://en.wikipedia.org/wiki/Brewster_Kahle*). In addition to websites, the Internet Archive preserves several million books, over a million pieces of video, 400,000 news programs from broadcast TV, over a million audio recordings, and over 100,000 live music concerts.

The Memento project has proposed a specification for using HTTP headers to perform "datetime negotiation" with the Wayback Machine and other archives of web pages, making it unnecessary for Memento to save anything on its own. Memento is implemented as a browser plug-in to "browse backwards in time" whenever older versions of pages are available from archives that use its specification. (VandeSompel 2010).

96. [Archives] People might still enjoy the many *Mona Lisa* parodies and recreations. See *http://www.megamonalisa.com*, *http://www.oddee.com/item_96790.aspx*, *http://www.chilloutpoint.com/art_and_design/the-best-mona-lisa-parodies.html*.

97. [Archives] (Brown and Duguid 2002).

98. [Museums] (Savodnik 2011).

99. [Computing] The set of content modules and their assembly structure for each kind of generated document conforms to a template or pattern that is called the document type model when it is expressed in XML.

100. [Business] Company intranets, wikis, and blogs are often used as knowledge management technologies; Lotus Notes and Microsoft SharePoint are popular commercial systems. See the case study in §10.7.2, "Knowledge Management for a Small Consulting Firm" (page 424).

101. [Business] In addition, the line between "preserving species" and "preserving marketing brands" is a fine one for zoos with celebrity animals, and in animal theme parks like Sea World, it seems to have been crossed. "Shamu" was the first killer whale (orca) to survive long in captivity and performed for several years at SeaWorld San Diego. Shamu died in 1971 but over forty years later all three US-based SeaWorld parks have Shamu shows and Shamu webcams.

102. [Archives] (Manyika et al. 2011).

103. [Museums] The College of Physicians of Philadelphia's Mütter Museum houses a novel collection of artifacts meant to "educate future doctors about anatomy and human medical anomalies." No museum in the world is like it; it contains display cases full of human skulls, abnormal fetuses in jars, preserved human bodies, a garden of medicinal herbs, and many other unique collections of resources.

However, one sub-collection best reflects the distinctive and idiosyncratic *selection* and arrangement of resources in the museum. Chevalier Jackson, a distinguished laryngologist, collected over 2,000 objects extracted from the throats of patients. Because of the peculiar focus and educational focus of this collection, and because there are few shared characteristics of "things people swallow that they should not," the characteristics and principles used to organize and describe the collection would be of little use in another organizing system. What other collection would include toys, bones, sewing needles, coins, shells, and dental material? It is hard to imagine that any other collection that would include all of these items plus fully annotated record of sex and approximate age of patient, the amount of time the extraction procedure took, the tool used, and whether or not the patient survived.

104. [LIS] Curation is a very old concept whose Medieval meaning focused on the "preservation and cure of souls" by a pastor, priest, or "curate" (Simpson and Weiner 1989). A set of related and systematized curation practices for some class of resources is often called a curation system, especially when they are embodied in technology.

105. [Archives] Information about which resources are most often interacted with in scientific or archival collections is essential in understanding resource value and quality.

106. [LIS] In memory institutions, the most common job titles include "curator" or "conservator." In for-profit contexts where "*governance*" is more common than "curation" job titles reflect that difference. In addition to "governance," job titles often include "recordkeeping," "compliance," or "regulatory" prefixes to "officer," "accountant," or "analyst" job classifications.

107. [CogSci] Because personal collections are strongly biased by the experiences and goals of the organizer, they are highly idiosyncratic, but still often embody well-thought-out and carefully executed curation activities (Kirsh 2000), (Jones 2007), (Marshall 2007),(Marshall 2008).

108. [Computing] (Bush 1945). Bush imagined that Memex users could share these packages of trails and that a profession of trailbuilders would emerge. However, he did not envision that the Memexes themselves could be interconnected, nor did he imagine that their contents could be searched computationally.

109. [Web] (Howe 2008).

110. [Web] The most salient example of this so called "community curation" activity is the work to maintain the Wikipedia open-source encyclopedia according to a curation system of roles and functions that governs how and under what conditions contributors can add, revise, or delete articles; receive notifications of changes to articles; and resolve editing disputes (Lovink and Tkacz 2011). Some museums and scientific data repositories also encourage voluntary curation to analyze and classify specimens or photographs (Wright 2010).

111. [Web] (Trant 2009b).

112. [Business] Some popular "community content" sites like Yelp where people rate local businesses have been criticized for allowing positive rating manipula-

tion. Yelp has also been criticized for allowing negative manipulation of ratings when competitors slam their rivals.

113. [Web] The resource might have been put someplace else when the site was reorganized or a new web server was installed. It is no longer the same resource because it will have another URI, even if its content did not change.

114. [Computing] All of these terms refer to types of web resources or techniques whose purpose is to mislead people into doing things or letting things be done to their computers that will cost them their money, time, privacy, reputation, or worse. We know too well what spam is. Phishing is a type of spam that directs recipients to a fake website designed to look like a legitimate one to trick them into entering account numbers, passwords, or other sensitive personal information. Malware, fakeware, or spyware sites offer tempting downloadable content that installs software designed to steal information from or take control of the visiting computer. Keyword stuffing, spamdexing, and META tag abuse are techniques that try to mislead search engines about the content of a resource by annotating it with false descriptions. Link farms or scraper sites contain little useful or original content and exist solely for the purpose of manipulating search engine rankings to increase advertising revenue. Similarly, cybersquatters register domain names with the hope of profiting from the goodwill of a trademark they do not own.

115. [Computing] (Brown 2009).

116. [Computing] (Diaz 2005), (Grimmelmann 2009).

117. [LIS] (Kim, Nofsinger, and Mohr 2009).

118. [Law] Data governance decisions are also often shaped by the need to conform to information or process model standards, or to standards for IT service management like the *Information Technology Infrastructure Library* (ITIL). See *http://www.itil-officialsite.com/*.

119. [Business] In this context, these management and maintenance activities are often described as "IT governance" (Weill and Ross 2004). Data classification is an essential IT governance activity because the confidentiality, competitive value, or currency of information are factors that determine who has access to it, how long it should be preserved, and where it should be stored at different points in its lifecycle.

120. [Business] (Turban et al. 2010).

121. [Computing] This master data must be continually "cleansed" to remove errors or inconsistencies, and "de-duplication" techniques are applied to ensure an authoritative source of data and to prevent the redundant storage of many copies of the same resource. Redundant storage can result in wasted time searching for the most recent or authoritative version, cause problems if an out-

dated version is used, and increase the risk of important data being lost or stolen. (Loshin 2008).

122. [Computing] (Cox et al. 2007).

123. [Law] Recently imposed requirements by the National Science Foundation (NSF), National Institute of Health (NIH) and other research granting agencies for researchers to submit "data management plans" as part of their proposals should make digital data curation a much more important concern (Borgman 2011). (NSF Data Management Plan Requirements: *http://www.nsf.gov/eng/general/dmp.jsp*).

Chapter 3
Resources in Organizing Systems

Robert J. Glushko
Daniel D. Turner
Kimra McPherson
Jess Hemerly

3.1 Introduction

This chapter builds upon the foundational concepts introduced in Chapter 1 to explain more carefully what we mean by **resource**. In particular, we focus on the issue of identity—what will be treated as a separate resource—and discuss the issues and principles we need to consider when we give each resource a name or identifier.

In §3.2, "Four Distinctions about Resources" (page 99) we introduce four distinctions we can make when we discuss resources: **domain**, **format**, **agency**, and **focus**. In §3.3, "Resource Identity" (page 109) we apply these distinctions as we discuss how resource identity is determined for physical resources, bibliographic resources, resources in information systems, as well as for *active resources* and "smart things." §3.4, "Naming Resources" (page 116) then tackles the problems and principles for naming: once we have identified resources, how do we name and distinguish them? Finally, §3.5, "Resources over Time" (page 123) considers issues that emerge with respect to resources over time.

3.1.1 What Is a Resource?

Resources are what we organize.

We introduced the concept of *resource* in §1.2.1, "The Concept of "Resource"" (page 8) with its ordinary sense of "anything of value that can support goal-oriented activity" and emphasized that a group of resources can be treated as a *collection* in an organizing system. And what do we mean by "anything of value," exactly? It might seem that the question of **identity**, of what a single resource is, should not be hard to answer. After all, we live in a world of resources, and finding, selecting, describing, arranging, and referring to them are everyday activities.

Nevertheless, even when the resources we are dealing with are tangible things, how we go about organizing them is not always obvious, or at least not obvious to each of us in the same way at all times. Not everyone thinks of them in the same way. Recognizing something in the sense of perceiving it as a tangible thing is only the first step toward being able to organize it and other resources like it. Which properties garner our attention, and which we use in organizing depends on our experiences, purposes, and context.

We add information to a resource when we name or describe it; it then becomes more than "it." We can describe the same resource in many different ways. At various times we can consider any given resource to be one of many members of a broad category, as one of the few members of a narrow category, or as a unique instance of a category with only one member. For example, we might recognize something as a piece of clothing, as a sock, or as the specific dirty sock with the hole worn in the heel from yesterday's long hike. However, even after we categorize something, we might not be careful how we talk about it; we often refer to two objects as "the same thing" when what we mean is that they are "the same type of thing." Indeed, we could debate whether a category with only one possible member is really a category, because it blurs an important distinction between particular items or instances and the class or type to which they belong.

The issues that matter and the decisions we need to make about resource instances and resource classes and types are not completely separable. Nevertheless, we will strive to focus on the former ones in this chapter and the latter ones in Chapter 6, *"Categorization: Describing Resource Classes and Types"*.

3.1.1.1 Resources with Parts

As tricky as it can be to decide what a resource is when you are dealing with single objects, it is even more challenging when the resources are objects or systems composed of other parts. In these cases, we must focus on the entirety of the object or system and treat it as a resource, treat its constituent parts as resources, and deal with the relationships between the parts and the whole, as we do with engineering drawings and assembly procedures.

How many things is a car? If you are imagining the car being assembled you might think of several dozen large parts like the frame, suspension, drive train, gas tank, brakes, engine, exhaust system, passenger compartment, doors, and other pre-assembled components. Of course, each of those components is itself made up of many parts—think of the engine, or even just the radio. Some sources have counted ten or fifteen thousand parts in the average car, but even at that precise granularity a lot of parts are still complex things. There are screws and wires and fasteners and on and on; really too many to count.

Ambiguity about the number of parts in the whole holds for information resources too; a newspaper can be considered a single resource but it might also consist of multiple sections, each of which contains separate stories, each of which has many paragraphs, and so on. From the typesetter's point of view, each character in a sentence can be taken as a distinct resource, selected from a font of similar resources.

3.1.1.2 Bibliographic Resources, Information Components, and "Smart Things" as Resources

Information resources generally pose additional challenges in their identification and description because their most important property is usually their content, which is not easily and consistently recognizable. Organizing systems for information resources in physical form, like those for libraries, have to juggle the duality of their tangible embodiment with what is inherently an abstract information resource; that is, the printed book versus the knowledge the book contains. Here, the organizing system emphasizes description resources or surrogates, like bibliographic records that describe the information content, rather than their physical properties.

Another important question in libraries is: What set of resources should be treated as the same work because they contain essentially similar intellectual or artistic content? We may talk about Shakespeare's play *Macbeth*, but what is this thing we call "Macbeth"? Is it a particular string of words, saved in a computer file or handwritten upon a folio? Is it the collection of words printed with some predetermined font and pagination? Are all the editions and printings of these words the same *Macbeth*? How should we organize the numerous live and recorded performances of plays and movies that share the *Macbeth* name? What about creations based on or inspired by *Macbeth* that do not share the title "Macbeth," like the Kurosawa film " *Kumonosu-jo* " (*Throne of Blood*) that transposes the plot to feudal Japan? Patrick Wilson proposed a genealogical analogy, characterizing a "work" as "a group or family of texts," with the idea that a creation like Shakespeare's *Macbeth* is the "ancestor of later members of the family."[124]

Information system designers and architects face analogous design challenges when they describe the "information components" in business or scientific organizing systems. Information content is intrinsically merged or confounded with structure and presentation whenever it is used in a specific instance and context. From a logical perspective, an order form contains information components for ITEM, CUSTOMER NAME, ADDRESS, and PAYMENT INFORMATION, but the arrangement of these components, their type font and size, and other non-semantic properties can vary a great deal in different order forms and even across a single information system that re-purposes these components for letters, delivery notices, mailing labels, and database entries.[125]

Similar questions about resource identity are posed by the emergence of ubiquitous or pervasive computing, in which information processing capability and connectivity are embedded into physical objects, in devices like smart phones, and in the surrounding environment. Equipped with sensors, radio-frequency identification (RFID) tags, GPS data, and user-contributed metadata, these "smart things" create a jumbled torrent of information about location and other properties that must be sorted into identified streams and then matched or associated with the original resource.

§3.3, "Resource Identity" (page 109) discusses the issues and methods for determining "what is a resource?" for physical resources as well as for the bibliographic resources, information components and "smart things" discussed here in §3.1.1.1, "Resources with Parts" (page 96).

3.1.2 Identity, Identifiers, and Names

The answer to the question posed in §3.1.1, "What Is a Resource?" (page 96) has two parts. The first part is *identity*: what thing are we treating as the resource? The second part is identification: differentiating between this single resource and other resources like it. These problems are closely related. Once you have decided what to treat as a resource, you create a name or an identifier so that you can refer to it reliably. A **name** is a label for a resource that is used to distinguish one from another. An **identifier** is a special kind of name assigned in a controlled manner and governed by rules that define possible values and naming conventions. For a digital resource, its identifier serves as the input to the system or function that determines its location so it can be retrieved, a process called **resolving** the identifier or **resolution**.

Choosing names and identifiers—be it for a person, a service, a place, a trend, a work, a document, a concept, etc.—is hardly straightforward. In fact, naming can often be challenging and is often highly contentious. Naming is made difficult by countless factors, including the audience that will need to access, share, and use the names, the limitations of language, institutional politics, and personal and cultural biases.

A common complication arises when a resource has more than one name or identifier. When something has more than one name each of the multiple names is a **synonym** or **alias**. A particular physical instance of a book might be called a hardcover or paperback or simply a text. George Furnas and his research collaborators called this issue of multiple names for the same resource or concept the "**vocabulary problem.**"[126]

Whether we call it a book or a text, the resource will usually have a Library of Congress catalog number as well as an ISBN as an *identifier*. When the book is in a carton of books being shipped from the publisher to a bookstore or library, that carton will have a bar-coded tracking number assigned by the delivery service, and a manifest or receipt document created by the publisher whose identifier associates the shipment with the customer. Each of these identifiers is unique with respect to some established scope or context.

A partial solution to the *vocabulary problem* is to use a **controlled vocabulary**. We can impose rules that standardize the way in which names and labels for resources are assigned in the first place. Alternatively, we can define mappings from terms used in our natural language to the authoritative or controlled terms. However, vocabulary control cannot remove all ambiguity. Even if a passport or national identity system requires authoritative full names rather than nicknames, there could easily be more than one Robert John Smith in the system.

Controlling the language used for a particular purpose raises other questions: Who writes and enforces these rules? What happens when organizing systems that follow different rules get compared, combined, or otherwise brought together in contexts different from those for which they were originally intended?

3.2 Four Distinctions about Resources

The nature of the resource is critical for the creation and maintenance of quality organizing systems. There are four distinctions we make in discussing resources: **domain**, **format**, **agency**, and **focus**. Figure 3.1, "Resource Domain, Format, Focus and Agency." depicts these four distinctions, perspectives or points of view on resources; because they are not independent, we cannot portray these distinctions as categories of resources.

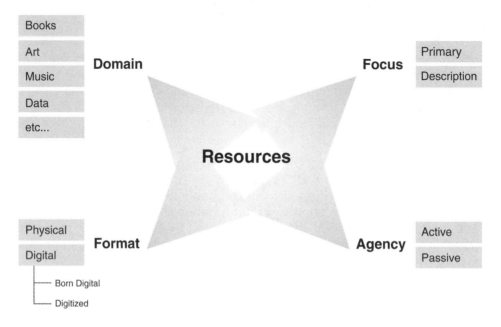

Figure 3.1. Resource Domain, Format, Focus and Agency.

3.2.1 Resource Domain

Every resource has some essence or type that distinguishes it from other resources, which we call the resource ***domain***. Domain is an intuitive notion that we can help define by contrasting it with the alternative of *ad hoc* or arbitrary groupings of resources that just happen to be in the same place at some moment, rather than being based on natural or intrinsic characteristics.

For physical resources, domains can be coarsely distinguished according to the type of matter of which they are made using properties that can be readily perceived. The top-level classification of all things into the animal, vegetable, and mineral kingdoms by Carl Linnaeus in 1735 is today deeply embedded in most languages and cultures to create a hierarchical system of domain categories.[127] Many aspects of this system of domain categories are determined by natural constraints on category membership that are manifested in patterns of shared properties; once a resource is identified as a member of one category it must also be a member of another with which it shares some but not all properties. For example, a marble statue in a museum must also be a kind of material resource, and a fish in an aquarium must also be a kind of animal resource.

For information resources, easily perceived properties are less reliable and correlated, so we more often distinguish domains based on semantic properties; the definitions of the "encyclopedia," "novel," and "invoice" resource types distinguish them according to their typical subject matter, or the type of content, rather than according to the great variety of physical forms in which we might encounter them. Arranging books by color or size might be sensible for very small collections, or in a photo studio, but organizing according to physical properties would make it extremely impractical to find books in a large library.

We can arrange types of information resources in a hierarchy but because the category boundaries are not sharp it is more useful to view domains of information resources on a continuum from weakly-structured narrative content to highly structured transactional content. This *framework*, called the *Document Type Spectrum* by Glushko and McGrath, captures the idea that the boundaries between resource domains, like those between colors in the rainbow, are easy to see for colors far apart in the spectrum but hard to see for adjacent ones.[128] (See the Sidebar, "The Document Type Spectrum" (page 101), and its corresponding depiction as Figure 3.2, "Document Type Spectrum.")

The Document Type Spectrum

Different domains or types of documents can be distinguished according to the extent to which their content is semantically prescribed, by the amount of internal structure, and by the correlations of their presentation and formatting to their content and structure. These three characteristics of content, structure, and presentation vary systematically from narrative document types like novels to transactional document types like invoices.

Narrative types are authored by people and are heterogeneous in structure and content, and their content is usually just prose and graphic elements. Their presentational characteristics carefully reinforce their structure and semantics; for example, the text of titles or major headings is large because the content is important, in contrast to the small text of footnotes. Transactional document types are usually created mechanically and, as a result, are homogeneous in structure and content; their content is largely "data" — strongly typed content with precise semantics that can be processed by computers.

In the middle of the spectrum are hybrid document types like textbooks, encyclopedias, and technical manuals that contain a mixture of narrative text and structured content in figures, data tables, code examples, and so on.

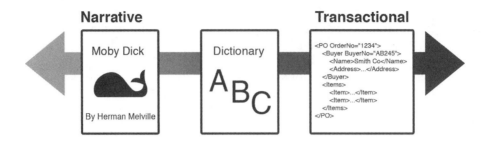

Figure 3.2. Document Type Spectrum.

3.2.2 Resource Format

Information resources can exist in numerous formats with the most basic format distinction being whether the resource is physical or digital. This distinction is most important when it comes to the implementation of a resource storage or preservation system because that is where physical properties are usually considerations, and very possibly constraints. This distinction is less important at the logical level when we design interactions with resources because it is often possible to use digital surrogates for the physical resources to overcome the constraints posed by their physical properties. When we search for cars or appliances in an online store it does not matter where the actual cars or appliances are located or how they are physically organized. (See the Sidebar, "The Three Tiers of Organizing Systems" (page 13)).

Many digital representations can be associated with either physical or digital resources, but it is important to know which one is the original or primary resource, especially for unique or valuable ones.

Today a great many resources in organizing systems are **born digital**. They are created in word processors and digital cameras, or by audio and video recorders. Other resources are produced in digital form by the many types of sensors in "smart things" and by the systems that create digital resources when they interact with barcodes, QR ("quick response") codes, RFID tags, or other mechanisms for tracking identity and location.[129]

Other digital resources are digitized ones created by **digitization**, the process for transforming an artifact whose original format is physical so that it can be stored and manipulated by a computer. We can digitize the printed word, photographs, blueprints and record albums. Printed text, for example, can be digitized by scanning the pages and employing character recognition software or simply by re-typing it.[130]

INFORMATION IQ

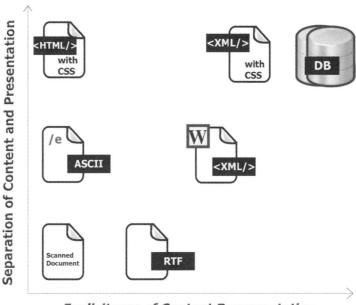

Figure 3.3. Information IQ.

There are a vast number of digital formats that differ in many ways, but we can coarsely compare them on two dimensions: the degree to which they distinguish information content from presentation or rendering, and the explicitness with which content distinctions are represented. Taken together, these two dimensions allow us to compare formats on their overall "Information IQ" —with the overarching principle being that "smarter" formats contain more computer-processable information, as illustrated in Figure 3.3, "Information IQ."

Simple digital formats for "plain text" documents contain only the characters that you see on your computer keyboard. *ASCII* is the most commonly used simple format, but ASCII is inadequate for most languages, which have larger character sets, and it also cannot handle mathematical characters.[131] The Unicode standard was designed to overcome these limitations.[132] (ASCII and Unicode are discussed in great detail in §8.3.1, "Notations" (page 340)).

Most document formats also explicitly encode a hierarchy of structural components, such as chapters, sections or semantic components like descriptions or procedural steps, and sometimes the appearance of the rendered or printed form.[133] Another important distinction to note is whether the information is encoded as a sequence of text characters so that it is human readable as well as computer readable. Encoding character content with XML, for example, allows for layering of intentional coding or *markup* interwoven with the "plain text" content. Because XML processors are required to support Unicode, any character can appear in an XML document. The most complex digital formats are those for multimedia resources and multidimensional data, where the data format is highly optimized for specialized analysis or applications.[134]

Digitization of non-text resources such as film photography, drawings, and analog audio and visual recordings raises a complicated set of choices about pixel density, color depth, sampling rate, frequency filtering, compression, and numerous other technical issues that determine the digital representation.[135] There may be multiple intended uses and devices for the digitized resource that might require different digitization approaches and formats. Moreover, downstream users of digitized resources often need to know the format in which the digital artifact has been created so they can reuse it as is or process it in other ways.

Some digital formats support interactions that are qualitatively different and more powerful than those possible with physical resources. Museums are using virtual world technology to create interactive exhibits in which visitors can fly through the solar system, scan their own bodies, and change gravity so they can bounce off walls. Sophisticated digital document formats can enable interactions with annotated digital images or video, 3-D graphics or embedded data sets. The Google Art Project contains extremely high resolution photographs of famous paintings that make it possible to see details that are undetectable under the normal viewing conditions in museums.[136]

Nevertheless, digital representations of physical resources can also lose important information and capabilities. The distinctive sounds of hip hop music produced by "scratching" vinyl records on turntables cannot be produced from digital MP3 music files.[137]

Copyright often presents a barrier to digitization, both as a matter of law and because digitization itself enables copyright enforcement to a degree not possible prior to the advent of digitization, by eliminating common forms of access and interactions that are inherently possible with physical printed books like the ability to give or sell them to someone else.[138]

3.2.3 Resource Agency

Agency, the extent to which a resource can initiate actions on its own is the third distinction we make about a resource. Another way to express this contrast is between passive resources that are acted upon and active resources that can initiate actions. Telephone answering and fax machines are agents because they are capable of independently responding to an outside stimulus, accepting and managing messages. An ordinary mercury thermometer is not capable of communicating its own reading, but a digital wireless thermometer or "weather station" can. Passive resources serve as nouns or operands, while active resources serve as verbs or operants.[139]

3.2.3.1 Passive or Operand Resources

Organizing systems that contain passive or operand resources are ubiquitous for the simple reason that we live in a world of physical resources that we identify and name in order to interact with them. ***Passive resources*** are usually tangible and static and thus they become valuable only as a result of some action or interaction with them.

Most organizing systems with physical resources or those that contain resources that are digitized equivalents treat those resources as passive. A printed book on a library shelf, a digital book in an e-book reader, a statue in a museum gallery, or a case of beer in a supermarket refrigerator only create value when they are checked out, viewed, or consumed. None of these resources exhibits any agency and cannot initiate any actions to create value on their own.

3.2.3.2 Active or Operant Resources

Active resources create effects or value on their own, sometimes when they initiate interactions with passive resources. Active resources can be people, other living resources, computational agents, active information sources, or web-based services. We can exploit computing capability, storage capacity and communication bandwidth to create active resources that can do things and support interactions that are impossible for ordinary physical passive resources.

Objects become active resources when they contain sensing or communication capabilities. RFID chips, which are essentially bar codes with built-in radio transponders, enable automated location tracking and context sensing. RFID Receivers are built into store shelves, loading docks, parking lots, and toll booths to detect when some RFID-tagged resource is at some meaningful location. RFID tags can be made "smarter" by having them record and transmit information from sensors that detect temperature, humidity, acceleration, and even biological contamination.[140]

Smart phones are *active resources* that can identify and share their own location, orientation, acceleration and a growing number of other *contextual parameters* to enable personalization of information services. Self-regulating appliances are active resources when they communicate with each other in a "smart building" to minimize energy consumption.

Many organizing systems on the web consist of collections or configurations of active digital resources. Interactions among these active resources often implement information-intensive business models where value is created by exchanging, manipulating, transforming, or otherwise processing information, rather than by manipulating, transforming, or otherwise processing physical resources.

Service Oriented Architecture (SOA) is an emerging design discipline for organizing active resources as functional business components that can be combined in different ways. SOA is generally implemented using web services that exchange XML documents in real-time information flows to interconnect the business service components.

A familiar design pattern for an organizing system composed from active digital resources is the "online store." The store can be analyzed as a composition or choreography in which some web pages display catalog items, others serve as "shopping carts" to assemble the order, and then a "checkout" page collects the buyer's payment and delivery information that gets passed on to other service providers who process payments and deliver the goods.

The web has enabled the novel application of human resources as active resources to carry out tasks of short duration that can be precisely described but which cannot be done reliably by computers. These tasks include image classification or annotation, spoken language transcription, and sentiment analysis. The people doing these tasks over the web are sometimes called "Mechanical Turks" by analogy to a fake chess playing machine from the 18th century that had a human hidden inside who was secretly moving the pieces.[141]

3.2.4 Resource Focus

A fourth contrast between types of resources distinguishes primary or original resources from resources that describe them. Any primary resource can have one or more description resources associated with it to facilitate finding, interacting with, or interpreting the primary one. Description resources are essential in organizing systems where the primary resources are not under its control and can only be accessed or interacted with through the description. Description resources are often called **metadata**.

The distinction between primary resources and description resources, or metadata, is deeply embedded in library science and traditional organizing systems whose collections are predominantly text resources like books, articles, or other documents. In these contexts description resources are commonly called bibliographic resources or catalogs, and each primary resource is typically associated with one or more description resources.

In business enterprises, the organizing systems for digital information resources, such as business documents, or data records created by transactions or automated processes, almost always employ resources that describe, or are associated with, large sets or classes of primary resources.[142]

The contrast between primary resources and description resources is very useful in many contexts, but when we look more broadly at organizing systems, it is often difficult to distinguish them, and determining which resources are primary and which are metadata is often just a decision about which resource is currently the **focus** of our attention.

For example, many people who use Twitter focus on the 140-character message body as the primary resource, while the associated metadata about the sender and the message (is it a forward, reply, link, and so on?) is less important to them. However, for firms in the growing ecosystem of services that use Twitter metadata to measure sender and brand impact, identify social networks, and assess trends, the focus is on the metadata, not the message content.[143]

As another example, the players on professional sports teams are human resources that we enjoy watching as they compete, but millions of people participate in fantasy sports leagues where teams consist of fantasy players that are simulated resources based on the statistics generated by the actual human players. Put another way, the associated resources in the actual sports are treated as the primary ones in the fantasy leagues.[144]

3.2.5 Resource Format x Focus

Applying the format contrast between physical and digital resources to the focus distinction between primary and descriptive resources yields a useful *framework* with four categories of resources (see Figure 3.4, "Resource Format x Focus.").

3.2.5.1 Physical Description of a Primary Physical Resource

The oldest relationship between descriptive resources and physical resources is when descriptions or other information about physical resources are themselves encoded in a physical form. Nearly ten thousand years ago in Mesopotamia small clay tokens kept in clay containers served as inventory information to count units of goods or livestock. It took 5000 years for the idea of stored tokens to evolve into Cuneiform writing in which marks in clay stood for the tokens and made both the tokens and containers unnecessary.[145] Printed cards

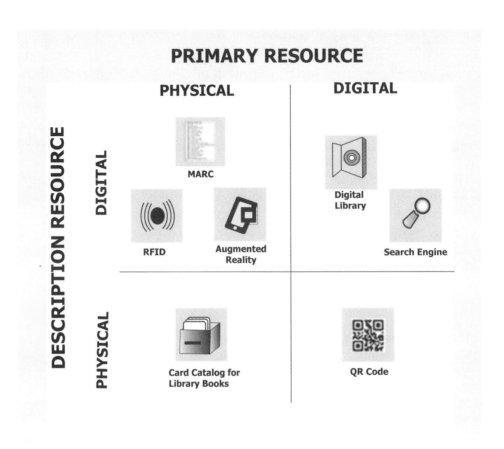

Figure 3.4. Resource Format x Focus.

served as physical description resources for books in libraries for nearly two centuries.[146]

3.2.5.2 Digital Description of a Primary Physical Resource

Here, the digital resource describes a physical resource. The most familiar example of this relationship is the online library catalog used to find the shelf location of physical library resources, which beginning in the 1960s replaced the physical cards with database records. The online catalogs for museums usually contain a digital photograph of the painting, item of sculpture, or other museum object that each catalog entry describes.

Digital description resources for primary physical resources are essential in supply chain management, logistics retailing, transportation, and every business model that depends on having timely and accurate information about where things are or about their current states. This digital description resource is created as a result of an interaction with a primary physical resource like a temperature sensor or with some secondary physical resource that is already associated with the primary physical resource like an RFID tag or barcode.

Augmented reality systems combine a layer of real-time digital information about some physical object to a digital view or representation of it. The yellow "first down" lines superimposed in broadcasts of football games are a familiar example. Augmented reality techniques that superimpose identifying or descriptive metadata have been used in displays to support the operation or maintenance of complex equipment, in smart phone navigation and tourist guides, in advertising, and in other domains where users might otherwise need to consult a separate information source. Advanced airplane cockpit technology includes heads-up displays that present critical data based on available instrumentation, including augmented reality runway lights when visibility is poor because of clouds or fog.

3.2.5.3 Digital Description of a Primary Digital Resource

Here, the digital resource describes a digital resource. This is the relationship in a digital library or any web-based organizing system and it makes it possible to access the primary digital resource directly from the digital secondary resource.

3.2.5.4 Physical Description of a Primary Digital Resource

This is the relationship implemented when we encounter an embedded QR barcode in newspaper or magazine advertisements, on billboards, sidewalks, t-shirts, or on store shelves. Scanning the QR code with a mobile phone camera can launch a website that contains information about a product or service, place an order for one unit of the pointed-to- item in a web catalog, dial a phone number, or initiate another application or service identified by the QR code.[147]

3.3 Resource Identity

Determining the identity of resources that belong in a domain, deciding which properties are important or relevant to the people or systems operating in that domain, and then specifying the principles by which those properties encapsulate or define the relationships among the resources are the essential tasks when building any organizing system. In organizing systems used by individuals or with small scope, the methods for doing these tasks are often *ad hoc* and unsystematic, and the organizing systems are therefore idiosyncratic and do not scale well. At the other extreme, organizing systems designed for institutional or industry-wide use, especially in information-intensive domains, require systematic design methods to determine which resources will have separate identities and how they are related to each other. These resources and their relationships are then described in conceptual models which guide the implementation of the systems that manage the resources and support interactions with them.[148]

3.3.1 Identity and Physical Resources

Our human visual and cognitive systems do a remarkable job at picking out objects from their backgrounds and distinguishing them from each other. In fact, we have little difficulty recognizing an object or a person even if we are seeing them from a novel distance and viewing angle or with different lighting, shading, and so on. When we watch a football game, we do not have any trouble perceiving the players moving around the field, and their contrasting uniform colors allow us to see that there are two different teams.

The perceptual mechanisms that make us see things as permanent objects with contrasting visible properties are just the prerequisite for the organizing tasks of identifying the specific object, determining the categories of objects to which it belongs, and deciding which of those categories is appropriate to emphasize. Most of the time we carry out these tasks in an automatic, unconscious way; at other times we make conscious decisions about them. For some purposes we consider a sports team as a single resource, as a collection of separate players for others, as offense and defense, as starters and reserves, and so on.[149]

Although we have many choices about how we can organize football players, all of them will include the concept of a single player as the smallest identifiable resource. We are never going to think of a football player as an intentional collection of separately identified leg, arm, head, and body resources because there are no other ways to "assemble" a human from body parts. Put more generally, there are some natural constraints on the organization of matter into parts or collections based on sizes, shapes, materials, and other properties that make us identify some things as indivisible resources in some domain.

3.3.2 Identity and Bibliographic Resources

Pondering the question of *identity* is something relatively recent in the world of librarians and catalogers. Libraries have been around for about 4000 years, but until the last few hundred years librarians created "bins" of headings and topics to organize resources without bothering to give each individual item a separate identifier or name. This meant searchers first had to make an educated guess as to which bin might house their desired information—"Histories"? "Medical and Chemical Philosophy"?—then scour everything in the category in a quest for their desired item. The choices were *ad hoc* and always local—that is, each cataloger decided the bins and groupings for each catalog.[150]

The first systematic approach to dealing with the concept of *identity* for bibliographic resources was developed by Antonio Panizzi at the British Museum in the mid-19th century. Panizzi wondered: How do we differentiate similar objects in a library catalog? His solution was a catalog organized by author name with an index of subjects, along with his newly concocted *Rules for the Compilation of the Catalogue*. This contained 91 rules about how to identify and arrange author names and titles and what to do with anonymous works. The rules were meant to codify how to differentiate and describe each singular resource in his library. Taken together, the rules serve to group all the different editions and versions of a work together under a single identity.[151]

The concept of identity for bibliographic resources was refined in the 1950s by Lubetzky, who enlarged the concept of "the work" to make it a more abstract idea of an author's intellectual or artistic creation. According to Lubetzky's principle, an audio book, a video recording of a play, and an electronic book should be listed each as distinct items, yet still linked to the original because of their overlapping intellectual origin.[152]

The distinctions put forth by Lubetzky, Svenonius and other library science theorists have evolved today into a four-step abstraction hierarchy (illustrated in Figure 3.5, "The Abstraction Hierarchy for Identifying Resources.") between the abstract **work**, an **expression** in multiple formats or genres, a particular **manifestation** in one of those formats or genres, and a specific physical **item**. The broad scope from the abstract work to the specific item is essential because organizing systems in libraries must organize tangible artifacts while expressing the conceptual structure of the domains of knowledge represented in their collections.

If we revisit the question "What is this thing we call *Macbeth*?" we can see how different ways of answering fit into this abstraction hierarchy. The most specific answer is that *"Macbeth"* is a specific **item**, a very particular and individual resource, like that dog-eared paperback with yellow marked pages that you owned when you read *Macbeth* in high school. A more abstract answer is that *Macbeth* is an idealization called a **work**, a category that includes all the plays, movies, ballets, or other intellectual creations that share a recognizable amount of the plot and meaning from the original Shakespeare play.

This hierarchy is defined in the *Functional Requirements for Bibliographical Records (FRBR)*, published as a standard by the International Federation of Library Associations and Institutions (IFLA).[153]

3.3.3 Identity and Information Components

In information-intensive domains, documents, databases, software applications, or other explicit repositories or sources of information are ubiquitous and essen-

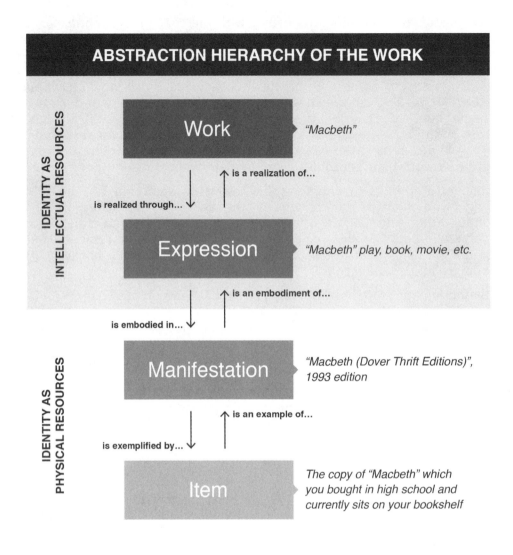

Figure 3.5. The Abstraction Hierarchy for Identifying Resources.

tial to the creation of value for the user, reader, consumer, or customer. Value is created through the comparison, compilation, coordination or transformation of information in some chain or choreography of processes operating on information flowing from one information source or process to another. These processes are employed in accounting, financial services, procurement, logistics, supply chain management, insurance underwriting and claims processing, legal and professional services, customer support, computer programming, and energy management.

The processes that create value in information-intensive domains are "glued together" by shared information components that are exchanged in documents, records, messages, or resource descriptions of some kind. Information components are the primitive and abstract resources in information-intensive domains. They are the units of meaning that serve as building blocks of composite descriptions and other information artifacts.

The value creation processes in information-intensive domains work best when their component parts come from a common *controlled vocabulary* for components, or when each uses a vocabulary with a granularity and semantic precision compatible with the others. For example, the value created by a personal health record emerges when information from doctors, clinics, hospitals, and insurance companies can be combined because they all share the same "patient" component as a logical piece of information.

This abstract definition of information components does not help identify them, so we will introduce some heuristic criteria: An "information component" can be (1) Any piece of information that has a unique label or identifier or (2) Any piece of information that is self-contained and comprehensible on its own.[154]

These two criteria for determining the identity of information components are often easy to satisfy through observations, interviews, and task analysis because people naturally use many different types of information and talk easily about specific components and the documents that contain them. Some common components (e.g., person, location, date, item) and familiar document types (e.g., report, catalog, calendar, receipt) can be identified in almost any domain. Other components need to be more precisely defined to meet the more specific semantic requirements of narrower domains. These smaller or more fine-grained components might be viewed as refined or qualified versions of the generic components and document types, like course grade and semester components in academic transcripts, airport codes and flight numbers in travel itineraries and tickets, and drug names and dosages in prescriptions.

Decades of practical and theoretical effort in conceptual modeling, relational theory, and database design have resulted in rigorous methods for identifying information components when requirements and business rules for information can be precisely specified. For example, in the domain of business transactions, required information like item numbers, quantities, prices, payment information, and so on must be encoded as a particular type of data—integer, decimal, Unicode string, etc.— with clearly defined possible values and that follows clear occurrence rules.[155]

Identifying components can seem superficially easy at the transactional end of the Document Type Spectrum (see the Sidebar in §3.2.1, "Resource Domain" (page 100)), with orders or invoices, forms requiring data entry, or other highly-structured document types like product catalogs, where pieces of information are typically labeled and delimited by boxes, lines, white space or other presentation features that encode the distinctions between types of content. For example, the presence of ITEM, CUSTOMER NAME, ADDRESS, and PAYMENT INFORMATION labels on the fields of an online order form suggests these pieces of information are semantically distinct components in a retail application. They follow the "self-contained and comprehensible" heuristic enough to interconnect the order management, payment, and delivery services that work together to carry out the transaction. In addition, these labels might have analogues in variable names in the source code that implements the order form, or as tags in a XML document created by the ordering application; <CustName>John Smith</CustName> and <Item>A-19</Item> in the order document can be easily identified when it is sent to the other services by the order management application.

But the theoretically grounded methods for identifying components like those of relational theory and normalization that work for structured data do not strictly apply when information requirements are more qualitative and less precise at the narrative end of the Document Type Spectrum. These information requirements are typical of narrative, unstructured and semi-structured types of documents, and information sources like those often found in law, education, and professional services. Narrative documents include technical publications, reports, policies, procedures and other less structured information, where semantic components are rarely labeled explicitly and are often surrounded by text that is more generic. Unlike transactional documents that depend on precise semantics because they are used by computers, narrative documents are used by people, who can ask if they aren't sure what something means, so there is less need to explicitly define the meaning of the information components. Occasional exceptions, such as where components in narrative documents are identified with explicit labels like NOTE and WARNING, only prove the rule.

3.3.4 Identity and Active Resources

Active resources (§3.4.3.2) initiate effects or create value on their own. In many cases an inherently passive physical resource like a product package or shipping pallet is transformed into an active one when it associated with an RFID tag or bar code. Mobile phones contain device or subscriber IDs so that any information they communicate can be associated both with the phone and often, through indirect reference, with a particular person. If the resource has an IP address, it is said to be part of the "Internet of Things."[156]

Organizing systems that create value from active resources often co-exist with or complement organizing systems that treat its resources as passive. In a traditional library, books sat passively on shelves and required users to read their spines to identify them. Today, some library books contain active RFID tags that make them dynamic information sources that self-identify by publishing their own locations. Similarly, a supermarket or department store might organize its goods as physical resources on shelves, treating them as passive resources; superimposed on that traditional organizing system is one that uses point-of-sale transaction information created when items are scanned at checkout counters to automatically re-order goods and replenish the inventory at the store where they were sold. In some stores the shelves contain sensors that continually "talk to the goods" and the information they gather can maintain inventory levels and even help prevent theft of valuable merchandise by tracking goods through a store or warehouse. The inventory becomes a collection of active resources; each item eager to announce its own location and ready to conduct its own sale.

Blogjects—objects that blog—and Tweetjects—objects that post messages to Twitter—are neologisms for active resources that are plugged into the social web. Blogjects don't write editorial commentary about their experiences, but they use APIs and customized programs to harness the information captured by sensors and RFID that then appears on blogs in the form of human-readable maps, charts, and text.[157]

Tweetjects are sensors that send information about measurements or events to a Twitter account. For example, Sparkfun Electronics sells a kit consisting of a soil sensor that sends information about the water level in the soil through an Arduino circuit board, converting thresholds to Twitter messages like, "Please water me, I'm thirsty!"[158]

The extent to which an active resource is "smart" depends on how much computing capability it has available to refine the data it collects and communicates. A large collection of sensors can transmit a torrent of captured data that requires substantial processing to distinguish significant events from those that reflect normal operation, and also from those that are statistical outliers with strange values caused by random noise. This challenge gets qualitatively more difficult as the amount of data grows to *big data* size, because a one in million event might be a statistical outlier that can be ignored, but if there are a thousand similar outliers in a billion sensor readings, this cluster of data probably reveals something important. On the other hand, giving every sensor the computing capability to refine its data so that it only communicates significant information might make the sensors too expensive to deploy.[159]

3.4 Naming Resources

Determining the identity of the thing, document, information component, or data item we need isn't always enough. We often need to give that resource a name, a label that will help us understand and talk about what it is. But naming isn't just the simple task of assigning a sequence of characters. In this section, we'll discuss why we name, some of the problems with naming, and the principles that help us name things in useful ways.

3.4.1 What's in a Name?

When a child is born, its parents give it a name, often a very stressful and contentious decision. Names serve to distinguish one person from another. Names also, intentionally or unintentionally, suggest characteristics or aspirations. The name given to us at birth is just one of the names we will be identified with during our lifetimes. We have nicknames, names we use professionally, names we use with friends, and names we use online. Our banks, our schools, and our governments will know who we are because of numbers they associate with our names. As long as it serves its purpose to identify you, your name could be anything.[160]

Resources other than people need names so we can find them, describe them, reuse them, refer or link to them, record who owns them, and otherwise interact with them. In many domains the names assigned to resources are also influenced or constrained by rules, industry practice, or technology considerations.

3.4.2 The Problems of Naming

Giving names to anything, from a business to a concept to an action, can be a difficult process and it is possible to do it well or do it poorly. The following section details some of the major challenges in assigning a name to a resource.

3.4.2.1 The Vocabulary Problem

Every natural language offers more than one way to express any thought, and in particular there are usually many words that can be used to refer to the same thing or concept. The words people choose to name or describe things are embodied in their experiences and context, so people will often disagree in the words they use. Moreover, people are often a bit surprised when it happens, because what seems like the natural or obvious name to one person isn't natural or obvious to another.[161]

Back in the 1980s in the early days of computer user interface design, George Furnas and his colleagues at Bell Labs conducted a set of experiments to measure how much people would agree when they named some resource or function.

The short answer: very little. Left to our own devices, we come up with a shockingly large number of names for a single common thing.

In one experiment, a thousand pairs of people were asked to "write the name you would give to a program that tells about interesting activities occurring in some major metropolitan area." Less than 12 pairs of people agreed on a name. Furnas called this phenomenon "the vocabulary problem," concluding that no single word could ever be considered the "best" name.[162]

3.4.2.2 Homonymy, Polysemy, and False Cognates

Sometimes the same word can refer to different resources—a "bank" can be a financial institution or the side of a river. When two words are spelled the same but have different meanings they are **homographs**; if they are also pronounced the same they are **homonyms**. If the different meanings of the homographs are related, they are called **polysemes**.

Resources with homonymous and polysemous names are sometimes incorrectly identified, especially by an automated process that can't use common sense or context to determine the correct referent. Polysemy can cause more trouble than simple homography because the overlapping meaning might obscure the misinterpretation. If one person thinks of a "shipping container" as being a cardboard box and orders some of them, while another person thinks of a "shipping container" as the large box carried by semi-trailers and stacked on cargo ships, their disagreement might not be discovered until the wrong kinds of containers arrive.[163]

Many words in different languages have common roots, and as a result are often spelled the same or nearly the same. This is especially true for technology words; for example, "computer" has been borrowed by many languages. The existence of these cognates and borrowed words makes us vulnerable to false cognates. When a word in one language has a different meaning and refers to different resources in another, the results can be embarrassing or disastrous. "*Gift*" is poison in German; "*pain*" is bread in French.

3.4.2.3 Names with Undesirable Associations

False cognates are a special category of words that make poor names, and there are many stories relating product marketing mistakes, where a product name or description translates poorly, into other languages or cultures, with undesirable associations.[164] Furthermore, these undesirable associations differ across cultures. For example, even though floor numbers have the straightforward purpose to identify floors from lowest to highest levels, most buildings in Western cultures skip the 13th floor because many people think 13 is an unlucky number. In many East and Southeast Asian buildings, the 4th floor is skipped. In China the number 4 is dreaded because it sounds like the word for "death," while 8 is prized because it sounds like the word for "wealth."

While it can be tempting to dismiss unfamiliar biases and beliefs about names and identifiers as harmless superstitions and practices, their implications are ubiquitous and far from benign. *Alphabetical ordering* might seem like a fair and non-discriminatory arrangement of resources, but because it is easy to choose the name at the top of an alphabetical list, many firms in service businesses select names that begin with "A," "AA," or even "AAA" (look in any printed service directory). A consequence of this bias is that people or resources with names that begin with letters late in the alphabet are systematically discriminated against because they are often not considered, or because they are evaluated in the context created by resources earlier in the alphabet rather than on their own merit.[165]

3.4.2.4 Names that Assume Impermanent Attributes

Many resources are given names based on attributes that can be problematic later if the attribute changes in value or interpretation.

Web resources are often referred to using URLs that contain the domain name of the server on which the resource is located, followed by the directory path and file name on the computer running the server. This treats the current location of the resource as its name, so the name will change if the resource is moved. It also means that resources that are identical in content, like those at an archive or mirror website, will have different names than the original even though they are exact copies. An analogous problem is faced by restaurants or businesses with street names or numbers in their names if they lose their leases or want to expand.[166]

Some dynamic web resources that are generated by programs have URIs that contain information about the server technology used to create them. When the technology changes, the URIs will no longer work.[167]

Other resources have names that include page numbers, which disappear or change when the resource is accessed in a digital form. For example, the standard citation format for legal opinions uses the page number from the printed volume issued by West Publishing, which has a virtual monopoly on the publishing of court opinions and other types of legal documents.[168]

Some resources have names that contain dates, years or other time indicators, most often to point to the future. The film studio named "20th Century Fox" took on that name in the 1930s to give it a progressive, forward-looking identity, but today a name with "20th Century" in it does the opposite.[169]

3.4.2.5 The Semantic Gap

The *semantic gap* is the difference in perspective in naming and description when resources are described by automated processes rather than by people.[170]

The semantic gap is largest when computer programs or sensors obtain and name some information in a format optimized for efficient capture, storage, decoding, or other technical criteria. The names—like *IMG20268.jpg* on a digital photo—might make sense for the camera as it stores consecutively taken photos but they are not good names for people. We may prefer names that describe the content of the picture, like *goldengatebridge.jpg.*

And if we try to examine the content of computer-created or sensor-captured resources, like a clip of music or a compiled software program, a human-language text rendering of the content simply looks like nonsense. It was designed to be interpreted by a computer program, not by a person.

3.4.3 Choosing Good Names and Identifiers

If someone tells you they are having dinner with their best friend, a cousin, someone with whom they play basketball, and their professional mentor from work, how many places at the table will be set? Anywhere from two to five; it's possible all those relational descriptions refer to a single person, or to four different people, and because "friend," "cousin," "basketball teammate" and "mentor" don't name specific people you'll have to guess who is coming to dinner.

If instead of descriptions you're told that the dinner guests are Bob, Carol, Ted, and Alice, you can count four names and you know how many people are having dinner. But you still can't be sure exactly which four people are involved because there are many people with those names.

The uncertainty is completely eliminated only if we use identifiers for the people rather than names. *Identifiers* are names that refer unambiguously to a specific person, place, or resource because they are assigned in a controlled way. Identifiers are often created as strings of numbers or letters rather than words to avoid the biases and associations that words can convey. For example, in some universities professors grade final exams that are identified with student numbers rather than names so that grades are assigned without the bias that could arise if the professor knows the student.

The distinction between *names* and *identifiers* for people is often not appreciated. (See the Sidebar, "Names {and, or, vs} Identifiers" (page 120)).

Names {and, or, vs} Identifiers

People change their names for many reasons: when they get married or divorced, because their name is often mispronounced or misspelled, to make a political or ethnic statement, or because they want to stand out. A few years ago, a football player with a large ego named Chad Johnson, which is the second most common surname in the US, decided to change his name to his player number of 85, becoming Chad "Ochocinco." He has an ochocinco.com website and uses the ochocinco name on Facebook and Twitter. In a bit of irony, when Ochocinco wanted to put Ocho Cinco on the back of his football jersey, the football league would not let him because his legal name doesn't have a space in it. That surely contributed to his decision to change his name back to Chad Johnson in 2012.

A similar name change with an unintended consequence was that of the American singer and musician Price Rogers Nelson, who adopted the stage name of Prince and released numerous highly successful record albums under that name. But because Prince wasn't a legal name change, the record label trademarked it for marketing purposes, which led to disputes about control. In response, "The Artist Formerly Known as Prince" invented a graphical symbol that merged the symbols for male and female. Unfortunately, even though it is a unique identifier, this symbol isn't represented in any standard character set, so it can't be printed here and can't be searched for on the web.

Some minor league sports teams have replaced the player names on jerseys with Twitter handles, which might be a good thing if their fans are into social media, but it must be strange for the announcers at the games when they say "@ifuentes4 just scored a goal."

When you go to coffee shops, you are often asked your name, which the cashier writes on the empty cup so that your drink can be identified after the *barista* makes it. They don't actually need your name; just as some establishments use a receipt number to distinguish orders, what they need is an identifier. So even if your name is Joe, you can tell them it is Thor, Wotan, Mercurio, El Greco, Clark Kent, or any other name that is likely to be a unique identifier for the minute it takes to make your beverage.[171]

3.4.3.1 Make Names Informative

The most basic principle of naming is to choose names that are informative, which makes them easier to understand and remember. It is easier to tell what a computer program or XML document is doing if it uses names like "ItemCost" and "TotalCost" rather than just "I" or "T." People will enter more consistent and reusable address information if a form asks explicitly for "Street," "City," and "PostalCode" instead of "Line1" and "Line2."

Identifiers can be designed with internal structure and semantics that conveys information beyond the basic aspect of pointing to a specific resource. An International Standard Book Number (ISBN) like "ISBN 978-0-262-07261-8" identifies a resource (07261="Document Engineering") and also reveals that the resource is a book (978), in English (0), and published by The MIT Press (262).[172]

The navigation points that mark intersections of radial signals from ground beacons or satellites that are crucial to aircraft pilots used to be meaningless five-letter codes. These identifiers were changed to make them suggest their locations; semantic landmark names made pilots less likely to enter the wrong names into navigation systems, For example, some of the navigation points near Orlando, Florida—the home of Disney World—are MICKI, MINEE, and GOO-FY.[173]

3.4.3.2 Use Controlled Vocabularies

One way to encourage good names for a given resource domain or task is to establish a **controlled vocabulary**. A *controlled vocabulary* can be thought of as a fixed or closed dictionary that includes all the terms that can be used in a particular domain. A controlled vocabulary shrinks the number of words used, reducing synonymy and homonymy and eliminating undesirable associations, leaving behind a set of words with precisely defined meanings and rules governing their use. Controlled vocabularies are applied in many organizing systems, from bibliographic languages that determine the ways books are catalogued in a library to business languages that define the set of information components that can be used in transactional documents.

A *controlled vocabulary* isn't simply a set of allowed words; it also includes their definitions and often specifies rules by which the vocabulary terms can be used and combined. Different domains can create specific controlled vocabularies for their own purposes, but the important thing is that the vocabulary be used consistently throughout that domain.[174]

For bibliographic resources important aspects of vocabulary control include determining the authoritative forms for author names, uniform titles of works, and the set of terms by which a particular subject will be known. In library science, the process of creating and maintaining these standard names and terms is known as ***authority control***. When evaluating what name to use for an author, librarians typically look for the name form that's used most commonly across that author's body of work while conforming to rules for handling prefixes, suffixes and other name parts that often cause name variations. For example, a name like that of Johann Wolfgang von Goëthe might be alphabetized as both a "G" name and a "V" name, but using "G" is the authoritative way. "See" and "see also" references then map the variations to the authoritative name. Similar rules are followed for identifying the authoritative form of titles when multiple translations and editions exist.[175]

Official authority files are maintained for many resource domains: a gazetteer associates names and locations and tells us whether we should be referring to Bombay or Mumbai; the Domain Name System (DNS) maps human-oriented domain and host names to their IP addresses; the Chemical Abstracts Service Registry assigns unique identifiers to every chemical described in the open scientific literature; numerous institutions assign unique identifiers to different categories of animal species.[176]

In some cases, authority files are created or maintained by a community, as in the case of MusicBrainz, an "open music encyclopedia" to which users contribute information about artists, releases, tracks, and other aspects of music. Music metadata is notoriously unreliable; one study found over 100 variations in the description of the *Knockin' on Heaven's Door* song (written by Bob Dylan) as recorded by Guns N' Roses.[177]

3.4.3.3 Allow Aliasing

A *controlled vocabulary* is extremely useful to people who use it, but if you are designing an organizing system for other people who do not or cannot use it, you need to accommodate the variety of words they will actually use when they seek or describe resources. The authoritative name of a certain fish species is *Amphiprion ocellaris*, but most people would search for it as "clownfish," "anemone fish," or even by its more familiar film name of *Nemo*.

Furnas suggests "unlimited aliasing" to connect the uncontrolled or natural vocabularies that people use with the controlled one employed by the organizing system. By this he means that there must be many alternate access routes to each word or function that a user is trying to find. For example, the birth name of the 42nd President of the United States of America is "William Jefferson Clinton," but web pages that refer to him as "Bill Clinton" are vastly more common, and searches for the former are redirected to the latter. A related mechanism used by search engines is spelling correction, essentially treating all the incorrect spellings as aliases of the correct one ("did you mean California?" when you typed "Claifornia").

3.4.3.4 Make Identifiers Unique or Qualified

Even though an identifier refers to a single resource, this doesn't mean that no two identifiers are identical. One military inventory system might use stock number 99 000 1111 to identify a 24-hour, cold-climate ration pack, while another inventory system, the same number could be used to identify an electronic radio valve. Each identifier is unique in its inventory system, but if a supply request gets sent to the wrong warehouse hungry soldiers could be sent radio valves instead of rations.[178] [179]

We can prevent or reduce identifier collisions by adding information about the *namespace*, the domain from which the names or identifiers are selected, thus creating what are often called *qualified names*. There are several dozen US cities named "Springfield" and "Washington," but adding state codes to mail addresses distinguishes them. Likewise, we can add prefixes to XML element names when we create documents that reuse components from multiple document types, distinguishing <book:Title> from <legal:Title>.

We can fix problems like these by qualifying or extending the identifier, or by creating a *globally unique identifier* (or GUID), one that will never be the same as another identifier in any organizing system anywhere else. One easy method to create a GUID is to use a URL you control and append a string to it, the same approach that gives every web page a unique address. GUIDs are often used to identify software objects, the resources in distributed systems, or data collections.[180]

Because they aren't created by an algorithm whose results are provably unique, we do not consider fingerprints, or other biometric information, to be globally unique identifiers for people, but for all practical purposes they are.[181]

3.4.3.5 Distinguish Identifying and Resolving

Library call numbers are identifiers that do not contain any information about where the resource can be found in the library stacks on in a digital repository. This separation enables this identification system to work when there are multiple copies in different locations, in contrast to URIs that serve as both identifiers and locations much of the time. When the identifier does not contain information about resource location, we need a way to interpret or "resolve" it to determine the location. With physical resources, *resolution* takes place with the aid of signs, maps, or other associated resources that describe the arrangement of resources in some physical environment; for example, you are here maps have a list of its buildings and associate each with a coordinate or other means of finding it on the map.. With digital resources, the resolver is a directory system or service that interprets an identifier and looks up its location or directly initiates the retrieval of the resource.

3.5 Resources over Time

Problems of "what is the resource?" and "how do we identify it?" are complex and often require ongoing work to ensure they are properly answered as the content and context of an organizing system evolves. As a result, we might need to know how a resource does or does not change over time (its *persistence*), whether its state and content come into play at a specified point in time (its *effectivity*), whether the resource is what it is said to be (its *authenticity*), and sometimes who has certified its authenticity over time (its *provenance*).

3.5.1 Persistence

Even if you have reached an agreement as to the meaning of "a thing" in your organizing system, you still face the question of the identity of the resource over time, or its **persistence**.

3.5.1.1 Persistent Identifiers

How long must an identifier last? Coyle gives the conventional, if unsatisfying, answer: "As long as it's needed."[182] In some cases, the time frame is relatively short. When you order a specialty coffee and the *barista* asks for your name, this identifier only needs to last until you pick up your order at the end of the counter. But other time frames are much longer. For libraries and repositories of scientific, economic, census, or other data the time frame might be "forever."

The design of a scheme for persistent identifiers must consider both the required time frame and the number of resources to be identified. When the Internet Protocol (IP) was designed in 1980, it contained a 32-bit address scheme, sufficient for over 4 billion unique addresses. But the enormous growth of the Internet and the application of IP addresses to resources of unexpected types have required a new addressing scheme with 128 bits.[183]

Recognition that URIs are often not persistent as identifiers for web-based resources led the Association of American Publishers (AAP) to develop the Digital Object Identifier (DOI) system. The location and owner of a digital resource can change, but its DOI is permanent.[184]

3.5.1.2 Persistent Resources

Even though persistence often has a technology dimension, it is more important to view it as a commitment by an institution or organization to perform activities over time to ensure that a resource is available when it is needed. Put another way, preservation (§2.5.2) and governance (§2.5.4) are activities carried out to ensure the outcome of persistence.

The subtle relationship between preservation and persistence raises some interesting questions about what it means for a resource to stay the same over time. One way to think of persistence is that a persistent resource is never changed. However, physical resources often require maintenance, repair, or restoration to keep them accessible and usable, and we might question whether at some point these activities have transformed them into different resources.[185] Likewise, digital resources require regular backup and migration to keep them available and this might include changing their digital format.

We might instead think of persistence more abstractly, and expect that persistent resources need only to remain functionally the same to support the same interactions at any point in their lifetimes even if their physical properties change. Active resources implemented as computational agents or web services might be re-implemented numerous times, but as long as they don't change their interfaces they can be deemed to be persistent from the perspective of any other resource that uses them. Similarly, many resources like online newspapers or blog feeds continually change their content but still could have persistent identifiers.

Some organizing systems closely monitor their resources and every interaction with them to prevent or detect tampering with them or other unauthorized changes. Some organizing systems, like those for software or legal documents, explicitly maintain every changed version to satisfy expectations of persistence because different users might not be relying on the same version. With digital resources determining whether two resources are the same or determining how they are related or derived from one another are very challenging problems.[186]

3.5.2 Effectivity

Many resources, or their properties, also have *effectivity*, meaning that they come into effect at a particular time and will almost certainly cease to be effective at some future date. Effectivity is sometimes known as time-to-live and it is generally expressed as a range of two dates. It consists of a date on which the resource is effective, and optionally a date on which the resource ceases to be effective, or becomes stale. For some types of resources, the effective date is the moment they are created, but for others, the effective date can be a time different from the moment of creation. For example, a law can be passed in November but not take effect until January 1 of the following year. An "effective date" is the counterpart of the "Best Before" date on perishable goods. That date indicates when a product goes bad, whereas an item's effective date is when it "goes good" and the resource that it supersedes needs to be disposed of or archived.

Effectivity concerns sometimes intersect with name authority control, because name changes for resources often are tied to particular dates and events. Some places that have been the site of civil unrest, foreign occupation, and other political disruptions have had many different names over time. Even if you always live in the same place, the answer to "what country do you live in?" can depend on when it is asked.[187]

In most cases effectivity implies persistence requirements because it is important to be able to determine and reconstruct the configuration of resources that was in effect at some prior time. A new tax might go into effect on January 1, but if the government audits your tax returns what matters is whether you followed the law that was in effect when you filed your returns.[188]

3.5.3 Authenticity

In ordinary use we say that something is **authentic** if it can be shown to be, or has come to be accepted as what it claims to be. The importance and nuance of questions about authenticity can be seen in the many words we have to describe the relationship between "the real thing" (the "original") and something else: copy, reproduction, replica, fake, phony, forgery, counterfeit, pretender, imposter, ringer, and so on.

It is easy to think of examples where authenticity of a resource matters: a signed legal contract, a work of art, a historical artifact, even a person's signature.

The creator or operator of an organizing system, whether human or machine, can authenticate a newly created resource. A third party can also serve as proof of authenticity. Many professional careers are based on figuring out if a resource is authentic.[189]

There is large body of techniques for establishing the identity of a person or physical resource. We often use judgments about the physical integrity of recorded information when we consider the integrity of its contents.

Digital authenticity is more difficult to establish. Digital resources can be reproduced at almost no cost, exist in multiple locations, carry different names on identical documents or identical names on different documents, and bring about other complications that do not arise with physical items. Technological solutions for ensuring digital authenticity include time stamps, watermarking, encryption, and digital signatures. However, while scholars generally trust technological methods, technologists are more skeptical of them because they can imagine ways for them to be circumvented or counterfeited. Even when a technologically sophisticated system for establishing authenticity is in place, we can still only assume the constancy of identity as far back as this system reaches in the "chain of custody" of the document.

3.5.4 Provenance

The idea that important documents must be created in an authenticatable manner and then preserved with an unbroken chain of custody goes back to ancient Rome. Notaries witnessed the creation of important documents, which were then protected to maintain their integrity or value as evidence. In organizing systems like museums and archives that preserve rare or culturally important

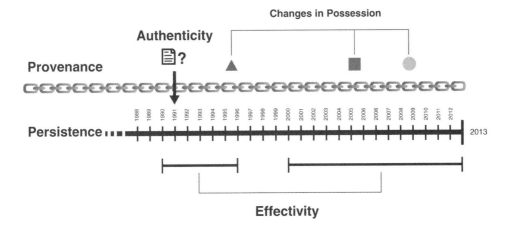

Figure 3.6. Resources over Time.

objects or documents this concern is expressed as the principle of **provenance**. This is the history of the ownership of a collection or the resources in it, where they have been and who has had access to the resources.

A uniquely Chinese technique in organizing systems is the imprinting of elaborate red seals on documents, books, and paintings that collectively record the provenance of ownership and the review and approval of the artifact by emperors or important officials.

Figure 3.6, "Resources over Time." portrays the relationships among the concepts of Persistence, Provenance, Effectivity, and Authenticity. A resource might have persistence over some time line, but an unbroken chain of custody that captures changes in possession enables questions about authenticity to be answered with authority. Effectivity emphasizes a particular segment on the time line or a starting point after which the resource is effective.

3.6 Key Points in Chapter Three

- We can consider a resource to be one of many members of a very broad category, as the unique instance of a category with only one member, or anywhere in between.

- The size of the category—the number of resources that are treated as equivalent—is determined by the properties or characteristics we consider when we examine the resource.

- More fine-grained organization reduces *recall*, the number of resources you find or retrieve in response to a query, but increases the *precision* of the recalled set, the proportion of recalled items that are relevant.

- Organizing systems for physical information resources emphasize description resources or surrogates like bibliographic records that describe the information content rather than their physical properties.

- Which resources are primary and which are metadata is often just a decision about which resource is the *focus* of our attention.

- It can be useful to view domains of information resources on the Document Type Spectrum from weakly-structured narrative content to highly structured transactional content.

- Organizing systems designed for institutional or industry-wide use require systematic design methods to determine which resources will have separate identities and how they are related to each other.

- The concept of identity for bibliographic resources has evolved into a four-step abstraction hierarchy between the abstract *work*, an *expression* in multiple formats or genres, a particular *manifestation* in one of those formats or genres, and a specific physical *item*.

- Resources become active resources when they contain sensing and communication capabilities.

- Organizing systems that create value from active resources often co-exist with or complement organizing systems that treat its resources as passive.

- If the resource has an IP address, it is said to be part of the "Internet of Things."

- The most basic principle of naming is to choose names that are informative.

- A *controlled vocabulary* can be thought of as a fixed or closed dictionary that includes all the terms that can be used unambiguously in a particular domain.

- Many resources are given names based on attributes that can be problematic later if the attribute changes in value or interpretation.

- An identifier is a special kind of name assigned in a controlled manner and governed by rules that define possible values and naming conventions. The design of a scheme for persistent identifiers must consider both the required time frame and the number of resources to be identified.

- Preservation and governance are activities carried out to ensure the outcome of persistence.

Notes

124. [LIS] (Wilson 1968, p. 9).

125. [Business] Separating information content from its structure and presentation is essential to re-purposing it for different scenarios, applications, devices, or users. The global information economy is increasingly driven by automated information exchange between business processes. When information flows efficiently from one type of document to another in this chain of related documents, the overlapping content components act as the "glue" that connects the information systems or web services that produce and consume the documents. (Glushko and McGrath 2005).

126. [CogSci] (Furnas, Landauer, Gomez, and Dumais 1987).

127. [Philosophy] Linnaeus is sometimes called the father of modern taxonomy (which is unfair to Aristotle) but he certainly deserves enormous credit for the systematic approach to biological classification that he proposed in *Systema Naturae*, published in 1735. This seminal work contains the familiar kingdom, class, order, family, genus, species hierarchy.

128. [Computing] (Glushko and McGrath 2005).

129. [Computing] (Kuniavsky 2010).

130. [Archives] Project Gutenberg, begun in 1971, was the first large-scale effort to digitize books; its thousands of volunteers have created about 40,000 digital versions of classic printed works. Systematic research in digital libraries began in the 1990s when the US National Science Foundation (NSF), the Advanced Research Projects Agency (ARPA), and NASA launched a Digital Library Initiative that emphasized the enabling technologies and infrastructure. At about the same time numerous pragmatic efforts to digitize library collections began, characterized by some as a race against time as old books in libraries were literally disintegrating and turning into dust. The Internet Archive, started in 1996, now has a collection of over 3 million texts and has estimated the cost of digitizing to be about $30 for the average book. Multiply this by the scores of millions of books held in the world's research libraries and it is easy to why many libraries endorsed Google's offer to digitize their collections.

131. [Computing] The ASCII scheme was standardized in the 1960s when computer memory was expensive and most computing was in English-speaking countries, so it is minimal and distinguishes only 128 characters. *American Standard Code for Information Interchange (ASCII)* is an ANSI specification. (See *http://en.wikipedia.org/wiki/ASCII*.)

132. [Computing] Unicode 6.0 (*http://www.unicode.org/*) has room to encode 109,449 characters for all the *writing systems* in the world, so a single standard

can represent the characters of every existing language, even "dead" ones like Sumerian and Hittite. Unicode encodes the scripts used in languages, rather than languages per se, so there only needs to one representation of the Latin, Cyrillic, Arabic, etc scripts that are used for writing multiple language. Unicode also distinguishes *characters* from *glyphs*, the different forms for the same character—enabling different *fonts* to be identified as the same character.

133. [Computing] Encoding of structure in documents is valuable because titles, sections, links and other structural elements can be leveraged to enhance the user interface and navigational interactions with the digital document and enable more precise information retrieval. Some uses of documents require formats that preserve their printed appearance. "Presentational fidelity" is essential if we imagine a banker or customs inspector carefully comparing a printed document with a computer-generated one to ensure they are identical.

134. [Computing] Text encoding specs are well-documented; see (*http://www.wotsit.org/list.asp?fc=10*).

135. [Computing] (Chapman and Chapman 2009).

136. [Museums] Numerous museums have created web collections, but a great many of them seem to have focused on the quantity of information they could put online rather than on the user experience they were creating. Perhaps not surprisingly, the ambitious use of virtual world technology to create novel forms of interaction described by (Rothfarb and Doherty 2007) reflects the highly interactive character of its host museum, the Exploratorium in San Francisco (*http://www.exploratorium.edu/*). Similarly, the Google Art Project (*http://googleartproject.com*) is notable for its goal of complementing and extending, rather than merely imitating, the museum visitor's encounter with artwork (Proctor 2011). A feature that let people create a "personal art collection" is very popular, enabling a fan of Vincent Van Gogh to bring together paintings that hang in different museums.

137. [Computing] However, scratching can be simulated using a smart phone or tablet app called djay. See *http://www.algoriddim.com/djay*.

138. [Law] As a result, digital books are somewhat controversial and problematic for libraries, whose access models were created based on the economics of print publication and the social contract of the copyright first sale doctrine that allowed libraries to lend printed books.. Digital books change the economics and first sale is not as well-established for digital works, which are licensed rather than sold (Aufderheide and Jaszi 2011). To protect their business models, many publishers are limiting the number of times e-books can be lent before they "self-destruct." Some librarians have called for boycotts of publishers in response (*http://boycottharpercollins.com*).

139. [Business] The opposing categories of operands and operants have their roots in debates in political economics about the nature of work and the creation of value (Vargo and Lusch 2004) and have more recently played a central role in the development of modern thinking about service design (Constantin and Lusch 1994), (Maglio et al. 2009). The concept of agency or operant resources is needed to bring resources that are active information sources, or computational in character, into the organizing system framework. This concept also lets us include living resources, or more specifically, humans, into discussions about organizing systems in a more general way that emphasizes their agency and de-emphasizes other characteristics that could otherwise be distracting.

140. [Computing] See (Allmendinger and Lombreglia 2005), (Want 2006).

141. [Web] Luis Von Ahn (von Ahn 2004) was the first to use the web to get people to perform "microwork" or "human computation" tasks when he released what he called "the ESP game" that randomly paired people trying to agree on labeling an image. Not long afterwards Amazon created the MTurk platform (*http://www.mturk.com*) that lets people propose microwork and others sign up to do it, and today there are both hundreds of thousands of tasks offered and hundreds of thousands of people offering to be paid to do them.

142. [Computing] For semi-structured or more narrative documents these descriptions might be authoring templates used in word processors or other office applications, document schemas in XML applications, style sheets, or other kinds of transformations that change one resource representation into another one. Primary resources that are highly and regularly structured are invariably organized in databases or enterprise information management systems in which a *data schema* specifies the arrangement and type of data contained in each field or component of the resource.

143. [Web] There are a large number of third-party Twitter apps. See *http://twitter.pbworks.com/w/page/1779726/Apps*. For a scholarly analysis see (Efron 2011).

144. [Business] The basic idea behind fantasy sports is quite simple. You select a team of existing players in any sport, and then compare their statistical performance against other teams similarly selected by other people. Fantasy sports appeal mostly to die-hard fans who study player statistics carefully before "drafting" their players. The global fantasy sports business for companies who organize and operate fantasy leagues is estimated as between 1 and 2 billion US dollars annually (Montague 2010).

145. [LIS] (Schmandt-Besserat 1997).

146. [LIS] The oldest known lists of books were created about 4000 years ago in Sumeria. The first use of cards in library catalogs was literal; when the revolutionary government of France seized private book collections, an inventory was

created starting in 1791 using the blank backs of playing cards. 110 years later the US Library of Congress began selling pre-printed catalog cards to libraries, but in the mid-1960s the creation of the *Machine-Readable Cataloging (MARC)* format marked the beginning of the end of printed cards. See (Strout 1956). The MARC standards are at *http://www.loc.gov/marc/*.

147. [LIS] We treat resource format and resource focus as distinct dimensions, so there are four categories here. This contrasts with David Weinberger's three "orders of order" that he proposes in the first chapter of a book called *Everything is Miscellaneous* (Weinberger 2007). Weinberger starts with the assumption that physical resources are inherently the primary ones, so the first "order of order" emerges when physical resources are arranged. The second "order of order" emerges when physical description resources are arranged, and the third "order of order" emerges when digital description resources for physical resources are arranged. Later in the book Weinberger mentions the use of bar codes associated with websites, a physical description of a digital resource, but because he started with the assumption that physical resources define the "first order" this example does not fit into his orders of order.

148. [Computing] These methods go by different names in different disciplines, including "data modeling," "systems analysis," and "document engineering" (e.g., (Kent 2012), (Silverston 2000), (Glushko and McGrath 2005). What they have in common is that they produce conceptual models of a domain that specify their components or parts and the relationships among these components or parts. These conceptual models are called "schemas" or "domain ontologies" in some modeling approaches, and are typically implemented in models that are optimized for particular technologies or applications.

149. [CogSci] Specifically, an NFL football team needs to be considered a single resource for games through the season and in playoffs, and 53 individual players for other situations, like the NFL draft or play-calling. The team and the team's roster can be thought of as resources, and the team's individual players are also resources that make up the whole team.

150. [LIS] (Denton 2007) is a highly readable retelling of the history of cataloging that follows four themes—the use of axioms, user requirements, the "work," and standardization and internationalization—culminating with their synthesis in the Functional Requirements for Bibliographic Records (FRBR).

151. [LIS] This was a surprisingly controversial activity. Many opposed Panizzi's efforts as a waste of time and effort because they assumed that "building a catalog was a simple matter of writing down a list of titles"(Denton 2007 p. 38).

152. [LIS] Seymour Lubetzky worked for the US Library of Congress from 1943-1960 where he tirelessly sought to simplify the proliferating mass of special case cataloging rules proposed by the American Library Association, be-

cause at the time the LOC had the task of applying those rules and making the catalog cards other libraries used. Lubetzky's book on *Cataloguing Rules and Principles* (Lubetzky 1953) bluntly asks "Is this rule necessary?" and was a turning point in cataloging.

153. [LIS] In between the abstraction of the **work** and the specific single **item** are two additional levels in the FRBR abstraction hierarchy. An **expression** denotes the multiple the multiple realizations of a work in some particular medium or notation, where it can actually be perceived. There are many editions and translations of *Macbeth*, but they are all the same expression, and they are a different expression from all of the film adaptations of *Macbeth*. A **manifestation** is the set of physical artifacts with the same expression. All of the copies of the Folger Library print edition of *Macbeth* are the same manifestation.

154. [Computing] This kind of advice can be found in many data or conceptual modeling texts, but this particular statement comes from (Glushko, Weaver, Coonan, and Lincoln 1988). Similar advice can also be found in the information science literature: "A unit of information...would have to be....correctly interpretable outside any context" (Wilson 1968, p. 18).

155. [Computing] A group of techniques collectively called "normalization" produces a set of tightly defined information components that have minimal redundancy and ambiguity. Imagine that a business keeps information about customer orders using a "spreadsheet" style of organization in which a row contains cells that record the date, order number, customer name, customer address, item ID, item description, quantity, unit price, and total price. If an order contains multiple products, these would be recorded on additional rows, as would subsequent orders from the same customer. All of this information is important to the business, but this way of organizing it has a great deal of redundancy and inefficiency. For example, the customer address recurs in every order, and the customer address field merges street, city, state and zip code into a large unstructured field rather than separating them as atomic components of different types of information with potentially varying uses. Similar redundancy exists for the products and prices. Canceling an order might result in the business deleting all the information it has about a particular customer or product.

Normalization divides this large body of information into four separate tables, one for customers, one for customer orders, one for the items contained in each order, and one for item information. This normalized information model encodes all of the information in the "spreadsheet style" model, but eliminates the redundancy and avoids the data integrity problems that are inherent in it.

Normalization is taught in every database design course. The concept and methods were proposed by (Codd 1970), who invented the relational data model, and has been taught to students in numerous database design textbooks like (Date 2003).

156. [Computing] The "Internet of Things" concept spread very quickly after it was proposed in 1999 by Kevin Ashton, who co-founded the Auto-ID center at MIT that year to standardize RFID and sensor information. For a popular introduction, see (Gershenfeld, Krikorian, and Cohen 2004). For a recent technical survey and a taxonomy of application domains and scenarios see (Atzori, Iera, and Morabito 2010).

157. [Computing] University of Southern California professor Julian Bleecker coined the term "Blogjects" to describe objects that blog (Bleecker 2006, p. 2). Bleecker's early example of a Blogject is Beatriz da Costa's Pigeon Blog. Da Costa, a Los Angeles—based artist working at the intersection of life sciences, politics, and technology, armed urban pigeons with pollution sensors and locative tracking devices, released them, and created a web interface—in this case Pigeon Blog—to display their flight patterns on Google Maps alongside the pollution levels in the air as they flew. "Whereas once the pigeon was an urban varmint whose value as a participant in the larger social collective was practically nil or worse, the Pigeon that Blogs now attains first-class citizen status" (Bleecker 2006, p. 5).

158. [Computing] IBM's Andy Stanford-Clark has been credited with coining the term when he wired his house with sensors, enabling appliances to send information to the house's Twitter account, @andy_house (MacManus, 2009, para. 4). The house plant kit: *http://www.sparkfun.com/products/10334*. See also *http://supermechanical.com/twine*.

159. [Computing] Pattern analysis can help escape this dilemma by enabling predictive modeling to make optimal use of the data. In designing smart things and devices for people, it is helpful to create a smart model in order to predict the kinds of patterns and locations relevant to the data collected or monitored. These allow designers to develop a set of dimensions and principles that will act as smart guides for the development of smart things. Modeling helps to enable automation, security, or energy efficiency, and baseline models can be used to detect anomalies. As for location, exact locations are unnecessary; use of a "symbolic space" to represent each "sensing zone"—e.g., rooms in a house—and an individual's movement history as a string of symbols—e.g., abcdegia—works sufficiently as a model of prediction. See (Das et al. 2002).

160. [Law] Well, maybe not anything. Books list traditional meanings of various names, charts rank names by popularity in different eras, and dozens of websites tout themselves as the place to find a special and unique name. See *http://www.ssa.gov/oact/babynames/* for historical trends about baby names in the US with an interactive visualization at *http://www.babynamewizard.com/voyager#*.

Different countries have rules about characters or words that may be used in names. In Germany, for example, the government regulates the names parents can give to their children; there's even a book, the *International Handbook of Forenames*, to guide them (Kulish 2009). In Portugal, the Ministry of Justice publishes lists of prohibited names (BBC News, 2007a). Meanwhile, in 2007, Swedish tax officials rejected a family's attempt to name their daughter Metallica (*http://news.bbc.co.uk/2/hi/6525475.stm*).

We can also change our names. Whether a woman takes on her husband's surname after marriage or, like the California man who changed his name to "Trout Fishing," we just find something that better suits us than the name given by our parents.

161. [Lingusitics] While you may think that certain terms are more obviously "good" than others, studies show that "there is no one good access term for most objects. The idea of an 'obvious,' 'self-evident,'' or 'natural' term is a myth!" (Furnas et al. 1987, p. 967).

162. [CogSci] The most common names for this service were activities, calendar and events, but in all over a hundred different names were suggested, including cityevents, whatup, sparetime, funtime, weekender, nightout, and many more, "People use a surprisingly great variety of words to refer to the same thing," Furnas wrote. "If everyone always agreed on what to call things, the user's word would be the designer's word would be the system's word. . . . Unfortunately, people often disagree on the words they use for things" (Furnas et al. 1987, p. 964).

163. [CogSci] This example comes from (Farish 2002), who analyzes "What's in a Name?" and suggests that multiple names for the same thing might be a good idea because non-technical business users, data analysts, and system implementers need to see things differently and no one standard for assigning names will work for all three audiences.

164. [Linguistics] See, for example, *Handbook of Cross-Cultural Marketing*, (Kaynak 1997). The Starbucks coffee chain seemingly goes out of its way to confuse its customers by calling the smallest of its three coffee sizes (12 ounces) the "tall" size, calling its 16-ounce size a "*grande*," and calling its largest a "*venti*," which is Italian for 20 (ounces). Outside of Starbucks, something that is "tall" is never also considered "small." Ironically, despite having about 20,000 stores in about 60 countries, Starbucks has none in Italy where *venti* would be in the local language.

165. [Business] See "As easy as YZX," *http://www.economist.com/node/760345*. In addition, the convention to list the co-authors of scientific publications in alphabetic order has been shown to affect reputation and employment by giving undeserved advantages to people whose names start with letters that come early in the alphabet. This bias might also affect admission to selective schools. (Efthyvoulou 2008).

166. [Business] The Kentucky Fried Chicken franchise solved this problem by changing its name to KFC, which you can now find in Beijing, Moscow, London and other locations not anywhere near Kentucky and where many people have probably never heard of the place.

167. [Web] Tim Berners-Lee, the founder of the web, famously argued that *Cool URIs Don't Change* (Berners-Lee 1998).

168. [Law] Any online citation to one of the West printed court reports will use the West format. However, when Mead Data wanted to use the West page numbers in its LEXIS online service to link to specific pages, West sued for copyright infringement. The citation for the West Publishing vs. Mead Data Central case is 799 F.2d 1219 (8th Cir 1986), which means that the case begins on page 1219 of volume 799 in the set of opinions from the 8th Circuit Court of Appeals that West published in print form. West won the case and Mead Data had to pay substantial royalties. Fortunately, this logic behind this decision was repudiated by the US Supreme Court a few years later in a case that West published as *Feist Publications, Inc., v. Rural Telephone Service Co., 499 U.S. 340 (1991)*, and West can no longer claim copyright on page numbers.

169. [Linguistics] When George Orwell gave the title "1984" to a novel he wrote in 1949 he intended it as a warning about a totalitarian future as the Cold War took hold in a divided Europe, but today 1984 is decades in the past and the title does not have the same impact.

170. [Computing] (Dorai and Venkatesh 2002).

171. [Business] Most common US surnames; *http://names.mongabay.com/most_common_surnames.htm*.

Chad Ochocinco story: *http://en.wikipedia.org/wiki/Chad_Ochocinco*.

The Artist Formerly Known as Prince: *http://en.wikipedia.org/wiki/Prince_%28musician%29*.

Fake names at Starbucks: *http://online.wsj.com/article/SB10001424053111904106704576582834147448392.html*.

Twitter on sports jerseys: : *http://www.forbes.com/sites/alexknapp/2011/12/30/pro-lacrosse-team-replaces-names-with-twitter-handles-on-jerseys/?partner=technology_newsletter*.

172. [Computing] Identifiers with meaningful internal structure are said to be structured or intelligent. Those that contain no additional information are sometimes said to be unstructured, opaque, or dumb. The 8 in the ISBN example is a check digit, not technically part of the identifier, that is algorithmically derived from the other digits to detect errors in entering the ISBN.

173. [Linguistics] (McCartney 2006).

174. [LIS] (Svenonius 2000) calls vocabulary control "the *sine qua non* of information organization" (p. 89). "The imposition of vocabulary control creates an artificial language out of a natural language" (p. 89), leaving behind an official, normalized set of terms and their uses.

175. [LIS] This mapping is "the means by which the language of the user and that of a retrieval system are brought into sync" (Svenonius 2000, p. 93) and allows an information-seeker to understand the relationship between, say, Samuel Clemens and Mark Twain. The Library of Congress maintains a list of standard, accepted names for authors, subjects, and titles called the *Name Authority File*. *http://id.loc.gov/authorities/names.html*.

176. [LIS] Pan-European Species Directory Infrastructure (PESI): *http://www.eu-nomen.eu/pesi*; Consortium for the Barcode of Life (CBOL): *http://www.barcoding.si.edu/*; NatureServe: *http://services.natureserve.org/BrowseServices/getSpeciesData/getSpeciesListREST.jsp*.

177. [Web] (Hemerly 2011).

178. [Law] This rations / radio confusion is described in (Wheatley 2004). In 2008 a similar mistake in managing inventory at a US military warehouse led to missile launch fuses being sent to Taiwan instead of helicopter batteries, causing a high-level diplomatic furor when the Chinese government objected to this as a treaty violation (Hoffman 2008).

179. [LIS] Organizing systems in libraries, museums, and businesses often give sequential accession numbers to resources when they are added to a collection, but these identifiers are of no use outside of the context in which they are assigned, as when a union catalog or merged database is created.

180. [Computing] A more general technique is to use the UUID standard, which standardizes some algorithms that generate 128-bit tokens that, for all practical purposes, will be unique for hundreds, if not thousands, of years.

181. [Computing] The *Organization for the Advancement of Structured Information Systems (OASIS)* XML Common Biometric Format (XCBF) was developed to standardize the use of biometric data like DNA, fingerprints, iris scans, and hand geometry to verify identity (*https://www.oasis-open.org/committees/tc_home.php?wg_abbrev=xcbf*).

182. [LIS] (Coyle 2006, p. 429).

183. [Computing] IP v6 for internet addresses. The threat of exhaustion was the motivation for remedial technologies, such as classful networks, Classless Inter-Domain Routing (CIDR) methods, and Network Address Translation (NAT) that extend the usable address space.

184. [Computing] Digital Object Identifier (DOI) system (*http://www.doi.org*). However, DOI has its issues too. It's a highly political, publisher-controlled system, not a universal solution to persistence.

185. [Philosophy] This is called the *Paradox of Theseus*, a philosophical debate since ancient times. Every day that Theseus's ship is in the harbor, a single plank gets replaced, until after a few years the ship is completely rebuilt: not a single original plank remains. Is it still the ship of Theseus? And suppose, meanwhile, the shipbuilders have been building a new ship out of the replaced planks? Is that the ship of Theseus? (Furner 2008, p. 6).

186. [Archives] See (Renear and Dubin 2003), (Wynholds 2011).

187. [Law] Consider the case of an elderly woman born in 1929 in Zemum, a district in the eastern European city of Belgrade, who has never moved. The place she lives has been part of seven different countries during her lifetime: Kingdom of Yugoslavia (1929-1941); Independent State of Croatia (1941-1945); Federal People's Republic of Yugoslavia (1945-1963); Socialist Federal Republic of Yugoslavia (1963-1992); Federal Republic of Yugoslavia (1992-2003); State Union of Serbia and Montenegro (2003-2006); Republic of Serbia (2007 - present). See *http://www.nationsonline.org/oneworld/hist_coun try_names.htm* for a list of formerly used country names and their effectivities.

188. [Business] Effectivity in the tax code is simple compared to that relating to documents in complex systems, like commercial aircraft. Because of their long lifetimes—the Boeing 737 has been flying since the 1960s—and continual upgrading of parts like engines and computers, each airplane has its own operating and maintenance manual that reflects changes made to the plane over time. Every change to the plane requires an update to the repair manual, making the old version obsolete. And while an aircraft mechanic might refer to "the 737 maintenance manual," each 737 aircraft actually has its own unique manual.

189. [Law] A notary public is used to verify that a signature on an important document, such as a mortgage or other contract, is authentic, much as signet rings and sealing wax once proved that no one has tampered with a document since it was sealed.

Chapter 4
Resource Description and Metadata

Robert J. Glushko
Kimra McPherson
Ryan Greenberg
Matthew Mayernik

4.1 Introduction

Click. A professional photographer standing on a mountainside takes a picture with a digital camera. What information should be recorded and associated with the recorded image of the mountain scene? Modern cameras assign an identifier to the stored photograph and they also capture the technical description of the image's production: the type of camera, lens, shutter speed, light sensitivity, aperture, and other settings.[190] Many modern cameras also record information about the geographic and temporal circumstances surrounding the image's creation: the date, time and location on Earth where the photograph is taken. When the image is transferred out of the camera and is published for all to see, it might be useful to record biographical information about the photographer to help viewers relate to the photographer and better understand the photograph's context. There may also be different licenses and copyright information to associate with the picture—who owns it and how it can be used.

Four 7-year old boys are selecting Lego blocks to complete their latest construction. The first boy is looking for "cylinder one-ers," another for "coke bottles," the third for "golder wipers," and the final boy is looking for "round one-bricks"? It turns out, they are all the same thing; each boy has devised his own set of descriptive terms for the tiny building blocks. Some of their many descriptions are based on color alone ("redder"), some on color and shape ("blue tunnel"), some on role ("connector"), some on common cultural touchstones ("light saber"). Others, like "jail snail" and "slug," seem unidentifiable—unless, of course, you happen to be inside the mind of a particular 7-year-old kid. That does not matter, so long as their descriptions allow the boys to understand each other.[191]

Digital photos and Lego blocks are very different, yet for our purposes these scenarios are both about resource description. Together both scenarios raise important questions about describing resources that we answer in this chapter: What is the purpose of resource description? What resource properties should be described? How are resource descriptions created? What makes a good resource description?

We begin with an overview of "resource description" (§4.2), which we propose as a broad concept that includes the narrower concepts of bibliographic descriptions and metadata. §4.3, "The Process of Describing Resources" (page 148) describes a 7-step process of describing resources that includes determining scope, focus and purposes, identifying resource properties, designing the description vocabulary, designing the description form and implementation, and creating and evaluating the descriptions. Because many principles and methods for resource description were developed for describing text resources in physical formats, in §4.4, "Describing Non-Text Resources" (page 173) we briefly discuss the issues that arise when describing museum and artistic resources, images, music, video, and contextual resources.

4.2 An Overview of Resource Description

We describe resources so that we can refer to them, distinguish among them, search for them, manage access to them, and preserve them. Each purpose might require different resource descriptions. We use resource descriptions in every communication and conversation, and they are the enablers of organizing systems.

4.2.1 Naming {and, or, vs.} Describing

Chapter 3, *"Resources in Organizing Systems"* discussed how to decide what things should be treated as resources and how names and identifiers distinguish one resource from another. Many names are literally resource descriptions, or once were. Among the most common surnames in English are descriptions of occupations (Smith, Miller, Taylor), descriptions of kinship relations (Johnson, Wilson, Anderson), and descriptions of appearance (Brown, White).[192]

Similarly, many other kinds of resources have names that are property descriptions, including buildings (Pentagon, White House), geographical locations (North America, Red Sea), and cities (Grand Forks, Baton Rouge).

In many cultures throughout the world, it has been very common for one spouse or the other to take on a name that describes their marital relationship. Historically, in many parts of the English-speaking world, married women have often referred to themselves using their husband's name; when Jane Smith married John Brown, her name became Jane Brown or Mrs. John Brown.[193]

Every resource can be given a name or identifier. Identifiers are especially efficient resource descriptions because, by definition, identifiers are unique over some domain or collection of resources. Names and identifiers do not typically describe the resource in any ordinary sense because they are usually assigned to the resource rather than recording a property of it.

However, the arbitrariness of names and identifiers means that they do not serve to distinguish resources for people who do not already know them. This is why we use what linguists call referring expressions or definite descriptions, like "the small black dog" rather than the more efficient "Blackie," when we are talking to someone who does not know that is the dog's name.[194]

Similarly, when we use a library catalog or search engine to locate a known resource, such as a particular book or document, we query for it using its name, or other specific information we know about it, to increase the likelihood that we can find it. In contrast, when we are looking for resources to satisfy an information need but do not have specific resources in mind, we query for them using descriptions of their content or other properties. In general, information retrieval can be characterized as comparing the description of a user's needs with descriptions of the resources that might satisfy them.

4.2.2 "Description" as an Inclusive Term

Up to now we have used the concept of "description" without defining it because we have most often used it in its ordinary sense to mean the visible or important features that characterize or represent something. However, the concept is sometimes used more precisely in the context of organizing systems, where resource description is often more formal, systematic, and institutional. In the library science context of "bibliographic description," a *descriptor* is one of the terms in a carefully designed language that can be assigned to a resource to designate its properties, characteristics, or meaning, or its relationships with other resources. In the contexts of conceptual modeling and information systems design, the terms in resource descriptions are also called keywords, index terms, attributes, attribute values, elements, data elements, data values, or "the vocabulary." In contexts where descriptions are less formal or more personal the description terms are often called labels or tags. Rather than attempt to make fine distinctions among these synonyms or near-synonyms, we will use "description" as an inclusive term except where conventional usage overwhelmingly favors one of the other terms.

All of these terms come from a relatively narrow semantic scope in which the purpose of description is to identify and characterize the essence, or *aboutness*, of a resource. This leaves out many kinds of information that can be associated with a resource to support additional purposes; for example, information that specifies access controls or possible uses of the resource, or information about actual uses. We describe many of these purposes and the types of information needed to enable them in §4.3.2, "Determining the Purposes" (page 155). We apply "resource description" in an expansive way to accommodate all of them.

Chapter 3 introduced the distinction of Resource Focus (page 106) to contrast primary resources with resources that describe them, which we called Description Resources. We chose this term as a more inclusive and more easily understood alternative to two terms that are well established in organizing systems for information resources: **bibliographic descriptions** and **metadata**. We will also distinguish resource description as a general concept from the narrower senses of tagging of web resources and the *Resource Description Framework (RDF)* language used to make statements about web resources and physical resources that can be identified on the Web.

4.2.2.1 Bibliographic Descriptions

The purposes and nature of bibliographic description are the foundation of library and information science and have been debated and systematized for nearly two centuries. Bibliographic descriptions characterize information resources and the entities that populate the bibliographic universe, which include works, editions, authors, and subjects. Despite the "biblio-" root, bibliographic descriptions are applied to all of the resource types contained in libraries, not just books. Note also that this definition includes not just the information resources being described as distinct instances, but also as sets of related instances and the nature of those relationships.[195]

A bibliographic description of an information resource is typically realized as a structured record in a standardized format that describes a specific resource. The earliest bibliographic records in the nineteenth century were those in book catalogs, which organized for each author a list of his authored books, with separate entries for each edition and physical copy. Relationships between books by different authors were described using cross-references.

The nature and extent of bibliographic descriptions were highly constrained by the book catalog format, which also made the process of description a highly localized one because every library or collection of resources created its own catalog. The adoption of printed cards as the unit of organization for bibliographic descriptions around the turn of the twentieth century made it easier to maintain the catalog, and also enabled the centralized creation of the records by the Library of Congress.

The computerization of bibliographic records made them easier to use as aids for finding resources. However, digitizing legacy printed card-oriented descriptions for online use was not a straightforward task because the descriptions had been created according to cataloging rules designed for collections of books and other physical resources and intended only for use by people.

4.2.2.2 Metadata

Metadata is often defined as "data about data," a definition that is nearly as ubiquitous as it is unhelpful. A more content-full definition of metadata is that it is structured description for information resources of any kind, which makes it a superset of *bibliographic description*.

The concept of metadata originated in information systems and database design in the 1970s, so it is much newer than that of bibliographic description. In addition, metadata has originally meant and still most often refers to descriptions of classes or collections of resources rather than descriptions of individual resources. The earliest metadata resources, called data dictionaries, documented the arrangement and content of data fields in the records used by transactional applications on mainframe computers. A more sophisticated type of metadata emerged as the documentation of the data models in database management systems, called database schemas, which described the structure of relational tables, attribute names, and legal data types and values for content.

In 1986, the *Standard Generalized Markup Language (SGML)* formalized the *Document Type Definition (DTD)* as a metadata form for describing the structure and content elements in hierarchical and hypertextual document models. SGML was largely superseded beginning in 1997 by the eXtensible Markup Language (XML), whose initial purpose was to bring SGML to the web to make web content more structured and computer-processable.[196]

Today, XML schemas and other web- and compute-friendly formats for resource description have broadened the idea of resource description far beyond that of bibliographic description to include the description of software components, business and scientific data sets, web services, and computational objects in both physical and digital formats. The resource descriptions themselves serve to enable discovery, reuse, access control, and the invocation of other resources needed for people or computational agents to effectively interact with the primary ones described by the metadata.[197]

The concept of metadata has more recently been extended to include the tags, ratings, bookmarks or other types of descriptions that individuals apply to individual photos, blog or news items, or any other web resource or physical resource with a web presence that can be annotated.

4.2.2.3 Tagging of Web-Based Resources

Tags are labels in the form of words or phrases that describe a resource. With the explosive growth of digital photos and videos, both kept in personal collections and shared online, the practice of tagging has emerged as a way to apply labels to content in order to describe and identify it. Sets of tags have become incredibly useful both in managing one's collection of websites or digital media, to share them with others, and to enable new types of interactions and services.[198] For example, users of **Last.fm** tag music with labels help describe its nature, era, mood, or genre, and Last.fm uses these tags to generate radio stations that play music similar to that tag and related tags.

But tagging has a downside. A lack of vocabulary control and a tendency for users to tag intuitively and spontaneously revives the vocabulary problem (§3.4) because one photographer's "tree" is another's "oak." Likewise, unsystematic word choice leads to morphological inconsistency (§5.4.3, "Relationships among Word Forms" (page 207)); the same photo might be tagged with "burning" and "trees" by one person and with "burn" and "tree" by another. This disparity in the descriptors people use to categorize the same or similar resources can turn systems that use tagging into a "tag soup" lacking in structure.[199]

Some social media sites have incorporated mechanisms to make the tagging activity more systematic and to reduce *vocabulary problems*. For example, on Facebook, users can indicate that a specific person is in an uploaded picture by clicking on the faces of people in photographs, typing the person's name, and then selecting the person from a list of Facebook friends whose names are formatted the way they appear on the friend's profile, Some social media systems suggest the most popular tags, perform morphological normalization, or allow users to arrange tags in bundles or hierarchies.[200]

4.2.2.4 Resource Description Framework (RDF)

The Resource Description Framework (RDF) is a standard model for making computer-processable statements about web resources; it is the foundation for the vision of the *Semantic Web*.[201] We have been using the word "resource" to refer to anything that is being organized. In the context of RDF and the web, however, "*resource*" means something more specific: a resource is anything that has been given a Uniform Resource Identifier (URI). URIs can take various forms, but you are probably most familiar with the URIs used to identify web pages, such as http://springfield-elementary.edu/. (You are probably also used to calling these URLs instead of URIs.) The key idea behind RDF is that we can use URIs to identify not only things "on" the web, like web pages, but also things "off" the web like people or countries. For example, we might use the URI http://springfield-elementary.edu/ to refer to Springfield Elementary itself, and not just the school's web page.

RDF models all descriptions as sets of "triples," where each *triple* consists of the resource being described (identified by a URI), a property, and a value. Properties are resources too, meaning they are identified by URIs. For example, the URI *http://xmlns.com/foaf/0.1/schoolHomepage* identifies a property defined by the "Friend of a Friend" project for relating a person to (the web page of) a school they attended. Values can be resources too, but they do not have to be: when a property takes simple values like numbers, dates, or text strings, these values do not have URIs and so are not resources.

Because RDF uses URIs to identify described resources, their properties, and (some) property values, the triples in a description can be connected into a network or "graph." Figure 4.1, "RDF Triples Arranged as a Graph." shows four triples that have been connected into a graph. Two of the triples describe Bart Simpson, who is identified using the URI of his Wikipedia page.[202] The other two describe Lisa Simpson. Two of the triples use the property age, which takes a simple number value. The other two use the property schoolHomepage, which takes a resource value, and in this case they happen to have the same resource (Springfield Elementary's home page) as their value.

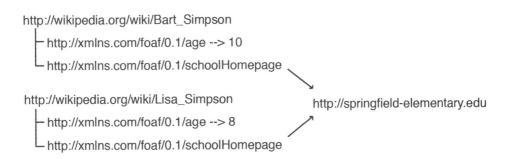

Figure 4.1. RDF Triples Arranged as a Graph.

Using URIs as identifiers for resources and properties allows descriptions modeled as RDF to be interconnected into a network of "linked data," in the same way that the web enabled information to be interconnected into a massive network of "linked documents." Proponents of RDF claim that this will greatly benefit knowledge discovery and inference.[203] But the benefits of RDF's highly prescriptive description form must be weighed against the costs; turning existing descriptions into RDF can be labor-intensive.

RDF can be used for bibliographic description, and some libraries are exploring whether RDF transformations of their legacy bibliographic records can be exposed and integrated with resource descriptions on the open web. This activity has raised technical concerns about whether the RDF model of description is sophisticated enough and more fundamental concerns about the desirability of losing control over library resources.[204]

4.2.3 Frameworks for Resource Description

The broad scope of resources to which descriptions can be applied and the different communities that describe them means that many **frameworks** and classifications have been proposed to help make sense of resource description.

The dominant historical view treats resource descriptions as a package of statements; this view is embodied in the printed library card catalog and its computerized analog in the MARC21 format (an exchange format for library catalog records), which contains many fields about the bibliographic characteristics of an object like author, title, publication year, publisher, and pagination. An alternate architecture for resource description focuses on each individual description or assertion about a single resource. This statement at a time view of resource is more typical when descriptions are assigned to web objects or resources, and much of the discussion about this view is framed in terms of the particular syntactic forms being used in RDF. Figure 4.2, "Architectures for Resource Description." contrasts these two alternatives.

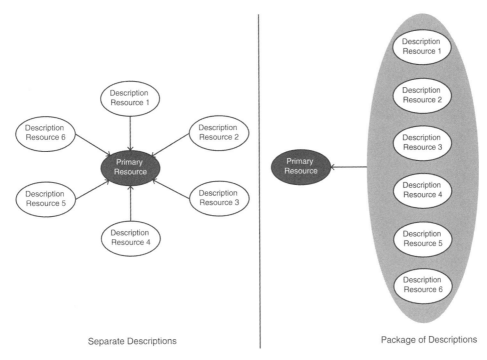

Separate Descriptions | Package of Descriptions

Resource Descriptions

Figure 4.2. Architectures for Resource Description.

In either case, these common ways of thinking about resource description emphasize—or perhaps even overemphasize—two implementation decisions. The first is whether to combine multiple resource descriptions into a structural package or to keep them as separate descriptive statements. The second is the choice of syntax in which the descriptions are encoded.

Both of these implementation decisions have important implications, but are secondary to the questions about the purposes of resource description, how resource properties are selected as the basis for description, how they are best created, and other logical or design considerations. In keeping with the fundamental idea of the discipline of organizing (introduced in §1.2.3.1, "The Concept of "Organizing Principle"" (page 12)), it is imperative to distinguish design principles from implementation choices. We treat the set of implementation decisions about character notations, syntax, and structure as the *form* of resource description and we will defer them as much as we can until Chapter 8, *"The Forms of Resource Descriptions"*.

In library and information science, it is very common to discuss resource descriptions using a classification proposed by Arlene Taylor, which distinguishes administrative, structural, and descriptive metadata.[205] A similar typology proposed by Gilliland breaks metadata down into five types: administrative, descriptive, preservation, use, and technical.[206] Both of these classifications imply a narrow notion of descriptive metadata that reflects the historical emphasis on bibliographic description, in contrast to our view that treats resource description as a more inclusive category. In addition, these classifications do not always distinguish between intrinsic and extrinsic properties (as we will see in §4.3.3, "Identifying Properties" (page 160)), and they often mix and match design and implementation considerations.

Resource description is not an end in itself. Its many purposes are all means for enabling and using an organizing system for some collection of resources. As a result, our framework for resource descriptions aligns with the activities of organizing systems we discussed in Chapter 2: selecting, organizing, interacting with, and maintaining resources.

4.3 The Process of Describing Resources

We prefer the general concept of resource description over the more specialized ones of bibliographic description and metadata because it makes it easier to see the issues that cut across the domains where those terms dominate. In addition, it enables us to propose more standard process that we can apply broadly to the use of resource descriptions in organizing systems. A shared vocabulary enables the sharing of lessons and best practices.

The process of describing resources involves several interdependent and iterative steps. We begin with a generic summary of the process to set the stage for a detailed step-by-step discussion.

1. **Determining Scope and Focus**

   Identifying resources to describe is the first step; this topic is covered in detail in §3.3, "Resource Identity" (page 109). The resource **domain** and **scope** circumscribe the describable properties and the possible purposes that descriptions might serve. The resource *focus* determines which are primary information resources and which ones are treated as the corresponding resource descriptions. Two important decisions at this stage are **granularity** of description—are we describing individual resources or collections of them?—and the **abstraction** level—are we describing resource instances, parts of them, or resource types?

2. **Determining Purposes**

Generally, the purpose of resource description is to support the activities common to all organizing systems: selecting, organizing, interacting with, and maintaining resources, as we saw in Chapter 2. The particular resource domain and the context in which descriptions are created and used imposes more specific requirements and constraints on the purposes that resource description can serve.

3. **Identifying Resource Properties**

    Once the purposes of description in terms of activities and interactions have been determined, the specific properties of the resources that are needed to enable them can be identified. The contrasts between intrinsic and extrinsic properties, and between static and dynamic properties, are useful to identify appropriate resource properties.

4. **Designing the Description Vocabulary**

    This step includes several logical and semantic decisions about how the resource properties will be described. What terms or element names should be used to identify the resource properties we have chosen to describe? Are there rules or constraints on the types of data or values that the property descriptions can assume? A good description vocabulary will be easy to assign when creating resource descriptions and easy to understand when using them.

5. **Designing the Description Form and Implementation**

    The logical and semantic decisions about the description vocabulary are reified by decisions about the notation, syntax and structure of the descriptions. Taken together, these decisions collectively determine what we call the **form** or **encoding** of the resource descriptions. The implementation of the descriptions involves decisions about how and where they are stored and the technology used to create, edit, store, and retrieve them.

6. **Creating the Descriptions**

    Resource descriptions are created by individuals, by informal or formal groups of people, or by automated or computational means. Some types of descriptions can only be created by people, some types of descriptions can only be created by automated or algorithmic techniques, and some can be created in either manner.

7. **Evaluating the Descriptions**

    The resource descriptions must be evaluated with respect to their intended purposes. The results of this evaluation will help determine which or the preceding steps need to be redone.

The next seven sub-sections discuss each of these steps in detail. A quick reference guide is Figure 4.3, "The Process of Describing Resources."

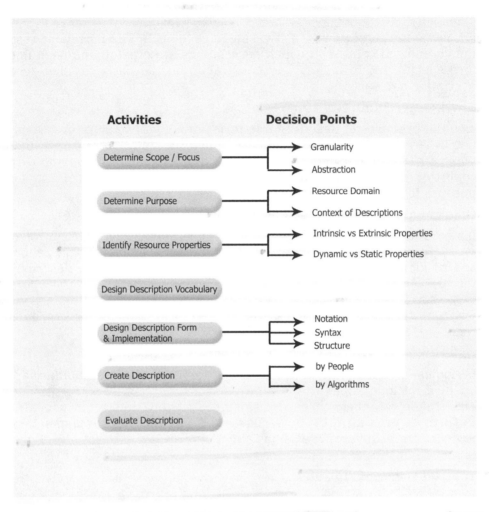

Figure 4.3. The Process of Describing Resources.

How explicit and systematic each step needs to be depends on the resource domain and scope, and especially on the intended users of the organizing system. If we look carefully, we can see most of these steps taking place even in very informal contexts, like the kids playing with Lego blocks with which we started this chapter. The goal of building things with the blocks leads the boys to identify which properties are most useful to analyze. They develop descriptions of the blocks that capture the specific values of the relevant properties. Finally, they evaluate their descriptions by using them when they play together; it becomes immediately obvious that a description is not serving its purpose when one boy hands a block to another that was not the one he thought he had asked for.

In contrast, the picture-taking scenario involves a much more explicit and systematic process of resource description. The resource properties, description vocabulary, and description form used automatically by the digital camera were chosen by an industry association and published as a technical specification implemented by camera and mobile phone manufacturers worldwide. If a professional photographer is taking the photo for commercial purposes, many of the other descriptions assigned to the image to identify ownership, rights management and syndication are likely to conform to formal specifications and be managed in institutional information systems.

The resource descriptions used by libraries, archives, and museums are typically created in an even more explicit and systematic manner. Like the descriptions of the digital photo, the properties, vocabulary, and form of the descriptions used by their organizing systems are governed by standards. However, there is no equivalent to the digital camera that can create these descriptions automatically. Instead, highly trained professionals create them meticulously.

A great many resources and their associated descriptions in business and scientific organizing systems are created by automated or computational processes, so the process of describing individual resources is not at all like that in libraries and other memory institutions. However, the process for designing the data models or schemas for the class of resources that will be generated is equally systematic and is typically performed by highly skilled data analysts and data modelers.

4.3.1 Determining the Scope and Focus

Which resources do we want to describe? As we saw in Chapter 3, determining what will be treated as a separate resource is not always easy, especially for resources with component parts and for information resources where the most important property is their content, which is not directly perceivable. Identifying the thing you want to describe as precisely as practical is the first step to creating a useful description.

In §3.2.4, "Resource Focus" (page 106), we introduced the contrast between primary resources and description resources, which we called resource focus. Determining the resource focus goes hand in hand with determining which resources we intend to describe; these often arbitrary decisions then make a huge difference in the nature and extent of resource description. One person's metadata is another person's data. For a librarian, the price of a book might be just one more attribute that is part of the book's record. For an accountant at a bookstore, the price of that book—both the cost to buy the book and the price at which it is then sold to customers—is critical information for staying in business. A scientist studying comparative anatomy preserves animal specimens and records detailed physical descriptions about them, but a scientist studying ecology or migration discards the specimens and focuses on describing the context in which the specimen was located.

4.3.1.1 Describing Instances or Describing Collections

It is simplest to think of a resource description as being associated with another individual resource. However, as discussed in Chapter 3, it can be challenging to determine what to treat as an individual resource when resources are themselves objects or systems that are composed of other parts or resources. For example, we sometimes describe a football team as a single resource and at other times we focus on each individual player. However, after we have decided on resource granularity, the question remains whether each resource needs a separate description.

Libraries and museums specialize in curating resource descriptions about the instances in their collections. Resource descriptions are also applied to classes or collections of resources (because a collection is also a resource; see §1.2.2, "The Concept of "Collection"" (page 10)). Archives and special collections of maps are typically assigned resource descriptions, but each document or map contained in the collection does not necessarily have its own bibliographic description. Similarly, business and scientific data sets are invariably described at collection-level granularity because they are often analyzed in their entirety.

Furthermore, the granularity of description for a collection of resources tends to differ for different users or purposes. Consider the information systems that commodity traders use to access descriptions of real resources in markets all over the world: some traders are concerned with weekly production in their region, while others are monitoring real-time global flows of precious metals and petroleum products. Many web pages, especially e-commerce product catalogs and news sites, are dynamically assembled and personalized from a large number of information resources and services that are separately identified and described in content management and content delivery systems. However, a highly complex collection of resources that comes together in a single page is treated as a single resource when that page appears in a list of search engine results. Moreover, all of the thousands of separately generated pages can be given a single description when a user creates a bookmark to make it easy to return to the home page of the site.

4.3.1.2 Abstraction in Resource Description

We can also associate resource descriptions with an entire type or domain of resources (see §2.5.2.4, "Preserving Resource Types" (page 73) and §3.2.1, "Resource Domain" (page 100)). A collection of resource descriptions is vastly more useful when every resource is described using common description elements or terms that apply to every resource. A *schema* (or model, or metadata standard) specifies the set of descriptions that apply to an entire resource type. Sometimes this schema, model, or standard is inferred from or imposed on a collection of existing resources to ensure more consistent definitions, but more often, it is used as a specification when the resources are created or generated in the first place (See "What about "Creating" Resources?" (page 50) in §2.1, "Introduction" (page 47)).

A relational database, for example, is easily conceptualized as a collection of records organized as one or more tables, with each record in its own row having a number of fields or attributes that contain some prescribed type of content. Each record or row in the database table is a description of a resource—an employee, a product, anything—and the individual attribute values, organized by the columns and rows of the table, are distinct parts of the description for some particular resource instance, like employee 24 or product 8012C.

Because the relational database schema serves as a model for the creation of resource descriptions, it is designed to restrict the descriptions to be simple and completely regular sets of attribute-value pairs. The database schema specifies the overall structure of the tables and especially their columns, which will contain the attribute values that describe each resource. An employee table might have columns for the attributes of employee ID, hiring date, department, and salary. A date attribute will be restricted to a value that is a date, while an employee salary will be restricted according to salary ranges established by the human resources department. This makes the name of the attribute and the constraints on attribute values into resource descriptions that apply to the entire class of resources described by the table.

The information resources that we commonly call documents are, by their nature, less homogeneous in content and structure than those that can be managed in databases. Document schemas, commonly represented in SGML or XML, usually allow for a mixture of data-like and textual descriptive elements. XML schema languages have greatly improved on SGML and XML by expressing the description of the document schema in XML itself, using the same syntax as the resource it describes, making it easy to create resources using the metadata as a template or pattern. As a result, XML schemas are often used as the specifications for XML resources created and used by information-intensive applications; in this context, they are often called XML vocabularies. XML schemas are often used to define web forms that capture resource instances (each filled-out form). XML schemas are also used to describe the interfaces to web services and other computational resources.[207]

It is often necessary to associate some descriptions with individual resources that are specific to that instance and other kinds of descriptions that reflect the abstract class to which the instance belongs. When a typical car comes off the assembly line, it has only one instance-level description that differentiates it from its peers: its vehicle identification number (VIN). Specific cars have individualized interior and exterior colors and installed options, and they all have a date and location of manufacture. Other description elements have values that are shared with many other cars of the same model and year, like suggested price and the additional option packages, or configurations that can be applied to it before it is delivered to a customer. Alternatively, any descriptive information that applies to multiple cars of the same model year could be part of a resource description at that level that is referred to rather than duplicated in instance descriptions.

4.3.1.3 Scope, Scale, and Resource Description

If we only had one thing to describe, we could use a single word to describe it: "it." We would not need to distinguish it from anything else. A second resource implies at least one more term in the description language: "not it." However, as a collection grows, descriptions must become more complex to distinguish not only between, but also among resources.

Every element or term in a description language creates a dimension, or axis, along which resources can be distinguished, or it defines a set of questions about resources. Distinctions and questions that arise frequently, such as "what is the name of the resource?", "who created it?", or "what type of content or matter does it contain?", need to be easy to address. Therefore, as a collection grows, the language for describing resources must become more rigorous, and descriptions created when the collection was small often require revision because they are no longer adequate for their intended purposes. The description language typically evolves from a simple list of descriptive terms to a glossary with definitions, to a highly controlled vocabulary with content rules for allowable values, and, finally, to a thesaurus in which each term is also defined with respect to its semantic relationships to other terms that are broader, narrower, or otherwise associated with it.[208]

This co-evolution of descriptive scope and description complexity is easy to see in the highly complex bibliographic descriptions created by professional catalogers. The commonly used *AACR2* cataloging standards distinguish 11 different categories of resources and specify several hundred descriptive elements.[209] Because the task of library resource description has been standardized at national and international levels, cataloging work is distributed among many describers whose results are shared. This principle of standardization has been the basis of centralized bibliographic description for a century.

Centralized resource description by skilled professionals works for libraries, but even in the earliest days of the web many library scientists and web authoring futurists recognized that this approach would not scale for describing web resources. In 1995, the Dublin Core metadata element set with only 15 elements was proposed as a vastly simpler description vocabulary that people not trained as professional catalogers could use.[210] Since then, the Dublin Core initiative has been highly influential in inspiring numerous other communities to create minimalist description vocabularies, often by simplifying vocabularies that had been devised by professionals for use by non-professionals. In this respect, we can also view the Dublin Core as part of the intellectual foundations for the "crowdsourcing" or "community curation" of resource descriptions by non-professionals (§2.5.3.3, "Social and Web Curation" (page 75)).

Of course, a simpler description vocabulary makes fewer distinctions than a complex one; replacing "author," "artist," "composer" and many other descriptions of the person or non-human resource responsible for the intellectual content of a resource with just "creator" results in a substantial loss of precision when the description is created and can cause misunderstanding when the descriptions are reused.[211]

The negative impacts of growing scope and scale on resource description can sometimes be avoided if the ultimate scope and scale of the organizing system is contemplated when it is being created. It would not be smart for a business with customers in six US states to create an address field in its customer database that only handled those six states; a more extensible design would allow for any state or province and include a country code. In general, however, just as there are problems in adapting a simple vocabulary as scope and scale increase, designing and applying resource descriptions that will work for a large and continuously growing collection might seem like too much work when the collection at hand is small.

4.3.2 Determining the Purposes

Resource description serves many purposes, and the mix of purposes and the resulting kinds of descriptions in any particular organizing system depends on the scope and scale of the resources being organized. We can identify and classify the most common purposes using the four activities that occur in every organizing system: selecting, organizing, interacting with, and maintaining resources (see Chapter 2).

4.3.2.1 Resource Description to Support Selection

Defining selection as the process by which resources are identified, evaluated, and then added to a collection in an organizing system emphasizes resource descriptions created by someone other than the person who is using them. We can distinguish several different ways in which resource description supports selection:

Discovery

What resources are available that might be added to a collection? New resources are often listed in directories, registries, or catalogs. Some types of resources are selected and acquired automatically through subscriptions or contracts.

Capability and Compatibility

Will the resource meet functional or interoperability requirements? Technology-intensive resources often have numerous specialized types of descriptions that specify their functions, performance, reliability, and other "-ilities" that determine if they fit in with other resources in an organizing system.[212] Some services have qualities of service levels, terms and conditions, or interfaces documented in resource descriptions that affect their compatibility and interoperability. Some resources have licensing or usage restrictions that might prevent the resources from being used effectively for the intended purposes.

Authentication

Is the resource what it claims to be? (§3.5.3, "Authenticity" (page 126)). Resource descriptions that can support authentication include technological ones like time stamps, watermarking, encryption, checksums, and digital signatures. The history of ownership or custody of a resource, called its provenance (§3.5.4, "Provenance" (page 126)), is often established through association with sales or tax records. Import and export certificates associated with the resource might be required to comply with laws designed to prevent the theft of antiquities or the transfer of technology or information with national security or foreign policy implications.

Appraisal

What is the value of this resource? What is its cost? At what rate does it depreciate? Does it have a shelf life? Does it have any associated ratings, rankings, or quality measures? Moreover, what is the quality of those ratings, rankings and measures?

We can also take the perspective of the person creating the resource description and consider his or her primary purpose, which is often to encourage the selection of the resource by someone else. This is what product marketing is about—devising names and descriptions to make a resource distinctive and attractive compared to alternatives. A fish once known as the Patagonian Toothfish became popular in American restaurants when a fish wholesaler began marketing it as the Chilean Sea Bass. Apple has consistently described its products to emphasize experiential or cultural properties, as compared with Intel or other PC manufacturers, whose descriptions emphasize technical specifications.[213]

4.3.2.2 Resource Description to Support Organizing

Often, the activities of organizing resources and designing interactions with them are intertwined, but they are logically separate. We define organizing as specifying the principles or rules for describing and arranging resources in order to create the capabilities on which interactions are based. This lets us treat the design and implementation of resource interactions as if those were separate and subsequent activities. For example, assigning keywords to documents that describe their contents is an organizing activity, while designing and implementing an information retrieval application that uses the keywords is the design of resource interactions.

Physical resources are often organized according to their tangible or perceivable properties like size, color, material of composition, or shape (§2.3.1.1, "Organizing with Properties of Physical Resources" (page 56)).[214] For other types of physical resources, however, such as hazardous materials, it is the descriptions and not the directly perceivable properties that determine or constrain how the resources are organized (§2.3.1.2, "Organizing with Descriptions of Physical Resources" (page 57)). Similarly, building codes or other regulations associated with physical resources can prescribe or prohibit particular resource arrangements. Rules governing the collection, integration, and analysis of personal information are also resource descriptions that influence the organization of information resources.

Any types of resources that have sortable identifiers can be organized using that descriptive element.

4.3.2.3 Resource Description to Support Interactions

Most discussions of the purposes of resource descriptions and metadata emphasize the interactions that are based on resource descriptions that have been intentionally and explicitly assigned. For bibliographic resources these interactions and the models of resource descriptions needed to support them have been formalized as the Functional Requirements for Bibliographic Records (FRBR).[215] FRBR presents four purposes that apply generically to organizing systems, not just bibliographic ones: Finding, Identifying, Selecting, and Obtaining resources.

Finding

What resources are available that "correspond to the user's stated search criteria" and thus can satisfy an information need? Before there were online catalogs and digital libraries, we found resources by referencing catalogs of printed resource descriptions incorporating the title, author, and subject terms as access points into the collection; the subject descriptions were the most important finding aids when the user had no particular resource in mind. Modern users accept that computerized indexing makes search possible over not only the entire description resource, but often over the entire content of the primary resource. Businesses search directories for descriptions of company capabilities to find potential partners, and they also search for descriptions of application interfaces that enable them to exchange information in an automated manner.

Identifying

Another purpose of resource description is to enable a user to confirm the identity of a specific resource or to distinguish among several that have some overlapping descriptions. In bibliographic contexts this might mean finding the resource that is identified by its citation. Computer processable resource descriptions like bar codes, QR codes, or RFID tags are also used to identify resources. In Semantic Web contexts, URIs serve this purpose.

Selecting

The user activity of using resource descriptions to support a choice of resource from a collection, not the institutional activity of selecting resources for the collection in the first place. Search engines typically use a short "text snippet" with the query terms highlighted as resource descriptions to support selection. People often select resources with the least restrictions on uses as described in a Creative Commons license.[216] A business might select a supplier or distributor that uses the same standard or industry reference model to describe its products or business processes because it is almost certain to reduce the cost of doing business with that business partner.[217]

Obtaining

Physical resources often require significant effort to obtain after they have been selected. Catching a bus or plane involves coordinating your current location and time with the time and location the resource is available. With information resources in physical form, obtaining a selected resource usually meant a walk through the library stacks. With digital information resources, a search engine returns a list of the identifiers of resources that can be accessed with just another click, so it takes little effort to go from selecting among the query results to obtaining the corresponding primary resource.[218]

Elaine Svenonius proposed that a fifth task be added to the FRBR list:

Navigation

If users are not able to specify their information needs in a way that the "finding" functionality requires, they should be able to use relational and structural descriptions among the resources to navigate from any resource to other ones that might be better. Svenonius emphasizes generalization, aggregation, and derivational relationships.[219] But in a truly semantic web, any relationship or property could serve as the navigation "highway" between resources.

What some authors call "structural metadata" can be used to support the related tasks of moving within multi-part digital resources like electronic books, where each page might have associated information about previous, next, and other related pages. Documents described using XML models can use XSLT and *XPath* to address and select data elements, sub-trees, or other structural parts of the document.[220]

The FRBR framework is the most recent formalization of the purposes of resource description that started in nineteenth century libraries.[221] This long history means it is not surprising that how we think about resource description still shows some bias toward interactions with physical bibliographic resources and the descriptions needed to obtain them. With physical resources, any interactions that take place once the primary resources are obtained are outside the scope of the organizing system because they are not directly supported by it.

With digital resources, on the other hand, many of the purposes of resource description are realized with the primary resources. These purposes usually involve processing of the resource content and structure: analysis, summarization, visualization, transformation, reuse, mixing, remixing... far too many purposes to list here. The core principle that underlies all of these purposes is that the variety and functions of the interactions with digital resources depends on the richness of their structural, semantic, and format description (See §2.4.2.2, "Value Creation with Digital Resources" (page 64)).

An important difference between interactions with physical resources and those with digital resources is how they use resource descriptions for access control. Resources sometimes have associated security classifications like "Top Secret" that restrict who can learn about their existence or obtain them. Nonetheless, if you get your hands on a top secret printed document, nothing can prevent you from reading it. Similarly, printed resources often have "All rights reserved" copyright notices that say that you cannot copy them, but nothing can prevent you from making copies with a copy machine. On the other hand, learning of the existence of a digital resource might be of little value if copyright or licensing restrictions prevent you from obtaining it. Moreover, obtaining a digital resource might be of no value if its content is only available using a password, decryption key, or other resource description that enforces access control directly rather than indirectly like the security classifications.

Another important difference between physical resources and digital ones is that interactions with the latter are easily recorded. Usage records from session logs, browsing, or downloading activities are resource descriptions that can be tied to payments for using the resources or analyzed to influence the selection and organizing of resources in future interactions.

4.3.2.4 Resource Description to Support Maintenance

Many types of resource descriptions that support selection (§4.3.2.1, "Resource Description to Support Selection" (page 155)) are also useful over time to support maintenance of specific resource and the collection to which they belong. In particular, technical information about resource formats and technology (software, computers, or other) needed to use the resources, and information needed to ensure resource integrity is often called "preservation metadata" in a maintenance context.[222]

Other types of resource descriptions more exclusively associated with maintenance activities include version information and effectivity or useful life information. Usage records are also valuable because they enable the identification of resources that are not being accessed, suggesting that they are no longer needed and can thus be safely archived or discarded.

4.3.3 Identifying Properties

Once the purposes of description have been established, we need to identify the specific properties of the resources that can satisfy those purposes. There are four reasons why this task is more difficult than it initially appears.

First, any particular resource might need many resource descriptions, all of which relate to different properties, depending on the interactions to be supported and the context in which they take place. Think about how we might describe something as simple as a chair. In your house, you might describe your chair based on the room it is in, e.g., "the kitchen chair." When you take the same chair to a potluck dinner at a friend's house, where all the chairs end up in the kitchen, it becomes "my chair," or "the wooden chair," or "the folding chair," or "the black chair with white trim." Maybe you inherited it, so when you talk to your family, you call it "grandma's chair." If you decide to sell it, you will describe it in a way that is intended to encourage someone to buy it, as an "all-oak antique kitchen chair in mint condition."

Second, different types of resources need to incorporate different properties in their descriptions. For resources in a museum, these might include materials and dimensions of pieces of art; for files and services managed by a network administrator, these include access control permissions; for electronic books or DVDs, they would include the digital rights management (DRM) code that expresses what you can and cannot do with the resource.

Third, as we briefly touched on in §4.3.1.3, "Scope, Scale, and Resource Description" (page 154), which properties participate in resource descriptions depends on who is doing the describing. It makes little sense to expect fine-grained distinctions and interpretations about properties from people who lack training in the discipline of organizing. We will return to this tradeoff in §4.3.6,

"Creating Resource Descriptions" (page 168) and again in §4.4.1, "Describing Museum and Artistic Resources" (page 173).

Fourth, what might seem to be the same property at a conceptual level might be very different at an implementation level. Many types of resources have a resource description that is a surrogate or summary in some respects of the primary resource. For photos, paintings, and other resources whose appearance is their essence, an appropriate summary description can be a smaller, reduced resolution or thumbnail photo of the original. This surrogate is simple to create and it is easy for users to understand its relationship to the primary resource. On the other hand, distilling a text down to a short summary or abstract is a skill unto itself. Time-based resources provide greater challenges for summary. Should the summary of a movie be a textual summary of the plot, a significant clip from the movie, a video summary, or something else altogether? How is a song summarized? Or a poem? Or a tree?

Two important dimensions for understanding and contrasting resource properties used in descriptions and organizing principles are property essence—whether the properties are intrinsically or extrinsically associated with the resource, and property persistence—the properties are static or dynamic. Taken together these two dimensions yield four categories of properties, as illustrated in Figure 4.4, "Property Essence x Persistence: Four Categories of Properties."

4.3.3.1 Intrinsic Static Properties

Intrinsic or implicit properties are inherent in the resource and can often be directly perceived or experienced. Static properties do not change their values over time. The size, color, shape, weight, material of composition, and texture of natural or manufactured objects are intrinsic and static properties that are often used to describe and organize physical resources. If a particular Lego is blue, it is set apart from all the not-blue Legos; a square Lego is physically different from a round one. When bibliographic resources were exclusively physical, their sizes and their number of pages were common physical properties in their descriptions.

Intrinsic physical properties are usually just part of resource descriptions. In many cases, physical properties describe only the surface layer of a resource, revealing little about what something is or its original intended purpose, what it means, or when and why it was created. These intrinsic static properties cannot be directly perceived. The author or creator of a resource, the context of its creation, and the duration of a song are other examples of intrinsic and static resource properties.

Intrinsic descriptions are often extracted or calculated by computational processes. For example, a computer program might calculate the frequency and distribution of words in some particular document. Those statistics about con-

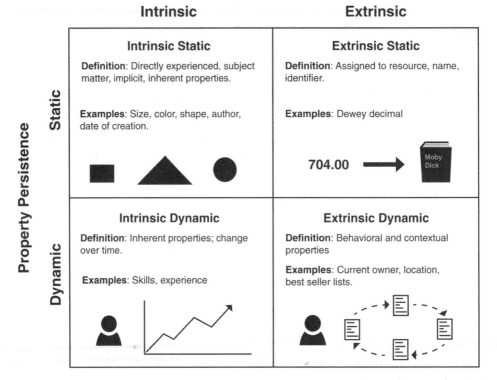

Property Essence

Intrinsic

Extrinsic

Intrinsic Static

Definition: Directly experienced, subject matter, implicit, inherent properties.

Examples: Size, color, shape, author, date of creation.

Extrinsic Static

Definition: Assigned to resource, name, identifier.

Examples: Dewey decimal

704.00

Intrinsic Dynamic

Definition: Inherent properties; change over time.

Examples: Skills, experience

Extrinsic Dynamic

Definition: Behavioral and contextual properties

Examples: Current owner, location, best seller lists.

Figure 4.4. Property Essence x Persistence: Four Categories of Properties.

tent properties would still be intrinsic descriptions even though an external process creates them. Similarly, "image signatures" or "audio fingerprints" are intrinsic descriptions (§4.4, "Describing Non-Text Resources" (page 173)).

Some relationships among resources are intrinsic and static, like the parent-child relationship or the sibling relationship between two children with the same parents. Part-whole or compositional relationships for resources with parts, both physical ones like manufactured objects and digital ones like hierarchical documents or databases, are also intrinsic static properties often used in resource descriptions. However, it is better to avoid treating resource relationships as properties, and instead express them as relations. Chapter 5, *"Describing Relationships and Structures"* discusses part-whole and other semantic relationships in great detail.

4.3.3.2 Extrinsic Static Properties

Extrinsic or explicit properties are assigned to a resource rather than being inherent in it. The name or identifier of a resource is often arbitrary but once assigned does not usually change. Arranging resources according to the alphabetical or numerical order of their descriptive identifiers is a common organizing principle. Classification numbers and subject headings assigned to bibliographic resources are extrinsic static properties, as are the serial numbers stamped on or attached to manufactured products.

For information resources that have a digital form, the properties of their printed or rendered versions might not be intrinsic. Some text formats completely separate content from presentation, and as a result, style sheets can radically change the appearance of a printed document or web page without altering the primary resource in any way. For example, were a different style applied to this paragraph to highlight it in bold or cast in 24-point font, its content would remain the same.

4.3.3.3 Intrinsic Dynamic Properties

Intrinsic dynamic properties change over time, such as developmental personal characteristics like a person's height and weight, skill proficiency, or intellectual capacity. Because these properties are not static, they are usually employed only to organize resources whose membership in the collection is of limited duration. Sports programs or leagues that segregate participants by age or years of experience are using intrinsic dynamic properties to describe and organize the resources.

4.3.3.4 Extrinsic Dynamic Properties

Extrinsic dynamic properties are in many ways arbitrary and can change because they are based on usage, behavior, or context. The current owner or location of a resource, its frequency of access, the joint frequency of access with other resources, its current popularity or cultural salience, or its competitive advantage over alternative resources are typical extrinsic and dynamic properties that are used in resource descriptions. A topical book described as a best seller one year might be found in the discount sales bin a few years later. A student's grade point average is an extrinsic dynamic property.

Many relationships between resources are extrinsic and dynamic properties, like that of best friend.

Resources are often described with ***cultural properties*** that derive from conventional language or culture, often by analogy, because they can be highly evocative and memorable.[223] For the Lego boys familiar with the *Star Wars* movies, "light saber" was just the obvious word for a long, neon tube with a handle.

However, someone who has never seen or heard of *Star Wars* would not understand this description, and he would describe the piece some other way. Sometimes a cultural description lasts longer than its salience, so it loses its power to evoke anything other than puzzlement about what it might mean.[224]

Contextual properties are those related to the situation or context in which a resource is described. Dey defines context as "any information that characterizes a situation related to the interactions between users, applications, and the surrounding environment."[225] This open-ended definition implies a large number of contextual properties that might be used in a description; crisper definitions of context might be "location + activity" or "who, when, where, why." Since context changes, context-based descriptors might be appropriate when assigned but can have limited persistence and effectivity (§3.5, "Resources over Time" (page 123)); the description of a document as "receipt of a recent purchase" will not be useful for very long.

Citations of one information resource by another are extrinsic static descriptions when they are in print form, but when they are published in digital libraries it is usually the case that "cited by" is a dynamic resource description. Similarly, any particular link from one web page to another is an extrinsic static description, but because many web pages themselves are highly dynamic, we can also consider links as dynamic as well. Citations and web links are discussed in more detail in Chapter 5.

4.3.4 Designing the Description Vocabulary

After we have determined the properties to use in resource descriptions, we need to design the description vocabulary: the set of words or values that represent the properties. §3.4, "Naming Resources" (page 116) discussed the problems of naming and proposed principles for good names, and since names are a very important resource description, much of what we said there applies generally to the design of the description vocabulary.

However, because the description vocabulary as a whole is much more than just the resource name, we need to propose additional principles or guidelines for this step. In addition, some new design questions arise when we consider all the resource descriptions as a set whose separate descriptions are created by many people over some period of time.

4.3.4.1 Principles of Good Description

In *The Intellectual Foundation of Information Organization*, Svenonius proposes a set of principles or "directives for design" of a description language.[226] Her principles, framed in the narrow context of bibliographic descriptions, still apply to the broad range of resource types we consider in this book.

User Convenience

Choose description terms with the user in mind; these are likely to be terms in common usage among the target audience.

Representation

Use descriptions that reflect the how the resources describe themselves; assume that self-descriptions are accurate.

Sufficiency and Necessity

Descriptions should have enough information to serve their purposes and not contain information that is not necessary for some purpose; this might imply excluding some aspects of self-descriptions that are insignificant.

Standardization

Standardize descriptions to the extent practical, but also use aliasing to allow for commonly used terms.

Integration

Use the same properties and terms for all types of resources whenever possible.

Any set of general design principles faces two challenges. The first is that implementing any principle requires many additional and specific context-dependent choices for which the general principle offers little guidance. For example, how does the principle of Standardization apply if multiple standards already exist in some resource domain? Which of the competing standards should be adopted, and why? The second challenge is that the general principles can sometimes lead to conflicting advice. The User Convenience recommendation to choose description terms in common use fails if the user community includes both ordinary people and scientists who use different terms for the same resources; whose "common usage" should prevail?

4.3.4.2 Who Uses the Descriptions?

Focus on the user of the descriptions. This is a core idea that we cannot overemphasize because it is implicit in every step of the process of resource description. All of the design principles in the previous section share the idea that the design of the description vocabulary should focus on the user of the descriptions. Are the resources being organized personal ones, for personal and mostly private purposes? In that case, the description properties and terms can be highly personal or idiosyncratic and still follow the design principles.

Similarly, when resource users share relevant knowledge, or are in a context where they can communicate and negotiate, if necessary, to identify the resources, their resource descriptions can afford to be less precise and rigorous than they might otherwise need to be. This helps explain the curious descriptions in the Lego story with which we began this chapter. The boys playing with the blocks were talking to each other with the Legos in front of them. If they had not been able to see the blocks the others were talking about, or if they had to describe their toys to someone who had never played with Legos before, their descriptions would have been quite different.

More often, however, resource descriptions can not assume this degree of shared context and must be designed for user categories rather than individual users: library users searching for books, business employees or customers using part and product catalogs, scientists analyzing the datasets from experiments or simulations. In each of these situations resource descriptions will need to be understood by people who did not create them, so the design of the description vocabulary needs to be more deliberate and systematic to ensure that its terms are unambiguous and sufficient to ensure reliable context-free interpretation. A single individual seldom has the breadth of domain knowledge and experience with users needed to devise a description vocabulary that can satisfy diverse users with diverse purposes. Instead, many people working together typically develop the required description vocabulary. We call the results institutional vocabularies, to contrast them with individual or cultural ones (We will discuss this contrast more fully in Chapter 6, *"Categorization: Describing Resource Classes and Types"*).

Some resource descriptions are designed to be used by computers or other machines, which seemingly reduces the importance of design principles that consider user preferences or common uses. However, the Standardization and Integration principles become more important for inter-machine communication because they enable efficient processing, reuse of data and software, and increased interoperability between organizing systems.[227]

4.3.4.3 Controlled Vocabularies and Content Rules

As we defined in §3.4.3.2, a ***controlled vocabulary*** is a fixed or closed set of description terms in some domain with precise definitions that is used instead of the vocabulary that people would otherwise use. For example, instead of the popular terms for descriptions of diseases or symptoms, medical researchers and teaching hospitals can use the National Library of Medicine controlled vocabulary (MeSH).[228]

We can distinguish a progression of vocabulary control: a glossary is a set of allowed terms; a thesaurus is a set of terms arranged in a hierarchy and annotated to indicate terms that are preferred, broader than, or narrower than other terms; an ontology expresses the conceptual relationships among the terms in a formal logic-based language so they can be processed by computers. We will say more about ontologies in Chapter 5.

Content rules are similar to controlled vocabularies because they also limit the possible values that can be used in descriptions. Instead of specifying a fixed set of values, content rules typically restrict descriptions by requiring them to be of a particular data type (integer, Boolean, Date, and so on). Possible values are constrained by logical expressions (e.g., a value must be between 0 and 99) or *regular expressions* (e.g., must be a string of length 5 that must begin with a number). Content rules like these are used to ensure valid descriptions when people enter them in web forms or other applications.

4.3.4.4 Vocabulary Control as Dimensionality Reduction

In most cases, a controlled vocabulary is a subset of the natural or uncontrolled vocabulary, but sometimes it is a new set of invented terms. This might sound odd until we consider that the goal of a controlled vocabulary is to reduce the number of descriptive terms assignable to a resource. Stated this way the problem is one of "dimensionality reduction," transforming a high-dimensional space into a lower-dimensional one. Reducing the number of components in a multidimensional description can be accomplished by many different statistical techniques that go by names like "feature extraction," "principle components analysis," "orthogonal decomposition," "latent semantic analysis," "multidimensional scaling," and "factor analysis."[229]

These techniques might sound imposing and they are computationally complex, but they all have the same simple concept at their core. What they do is analyze the correlations between resource descriptions to transform a large set into a much smaller set of uncorrelated ones. In a way this implements the principle of Sufficiency and Necessity we mentioned in §4.3.4.1, "Principles of Good Description" (page 164) because it eliminates description dimensions or properties that do not contribute much to distinguishing the resources.

Here is an oversimplified example that illustrates the idea. Suppose we have a collection of resources, and every resource described as "big" is also described as "red," and every "small" resource is also "green." This perfect correlation between color and size means that either of these properties is sufficient to distinguish "big red" things from "small green" ones, and we do not need clever algorithms to figure that out. But if we have thousands of properties and the correlations are only partial, we need the sophisticated statistical approaches to choose the optimal set of description properties and terms, and in some techniques the dimensions that remain are called "latent" or "synthetic" ones because they are statistically optimal but do not map directly to resource properties.

4.3.5 Designing the Description Form

By this step in the process of resource description we have made numerous important decisions about which resources to describe, the purposes for which we are describing them, and the properties and terms we will use in the descriptions. As much as possible we have described the steps at a conceptual level and postponed discussion of implementation considerations about the notation, syntax, and deployment of the resource descriptions separately or in packages. Separating design from implementation concerns is an idealization of the process of resource description, but is easier to learn and think about resource description and organizing systems if we do. We discuss these implementation issues in Chapter 8, *"The Forms of Resource Descriptions"*.

Sometimes we have to confront legacy technology, existing or potential business relationships, regulations, standards conformance, performance requirements, or other factors that have implications for how resource descriptions must or should be implemented, stored, and managed. We will take this more pragmatic perspective in Chapter 10, *The Organizing System Roadmap,* but until then, we will continue to focus on design issues and defer discussion of the implementation choices.

4.3.6 Creating Resource Descriptions

Resource descriptions can be created by professionals, by the authors or creators of resources, by users, or by computational or automated means. From the traditional perspective of library and information science with its emphasis on bibliographic description, these modes of creation imply different levels of description complexity and sophistication; Taylor and Joudrey suggest that professionals create **rich** descriptions, untrained users at best create **structured** ones, and automated processes create **simple** ones.

This classification reflects a disciplinary and historical bias more than reality. "Simple" resource descriptions are "no more than data extracted from the resource itself... the search engine approach to organizing the web through automated indexing techniques."[230] It might be fair to describe an inverted index implementation of a Boolean information retrieval model as simple, but it is clearly wrong to consider what Google and other search engines do to describe and retrieve web resources as simple.[231] A better notion of levels of resource description is one based on the amount of interpretation imposed by the description, an approach that focuses on the descriptions themselves rather than on their methods of creation. We will discuss this sort of approach in §4.4.1, "Describing Museum and Artistic Resources" (page 173) in the context of describing museum and artistic resources.

Professionally-created resource descriptions, author- or user-created descriptions, and computational or automated descriptions each have strengths and limitations that impose tradeoffs. A natural solution is to try to combine desirable aspects from each in hybrid approaches. For example, the vocabulary for a new resource domain may arise from tagging by end users but then be refined by professionals, lay classifiers may create descriptions with help from software tools that suggest possible terms, or software that creates descriptions can be improved by training it with human-generated descriptions.

Often existing resource descriptions can or must be transformed or enhanced to meet the ongoing needs of an organizing system, and sometimes these processes can be automated. We will defer further discussion of those situations to Chapter 9, *"Interactions with Resources"*. In the discussion that follows we focus on the creation of new resource descriptions where none yet exist.

4.3.6.1 Resource Description by Professionals

Before the web made it possible for almost anyone to create, publish, and describe their own resources and to describe those created and published by others, resource description was generally done by professionals in institutional contexts. Professional indexers and catalogers described bibliographic and museum resources after having been trained to learn the concepts, controlled descriptive vocabularies, and the relevant standards. In information systems domains professional data and process analysts, technical writers, and others created similarly rigorous descriptions after receiving analogous training. We have called these types of resource descriptions institutional ones to highlight the contrast between those created according to standards and those created informally in *ad hoc* ways, especially by untrained or undisciplined individuals.[232]

4.3.6.2 Resource Description by Authors or Creators

The author or creator of a resource can be presumed to understand the reasons why and the purposes for which the resource can be used. And, presumably, most authors want to be read, so they will describe their resources in ways that will appeal to and be useful to their intended users. However, these descriptions are unlikely to use the controlled vocabularies and standards that professional catalogers would use.

4.3.6.3 Resource Description by Users

Today's web contains a staggering number of resources, most of which are primary information resources published as web content, but many others are resources that stand for "in the world" physical resources. Most of these resources are being described by their users rather than by professionals or by their authors. These "at large" users are most often creating descriptions for their own benefit when they assign tags or ratings to web resources, and they are unlikely to use standard or controlled descriptors when they do so.[233] The resulting variability can be a problem if creating the description requires judgment on the tagger's part. Most people can agree on the length of a particular music file but they may differ wildly when it comes to determining to which musical genre that file belongs. Fortunately most web users implicitly recognize that the potential value in these "Web 2.0" or "user-generated content" applications will be greater if they avoid egocentric descriptions. In addition, the statistics of large sample sizes inevitably leads to some agreement in descriptions on the most popular applications because idiosyncratic descriptions are dominated in the frequency distribution by the more conventional ones.[234]

We are not suggesting that professional descriptions are always of high quality and utility, and socially produced ones are always of low quality and utility.[235] Rather, it is important to understand the limitations and qualifications of descriptions produced in each way. Tagging lowers the barrier to entry for description, making organizing more accessible and creating descriptions that reflects a variety of viewpoints. However, when many tags are associated with a resource, it increases *recall* while decreasing *precision*.

4.3.6.4 Computational and Automated Resource Description

When a digital camera takes a picture, it creates a description in the EXIF file format using properties associated with the camera and its settings, as well as some properties of the context in which the photo is taken. (See Figure 4.5, "Contrasting Descriptions for a Work of Art." for an example). Creating the description by hand would be laborious, especially if constructed retroactively. The downside, however, is that the automated description does not capture the meaning or purpose of the photo. The automated description might contain information about time and place, but not that people in the picture were on a honeymoon vacation. The difference between automated and human description is called the *semantic gap* (§3.4.2.5).

Some computational approaches create resource descriptions that are similar in purpose to those created by human describers. For example, Hu and Lui created a text mining and summarization system for customer comments about products for sale on the web. Thousands of comments about a particular digital camera are reduced to a list of the most important features.[236] People shopping for books at **Amazon.com** get insights about a book's content and distinctiveness from the statistically improbable phrases that it has identified by comparing all the books for which it has the complete text.[237]

Of course, all information retrieval systems compare a description of a user's needs with descriptions of the resources that might satisfy them. IR systems differ in the resource properties they emphasize; word frequencies and distributions for documents in digital libraries, links and navigation behavior for web pages, acoustics for music, and so on. These different property descriptions determine the comparison algorithms and the way in which relevance or similarity of descriptions is determined. We say a lot more about this in §4.4, "Describing Non-Text Resources" (page 173) and in Chapter 9.

4.3.7 Evaluating Resource Descriptions

Evaluation is implicit in many of the activities of organizing systems we described in Chapter 2, *"Activities in Organizing Systems"* and is explicit when we maintain a collection of resources over time. In this section, we focus on the narrower problem of evaluating resource descriptions.

Evaluating means determining *quality* with respect to some criteria or dimensions. Many different sets of criteria have been proposed, but the most commonly used ones are accuracy, completeness, and consistency.[238] Other typical criteria are timeliness, interoperability, and usability. It is easy to imagine these criteria in conflict; efforts to achieve accuracy and completeness might jeopardize timeliness; enforcing consistency might preclude modifications that would enhance usability.

The *quality* of the outcome of the multi-step process proposed in this chapter is a composite of the *quality* created or squandered at each step. A scope that is too granular or abstract, overly ambitious or vague intended purposes, a description vocabulary that is hard to use, or giving people inadequate time to create good descriptions can all cause quality problems, but none of these decisions is visible at the end of the process where users interact with resource descriptions.

4.3.7.1 Evaluating the Creation of Resource Descriptions

When professionals create resource descriptions in a centralized manner, which has long been the standard practice for many resources in libraries, there is a natural focus on *quality* at the point of creation to ensure that the appropriate controlled vocabularies and standards have been used. However, the need for resource description generalizes to resource domains outside of the traditional bibliographic one, and other *quality* considerations emerge in those contexts.

Resource descriptions in private sector firms are essential to running the business and in interacting efficiently with suppliers, partners, and customers. Compared to the public sector, there is much greater emphasis on the economics and strategy of resource description.[239] What is the value of resource description? Who will bear the costs of producing them? Which of the competing industry standards will be followed? Some of these decisions are not free choices as much as they are constraints imposed as a condition of doing business with a dominant economic partner, which is sometimes a governmental entity.[240]

In both the public and private sectors there is increased use of computational techniques for creating resource descriptions because the number of resources to be described is simply too great to allow for professional description. A great deal of work in text data mining, web page classification, semantic enrichment, and other similar research areas is already under way and is significantly lowering the cost of producing useful resource descriptions. Some museums have embraced approaches that automatically create user-oriented resource descriptions and new user interfaces for searching and browsing by transforming the professional descriptions in their internal collections management systems.[241] Google's ambitious project to digitize millions of books has been criticized for the quality of its algorithmically extracted resource descriptions, but we can expect that computer scientists will put the Google book corpus to good use as a research test bed to improve the techniques.[242]

Web 2.0 applications that derive their value from the aggregation and interpretation of user-generated content can be viewed as voluntarily ceding their authority to describe and organize resources to their users, who then tag or rate them as they see fit. In this context the consistency of resource description, or the lack of it, becomes an important issue, and many sites are using technology or incentives to guide users to create better descriptions.

4.3.7.2 Evaluating the Use of Resource Descriptions

The user's perspective is embodied in the FRBR statement of the purposes of bibliographic description (§4.3.2.3, "Resource Description to Support Interactions" (page 157)), but the problems of resource description on the web have highlighted this point of view. The most important quality criteria are now functional ones—do the resource descriptions satisfy their intended purposes in a usable way?

In many ways, the answer is a disappointing no. In one of the earliest revisions to the original HTML specification, a <META> tag was added to allow website creators to define a set of key terms to describe a website or web page, thus helping the site's position in search rankings when a user searched for one or more of those terms. However, it soon became obvious that it was possible to "game" the META tag by adding popular terms even though they did not accurately describe the page. Today search engines ignore the <META> tag for ranking pages, but many other techniques that use false *resource* descriptions continue to plague web users. (See §2.5.3.3).

The design of a description vocabulary circumscribes what can be said about a resource, so it is important to recognize that it implicitly determines what cannot be said as well, with unintended negative consequences for users. The *resource* description schema implemented in a physician's patient management system defines certain types of recordable information about a patient's visit—the date of the visit, any tests that were ordered, a diagnosis that was made, a referral to a specialist. The schema, and its associated workflow, impose constraints that affect the kinds of information medical professionals can record and the amount of space they can use for those descriptions. Moreover, such a schema might also eliminate vital unstructured space that paper records can provide, where doctors communicate their rationale for a diagnosis or decision without having to fit it into any particular box.

4.3.7.3 The Importance of Iterative Evaluation

The inevitable conflicts between *quality* goals mean that there will be compromises among the *quality* criteria. Furthermore, increasing *scale* in an organizing system and the steady improvements of computational techniques for resource description imply that the nature of the compromise will change over time. As a result, a single evaluation of resource descriptions at one moment in time will not suffice.

This makes usage records, navigation history, and transactional data extremely important kinds of resource descriptions because they enable you to focus efforts on improving *quality* where they are most needed. Furthermore, for organizing systems with many types of resources and user communities, this information can enable the tailoring of the nature and extent of resource description to find the right balance between "rich and comprehensive" and "simple and efficient" approaches. Each combination of resource type and user community might have a different solution.

The idea that *quality* is a property of an end-to-end process is embodied in the "quality movement" and statistical process control for industrial processes but it applies equally well to resource description.[243] Explicit feedback from users or implicit feedback from the records of their resource interactions needs are essential as we iterate through the design process and revisit the decisions made there.

4.4 Describing Non-Text Resources

Many of the principles and methods for resource description were developed for describing text resources in physical formats. Those principles have had to evolve to deal with different types of resources that people want to describe and organize, from paintings and statues to MP3s, JPEGs, and MPEGs.

Some descriptions for non-text resources are text-based, and are most often assigned by people. Other descriptions are in non-text formats are extracted algorithmically from the content of the non-text resource. These latter content-based resource descriptions capture intrinsic technical properties but cannot (yet) describe "aboutness" in a reliably complete manner.

4.4.1 Describing Museum and Artistic Resources

The problems associated with describing multimedia resources are not all new. Museum curators have been grappling with them since they first started to collect, store, and describe artifacts hundreds of years ago. Many artifacts may represent the same work (think about shards of pottery that may once have been part of the same vase). The materials and forms do not convey semantics on their own. Without additional research and description, we know nothing about the vase; it does not come with any sort of title page or tag that connects it with a 9th-century Mayan settlement. Since museums can acquire large batches of artifacts all at once, they have to make decisions about which resources they can afford to describe and how much they can describe them.

The German art historian Erwin Panofsky first codified one approach to these problems of description. In his classic *Studies in Iconology*, he defined three levels of description that can be applied to an artistic work or museum artifact:

Primary subject matter

At this level, we describe the most basic elements of a work in a generic way that would be recognizable by anyone regardless of expertise or training. The painting *The Last Supper*, for example, might be described as "13 people having dinner."

Secondary subject matter

Here, we introduce a level of basic cultural understanding into a description. Someone familiar with a common interpretation of the Bible, for example, could now see *The Last Supper* as representing Jesus surrounded by his disciples.

Intrinsic meaning or interpretation

At this level, context and deeper understanding come into play—including what the creator of the description knows about the situation in which the work was created. Why, for example, did this particular artist create this particular depiction of *The Last Supper* in this way? Panofsky posited that professional art historians are needed here, because they are the ones with the education and background necessary to draw meaning from a work.[244]

In other words, Panofsky saw the need for many different types of descriptors—including physical, cultural, and contextual—to work together when making a full description of an artifact.

Professionals who create descriptions of museum and artistic resources, architecture and other cultural works typically use the VRA Core from the Library of Congress, or the Getty Trust *Categories for the Description of Works of Art* (CDWA), a massive controlled vocabulary with 532 categories and subcategories. A CDWA-Lite has been developed to create a very small subset for use by non-specialists.[245]

The contrasts between descriptions created by technology and those created by people are striking. Figure 4.5, "Contrasting Descriptions for a Work of Art." shows the EXIF description created by a digital camera of a marble statue,

EXIF Summary

Make	NIKON CORPORATION
Model	NIKON D90
Aperture	9
Exposure Time	1/320 (0.003125 sec)
Lens	ID AF-S DX VR Zoom-Nikkor 18-105mm f/3.5-5.6G ED
Focal Length	21.0 mm
Flash	Auto, Did not fire
File Size	4.7 MB
File Type	JPEG
Image Height	4288
Image Width	2848
Date & Time	2012:12:03 10:31:14

3 Levels

Primary
Marble statue of nude woman standing on a seashell.

Secondary
Statue made in 2005 by Lucio Carusi of Carrara, Italy, titled "Venus", made of local marble.

Interpretive
This is a 3d transformation of the 1486 painting by Italian painter Sondro Botticelli, titled "The Birth of Venus", now in the Uffizi Gallery in Florence. Carusi's Venus is substantially slimmer in proportions than Botticelli's because of changing notions of female beauty.

Figure 4.5. Contrasting Descriptions for a Work of Art.

along with some descriptions of the statue that conform to Panofsky's three-level scheme for describing works of art.

4.4.2 Describing Images

Digital cameras, including those in cell phones, take millions of photos each day. Unlike the images in museums and galleries, most of these images receive few descriptions beyond those created by the device that made them. Nevertheless, a great many of them end up with some limited descriptions in Facebook, Instagram, Flickr, Picasa, DeviantArt, or others of the numerous places where people share images, or in professional image applications like Light Room. All of these sites provide some facilities for users to assign tags to images or arrange them in named groups.

Computer image analysis techniques are increasingly used to create content-based descriptions. The "visual signature" of an image is extracted from low-level features like color, shape, texture, and luminosity, which are then used to distinguish significant regions and objects. Image similarity is computed to create categories of images that contain the same kinds of objects or settings.[246]

For computers to identify the objects or people in images—creating the kinds of resource descriptions that people want—requires training with tags or labels. Louis van Ann devised a clever way to collect large amounts of labeled images with a web-based game that randomly pairs people to suggest labels or tags for an image. Typically, the obvious choices are removed from contention, so a photo of a bird against a blue sky might already strike "bird" and "sky" from the set of acceptable words, leaving users to suggest words such as "flying" and "cloudless."[247] This technique was later adopted by Google to improve its image search. An analogous effort to automatically identify people in Facebook photos uses photos where people identified themselves or others in photo.

4.4.3 Describing Music

Some parts of describing a song are not that different from describing text: You might want to pull out the name of the singer and/or the songwriter, the length of the song, or the name of the album on which it appears. But what if you wanted to describe the actual content of the song? You could write out the lyrics, but describing the music itself requires a different approach. A DJ, for example, might care greatly about the beats per minute in each song. If you are making a playlist for a road trip, you might be seeking songs that you would describe as "good for driving" —though you would have to figure out what "good for driving" means first, which is a highly subjective description. If you are looking for recommendations for new bands, you might want to know how to find music that is somehow like music you already know you love.

Several people and companies working in multimedia have explored different processes for how songs are described. On the heavily technological side, software applications such as Shazam and Midomi can create a content-based "audio fingerprint" from a snippet of music. Audio fingerprinting renders a digital description of a piece of music, which a computer can then interpret and compare to other digital descriptions in a library.[248]

On the other hand, the online radio service Pandora uses music experts, not computers, to create text-based descriptions. The company employs an army of coders, including trained musicologists, who listen to individual pieces of music and determine which words from Pandora's highly controlled vocabulary for musical description apply to a given song. The result is Pandora's "Music Genome," an algorithm that ultimately recommends songs for its users by stripping down the songs they say they like to their component parts and suggesting, for example, more songs with "driving bass" or "jangly guitars."[249]

4.4.4 Describing Video

Video is yet another resource domain where work to create resource descriptions to make search more effective is ongoing. Video analytics techniques can segment a video into shorter clips described according to their color, direction of motion, size of objects, and other characteristics. Identifying anomalous events and faces of people in video has obvious applications in security and surveillance.[250] Identifying specific content details about a video currently takes a significant amount of human intervention, though it is possible that image signature-matching algorithms will take over in the future because they would enable automated ad placement in videos and television.[251]

4.4.5 Describing Resource Context

As we discussed in §3.4, "Naming Resources" (page 116), sensors are now making all sorts of objects "smarter," capable of reporting their status, their location, or other important descriptive data. Many applications of smart resources are still in their infancy, and that makes them interesting to study for how descriptions can be created automatically and processed (automatically, by people, or both) down the line.

Some sensors create relatively simple descriptions: A pass that registers a car's location at a toll booth, for example, does not need to do much besides communicate that the particular sensor has arrived at some location. In essence, it acts as an identifier.

The information created or tracked by sensors can be more complex. Some sensors can calculate location using GPS coordinates and satellite tracking, while others can take readings of temperature, pollution, or other environmental measurements. These readings can be used separately or combined into richer and more detailed descriptions of a resource or event. The tradeoffs in creating these descriptions likely sound familiar by now: More descriptors can create a fuller and more accurate picture of the world, but they require more processing power not only to collect the necessary information but also to render it into a meaningful form.[252]

4.5 Key Points in Chapter Four

- Resource description is not an end in itself. Its many purposes are all means for enabling and using an organizing system for some collection of resources.

- The process of describing resources involves several interdependent and iterative steps, including determining scope, focus and purposes, identifying resource properties, designing the description vocabulary, designing the description form and implementation, and creating and evaluating the descriptions.

- In different contexts, the terms in resource descriptions are called keywords, index terms, attributes, attribute values, elements, data elements, data values, or "the vocabulary," labels, or tags.

- The dominant historical view treats resource descriptions as a package of statements, an alternate framework focuses on each individual description or assertion about a single resource.

- A bibliographic description of an information resource is most commonly realized as a structured record in a standard format that describes a specific resource.

- The Functional Requirements for Bibliographic Records (FRBR) presents four purposes that apply generically: Finding, Identifying, Selecting, and Obtaining resources.

- Metadata is structured description for information resources of any kind, which makes it a superset of bibliographic description.

- The Standard Generalized Markup Language (SGML) introduced the Document Type Definition (DTD) for describing the structure and content elements in hierarchical document models. SGML was largely superseded by the eXtensible Markup Language (XML).

- The Resource Description Framework (RDF) is a language for making computer-processable statements about web resources that is the foundation for the vision of the Semantic Web.

- RDF can be used for bibliographic description, and some libraries are exploring whether RDF transformations of their legacy bibliographic records can be exposed and integrated with resource descriptions on the open web.

- A collection of resource descriptions is vastly more useful when every resource is described using common description elements or terms that apply to every resource; this specification is most often called a schema or model.

- A relational database schema is designed to restrict resource descriptions to be simple and completely regular sets of attribute-value pairs.

- XML schemas are often used to define web forms that capture resource instances, and are also used to describe the interfaces to web services and other computational resources.

- When the task of resource description is standardized, the work can be distributed among many describers whose results are shared. This is the principle on which centralized bibliographic description has been based for a century.

- Any particular resource might need many resource descriptions, all of which relate to different properties, depending on the interactions that need to be supported and the context in which they take place.

- The variety and functions of the interactions with digital resources depends on the richness of their structural, semantic, and format description.

- Two important dimensions for understanding and contrasting resource properties are whether the properties are intrinsically or extrinsically associated with the resource, and whether the properties are static or dynamic.

- Design of the description vocabulary should focus on the user of the descriptions. Svenonius proposes five principles for a description vocabulary: user convenience, representation, sufficiency and necessity, standardization, and integration.

- A *controlled vocabulary* is a fixed or closed set of description terms in some domain with precise definitions that is used instead of the vocabulary that people would otherwise use.

- Professionally created resource descriptions, author or user created descriptions, and computational or automated descriptions each have strengths and limitations that impose tradeoffs.

- Information retrieval is characterized as comparing a description of a user's needs with descriptions of the resources that might satisfy them. Different property descriptions determine the comparison algorithms and the way in which relevance or similarity of descriptions is determined.

- The most commonly used criteria for evaluating resource descriptions are accuracy, completeness, and consistency. Other typical criteria are timeliness, interoperability, and usability.

- Sensors that assign more resource descriptors can create a fuller and more accurate picture of the world, but they require more processing power to collect the necessary information and render it into a meaningful form.

Notes

190. [Computing] Most digital cameras use the Exchangeable Image File Format (EXIF). The best source of information about it looks like its Wikipedia entry. *http://en.wikipedia.org/wiki/Exchangeable_image_file_format.*

191. [CogSci] This is much more than just a "kids say the darndest things" story (see *http://en.wikipedia.org/wiki/Kids_Say_the_Darndest_Things*). Giles Turnbull (Turnbull 2009) noticed that his kids never used the official names for Lego blocks (e.g. Brick 2x2). He then asked other kids what their names were for 32 types of Lego blocks. His survey showed that the kids mostly used different names, but each created names that followed some systematic principles. The most standard name was the "light saber," used by every kid in Turnbull's sample.

192. [Linguistics] (Reaney and Wilson 1997) classify surnames as local, surnames of relationship, surnames of occupation or office, and nicknames. The dominance of occupational names reflects the fact that there are fewer occupations than places. While there are only a handful of kinship relationships used in surnames (patronymic or father-based names are most common), because the surname includes the father's name there is more variation than for occupations.

193. [Linguistics] This odd convention is preserved today in wedding invitations, causing some feminist teeth gnashing (Geller 1999).

194. [CogSci] See (Donnellan 1966). A contemporary analysis from the perspective of cognitive science is (Heller, Gorman, and Tanenhaus 2012).

195. [LIS] An excellent source for both the history and theory of bibliographic description is *The Intellectual Foundation of Information Organization* by Elaine Svenonius (Svenonius 2000). She divides bibliographic descriptions into "those that describe information from those that describe its documentary embodiments," contrasting conceptual or subject properties from those that describe physical properties (p. 54). A more radical contrast was proposed by (Wilson 1968, p. 25), who distinguished descriptions according to the kind of bibliographic control they enabled. "Descriptive control" is objective and straightforward, "lining up a population of writings in any arbitrary order." "Exploitative control," defined as "the ability to make the best use of a body of writings," requires descriptions that evaluate resources for their suitability for particular uses. Wilson argued that descriptive control was a poor substitute for exploitative control, but recognized that evaluative descriptions were more difficult to create.

196. [Computing] (Rubinsky and Maloney 1997) capture this transitional perspective. A more recent text on XML is (Goldberg 2008).

197. [Computing] See (Sen 2004), (Laskey 2005).

198. [Web] See (Marlow, Naaman, Boyd, and Davis 2006). These authors propose a conceptual model of tagging that includes (1) tags assigned to a specific resource, (2) connections or links between resources, and (3) connections or links between users and explain how any two of these can be used to infer information about the other.

199. [Web] (Hammond, Hanney, Lund, and Scott 2004) coined the phrase "tag soup" in an review of social bookmarking tools written early in the tagging era that remains insightful today. Many of the specific tools are no longer around, but the reasons why people tag are still the same.

200. [Web] Making tagging more systematic leads to "tag convergence" in which the distribution of tags for a particular resource stabilizes over time (Golder and Huberman 2006). Consider three things a user might do if his tag does not match the suggested tags; (1) Change the tag to conform? (2) Keep the tag to influence the group norm? (3) Add the proposed tag but keep his tag as well?

201. [Web] The official source for all things RDF is the W3C RDF page at *http://www.w3.org/RDF/*.

202. [Web] Some argue that the resource being described is thus Bart Simpson's Wikipedia page, not Bart Simpson himself. Whether or not that is an important distinction is a controversial question among RDF architects and users.

203. [Web] (Heath and Bizer 2011) and linkeddata.org are excellent sources.

204. [LIS] (Byrne and Goddard 2010) present a balanced analysis of the cultural and technical obstacles to the adoption of RDF and linked data in libraries. (Yee 2009) is a highly specific technical demonstration of converting bibliographic descriptions to RDF. A detailed analysis / rebuttal of Yee's article is at *http://futurelib.pbworks.com/w/page/13686677/YeeRDF*.

205. [LIS] Taylor's book on *The Organization of Information*, now in its 3rd edition (with co-author Daniel Joudrey), has been widely used in library science programs for over a decade.

206. [LIS] (Gilliland-Swetland 2000).

207. [Computing] Web services are generally implemented using XML documents as their inputs and outputs. The interfaces to web services are typically described using an XML vocabulary called *Web Services Description Language (WSDL)*. See (Erl 2005b), especially Ch. 3, "Introduction to Web Services Technologies."

208. [LIS] Creating descriptions that can keep pace with the growth of a collection has been an issue for librarians for years, as libraries moved away from de-

scribing simply "whatever came across a cataloger's desk" to cataloging resources for a national and even international audience (Svenonius 2000, p. 31).

209. [LIS] The Anglo-American Cataloguing Rules (AACR2) have rules for books, pamphlets, and printed sheets; cartographic materials; manuscripts and manuscript collections; music; sound recordings; motion pictures and video recordings; graphic materials; electronic resources; 3-D artifacts; microforms; and continuing resources. The Concise AACR2 (4th Edition) is the most accessible treatment of these very complex rules (Gorman 2004). The *Resource Description and Access (RDA)* vocabularies have been proposed as the successor to AACR2 and make even finer distinctions among resource types. See *http://rdvocab.info/vocabulary/list.html*.

210. [LIS] See the Dublin Core Metadata Initiative (DCMI) at *http://dublincore.org/*.

211. [CogSci] The semantic "bluntness" of a minimalist vocabulary is illustrated by the examples for use of the "creator" element in an official Dublin Core user guide (Hillmann 2005) that shows "Shakespeare, William" and "Hubble Telescope" as creators.

212. [Computing] The Intel Core 2 Duo Processor has detailed specifications (*http://www.intel.com/products/processor/core2duo/specifications.htm*) and seven categories of technical documentation: application notes, datasheets, design guides, manuals, updates, support components, and white papers (*http://www.intel.com/design/core2duo/documentation.htm*).

213. [Business] Real estate advertisements are notorious for their creative descriptions; a house "convenient to transportation" is most likely next to a busy highway, and a house in a "secluded location" is in a remote and desolate part of town.

214. [CogSci] Typically, this takes place in an unanalyzed or unreflective manner. We can stack boxes on top of each other only if they are of certain relative and absolute sizes. Even if we consciously focus on resource properties when we follow organizing principles, our experience is that of directly arranging the resources, not organizing them on the basic of implicit resource descriptions. Even in the case when the physical resources have descriptions of their sizes and other properties (like labels on boxes or in clothes), when we arrange boxes or clothes, it is still the primary resources that we are organizing, not these descriptions.

215. [LIS] We encountered FRBR several times in previous chapters (especially in §3.1.1.2, "Bibliographic Resources, Information Components, and "Smart Things" as Resources" (page 97)) where we asked "what is this thing we call 'Macbeth'" and described FRBR's four-level abstraction hierarchy of the "work."

216. [Law] The Creative Commons nonprofit organization defines six kinds of copyright licenses that differ in the extent they allow commercial uses or modifications of an original resource (see *http://creativecommons.org/licenses/*). The Flickr photo sharing application is a good example of a site where a search for reusable resources can use the Creative Commons licenses to filter the results (*http://www.flickr.com/creativecommons/*).

217. [Business] Using the same standards to describe products or to specify the execution of business processes can facilitate the implementation and operation of information-intensive business models because information can then flow between services or firms without human intervention. In turn this enables the business to become more demand or event-driven rather than forecast driven, making it a more "adaptive," "agile," or "on demand" enterprise. See (Glushko and McGrath 2005), especially Ch. 5, *How Models and Patterns Evolve.*

218. [Web] For new resources, the labor-intensive cost of traditional bibliographic description is less justifiable when you can follow a link from a resource description to the digital resource it describes and quickly decide its relevance. That is, web search engines demonstrate that algorithmic analysis of the content of information resources can make them self-describing to a significant degree, reducing the need for bibliographic description.

219. [LIS] (Svenonius 2000, pages 18-19).

220. [Computing] Ken Holman's *Definitive XSLT and XPath* (Holman 2001) is the book to get started on with XPath, and no one has taught more people about XPath than Holman. The first five hours of a 24-hour video course on *Practical Transformation Using XSLT and XPath* is available for free at *http://www.udemy.com/practical-transformation-using-xslt-and-xpath.*

221. [LIS] There are three members of the "FRBR family." One family is the "Group 1 entities" —Work, Expression, Manifestation, and Item—which are used to define classes of intellectual products and their relationships to each other. The "Group 2 entities" are responsible for the creation or custodianship of the Group 1 entities — Person, Family, and Corporate Body. The Group 2 model and requirements have been developed further as the Functional Requirements for Authority Data (FRAD) to enable catalogs to answer questions about the relationships between corporate entities or collaborators; see *http://www.ifla.org/publications/functional-requirements-for-authority-data* and *http://archive.ifla.org/VII/d4/wg-franar.htm#Authority.* The "Group 3 entities" are the subject descriptions for Group 1 and Group 2; see the Functional Requirements for Subject Authority Data (FRSAD) at *http://www.ifla.org/node/1297.*

222. [LIS] The PREMIS standard for preservation metadata is maintained by the US Library of Congress at *http://www.loc.gov/standards/premis/.* A good

place is to start is the 2011 PREMIS Data Dictionary (*http://www.loc.gov/standards/premis/v2/premis-2-1.pdf*).

223. [Linguistics] Consider how many events are named by appending a "-gate" suffix to imply that there is something scandalous or unethical going on that is being covered up. This cultural description is not immediately meaningful to anyone who does not know about the break-in at the headquarters of the Democratic National Committee headquarters at the Watergate hotel and subsequent cover-up that led to the 1974 resignation of US President Richard Nixon. A list of "-gate" events is maintained at *http://en.wikipedia.org/wiki/List_of_scandals_with_%22-gate%22_suffix*.

224. [Linguistics] A particular type of geometrically patterned Turkish rug came to be known as a "Holbein carpet" after the German Renaissance painter Hans Holbein, who often depicted the rugs in his work. Holbein was very famous in his time, and his commissioned paintings of the English King Henry VIII have Henry standing on such rugs. But the rugs themselves existed (and were even painted by others) long before Holbein painted them, and today Holbein is much less famous than he once was. (*http://en.wikipedia.org/wiki/Holbein_carpet*).

225. [Computing] (Dey 2001) further defines the "environment" of context as places, people, and things, and for each of "entities" there are four categories of context information: location, identity, status (or activity), and time. This *framework* thus yields 12 dimensions for describing the context of an environment.

226. [LIS] (Svenonius 2000, Ch. 5).

227. [Computing] (Laskey 2005).

228. [LIS] *http://www.ncbi.nlm.nih.gov/mesh/*.

229. [Computing] We cannot cite all of mathematical statistics in one short endnote, but if you are inclined to learn more, (Mardia, Kent, and Bibby 1980) and (Lee and Verleysen 2007) are the kindest and gentlest resources. If we look very generously at "dimensionality reduction" we might even consider the indexing step of eliminating "stop words" to be a form of dimensionality reduction. Stop words appear with such high frequency that they have no discriminating power, so they are discarded from queries and not part of the description of the indexed documents.

230. [LIS] (Taylor and Joudrey 2009), p. 91.

231. [Computing] See Ch. 4 of (Buttcher, Clarke, and Cormack 2010) for a description of a simple Boolean information retrieval model and Chapter 14 and 15 for descriptions of Google-scale ones. For a popular discussion of the Google algorithm see (Levy 2010).

232. [Business] Many institutional organizing systems are subject to a single centralized or governmental authority that can impose principles for describing and arranging resources. Examples of organizing systems where resources are described using standard centralized principles are:

Libraries that use national bibliographic standards to satisfy requirements set by industry associations or other accreditation bodies such as the Association of College and Research Libraries (ACRL). (*http://ala.org/acrl*)

Companies that follow industry standards for information or process models, product classification or identification to be eligible for government business (Shah and Kesan 2006).

Legislative documents that conform to National or European Community standards for structure, naming, and description (Biasiotti 2008).

The *Internet Corporation for Assigned Names and Numbers (ICANN)* and its policies for operating the Domain Name System (DNS) make it possible for every website to be located using its logical name (like "berkeley.edu" rather than using an IP address like 169.229.131.81). (*http://www.icann.org/*)

In other domains multiple organizations or institutions have the authority to impose principles of resource description. Sometimes this authority derives from the voluntary collaboration of multiple autonomous parties who set and conform to standards because they benefit from being able to share resources or information about resources. Examples of organizing systems where resources are described using standardized decentralized principles are:

Firms that establish company-wide standards for their information resources, typically including the organization and management of source content, document type models, and a style guide that applies to print and web documents.

Firms that participate in the OASIS (*http://www.oasis-open.org/*) or the W3C (*http://www.w3.org/*) industry consortia to establish specifications or technical recommendations for their information systems or web services).

233. [LIS] Many organizing systems describe and arrange their physical or information resources in *ad hoc* ways because the person or institution determining the arrangement is completely autonomous. This is the domain of organizing systems embraced by David Weinberger in *Everything is Miscellaneous* (Weinberger 2007).

234. [Web] (Sen et al. 2006) analyze the effects of four tag selection algorithms used in sites that allow user tags on vocabulary evolution (more often called "tag convergence" in the literature), tag utility, tag adoption, and user satisfaction.

235. [CogSci] But in an often-cited essay (Doctorow, 2001) provocatively titled "Metacrap: Putting the torch to seven straw-men of the meta-utopia," Cory Doctorow argues that much human-created metadata **is** of low quality because "people lie, people are lazy, people are stupid, mission impossible—know thyself, schemas are not neutral, metrics influence results, (and) there is more than one way to describe something."

236. [Computing] (Hu and Lui 2004).

237. [Computing] *http://www.amazon.com/gp/search-inside/sipshelp.html/*.

238. [LIS] (Park 2009).

239. [Business] However, these concerns are rapidly becoming more important in the public sector. In particular, many public universities in the US are struggling with cuts in state and federal funding that are affecting library services and practices.

240. [Business] A firm like Wal-Mart with enormous market power can dictate terms and standards to its suppliers because the long-term benefits of a Wal-Mart contract usually make the initial accommodation worthwhile. Likewise, governments often require their suppliers to conform to open standards to avoid lock-in to proprietary technologies. More generally, economists use the concept of the "mode of exchange" in a business relationship to include the procedures and norms that govern routine behavior between business partners. An "exit" mode is one in which the buyer makes little long-term commitment to a supplier, and problems with a supplier cause the buyer to find a new one. In contrast, in "voice" mode there is much greater commitment and communication between the parties, usually leading to improved processes and designs. See (Helper and McDuffie 2003).

241. [Museums] (Schmitz and Black 2008).

242. [Computing] (Nunberg 2009) called the quality of Google's metadata "a disaster for scholars," but (Sag 2012) argues that the otherwise neglected "orphan works" in the Google corpus are "grist for the data mill."

243. [Business] The modern "quality movement" grew out of the efforts of the US to rebuild Japan after the Second World War and its "Bible" was Juran's 1951 *Quality Control Handbook.* The central idea is that *quality* cannot be tested in by inspecting the final products. Instead, *quality* is achieved through process control—measuring and removing the variability of every process needed to create the products.

244. [Museums] (Panofsky 1972).

245. [Museums] For CDWA, see *http://www.getty.edu/research/publica tions/electronic_publications/cdwa/*.

For CDWA-Lite, see *http://www.getty.edu/research/publications/elec tronic_publications/cdwa/cdwalite.pdf*.

246. [Computing] See (Datta et al. 2008). The company Idée is developing a variety of image search algorithms, which use image signatures and measures of visual similarity to return photos similar to those a user asks to see. The company's Multicolr search, for example, returns a set of stock photos with similar color combinations to the ones selected dynamically by the user. See *http:// www.ideeinc.com/*.

247. [Web] (von Ahn and Dabbish 2008).

248. [Computing] (Cano et al. 2005).

249. [Computing] (Walker 2009).

250. [Computing] (Regazzoni et al. 2010) introduce a special issue in IEEE *Signal Processing on visual analytics*.

251. [Business] One organization that sees a future in assembling better descriptions of video content is the United States' National Football League (NFL), whose vast library of clips can not only be used to gather plays for highlight reels and specials but can also be monetized by pointing out when key advertisers' products appear on film. Currently, labeling the video requires a person to watch the scenes and tag elements of each frame, but once those tags have been created and sequenced along with the video, they can be more easily searched in computerized, automated ways (Buhrmester 2007).

252. [Business] One interesting service that uses sensors to create descriptions of location is the NextBus transportation tracking service in San Francisco, which tells transit riders exactly when vehicles will be arriving at particular stops. NextBus uses sensors to track the GPS coordinates of buses and trains, then compares that to route and information from transportation providers and estimates the time it will take for a vehicle to arrive at some selected location. To offer information that will be useful to riders, NextBus must figure out how to describe the location of a vehicle and the distance between that location and some intended target, as well as creating descriptions of transit routes (name, number, and/or direction of travel) and particular stops along the route. In some areas, NextBus incorporates multiple descriptors for a given stop by allowing users to search by route, by location, or by an ID number assigned to the stop.

Chapter 5
Describing Relationships and Structures

Robert J. Glushko
Matthew Mayernik
Alberto Pepe
Murray Maloney

5.1 Introduction

We can consider a family to be a collection of people affiliated by some connections with each other such as common ancestors or a common residence. The Simpson family includes a man named Homer and a woman named Marge, the married parents of three sibling children, a boy named Bart and two girls, Lisa and Maggie. This is a magical family that speaks many languages, but always uses the language of the local television station. In the English-speaking Simpson family, the boy describes his parents as his father and mother and his two siblings as his sisters. In the Spanish speaking Simpson family the boy refers to his parents as *su padre y su madre* and his sisters are *las hermanas*. In the Chinese Simpson family Lisa and Maggie refer to each other according to their relative ages; Lisa, the elder sister as *jiě jie* and, Maggie, the younger sister as *mèi mei*.[253]

Kinship relationships are ubiquitous and widely studied, and the names and significance of kinship relations like "is parent of" or "is sibling of" are familiar ones, making kinship a good starting point for understanding **relationships** in organizing systems.[254] An organizing system can make use of existing relationships among resources, or it can create relationships by applying organizing principles to arrange the resources. Organizing systems for digital resources or digital description resources are the most likely to rely on explicit relationships to enable interactions with the resources.

In a classic book called *Data and Reality*, William Kent defines a **relationship** as "an association among several things, with that association having a particular significance."[255] "The things being associated," the components of the relationship, are people in kinship relationships but more generally can be any type of resource (Chapter 3), when we relate one resource instance to another. When we describe a resource (Chapter 4), the components of the relationship are a primary resource and a description resource. If we specify sets of relationships that go together, we are using these common relationships to define resource types or classes, which more generally are called categories (Chapter 6). We can then use resource types as one or both the components of a relationship when we want to further describe the resource type or to assert how two resource types go together to facilitate our interactions with them.

We begin with a more complete definition of relationship and introduce five perspectives for analyzing them: semantic, lexical, structural, architectural, and implementation. We then discuss each perspective, introducing the issues that each emphasizes, and the specialized vocabulary needed to describe and analyze relationships from that point of view. We apply these perspectives and vocabulary to analyze the most important types of relationships in organizing systems.

5.2 Describing Relationships: An Overview

The concept of a relationship is pervasive in human societies in both informal and formal senses. Humans are inescapably related to generations of ancestors, and in most cases they also have social networks of friends, co-workers, and casual acquaintances to whom they are related in various ways. We often hear that our access to information, money, jobs, and political power is all about "who you know," so we strive to "network" with other people to build relationships that might help us expand our access. In information systems, relationships between resources embody the organization that enables finding, selection, retrieval, and other interactions.

Most organizing systems are based on many relationships to enable the system to satisfy some intentional purposes with individual resources or the collection as a whole. In the domain of information resources, common resources include web pages, journal articles, books, data sets, metadata records, and XML documents, among many others. Important relationships in the information domain that facilitate purposes like finding, identifying, and selecting resources include "is the author of," "is published by," "has publication date," "is derived from," "has subject keyword," "is related to," and many others.

When we talk about relationships we specify both the resources that are associated along with a name or statement about the reason for the association. Just identifying the resources involved is not enough because several different relationships can exist among the same resources; the same person can be your brother, your employer, and your landlord. Furthermore, for many relationships the directionality or ordering of the participants in a relationship statement matters; the person who is your employer gives a paycheck to you, not vice versa. Kent points out that when we describe a relationship we sometimes use whole phrases, such as "is-employed-by," if our language does not contain a single word that expresses the meaning of the relationship.

We can analyze relationships from several different perspectives:

Semantic perspective
> The semantic perspective is the most essential one; it characterizes the meaning of the association between resources.

Lexical perspective
> The lexical perspective focuses on how the conceptual description of a relationship is expressed using words in a specific language.

Structural perspective
> The structural perspective analyzes the actual patterns of association, arrangement, proximity, or connection between resources.

Architectural perspective
> The architectural perspective emphasizes the number and abstraction level of the components of a relationship, which together characterize its complexity.

Implementation perspective
> The implementation perspective considers how the relationship is implemented in a particular notation and syntax and the manner in which relationships are arranged and stored in some technology environment.

The remainder of this chapter is organized around a discussion of these five perspectives in the order listed here.

5.3 The Semantic Perspective

In order to describe relationships among resources, we need to understand what the relations mean. This **semantic perspective** is the essence of relationships and explains why the resources are related, relying on information that is not directly available from perceiving the resources.[256] In our Simpson family example, we noted that Homer and Marge are related by marriage, and also by their relationship as parents of Bart, Lisa, and Maggie, and none of these relationships are directly perceivable.

Semantic relationships are commonly expressed with a predicate with one or more arguments. A *predicate* is a verb phrase template for specifying properties of objects or a relationship among objects. In many relationships the predicate is an action or association that involves multiple participants that must be of particular types, and the arguments define the different roles of the participants.[257]

We can express the relationship between Homer and Marge Simpson using a *predicate(argument(s))* syntax as follows:

is-married-to (Homer Simpson, Marge Simpson)

The sequence, type, and role of the arguments are an essential part of the relationship expression. The sequence and role are explicitly distinguished when predicates that take two arguments are expressed using a *subject-predicate-object* syntax that is often called a *triple* because of its three parts:

Homer Simpson → is-married-to → Marge Simpson

However, we have not yet specified what the "is-married-to" relationship means. People can demonstrate their understanding of "is-married-to" by realizing that alternative and semantically equivalent expressions of the relationship between Homer and Marge might be:

Homer Simpson → is-married-to → Marge Simpson
Homer Simpson → is-the-husband-of → Marge Simpson
Marge Simpson → is-married-to → Homer Simpson
Marge Simpson → is-the-wife-of → Homer Simpson

Going one step further, we could say that people understand the equivalence of these different expressions of the relationship because they have semantic and linguistic knowledge that relates some representation of "married," "husband," "wife," and other words. None of that knowledge is visible in the expressions of the relationships so far, all of which specify concrete relationships about individuals and not abstract relationships between resource classes or concepts. We have simply pushed the problem of what it means to understand the expressions into the mind of the person doing the understanding.

We can be more rigorous and define the words used in these expressions so they are "in the world" rather than just "in the mind" of the person understanding them. We can write definitions about these resource classes:[258]

- The conventional or traditional marriage relationship is a consensual lifetime association between a husband and a wife, which is sanctioned by law and often by religious ceremonies;
- A husband is a male lifetime partner considered in relation to his wife; and
- A wife is a female lifetime partner considered in relation to her husband.

Definitions like these help a person learn and make some sense of the relationship expressions involving Homer and Marge. However, these definitions are not in a form that would enable someone to completely understand the Homer and Marge expressions; they rely on other undefined terms (consensual, law, lifetime, etc.), and they do not state the relationships among the concepts in the definitions.[259] Furthermore, for a computer to understand the expressions, it needs a computer-processable representation of the relationships among words and meanings that makes every important semantic assumption and property precise and explicit. We will see what this takes starting in the next section.

5.3.1 Types of Semantic Relationships

In this discussion we will use "entity type," "class," "concept," and "resource type" as synonyms. **Entity type** and **class** are conventional terms in data modeling and database design, "concept" is the conventional term in computational or cognitive modeling, and we use "resource type"when we discuss organizing systems. Similarly, we will use "entity occurrence," **instance,** and "resource instance" when we refer to one thing rather than to a class or type of them.

There is no real consensus on how to categorize semantic relationships, but these three broad categories are reasonable for our purposes:

Inclusion
   One entity type contains or is comprised of other entity types; often expressed using "is-a," "is-a-type-of," "is-part-of," or "is-in" predicates.

Attribution
   Asserting or assigning values to properties; the predicate depends on the property: "is-the-author-of," "is-married-to," "is-employed-by," etc.

Possession
> Asserting ownership or control of a resource; often expressed using a "has" predicate, such as "has-serial-number-plate."[260]

All of these are fundamental in organizing systems, both for describing and arranging resources themselves, and for describing the relationships among resources and resource descriptions.

5.3.1.1 Inclusion

There are three different types of inclusion relationships: class inclusion, meronymic inclusion, and topological inclusion. All three are commonly used in organizing systems.

Class Inclusion is the fundamental and familiar "**is-a**," "**is-a-type-of**," or "**subset**" relationship between two entity types or classes where one is contained in and thus more specific than the other more generic one.

> **Meat → is-a → Food**

A set of interconnected class inclusion relationships creates a hierarchy, which is often called a *taxonomy*.

> **Meat → is-a → Food**
> **Dairy Product → is-a → Food**
> **Cereal → is-a → Food**
> **Vegetable → is-a → Food**
> **Beef → is-a → Meat**
> **Pork → is-a → Meat**
> **Chicken → is-a → Meat**
> **Ground Beef → is-a → Beef**
> **Steak → is-a → Beef**
> ...

A visual depiction of the taxonomy makes the class hierarchy easier to perceive. See Figure 5.1, "A Partial Taxonomy of Food."

Each level in a taxonomy subdivides the class above it into sub-classes, and each sub-class is further subdivided until the differences that remain among the members of each class no longer matter for the interactions the organizing system needs to support. We discuss the design of hierarchical organizing systems in §6.3, "Principles for Creating Categories."

All of the examples in the current section have expressed abstract relationships between classes, in contrast to the earlier concrete ones about Homer and Marge, which expressed relationships between specific people. Homer and Marge are instances of classes like "married people," "husbands," and "wives." When we make an assertion that a particular instance is a member of class, we

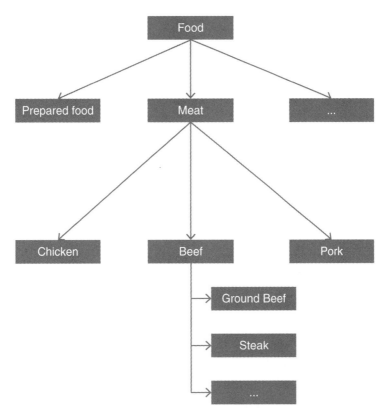

A PARTIAL TAXONOMY OF FOOD

Figure 5.1. A Partial Taxonomy of Food.

are ***classifying*** the instance. ***Classification*** is a class inclusion relationship between an instance and a class rather than between two classes. (We discuss Classification in detail in Chapter 7).

Homer Simpson → is-a → Husband

This is just the lowest level of the class hierarchy in which Homer is located at the very bottom; he is also a man, a human being, and a living organism (in cartoon land, at least).[261] You might now remember the bibliographic class inclusion hierarchy we discussed in §3.3.2, "Identity and Bibliographic Resources" (page 110); a specific physical *item* like your dog-eared copy of *Macbeth* is also a particular **manifestation** in some format or genre, and this *expression* is one of many for the abstract **work.**

Part-whole inclusion or *meronymic inclusion* is a second type of inclusion relationship. It is usually expressed using "is-part-of," "is-partly," or with other similar predicate expressions. Winston, Chaffin, and Herrmann identified **six** distinct types of part-whole relationships:[262]

- *Component-Object* is the relationship type when the part is a separate component that is arranged or assembled with other components to create a larger resource. In §3.1.1.1, "Resources with Parts," we used as an example the component-object relationship between an engine and a car:

  The Engine → is-part-of → the Car

  The components of this type of part-whole relationship need not be physical objects; "Germany is part of the European Union" expresses a component-object relationship. What matters is that the component is identifiable on its own as an integral entity and that the components follow some kind of patterned organization or structure when they form the whole. Together the parts form a composition, and the parts collectively form the whole. A car that lacks the engine part will not work.

- *Member-Collection* is the part-whole relationship type where "is-part-of" means "belongs-to," a weaker kind of association than component-object because there is no assumption that the component has a specific role or function in the whole.

  The Book → is-part-of → the Library

  The members of the collection exist independently of the whole; if the whole ceases to exist the individual resources still exist.

  The Slice → is-part-of → the Pie

- *Portion-Mass* is the relationship type when all the parts are similar to each other and to the whole, unlike either of the previous types where engines are not tires or cars, and books are not like record albums or libraries.

  The Slice → is-part-of → the Pie

- *Stuff-Object* relationships are most often expressed using "is-partly" or "is-made-of" and are distinguishable from component-object ones because the stuff cannot be separated from the object without altering its identity. The stuff is not a separate ingredient that is used to make the object; it is a constituent of it once it is made.

  Wine → is-partly → Alcohol

- *Place-Area* relationships exist between areas and specific places or locations within them. Like members of collections, places have no particular functional contribution to the whole.

  The Everglades → are-part-of → Florida

- *Feature-Activity* is a relationship type in which the components are stages, phases, or sub activities that take place over time. This relationship is similar to component-object in that the components in the whole are arranged according to a structure or pattern.

  Overtime → is-part-of → a Football Game

A seventh type of part-whole relationship called *Phase-Activity* was proposed by Storey.[263]

- *Phase-Activity* is similar to *feature-activity* except that the phases do not make sense as standalone activities without the context provided by the activity as a whole.

  Paying → is-part-of → Shopping

Topological*, *Locative* and *Temporal Inclusion is a third type of *inclusion relationship* between a container, area, or temporal duration and what it surrounds or contains. It is most often expressed using "is-in" as the relationship. However, the entity that is contained or surrounded is not a part of the including one, so this is not a *part-whole* relationship.

  The Vatican City → is-in → Italy
  The meeting → is-in → the afternoon

5.3.1.2 Attribution

In contrast to inclusion expressions that state relationships between resources, *attribution* relationships assert or assign values to properties for a particular resource. In Chapter 4 we used "attribute" to mean "an indivisible part of a resource description" and treated it as a synonym of "property." We now need to be more precise and carefully distinguish between the type of the *attribute* and the *value* that it has. For example, the color of any object is an *attribute* of the object, and the value of that attribute might be "green."

Some frameworks for semantic modeling define "attribute" very narrowly, restricting it to expressions with predicates with only one argument to assert properties of a single resource, distinguishing them from relationships between resources or resource types that require two arguments:[264]

  Martin the Gecko → is-small
  Martin the Gecko → is-green

However, it is always possible to express statements like these in ways that make them into relationships with two arguments:

Martin → has-size → small
Martin → has-skin-color → green

Dedre Gentner notes that this supposed distinction between one-predicate attributes and two-predicate relationships depends on context.[265] For example, small can be viewed as an attribute, **X → is-small,** or as a relationship between X and some standard or reference Y, **X → is-smaller-than → Y.**

Another somewhat tricky aspect of attribution relationships is that from a semantic perspective, there are often many different ways of expressing equivalent attribute values.

Martin → has-size → 6 inches
Martin → has size → 152 mm

These two statements express the idea that Martin is small. However, many implementations of attribution relationships treat the attribute values literally. This means that unless we can process these two statements using another relationship that expresses the conversion of inches to mm, the two statements could be interpreted as saying different things about Martin's size.

Finally, we note that we can express attribution relationships about other relationships, like the date a relationship was established. Homer and Marge Simpson's wedding anniversary is an attribute of their "is-married-to" relationship.

The semantic distinctions between attributes and other types of relationships are not strong ones, but they can be made clearer by implementation choices. For example, XML attributes are tightly coupled to a containing element, and their literal values are limited to atomic items of information. In contrast, inclusion relationships are expressed by literal containment of one XML element by another.

5.3.1.3 Possession

A third distinct category of semantic relationships is that of possession. *Possession* relationships can seem superficially like part-whole ones:

Bob → has → a car
A car → has → wheels

However, in the second of these relationships "has" is an elliptical form of "has as a part," expressing a component-object relationship rather that one of possession.

The concept of possession is especially important in institutional organizing systems, where questions of ownership, control, responsibility and transfers of ownership, control, and responsibility can be fundamental parts of the interactions they support. However, possession is a complex notion, inherently connected to societal norms and conventions about property and kinship, making it messier than institutional processes might like. Possession relationships also imply duration or persistence, and are often difficult to distinguish from relationships based on habitual location or practice. Miller and Johnson-Laird illustrate the complex nature of possession relationships with this sentence, which expresses three different types of them:[266]

- **He owns an umbrella but she's borrowed it, though she doesn't have it with her.**

5.3.2 Properties of Semantic Relationships

Semantic relationships can have numerous special properties that help explain what they mean and especially how they relate to each other. In the following sections we briefly explain those that are most important in systems for organizing resources and resource descriptions.

5.3.2.1 Symmetry

In most relationships the order in which the subject and object arguments are expressed is central to the meaning of the relationship. If X has a relationship with Y, it is usually not the case that Y has the same relationship with X. For example, because "is-parent-of" is an *asymmetric* relationship, only the first of these relationships holds:

> **Homer Simpson → is-parent-of → Bart Simpson (TRUE)**
> **Bart Simpson → is-parent-of → Homer Simpson (NOT TRUE)**

In contrast, some relationships are *symmetric* or *bi-directional*, and reversing the order of the arguments of the relationship predicate does not change the meaning. As we noted earlier, these two statements are semantically equivalent because "is-married-to" is symmetric:

> **Homer Simpson → is-married-to → Marge Simpson**
> **Marge Simpson → is-married-to → Homer Simpson**

We can represent the **symmetric** and *bi-directional* nature of these relationships by using a double-headed arrow:

> **Homer Simpson ⇔ is-married-to ⇔ Marge Simpson**

5.3.2.2 Transitivity

Transitivity is another property that can apply to semantic relationships. When a relationship is transitive, if X and Y have a relationship, and Y and Z have the same relationship, then X also has the relationship with Z. Any relationship based on ordering is transitive, which includes numerical, alphabetic, and chronological ones as well as those that imply qualitative or quantitative measurement. Because "is-taller-than" is transitive:

Homer Simpson → is-taller-than → Bart Simpson
Bart Simpson → is-taller-than → Maggie Simpson

implies that:

Homer Simpson → is-taller-than → Maggie Simpson

Inclusion relationships are inherently transitive, because just as "is-taller-than" is an assertion about relative physical size, "is-a-type of" and "is-part-of" are assertions about the relative sizes of abstract classes or categories.[267]

Transitive relationships enable inferences about class membership or properties, and allow organizing systems to be more efficient in how they represent them since transitivity enables implicit relationships to be made explicit only when they are needed.

5.3.2.3 Equivalence

Any relationship that is both symmetric and transitive is an *equivalence* relationship; "is-equal-to" is obviously an equivalence relationship because if A=B then B=A and if A=B and B=C, then A=C. Other relationships can be equivalent without meaning "exactly equal," as is the relationship of "is-congruent-to" for all triangles.

We often need to assert that a particular class or property has the same meaning as another class or property or that it is generally substitutable for it. We make this explicit with an equivalence relationship.

Sister (English) ⇔ is-equivalent-to ⇔ Hermana (Spanish)
Sister (English) ⇔ is-equivalent-to ⇔ Hermana (Spanish)

5.3.2.4 Inverse

For asymmetric relationships, it is often useful to be explicit about the meaning of the relationship when the order of the arguments in the relationship is reversed. The resulting relationship is called the ***inverse*** or the converse of the first relationship. If an organizing system explicitly represents that:

Is-child-of → is-the-inverse-of → Is-parent-of

We can then conclude that:

Bart Simpson → is-child-of → Homer Simpson .

5.3.3 Ontologies

We now have described types and properties of semantic relationships in enough detail to return to the challenge we posed earlier: what information is required to fully understand relationships? This question has been asked and debated for decades and we will not pretend to answer it to any extent here. However, we can sketch out some of the basic parts of the solution.

Let us begin by recalling that a *taxonomy* captures a system of class inclusion relationships in some domain. But as we have seen, there are a great many kinds of relationships that are not about class inclusion. All of these other types of relationships represent knowledge about the domain that is potentially needed to understand statements about it and to make sense when more than one domain of resources or activities comes together.

For example, in the food domain whose partial taxonomy appears in §5.3.1, "Types of Semantic Relationships" (page 193), we can assert relationships about properties of classes and instances, express equivalences about them, and otherwise enhance the representation of the food domain to create a complex network of relationships. In addition, the food domain intersects with food preparation, agriculture, commerce, and many other domains. We also need to express the relationships among these domains to fully understand any of them.

> **Hamburger → is-equivalent-to → Ground Beef**
> **Hamburger → is-prepared-by → Grilling**
> **Grilling → is-a-type-of → Food Preparation**
> **Hamburger Sandwich → is-a-type-of → Prepared Food**
> **BigMac → is-a → Hamburger Sandwich**
> **A bun → is-part-of → Hamburger Sandwich**
> **A bun → is-partly → flour**
> **Temperature → is-a-measure-of → Grilling**
> **Rare → is-a → State of Food Preparation**
> **Well-done → is-a → State of Food Preparation**
> **Meat → is-preserved-by → Freezing**
> **Thawing → is-the-inverse-of → Freezing**
> **...**

In this simple example we see that class inclusion relationships form a kind of backbone to which other kinds of relationships attach. We also see that there are many potentially relevant assertions that together represent the knowledge

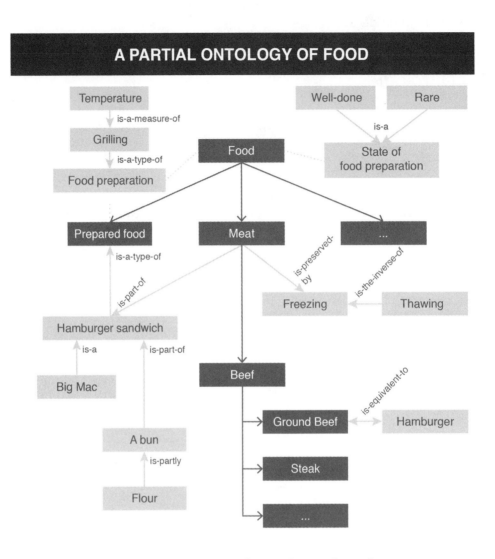

Figure 5.2. A Partial Ontology of Food.

that just about everyone knows about food and related domains. A network of relationships like these creates a resource that is called an *ontology*.[268] A visual depiction of the ontology illustrates this idea that it has a taxonomy as its conceptual scaffold. See Figure 5.2, "A Partial Ontology of Food."

There are numerous formats for expressing ontologies, but many of them have recently converged to or are based on the *Web Ontology Language (OWL)*, the developed by the W3C. OWL ontologies use a formal logic-based language that builds on RDF (§4.2.2.3, "Tagging of Web-Based Resources" (page 144)) to define resource classes and assign properties to them in rigorous ways, arrange them in a class hierarchy, establish their equivalence, and specify the properties of relationships.[269]

Ontologies are essential parts in some organizing systems, especially information-intensive ones where the scope and scale of the resources require an extensive and controlled description vocabulary (See §4.3, "The Process of Describing Resources" (page 148)). The most extensive ontology ever created is Cyc, born in 1984 as an artificial intelligence research project. Three decades later, the latest version of the Cyc ontology contains several hundred thousand terms and millions of assertions that interrelate them.[270]

5.4 The Lexical Perspective

The semantic perspective for analyzing relationships is the fundamental one, but it is intrinsically tied to the lexical one because a relationship is always expressed using words in a specific language. For example, we understand the relationships among the concepts or classes of "food," "meat," and "beef" by using the words "food," "meat," and "beef" to identify progressively smaller classes of edible things in a class hierarchy.

The connection between concept and words is not so simple. In the Simpson family example with which we began this chapter, we noted with "father" and "padre" that languages differ in the words they use to describe particular kinship relationships. Furthermore, we pointed out that cultures differ in which kinship relationships are conceptually distinct, so that languages like Chinese make distinctions about the relative ages of siblings that are not made in English.[271] This is not to suggest that an English speaker cannot notice the difference between his older and younger sisters, only that this distinction is not lexicalized—captured in a single word—as it is in Chinese. This "missing word" in English from the perspective of Chinese is called a "lexical gap."[272]

Earlier in this book we discussed the naming of resources (§3.4.2, "The Problems of Naming" (page 116)) and the design of a vocabulary for resource description (§4.3.1.3, "Scope, Scale, and Resource Description" (page 154)), and we explained how increasing the scope and scale of an organizing system made it essential to be more systematic and precise in assigning names and descriptions. We need to be sure that the terms we use to organize resources capture the similarities and differences between them well enough to support our interactions with them. After our discussion about semantic relationships in this chapter, we now have a clearer sense of what is required to bring like things together, keep different things separate, and to satisfy any other goals for the organizing system.

For example, if we are organizing cars, buses, bicycles, and sleds, all of which are vehicles, there is an important distinction between vehicles that are motorized and those that are powered by human effort. It might also be useful to distinguish vehicles with wheels from those that lack them. Not making these distinctions leaves an unbalanced or uneven organizing system for describing the semantics of the vehicle domain. However, only the "motorized" concept is lexicalized in English, which is why we needed to invent the "wheeled vehicle" term in the second case.[273]

Simply put, we need to use words effectively in organizing systems. To do that, we need to be careful about how we talk about the relationships among words and how words relate to concepts. There are two different contexts for those relationships. First, we need to discuss relationships among the meanings of words. Second, we need to discuss relationships among the form of words.

5.4.1 Relationships among Word Meanings

There are several different types of relationships of word meanings. Not surprisingly, in most cases they parallel the types of relationships among concepts that we described in §5.3, "The Semantic Perspective" (page 192).

5.4.1.1 Hyponymy and Hyperonymy

When words encode the semantic distinctions expressed by class inclusion, the word for the more specific class in this relationship is called the *hyponym*, while the word for the more general class to which it belongs is called the *hypernym*. George Miller suggested an exemplary formula for defining a hyponym as its hypernym preceded by adjectives or followed by relative clauses that distinguish it from its *co-hyponyms*, mutually exclusive subtypes of the same hypernym.

hyponym = {adjective+} hypernym {distinguishing clause+}

For example, robin is a hyponym of bird, and could be defined as "a migratory bird that has a clear melodious song and a reddish breast with gray or black upper plumage." This definition does not describe every property of robins, but it is sufficient to differentiate robins from bluebirds or eagles.[274]

5.4.1.2 Metonymy

Part-whole or meronymic semantic relationships have lexical analogues in *metonomy*, when an entity is described by something that is contained in or otherwise part of it. A country's capital city or a building where its top leaders reside is often used as a metonym for the entire government: "The White House announced today..." Similarly, important concentrations of business activity are often metonyms for their entire industries: "Wall Street was bailed out again..."

5.4.1.3 Synonymy

Synonymy is the relationship between words that express the same semantic concept.The strictest definition is that *synonyms* "are words that can replace each other in some class of contexts with insignificant changes of the whole text's meaning."[275] This is an extremely hard test to pass, except for acronyms or compound terms like "USA," "United States," and "United States of America" that are completely substitutable.

Most synonyms are not *absolute synonyms* like the aforementioned, and instead are considered *propositional synonyms*. *Propositional synonyms* are not identical in meaning, they are equivalent enough in most contexts in that substituting one for the other will not change the truth value of the sentence that uses them. This weaker test lets us treat word pairs as synonyms even though their meanings differ in subtle ways. For example, if we know that Lisa Simpson plays the violin, because "violin" and "fiddle" are propositional synonyms, no one would disagree with an assertion that Lisa Simpson can play the fiddle.

An unordered set of synonyms is often called a *synset*, a term first used by the WordNet "semantic dictionary" project started in 1985 by George Miller and others at Princeton's Cognitive Science program.[276] Instead of using spelling as the primary organizing principle for words, WordNet uses their semantic properties and relationships to create a network that captures the idea that words and concepts are an inseparable system. Synsets are interconnected by both semantic relationships and lexical ones, enabling navigation in either space.[277]

5.4.1.4 Polysemy

We introduced the lexical relationship of *polysemy*, when a word has several different meanings or senses, in the context of problems with names (§3.4.2.2, "Homonymy, Polysemy, and False Cognates" (page 117)). For example, the word "bank" can refer to any number of objects and activities: river bank, money bank, bank shots in basketball and billiards, an aircraft maneuver, to name a few.[278]

Polysemy is represented in WordNet by including a word in multiple synsets. This enables WordNet to be an extremely useful resource for sense disambiguation in natural language processing research and applications. When a polysemous word is encountered, it and the words that are nearby in the text are looked up in WordNet. By following the lexical relationships in the synset hierarchy, a "synset distance" can be calculated. The smallest semantic distance between the words, which identifies their most semantically specific hypernym, can be used to identify the correct sense.[279]

5.4.1.5 Antonymy

Antonymy is the lexical relationship between two words that have opposite meanings. Antonymy is a very salient lexical relationship, and for adjectives it is even more powerful than synonymy. In word association tests, when the probe word is a familiar adjective, the most common response is its antonym; a probe of "good" elicits "bad," and vice versa. Like synonymy, antonomy is sometimes exact and sometimes more graded.[280]

Contrasting or **binary antonyms** are used in mutually exclusive contexts where one or the other word can be used, but never both. For example, "alive" and "dead" can never be used at the same time to describe the state of some entity, because the meaning of one excludes or contradicts the meaning of the other.

Other antonymic relationships between word pairs are less semantically sharp because they can sometimes appear in the same context as a result of the broader semantic scope of one of the words. "Large" and "small," or "old" and "young" generally suggest particular regions on size or age continua, but "how large is it?" or "how old is it?" can be asked about resources that are objectively small or young.[281]

5.4.2 Thesauri

The words that people naturally use when they describe resources reflect their unique experiences and perspectives, and this means that people often use different words for the same resource and the same words for different ones. Guiding people when they select description words from a *controlled vocabulary* is a partial solution to this *vocabulary problem* (§3.4.2.1, "The Vocabulary Problem" (page 116)) that becomes increasingly essential as the scope and scale of the organizing system grows. A **thesaurus** is a reference work that organizes words according to their semantic and lexical relationships. Thesauri are often used by professionals when they describe resources.

Thesauri have been created for many domains and subject areas. Some thesauri are very broad and contain words from many disciplines, like the Library of Congress Subject Headings (LOC-SH) used to classify any published content. Other commonly used thesauri are more focused, like the *Art and Architecture Thesaurus (AAT)* developed by the Getty Trust and the Legislative Indexing Vocabulary developed by the Library of Congress.[282]

We can return to our simple food taxonomy to illustrate how a thesaurus annotates vocabulary terms with lexical and semantic relationships. The class inclusion relationships of *hypernomy* and *hyponymy* are usually encoded using BT ("broader term") and NT ("narrower term"):

Food BT Meat
Beef NT Meat

The BT and NT relationships in a thesaurus create a hierarchical system of words, but a thesaurus is more than a lexical taxonomy for some domain because it also encodes additional lexical relationships for the most important words. Many thesauri emphasize the cluster of relationships for these key words and de-emphasize the overall lexical hierarchy.

Because the purpose of a thesaurus is to reduce synonymy, it distinguishes among synonyms or near-synonyms by indicating one of them as a preferred term using UF ("used for"):

Food UF Sustenance, Nourishment

A thesaurus might employ USE as the inverse of the UF relationship to refer from a less preferred or variant term to a preferred one:

Victuals USE Food

Thesauri also use RT ("related term" or "see also") to indicate terms that are not synonyms but which often occur in similar contexts:

Food RT Cooking, Dining, Cuisine

5.4.3 Relationships among Word Forms

The relationships among word meanings are critically important. Whenever we create, combine, or compare resource descriptions we also need to pay attention to relationships between word forms. These relationships begin with the idea that all natural languages create words and word forms from smaller units. The basic building blocks for words are called *morphemes* and can express semantic concepts (when they are called *root words*) or abstract concepts like "pastness" or "plural"). The analysis of the ways by which languages combine *morphemes* is called *morphology*.[283]

Morphological analysis of a language is heavily used in text processing to create indexes for information retrieval; for example, *stemming* (discussed in more detail in Chapter 9) is morphological processing which removes prefixes and suffixes to leave the root form of words. Similarly, simple text processing applications like hyphenation and spelling correction solve word form problems using roots and rules because it is more scalable and robust than solving them using word lists. Many misspellings of common words (e.g., "pain") are words of lower frequency (e.g., "pane"), so adding "pane" to a list of misspelled words would occasionally identify it incorrectly. In addition, because natural languages are generative and create new words all the time, a word list can never be complete; for example, when "flickr" occurs in text, is it a misspelling of "flicker" or the correct spelling of the popular photo-sharing site?

5.4.3.1 Derivational Morphology

Derivational morphology deals with how words are created by combining morphemes. *Compounding*, putting two "free morphemes" together as in "batman" or "catwoman," is an extremely powerful mechanism. The meaning of some compounds is easy to understand when the first morpheme qualifies or restricts the meaning of the second, as in "birdcage" and "tollbooth."[284] However, many compounds take on new meanings that are not as literally derived from the meaning of their constituents, like "seahorse" and "batman."

Other types of derivations using "bound" morphemes follow more precise rules for combining them with "base" morphemes. The most common types of bound morphemes are prefixes and suffixes, which usually create a word of a different part-of-speech category when they are added. Familiar English prefixes include "a-," "ab-," "anti-," "co-," "de-," "pre-," and "un-." Among the most common English suffixes are "-able," "-ation," "-ify," "ing," "-ity," "-ize," "-ment," and "-ness." Compounding and adding prefixes or suffixes are simple mechanisms, but very complex words like "unimaginability" can be formed by using them in combination.

5.4.3.2 Inflectional Morphology

Inflectional mechanisms change the form of a word to represent tense, aspect, agreement, or other grammatical information. Unlike derivation, inflection never changes the part-of-speech of the base morpheme. The **inflectional morphology** of English is relatively simple compared with other languages.[285]

5.5 The Structural Perspective

The *structural perspective* analyzes the association, arrangement, proximity, or connection between resources without primary concern for their meaning or the origin of these relationships.[286] We take a structural perspective when we define a family as "a collection of people" or when we say that a particular family like the Simpsons has five members. Sometimes all we know is that two resources are connected, as when we see a highlighted word or phrase that is pointing from the current web page to another. At other times we might know more about the reasons for the relationships within a set of resources, but we still focus on their structure, essentially merging or blurring all of the reasons for the associations into a single generic notion that the resources are connected. We do this when we analyze communication or interaction patterns to determine the number of "degrees of separation" between any pair of resources.[287]

Many types of resources have internal structure in addition to their structural relationships with other resources. Of course, we have to remember (as we discussed in §3.3, "Resource Identity" (page 109)) that we often face arbitrary choices about the abstraction and granularity with which we describe the parts that make up a resource and whether some combination of resource should also be identified as a resource. This is not easy when you are analyzing the structure of a car with its thousands of parts, and it is ever harder with information resources where there are many more ways to define parts and wholes. However, an advantage for information resources is that their internal structural descriptions are usually highly "computable," something we consider in depth in Chapter 9, *"Interactions with Resources"*.

5.5.1 Intentional, Implicit, and Explicit Structure

In the discipline of organizing we emphasize "intentional structure" created by people or by computational processes rather than accidental or naturally-occurring structures created by physical, geological, biological or genetic processes. We acknowledged in §1.2.3, "The Concept of "Intentional Arrangement"" (page 10) that there is information in the piles of debris left after a tornado or tsunami and in the strata of the Grand Canyon. Similarly, we can perceive a pattern of stars and name it Orion or the Big Dipper, but this structural organization only exists from our galactic point of view; the stars that make up these constellations are at significantly different distances from Earth. These structural patterns might be of interest to meteorologists, geologists, astronomers or others but because they were not created by an identifiable agent following one or more organizing principles, they are not our primary focus.

Some organizing principles impose very little structure. For a small collection of resources, co-locating them or arranging them near each other might be sufficient organization. We can impose two- or three-dimensional coordinate systems on this "implicit structure" and explicitly describe the location of a resource as precisely as we want, but we more naturally describe the structure of resource locations in relative terms. In English we have many ways to describe the structural relationship of one resource to another: "in," "on," "under," "behind," "above," "below," "near," "to the right of," "to the left of," "next to," and so on. Sometimes several resources are arranged or appear to be arranged in a sequence or order and we can use positional descriptions of structure: a late 1990s TV show described the planet Earth as "the third rock from the Sun."[288]

We pay most attention to intentional structures that are explicitly represented within and between resources because they embody the design or authoring choices about how much implicit or latent structure will be made explicit. Structures that can be reliably extracted by algorithms become especially important for very large collections of resources whose scope and scale defy structural analysis by people.

5.5.2 Structural Relationships within a Resource

We almost always think of human and other animate resources as unitary entities. Likewise, many physical resources like paintings, sculptures, and manufactured goods have a material integrity that makes us usually consider them as indivisible. For an information resource, however, it is almost always the case that it has or might have had some internal structure or sub-division of its constituent data elements.

In fact, since all computer files are merely encodings of bits, bytes, characters and strings, we can say with some certainty that most digital resources exhibit some internal structure, even if that structure is only discernible by software agents. The internal formats of word processing files, for example, have changed many times since their invention in the mid-twentieth century, converging on XML in the early twenty-first century.

When an author writes a document, he or she gives it some internal organization with its title, section headings, typographic conventions, page numbers, and other mechanisms that identify its parts and their significance or relationship to each other. The lowest level of this structural hierarchy, usually the paragraph, contains the text content of the document. Sometimes the author finds it useful to identify types of content like glossary terms or cross-references within the paragraph text. Document models like these that mix structural description with content "nuggets" in the text are said to contain **mixed content** (See the Sidebar.)

In data-intensive or transactional domains, document instances tend to be homogeneous because they are produced by or for automated processes, and their information components will appear predictably in the same structural relationships with each other. These structures typically form a hierarchy expressed in an XML schema or word processing style template. XML documents describe their component parts using content-oriented elements like <ITEM>, <NAME>, and <ADDRESS>, that are themselves often aggregate structures or containers for more granular elements. The structures of resources maintained in databases are typically less hierarchical, but the structures are precisely captured in database schemas.

> ## Mixed Content
>
> **Mixed content** distinguishes XML from other data representation languages. It is this structural feature, combined with the fact that child nodes in the XML Infoset (§8.2.2.2) are ordered, that makes it possible for XML documents to function both as human reader-oriented, textual documents and as structured data formats. It allows us to use natural language in writing descriptions while still enabling us to identify content by type by embedding markup to enclose "semantic nuggets" in otherwise undifferentiated text.[289]
>
> The *Guidelines for Electronic Text Encoding and Interchange*, produced by the Text Encoding Initiative (TEI), for example, includes a set of elements and attributes for *Names, Dates, People and Places*.[290]

The internal parts of XML documents can be described, found and selected using the XPath language, which defines the structures and patterns used by XML forms, queries, and transformations. The key idea used by XPath is that the structure of XML documents is a tree of information items called nodes, whose locations are described in terms of the relationships between nodes. The relationships built into XPath, which it calls axes, include self, child, parent, following, and preceding, making it very easy to specify a structure-based query like "find all sections in Chapter 1 through Chapter 5 that have at least two levels of subsections."[291] In addition, tools like Schematron take advantage of XPath's structural descriptions to test assertions about a document's structure and content. For example, a common editorial constraint might be that a numbered list must have at least three items.[292]

In more qualitative, less information-intensive and more experience-intensive domains, we move toward the narrative end of the Document Type Spectrum, and document instances become more heterogeneous because they are produced by and for people (See the Sidebar, "The Document Type Spectrum" (page 101) in §3.2.1). The information conveyed in the documents is conceptual or thematic rather than transactional, and the structural relationships between document parts are much weaker. Instead of precise structure and content rules, there is usually just a shallow hierarchy marked up with Word processing or HTML tags like <HEAD>, <H1>, <H2>, and <LIST>.

Structural Metadata

Structural metadata, in the form of a schema for a database or document, describes a class of information resource, and may also prescribe grammatical details of inclusion and attribution relationships among the components. For example, the chapters of this book contain four levels of subsections. Each of those sections contains a title, some paragraphs and other text blocks, and subordinate sections. The textual content of the paragraphs includes highlighted terms and phrases that are defined *in situ* and referenced again in the glossary and index; there are also bibliographic citations that are reflected in the bibliography and index. We can discover these characteristics of a book through observation, but we could also examine its structural metadata, in its schema.

The schema most commonly used for producing technical books is called DocBook; it describes every XML element and attribute and prescribes their grammatical forms. The schema lets us know that a formal paragraph must include a title, and that a title may contain emphasis. A schema can also describe and prescribe the lexical value space of a postal code, or require that every list must have at least three items. The DocBook schema is well-documented and has been production-tested in institutional publishing contexts for over twenty years.[293]

Structural metadata allows us to describe and prescribe relations among database tables, within the chapters of a book, or among parts in an inventory management system. The schema for HTML, for example, informs us that the <A> element can be used to signal a hypertext link-end; whether that link-end is an anchor or a target, or both, depends on the combination of values assigned to attributes. In HTML, the optional REL attribute may contain a value that signals purpose of a hypertext link, and any HTML element may include a CLASS attribute value that may be used as a CSS selector for the purposes of formatting.

The usefulness of any given schema is often a function of precision with which we may make useful statements based upon the descriptions and prescriptions it offers. Institutional schemas tend to be more prescriptive and restrictive, stressing professional orthodoxy and conformance to controlled vocabularies. Schemas for the information content in social and informal applications tend to be less prescriptive. Whether and how we use structural metadata is a tradeoff. Structural metadata is essential to enable quality control and maintenance in information collection and publishing processes, but someone has to do the work to create it.

The internal structural hierarchy in a resource is often extracted and made into a separate and familiar description resource called the "table of contents" to support finding and navigation interactions with the primary resource. In a printed media context, any given content resource is likely to only be presented once, and its page number is provided in the table of contents to allow the reader to locate the chapter, section or appendix in question. In a hypertext media context, a given resource may be a chapter in one book while being an appendix in another. Some tables of contents are created as a static structural description, but others are dynamically generated from the internal structures whenever the resource is accessed. In addition, other types of entry points can be generated from the names or descriptions of content components, like selectable lists of tables, figures, maps, or code examples.

Identifying the components and their structural relationships in documents is easier when they follow consistent rules for structure (e.g., every non-text component must have a title and caption) and presentation (e.g., *hypertext links* in web pages are underlined and change cursor shapes when they are "moused over") that reinforce the distinctions between types of information components. Structural and presentation features are often ordered on some dimension (e.g., type size, line width, amount of white space) and used in a correlated manner to indicate the importance of a content component.[294]

Many indexing algorithms treat documents as "bags of words" to compute statistics about the frequency and distribution of the words they contain while ignoring all semantics and structure. In Chapter 9, we contrast this approach with algorithms that use internal structural descriptions to retrieve more specific parts of documents.

5.5.3 Structural Relationships between Resources

Many types of resources have "structural relationships" that interconnect them. Web pages are almost always linked to other pages. Sometimes the links among a set of pages remain mostly within those pages, as they are in an e-commerce catalog site. More often, however, links connect to pages in other sites, creating a link network that cuts across and obscures the boundaries between sites.

The links between documents can be analyzed to infer connections between the authors of the documents. Using the pattern of links between documents to understand the structure of knowledge and of the intellectual community that creates it is not a new idea, but it has been energized as more of the information we exchange with other people is on the web or otherwise in digital formats. An important function in Google's search engine is the **page rank** algorithm that calculates the relevance of a page in part using the number of links that point to it while giving greater weight to pages that are themselves linked to often.[295]

Web-based social networks enable people to express their connections with other people directly, bypassing the need to infer the connections from links in documents or other communications.

5.5.3.1 Hypertext Links

The concept of read-only or follow-only structures that connect one document to another is usually attributed to Vannevar Bush in his seminal 1945 essay titled "As We May Think." Bush called it "associative indexing," defined as "a provision whereby any item may be caused at will to select immediately and automatically another."[296] The "item" connected in this way was for Bush most often a book or a scientific article. However, the anchor and destination of a hypertext link can be a resource of any granularity, ranging from a single point or character, a paragraph, a document, or any part of the resource to which the ends of link are connected. The anchor and destination of a web link are its structural specification, but we often need to consider links from other perspectives. (See the Sidebar, "Perspectives on Hypertext Links" (page 215)).

Theodor Holm Nelson, in a book intriguingly titled *Literary Machines*, renamed associative indexing as "hypertext" decades later, expanding the idea to make it a writing style as well as a reading style.[297] Nelson urged writers to use hypertext to create non-sequential narratives that gave choices to readers, using a novel technique for which he coined the term "transclusion." [298]

At about the same time, and without knowing about Nelson's work, Douglas Engelbart's *Augmenting the Human Intellect*, described a future world in which professionals equipped with interactive computer displays utilize an information space consisting of a cross-linked resources.[299]

In the 1960s, computers lacked graphic displays and were primarily employed to solve complex mathematical and scientific problems that might take minutes, hours or even days to complete, Nelson's and Engelbart's visions of hypertext-based personal computing may have seemed far-fetched. In spite of this, by 1968, Engelbart and his team demonstrated human computer interface including the mouse, hypertext, and interactive media, along with a set of guiding principles.[300]

Hypertext links are now familiar structural mechanisms in information applications because of the World Wide Web, proposed in 1989 by Tim Berners-Lee and Robert Cailliau.[301] They invented the methods for encoding and following *hypertext links* using the now popular HyperText Markup Language (HTML).[302] The resources connected by HTML's hypertext links are not limited to text or documents. Selecting a hypertext link can invoke a connected resource that might be a picture, video, or interactive application.[303]

By 1993, personal computers, with a graphic display, speakers and a mouse pointer, had become ubiquitous. NCSA Mosaic is widely credited with popularizing the World Wide Web and HTML in 1993, by introducing inline graphics, audio and video media, rather than having to link to media segments in a separate window.[304] The team in Joseph Hardin's lab at NCSA recognized that adding the ability to transclude images and other media would transform the World Wide Web from a text-only viewer with links to a new publishing paradigm, a "networked landscape" with hypertext signposts to guide the way. On 12 November 1993, the first full release of NCSA Mosaic on the world's three most popular operating systems (X Windows, Microsoft Windows and Apple Macintosh) enabled the general public to access the network with a graphical browser.[305] Since browsers made them familiar, hypertext links have been used in other computing applications as structure and navigation mechanisms.

Perspectives on Hypertext Links

A lexical perspective on hypertext links concerns the words that are used to signal the presence of a link or to encode its type. In web contexts, the words in which a structural link is embedded are called the *anchor text*. More generally, rhetorical structure theory analyzes how different conventions or signals in texts indicate relationships between texts or parts of them, like the subtle differences in polarity among "see," "see also," and "but see" as citation signals.[306]

Many hypertext links in web pages are purely structural because they lack explicit representation of the reason for the relationship. When it is evident, this semantic property of the link is called the *link type*.[307]

An architectural perspective on links considers whether links are *one-way* or *bi-directional*. When a bi-directional link is created between an anchor and a destination, it is as though a one-way link that can be followed in the opposite direction is automatically created. Two one-way links serve the same purpose, but the return link is not automatically established when the first one is created. A second architectural consideration is whether links are *binary*, connecting one anchor to one destination, or **n-ary**, connecting one anchor to multiple types of destinations.[308] (See §5.6).

A "front end" or "surface" implementation perspective on hypertext links concerns how the presence of the link is indicated in a user interface; this is called the "link marker"; underlining or coloring of clickable text are conventional markers for web links.[309] A "back end" implementation issue is whether links are contained or embedded in the resources they link or whether they are stored separately in a "link base."[310] (See §5.7).

5.5.3.2 Analyzing Link Structures

We can portray a set of links between resources graphically as a pattern of boxes and links. Because a link connection from one resource to another need not imply a link in the opposite direction, we distinguish one-way links from explicitly bi-directional ones.

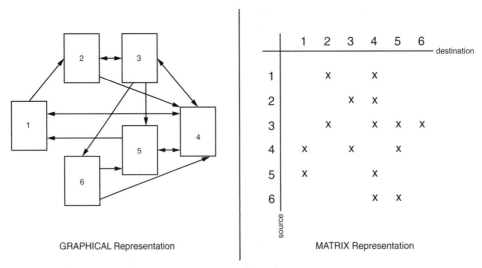

Representing Link Structures

Figure 5.3. Representing Link Structures.

A graphical representation of link structure is shown on the left panel of figure Figure 5.3, "Representing Link Structures.". For a small network of links, a diagram like this one makes it easy to see that some resources have more incoming or outgoing links than other resources. However, for most purposes we leave the analysis of link structures to computer programs, and there it is much better to represent the link structures more abstractly in matrix form. In this matrix the resource identifiers on the row and column heads represent the source and destination of the link. This is a full matrix because not all of the links are symmetric; a link from resource 1 to resource 2 does not imply one from 2 to 1.

A matrix representation of the same link structure is shown on the right panel of figure Figure 5.3, "Representing Link Structures.". This representation models the network as a directed graph in which the resources are the vertices and the relationships are the edges that connect them. We now can apply graph algorithms to determine many useful properties. A very important property is *reachability*, the "can you get there from here" property.[311] Other useful properties include the average number of incoming or outgoing links, the average distance between any two resources, and the shortest path between them.

5.5.3.3 Bibliometrics, Shepardizing, and Social Network Analysis

Information scientists began studying the structure of scientific citation, now called *bibliometrics*, nearly a century ago to identify influential scientists and publications. This analysis of the flow of ideas through publications can identify "invisible colleges" of scientists who rely on each other's research, and recognize the emergence of new scientific disciplines or research areas. Universities use bibliometrics to evaluate professors for promotion and tenure, and libraries use it to select resources for their collections.[312]

The expression of citation relationships between documents is especially nuanced in legal contexts, where the use of legal cases as precedents makes it essential to distinguish precisely where a new ruling lies on the relational continuum between "Following" and "Overruling" with respect to a case it cites. The analysis of legal citations to determine whether a cited case is still good law is called **Shepardizing** because lists of cases annotated in this way were first published in the late 1800s by Frank Shepard, a salesman for a legal publishing company.[313]

Facebook's multi-billion dollar valuation after its 2012 initial public offering is based on its ability to exploit the structure of a person's social network to personalize advertisements for people and their "friends" to whom they are connected. Many computer science researchers are working to determine the important characteristics of people and relationships that best identify the people whose activities or messages influence others to spend money.[314]

5.6 The Architectural Perspective

The architectural perspective emphasizes the number and abstraction level of the components of a relationship, which together characterize the complexity of the relationship. We will briefly consider three architectural issues: degree (or arity), cardinality, and directionality.

5.6.1 Degree

The *degree* or *arity* of a relationship is the number of entity types or categories of resources in the relationship. This is usually, though not always, the same as the number of arguments in the relationship expression.

Homer Simpson (husband) ⇔ is-married-to ⇔ Marge Simpson (wife)

is a relationship of degree 2, a **binary** relationship between two entity types, because the "is-married-to" relationship as we first defined it requires one of the arguments to be of entity type "husband" and one of them to be of type "wife."

Now suppose we change the definition of marriage to allow the two participants in a marriage to be any instance of the entity type "person." The relationship expression looks exactly the same, but its degree is now *unary* because only 1 entity type is needed to instantiate the two arguments:

Homer Simpson (person) ⇔ is-married-to ⇔ Marge Simpson (person)

Some relationships are best expressed as *ternary* ones that involve three different entity types. An example that appears in numerous data modeling books is one like this:

Supplier → provides → Part → assembled-in → Product

It is always possible to represent ternary relationships as a set of binary ones by creating a new entity type that relates to each of the others in turn. This new entity type is called a dummy in modeling practice.

Supplier → provides → DUMMY
Part → provided-for → DUMMY
DUMMY → assembled-in → Product

This transformation from a sensible ternary relationship to three binary ones involving a DUMMY entity type undoubtedly seems strange, but it enables all relationships to be binary while still preserving the meaning of the original ternary one. Making all relationships binary makes it easier to store relationships and combine them to discover new ones.

5.6.2 Cardinality

The *cardinality* of a relationship is the number of instances that can be associated with each entity type in a relationship. At first glance this might seem to be degree by another name, but it is not.

Cardinality is easiest to explain for binary relationships. If we return to Homer and Marge, the binary relationship that expresses that they are married husband and wife is a **one-to-one** relationship because a husband can only have one wife and a wife can only have one husband (at a time, in monogamous societies like the one in which the Simpsons live).

In contrast, the "is-parent-of" relationship is one-to-many, because the meaning of being a parent makes it correct to say that:

Homer Simpson → is-parent-of → Bart AND Lisa AND Maggie

As we did with the ternary relationship in §5.6.1, "Degree" (page 217), we can transform this more complex relationship architecture to a set of simpler ones by restricting expressions about being a parent to the one-to-one cardinality.

Homer Simpson → is-parent-of → Bart
Homer Simpson → is-parent-of → Lisa
Homer Simpson → is-parent-of → Maggie

The one-to-many expression brings all three of Homer's children together as arguments in the same relational expression, making it more obvious that they share the same relationship than in the set of separate and redundant one-to-one expressions.

5.6.3 Directionality

The *directionality* of a relationship defines the order in which the arguments of the relationship are connected. A *one-way* or *uni-directional* relationship can be followed in only one direction, whereas a *bi-directional* one can be followed in both directions.

All symmetric relationships (§5.3.2.1, "Symmetry" (page 199)) are bi-directional, but not all bi-directional relationships are symmetric. A relationship between a manager and an employee that he manages is "employs," a different meaning than the "is-employed-by" relationship in the opposite direction. As in this example, the relationship is often lexicalized in only one direction.

5.7 The Implementation Perspective

Finally, the *implementation perspective* on relationships considers how a relationship is realized or encoded in a technology context. The implementation perspective contrasts strongly with the conceptual, structural, and architectural perspectives, which emphasize the meaning and abstract structure of relationships. The implementation perspective is a superset of the lexical perspective, because the choice of the language in which to express a relationship is an implementation decision. However, most people think of implementation as all of the decisions about technological form rather than just about the choice of words.

In this book we focus on the fundamental issues and challenges that apply to all organizing systems, and not just on information-intensive ones that rely extensively on technology. Even with this reduced scope, there are some critical implementation concerns about the notation, syntax, and deployment of the relationships and other descriptions about resources. We briefly introduce some of these issues here and then discuss them in detail in Chapter 8, "*The Forms of Resource Descriptions*".

5.7.1 Choice of Implementation

The choice of implementation determines how easy it is to understand and process a set of relationships. For example, the second sentence of this chapter is a natural language implementation of a set of relationships in the Simpson family:

The Simpson family includes a man named Homer and a woman named Marge, the married parents of three sibling children, a boy named Bart and two girls, Lisa and Maggie.

A subject-predicate-object syntax makes the relationships more explicit:

Example 5.1. Subject-predicate syntax

Homer Simpson → **is-married-to** → **Marge Simpson**
Homer Simpson → **is-parent-of** → **Bart**
Homer Simpson → **is-parent-of** → **Lisa**
Homer Simpson → **is-parent-of** → **Maggie**
Marge Simpson → **is-married-to** → **Homer Simpson**
Marge Simpson → **is-parent-of** → **Bart**
Marge Simpson → **is-parent-of** → **Lisa**
Marge Simpson → **is-parent-of** → **Maggie**
Bart Simpson → **is-a** → **Boy**
Lisa Simpson → **is-a** → **Girl**
Maggie Simpson → **is-a** → **Girl**

In the following example of a potential XML implementation syntax, we emphasize class inclusion relationships by using elements as containers, and the relationships among the members of the family are expressed explicitly through references, using XML's ID and IDREF attribute types:[315]

Example 5.2. An XML implementation syntax

```
<Family name="Simpson">
   <Parents children="Bart Lisa Maggie">
      <Father name="Homer" spouse="Marge"  />
      <Mother name="Marge" spouse="Homer"  />
   </Parents>
   <Children parents="Homer Marge" >
      <Boy name="Bart" siblings="Lisa Maggie" />
      <Girl name="Lisa" siblings="Bart Maggie" />
      <Girl name="Maggie" siblings="Bart Lisa" />
   </Children>
</Family>
```

None of the models we have presented so far in this chapter represents the complexities of modern families that involve multiple marriages and children from more than one marriage, but they are sufficient for our limited demonstration purposes.

5.7.2 Syntax and Grammar

The *syntax* and *grammar* of a language consists of the rules that determine which combinations of its words are allowed and are thus grammatical or **well-formed.** Natural languages differ immensely in how they arrange nouns, verbs, adjectives, and other parts of speech to create sentences. Conformance to these rules makes the sentence syntactically compliant but does not mean that an expression is semantically comprehensible; the classic example is Chomsky's anomalous sentence:

- **Colorless green ideas sleep furiously**

Any meaning this sentence has is odd, difficult to visualize, and outside of readily accessible experience, but anyone who knows the English language can recognize that it follows its syntactic rules, as opposed to this sentence, which breaks them and seems completely meaningless:

- **Ideas colorless sleep furiously green**[316]

5.7.3 Requirements for Implementation Syntax

The most basic requirement for implementation syntax is that it can represent all the expressions that it needs to express. For the examples in this chapter we used an informal combination of English words and symbols (arrows and parentheses) that you could understand easily, but simple language is incapable of expressing most of what we readily say in English. But this benefit of natural language only accrues to people, and the more restrictive and formal syntax is easier to understand for computers.

A second consideration is that the implementation can be understood and used by its intended users. We can usually express a relationship in different languages while preserving its meaning, just as we can usually implement the same computing functionality in different programming languages. From a semantic perspective these three expressions are equivalent:

> **My name is Homer Simpson**
> **Mon nom est Homer Simpson**
> **Mein name ist Homer Simpson**

However, whether these expressions are equivalent for someone reading them depends on which languages they understand.

An analogous situation occurs with the implementation of web pages. HTML was invented as a language for encoding how web pages look in a browser, and most of the tags in HTML represent the simple structure of an analogous print document. Representing paragraphs, list items and numbered headings with <P> and <LI> and <Hn> makes using HTML so easy that school children can create web pages. However, the "web for eyes" implemented using HTML is of less efficient or practical for computers that want to treat content as product catalogs, orders, invoices, payments, and other business transactions and information that can be analyzed and processed. This "web for computers" is best implemented using domain-specific vocabularies in XML.

5.8 Relationships in Organizing Systems

In the previous sections as we surveyed the five perspectives on analyzing relationships we mentioned numerous examples where relationships had important roles in organizing systems. In this final section we examine three contexts for organizing systems where relationships are especially fundamental; the *Semantic Web* and Linked Data, bibliographic organizing systems, and situations involving system integration and interoperability.

5.8.1 The Semantic Web and Linked Data

In a classic 2001 paper, Tim Berners-Lee laid out a vision of a *Semantic Web* in which all information could be shared and processed by automated tools as well as by people.[317] The essential technologies for making the web more semantic and relationships among web resources more explicit are applications of XML, including RDF (§4.2.2.3, "Tagging of Web-Based Resources" (page 144)), and OWL (§5.3.3, "Ontologies" (page 201)). Many tools have been developed to support more semantic encoding, but most still require substantial expertise in semantic technologies and web standards.[318] More likely to succeed are applications that aim lower, not trying to encode all the latent semantics in a document or web page. For example, some wiki and blogging tools contain templates for semantic annotation, and Wikipedia has thousands of templates and "info boxes" to encourage the creation of information in content-encoded formats.

The "Linked Data" movement is an extension of the *Semantic Web* idea to reframe the basic principles of the web's architecture in more semantic terms. Instead of the limited role of links as simple untyped relationships between HTML documents, links between resources described by RDF can serve as the bridges between islands of semantic data, creating a Linked Data network or cloud.[319]

5.8.2 Bibliographic Organizing Systems

Much of our thinking about relationships in organizing systems for information comes from the domain of bibliographic cataloging of library resources and the related areas of classification systems and descriptive thesauri. Bibliographic relationships provide an important means to build structure into library catalogs.[320]

Bibliographic relationships are common among library resources. Smiraglia and Leazer found that approximately 30% of the works in the *Online Computer Library Center (OCLC)* WorldCat union catalog have associated derivative works. Relationships among items within these bibliographic families differ, but the average family size for those works with derivative works was found to be 3.54 items. Moreover, "canonical" works that have strong cultural meaning and influence, such as "the plays of William Shakespeare" and *The Bible*, have very large and complex bibliographic families.[321]

5.8.2.1 Tillett's Taxonomy and FRBR

Barbara Tillett, in a study of 19th and 20th century catalog rules, found that many different catalog rules have existed over time to describe bibliographic relationships. She developed a taxonomy of bibliographic relationships that includes equivalence, derivative, descriptive, whole-part, accompanying, sequential or chronological, and shared characteristic. These relationship types span the relationship perspectives defined in this chapter; equivalence, derivative, and description are semantic types; whole-part and accompanying are part semantic and part structural types; sequential or chronological are part lexical and part structural types; and shared characteristics are part semantic and part lexical types.[322]

Smiraglia expanded on Tillett's derivative relationship to create seven subtypes: simultaneous derivations, successive derivations, translations, amplifications, extractions, adaptations, and performances.[323]

In §3.3.2, "Identity and Bibliographic Resources," we briefly mentioned the four-level abstraction hierarchy for resources introduced in the Functional Requirements for Bibliographic Records report. FRBR was highly influenced by Tillett's studies of bibliographic relationships, and prescribes how the relationships among resources at different levels are to be expressed (work-work, expression-expression, work-expression, expression-manifestation, and so on).

5.8.2.2 Resource Description and Access (RDA)

Many cataloging researchers have recognized that online catalogs do not do a very good job of encoding bibliographic relationships among items, both due to catalog display design and to the limitations of how information is organized within catalog records.[324] Author name authority databases, for example, provide information for variant author names, which can be very important in finding all of the works by a single author, but this information is not held within a catalog record. Similarly, MARC records can be formatted and displayed in web library catalogs, but the data within the records are not available for re-use, re-purposing, or re-arranging by researchers, patrons, or librarians.

The Resource Description and Access (RDA) next-generation cataloging rules are attempting to bring together disconnected resource descriptions to provide more complete and interconnected data about works, authors, publications, publishers, and subjects.

RDA utilizes RDF to declare and store relationships among bibliographic materials.[325]

5.8.2.3 RDA and the Semantic Web

The move in RDA to encode bibliographic data in RDF stems from the desire to make library catalog data more web-accessible. As web-based data mash-ups, application programming interfaces (APIs), and web searching are becoming ubiquitous and expected, library data are becoming increasingly isolated. The developers of RDA see RDF as the means for making library data more widely available online.[326]

In addition to simply making library data more web accessible, RDA seeks to leverage the distributed nature of the Semantic Web. Once rules for describing resources, and the relationships between them, are declared in RDF syntax and made publicly available, the rules themselves can be mixed and mashed up. Creators of information systems that use RDF can choose elements from any RDF schema. For example, we can use the Dublin Core metadata schema (which has been aligned with the RDF model) and the Friend of a Friend (FOAF) schema (a schema to describe people and the relationships between them) to create a set of metadata elements about a journal article that goes beyond the standard bibliographic information. RDA's process of moving to RDF is well underway.[327]

5.8.3 Integration and Interoperability

Integration is the controlled sharing of information between two (or more) business systems, applications, or services within or between firms. Integration means that one party can extract or obtain information from another one, it does not imply that the recipient can make use of the information.

Interoperability goes beyond integration to mean that systems, applications, or services that exchange information can make sense of what they receive. Interoperability can involve identifying corresponding components and relationships in each system, transforming them syntactically to the same format, structurally to the same granularity, and semantically to the same meaning.

For example, an Internet shopping site might present customers with a product catalog whose items come from a variety of manufacturers who describe the same products in different ways. Likewise, the end-to-end process from customer ordering to delivery requires that customer, product and payment information pass through the information systems of different firms. Creating the necessary information mappings and transformations is tedious or even impossible if the components and relationships among them aren't formally specified for each system.

In contrast, when these models exist as data or document schemas or as classes in programming languages, identifying and exploiting the relationships between the information in different systems to achieve interoperability or to merge different classification systems can often be completely automated. Because of the substantial economic benefits to governments, businesses, and their customers of more efficient information integration and exchange, efforts to standardize these information models are important in numerous industries. Chapter 9, "*Interactions with Resources*" will dive deeper into interoperability issues, especially those that arise in business contexts.

5.9 Key Points in Chapter Five

- A relationship is "an association among several things, with that association having a particular significance."
- Just identifying the resources involved is not enough because several different relationships can exist among the same resources.
- Most relationships between resources can be expressed using a subject-predicate-object model.
- For a computer to understand relational expressions, it needs a computer-processable representation of the relationships among words and meanings that makes every important semantic assumption and property precise and explicit.
- Three broad categories of semantic relationships are inclusion, attribution, and possession.
- A set of interconnected class inclusion relationships creates a hierarchy called a taxonomy.
- Classification is a class inclusion relationship between an instance and a class.

- Ordering and inclusion relationships are inherently transitive, enabling inferences about class membership and properties.
- Class inclusion relationships form a framework to which other kinds of relationships attach, creating a network of relationships called an ontology.
- When words encode the semantic distinctions expressed by class inclusion, the more specific class is called the hyponym; the more general class is the hypernym.
- A thesaurus uses lexical relationships to suggest which terms to use.
- Morphological analysis of how words in a language are created from smaller units is heavily used in text processing.
- Many types of resources have internal structure in additional to their structural relationships with other resources.
- The XPath language defines the structures and patterns in XML documents used by XML forms, queries, and transformations.
- Many hypertext links are purely structural because there is no explicit representation of the reason for the relationship.
- Using the pattern of links between documents to understand the structure of knowledge and the structure of the intellectual community that creates it is an idea that is nearly a century old.
- The essential technologies for making the web more semantic and relationships among web resources more explicit are XML, RDF, and OWL.
- Much of our thinking about relationships in organizing systems for information comes from the domain of bibliographic cataloging of library resources and the related areas of classification systems and descriptive thesauri.
- The Resource Description and Access (RDA) next-generation cataloging rules are attempting to bring together disconnected resource descriptions.
- Integration is the controlled sharing of information between two (or more) business systems, applications, or services within or between firms.
- Interoperability goes beyond integration to mean that systems, applications, or services that exchange information can make sense of what they receive.

Notes

253. [Business] *The Simpsons* TV show began in 1989 and is now the longest running scripted TV show ever. The official website is *http://www.thesimp sons.com*. The show is dubbed into French, Italian and Spanish for viewers in Quebec, France, Italy, Latin America and Spain. *The Simpsons Movie* has been dubbed into Mandarin Chinese and Cantonese. (Yes, we know that Bart actually

calls his father by his first name, but that would mess up our example here.) For more information about Mandarin kinship terms see *http://mandarin.about.com/od/vocabularylists/tp/family.htm*.

254. [CogSci] Kinship can be studied from both anthropological and biological perspectives, which differ to the degree to which they emphasize social relationships and genetic ones. Kinship has been systematically studied since the nineteenth century: (Morgan 1871/1997) developed a system of kinship classification still taught today. A detailed interactive web tutorial developed by Brian Schwimer can be found at *http://umanitoba.ca/faculties/arts/anthropology/kintitle.html*.

255. [Computing] Kent's *Data and Reality* was first published in 1978 with a second edition in 1998. Kent was a well-known and well-liked researcher in data modeling at IBM, and his book became a cult classic. In 2012, seven years after Kent's death, a third edition (Kent and Hoberman 2012) came out, slightly revised and annotated but containing essentially the same content as the book from 34 years earlier because its key issues about data modeling are timeless.

256. [CogSci] "Semantic" is usually defined as "relating to meaning or language" and that doesn't seem helpful here. "Homer is married to Marge" is a semantic assertion, but "Homer is standing next to Marge" is not.

257. [CogSci] For decades important and vexing questions have been raised about the specificity of these predicate-argument associations and how or when the semantic constraints they embody combine with syntactic and contextual constraints during the process of comprehending language. Consider how "While in the operating room, the surgeon used a knife to cut the ___" generates a different expectancy from the same predicate and agent in "While at the fancy restaurant, the surgeon used a knife to cut the ___." See (Elman 2009).

258. [Law] This book is not the place for the debate over the definition of marriage. We aren't bigots; we just don't need this discussion here. If these definitions upset you here, you will feel better in §5.6.1.

259. [CogSci] Typically, when people use language they operate on the assumption that everyone shares their model of the world, providing the common ground that enables them to communicate. As we saw in Chapter 3, *"Resources in Organizing Systems"* and Chapter 4, *"Resource Description and Metadata"*, (because of the *vocabulary problem* and different purposes for using resources and language) this assumption is often wrong, This paves the way for serious misunderstandings, since what is assumed to be shared knowledge may not really be shared or understood the same way.

260. [CogSci] See (Chaffin and Herrmann 1984), (Storey 1993).

261. [CogSci] Which of these classifications is most relevant depends on the context. In addition, there might be other Homer Simpsons who are not cartoon characters or who are not married, so we might have to disambiguate this homonymy to make sure we referring to the intended Homer Simpson.

262. [CogSci] (Winston, Chaffin, and Herman 1987).

263. [CogSci] (Storey 1993).

264. [Business] Martin is the animated gecko who is the advertising spokesman for Geico Insurance (*http://www.geico.com/*). Martin's wit and cockney accent make him engaging and memorable, and a few years ago he was voted the favorite advertising icon in the US.

265. [CogSci] (Gentner 1983).

266. [Linguistics] (Miller and Johnson-Laird 1976, p 565).

267. [Linguistics] An example of transitivity in meronymic relationships is: (1) the carburetor is part of the engine, (2) the engine is part of the car, (3) therefore, the carburetor is part of the car. Some people have argued that meronomy isn't transitive, but a closer look at their supposed counter-examples suggests that they have confused different types of meronymic relationships. See Section 5 in (Winston, Chaffin, and Herman 1987).

268. [Philosophy] "Ontology" is a branch of philosophy concerned with what exists in reality and the general features and relations of whatever that might be (Hofweber 2009). Computer science has adopted "ontology" to refer to any computer-processable resource that represents the relationships among words and meanings in some knowledge domain. See (Gruber 1993), (Guarino 1998).

269. [Web] Web Ontology Language (OWL) *http://www.w3.org/2004/OWL/*.

270. [Computing] *http://www.cyc.com/*.

271. [Linguistics] Languages and cultures differ in how they distinguish and describe kinship, so Bart might find the system of family organization easier to master in some countries and cultures and more difficult in others.

272. [Linguistics] It isn't quite this simple, because it depends on how we define "word" —polar bear and sea horse aren't lexicalized but they are a single meaning-bearing unit because we don't decompose and reassemble meaning from the two separate words. These "lexical gaps" differ from language to language, whereas "conceptual gaps" —the things we can't think of or directly experience, like the pull of gravity— may be innate and universal. We revisit this issue as "linguistic relativity" in Chapter 6. (See Bentivogli and Pianta 2000).

273. [Linguistics] This example comes from (Fellbaum 2010, pages 236-237). German has a word *Kufenfahrzeug* for vehicle on runners.

274. [Linguistics] (Miller 1998).

275. [Linguistics] (Bolshakov and Gelbukh 2004), p, 314. The quote continues "The references to 'some class' and to 'insignificant change' make this definition rather vague, but we are not aware of any significantly stricter definition. Hence the creation of synonymy dictionaries, which are known to be quite large, is rather a matter of art and insight."

276. [CogSci] George Miller made many important contributions to the study of mind and language during his long scientific career. His most famous article, "The Magical Number Seven, Plus or Minus Two" (Miller 1956), was seminal in its proposals about information organization in human memory, even though it is one of the most misquoted scientific papers of all time. Relatively late in his career Miller began the WordNet project to build a semantic dictionary, which is now an essential resource in natural language processing applications. See *http://wordnet.princeton.edu/*.

277. [Business] This navigation is easiest to carry out using the commercial product called "The Visual Thesaurus" at *http://www.visualthesaurus.com/*.

278. [Linguistics] These contrasting meanings for "bank" are clear cases of polysemy, but there are often much subtler differences in meaning that arise from context. The verb "save" seems to mean something different in "The shopper saved..." versus "The lifeguard saved..." although they overlap in some ways. (Fillmore and Atkins 2000) and others have proposed definitions of polysemy, but there is no rigorous test for determining when word meanings diverge sufficiently to be called different senses.

279. [Computing] Many techniques for using WordNet to calculate measures of semantic similarity have been proposed. See (Budanitsky and Hirst 2006).

280. [Linguistics] See (Gross and Miller, 1990).

281. [Linguistics] This type of "lexical asymmetry" is called "markedness." The broader or dominant term is the unmarked one and the narrower one is the marked one. See (Battistella 1996).

282. [LIS] *http://www.loc.gov/library/libarch-thesauri.html*, *http://www.getty.edu/research/tools/vocabularies/aat/index.html*.

283. [Linguistics] Languages differ a great deal in morphological complexity and in the nature of their morphological mechanisms. Mandarin Chinese has relatively few morphemes and few grammatical inflections, which leads to a huge number of homophones. English is pretty average on this scale. A popular textbook on morphology is (Haspelmath and Sims 2010).

284. [LIS] These so-called endocentric compounds essentially mean what the morphemes would have meant separately. But if a '"birdcage" is exactly a "bird

cage," what is gained by creating a new word? This question has long been debated in subject classification, where it is framed as the contrast between "pre-coordination" and "post-coordination." For example, is it better to pre-classify some resources as about "Sports Gambling" or should such resources be found by intersecting those classified as about "Sports" and about "Gambling." See (Svenonius 2000, pages 187-192).

285. [Linguistics] English nouns have plural (book/books) and possessive forms (the professor's book), adjectives have comparatives and superlatives (big/bigger/biggest), and regular verbs have only four inflected forms (see *http://cla.calpoly.edu/~jrubba/morph/morph.over.html*). In contrast, in Classical Greek each noun can have 11 word forms, each adjective 30, and every regular verb over 300 (Anderson 2001).

286. [Computing] Of the five perspectives on relationships in this chapter, the structural one comes closest to the meaning of "relation" in mathematics and computer science, where a relation is a set of ordered elements ("tuples") of equal degree (§5.6.1, "Degree" (page 217)). A binary relation is a set of element pairs, a ternary relation is a set of 3-tuples, and so on. The elements in each tuple are "related" but they do not need to have any "significant association" or "relationship" among them.

287. [Computing] (Travers and Milgram 1969) was the groundbreaking study that demonstrated what they called the "small world problem" by which any two arbitrarily selected people were separated by an average of fewer than six links. See (Markoff and Sengupta 2011) for a recent article that describes a similar study using Facebook data. See *http://oracleofbacon.org/* for a web-based demonstration based on actor Kevin Bacon's remarkable variety of roles and hence fellow actors in his movies.

288. [CogSci] This seems like an homage to Jimi Hendrix based on the title from a 1967 song, *Third Stone from the Sun* http://en.wikipedia.org/wiki/Third_Stone_from_the_Sun.

289. [Computing] The subfield of natural language processing called "named entity recognition" has as its goal the creation of mixed content by identifying people, companies, organizations, dates, trademarks, stock symbols, and so on in unstructured text.

290. [Computing] *http://www.tei-c.org/release/doc/tei-p5-doc/en/html/ND.html*.

291. [Computing] See (Holman 2001) or (Tidwell 2008).

292. [Computing] See (van der Vlist 2007) and schematron.org for overviews. See (Hamilton and Wood 2012) for a detailed case study.

293. [Computing] (Walsh 2010).

294. [CogSci] These layout and typographic conventions are well known to graphic designers (Williams 2008) but are also fodder for more academic treatment in studies of visual language or semiotics (Crow 2010).

295. [Web] (Page, Brin, Motwani, and Winograd 1999) describes Page Rank when its inventors were computer science graduate students at Stanford. It isn't a coincidence that the technique shares a name with one of its inventors, Google co-founder and CEO Larry Page. (Langville and Meyer 2012) is an excellent textbook. The ultimate authority about how page rank works is Google; see Matt Cutts at *http://www.google.com/competition/howgooglesearchworks.html*.

296. [Computing] (Bush 1945). "Wholly new forms of encyclopedias will appear, ready made with a mesh of associative trails running through them..." See *http://www.theatlantic.com/magazine/archive/1945/07/as-we-may-think/303881/*.

297. [Computing] (Nelson 1981). Also see Computer Lib/Dream Machines (Nelson 1974) for an early example of Nelson's non-linear book style.

298. [Computing] The inclusion, by hypertext reference, of a resource or part of a resource into another resource is called **transclusion**. Transclusion is normally performed automatically, without user intervention. The inclusion of images in web documents is an example of transclusion. Transclusion is a frequently used technique in business and legal document processing, where re-use of consistent and up-to-date content is essential to achieve efficiency and consistency.

299. [Computing] (Engelbart 1963) Douglas Engelbart credits Bush's "As We May Think" article as his direct inspiration. Engelbart was in the US Navy, living in a hut in the South Pacific during the last stages of WWII when he read *The Atlantic* monthly magazine in which Bush's article was published.

300. [Computing] Doug Engelbart's demonstration has been called the Mother of All Demos and can be seen in its entirety at *http://sloan.stanford.edu/MouseSite/1968Demo.html*.

301. [Web] (Gillies and Cailliau 2000).

302. [Web] Most web links are very simple in structure. The anchor text in the linking document is wrapped in <A> and </A> tags, with an HREF (hypertext reference) attribute that contains the URI of the link destination if it is in another page, or a reference to an ID attribute if the link is to a different part of the same page. HTML also has a <LINK> tag, which, along with <A> have REL (relationship) and REV (reverse relationship) attributes that enable the encoding of typed relationships in links. In a book context for example, link relationships and reverse relations include obvious candidates such as next, previous, parent, child, table of contents, bibliography, glossary and index.

303. [Computing] Using hypertext links as interaction controls is the modern dynamic manifestation of cross references between textual commentary and illustrations in books, a mechanism that dates from the 1500s (Kilgour 1998). Hypertext links can be viewed as state transition controls in distributed collections of web-based resources; this design philosophy is known as Representational State Transfer (REST). See (Wilde and Pautasso 2011).

304. [Web] Mosaic was developed in Joseph Hardin's lab at the National Center for Supercomputing Applications (NCSA), hosted by the University of Illinois, at Urbana/Champaign by Marc Andreesen, Eric Bina and a team of student programmers. Mosaic was initially developed on the Unix X Window System, which made it immediately available on a wide variety of Unix and Linux systems. See *http://www.ncsa.illinois.edu/Projects/mosaic.html*.

305. [Web] (Schatz and Hardin 1994).

306. [Linguistics] See (Lorch 1989), (Mann and Thomson 1988). For example, an author might use "See" as in "See (Glushko et al. 2013)" when referring to this chapter if it is consistent with his point of view. On the other hand, that same author could use "but" as a contrasting citation signal, writing "But see (Glushko et al. 2013)" to express the relationship that the chapter disagrees with him.

307. [Computing] Before the web, most hypertexts implementations were in stand-alone applications like CD-ROM encyclopedias or in personal information management systems that used "cards" or "notes" as metaphors for the information units that were linked together, typically using rich taxonomies of *link types*. See (Conklin 1987), (Conklin and Begeman 1988), and (DeRose 1989).

308. [Computing] Many of the pre-web hypertext designs of the 1980s and 1990s allowed for n-ary links. The Dexter hypertext reference model (Halasz and Schwartz 1994) elegantly describes the typical architectures. However, there is some ambiguity in use of the term binary in hypertext link architectures. One-to-one vs. one-to-many is a cardinality distinction, and some people reserve binary to discussion about degree. See §5.6, "The Architectural Perspective" (page 217).

309. [Web] See (Weinreich, Obendorf, and Lamersdorf 2001).

310. [Web] See (Brailsford 1999), (Wilde and Lowe 2002).

311. [Computing] Reachability is determined by calculating the transitive closure of the link matrix. A classic and well written explanation is (Agrawal, Borgida, and Jagadish 1989).

312. [LIS] Eugene Garfield developed many of the techniques for studying scientific citation and he has been called the "grandfather of Google" (*http://blog.lib.uiowa.edu/hardinmd/2010/07/12/eugene-garfield-librarian-*

grandfather-of-google/) because of Google's use of citation patterns to determine relevance. See (Garfield, Cronin, and Atkins 2000) for a set of papers that review Garfield's many contributions. See (Bar-Ilan 2008) and (Neuhaus and Daniel 2008) for recent reviews of data sources and citation metrics.

313. [Law] Shepard first put adhesive stickers into case books, then published lists of cases and their citations. Shepardizing is a big business for Lexis/Nexis and Westlaw (where the technique is called "KeyCite").

314. [Computing] See (Watts 2004) for a detailed review of the theoretical foundations. See (Wu 2012) for applications in web-based social networks.

315. [Computing] We are assuming a schema that establishes that the name attributes are of type ID and that the other attributes are of type IDREFS. This schema allows for polygamy, the possibility of multiple values for the spouse attribute. Restrictions on the number of spouses can be enforced with Schematron. (Also see the Sidebar, "Inclusions and References" (page 332)).

316. [CogSci] (Chomsky 1957) used these now famous sentences to motivate the distinction between syntax and semantics. He argued that since the probability in both cases that the words had previously occurred in this order was essentially zero, statistics of word occurrence could not be part of language knowledge. There is a fascinating analysis of these sentences in Wikipedia. *http://en.wiki pedia.org/wiki/Colorless_green_ideas_sleep_furiouslyendnote.*

317. [Web] (Berners-Lee, Hendler, and Lassila, 2001) is the classic paper, and (Shadbolt, Hall, and Berners-Lee 2006) is something of a revisionist history.

Somewhat ironically, the web was not semantic from the beginning because Berners-Lee made a conscious decision to implement web documents using HTML, a presentation-oriented markup language, rather than require markup to be content-oriented. Designing HTML to be conceptually simple and easy to implement rather than general and powerful led to its rapid adoption after invention of the *NCSA* Mosaic graphical browser. Web documents encoded using HTML are capable of expressing sophisticated assertions and relationships using REL and REV attributes, but content creators rarely do so because browser makers have not provided useful interactions for well-known link relation types.

318. [Computing] For example, Protégé a free, open-source platform with a suite of tools to construct domain models and knowledge-based applications with ontologies. (See *http://protege.stanford.edu/*)

319. [Web] See *http://linkeddata.org/* and §8.3.3, "Syntax" (page 344).

320. [LIS] Barbara Tillett has written extensively about the theory of bibliographic relationships; (Tillett 2001) is an especially useful resource because it is a chapter in a comprehensive discussion ambitiously titled *Relationships in the Organization of Knowledge* (Bean and Green 2001).

321. [LIS] (Smiraglia and Leazer 1999).

322. [LIS] (Tillett 1991, 1992).

323. [LIS] (Smiraglia 1994).

324. [LIS] (Tillett 2005).

325. [LIS] See Section 8.1.3.1.

326. [LIS] See (Coyle 2010a).

327. [LIS] The FRBR entities, RDA data elements, and RDA value vocabularies have been defined in alignment with RDF using the Simple Knowledge Organization System (SKOS). SKOS is an "RDF-compliant language specifically designed for term lists and thesauri" (Coyle 2010b). The SKOS website provides lists of registered RDF metadata schemas and vocabularies. From these, information system designers can create application profiles for their resources, selecting elements from multiple schemas, including FRBR and RDA vocabularies.

Chapter 6
Categorization: Describing Resource Classes and Types

Robert J. Glushko
Rachelle Annechino
Jess Hemerly
Longhao Wang

6.1 Introduction

For nearly two decades, a TV game show called *Pyramid* aired in North America. The show featured two competing teams, each team consisting of two contestants: an ordinary civilian contestant and a celebrity. In the show's first round, both teams' members viewed a pyramid-shaped sign that displayed six category titles, some straightforward like "Where You Live" and others less conventional like "Things You Need to Feed." Each team then had an opportunity to compete for points in 30-second turns. The goal was for one team member to gain points by identifying a word or phrase related to the category from clues provided by the other team member. For example, a target phrase for the "Where You Live" category might be "zip code," and the clue might be "Mine is 94705." "Things you Need to Feed" might include both "screaming baby" and "parking meter."

The team that won the first round advanced to the "Winner's Circle," where the game was turned around. This time, only the clue giver was shown the category name and had to suggest concepts or instances belonging to that category so that the teammate could guess the category name. Clues like "alto," "soprano," and "tenor" would be given to prompt the teammate to guess "Singing Voices" or "Types of Singers."

As the game progressed, the categories became more challenging. It was interesting and entertaining to hear the clue receiver's initial guess and how subsequent guesses changed with more clues. The person giving clues would often become frustrated, because to them their clues seemed obvious and discriminating but would seem not to help the clue receivers in identifying the category. Viewers enjoyed sharing in these moments of vocabulary and category confusion.

The *Pyramid* TV game show developers created a textbook example for teaching about categories—groups or classes of things, people, processes, events or anything else that we treat as equivalent—and categorization—the process of assigning instances to categories. The game is a useful analog for us to illustrate many of the issues we discuss in this chapter. The Pyramid game was challenging, and sometimes comical, because people bring their own experiences and biases to understanding what a category means, and because not every instance of a category is equally typical or suggestive. How we organize reflects our thinking processes, which can inadvertently reveal personal characteristics that can be amusing in a social context. Hence, the popularity of the *Pyramid* franchise, which began on CBS in 1973 and has been produced in 20 countries.

Many texts in library science introduce categorization via cataloging rules, a set of highly prescriptive methods for assigning resources to categories that some describe and others satirize as "mark 'em and park 'em." Similarly, many texts in computer science discuss the process of defining the categories needed to create, process, and store information in terms of programming language constructs: "here's how to define an abstract type, and here's the data type system."[328] We take a very different approach in this chapter. In the following sections, we discuss how and why we create categories, reviewing some important work in philosophy, linguistics, and cognitive psychology so that we can better understand how categories are created and used in organizing systems. We discuss how the way we organize differs when we act as individuals or as members of social, cultural, or institutional groups; later we share principles for creating categories, design choices and implementation experience. As usual, we close the chapter with a summary of the key points.

6.2 The What and Why of Categories

Categories are *equivalence classes*, sets or groups of things or abstract entities that we treat the same. This does not mean that every instance of a category is identical, only that from some perspective, or for some purpose, we are treating them as equivalent based on what they have in common. When we consider something as a member of a category, we are making choices about which of its properties or roles we are focusing on and which ones we are ignoring. We do this automatically and unconsciously most of the time, but we can also do it in an explicit and self-aware way.[329]

When we encounter objects or situations, recognizing them as members of a category helps us know how to interact with them. For example, when we enter an unfamiliar building we might need to open or pass through an entryway that we recognize as a door. We might never have seen that particular door before, but it has properties and affordances that we know that all doors have; it has a doorknob or a handle; it allows access to a larger space; it opens and closes. By mentally assigning this particular door to the "doors" category we distinguish it from "windows," a category that also contains objects that sometimes have handles and that open and close, but which we do not normally pass through to enter another space. Categorization judgments are therefore not just about what is included in a class, but also about what is excluded from a class. Nevertheless, the category boundaries are not sharp; a "Dutch door" is divided horizontally in half so that the bottom can be closed like a door while the top can stay open like a window.

Categories are **cognitive and linguistic models** for applying prior knowledge; creating and using categories are essential human activities. Categories enable us to relate things to each other in terms of similarity and dissimilarity and are involved whenever we perceive, communicate, analyze, predict, or classify. Without categories, we would perceive the world as an unorganized blur of things with no understandable or memorable relation to each other. Every wall-entry we encounter would be new to us, and we would have to discover its properties and supported interactions as though we had never before encountered a door. Of course, we still often need to identify something as a particular instance, but categories enable us to understand how it is equivalent to other instances. We can interchangeably relate to something as specific as "the wooden door to the main conference room" or more generally as "any door."

All human languages and cultures divide up the world into categories. How and why this takes place has long been debated by philosophers, psychologists and anthropologists. One explanation for this differentiation is that people recognize structure in the world, and then create categories of things that "go together" or are somehow similar. An alternative view says that human minds make sense of the world by imposing structure on it, and that what goes together or seems similar is the outcome rather than a cause of categorization. Bulmer framed the contrast in a memorable way by asking which came first, the chicken (the objective facts of nature) or the egghead (the role of the human intellect).[330]

A secondary and more specialized debate going on for the last few decades among linguists. cognitive scientists, and computer scientists concerns the extent to which the cognitive mechanisms involved in category formation are specialized for that purpose rather than more general learning processes.[331]

Even before they can talk, children behave in ways that suggest they have formed categories based on shape, color, and other properties they can directly perceive in physical objects.[332] People almost effortlessly learn tens of thousands of categories embodied in the culture and language in which they grow up. People also rely on their own experiences, preferences, and goals to adapt cultural categories or create entirely individual ones that they use to organize resources that they personally arrange. Later on, through situational training and formal education, people learn to apply systematic and logical thinking processes so that they can create and understand categories in engineering, logistics, transport, science, law, business, and other institutional contexts.

These three contexts of **cultural, individual,** and **institutional categorization** share some core ideas but they emphasize different processes and purposes for creating categories, so they are a useful distinction.[333] Cultural categorization can be understood as a natural human cognitive ability that serves as a foundation for both informal and formal organizing systems. Individual categorization tends to grow spontaneously out of our personal activities. Institutional categorization responds to the need for formal coordination and cooperation within and between companies, governments, and other goal-oriented enterprises.

6.2.1 Cultural Categories

Cultural categories are the archetypical form of categories upon which individual and institutional categories are usually based. Cultural categories tend to describe our everyday experiences of the world and our accumulated cultural knowledge. Such categories describe objects, events, settings, internal experiences, physical orientation, relationships between entities, and many other aspects of human experience. Cultural categories are acquired primarily, with little explicit instruction, through normal exposure of children with their caregivers; they are associated with language acquisition and language use within particular cultural contexts.

Two thousand years ago Plato wrote that living species could be identified by "carving nature at its joints," the natural boundaries or discontinuities between types of things where the differences are the largest or most salient. Plato's metaphor is intuitively appealing because we can easily come up with examples of perceptible properties or behaviors of physical things that go together that make some ways of categorizing them seem more natural than others.[334]

Natural languages rely heavily on nouns to talk about categories of things because it is useful to have a shorthand way of referring to a set of properties that co-occur in predictable ways.[335] For example, in English (borrowed from Portuguese) we have a word for "banana" because a particular curved shape, greenish-yellow or yellow color, and a convenient size tend to co-occur in a familiar edible object, so it became useful to give it a name. The word "banana" brings together this configuration of highly interrelated perceptions into a unified concept so we do not have to refer to bananas by listing their properties.[336]

Languages differ a great deal in the words they contain and also in more fundamental ways that they require speakers or writers to attend to details about the world or aspects of experience that another language allows them to ignore. This idea is often described as *linguistic relativity*. (See the Sidebar).

Linguistic Relativity

Linguistic diversity led Benjamin Whorf, in the mid 20th century, to propose an overly strong statement of the relationships among language, culture, and thought. Whorf argued that the particularities of one's native language determine how we think and what we can think about. Among his extreme ideas was the suggestion that, because some Native American languages lacked words or grammatical forms that refer to what we call "time" in English, they could not understand the concept. More careful language study showed both parts of the claim to be completely false.

Nevertheless, even though academic linguists have discredited strong versions of Whorf's ideas, less deterministic versions of **linguistic relativity** have become influential and help us understand cultural categorization. The more moderate position was crisply characterized by Roman Jakobson, who said that "languages differ essentially in what they *must* convey and not in what they *may* convey." In English one can say "I spent yesterday with a neighbor." In languages with grammatical gender, one must choose a word that identifies the neighbor as male or female.[337]

For example, speakers of the Australian aboriginal language, Guugu Yimithirr, don't use concepts of left and right, but rather use compass-point directions. Where in English we might say to a person facing north, "Take a step to your left," they would use their term for west. If the person faced south, we would change our instruction to "right," but they would still use their term for west.

Imagine how difficult it would be for a speaker of Guugu Yimithirr and a speaker of English to collaborate in organizing a storage room or a closet.[338]

It is not controversial to notice that different cultures and language communities have different experiences and activities that give them contrasting knowledge about particular domains. No one would doubt that university undergraduates in Chicago would think differently about animals than inhabitants of Guatemalan rain forests, or even that different types of "tree experts" (taxonomists, landscape workers, and tree maintenance personnel) would categorize trees differently.[339]

6.2.2 Individual Categories

Individual categories are created in an organizing system to satisfy the *ad hoc* requirements that arise from a person's unique experiences, preferences, and resource collections. Unlike cultural categories, which usually develop slowly and last a long time, individual categories are created by intentional activity, in response to a specific situation, or to solve an emerging organizational challenge. As a consequence, the categories in individual organizing systems generally have short lifetimes and rarely outlive the person who created them.[340]

Individual categories draw from cultural categories but differ in two important ways. First, individual categories sometimes have an imaginative or metaphorical basis that is meaningful to the person who created them but which might distort or misinterpret cultural categories. Second, individual categories are often specialized or synthesized versions of cultural categories that capture particular experiences or personal history. For example, a person who has lived in China and Mexico, or lived with people from those places, might have highly individualized categories for foods they like and dislike that incorporate characteristics of both Chinese and Mexican cuisine.

Individual categories in organizing systems also reflect the idiosyncratic set of household goods, music, books, website bookmarks, or other resources that a person might have collected over time. The organizing systems for financial records, personal papers, or email messages often use highly specialized categories that are shaped by specific tasks to be performed, relationships with other people, events of personal history, and other highly individualized considerations.

Traditionally, ***individual categorization*** systems were usually not visible to, or shared with, others, whereas, this has become an increasingly common situation for people using web-based organizing system for pictures, music, or other personal resources. On websites like the popular Flickr site for photos, people typically use existing cultural categories to tag their photos as well as individual ones that they invent. In particular, the typical syntactic constraint that tags are delimited by white space encourages the creation of new categories by combining existing category names using concatenation and camel case conventions; photos that could be categorized as "Berkeley" and "Student" are thus tagged as "BerkeleyStudent." Similar generative processes for creating individual category names are used with Twitter "hashtags" where tweets about events are often categorized with an *ad hoc* tag that combines an event name and a year identifier like "#NBAFinals12." Web-based documents and product pages in web catalogs are commonly categorized with "ReadThis" and "BuyThis" tags that are meaningful for the individuals who created those categories for themselves, but which are not very informative for anyone else.

6.2.3 Institutional Categories

In contrast to cultural categories that are created and used implicitly, and to individual categories that are used by people acting alone, "institutional categories" are created and used explicitly and rationally, and most often by many people or computational agents in coordination with each other. Institutional categories are most often created in abstract and information-intensive domains where unambiguous and precise categories are needed to regulate and systematize activity, to enable information sharing and reuse, and to reduce transaction costs. Furthermore, instead of describing the world as it is, institutional categories are usually defined to change or control the world by imposing semantic models that are more formal and arbitrary than those in cultural categories. Laws, regulations, and standards often specify institutional categories, along with decision rules for assigning resources to new categories, and behavior rules that prescribe how people must interact with them.[341] The rigorous definition of institutional categories enables **classification:** the systematic assignment of resources to categories in an organizing system.

Institutional categorization stands apart from individual categorization primarily because it invariably requires significant efforts to reconcile mismatches between existing individual categories, where those categories embody useful working or contextual knowledge that is lost in the move to a formal institutional system.[342]

Institutional categorization efforts must also overcome the vagueness and inconsistency of cultural categories because the former must often conform to stricter logical standards to support inference and meet legal requirements. Furthermore, institutional categorization is usually a process that must be accounted for in a budget and staffing plans. While some kinds of institutional categories can be devised or discovered by computational processes, most of them are created through the collaboration of many individuals, typically from various parts of an organization or from different firms.[343] The different business or technical perspectives of the participants are often the essential ingredients in developing robust categories that can meet carefully identified requirements. And as requirements change over time, institutional categories must often change as well, implying version control, compliance testing, and other formal maintenance and governance processes.

Some institutional categories that initially had narrow or focused applicability have found their way into more popular use and are now considered cultural categories. A good example is the periodic table in chemistry, which Mendeleev developed in 1869 as a new system of categories for the chemical elements. The periodic table proved essential to scientists in understanding their properties and in predicting undiscovered ones. Today the periodic table is taught in elementary schools, and many things other than elements are commonly organized using a graphical structure that resembles the periodic table of elements in chemistry, including sci-fi films and movies, desserts, and superheroes.[344]

6.2.4 A "Categorization Continuum"

As we have seen, the concepts of cultural, individual, and institutional categorization usefully distinguish the primary processes and purposes for creating categories. However, these three kinds of categories can fuse, clash, and recombine with each other. Rather than viewing them as having precise boundaries, we might view them as regions on a continuum of categorization activities and methods.

Consider a few different perspectives on categorizing animals as an example. Scientific institutions categorize animals according to explicit, principled classification systems, such as the Linnaean taxonomy that assigns animals to a phylum, class, order, family, genus and species. Cultural categorization practices cannot be adequately described in terms of a master taxonomy, and are more fluid, converging with principled taxonomies sometimes, and diverging at other times. While human beings are classified within the animal kingdom in biological classification systems, people are usually not considered animals in most cultural contexts. Sometimes a scientific designation for human beings, *homo sapiens* is even applied to human beings in cultural contexts, since the genus-species taxonomic designation has influenced cultural conceptions of people and (other) animals over the years.

Animals are also often culturally categorized as pets or non-pets. The category "pets," in the US mainstream, commonly includes dogs, cats, and fish. A pet cat might be categorized at multiple levels that incorporate individual, cultural, and institutional perspectives on categorization—as an "animal" (cultural/institutional), as a "mammal" (institutional), as a "domestic short-hair" (institutional) as a "cat" (cultural), and as a "troublemaker" or a "favorite" (individual), among other possibilities, in addition to being identified individually by one or more pet names. Furthermore, not everyone experiences pets as just dogs, cats and fish.

Some people have relatively unusual pets, like pigs. For individuals who have pet pigs or who know people with pet pigs, "pigs" may be included in the "pets" category. If enough people have pet pigs, eventually "pigs" could be included in mainstream culture's pet category.

It is not possible to entirely separate individual, cultural and institutional perspectives on categorization. Individuals form subcultures and contribute to institutions; culture influences individuals and institutions; institutions influence individuals and culture.

Categorization skewed toward cultural perspectives incorporate relatively traditional categories, such as those learned implicitly from social interactions, like mainstream understandings of what kinds of animals are "pets," while categorization skewed toward institutional perspectives emphasizes explicit, formal categories, like the categories employed in biological classification systems.

A final example that demonstrates the interplay and conflict between the different contexts of categorization involves the vehicle categories in the US *Corporate Average Fuel Economy (CAFE)* standards. The CAFE standards sort vehicles into "passenger car" and "light truck" categories and impose higher minimum fuel efficiency requirements for cars because trucks have different typical uses.

When CAFE standards were first introduced in 1975, the vehicles classified as light trucks were generally used for "light duty" farming and manufacturing purposes. "Light trucks" might be thought of as a "sort of" in-between category —a light truck is not really a car, but sufficiently unlike a prototypical truck to qualify the vehicle's categorization as "light." Formalizing this sense of in-between-ness by specifying features that define a "car" and a "light truck" is the only way to implement a consistent, transparent fuel efficiency policy that makes use of informal, graded distinctions between vehicles.

A manufacturer whose average fuel economy for all the vehicles it sells in a year falls below the CAFE standards has to pay penalties. This encourages them to produce "sport utility vehicles" (SUVs) that adhere to the CAFE definitions of light trucks but which most people use as passenger cars. Similarly, the PT Cruiser, a retro-styled hatchback produced by Chrysler from 2000-2010, strikes many people as a car. It looks like a car; we associate it with the transport of passengers rather than with farming; and in fact it is formally classified as a car under emissions standards. But like SUVs, in the CAFE classification system, the PT Cruiser is a light truck.

CAFE standards have evolved over time, becoming a theater for political clashes between holistic cultural categories and formal institutional categories, which plays out in competing pressures from industry, government, and political organizations. Furthermore, CAFE standards and manufacturers' response to them are influencing cultural categories, such that our cultural understanding of what a car looks like is changing over time as manufacturers design vehicles like the PT Cruiser with car functionality in unconventional shapes to take advantage of the CAFE light truck specifications.[345]

§6.2, "The What and Why of Categories" (page 237) explained what categories are and the contrasting cultural, individual, and institutional contexts and purposes for which categories are created. In doing so, a number of different principles for creating categories were mentioned, mostly in passing.

6.3 Principles for Creating Categories

We now take a systematic look at principles for creating categories, including: enumeration, single properties, multiple properties and hierarchy, family resemblance, similarity, theory and goal-based categorization.

6.3.1 Enumeration

The simplest principle for creating a category is *enumeration*; any resource in a finite or countable set can be deemed a category member by that fact alone. This principle is also known as *extensional definition*, and the members of the set are called the *extension*. Many institutional categories are defined by enumeration as a set of possible or legal values, like the 50 states in the US or the ISO currency codes (ISO 4217).

Enumerative categories enable membership to be unambiguously determined because a value like state name or currency code is either a member of the category or it isn't. But there comes a size when enumerative definition is impractical or inefficient, and the category either must be sub-divided or be given a definition based on principles other than enumeration.

For example, for millennia we earthlings have had a cultural category of "planet" as a "wandering" celestial object, and because we only knew of planets in our own solar system, the planet category was defined by enumeration: Mercury, Venus, Earth, Mars, Jupiter, and Saturn. When the outer planets of Uranus, Neptune, and Pluto were identified as planets in the 18th-20th centuries, they were added to this list of planets without any changes in the cultural category. But in the last couple of decades many heretofore unknown planets outside our solar system have been detected, making the set of planets unbounded, and definition by enumeration no longer works.

The International Astronomical Union (IAU) thought it solved this category crisis in 2006 by proposing a definition of planet as "a celestial body that is (a) in orbit around a star, (b) has sufficient mass for its self-gravity to overcome rigid body forces so that it assumes a hydrostatic equilibrium (nearly round) shape, and (c) has cleared the neighbourhood around its orbit." Unfortunately, Pluto does not satisfy the third requirement, so it no longer is a member of the planet category, and instead is now called an "inferior planet."[346]

6.3.2 Single Properties

It is intuitive and useful to think in terms of properties when we identify instances and when we are describing instances (as we saw in §3.3, "Resource Identity" (page 109) and in Chapter 4, *"Resource Description and Metadata"*). Therefore, it should also be intuitive and useful to consider properties when we analyze more than one instance to compare and contrast them so we can determine which sets of instances can be treated as a category or *equivalence class*. Categories whose members are determined by one or more properties or rules follow the principle of **intensional definition**, and the defining properties are called the **intension**.[347]

Any **single property** of a resource can be used to create categories, and the easiest ones to use are often the intrinsic static properties. As we discussed in Chapter 4, *"Resource Description and Metadata"*, intrinsic static properties are those inherent in a resource that never change. The size, color, shape, weight, material of composition, and texture of natural or manufactured objects are intrinsic and static properties that can be used to arrange physical resources. For example, an organizing system for a personal collection of music that is based on the intrinsic static property of physical format might use categories for CDs, DVDs, vinyl albums, 8-track cartridges, reel-to-reel tape and tape cassettes.[348] Using a single property is most natural to do when the properties can take on only a small set of discrete values like music formats, and especially when the property is closely related to how the resources are used, as they are with the music collection where each format requires different equipment to listen to the music. Each value then becomes a subcategory of the music category.

The author, date, and location of creation of an intellectual resource cannot be directly perceived but they are also intrinsic static properties. The subject matter or purpose of a resource, its "what it is about" or "what it was originally for," are also intrinsic static properties that are not directly perceivable, especially for information resources.

The name or identifier of a resource is often arbitrary but once assigned normally does not change, making it an extrinsic static property. Any collection of resources with alphabetic or numeric identifiers as an associated property can use sorting order as an organizing principle to arrange spices, books, personnel records, etc., in a completely reliable way. Some might argue whether this organizing principle creates a category system, or whether it simply exploits the ordering inherent in the identifier notation. For example, with alphabetic identifiers, we can think of alphabetic ordering as creating a recursive category system with 26 (A-Z) top-level categories, each containing the same number of second-level categories, and so on until every instance is assigned to its proper place.[349]

Some resource properties are both extrinsic and dynamic because they are based on usage or behaviors that can be highly context-dependent. The current owner or location of a resource, its frequency of access, the joint frequency of access with other resources, or its current rating or preference with respect to alternative resources are typical extrinsic and dynamic properties that can be the basis for arranging resources and defining categories.

These properties can have a large number of values or are continuous measures, but as long as there are explicit rules for using property values to determine category assignment the resulting categories are still easy to understand and use. For example, we naturally categorize people we know on the basis of their current profession, the city where they live, their hobbies, or their age. Properties with a numerical dimension like "frequency of use" are often transformed into a small set of categories like "frequently used," "occasionally used," and "rarely used" based on the numerical property values.[350]

While there are an infinite number of logically expressible properties for any resource, most of them would not lead to informative and useful categories. Therefore, it is important to choose properties that are psychologically or pragmatically relevant for the resource domain being categorized. Whether something weighs more or less than 5000 pounds is a poor property to apply to things in general, because it puts cats and chairs in one category, and buses and elephants in another.[351]

To summarize: The most useful single properties to use for creating categories for an organizing system are those that are formally assigned, objectively measurable and orderable, or tied to well-established cultural categories, because the resulting categories will be easier to understand and describe.

If only a single property is used to distinguish among some set of resources and to create the categories in an organizing system, the choice of property is critical because different properties often lead to different categories. Using the age property, Bill Gates and Mark Zuckerberg are unlikely to end up in the same category of people. Using the wealth property, they most certainly would. Furthermore, if only one property is used to create a system of categories, any category with a large numbers of items in it will lack coherence because differences on other properties will be too apparent, and some category members will not fit as well as the others.

6.3.3 Multiple Properties

Organizing systems often use multiple properties to define categories. There are three different ways in which to do this that differ in the scope of the properties and how essential they are in defining the categories.

6.3.3.1 Multi-Level or Hierarchical Categories

If you have many shirts in your closet (and you are a bit compulsive or a "neat freak"), instead of just separating your shirts from your pants using a single property (the part of body on which the clothes are worn) you might arrange the shirts by style, and then by sleeve length, and finally by color. When all of the resources in an organizing system are arranged using the same sequence of resource properties, this creates a *logical hierarchy*, a multi-level category system.

If we treat all the shirts as the collection being organized, in the shirt organizing system the broad category of shirts is first divided by style into categories like "dress shirts," "work shirts," "party shirts," and "athletic or sweatshirts." Each of these style categories is further divided until the categories are very narrow ones, like the "white long-sleeve dress shirts" category. A particular shirt ends up in this last category only after passing a series of property tests along the way: it is a dress shirt, it has long sleeves, and it is white. Each test creates more precise categories in the intersections of the categories whose members passed the prior property tests.

Put another way, each subdivision of a category takes place when we identify or choose a property that differentiates the members of the category in a way that is important or useful for some intent or purpose. Shirts differ from pants in the value of the "part of body" property, and all the shirt subcategories share this "top part" value of that property. However, shirts differ on other properties that determine the subcategory to which they belong. Even as we pay attention to these differentiating properties, it is important to remember the other properties, the ones that members of a category at any level in the hierarchy have in common with the members of the categories that contain it. These properties are often described as "inherited" or "inferred" from the broader category.[352] For example, just as every shirt shares the "worn on top part of body" property, every item of clothing shares the "can be worn on the body" property, and every resource in the "shirts" and "pants" category inherits that property.

Each differentiating property creates another level in the category hierarchy, which raises an obvious question: How many properties and levels do we need? In order to answer this question we must reflect upon the shirt categories in our closet. Our organizing system for shirts arranges them with the three properties of style, sleeve length, and color; some of the categories at the lowest level of the resulting hierarchy might have only one member, or no members at all. You might have yellow or red short-sleeved party shirts, but probably don't have yellow or red long-sleeved dress shirts, making them empty categories Obviously, any category with only one member does not need any additional properties to tell the members apart, so a category hierarchy is logically complete if every resource is in a category by itself.

However, even when the lowest level categories of our shirt organizing system have more than one member, we might choose not to use additional properties to subdivide it because the differences that remain among the members do not matter to us for the interactions the organizing system needs to support. Suppose we have two long-sleeve white dress shirts from different shirt makers, but whenever we need to wear one of them, we ignore this property. Instead, we just pick one or the other, treating the shirts as completely equivalent or substitutable. When the remaining differences between members of a category do not make a difference to the users of the category, we can say that the organizing system is pragmatically, or practically complete even if it is not yet logically complete. That is to say, it is complete "for all intents and purposes."

On the other hand, consider the shirt section of a big department store. Shirts there might be organized by style, sleeve length, and color as they are in our home closet, but would certainly be further organized by shirt maker and by size to enable a shopper to find a Marc Jacobs long-sleeve blue dress shirt of size 15/35. The department store organizing system needs more properties and a deeper hierarchy for the shirt domain because it has a much larger number of shirt instances to organize and because it needs to support many shirt shoppers, not just one person whose shirts are all the same size.

6.3.3.2 Different Properties for Subsets of Resources

A different way to use multiple resource properties to create categories in an organizing system is to employ different properties for distinct subsets of the resources being organized. This contrasts with the strict multi-level approach in which every resource is evaluated with respect to every property. Alternatively, we could view this principle as a way of organizing multiple domains that are conceptually or physically adjacent, each of which has a separate set of categories based on properties of the resources in that domain. This principle is used for most folder structures in computer file systems and by many email applications; you can create as many folder categories as you want, but any resource can only be placed in one folder.

The contrasts between intrinsic and extrinsic properties, and between static and dynamic ones, are helpful in explaining this method of creating organizing categories. For example, you might organize all of your clothes using intrinsic static properties if you keep your shirts, socks, and sweaters in different drawers and arrange them by color; extrinsic static properties if you share your front hall closet with a roommate, so you each use only one side of that closet space; intrinsic dynamic properties if you arrange your clothes for ready access according to the season; and, extrinsic dynamic properties if you keep your most frequently used jacket and hat on a hook by the front door.[353]

If we relax the requirement that different subsets of resources use different organizing properties and allow any property to be used to describe any resource, the loose organizing principle we now have is often called *tagging*. Using any property of a resource to create a description is an uncontrolled and often unprincipled principle for creating categories, but it is increasingly popular for organizing photos, web sites, email messages in gmail, or other web-based resources. We discuss tagging in more detail in §4.2.2.3, "Tagging of Web-Based Resources."

6.3.3.3 Necessary and Sufficient Properties

A large set of resources does not always require many properties and categories to organize it. Some types of categories can be defined precisely with just a few **essential** properties. For example, a prime number is a positive integer that has no divisors other than 1 and itself, and this category definition perfectly distinguishes prime and not-prime numbers no matter how many numbers are being categorized. "Positive integer" and "divisible only by 1 and itself" are **necessary** or **defining** properties for the prime number category; every prime number must satisfy these properties. These properties are also *sufficient* to establish membership in the prime number category; any number that satisfies the necessary properties is a prime number. Categories defined by necessary and sufficient properties are also called **monothetic**. They are also sometimes called *classical categories* because they conform to Aristotle's theory of how categories are used in logical deduction using syllogisms.[354] (See the Sidebar, "The Classical View of Categories" (page 250)).

Theories of categorization have evolved a great deal since Plato and Aristotle proposed them over two thousand years ago, but in many ways we still adhere to classical views of categories when we create organizing systems because they can be easier to implement and maintain that way.

An important implication of necessary and sufficient category definition is that every member of the category is an equally good member or example of the category; every prime number is equally prime. Institutional category systems are often designed to have necessary and sufficient properties because it makes them conceptually simple and gives them a straightforward implementation in technologies like database schemas, decision trees, and classes in programming languages.

> ## The Classical View of Categories
>
> The classical view is that categories are defined by necessary and sufficient properties. This theory has been enormously influential in Western thought, and is embodied in many organizing systems, especially those for information resources. This principle of defining categories is conceptually simple and has a straightforward implementation in technologies like database schemas, decision trees, and classes in programming languages.
>
> However, as we will explain, we cannot rely on this principle to create categories in many domains and contexts because there are not necessary and sufficient properties. As a result, many psychologists, cognitive scientists, and computer scientists who think about categorization have criticized the classical theory.
>
> We think this is unfair to Aristotle, who proposed what we now call the classical theory primarily to explain how categories underlie the logic of deductive reasoning: All men are mortal; Socratesis a man; Therefore, Socrates is mortal. People are wrong to turn Aristotle's thinking around and apply it to the problem of inductive reasoning, how categories are created in the first place. But this isn't Aristotle's fault; he was not trying to explain how natural cultural categories arise.

Consider the definition of an address as requiring a street, city, governmental region, and postal code. Anything that has all of these information components is therefore considered to be a valid address, and anything that lacks any of them will not be considered to be a valid address. If we refine the properties of an address to require the governmental region to be a state, and specifically one of the United States Postal Service's list of official state and territory codes, we create a subcategory for US addresses that uses an enumerated category as part of its definition. Similarly, we could create a subcategory for Canadian addresses by exchanging the name "province" for state, and using an enumerated list of Canadian province and territory codes.

6.3.4 The Limits of Property-Based Categorization

Property-based categorization works tautologically well for categories like "prime number" where the category is defined by necessary and sufficient properties. Property-based categorization also works well when properties are conceptually distinct and the value of a property is easy to perceive and examine, as they are with man-made physical resources like shirts.

Historical experience with organizing systems that need to categorize information resources has shown that basing categories on easily perceived properties is often not effective. There might be indications "on the surface" that suggest the "joints" between types of information resources, but these are often just presentation or packaging choices, That is to say, neither the size of a book nor the color of its cover are reliable cues for what it contains. Information resources have numerous descriptive properties like their title, author, and publisher that can be used more effectively to define categories, and these are certainly useful for some kinds of interactions, like finding all of the books written by a particular author or published by the same publisher. However, for practical purposes, the most useful property of an information resource is its **aboutness**, which may not be objectively perceivable and which is certainly hard to characterize.[355] Any collection of information resources in a library or document filing system is likely to be about many subjects and topics, and when an individual resource is categorized according to a limited number of its content properties, it is at the same time not being categorized using the others.

When the web first started, there were many attempts to create categories of web sites, most notably by Yahoo! As the web grew, it became obvious that search engines would be vastly more useful because their near real-time text indexes obviate the need for *a priori* assignment of web pages to categories. Rather, web search engines represent each web page or document in a way that treats each word or term they contain as a separate property.

Considering every distinct word in a document as a property stretches our notion of property to make it very different from the kinds of properties we have discussed in the previous two sections of this chapter. We do not need that generality yet, so we will defer further discussion of document representation for search engines until Chapter 8 and stick with our more intuitive and limited concept of property.

6.3.5 Family Resemblance

In general, categorization based on explicit and logical consideration of properties is much less effective, and sometimes not even possible for domains where properties lack one or more of the characteristics of separability, perceptibility, and necessity. Instead, we need to categorize using properties in a statistical rather than a logical way to come up with some measure of resemblance or similarity between the resource to be categorized and the other members of the category.

Consider a familiar category like "bird." All birds have feathers, wings, beaks, and two legs. But there are thousands of types of birds, and they are distinguished by properties that some birds have that other birds lack: most birds can fly, most are active in the daytime, some swim, some swim underwater; some have webbed feet. These properties are correlated, a consequence of natural selection that conveys advantages to particular configurations of characteristics;

birds that live in trees have different wings and feet than those that swim, for example. In the end, there is no single set of properties that are both necessary and sufficient to categorize a bird.

There are three related consequences of this complex distribution of properties for birds and for many other categories in cultural or natural (as opposed to man-made) domains. The first is an effect of **typicality** or **centrality** that makes some members of the category better examples than others, even if they share most properties. Most people consider a robin to be a more typical bird than a penguin.[356] Or try to define "friend" and ask yourself if all of the people you consider friends are equally good examples of the category. This effect is also described as "gradience" in category membership and reflects the extent to which the most characteristic properties are shared.

A second consequence is that the sharing of some but not all properties creates what we call **family resemblances** among the category members; just as biological family members do not necessarily all share a single set of physical features but still are recognizable as members of the same family. This idea was first proposed by the 20th century philosopher Ludwig Wittgenstein, who used "games" as an example of a category whose members resemble each other according to shifting property subsets. (See the Sidebar "What Is a Game?" (page 252)).[357]

What Is a Game?

Ludwig Wittgenstein (1889-1951) was a philosopher who thought deeply about mathematics, the mind, and language. In 1999 his *Philosophical Investigations* was ranked as the most important book of 20th century philosophy in a poll of philosophers.[358] In that book, Wittgenstein uses "game" to argue that many concepts have no defining properties, and that instead there is a "complicated network of similarities overlapping and criss-crossing: sometimes overall similarities, sometimes similarities of detail." He contrasts board games, card games, ball games, games of skill, games of luck, games with competition, solitary games, and games for amusement. Wittgenstein notes that not all games are equally good examples of the category, and jokes about teaching children a gambling game with dice because he knows that this is not the kind of game that the parents were thinking of when they asked him to teach their children a game.

The third consequence, when categories do not have necessary features for membership, is that the boundaries of the category are not fixed; the category can be stretched and new members assigned as long as they resemble incumbent members. Personal video games and multiplayer online games like World of Warcraft did not exist in Wittgenstein's time but we have no trouble recognizing them as games and neither would Wittgenstein, were he alive. Recall that in Chapter 1 we pointed out that the cultural category of "library" has been repeatedly extended by new properties, as when Flickr is described as a web-based photo-sharing library. Categories defined by family resemblance or multiple and shifting property sets are termed **polythetic**.

We conclude that instead of using properties one at a time to assign category membership, we can use them in a composite or integrated way to determine *similarity*. Something is categorized as an A and not a B if it is more similar to A's best or most typical member rather than it is to B's.[359]

6.3.6 Similarity

Similarity is a very flexible notion whose meaning depends on the domain within which we apply it.[360] To make similarity a useful mechanism for categorization we have to specify how the similarity measure is determined. There are four major psychological approaches that propose different functions for computing similarity: feature- or property-based, geometry-based, alignment-based, and transformational.[361] Each of these psychological definitions or models of similarity has analogues in or can be applied to organizing systems.

An influential model of feature-based similarity calculation is the contrast model proposed by Amos Tversky. This model matches the features or properties of the two things being compared and computes a similarity measure according to three sets of features: those they share, those the first has that the second lacks, and those that the second has that the first lacks. The similarity that results from the set of shared features is reduced by the two sets of distinctive features. The weights or importance assigned to each of these three sets can be adjusted to explain how items are assigned to a set of categories.

We often use a heuristic version of feature-based similarity calculation when we create multi-level or hierarchical category systems to ensure that the categories at each level are at the same level of abstraction or breadth. For example, if we were organizing a collection of musical instruments, it would not seem correct to have subcategories of "woodwind instruments," "violins," and "cellos" because the feature-based similarity among the categories is not the same for all pairwise comparisons among the categories; violins and cellos are simply too similar to each other to be separate categories given woodwinds as a category.

Geometric models are a second type of similarity framework, in which items are represented as points in a multi-dimensional feature- or property-space and similarity is calculated by measuring the distance between them. How distance is measured depends on the type of properties that characterize a domain. When properties that are psychologically or perceptually combined, a Euclidean distance function best accounts for category judgments; but when properties can be conceptually separated, a "city block" distance function works best to explain psychological data, because that ensures that each property value contributes its full amount. Geometric similarity functions are commonly used by search engines; if a query and document are each represented as a vector of search terms, relevance is determined by the distance between the vectors in the "document space." We will discuss how this works in greater detail in Chapter 9, *"Interactions with Resources"*.

Alignment-based similarity models have been proposed for domains in which the items to be categorized are characterized by abstract or complex relationships with their features and with each other. For example, some categories are best understood as metaphors that have become conventionalized, and category judgments are made by aligning and projecting aspects of one item or entity onto another. With this model an entity need not be understood as inherently possessing features shared in common with another entity. Rather, people project features from one thing to another in a search for congruities between things, much as clue receivers in the second round of the *Pyramid* game search for congruities between examples provided by the clue giver in order to guess the target category. For example, a clue like "screaming baby" can suggest many categories, as can "parking meter." But the likely intersection of the interactions one can have with babies and parking meters is that they are both "Things you need to feed."

Transformational models for calculating similarity assume that the similarity between two things is inversely proportional to the complexity of the transformation required to turn one into the other. For example, one way to perform the **name matching** task of determining when two different strings denote the same person, object, or other named entity is to calculate the "edit distance" between them, the number of changes required to transform one into the other. Two strings with a short edit distance might be variant spellings or misspellings of the same name.[362]

6.3.7 Theory-Based Categories

Another principle for creating categories is organizing things in ways that fit a theory or story that makes a particular categorization sensible. A **theory-based category** can win out even if "family resemblance" or "similarity" with respect to visible properties would lead to a different category assignment. For example, whales are categorized as mammals by biologists even though they share their most visible properties with fish because the theory of "mammalness" emphasizes the property of nursing with mother's milk.

Theory-based categories based on origin or causation are especially important with highly inventive and computational resources because unlike natural kinds of physical resources, little or none of what they can do or how they behave is visible on the surface (see §2.4.1, "Affordance and Capability" (page 61)). Consider all of the different appearances and form factors of the resources that we categorize as "computers" —their essence is that they all compute, an invisible or theory-like principle that does not depend on their visible properties.[363]

6.3.8 Goal-Derived Categories

A final principle for creating categories is to organize resources that go together in order to satisfy a goal. Consider the category "Things to take from a burning house," an example that cognitive scientist Lawrence Barsalou termed an ad hoc or **goal-derived** category.[364] What things would you take from your house if your neighborhood were burning? Possibly your cat, your wallet and checkbook, your important papers like birth certificates and passports, and grandma's old photo album, and anything else you think is important, priceless, or irreplaceable—as long as you can carry it. These items have almost no discernible properties in common, except for somehow being your most precious possessions. The category is derived or induced by a particular goal in some specified context.

Similarly, a small towel, a music player with headphones, and a bottle of water have no properties in common but they could be organized together because they are members of "things used at the gym when working out" category. This category would fit very well with the many *ad hoc* categories that gave contestants so much trouble on the *Pyramid* game show.

6.4 Category Design Issues and Implications

We have previously discussed the most important principles for creating categories: resource properties, similarity, and goals. When we use one or more of these principles to develop a system of categories, we must make decisions about its depth and breadth. Here, we examine the idea that some levels of abstraction in a system of categories are more basic or natural than others. We also consider how the choices we make affect how we create the organizing system in the first place, and how they shape our interactions when we need to find some resources that are categorized in it.

6.4.1 Category Abstraction and Granularity

We can identify any resource as a unique instance or as a member of a class of resources. The size of this class—the number of resources that are treated as equivalent—is determined by the properties or characteristics we consider when we examine the resources in some domain. The way we think of a resource domain depends on context and intent, so the same resource can be thought of abstractly in some situations and very concretely in others. As we discussed in Chapter 4, *"Resource Description and Metadata"*, this influences the nature and extent of resource description, and as we've seen in this chapter, it then influences the nature and extent of categories we can create.

Consider the regular chore of putting away clean clothes. We can consider any item of clothing as just that—a member of a broad category whose members are any kind of garment that a person might wear. Using one category for all clothing, that is, failing to distinguish among the various items in any useful or practical way would likely mean that we would keep our clothes in a big unorganized pile.

However, we cannot wear any random combination of clothing items—we need a shirt, a pair of pants, socks, and so on. Clearly, our indiscriminate clothing category is too broad for most purposes. So instead, most people organize their clothes in more fine-grained categories that fit the normal pattern of how they wear clothes. For example, everyone probably separates their shirts, pants, and socks when they put away their clothes after doing their laundry. Some pants and shirts may merit wooden hangers; others may rest in special drawers.

In §6.3.2, "Single Properties" (page 245) we described an organizing system for the shirts in our closet, so let's talk about socks instead. When it comes to socks, most people think that the basic unit is a pair because they always wear two socks at a time. If you are going to need to find socks in pairs, it seems sensible to organize them into pairs when you are putting them away. Some people might further separate their dress socks from athletic ones, and then sort these socks by color or material, creating a hierarchy of sock categories analogous to the shirt categories in our previous example. We note, parenthetically, that not everyone works this hard when putting their clothes away; some people toss all the single, unpaired socks in a drawer and then rummage around when they need to find a matching pair of socks. People differ in their preferences or tolerances for the amount of granularity in an organizing system and we need to expect and respect these differences.

Questions of resource abstraction and granularity also emerge whenever the information systems of different firms, or different parts of a firm, need to exchange information or be merged into a single system. All parties must define the identity of each thing in the same way, or in ways that can be related or mapped to each other either manually or electronically.

For example, how should a business system deal with a customer's address? Printed on an envelope, "an address" typically appears as a comprehensive, multi-line text object. Inside an information system, however, an address is stored as separate information components for each printed line, or as a set of distinctly identifiable information components. This fine-grained organization makes it easier to sort customers by city or postal codes, for sales and marketing purposes. Incompatibilities in the abstraction and granularity of these information components, and the ways in which they are presented and reused in documents, will cause interoperability problems when businesses need to share information, some of which may be difficult to detect because of the *vocabulary problem*.[365]

6.4.2 Basic or Natural Categories

We can describe category abstraction in terms of a hierarchy of **superordinate**, **basic**, and **subordinate** category levels. "Clothing," for example, is a superordinate category, "shirts" and "socks" are basic categories, and "white long-sleeve dress shirts" and "white wool hiking socks" are subordinate categories. Members of basic level categories like "shirts" and "socks" have many perceptual properties in common, and are more strongly associated with motor movements than members of superordinate categories. Members of subordinate categories have many common properties, but these properties are also shared by members of other subordinate categories at the same level of abstraction in the category hierarchy. That is, while we can identify many properties shared by all "white long-sleeve dress shirts," many of them are also properties of "blue long-sleeve dress shirts" and "black long-sleeve pullover shirts."

Psychological research suggests that some levels of abstraction in a system of categories are more basic or natural than others. An implication for organizing system design is that basic level categories are highly efficient in terms of the cognitive effort they take to create and use.[366]

6.4.3 The Recall and Precision Tradeoff

The abstraction level we choose determines how precisely we identify resources. When we want to make a general claim, or communicate that the scope of our interest is broad, we use superordinate categories, as when we ask, "How many animals are in the San Diego Zoo?" But we use precise subordinate categories when we need to be specific: "How many adult emus are in the San Diego Zoo today?"

If we return to our clothing example, finding a pair of white wool hiking socks is very easy if the organizing system for socks creates fine-grained categories. When resources are described or arranged with this level of detail, a similarly detailed specification of the resources you are looking for yields precisely what you want. When you get to the place where you keep white wool hiking socks, you find all of them and nothing else. On the other hand, if all your socks are tossed unsorted into a sock drawer, when you go sock hunting you might not be able to find the socks you want and you will encounter lots of socks you do not want. But you won't have put time into sorting them, which many people don't enjoy doing; you can spend time sorting or searching depending on your preferences.

If we translate this example into the jargon of information retrieval, we say that more fine-grained organization reduces **recall**, the number of resources you find or retrieve in response to a query, but increases the **precision** of the recalled set, the proportion of recalled items that are relevant. Broader or coarse-grained categories increase recall, but lower precision. We are all too familiar with this hard bargain when we use a web search engine; a quick one-word query results in many pages of mostly irrelevant sites, whereas a carefully crafted multi-word query pinpoints sites with the information we seek. We will discuss recall, precision, and evaluation of information retrieval more extensively in Chapter 9, *"Interactions with Resources"*.

This mundane example illustrates the fundamental tradeoff between organization and retrieval. A tradeoff between the investment in organization and the investment in retrieval persists in nearly every organizing system. The more effort we put into organizing resources, the more effectively they can be retrieved. The more effort we are willing to put into retrieving resources, the less they need to be organized first. The allocation of costs and benefits between the organizer and retriever differs according to the relationship between them. Are they the same person? Who does the work and who gets the benefit?

6.4.4 Category Audience and Purpose

The ways in which people categorize depend on the goals of categorization, the breadth of the resources in the collection to be categorized, and the users of the organizing system. Suppose that we want to categorize languages. Our first step might be determining what constitutes a language, since there is no widespread agreement on what differentiates a language from a dialect, or even on whether such a distinction exists.

What we mean by "English" and "Chinese" as categories can change depending on the audience we are addressing and what our purpose is, however.[367] A language learning school's representation of "English" might depend on practical concerns such as how the school's students are likely to use the language they learn, or on which teachers are available. For the purposes of a school teaching global languages, one of the standard varieties of English (which are associated with more political power), or an amalgamation of standard varieties might be thought of as an instance ("English") of the category "Languages."

Similarly, the category structure in which "Chinese" is situated can vary with context. While some schools might not conceptualize "Chinese" as a category encompassing multiple linguistic varieties, but rather as a single instance within the "Languages" category, another school might teach its students Mandarin, Wu, and Cantonese as dialects within the language category "Chinese," that are unified by a single standard *writing system*. In addition, a linguist might consider Mandarin, Wu, and Cantonese to be mutually unintelligible, making them separate languages within the broader category "Chinese" for the purpose of creating a principled language classification system.

In fact languages can be categorized in multitude of ways. If we are concerned with linguistic diversity and the survival of minority languages, we might categorize some languages as endangered in order to mobilize language preservation efforts. We could also categorize languages in terms of shared linguistic ancestors ("Romance languages," for example), in terms of what kinds of sounds they make use of, by how well we speak them, by regions they are commonly spoken in, whether they are signed or unsigned, and so on. We could also expand our definition of the languages category to include artificial computer languages, or body language, or languages shared by people and their pets—or thinking more metaphorically, we might include the language of fashion.

If people could only categorize in a single way, the *Pyramid* game show, where contestants guess what category is illustrated by the example provided by a clue giver, would pose no challenge. The creative possibilities provided by categorization allow people to order the world and refer to interrelationships among conceptions through a kind of allusive shorthand. When we talk about the language of fashion, we suggest that in the context of our conversation, instances like "English," "Chinese," and "fashion" are alike in ways that distinguish them from other things that we would not categorize as languages.

6.5 Implementing Categories

We have emphasized the intellectual choices and challenges that arise in the design of a system of categories because, at their essence, categories are conceptual or mental constructs. We use categories in a mostly invisible way when we communicate, solve problems, or organize our kitchens and clothes closets. Sometimes categories are more apparent, as when we see signs and labels in the aisles of department or grocery stores to help us find things, when we put our socks and t-shirts in different dresser drawers, or when we create a system of folders and directories in our file cabinets or on our personal computers.

The most visible implementations of a category system are usually those for institutional categories, especially those that are embodied in the organizing systems for information resources where category membership can be verified by technology and the boundaries between categories are precise. In this final section of the chapter we briefly discuss some of the most important technologies for implementing categories, contrasting those that are appropriate for categories where membership is defined using properties with those that work for categories defined on the basis of similarity.

6.5.1 Implementing Classical Categories

The most conceptually simple and straightforward implementation of categories in technologies for organizing systems adopts the **classical view of categories** based on necessary and sufficient features. This approach results in prescriptive categories with explicit and clear boundaries. Classifying items into the categories is objective and deterministic and supports a well-defined notion of *validation* to determine unambiguously whether some instance is a member of the category.

The most direct way to implement classical categories is as a **decision tree**. A simple decision tree is an algorithm for determining a decision by making a sequence of logical or property tests. For example, we can classify numbers as prime or not with two tests: is it greater than 1, and does it have any divisors other than itself and 1. More complex categories need more tests. We can model the CAFE fuel econobeamy standards (§6.2.4, "A "Categorization Continuum"" (page 242)) that assign vehicles to "car," "truck," and "light truck" categories using a decision tree whose differentiating tests are (1) the maximum number of passengers (cars have 10 or fewer), (2) off-road capability (cars do not have it), and (3) weight (trucks weigh at least 6000 pounds), and (4) function (numerous sub-tests that classify vehicles as trucks even if they weigh less than 6000 pounds).[368]

Precisely because natural language embodies cultural categories, it is not the optimal representational format for formally defined institutional categories. Categories defined using natural language can easily be incomplete, inconsistent, or ambiguous, so they are sometimes defined using "simplified writing" or "business rules" that in the aggregate create a decision tree or network that reliably classifies instances.[369] However, the vast majority of institutional category systems are still specified with natural language, despite its ambiguities. Sometimes this is even intentional to allow institutional categories embodied in laws to evolve in the courts and to accommodate technological advances.[370]

Data schemas that specify data entities, elements, identifiers, attributes, and relationships in databases and XML document types on the transactional end of the Document Type Spectrum (§3.2.1) are implementations of the categories needed for the design, development and maintenance of information organization systems. Like the classical model of categorization, data schemas tend to rigidly define resources. "Rigid" might sound negative, but a rigidly defined resource is also precisely defined. Precise definition is essential when creating, capturing, and retrieving data and when information about resources in different organizing systems needs to be combined or compared.[371]

The 100 or so standard document types of the *Universal Business Language (UBL)* (mentioned briefly in §7.1.5.2) are XML schemas that define basic level categories like orders, invoices, payments, and receipts that many people are familiar with from their personal experiences of shopping and paying bills. UBL's vast library of information components enables the design of very specific or subordinate level transactional document types like "purchase order for industrial chemicals when buyer and seller are in different countries." At the other end of the abstraction hierarchy are document types like "fill-in-the-blank" legal forms for any kind of contract.

In object-oriented programming languages, *classes* are schemas that serve as templates for the creation of objects. A class in a programming language is analogous to a database schema that specifies the structure of its member instances, in that the class definition specifies how instances of the class are constructed in terms of data types and possible values. Programming classes may also specify whether data in a member object can be accessed, and if so, how.[372]

6.5.2 Implementing Categories That Do Not Conform to the Classical Theory

Unlike transactional document types, which can be prescriptively defined as *classical categories* because they are often produced and consumed by automated processes, narrative document types are usually descriptive in character. We do not classify something as a novel because it has some specific set of properties and content types. Instead, we have a notion of typical novels and their characteristic properties, and some things that are considered novels are far from typical in their structure and content.[373]

Nevertheless, categories like narrative document types can sometimes be implemented using document schemas that impose only a few constraints on structure and content. Unlike a schema for a purchase order that uses *regular expressions*, strongly data typed content and enumerated code lists to validate the value of required elements that must occur in a particular order, a schema for a narrative document type would have much optionality, be flexible about order, and expect only text in its sections, paragraphs and headings. Even very lax document schemas can be useful in making content management, reuse, and formatting more efficient.

Category types that are furthest in character from the classical model are those that are not defined using properties in any explicit way. We do not use technology to help us understand cultural categories like "friend" or "game" that rely on some notion of similarity to determine category membership. However, there are technologies that can create a system of categories that uses similarity as its basis.

In particular, **Machine learning** is a subfield of computer science that develops and applies algorithms that accomplish tasks that are not explicitly programmed; creating categories and assigning items to them is an important subset of machine learning. Two subfields of machine learning that are particularly relevant to organizing systems are **supervised** and **unsupervised** learning. In supervised learning, a machine learning program is trained by giving it sample items or documents that are labeled by category, and the program learns to assign new items to the correct categories. In unsupervised learning, the program gets the samples but has to come up with the categories on its own by discovering the underlying correlations between the items; that is why unsupervised learning is sometimes called **statistical pattern recognition**. This generally takes longer, since the program isn't given correct answers to use in improving its performance, as it is in the supervised case. As we pointed out in §6.2.1, "Cultural Categories" (page 238), we learn most of our cultural categories without any explicit instruction about them, so it is not surprising that computational models of categorization developed by cognitive scientists often employ unsupervised statistical learning methods. We will now briefly discuss unsupervised learning and return to supervised learning in Chapter 7, "*Classification: Assigning Resources to Categories*".

There are far too many unsupervised learning techniques for categorization to even mention them all, let alone describe how they work. The ones that are most relevant for us are called *clustering* techniques, which share the same goal and a few basic methods. Clustering techniques share the goal of creating meaningful categories from a collection of items whose properties are hard to directly perceive and evaluate; this is especially true with large collections of heterogeneous documents, where goals might be to find categories of documents with the same topics, genre, sentiment, or other characteristic that cannot easily be reduced to specific property tests.

The first shared method is that clustering techniques start with an initially uncategorized set of items or documents from which some measures of inter-item similarity can be calculated.[374]

The second shared method is that categories are created by putting items that are most similar into the same category. Hierarchical clustering approaches start with every item in its own category. Other approaches, notably one called "K-means clustering," start with a fixed number of K categories initialized with a randomly chosen item or document.

The third shared method is refining the system of categories by iterative similarity recalculation each time an item is added to a category. Approaches that start with every item in its own category create a hierarchical system of categories by merging the two most similar categories, recomputing the similarity between the new category and the remaining ones, and repeating this process until all the categories are merged into a single category at the root of a category tree. Techniques that start with a fixed number of categories do not create new ones but instead repeatedly recalculate the "center" of the category by adjusting its property representation to the average of all its members after a new member is added.[375]

The end result of clustering is a statistically optimal set of categories in which the similarity of all the items within a category is larger than the similarity of items that belong to different categories. This is a statistical result produced by a computer, and there is no guarantee that the categories are meaningful ones that can be named and used by people. In the end, clustering relies on the data analyst or information scientist to make sense of the clusters if they are to be used to classify resources. In many cases it is better to start with categories created by people and then teach them to computers that can use supervised learning techniques to assign new resources to the categories.

6.6 Key Points in Chapter Six

- Categories are **equivalence classes**: sets or groups of things or abstract entities that we treat the same.

- The size of the equivalence class is determined by the properties or characteristics we consider.

- We can describe category abstraction in terms of a hierarchy of **superordinate**, **basic**, and **subordinate** category levels.

- Any particular collection of resources can be organized using a combination of intrinisic, extrinsic, static and dynamic resource properties.

- Broader or coarse-grained categories increase **recall**, but lower **precision.**

- Some types of categories can be defined precisely with just a few *necessary and sufficient* properties.

- An important implication of necessary and sufficient category definition is that every member of the category is an equally good member or example of the category.

- Any collection of resources with sortable identifiers (alphabetic or numeric) as an associated property can benefit from using sorting order as an organizing principle.

- A sequence of organizing decisions based on a fixed ordering of resource properties creates a **hierarchy**, a multi-level category system.

- Sharing some but not all properties is akin to **family resemblances** among the category members.

- We use properties one at a time to assign category membership.

- We use properties in a composite or integrated way to determine **similarity.**

- To make similarity a useful mechanism for categorization we have to specify how similarity is measured.

- For most purposes, the most useful property of information resources for categorizing them is their **aboutness**, which is not directly perceivable and which is hard to characterize.

- Cultural, individual, and institutional categorization share some core ideas but they emphasize different processes and purposes for creating categories.

- Languages differ a great deal in the words they contain and also in more fundamental ways by which they organize words into grammatical categories.

- Individual categories are created by intentional activity that usually takes place in response to a specific situation.

- Institutional categories are most often created in abstract and information-intensive domains where unambiguous and precise categories are needed.

- The rigorous definition of institutional categories enables **classification**, the systematic assignment of resources to categories in an organizing system.

- The most conceptually simple and straightforward implementation of categories in technologies for organizing system adopts the classical view of categories based on necessary and sufficient features.

Notes

328. [CogSci] Cataloging and programming are important activities that need to be done well, and prescriptive advice is often essential. However, we believe that understanding how people create psychological and linguistic categories can help us appreciate that cataloging and information systems design are messier and more intellectually challenging activities than we might otherwise think.

329. [CogSci] Cognitive science mostly focuses on the automatic and unconscious mechanisms for creating and using categories. This disciplinary perspective emphasizes the activation of category knowledge for the purpose of making inferences and "going beyond the information given," to use Bruner's classic phrase (Bruner 1957). In contrast, the discipline of organizing focuses on the explicit and self-aware mechanisms for creating and using categories because by definition, organizing systems serve intentional and often highly explicit purposes. Organizing systems facilitate inferences about the resources they con-

tain, but the more constrained purposes for which resources are described and arranged makes inference a secondary goal.

Cognitive science is also highly focused on understanding and creating computational models of the mechanisms for creating and using categories. These models blend data-driven or bottom-up processing with knowledge-driven or top-down processing to simulate the time course and results of categorization at both fine-grained scales (as in word or object recognition) and over developmental time frames (as in how children learn categories). The discipline of organizing can learn from these models about the types of properties and principles that organizing systems use, but these computational models are not a primary concern to us in this book.

330. [CogSci] However, even the way this debate has been framed is a bit controversial. Bulmer's chicken, the "categories are in the world" position, has been described as empirical, environment-driven, bottom-up, or objectivist, and these are not synonymous. Likewise, the "egghead" position that "categories are in the mind" has been called rational, constructive, top-down, experiential, and embodied—and they are also not synonyms. See (Bulmer 1970). See also (Lakoff 1990), (Malt 1995).

331. [CogSci] Is there a "universal grammar" or a "language faculty" that imposes strong constraints on human language and cognition? (Chomsky 1965) and (Jackendoff 1996) think so. Such proposals imply cognitive representations in which categories are explicit structures in memory with associated instances and properties. In contrast, generalized learning theories model category formation as the adjustment of the patterns and weighting of connections in neural processing networks that are not specialized for language in any way. Computational simulations of semantic networks can reproduce the experimental and behavioral results about language acquisition and semantic judgments that have been used as evidence for explicit category representations without needing anything like them. (Rogers and McClelland 2008) thoroughly review the explicit category models and then show how relatively simple learning models can do without them.

332. [CogSci] The debates about human category formation also extend to issues of how children learn categories and categorization methods. Most psychologists argue that category learning starts with general learning mechanisms that are very perceptually based, but they don't agree whether to characterize these changes as "stages" or as phases in a more complex dynamical system. Over time more specific learning techniques evolve that focus on correlations among perceptual properties (things with wings tend to have feathers), correlations among properties and roles (things with eyes tend to eat), and ultimately correlations among roles (things that eat tend to sleep). See (Smith and Thelen 2003).

333. [CogSci] These three contexts were proposed by (Glushko, Maglio, Matlock, and Barsalou 2008), who pointed out that cognitive science has focused on cultural categorization and largely ignored individual and institutional contexts. They argue that taking a broader view of categorization highlights dimensions on which it varies that are not apparent when only cultural categories are considered. For example, institutional categories are usually designed and maintained using prescriptive methods that have no analogues with cultural categories.

334. [Philosophy] This quote comes from Plato's *Phaedrus* dialogue, written around 370 BCE. Contemporary philosophers and cognitive scientists in discussions about whether "natural kinds" exist commonly invoke it. For example, see (Campbell, O'Rourke, and Slater 2011), and (Hutchins 2010). (Atran 1987) and others have argued that the existence of perceptual discontinuities is not sufficient to account for category formation. Instead, people assume that members of a biological category must have an essence of co-occurring properties and these guide people to focus on the salient differences, thereby creating categories. Property clusters enable inferences about causality, which then builds a framework on which additional categories can be created and refined. For example, if "having wings" and "flying" are co-occurring properties that suggest a "bird" category, wings are then inferred as the causal basis of flying, and wings become more salient.

335. [Linguistics] Pronouns, adjectives, verbs, adverbs, prepositions, conjunctions, particles, and numerals and other "parts of speech" are also grammatical categories, but nouns carry most of the semantic weight.

336. [CogSci] In contrast, the set of possible interactions with even a simple object like a banana is very large. We can pick, peel, slice, smash, eat, or throw a banana, so instead of capturing this complexity in the meaning of banana it gets parceled into the verbs that can act on the banana noun. Doing so requires languages to use verbs to capture a broader and more abstract type of meaning that is determined by the nouns they are combined with. Familiar verbs like "set," "put," and "get" have dozens of different senses as a result because they go with so many different nouns. We set fires and we set tables, but fires and tables have little in common. The intangible character of verbs and the complexity of multiple meanings make it easier to focus instead on their associated nouns, which are often physical resources, and create organizing systems that emphasize the latter rather than the former. We create organizing systems that focus on verbs when we are categorizing actions, behaviors, or services where the resources that are involved are less visible or less directly involved in the supported interactions.

337. [Linguistics] Many languages have a system of grammatical gender in which all nouns must be identified as masculine or feminine using definite arti-

cles (*el* and *la* in Spanish, *le* and *la* in French, and so on) and corresponding pronouns. Languages also contrast in how they describe time, spatial relationships, and in which things are treated as countable objects (one ox, two oxen) as opposed to substances or mass nouns that do not have distinct singular and plural forms (like water or dirt). (Deutscher 2011) carefully reviews and discredits the strong Whorfian view and makes the case for a more nuanced perspective on linguistic relativity. He also reviews much of Lera Boroditsky's important work in this area. George Lakoff's book with the title *Women, Fire, and Dangerous Things* (Lakoff 1990) provocatively points out differences in gender rules among languages; in an aboriginal language called Dyirbal many dangerous things, including fire have feminine gender, meanwhile "fire" is masculine in Spanish (*el feugo*) and French (*le feu*).

338. [CogSci] This analysis comes from (Haviland 1998). More recently, Lera Boroditsky has done many interesting studies and experiments about linguistic relativity. See (Boroditksy 2003) for an academic summary and (Boroditsky 2010, 2011) for more popular treatments.

339. [CogSci] (Medin et al. 1997).

340. [LIS] The personal archives of people who turn out to be famous or important are the exception that proves this rule. In that case, the individual's organizing system and its categories are preserved along with their contents.

341. [Law] Consider how the cultural category of "killing a person" is refined by the legal system to distinguish manslaughter and different degrees of murder based on the amount of intentionality and planning involved (e.g., first and second degree murder) and the roles of people involved with the killing (accessory). In general, the purpose of laws is to replace coarse judgments of categorization based on overall similarity of facts with rule-based categorization based on specific dimensions or properties.

342. [Business] And often the particularities or idiosyncrasies of individual categorization systems capture user expertise and knowledge that is not represented in the institutional categories that replace them. Many of the readers of this book are information professionals whose technological competence is central to their work and which helps them to be creative. But for a great many other people, information technology has enabled the routinization of work in offices, assembly lines, and in other jobs where new institutionalized job categories have "downskilled" or "deskilled" the nature of work, destroying competence and engendering a great deal of resistance from the affected workers.

343. [Business] Similar technical concerns arise in within-company and multi-company standardization efforts, but the competitive and potentially anti-competitive character of the latter imposes greater complexity by introducing considerations of business strategy and politics. Credible standards-making in

multi-company contexts depends on an explicit and transparent process for gathering and prioritizing requirements, negotiating specifications that satisfy them, and ensuring conformant implementations—without at any point giving any participating firm an advantage. See the OASIS Technical Committee Process for an example (*https://www.oasis-open.org/policies-guidelines/tc-process*) and (Rosenthal et al. 2004) for an analysis of best practices.

344.   [CogSci]   *http://www.wired.com/geekmom/2012/03/the-periodic-tables-of-everything-but-elements/*.

345. [Business] The Corporate Average Fuel Economy (CAFE) standards have been developed by the US National Highway Traffic Safety Administration (*http://www.nhtsa.gov/fuel-economy*) since 1975. For a careful and critical assessment of CAFE, including the politics of categorization for vehicles like the PT Cruiser, see the 2002 report from the Committee on the Effectiveness and Impact of Corporate Average Fuel Economy (CAFE) Standards, National Research Council.

346. [LIS] International Astronomical Union (IAU) (iau.org) published its new definition of planet in August 2006.Changing the definition of a significant cultural category generated a great deal of controversy and angst among ordinary non-scientific people. A typical headline was "Pluto's demotion has schools spinning," describing the outcry from elementary school students and teachers about the injustice done to Pluto and the disruption on the curriculum. A public television documentary in 2011 called *The Pluto Files* retells the story (Nova 2011).

347. [Philosophy] The distinction between intension and extension was introduced by Gottlob Frege, a German philosopher and mathematician (Frege 1892). You might be thinking here that enumeration or extensional definition of a category is also a property test; is not "being a state" a property of California? But statehood is not a property precisely because "state" is defined by extension, which means the only way to test California for statehood is to see if it is in the list of states.

348. [CogSci] The number of resources in each of these categories depends on the age of the collection and the collector. We could be more precise here and say "single atomic property" or otherwise more carefully define "property" in this context as a characteristic that is basic and not easily or naturally decomposable into other characteristics. It would be possible to analyze the physical format of a music resource as a composition of size, shape, weight, and material substance properties, but that is not how people normally think. Instead, they treat physical format as a single property as we do in this example.

349. [CogSci] We need to think of alphabetic ordering or any other organizing principle in a logical way that does not imply any particular physical implemen-

tation. Therefore, we do not need to consider which of these alphabetic categories exist as folders, files, or other tangible partitions.

350. [CogSci] Another example: rules for mailing packages might use either size or weight to calculate the shipping cost, and whether these rules are based on specific numerical values or ranges of values, the intent seems to be to create categories of packages.

351. [CogSci] If you try hard, you can come up with situations in which this property is important, as when the circus is coming to the island on a ferry or when you are loading an elevator with a capacity limit of 5000 pounds, but it just isn't a useful or psychologically salient property in most contexts.

352. [Computing] Many information systems, applications, and programming languages that work with hierarchical categories take advantage of this logical relationship to infer inherited properties when they are needed rather than storing them redundantly.

353. [Business] Similarly, clothing stores use intrinsic static properties when they present merchandise arranged according to color and size; extrinsic static properties when they host branded displays of merchandise; intrinsic dynamic properties when they set aside a display for seasonal merchandise, from bathing suits to winter boots; and extrinsic dynamic properties when a display area is set aside for "Today's Special."

354. [Philosophy] Aristotle did not call them classical categories. That label was bestowed about 2300 years later by (Smith and Medin 1981).

355. [LIS] We all use the word "about" with ease in ordinary discourse, but "aboutness" has generated a surprising amount of theoretical commentary about its typically implicit definition, starting with (Hutchins 1977) and (Maron 1977) and relentlessly continued by (Hjørland 1992, 2001).

356. [CogSci] Typicality and centrality effects were studied by Rosch and others in numerous highly influential experiments in the 1970s and 1980s. Good summaries can be found in (Mervis and Rosch 1981), (Rosch 1999), and in Chapter 1 of (Rogers and McClelland 2008).

357. [Philosophy] An easy to find source for Wittgenstein's discussion of "game" is (Wittgenstein 2002) in a collection of core readings for cognitive psychology (Levitin 2002).

358. [Philosophy] The philosopher's poll that ranked Wittgenstein's book #1 is reported by (Lackey 1999).

359. [CogSci] The exact nature of the category representation to which the similarity comparison is made is a subject of ongoing debate in cognitive science. Is it a **prototype**, a central tendency or average of the properties shared by cate-

gory members, or it one or more **exemplars,** particular members that typify the category. Or is it neither, as argued by connectionist modelers who view categories as patterns of network activation without any explicitly stored category representation? Fortunately, these distinctions do not matter for our discussion here. A recent review is (Rips, Smith, and Medin 2012).

360. [CogSci] Some people consider that the concept of similarity is itself meaningless because there must always be some basis, some unstated set of properties, for determining whether two things are similar. If we could identify those properties and how they are used, there would not be any work for a similarity mechanism to do. Another situation where similarity has been described as a "mostly vacuous" explanation for categorization is with abstract categories or metaphors. Goldstone says "an unrewarding job and a relationship that can't be ended may both be metaphorical prisons... and may seem similar in that both conjure up a feeling of being trapped... but this feature is almost as abstract as the category to be explained." (Goldstone 1994), p. 149.

361. [CogSci] (Medin, Goldstone, and Gentner 1993).

362. [Computing] The "strings" to be matched can themselves be transformations. The "soundex" function is very commonly used to determine if two words could be different spellings of the same name. It "hashes" the names into phonetic encodings that have fewer characters than the text versions. See (Christen 2006) and *http://www.searchforancestors.com/utility/soundex.html* to try it yourself.

363. [CogSci] The emergence of theory-based categorization is an important event in cognitive development that has been characterized as a shift from "holistic" to "analytic" categories or from "surface properties" to "principles." See (Carey and Gelman 1991) (Rehder and Hastie 2004).

364. [CogSci] (Barsalou 1983).

365. [Computing] Consider what happens if two businesses model the concept of "address" in a customer database with different granularity. One may have a coarse "Address" field in the database, which stores a street address, city, state, and Zip code all in one block, while the other stores the components "StreetAddress," "City," and "PostalCode" In separate fields. The more granular model can be automatically transformed into the less granular one, but not vice versa (Glushko and McGrath 2005).

366. [CogSci] (Rosch 1999) calls this the principle of cognitive economy, that "what one wishes to gain from one's categories is a great deal of information about the environment while conserving finite resources as much as possible. [...] It is to the organism's advantage not to differentiate one stimulus from another when that differentiation is irrelevant to the purposes at hand." (Pages 3-4.)

367. [Linguistics] For example, some linguists think of "English" as a broad category encompassing multiple languages or dialects, such as "Standard British English," "Standard American English," and "AppalachianEnglish."

368. [CogSci] Even though they are not classical categories, we might also model goal-derived categories as decision trees by ordering the decisions to ensure that any sub-goals are satisfied according to their priority. We could understand the category "Things to take from a burning house" by first asking the question "Are there living things in the house?" because that might be the most important sub-goal. If the answer to that question is "yes," we might proceed along a different path than if the answer is "no." Similarly, we might put a higher priority on things that cannot be replaced (Grandma's photos) than those that can (passport).

369. [CogSci] Institutional uses of decision trees can also sometimes be thought of as models of goal-derived categories. For example, the US Department of Health and Human Services (HHS) uses several decision trees as part of its efforts to ensure that research programs funded by the department do not harm human subjects. The chart *http://www.hhs.gov/ohrp/humansubjects/guid ance/decisioncharts.htm#c1* for example, is used to determine whether a program can be classified as research involving human subjects, which would mean that the program would have to be reviewed by an Institutional Review Board (IRB).

370. [Law] When the US Congress revised copyright law in 1976 it codified a "fair use" provision to allow for some limited uses of copyrighted works, but fair use in the digital era is vastly different today; website caching to improve performance and links that return thumbnail versions of images are fair uses that were not conceivable when the law was written. A law that precisely defined fair uses using contemporary technology would have quickly become obsolete, but one written more qualitatively to enable interpretation by the courts has remained viable. See (Samuelson 2009).

371. [Computing] For example, in a traditional relational database, each table contains a field, or combination of fields, known as a primary key, which is used to define and restrict membership in the table. A table of email messages in a database might define an email message as a unique combination of sender address, recipient address, and date/time when the message was sent, by enforcing a primary key on a combination of these fields. Similar to category membership based on a single, monothetic set of properties, membership in this email message table is based on a single set of required criteria. An item without a recipient address cannot be admitted to the table. In categorization terms, the item is not a member of the "email message" class because it does not have all the properties necessary for membership.

372. [Computing] Like *data schemas*, programming classes specify and enforce rules in the construction and manipulation of data. However, programming classes, like other implementations that are characterized by specificity and rule enforcement, can vary widely in the degree to which rules are specified and enforced. While some class definitions are very rigid, others are more flexible. Some languages have abstract types that have no instances but serve to provide a common ancestor for specific implemented types.

373. [CogSci] The existence of chapters might suggest that an item is a novel; however, a lack of chapters need not automatically indicate that an item is not a novel. Some novels are hypertexts that encourage readers to take alternative paths. Many of the writings by James Joyce and Samuel Beckett are "stream of consciousness" works that lack a coherent plot, yet they are widely regarded as novels.

374. [Computing] Some approaches represent each item as a vector of property values; documents are usually represented as vectors of frequency-weighted terms; in either case the items can be represented as points in a multidimensional space of these properties. Similarity can then be calculated by measuring the distance between items in this space. A popular text on *machine learning* is (Witten, Frank, and Hall 2011).

Other approaches start more directly with the similarity measure, obtained either by direct judgments of the similarity of each pair of items or by indirect measures like the accuracy in deciding whether two sounds, colors, or images are the same or different. The assumption is that the confusability of two items reflects how similar they are.

375. [Computing] Unlike hierarchical clustering methods that have a clear stopping rule when they create the root category, k-means clustering methods run until the centroids of the categorize stabilize. Furthermore, because the k-means algorithm is basically just hill-climbing, and the initial category "seed" items are random, it can easily get stuck in a local optimum. So it is desirable to try many different starting configurations for different choices of K.

Chapter 7
Classification: Assigning Resources to Categories

Robert J. Glushko
Jess Hemerly
Vivien Petras
Michael Manoochehri
Longhao Wang

7.1 Introduction

Classification, the systematic assignment of resources to intentional categories, is the focus of this chapter. In Chapter 6, *"Categorization: Describing Resource Classes and Types"*, we described categories as cognitive and linguistic models for applying prior knowledge and we discussed a set of principles for creating categories and category systems. We explained how cultural categories serve as the foundations upon which individual and institutional categories are based. Institutional categories are most often created in abstract and information-intensive domains where unambiguous and precise categories enable *classification* to be purposeful and principled.

A system of categories and its attendant rules or access methods are typically called a ***classification scheme*** or just the ***classifications***. A system of categories captures the distinctions and relationships among its resources that are most important in a domain and for a particular context of use, creating a reference model or conceptual roadmap for its users. This classification creates the structure and support for the interactions that human or computational agents perform. For example, research libraries and bookstores do not use the same classifications to organize books, but the categories they each use are appropriate for their contrasting types of collections and the different kinds of browsing and searching activities that take place in each context. Likewise, the scientific classifications for animals used by biologists contrast with those used in pet stores because the latter have no need for the precise differentiation enabled by the former.

Most of the chapter is a survey of topics that span the broad range of how classifications are used in organizing systems. These include enumerative classification, faceted classification, activity-based classification, and computational classification. Because classification and standardization are closely related, we also analyze standards and standards making as they apply to organizing systems. Throughout, we observe how personal, institutional, cultural, linguistic, political, religious and even artistic biases can affect otherwise principled and purposeful classification schemes.

7.1.1 Classification vs. Categorization

Classification requires a system of categories, so not everyone distinguishes classification from categorization. Batley, for example, says classification is "imposing some sort of structure on our understanding of our environment," a vague definition that applies equally well to categorization.[376]

In the discipline of organizing, the definition of classification is narrower and more formal. The contrasts among cultural, individual, and institutional categories in §6.2, "The What and Why of Categories" (page 237) yield a precise definition of **classification: The systematic assignment of resources to a system of intentional categories, often institutional ones.** This definition highlights the intentionality behind the system of categories, the systematic processes for using them, and implies the greater requirements for *governance* and *maintenance* that are absent for cultural categories and most individual ones.

7.1.2 Classification vs. Tagging

Precise and reliable classification is possible when the shared properties of a collection of resources are used in a principled and systematic manner. This method of classification is essential to satisfy institutional and commercial purposes. However, this degree of rigor might be excessive for personal classifications and for classifications of resources in social or informal contexts.

Instead, a weaker approach to organizing resources is to use any property of a resource and any vocabulary to describe it, regardless of how well it differentiates it from other resources to create a system of categories. This method of organizing resources is most often called **tagging** (§4.2.2.3), but it has also been called *social classification.*[377] Tagging is often used in personal organizing systems, but is social when it serves goals to convey information, develop a community, or manage reputation. Regardless of its name, however, tagging is popular for organizing and rating photos, websites, email messages, or other web-based resources or web-based descriptions of physical resources like stores and restaurants.

The distinction between classification and tagging was blurred when Thomas Vander Wal coined the term "folksonomy" —combining "folk" and "taxonomy" (which is a classification; see §5.3.1.1, "Inclusion" (page 194)) —to describe the collection of tags for a particular web site or application.[378] Folksonomies are often displayed in the form of a *tag cloud,* where the frequency with which the tag is used throughout the site determines the size of the text in the tag cloud. The tag cloud emerges through the bottom-up aggregation of user tags and is a statistical construct, rather than a semantic one.[379]

Tagging seems insufficiently principled to be considered classification. Tagging a photo as "red" or "car" is an act of resource description, not classification, because the other tags that would serve as the alternative classifications are unspecified. Furthermore, when tagging principles are followed at all, they are likely to be idiosyncratic ones that were not pre-determined or arrived at through an analysis of goals and requirements.

Noticeably, some uses of tags treat them as category labels, turning tagging into classification. Many websites and resources encourage users to assign "Like" or "+1" tags to them, and because these tags are pre-defined, they are category choices in an implied classification system; for example, we can consider "Like" as an alternative to a "Not liked enough" category.

When users or communities establish sets of principles to govern their tagging practices, tagging is even more like classification. Such a tagging system can be called a *tagsonomy*, a neologism we have invented to describe more systematic tagging. For example, a tagsonomy could predetermine tags as categories to be assigned to particular contents of a blog post, or specify the level of abstraction and granularity for assigning tags without predetermining them (§6.4, "Category Design Issues and Implications" (page 255)). Some people use multiple user accounts for the same application to establish distinct personas or contexts (e.g., personal vs. business photo collections) as a way to make their tagsonomies more distinct.

Making these decisions about tagging content and form and applying them in the tagging process transforms an *ad hoc* set of tags into a principled tagsonomy. When tagging is introduced in a business setting, more pragmatic purposes and more systematic tagging—for example, by using tags from lists of departments or products—also tends to create tagsonomic classification.[380]

7.1.3 Classification vs. Physical Arrangement

We have often stressed the principle in the discipline of organizing that logical issues must be separated from implementation issues (see §1.2.3.1, "The Concept of "Organizing Principle"" (page 12), §4.3.5, "Designing the Description Form" (page 167), and §5.7, "The Implementation Perspective " (page 219)). With classification we separate the conceptual act of assigning a resource to a category from the subsequent but often incidental act of putting it in some physical or digital storage location. This focus on the logical essence of classification is elegantly expressed in a definition by Gruenberg: **Classification** is "a higher order thinking skill requiring the fusion of the naturalist's eye for relationships...with the logician's desire for structured order...the mathematician's compulsion to achieve consistent, predictable results...and the linguist's interest in explicit and tacit expressions of meaning."[381]

Taking a conceptual or cognitive perspective on classification contrasts with much conventional usage in library science, where classification is mostly associated with arranging tangible items on shelves, emphasizing the "parking" function that realizes the "marking" function of identifying the category to which the resource belongs.[382]

From a library science or collection curation perspective, it seems undeniable that when the resources being classified are physical or tangible things such as books, paintings, animals, or cooking pots, the end result of the classification activity is that some resource has been placed in some physical location. Moreover, the placement of physical resources can be influenced by the physical context in which they are organized. Once placed, the physical context often embodies some aspects of the organization when similar or related resources are arranged in nearby locations. In libraries and bookstores, this adjacency facilitates the serendipitous discovery of resources, as anyone well knows who has found an interesting book by browsing the shelves.

It might seem natural to identify storage locations with the classes used by the classification system. Just as we might think of a location in the zoo as the "lion habitat," we can put a "QC" sign on a particular row of shelves in a library where books about physics are arranged.

However, once we broaden the scope of organizing to include digital resources, it is clear that we rely on their logical classifications when we interact with them, not whether they reside on a computer in Berkeley or Bangalore. It is better to emphasize that a classification system is foremost a specification for the logical arrangement of resources because there are usually many possible and often arbitrary mappings of logical references to physical locations.

7.1.4 Classification Schemes

A classification scheme is a realization of one or more organizing principles. Physical resources are often classified according to their tangible or perceivable properties. As we discussed in §6.3.2, "Single Properties" (page 245) and §6.3.3, "Multiple Properties" (page 247), when properties take on only a small set of discrete values, a classification system naturally emerges in which each category is defined by one property value or some particular combination of property values. Classification schemes in which all possible categories to which resources can be assigned are defined explicitly are **enumerative**. For example, the enumerative classification for a personal collection of music recorded on physical media might have categories for CDs, DVDs, vinyl albums, 8-track cartridges, reel-to-reel tape and tape cassettes; every music resource fits into one and only one of these categories.

When multiple resource properties are considered in a fixed sequence, each property creates another level in the system of categories and the classification scheme is *hierarchical* or **taxonomic**. (See §5.3.1.1, "Inclusion" (page 194).) In §6.3.3.1, "Multi-Level or Hierarchical Categories" (page 247) we described a hierarchical scheme for organizing shirts in a clothes closet that arranges the shirts by style, and then by sleeve length, and finally by color; an example of the fine-grained categories at the lowest level in this classification is "white long-sleeved dress shirts."

For information resources, their "aboutness" is usually more important than their physical properties. For example, a professor planning a new course might organize candidate articles for the syllabus in a fixed set of categories, one for each potential lecture topic. It can be challenging to enumerate all the subjects or topics that a collection of resources might be about. The Library of Congress Classification (LCC) is a hierarchical and enumerative scheme with a very detailed set of subject categories because books can be about almost anything. We discuss the LCC more in §7.3, "Bibliographic Classification" (page 289).

In addition to or instead of their "aboutness," information resources are sometimes organized using intrinsic properties like author names or creation dates. Our professor might primarily organize his collection of articles by author name, and when he plans a new course, he might put those he selects for the syllabus into a classification system with one category for every scheduled lecture.

Because names and dates can take on a great many values, an organizing principle like *alphabetical* or *chronological* ordering is unlikely to enumerate in advance an explicit category for each possible value. Instead, we can consider these organizing principles as creating an **implicit or latent** classification system in which the categories are generated only as needed. For example, the Q category only exists in an alphabetical scheme if there is a resource whose name starts with Q.

Many resource domains have multiple properties that might be used to define a classification scheme. For example, wine can be classified by type of grape (varietal), color, flavor, price, winemaker, region of origin (appellation), blending style, and other properties. Furthermore, people differ in their knowledge or preferences about these properties; some people choose wine based on its price and varietal, while others studiously compare winemakers and appellations. Each order of considering the properties creates a different hierarchical classification, and using all of them would create a very deep and unwieldy system. Moreover, many different hierarchies might be required to satisfy divergent preferences. An alternative classification scheme for domains like these is **faceted** classification, a type of classification system that takes a set of resource properties and then generates only those categories for combinations that actually occur.

In library science a classification system that builds categories by combination of facets is sometimes also called ***analytico-synthetic***. The most common types of facets are enumerative (mutually exclusive); Boolean (yes or no); hierarchical or taxonomic (logical containment); and spectrum (a range of numerical values). We discuss *faceted classification* in detail in §7.4, "Faceted Classification" (page 293) because it is very frequently used in online classifications. Faceted schemes enable easier search and browsing of large resource collections like those for retail sites and museums than hierarchical enumerative schemes.

The *Dewey Decimal Classification (DDC)* is a highly enumerative classification system that also uses faceted properties; we will discuss it more in §7.3, "Bibliographic Classification" (page 289).

7.1.5 Classification and Standardization

Classifications impose order on resources. Standards do the same by making distinctions, either implicitly or explicitly, between "standard" and "nonstandard" ways of creating, organizing, and using resources. Classification and standardization are not identical, but they are closely related. Some classifications become standards, and some standards define new classifications.

Institutional categories (§6.2.3) are of two broad types.

7.1.5.1 Institutional Taxonomies

Institutional taxonomies are classifications designed to make it more likely that people or computational agents will organize and interact with resources in the same way. Among the thousands of standards published by the *International Organization for Standardization (ISO)* are many institutional taxonomies that govern the classification of resources and products in agriculture, aviation, construction, energy, healthcare, information technology, transportation, and almost every other industry sector.[383]

Institutional taxonomies are especially important in libraries and knowledge management. The Dewey Decimal Classification (DDC) and Library of Congress Classification (LCC) enable different libraries to arrange books in the same categories, and the *Diagnostic and Statistical Manual of Mental Disorders* (DSM) in clinical psychology enables different doctors to assign patients to the same diagnostic and insurance categories.[384]

7.1.5.2 Institutional Semantics

Systems of ***institutional semantics*** offer precisely defined abstractions or information components (§3.3.3, "Identity and Information Components" (page 111)) needed to ensure that information can be efficiently exchanged and used. Organizing systems that use different information models often cannot share and combine information without tedious negotiation and excessive rework.

Automating transactions with suppliers and customers in a supply chain requires that all the parties use the same data format or formats that can be transformed to be interoperable. Retrofitting or replacing these applications to enable efficient interoperability is often possible, and it is usually desirable for the firm to develop or adopt enterprise standards for information exchange models rather than pay the recurring transaction costs to integrate or transform incompatible formats.

An example of a system of institutional semantics is the Universal Business Language (UBL) a library of about 2000 semantic "building blocks" for common concepts like "Address," "Item," "Payment," and "Party" along with nearly 100 document types assembled from the standard components. UBL is widely used to facilitate the automated exchange of transactional documents in procurement, logistics, inventory management, collaborative planning and forecasting, and payment.[385]

Standard semantics are especially important in industries or markets that have significant network effects where the value of a product depends on the number of interoperable or compatible products—these include much of the information and service economies.

7.1.5.3 Specifications vs. Standards

Implementing an organizing system of significant scope and complexity in a robust and maintainable fashion requires precise descriptions of the resources it contains, their formats, the classes, relations, structures and collections in which they participate, and the processes that ensure their efficient and effective use. Rigorous descriptions like these are often called "specifications" and there are well-established practices for developing good ones.

There is a subtle but critical distinction between "specifications" and "standards." Any person, firm, or *ad hoc* group of people or firms can create a specification and then use it or attempt to get others to use it.[386] In contrast, a standard is a published specification that is developed and maintained by consensus of all the relevant stakeholders in some domain by following a defined and transparent process, usually under the auspices of a recognized standards organization.[387] In addition, implementations of standards often are subject to conformance tests that establish the completeness and accuracy of the implementation. This means that users can decide either to implement the specification themselves or choose from other conforming implementations.

The additional rigor and transparency when specifications are developed and maintained through a standards process often makes them fairer and gives them more legitimacy. Governments often require or recommend these *de jure* standards, especially those that are "open" or "royalty free" because they are typically supported by multiple vendors, minimizing the cost of adoption and maximizing their longevity. For example, work on UBL has gone on for over a decade in a technical committee under the auspices of a standards development consortium called the Organization for the Advancement of Structured Information Standards (OASIS), which has developed scores of standards for web services and information-intensive industries.

Despite these important distinctions between "specifications" and "standards," however, in conventional usage "standard" is often simply a synonym for "dominant or widely-adopted specification." These *de facto* standards, in contrast with the *de jure* standards created by standards organizations, are typically created by the dominant firm or firms in an industry, by a new firm that is first to use a new technology or innovative method, or by a non-profit entity like a foundation that focuses on a particular domain.[388] *De facto* standards and *ad hoc* standards often co-exist and compete in "standards wars," especially in information-intensive domains and industries with rapid innovation.[389]

For example, the Dewey Decimal Classification (DDC) is the world's most widely used library classification system, and most people treat it as a standard. In fact, the DDC is proprietary and it is maintained and licensed for use by the Online Computer Library Center (OCLC). Similarly, the DSM is maintained and published by the American Psychiatric Association (APA) and it earns the APA many millions of dollars a year.

In contrast, *de jure* standards include the Library of Congress Classification (LCC), developed under the auspices of the US government, the familiar MARC record format used in online library catalogs (ISO 2709), and its American counterpart ANSI Z39.2.[390]

As a result, even though it would be technically correct to argue that "while all standards are specifications, not all specifications are standards," this distinction is hard to maintain in practice.

7.1.5.4 Mandated Classifications

Standards are often imposed by governments to protect the interests of their citizens by coordinating or facilitating activities that might otherwise not be possible or safe. Some of them primarily concern public or product safety and are only tangentially relevant to systems for organizing information. Others are highly relevant, especially those that specify the formats and content of information exchange; many European governments require firms doing business with the government to adopt UBL.[391]

Other government standards that are important in organizing systems are those that express requirements for classification and retention of auditing information for financial activities, such as the *Sarbanes-Oxley Act*, or for non-retention of personal information, such as HIPAA and FERPA.[392]

7.2 Understanding Classification

Classifications arrange resources to support discovery, selection, combination, integration, analysis, and other purposeful activity in every organizing system. A classification of diseases facilitates diagnosis and development of medical procedures, as well as accounting and billing. In addition, classifications facilitate understanding of a domain by highlighting the important resources and relationships in it, supporting the training of people who work in the domain and their acquisition of specialized skills for it.

In the discipline of organizing we consider classification to be systematic when it follows principles that govern the structure of categories and their relationships. However, being systematic and principled does not necessarily ensure that a classification will be unbiased or satisfy all users' requirements. For example, the zoning, environmental, economic development, and political district classifications that overlay different parts of a city determine the present and future allocation of services and resources, and over time influence whether the city thrives or decays. These classifications reflect tradeoffs and negotiations among numerous participants, including businesses, lobbyists, incumbent politicians, donors to political parties, real estate developers, and others with strong self-interests.

7.2.1 Classification Is Purposeful

Categories often arise naturally, but by definition classifications do not because they are systems of categories that have been intentionally designed for some purpose. Every classification brings together resources that go together, and in doing so differentiates among them. However, bringing resources together would be pointless without reasons for finding, accessing, and interacting with them later.

7.2.1.1 Classifications Are Reference Models

A classification creates a semantic or conceptual roadmap to a domain by highlighting the properties and relationships that distinguish the resources in it. This reference model facilitates learning, comprehension, and use of organizing systems within the domain. Standard classifications like those used in libraries enable people to rely on one system that they can use to locate resources in many libraries. Standard business, job, and product classifications enable the reliable collection, analysis, and interchange of economic data and resources.[393]

7.2.1.2 Classifications Support Interactions

A classification creates structure in the organizing system that increases the variety and capability of the interactions it can support. With physical resources, classification increases useful co-location; in kitchens, for example, keeping resources that are used together near each other (e.g. baking ingredients) makes cooking and cleanup more efficient (see "activity-based" classification in §7.5).

Classification makes systems more usable when it is manifested in the arrangement of resource descriptions or controls in user interface components like list boxes, tabs, buttons, function menus, and structured lists of search results.[394]

A typical mapping between the logic of a classification scheme and a user interface is illustrated in Figure 7.1, "Classification and Interactions."

How a business classifies its product or service strongly influences whether a customer can find it; this is the essential task of marketing.The business of "search engine optimization" exists to help a firm with a web presence choose the categories and descriptive terms that will improve its ranking in search results and attract the number of types of customer it desires.[395] How a customer interacts with a supplier is influenced by how the supplier classifies its offerings in its shopping aisles or catalogs; the "science of shopping" uses creative classifications and co-location of goods to shape browsing behavior and encourage impulse buying.[396] In business-to-business contexts, standard classifications for

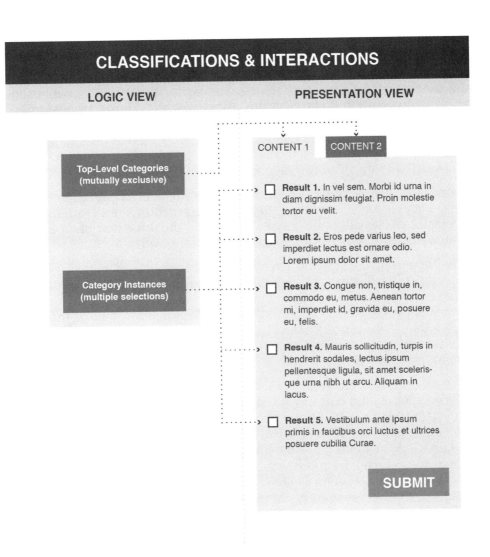

Figure 7.1. Classification and Interactions.

business processes and their application interfaces enable firms to more easily build and maintain supply chains and distribution networks that interconnect many business partners.[397]

7.2.2 Classification Is Principled

§6.3, "Principles for Creating Categories" (page 244) explained principles for creating categories, including enumeration, single properties, multiple properties and hierarchy, family resemblance, similarity, theory and goal-based categorization. It logically follows that the principles considered in designing categories are embodied in classifications that use those categories. However, when we say, "classification is principled," we are going further to say that the processes of assigning resources to categories and maintaining the classification scheme over time must also follow principles.

The design and use of a classification system involves many choices about its purposes, scope, scale, intended lifetime, extensibility, and other considerations. Principled classification means that once those design choices are made they should be systematically and consistently followed.

Principled does not necessarily equate to "good," because many of the choices can be arbitrary and others may involve tradeoffs that depend on the nature of the resources, the purposes of the classification, the amount of effort available, and the capabilities of the people doing the classification and of the people using it (see §6.4, "Category Design Issues and Implications" (page 255)). Every classification system is biased in one way or another (see §7.3, "Bibliographic Classification" (page 289)).

Consider the classifications of resources in a highly-organized kitchen. Tableware (forks, spoons and cutlery) is usually kept together in a single drawer, separated by utensil type with a flatware organizer. Dishes are stacked on a cabinet shelf. Pots and pans are nested to save space, spices are alphabetized in a spice rack, items used for baking are on the same shelf, and coffee is next to the coffee maker. Items used frequently may be in more accessible areas—on top in drawers, lower cabinets, and shelves—than items used infrequently, which end up on high shelves or pushed to the back of cabinets. This classification system is not documented with a written specification and the person who created and uses it did not study principles of kitchen classification in school, but when she cleans up the kitchen after making a meal, everything goes back where it came from, making it easy to find necessary resources the next time she cooks. Other people might have different classifications of kitchen resources, and some people might use much simpler classification schemes because they do not cook often and do not mind rummaging around to find what they need when they do.

On the other hand, complex institutional classification systems like those used in libraries or government agencies are implemented with detailed specifications, methods, and guidelines. The people who apply them probably did study them in school or received extensive on-the-job training to ensure they apply them correctly and consistently.

7.2.2.1 Principles Embodied in the Classification Scheme

Some of the most important principles that lead us to say that classification is principled are those that guide the design of the classification scheme in the first place. These principles are fundamental in the discipline of library science but they apply more broadly to other domains.

The *warrant* principle concerns the justification for the choice of categories and the names given to them. The principle of **literary warrant** holds that a classification must be based only on the specific resources that are being classified. In the library context, this *ad hoc* principle that builds a classification from a particular collection principle is often posed in opposition to a more philosophical or epistemological perspective, first articulated by Francis Bacon in the seventeenth century, that a classification should be universal and must handle all knowledge and all possible resources.[398] The principle of **scientific warrant** argues that only the categories recognized by the scientists or experts in a domain should be used in a classification system, and it is often opposed by the principle of **user** or **use warrant**, which chooses categories and descriptive terms according to their frequency of use by everyone, not just experts.[399] With classifications of physical resources like those in a kitchen, we see **object warrant**,

together, but more frequently the justifying princi-
int, where resources are organized based on how

l in a classification scheme concerns the breadth
erarchy. We discussed this in §6.4, "Category De-
(page 255) but in the context of classification this
ications and is framed as the extent to which the
.3, "Classification vs. Physical Arrangement" (page
broadly or precisely depends largely on the varie-
sources that the system of categories has been de-
of the diversity of resources for a sale in a depart-
ation is necessary to accommodate everything in
l be grouped together in a few aisles on a single
store or a wholesale kitchen supply store for res-
more precisely because of the restricted resource
tise of those who want to buy things there. An en-
d just to knives, organized by knife type, manufac-
er categories that are not used in the kitchen sec-
00

ness of a classification scheme increases the simi-
signed to the same category and sharpens the dis-
in different categories. However, when different
ned, mismatches in their precision or granularity

can create challenges (see §9.3, "Organizing Resources for Interactions" (page 372)).

7.2.2.2 Principles for Assigning Resources to Categories

The **uniqueness principle** means the categories in a classification scheme are mutually exclusive. Thus, when a logical concept is assigned to a particular category, it cannot simultaneously be assigned to another category. Resources, however, can be assigned several categories if they embody several concepts represented by those different categories. This can present a challenge when a physical storage solution is based on storing resources according to its assigned category in a logical classification system. This is not a serious problem for resource types like technical equipment or tools, for which the properties used to classify them are highly salient, and that have very narrow and predictable contexts of use. It is also not a problem for highly-specialized information resources like scientific research reports or government economic data, which might end up in only one specialized class. However, many resources are inherently more difficult to classify because they have less salient properties or because they have many more possible uses.

We face this kind of problem all the time. For example, should we store a pair of scissors in the kitchen or in the office? One solution is to buy a second pair of scissors so that scissors can be kept in both locations where they are typically used, but this is not practical for many types of resources and this principle would be difficult to apply in a systematic manner.

Many books are about multiple subjects. A self-help book about coping with change in a business setting might reasonably be classified as either about applied psychology or about business. It is not helpful that book titles are often poor clues to their content; *Who Moved My Cheese?* is in fact a self-help book about coping with change in a business setting. Its Library of Congress Classification is BF 637, "Applied Psychology," and at UC Berkeley it is kept in the business school library.

The general solution to satisfying the *uniqueness principle* in library classifications when resources do not clearly fit in a single category is to invent and follow a detailed set of often arbitrary rules. Usually, the primary subject of the book is used for assigning a category, which will then determine the book's place on a shelf. However, a rule might also state that if a book treats two subjects equally, the subject that is covered first determines the classification. For some classifications a "table of preference" can trump other rules at the last minute. Not surprisingly, the rules for categorizing books take a long time to learn and are not always easy to apply.[401]

7.2.2.3 Principles for Maintaining the Classification over Time

The classification schemes in your kitchen or closet are deconstructed and disappear when you move and take your possessions to a different house or apartment. Your efforts to re-implement the classifications will be influenced by the configuration of shelves and cabinets in your new residence, so they will not be exactly the same. Most personal classifications are created in response to a specific situation to solve an emerging organizational challenge. As a consequence, personal classification systems change in an *ad hoc* or opportunistic manner during their limited lifetimes.

In contrast, the institutional classification schemes for many library resources, culturally or scientifically-important artifacts, and much of the information created or collected by businesses, governments and researchers might have useful lives of decades or centuries. Classification systems like these can only be changed incrementally to avoid disruption of the work flows of the organization. We described maintaining resources as an activity in all organizing systems (§2.5, "Maintaining Resources" (page 68)) and the issues of persistence, effectivity, authenticity, and provenance that emerge with resources over time (§3.5, "Resources over Time" (page 123)). Much of this previous discussion applies in a straightforward manner to maintaining classifications over time.

However, some additional issues arise with classifications over time. The most important one is that the meaning of an underlying category can change, along with its relative and absolute importance with respect to the other categories in the classification system. Categories sometimes change slowly, but they can also change quickly and radically as a result of technological, process, or geopolitical innovation or events. Entirely new types of resources and bodies of knowledge can appear in a short time. Consider what the categories of "travel," "entertainment," "computing," and "communication" mean today compared to just a decade or two ago.

Changes in the meaning of the categories in a classification threaten its ***integrity***, the principle that categories should not move within the structure of the classification system.[402] One way to maintain integrity while adapting to the dynamic and changing nature of knowledge is to define a new version of a classification system while allowing earlier ones to persist, which preserves resource assignments in the previous version of the classification system while allowing it to change in the new one. If we adopt a logical perspective on classification (§7.1.2, "Classification vs. Tagging" (page 274)) that dissociates the conceptual assignment of resources to categories from their physical arrangement, there is no reason why a resource cannot have contrasting category assignments in different versions of a classification.

However, the conventional library with collections of physical resources cannot easily abandon its requirement to use a classification to arrange books on shelves in specific places so they can be located, checked out, and returned to the same location. This constraint does not preclude the versioning of library classifications, but it increases the inertia and limits the degree of change when revisions are made because of the cost and coordination considerations of rearranging books in all the world's libraries.

A related principle about maintaining classifications over time is **flexibility**, the degree to which the classification can accommodate new categories. Computer scientists typically describe this principle as **extensibility**, and library scientists sometimes describe it as **hospitality**. In any case the concern is the same and we are all familiar with it. When you buy a bookshelf, clothes wardrobe, file cabinet, or computer, it makes sense to buy one that has some extra space to accommodate the books, clothes, or files you will acquire over some future timeframe. As with other choices that need to be made about organizing systems, how much extra space and "organizing room" you will acquire involves numerous tradeoffs.

Classification schemes can increase their flexibility by creating extra "logical space" when they are defined. Library classifications accomplish this by using naming or numbering schemes for classification that can be extended easily to create new subcategories.[403] Classification schemes in information systems can also anticipate the evolution of document or database schemas.[404]

7.2.3 Classification Is Biased

The discipline of organizing is fundamentally about choices of properties and principles for describing and arranging resources. We discussed choices about describing resources in §4.3, "The Process of Describing Resources" (page 148), choices for creating resource categories in §6.3, "Principles for Creating Categories" (page 244), and choices for creating classifications in this chapter. The choices made reflect the purposes, experiences, professions, politics, values, and other characteristics and preferences of the people making them. As a result, every system of classification is biased because it takes a point of view that is a composite of all of these influences.

This claim might seem surprising, because many classification systems are formal and institutional, created by governments or firms participating in standards organizations. We expect these classifications to be impartial and objective.

Consider the classification of people as "employed" or "unemployed." Many people think that any employable person who is not currently employed would be counted as unemployed. But the US government's Department of Labor only counts someone as unemployed if they have actively looked for work in the past month, effectively removing anyone who has given up on finding work from the unemployed category by assigning them to a "discouraged worker" category. In 2012 this classification scheme allowed the government to report that unemployment was about 8% and falling, when in fact it was closer to 20% and rising. The political implications of this classification are substantial.[405]

Bowker and Star have written extensively about biases in classification systems but acknowledge that many people do not see them:

Information scientists work every day on the design, delegation and choice of classification systems and standards, yet few see them as artifacts embodying moral and aesthetic choices that in turn craft people's identities, aspirations and dignity.[406]

Bowker and Star describe many examples where seemingly neutral and benign classifications implement controversial assumptions. A striking example is found in the ethnic classifications of the United States Census and the categories to which US residents are required to assign themselves. These categories have changed nearly every decade since the first census in 1790 and strongly reflect political goals, prevailing cultural sensitivities or lack thereof, and non-scientific considerations. Some recent changes included a "multi-racial" category, which some people viewed as empowering, but which was attacked by African-American and Hispanic civil rights groups as diluting their power.[407]

A more positive way to think about bias in classification is that the choices made in an organizing system about resource selection, description, and arrangement come together to convey the values of the organizers. This makes a classification a rhetorical or communicative vehicle for establishing credibility and trust with those who interact with the resources in the classification. Seen in this light, an objective or neutral classification is not just hard to achieve, but also somewhat undesirable because it gives up the opportunity to interpret the resources in some creative way. Melanie Feinberg makes the point that "fair trade" or "green" supermarkets differentiate themselves by a relatively small proportion of the goods they offer compared with ordinary stores, but these particular items signal the values that their customers care most about.[408]

Bias is clearly evident in the most widely used bibliographic classifications, the Library of Congress and the Dewey Decimal, which we discuss in the next section.

7.3 Bibliographic Classification

Much of our thinking about classification comes from the bibliographic domain. Libraries and the classification systems for the resources they contain have been evolving for millennia.[409] We will briefly describe the most important systems for bibliographic classification, especially the Dewey Decimal Classification (DDC) and *Library of Congress Classification (LCC)* systems. However, there are several important ways in which bibliographic classification is distinctive and we will discuss those first:

- Scale, Complexity, and Degree of Standardization: Department stores and supermarkets typically offer tens of thousands of different items (as measured by the number of "stock keeping units" or SKUs), and popular online commerce sites like Amazon.com and eBay are of similar scale. However, the standard product classification system for supermarkets has only about 300 categories.[410] The classifications for online stores are typically deeper than those for physical stores, but they are highly idiosyncratic and nonstandard. In contrast, scores of university libraries have five million or more distinct items in their collections, and they almost all use the same standard bibliographic classification system that has about 300,000 distinct categories.[411]

- Legacy of Physical Arrangement, User Access, and Re-Shelving. A corollary to the previous one that distinguishes bibliographic classification systems is that they have long been shaped and continue to be shaped by the legacy of physical arrangement, user access to the storage locations, and re-shelving that they support. These requirements constrain the evolution and extensibility of bibliographic classifications, making them less able to keep pace with changing concepts and new bodies of knowledge. Amazon classifies the products it sells in huge warehouses, but its customers do not have to pick out their purchases there, and most goods never return to the warehouse. Amazon can add new product categories and manage the resources in warehouses far more easily than libraries can.

With digital libraries, constraints of scale and physical arrangement are substantially eliminated, because the storage location is hidden from the user and the resources do not need to be returned and re-shelved. However, when users can search the entire content of the library, as they have learned to expect from the web, they are less likely to use the bibliographic classification systems that have painstakingly been applied to the library's resources.

7.3.1 The Dewey Decimal Classification

The Dewey Decimal Classification (DDC) is the world's most widely used bibliographic system, applied to books in over 200,000 libraries in 135 countries. It is a proprietary and *de facto* standard, and it must be licensed for use from the Online Computer Library Center (OCLC).[412] In 1876, Melvil Dewey invented the DDC when he was hired to manage the Amherst College library immediately after graduating. Dewey was inspired by Bacon's attempt to create a universal classification for all knowledge and considered the DDC as a numerical overlay on Bacon with 10 main classes, each divided into 10 more, and so on. Despite

```
200 Religion
  210 Natural Theology
  220 Bible
  230 Christian theology
  240 Christian moral and devotional theology
  250 Christian orders and local church
  260 Christian social theology
  270 Christian church history
  280 Christian sects and denominations
  290 Other religions
```

Figure 7.2. "Religion" in Dewey Decimal Classification.

his explicit rejection of literary warrant, however, Dewey's classification was strongly influenced by the existing Amherst collection, which reflected Amherst's focus on the time on the "education of indigent young men of piety and talents for the Christian ministry."[413]

The resulting nineteenth century Western bias in the DDC's classification of religion seems almost startling today, where it persists in the 23rd revision (see Figure 7.2, ""Religion" in Dewey Decimal Classification."). "Religion" is one of the 10 main classes, the 200 class, with nine subclasses, Six of these nine subclasses are topics with "Christian" in the name; one class is for the *Bible* alone; and another section is entitled "Natural theology." Everything else related to the world's many religions is lumped under 290, "Other religions."

The notational simplicity of a decimal system makes the DDC easy to use and easy to subdivide existing categories, So-called subdivision tables allow facets for language, geography or format to be added to many classes, making the classification more specific. But the overall system is not very hospitable to new areas of knowledge.

7.3.2 The Library of Congress Classification

The US Library of Congress is the largest library in the world today, but it got off to a bad start after being established in 1800. In 1814, during the War of 1812, British troops burned down the US Capitol building where the library was located and the 3000 books in the collection went up in flames.[414] The library was restarted a year later when Congress purchased the personal library of former president Thomas Jefferson, which was over twice the size of the collection that the British burned. Jefferson was a deeply intellectual person, and unlike the narrow historical and legal collection of the original library, Jefferson's library reflected his "comprehensive interests in philosophy, history, geography, science, and literature, as well as political and legal treatises."[415]

```
A -- GENERAL WORKS
B -- PHILOSOPHY. PSYCHOLOGY. RELIGION
C -- AUXILLARY SCIENCES OF HISTORY (GENERAL)
D -- WORLD HISTORY (EXCEPT AMERICAN HISTORY)
E -- HISTORY: AMERICA
F -- HISTORY: AMERICA
G -- GEOGRAPHY. ANTHROPOLOGY. RECREATION
H -- SOCIAL SCIENCE
J -- POLITICAL SCIENCE
K -- LAW
L -- EDUCATION
M -- MUSIC
N -- FINE ARTS
P -- LANGUAGE AND LITERATURE
Q -- SCIENCE
R -- MEDICINE
S -- AGRICULTURE
T -- TECHNOLOGY
U -- MILITARY SCIENCE
V -- NAVAL SCIENCE
Z -- BIBLIOGRAPHY. LIBRARY SCIENCE
```

Figure 7.3. Top Level Categories in the Library of Congress Classification.

Restarting the Library of Congress around Jefferson's personal collection and classification had an interesting implication. When Herbert Putnam formally created the Library of Congress Classification (LCC) in 1897, he meant it not as a way to organize all the world's knowledge, but to provide a practical way to organize and later locate items within the Library of Congress's collection. However, despite Putnam's commitment to literary warrant, the breadth of Jefferson's collection made the LCC more intellectually ambitious than it might otherwise had been, and probably contributed to its dominant adoption in university libraries.

The LCC has 21 top-level categories, identified by letters instead of using numbers like the DDC (see Figure 7.3, "Top Level Categories in the Library of Congress Classification."). Each top-level category is divided into about 10-20 subclasses, each of which is further subdivided. The complete LCC and supporting information takes up 41 printed volumes.

Bias is apparent in the LCC as it is in the DDC, but is somewhat more subtle. A library for the US emphasizes its own history. "Naval science" was vastly more important in the 1800s when it was given its own top level category, separated from other resources about "Military science" (which had a subclass for "Cavalry").[416]

The LCC is highly enumerative, and along with the uniqueness principle, this creates distortions over time and sometimes requires contortions to incorporate new disciplines.[417]

7.3.3 The BISAC Classification

A very different approach to bibliographic classification is represented in the *Book Industry Standards Advisory Committee classification (BISAC)*. BISAC is developed by the Book Industry Study Group (BISG), a non-profit industry association that "develops, maintains, and promotes standards and best practices that enable the book industry to conduct business more efficiently." The BISAC classification system is used by many of the major businesses within the North American book industry, including Amazon, Baker & Taylor, Barnes & Noble, Bookscan, Booksense, Bowker, Indigo, Ingram and most major publishers.[418]

The BISAC classifications are used by publishers to suggest to booksellers how a book should be classified in physical and online bookstores. Because of its commercial and consumer focus, BISAC follows a principle of use warrant, and its categories are biased toward common language usage and popular culture. Some top-level BISAC categories, including Law, Medicine, Music, and Philosophy, are also top-level categories in the LCC. However, BISAC also has top-level categories for Comics & Graphic Novels. Cooking, Juvenile Fiction, Pets, and True Crime.

The differences between BISAC and the LCC are understandable because they are used for completely different purposes and generally have little need to come into contact. But this changed in 2004, when Google began its ambitious project to digitize the majority of the world's books (See the Sidebar, "What Is a Library?" (page 21) in §1.3.1.2). Much to the dismay of many people in the library and academic community, Google initially classified books using BISAC rather than the LCC.[419]

In addition, some new public libraries have adopted BISAC rather than the DDC because they feel the former makes the library friendlier to its users. Some librarians believe that their online catalogs need to be more like web search engines, so a less precise classification that uses more familiar category terms seems like a good choice.[420]

7.4 Faceted Classification

We have noted several times that strictly enumerative classifications constrain how resources are assigned to categories and how the classification can evolve over time. **Faceted classifications** are an alternative that overcome some of these limitations. In a faceted classification system, each resource is described using properties from multiple facets, but an agent searching for resources does not need to consider all of the properties (and consequently the facets) and does not need to consider them in a fixed order, which an enumerative hierarchical classification requires. Faceted classifications are especially useful in web user interfaces for online shopping or for browsing a large and heterogeneous museum collection. The process of considering facets in any order and ignoring those that are not relevant implies a dynamic organizational structure that makes selection both flexible and efficient. We can best illustrate these advantages with a shopping example in a domain that we are familiar with from §6.3.3, "Multiple Properties" (page 247).

If a department store offers shirts in various styles, colors, sizes, brands, and prices, shoppers might want to search and sort through them using properties from these facets in any order. However, in a physical store, this is not possible because the shirts must be arranged in actual locations in the store, with dress shirts in one area, work shirts in another, and so on.

Assume that the shirt store has shirts in four styles: dress shirts, work shirts, party shirts, and athletic shirts. The dress shirts come in white and blue, the work shirts in white and brown, and the party and athletic shirts come in white, blue, brown, and red. White dress shirts come in large and medium sizes.

Suppose we are looking for a white dress shirt in a large size. We can think of this desired shirt in two equivalent ways, either as a member of a category of "large white dress shirts" or a shirt with "dress," "white," and "large" values on style, color, and size facets. Because of the way the shirts are arranged in the physical store, our search process has to follow a hierarchical structure of categories. We go to the dress shirt section, find the white shirts, and then look within the white shirts for a large one. This process corresponds to the hierarchy shown in Figure 7.4, "Enumerative Classification with Style Facet Followed by Color Facet."

Although unlikely, a store might choose to organize its shirts by color. In our search for a "white dress shirt in a large size," if we consider the color first, because shirts come in four colors, there are four color categories to choose from. When we choose the white shirts, there is no category for work shirts because there are no work shirts that come in white. We then choose the dress shirts, and then finally find the large one. (Figure 7.5, "Enumerative Classification with Color Facet Followed by Style Facet.")

This department store example shows that for a physical organization, one property facet guides the localization of resources; all other facets are subordinated under the primary organizing property. In hierarchical enumerative classifications, this means that the primary organizing facet determines the primary form of access. The shirts are either organized by style and then color, or by color then style, which enforces an inflexible query strategy (either first by style or first by color).

ENUMERATIVE CLASSIFICATION WITH FACETS

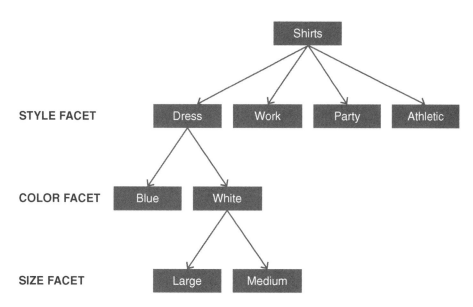

Figure 7.4. Enumerative Classification with Style Facet Followed by Color Facet.

In an online store, however, descriptions of the shirts are being searched and sorted instead of the real shirts, and different organizations are possible. When the shirts are described using a faceted classification system, we treat all facets independently, i.e. they can all be the primary facet.

We can enumerate all the properties needed to assign resources appropriately, but we create the categories (i.e. combination of properties from different facets) only if they are needed to sort resources with a particular combination of properties.

An additional aspect of the flexibility of faceted classification is that a facet can be left out of a resource description if it is not needed or appropriate. For example, because party shirts are often multi-colored with exotic patterns, it is not that useful to describe their color. Likewise, certain types of athletic shirts might be very loose-fitting, and as a result not be given a size description, but

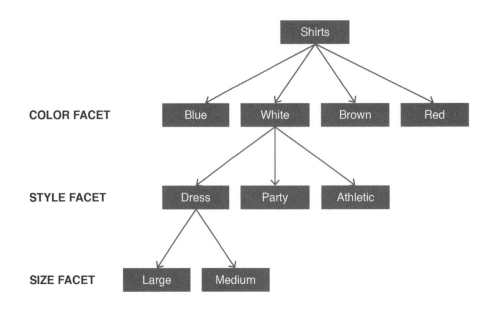

ENUMERATIVE CLASSIFICATION WITH FACETS

Figure 7.5. Enumerative Classification with Color Facet Followed by Style Facet.

their color is important because it is tied to a particular team. Figure 7.6, "Faceted Classification." shows how these two resource types can be classified with the faceted Shirt classification. Resource 1 describes a party shirt in medium; resource 2 describes an athletic shirt in blue without information about size.

A faceted classification scheme like that shown in Figure 7.6, "Faceted Classification." eliminates the requirement for predetermining a combination and or-

Figure 7.6. Faceted Classification.

dering of facets like those in Figure 7.4, "Enumerative Classification with Style Facet Followed by Color Facet." and Figure 7.5, "Enumerative Classification with Color Facet Followed by Style Facet." Instead, imagine a shirt store where you decide when you begin shopping which facets are important to you ("show me all the medium party shirts," "show me the blue athletic shirts") instead of having to adhere to whatever predetermined (pre-combined) enumerative classification the store came up with. In a digital organizing system, faceted classification enables highly flexible access because prioritizing different facets can dynamically reorganize how the collection is presented.

7.4.1 Foundations for Faceted Classification

In library and information science texts it is common to credit the idea of faceted classification to S.R. Ranganathan, a Hindu mathematician working as a librarian. Ranganathan had an almost mystical motivation to classify everything in the universe with a single classification system and notation, considering it his dharma (the closest translation in English would be "fundamental duty" or "destiny"). Facing the limitations of Dewey's system, where an item's essence had to first be identified and then the item assigned to a category based on that essence, Ranganathan believed that all bibliographic resources could be organized around a more abstract variety of aspects.

In 1933 Ranganathan proposed that a set of five and only five facets applied to all knowledge:

Personality
　　The type of thing.

Matter
　　The constituent material of the thing.

Energy
　　The action or activity of the thing.

Space
　　Where the thing occurs.

Time
　　When the thing occurs.

This classification system is known as colon classification because the notation used for resource identifiers uses a colon to separate the values on each facet. These values come from tables of categories and subcategories, making the call number very compact. Colon classification is most commonly used in libraries in India.[421]

For example, a book on "research in the cure of tuberculosis of lungs by x-ray conducted in India in 1950" has a Personality facet value of Medicine, a Matter facet value of Lungs with tuberculosis, an Energy facet value of Treatment using X-rays, a Space facet value of India, and a Time facet value of 1950. When the alphanumeric codes for these values are looked up in the classification tables, the composed call number is L,45;421:6;253:f.44'N5.[422]

Ranganathan deserves credit for implementing the first faceted classification system, but people other than librarians generally credit the idea to Nicolas de

Condorcet, a French mathematician and philosopher. About 140 years before Ranganathan, Condorcet was concerned that "systems of classification that imposed a given interpretation upon Nature ... represented an insufferable obstacle to... scientific advance." Condorcet thus proposed a flexible classification scheme for "arranging a large number of subjects in a system so that we may straightway grasp their relations, quickly perceive their combinations, and readily form new combinations."[423]

Condorcet's system was based on five major facet categories, divided into 10 terms each, yielding 10^5 or 100,000 combinations:

Objects
> domains of study.

Methods
> for studying objects and describing the knowledge gained.

Points of view
> for studying objects.

Uses and utility
> of knowledge.

Ways
> in which knowledge can be acquired.[424]

Condorcet and Ranganathan proposed different facets, but both hoped that their five top-level facets would be sufficient for a universal classification system. People have generally rejected the idea of universal facets, but Ranganathan's proposals continue to influence the development of the *Library of Congress Subject Headings* (LCSH).[425]

Today faceted classification is most commonly used in narrow domains, each with its own specific facets. This makes intuitive sense because even if resources can be distinguished with a general classification, doing so requires lengthy notations, and it is much harder to add to a general classification than to a classification created specifically for a single subject area. We could probably figure out a way to describe shirts using the PMEST facets, but style, color, and size seem more natural.

7.4.2 Faceted Classification in Description

Elaine Svenonius defines facets as "groupings of terms obtained by the first division of a subject discipline into homogeneous or semantically cohesive categories."[426] The relationships between these facets results in a controlled vocabulary (§3.1.2) governing the resources we are organizing. From this controlled vocabulary we can generate many structured descriptions that are complex but formally structured and enable us to describe things for which terms do not yet exist.

Getty's Art & Architecture Thesaurus (AAT) is a robust and widely used *controlled vocabulary* consisting of generic terms used to describe artifacts, objects, places and concepts in the domains of "art, architecture, and material culture."[427] The AAT was developed in the mid-1980s and released as a book until 1997, when those maintaining it realized that the vocabulary was so large and changed so frequently that users would be better served by a dynamic online version that could change easily, rather than by a printed book bound to a publishing cycle.

AAT is a thesaurus with a faceted hierarchical structure. The AAT's facets are "conceptually organized in a scheme that proceeds from abstract concepts to concrete, physical artifacts:"

Associated Concepts
Concepts, philosophical and critical theory, and phenomena, such as "love" and "nihilism."

Physical Attributes
Material characteristics that can be measured and perceived, like "height" and "flexibility."

Styles and Periods
Artistic and architectural eras and stylistic groupings, such as "Renaissance" and "Dada."

Agents
Basically, people and the various groups and organizations with which they identify, whether based on physical, mental, socio-economic, or political characteristics—e.g., "stonemasons" or "socialists."

Activities
Actions, processes, and occurrences, such as "body painting" and "drawing." These are different from the "Objects" facet, which may also contain "body painting" but there in terms of the actual work itself, not the process of creation.

Materials
Concerned with the actual substance of which a work is made, like "metal" or "bleach." "Materials" differ from "Physical Attributes" in that the latter is more abstract than the former.

Objects
The largest facet, "Objects" contains the actual works, like "sandcastles" and "screen prints."

Within each facet is a strict hierarchical structure drilling down from broad term to very specific instance. For example, let's look at where we would find "patent leather" in the hierarchy (Figure 7.7, ""Patent Leather" in the Art & Architecture Thesaurus."):[428]

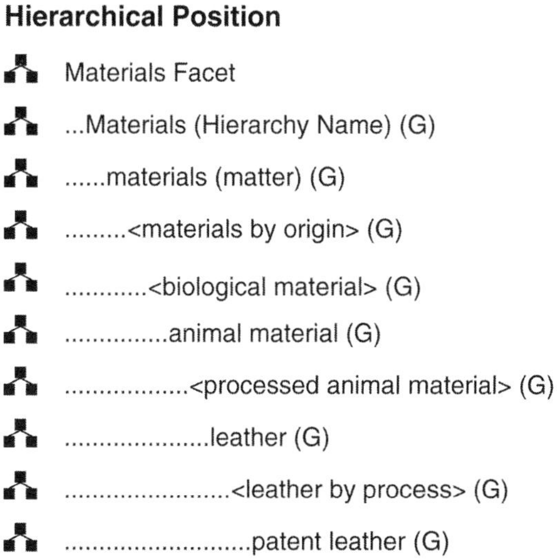

Hierarchical Position

- Materials Facet
- ...Materials (Hierarchy Name) (G)
- ......materials (matter) (G)
- ....<materials by origin> (G)
- ....<biological material> (G)
- ....animal material (G)
- ....<processed animal material> (G)
- ....leather (G)
- ....<leather by process> (G)
- ....patent leather (G)

Figure 7.7. "Patent Leather" in the Art & Architecture Thesaurus.

We can see from this example how a particular instance may be described on a number of dimensions for the purpose of organizing the item and retrieving information about it. And by using a standard *controlled vocabulary*, catalogers and indexers make it easier for users to understand and adapt to the way things are organized for the purpose of finding them.

7.4.3 A Classification for Facets

There are four major types of facets.

Enumerative facets
> Have mutually exclusive possible values. In our online shirt store, "Style" is an enumerative facet whose values are "dress," "work," "party," and "athletic."

Boolean facets
> Take on one of two values, yes (true) or no (false) along some dimension or property. On a sportswear website, "Waterproof" would be a Boolean facet because an item of clothing is either waterproof or it is not.

Hierarchical facets
> Organize resources by logical inclusion (§5.3.1.1). At Williams-Sonoma's website, the top-level facet includes "Cookware," "Cooks' Tools," and "Cutlery." At wine.com the "Region" facet has values for "US," "Old World," and "New World," each of which is further divided geographically. Also, ***taxonomic facets***. [429]

Spectrum facets
> Assume a range of numerical values with a defined minimum and maximum. Price and date are common spectrum facets. The ranges are often modeled as mutually exclusive regions (potential price facet values might include "$0 - $49," "$50 - $99," and "$100 - $149").

7.4.4 Designing a Faceted Classification System

It is important to be systematic and principled when designing a faceted classification. In some respects the process and design concerns overlap with those for describing resources, and much of the advice in §4.3, "The Process of Describing Resources" (page 148) is relevant here.[430]

7.4.4.1 Design Process for Faceted Classification

We advocate a five step process for designing a faceted classification system.

1. **Scoping.**

   Define the purposes of the classification (§4.3.2, "Determining the Purposes" (page 155), §7.2.1, "Classification Is Purposeful" (page 282)) and specify the collection of concepts or resources to be classified.

2. **Choosing values for each facet.**

   For each facet, determine its logical type (§7.4.3, "A Classification for Facets" (page 301)) and possible values. Specify the order of the values for each facet so that they make sense to users; useful orderings are alphabetical, chronological, procedural, size, most popular to least popular, simple to complex, and geographical or topological.

3. **Identifying facets.**

   Analyze and describe a representative sample of resource instances to identify properties or dimensions as candidate facets (See §4.3.3, "Identifying Properties" (page 160)).

4. **Designing the facet hierarchy and grammar.**

   Examine the relationships between the facets to create subfacets if necessary. Determine how the facets will be combined to generate the classifications.

5. **Validation, Iteration and Refinement.**

   Test the classification on new instances, and revise the facets, facet values, and facet grammar as needed.

7.4.4.2 Design Principles and Pragmatics

Here is some more specific advice about selecting and designing facets and facet values:

Orthogonality

   Facets should be independent dimensions, so a resource can have values of all of them while only having one value on each of them. In an online kitchen store, one facet might be "Product" and another might be "Brand." A particular item might be classified as a "Saucepan" in the "Product" facet and as "Calphalon" in the "Brand" one. Other saucepans might have other brands, and other Calphalon products might not be saucepans, because Product and Brand are orthogonal.

Semantic Balance

   Top-level facets should be the properties that best differentiate the resources in the classification domain. The values should be of equal semantic scope so that resources are distributed among the subcategories. Subfacets of "Cookware" like "Sauciers and Saucepans" and "Roasters and Brasiers" are semantically balanced as they are both named and grouped by cooking activity.[431]

Coverage

   The values of a facet should be able of classifying all instances within the intended scope.

Scalability

   Facet values must accommodate potential additions to the set of instances. Including an "Other" value is an easy way to ensure that a facet is flexible and hospitable to new instances, but it not desirable if all new instances will be assigned that value.

Objectivity

Although every classification has an explicit or implicit bias (§7.2.3, "Classification Is Biased" (page 288)), facets and facet values should be as unambiguous and concrete as possible to enable reliable classification of instances.

Normativity

To make a faceted classification as useful by as many people as possible, the terms used for facets and facet values should not be idiosyncratic, metaphorical, or require special knowledge to interpret.[432]

As we will see in §7.6, "Computational Classification" (page 305), classification can sometimes be done by computers rather than by people. Computer algorithms can analyze resource properties and descriptions to identify dimensions on which resources differ and the most frequent descriptive terms, which can then be used to design a faceted classification scheme. Resources can then be assigned to the appropriate categories, either without human intervention or in collaboration with a human who trains the algorithm with classified instances.

7.5 Classification by Activity Structure

Institutional classification systems are often strongly hierarchical and taxonomic because their many users come to them for diverse purposes, making a context-free or semantic organization the most appropriate. However, in narrow domains that offer a more limited variety of uses it can be much more effective to classify resources according to the tasks or activities they support. A task or activity-based classification system is called a **taskonomy**, a term invented by anthropologists Janet Dougherty and Charles Keller after their ethnographic study of how blacksmiths organized their tools. Instead of keeping things together according to their semantic relationships in what Donald Norman called "hardware store organization," the blacksmiths arranged tools in locations where they were used— "fire tools," "stump tools," "drill press rack tools," and so on.[433]

Personal organizing systems are often taskonomic. Think about the way you cook when you are following a recipe. Do you first retrieve all the ingredients from their storage places, and arrange them in activity-based groups in the preparation area?[434]

Looking at the relationship between tasks and tools in this way can help a cook determine the best way to organize tools in a kitchen. Cutting items would necessarily be kept together near a prep area; having to run across the kitchen to another area where a poultry knife is kept with, say, chicken broth would be detrimental to the cook's workflow. It would make far more sense to have all of the items for the task of cutting in a single area.

The intentional arrangement of tools in a working kitchen might look something like Table 7.1:

Table 7.1. A cook's taskonomy

Prep	Oven	Stove
Poultry knife	Oven mitts	Pots and pans
Paring knife	Baking sheets	Wooden spoons
Vegetable knife	Aluminum foil	Wok
Cutting board	Parchment paper	
	Roasting pan	

7.6 Computational Classification

In §6.5.2, "Implementing Categories That Do Not Conform to the Classical Theory" (page 261) we briefly discussed the use of the machine learning technique known as clustering to create a system of categories for classifying a set of resources or documents for which measures of inter-item similarity can be calculated. Clustering programs do not start with a set of resources that are already classified, making them **unsupervised** techniques. The categories they create maximize the similarity of resources within a category and maximize the differences between them, but these statistically-designed categories are not always meaningful ones that can be named and used by people. We ended Chapter 6 by suggesting that it is often better to start with a designed classification scheme and then train computers with **supervised** learning techniques to assign new resources to the categories.

A familiar example of supervised machine learning to classify resources is email spam filtering. Messages are classified as SPAM or HAM (i.e., non-SPAM); the former are sent to a SPAM folder, while the latter head to your inbox. We can describe this technique generically as follows:

1. **Create the training set**

   First, the algorithm is provided with emails that have been assigned to the SPAM and HAM categories. These labeled instances make up the **training set**. The training set can be created explicitly for training the classification algorithm, or extracted from regular email activity when people sort their email or select a "report spam" button in their email program.

2. **Select features**

   The algorithm is given a set of pre-defined "features" of the email messages, some from the message metadata like the sender's email address or the number of recipients, and some from the message content, like the presence of words that appear in SPAM messages with higher frequency than in HAM messages (like "pharmaceutical" or "beneficiary"). Different algorithms use different features, so the "feature selection" task is a pre-requisite step.[435]

3. **Analyze for presence of features**

   The algorithm examines each message and stores the components reflecting the presence or absence of the pre-defined features.

4. **Learn**

   The algorithm modifies itself (i.e. "**learns**") based on the training set to adjust the weight given to each feature until it can correctly assign (most of) them into the categories they belonged to in the training set.

5. **Remove the training wheels**

   The algorithm is now ready to classify new uncategorized messages to the SPAM or HAM categories.[436]

How the algorithm "learns" depends on the specific machine learning algorithm.[437] The choice of algorithm is called "model selection."[438]

7.7 Key Points in Chapter Seven

- Classification is the systematic assignment of resources to a system of intentional categories, often institutional ones.

- Every classification brings together resources that go together, and in doing so differentiates among them.

- A classification system is foremost a specification for the logical arrangement of resources because there are usually many possible and often arbitrary mappings of logical locations to physical ones.

- A classification creates structure in the organizing system that increases the variety and capability of the interactions it can support.

- Classifications are always biased by the purposes, experiences, professions, politics, values, and other characteristics and preferences of the people making them.

- Classification schemes in which all possible categories to which resources can be assigned are defined explicitly are called **enumerative.**

- When multiple resource properties are considered in a fixed sequence, each property creates another level in the system of categories and the classification scheme is **hierarchical** or **taxonomic.**

- Classification and standardization are not identical, but they are closely related. Some classifications become standards, and some standards define new classifications.

- A standard is a published specification that is developed and maintained by consensus of all the relevant stakeholders in some domain by following a defined and transparent process.

- Standard semantics are especially important in industries or markets that have significant network effects where the value of a product depends on the number of interoperable or compatible products.

- The principle of **literary warrant** holds that a classification must be based only on the specific resources that are being classified.

- The general solution to satisfying the uniqueness principle in library classifications when resources do not clearly fit in a single category is to invent and follow a detailed set of often-arbitrary rules.

- Categories sometimes change slowly, but they can also change quickly and radically as a result of technological, process, or geopolitical innovation or events.

- **Flexibility**, **extensibility**, and **hospitality** are synonyms for the degree to which the classification can accommodate new resources.

- Bibliographic classification is distinctive because of a legacy of physical arrangement and its scale and complexity.

- **Faceted** classification systems enumerate all the categories needed to assign resources appropriately, but instead of combining them in advance in a fixed hierarchy, they are applied only if they are needed to sort resources with a particular combination of properties.

- Most tagging seems insufficiently principled to be considered classification, except when tags are treated as category labels or when decisions that make tagging more systematic turn a set of tags into a **tagsonomy.**

- A task or activity-based classification system is called a **taskonomy**.

- **Supervised** learning techniques start with a designed classification scheme and then train computers to assign new resources to the categories.

Notes

376. [LIS] (Batley 2005 p. 1).

377. [Web] (Hammond et al. 2004) note that the "unstructured (or better, free structured) approach to classification with users assigning their own labels is

variously referred to as a folksonomy, folk classification, ethnoclassification, distributed classification, or social classification."

378. [Web] Thomas Vander Wal invented the term "folksonomy" in 2004, and the term quickly gained traction. His personal account of the creation and dispersion of the term is (Vander Wal 2007).

379. [Computing] See (Halvey and Keane 2007, Sinclair and Cardrew-Hall 2007) for analyses of the usability of different presentations, and (Kaser and Lemire 2007) for algorithms for drawing tag clouds.

380. [Business] See (Millen, Feinberg, and Kerr 2006), (John and Seligmann 2006).

381. [LIS] Gruenberg wrote this definition over a decade ago as a University of Illinois PhD student in an unpublished paper titled "Faceted Classification, Facet Analysis, and the Web" that was found by a web search by the first author of this chapter in 2005. When this chapter was being written several years later, the paper was no longer on the web, but a copy was located at Illinois by Matthew Beth on a backup disk.

382. [LIS] This is reflected in library call numbers, which assign a unique number to books to designate the order in which they are shelved. Most American libraries use a classification system as part of their call number, composing it from a class number of the classification and a unique identifier (derived from the author name and title), which identifies the book within the class, often using a system called Cutter numbers. See *http://www.itsmarc.com/crs/merged Projects/cutter/cutter/general_information_cutter.htm*.

383. [Business] The most "standard" of all standards organization is the International Organization for Standardization (ISO), whose members are themselves national standards organizations, which as a result gives the nearly 20,000 ISO standards the broadest and most global coverage. See *http://ISO.org*. In addition, there are scores of other national and industry-specific standards bodies whose work is potentially relevant to organizing systems of the sorts discussed in this book. We encounter these kinds of standards every day in codes for countries, currencies, and airports, in file formats, in product barcodes, and in many other contexts.

384. [LIS] Dewey Decimal Classification: *http://www.oclc.org/dewey/DDC*.

Similarly, the DSM is maintained and published by the American Psychiatric Association (APA) and it earns the many millions of dollars a year.

385. [Business] All the finished work of OASIS is freely available at *https://www.oasis-open.org*; the UBL committee is at *https://www.oasis-open.org/committees/tc_home.php?wg_abbrev=ubl*.

386. [Business] It might be possible for a small number of people to agree on an organizing system that meets the needs of each participant. But obviously the potential for conflict increases when more people are involved, and "bottom-up" *ad hoc* negotiations to resolve every disagreement between every pair of participants just are not feasible. Instead, for a large-scale organizing system, standards are usually decided by entities that have the authority to coordinate actions and prevent conflicts by imposing a single solution on all the participants in a "top-down" manner. (Rosenthal, Seligman, and Renner 2004) call this the "person-concept" tradeoff, which we can paraphrase as "a few people can agree on a lot, but a lot of people can only agree on a little."

This authority can come from many different sources, but they can be roughly categorized as "authority from power" and "authority from consensus." Often the economic dominance of a firm allows it to control how business gets done in its industry. One key part of that is establishing specifications for data formats and classification schemes in organizing systems, which usually means requiring other firms to use the ones developed by the dominant firm for its own use. This ensures the continued efficiency of their own business processes while making it harder for other firms to challenge their market power.

In contrast, consensus is the authority mechanism embodied in the workings of the open source community, where the freedom to view and change data formats and code that uses them encourages cooperation and adoption. Consensus also underlies the authority of voluntary standards activities, where firms work together under the auspices of a standards body and agree to follow its procedures for creating, ratifying, and implementing standards.

387. [Business] International and national standards bodies derive their authority from the authority of the governments that created them. But standards organizations arguably derive most of their authority from the collective power of their members, because many influential standards organizations like OASIS, W3C, OMG, and IETF are not chartered or sponsored by governments. In addition, firms often create *ad hoc* "quasi-standards" organizations or "communities of interest" to facilitate relatively short-term cooperative standards-making activities that in the former case would otherwise be prohibited by anti-trust considerations. Finally, at the extreme "lightweight" end of the standards-making continuum, the codification of simple and commonly used information models as "microformats" depends on authority that emerges from the collaboration of individuals rather than firms.

388. [Business] Often a standard evolves from an existing specification submitted to a standards organization by the firm that created it. In other cases, the specifications used by a dominant firm becomes a de-facto standard by other firms in its industry, and it is never submitted to a formal standards-making process.

389. [Business] Standards "wars" tend to occur when different firms or groups of firms develop two or more standards that tend to address the same needs. Not surprisingly, the competing standards are often incompatible on purpose. At first this lets each standard attract customers with features not enabled by the other, but it ends up locking them in by imposing switching costs. See (Shapiro and Varian, 1998).

390. [LIS] Even so, the LCC is not "open" standard. You can browse the classifications on the LOC site, but to get them packaged as a book or complete digital resource you have to pay for them.

391. [Law] Governments have inherently long time horizons for their actions, they need to serve all citizens fairly and without discrimination, and they (should seek to) minimize cost to taxpayers. Each of these principles is an independent argument for standards and taken together they make a very strong one. Indeed, one the founding goals in the US Constitution is to protect the public interest, and this is enabled in Article I, Section 8 by granting Congress the power to set standards "of Weights and Measures" to facilitate commerce. Setting standards is a key role of the National Institute of Standards and Technology (NIST), part of the Department of Commerce, and other departments have similar standards-setting responsibilities and agencies, like the Food and Drug Administration (FDA) in the Department of Health and Social Services. In addition, independent government agencies like the Federal Communications Commission (FCC) and Federal Trade Commission (FTC) set numerous standards that are relevant to information organizing systems. And of course, the Library of Congress (LOC) maintains procedures and standards needed "to sustain and preserve a universal collection of knowledge... for future generations" (LOC.gov/about).

392. [Business] The *Sarbanes-Oxley Act* is *US Public Law 107-204*, *http://www.sec.gov/about/laws/soa2002.pdf*.

The definitive source for the *Health Insurance Portability and Accountability Act* (HIPAA) is the US Department of Health & Human Services, *http://www.hhs.gov/ocr/privacy/hipaa/understanding/index.html*.

The definitive source for the *Family Educational Rights and Privacy Act* (FERPA) is the US Department of Education, *http://www2.ed.gov/policy/gen/guid/fpco/ferpa/index.html*.

Complying with government regulations like these can be expensive and difficult, and many companies, especially smaller ones, complain about the cost. On the other hand, the argument can be made that investing in a rigorous system for organizing information can provide competitive advantages, turning the compliance burden into a competitive weapon (see Taylor 2006).

393. [Business] Examples are the North American Industry Classification System (NAICS) developed by the US Census Bureau, *http://www.census.gov/eos/www/naics/*, and the United Nations Standard Products and Services Code (UNSPC), *http://www.unspsc.org/*.

394. [Web] The application of classification and organizing principles more generally to the design of user interfaces to facilitate information access, navigation, and use is often called "Information Architecture." See (Morville and Rosenfeld 2006).

395. [Web] (Grappone and Couzin 2011) is a search engine optimization "cookbook" for do-it-yourselfers. See (Malaga 2008) for a critique of typical SEO practices.

396. [Business] See (Gladwell 1996), (Schwartz 2005), (Underhill 2008).

397. [Business] The RosettaNet standards are used by thousands of firms as specifications and implementations of business-to-business processes in several industries, especially component manufacturing and electronics. The specifications are defined using a three-level hierarchy of process clusters, segments, and partner interface processes (PIPs) to enable firms to find a level of process abstraction that works best for them. See *http://RosettaNet.org*.

398. [LIS] See (Gaukroger 2001) and (Weinberger 1985) for an introduction to Bacon's philosophy, and (Miksa 1984) for an analysis of Bacon's influence on systems of library classification.

399. [LIS] (Svenonius 2000, Ch. 8).

400. [CogSci] Very detailed classification of knives are at *http://www2.knifecenter.com/knifecenter/kitchen/* and *http://kitchenknives.com/*.

401. [LIS] For example, the introductory text for the Dewey Decimal Classification (DDC) is 38 pages long (*http://www.oclc.org/dewey/resources/scholar.htm*). A full set of online training modules "focused on the needs of experienced librarians needing Dewey application training" runs 30 hours (*http://www.oclc.org/dewey/resources/teachingsite/courses/default.htm*).

402. [LIS] (Taylor and Joudrey 2009, p. 392) define integrity as the stability of notations (class identifiers) in a classification so that resources are never given new notations when the category meaning changes. This is especially pertinent in a physical world where class notations are affixed to resources (books in a traditional library, for example) and where the changing of meaning would necessitate the changing of many numbers.

403. [LIS] For example, the Universal Decimal Classification (UDC) intentionally left the main class 4 blank in order to have space for currently unknown subjects on the highest hierarchy level. (*http://www.udcc.org/udcsummary/php/*

index.php). The Library of Congress Classification (LCC) also left space on the highest hierarchical level by not using all letters in the alphabet. Classifications also leave spaces in the enumeration of more specific classes.

404. [Computing] (Rahm and Bernstein 2006) provide a crisp introduction to the challenges and approaches for changing deployed schemas in databases, conceptual models, ontologies, XML schemas, and software application interfaces. They operate an online bibliography on schema evolution that contains several hundred sources. See *http://se-pubs.dbs.uni-leipzig.de/*.

405. [Law] See *How the Government Measures Unemployment, http://www.bls.gov/cps/cps_htgm.htm* from the Department of Labor's Bureau of Labor Statistics, and a critical commentary about the measurement scheme titled *Making 9 Million Jobless Vanish: How the Government Manipulates Unemployment Statistics* at *http://danielamerman.com/articles/2012/WorkC.html*.

406. [LIS] (Bowker and Star 2000, p. 4).

407. [LIS] See the Wikipedia entry *Race and ethnicity in the United States census, http://en.wikipedia.org/wiki/Race_and_ethnicity_in_the_United_States_Census*, and (Lee 1993) for arguments against any racial categorization because of the "political motivations and non-scientific character of the classifications."

408. [Business] (Feinberg 2012).

409. [LIS] (Taylor and Joudrey 2009, Ch. 3) is a historical review of library classification. (Svenonius 2000) reviews the evolution of the theoretical foundations. (Kilgour 1998) focuses on the evolution of the book and the story of the co-evolution of libraries and classification comes along for the ride.

410. [Business] Supermarkets typically carry anywhere from 15,000 to 60,000 SKUs (depending on the size of the store), and may offer a service deli, a service bakery, and/or a pharmacy. 300 standard product categories (*http://www.fmi.org/research-resources/supermarket-facts*).

411. [LIS] *http://www.ala.org/tools/libfactsheets/alalibraryfactsheet22*.

412. [LIS] Dewey Decimal Classification: *http://www.oclc.org/dewey/*.

413. [LIS] *https://www.amherst.edu/aboutamherst/history*. Today Amherst is aggressively co-ed and secular.

414. [CogSci] That was not a typo. The "War of 1812" lasted well into 1815. The persistence of an inaccurate name for this war reflects its unique characteristics. Wars (in the English language) are generally named for the location of the fighting or the enemy being fought (the Mexican-American War, the Korean War, the Vietnam War, the Iraq War), or for a particular ideal or ambition (the

Revolutionary War, the Civil War). The War of 1812 does not satisfy any of these naming conventions; the war was fought across a huge range of geography from eastern Canada to Louisiana, between a diverse range of groups from Canadians and Native American tribes, with national armies getting involved very late in the war. While nominally fought over freedom the seas, the war quickly morphed into one about territorial ambition in North America. Of course, if the world were a place where people could agree on naming standards for wars, it is likely we would no longer have wars. See *http://en.wikipedia.org/wiki/List_of_wars_involving_the_United_States*.

415. [LIS] (Miksa 1984, p. 3).

416. [LIS] See Clay Shirky, *Ontology is Overrated: Categories, Links, and Tags* for additional examples *http://shirky.com/writings/ontology_overrated.html*.

417. [Computing] Where's computer science? It might seem odd today that a discipline this broad and important does not have its own second level category under the Q of science, but because computer science was first taught in math departments, the LCC has it as the QA76 subclass of mathematics, which is QA.

418. [Business] The Book Industry Study Group (BISG) first and foremost is focused on resource description and classification as means to business ends; this purpose contrasts with goals of DDC or LOC. BISG classifications are used for barcodes and shipping labels to support supply chain and inventory management, marketing, and promotion activities. See *http://www.bisg.org/*.

419. [Business] See (Pope and Holley 2011), (Samuelson 2010).

420. [LIS] What some call the "Perry Rebellion" or the "Dewey Dilemma" began in 2007 when the new Perry Branch Library in Gilbert, Arizona opened with its books classified using the BISAC rather than Dewey classifications. (Fister 2009). This is a highly inflamed controversy that pits advocates of customer service and usability against the library establishment, which despises the idea of turning to retailing as inspiration when designing and operating a library. Even if BISAC gets more widely adopted in public libraries it is unimaginable that it can be used in research libraries.

421. [LIS] (Ranganathan 1967). (Satija 2001). See (Svenonius 2000, p. 174-176) for a quick introduction.

422. [LIS] Wikipedia article at *http://en.wikipedia.org/wiki/Colon_classification*.

423. [Business] (Baker 1962). The first quote is on page 104; the second one is on page 100. This article contains Condorcet's 1805 essay in French, but fortunately for us Baker's analysis is in English, This motivation of Condorcet's classification scheme sounds like the description of a data warehouse or business

intelligence system in which transactional data can be "sliced and diced" into new combinations to answer questions in support of strategic decision-making. See (Watson and Wixon 2007).

424. [LIS] See Joacim Hansson, *Condorcet and the Origins of Faceted Classification,* *http://documentationandlibrarianship.blogspot.com/2011/02/condorcet-and-origins-of-faceted.html.*

425. [LIS] LCSH uses facets for Topic, Place, Time, and Form (but they can be ordered in a variety of ways, not as rigidly as PMEST. (Anderson and Hoffman 2006) argue for a fully faceted syntax in LCSH.

426. [LIS] (Svenonius 2000, p. 140).

427. [Museums] The Getty AAT is online at *http://www.getty.edu/research/tools/vocabularies/aat/index.html.*

428. [Museums] This section of the thesaurus comes from *http://www.getty.edu/vow/AATFullDisplay?find=leather8log ic=AND8note=8english=N8prev_page=18subjectid=300193362.*

429. [CogSci] You might have thought that the US was in the new world, but according to wine.com, the new world of wine includes Australia, New Zealand, Argentina, Chile, and South Africa. The geography under the US facet is equally distorted by the uneven distribution of quality wine making regions, so the values of that facet are California. Oregon, Washington, and Other US.

430. [LIS] Denton, William. *How to Make a Faceted Classification and Put It On the Web* Nov. 2003. *http://www.miskatonic.org/library/facet-web-howto.html.* See also (Spiteri 1998).

431. [Linguistics] Should remind you of issues of lexical gap in §5.4, "The Lexical Perspective" (page 203).

432. [CogSci] Semantic balance is a bit hard to define, but you can often tell when facet values are not balanced. A cookware facet whose values include saucepans, frying pans, stock pots, and pizza pans will not evenly distribute resources across the facets.

433. [CogSci] See (Dougherty and Keller 1985) for the ethnography of blacksmithing, and also (Norman 2006), who extends the taskonomy idea to the design of user interfaces for cell phones and other computing devices. You probably have not worked as blacksmith, but you have certainly used taskonomic classification. For example. a student writing a term paper or doing a course project checks out books from the library's taxonomic classification system (or prints them out from the web) and then organizes them in piles on a desk or on the floor according to the plan for the paper or project. Some of the original classification might persist, but the emphasis clearly shifts toward getting work done.

When the task is completed the books go back to the library and are put back into the context-free taxonomy.

434. [CogSci] See (Kirsh 1995) for theoretical motivation and a classification scheme for the "intelligent use of space," and (de Leon 2003) for an example of cooking ethnography.

435. [Computing] A straightforward method is to run the *machine learning* algorithms using different sets of features, and select the set of features that yields the best result. Because this method "wraps" around the machine learning algorithm itself, it is named "**wrapper method**." However, it can be very computationally expensive to run machine learning algorithms multiple times, especially when the number of features are large. A faster alternative is the so-called **filter methods**. In filter methods, one computes how "informative" or "predictive" a feature is to a category. For instance, an email with word "lottery" is more likely to be SPAM than "metadata." The numeric measures frequently used for such purpose are *correlation* and *mutual information*. Filter method is less computationally expensive than wrapper method, but in general does not perform as well as wrapper method.

436. [Computing] See (Blanzieri and Bryl 2009) for a review of the spam problem and the policy and technology methods for fighting it. (Upsana and Chakravarty 2010) is somewhat more recent and more narrowly focused on text classification techniques.

437. [Computing] The "Naïve Bayes" model is based on the assumption that the features are conditionally independent of each other. Based on the training set, the probability of features conditional on categories is estimated; and then using Bayes' Theorem, the probability of categories conditional on features is inferred. Although the assumption of conditional independent is not met in reality, Naïve Bayes works surprisingly well in practice.

Decision trees are another popular class of algorithms for classification. In the ID3 algorithm, during the learning process the training set is repeatedly split into subsets based on the feature that yielded the highest information gain. Information gain is a concept borrowed from information theory. Intuitively, the higher the information gain, the greater the difference in the distribution of the subsets.

Support vector machine (SVM) approaches work by constructing a plane that maximally separates the positive and negative training samples. The SVM is commonly regarded as one of the most effective off-the-shelf classification algorithms.

438. [Computing] **Cross validation** is the method commonly used for model selection. It works as follows: the entire labeled data set is divided into training subset and holdout validation set. The commonly used ratio of the divide is 70%

for training and 30% for holdout validation. To compare different *machine learning* algorithms, one runs each of these algorithms on the training subset, and tests the training result on the holdout cross validation set. The algorithm that yields the best performance on the cross validation set is selected.

Chapter 8
The Forms of Resource Descriptions

Ryan Shaw
Murray Maloney

8.1 Introduction

Throughout this book, we have emphasized the importance of separately considering fundamental organizing principles, application-specific concepts, and details of implementation. The three-tier architecture we introduced in §1.2.3.1 is one way to conceptualize this separation. In §5.7, we contrasted the implementation-focused perspective for analyzing relationships with other perspectives that focus on the meaning and abstract structure of relationships. In this chapter, we present this contrast between conceptualization and implementation in terms of separating the *content* and *form* of resource descriptions.

In the previous chapters, we have considered principles and concepts of organizing in many different contexts, ranging from personal organizing systems to cultural and institutional ones. We have noted that some organizing systems have limited scope and expected lifetime, such as a task-oriented personal organizing system, like a shopping list. Other organizing systems support broad uses that rely on standard categories developed through rigorous processes, like a product catalog.

By this point you should have a good sense of the various conceptual issues you need to consider when deciding how to describe a resource in order to meet the goals of your organizing system. Considering those issues will give you some sense of what the content of your descriptions should be. In order to focus on the conceptual issues, we have deferred discussion of specific implementation issues. Implementation involves choosing the specific form of your descriptions, and that is the topic of this chapter.

We can approach the problem of how to form resource descriptions from two perspectives: structuring and writing. From one perspective, resource descriptions are things that are *used* by both people and computational agents. From this perspective, choosing the form of resource descriptions is a kind of design. This is easy to see for certain kinds of resource descriptions, like the signs and maps found in physical environments like airport terminals, public libraries, and malls. In these spaces, resource descriptions are quite literally designed to help people orient themselves and find their way. But any kind of resource description, not just those embedded in the built environment, can be viewed as a designed object. Designing an object involves making decisions about how it should be structured so that it can best be used for its intended purpose. From a design perspective, choosing the form of a resource description means making decisions about its *structure*.

In §5.5, "The Structural Perspective" (page 208), we took a structural perspective on resources and the relationships among them. In this chapter, we will take a structural perspective on resource *descriptions*. The difference is subtle but important. A structural perspective on resource *relationships* focuses on how people or computational processes associate, arrange, and connect those resources. A structural perspective on resource *descriptions* focuses on how those associations, arrangements, and connections are explicitly represented or implemented in the descriptions we create. Mismatches between the structure imposed on the resources being organized and the structure of the descriptions used to implement that organization could result in an organizing system that is complex, inefficient, and difficult to maintain, as you will see in our first example.

The structures of resource descriptions enable or inhibit particular ways of interacting with those descriptions, just as the descriptions themselves enable or inhibit particular ways of interacting with the described resources (see §2.4, "Designing Resource-Based Interactions" (page 61), and Chapter 9, "*Interactions with Resources*"). Keep in mind that resource descriptions are themselves information resources. So, much of what we will say in this chapter is applicable to the structures and forms of information resources in general. Put another way, the structure and form of information resources informs the design of resource descriptions.

From another perspective, creating resource descriptions is a kind of "writing." I may describe something to you orally, but such a description might not be very useful to an organizing system unless it were transcribed. Organizing systems need persistent descriptions, and that means they need to be written. In that sense, choosing the form of a resource description means making decisions about *notation* and *syntax*.

Modern Western culture tends to make a sharp distinction between designing and writing, but there are areas where this distinction breaks down, and the creation of resource descriptions in organizing systems is one of them. In the following sections, we will use designing and writing as two lenses for looking at the problem of how to choose the form of resource descriptions. Specifically, we will examine the spectrum of options we have for structuring descriptions, and the kinds of syntaxes we have for writing those descriptions.

8.2 Structuring Descriptions

Choosing how to structure resource descriptions is a matter of making principled and purposeful design decisions in order to solve specific problems, serve specific purposes, or bring about some desirable property in the descriptions. Most of these decisions are specific to a *domain*: the particular context of application for the organizing system being designed and the kinds of interactions with resources it will enable. Making these kinds of context-specific decisions results in a model of that domain (see §4.3.1.2, "Abstraction in Resource Description" (page 152)).

Over time, many people have built similar kinds of descriptions. They have had similar purposes, desired similar properties, and faced similar problems. Unsurprisingly, they have converged on some of the same decisions. When common sets of design decisions can be identified that are not specific to any one domain, they often become systematized in textbooks and in design practices, and may eventually be designed into standard formats and architectures for creating organizing systems. These formally recognized sets of design decisions are known as **abstract models** or **metamodels**. Metamodels describe structures commonly found in resource descriptions and other information resources, regardless of the specific domain. While any designer of an organizing system will usually create a model of her specific domain, she usually will not create an entirely new metamodel but will instead make choices from among the metamodels that have been formally recognized and incorporated into existing standards. The resulting model is sometimes called a "domain-specific language." Reusing standard metamodels can bring great economical advantages, as developers can reuse tools designed for and knowledge about these metamodels, rather than having to start from scratch.

Al	A	B	C	A	●	C	Al Un	M	Mb Hd	Un Pa Ch In	Qd B	A C E F	Un Mt
Un	D	E	F	D	E	F	Na Pa	● Wf	Al ● Jp Oc Mu	x W	B D	x Ot En Ft	
Na	G	H	I	G	H	I	0 0	0 ● ●	0 0	0 0	0 0	0 0	0 ●	● ●
Pa	K	L	M	K	L	M	1 1	1 1 1	1 1	1 ●	1 1	1 1	1 1	1 1
	N	O	●	N	O	P	2 2	2 2 2	2 2	2 2	●2	2 2	2 2	2 2
Jp	Q	R	S	Q	R	S	3 3	3 3 3	●3	3 3	3 3	3 3	●3	3 3
Ch														
Oc	a	b	c	a	b	c	●4	4 4 4	4 4	4 4	4 ●	4 4	4 4	4 4
In	d	e	f	d	e	f	5 5	5 5 5	5 ●	5 5	5 5	5 5	5 5	5 5
Mu	g	h	i	g	h	●	6 ●	6 6 6	6 6	●6	6 6	6 ●	6 6	6 6
●	k	l	m	k	l	m	7 7	7 7 7	7 7	7 7	7 7	7 7	7 7	7 7
B	n	o	p	n	o	p	8 8	8 8 8	8 8	8 8	8 8	●8	8 8	8 8
W	q	●	s	q	r	s	9 9	●9 9	9 9	9 9	9 9	9 9	9 9	9 9

Figure 8.1. A Batten Card.

In the following sections, we examine some common kinds of structures used as the basis for metamodels. But first, we consider a concrete example of how the structure of resource descriptions supports or inhibits particular uses. As we explained in Chapter 1, the concept of a resource de-emphasizes the differences between physical and digital things in favor of focusing on how things, in general, are used to support goal-oriented activity. Different kinds of books can be treated as information resources regardless of the particular mix of tangible and intangible properties they may have. Since resource descriptions are also information resources, we can similarly consider how their structures support particular uses, independent of whether they are physical, digital, or a mix of both.

During World War II, a British chemist named W. E. Batten developed a system for organizing patents.[439] The system consisted of a language for describing the product, process, use, and apparatus of a patent, and a way of using punched cards to record these descriptions. Batten used cards printed with matrices of 800 positions (see Figure 8.1). Each card represented a specific value from the vocabulary of the description language, and each position corresponded to a particular patent. To describe patent #256 as covering *extrusion of polythene to produce cable coverings*, one would first select the cards for the values *polythene*, *extrusion*, and *cable coverings*, and then punch each card at the 256th position. The description of patent #256 would thus extend over these three cards.

The advantage of this structure is that to find patents covering *extrusion of polythene* (for any purpose), one needs only to select the two cards corresponding to those values, lay one on top of the other, and hold them up to a light. Light will shine through wherever there is a position corresponding to a patent described using those values. Patents meeting a certain description are easily found due to the structure of the cards designed to describe the patents.

Of course, this system has clear disadvantages as well. Finding the concepts associated with a particular patent is tedious, because every card must be inspected. Adding a new patent is relatively easy as long as there is an index that allows the cards for specific concepts to be located quickly. However, once the cards run out of space for punching holes, the whole set of cards must be duplicated to accommodate more patents: a very expensive operation. Adding new concepts is potentially easy: simply add a new card. But if we want to be able to find existing patents using the new concept, all the existing patents would have to be re-examined to determine whether their positions on the new card should be punched: also an expensive operation.

The structure of Batten's cards supported rapid selection of resources given a partial description. The kinds of structures we will examine in the following sections are not quite so elaborate as Batten's cards. But like the cards, each kind of structure supports more efficient mechanical execution of certain operations, at the cost of less efficient execution of others.

8.2.1 Kinds of Structures

Sets, lists, dictionaries, trees, and graphs are kinds of structures that can be used to form resource descriptions. As we shall see, each of these kinds is actually a family of related structures. These structures are *abstractions*: they describe formal structural properties in a general way, rather than specifying an exact physical or textual form. Abstractions are useful because they help us to see common properties shared by different specific ways of organizing information. By focusing on these common properties, we can more easily reason about the operations that different forms support and the affordances that they provide, without being distracted by less relevant details.

8.2.1.1 Blobs

The simplest kind of structure is no structure at all. Consider the following description of a book: *Sebald's novel uses a walking tour in East Anglia to meditate on links between past and present, East and West.*[440] This description is an unstructured text expression with no clearly defined internal parts, and we can consider it to be a **blob**. Or, more precisely, it has structure, but that structure is the underlying grammatical structure of the English language, and none of that grammatical structure is explicitly represented in a surface structure when the sentence is expressed. As readers of English we can interpret the sentence as a description of the subject of the book, but to do this mechanically is difficult.[441] On the other hand, such a written description is relatively easy to create, as the describer can simply use natural language.

A blob need not be a blob of text. It could be a photograph of a resource, or a recording of a spoken description of a resource. Like blobs of text, blobs of pixels or sound have underlying structure that any person with normal vision or hearing can understand easily.[442] But we can treat these blobs as unstructured, because none of the underlying structure in the visual or auditory input is explicit, and we are concerned with the ways that the structures of resource descriptions support or inhibit mechanical or computational operations.[443]

8.2.1.2 Sets

The simplest way to structure a description is to give it parts and treat them as a **set**. For example, the description of Sebald's novel might be reformulated as a set of terms: *Sebald, novel, East Anglia, walking, history.* Doing this has lost much of the meaning, but something has been gained: we now can easily distinguish *Sebald* and *walking* as separate items in the description.[444] This makes it easier to find, for example, all the descriptions which include the term *walking*. (Note that this is different from simply searching through blob-of-text descriptions for the word *walking*. When treated as a set, the description *Fiji, fire walking, memoir* does not include the term *walking*, though it does include the term *fire walking*.)

Sets make it easy to find intersections among descriptions. Sets are also easy to create. In §7.1.2, "Classification vs. Tagging" (page 274) we looked at "folksonomies," organizing systems in which non-professional users create resource descriptions. In these systems, descriptions are structured as sets of "tags." To find resources, users can specify a set of tags to obtain resources having descriptions that intersect at those tags. This is more valuable if the tags come from a *controlled vocabulary*, making intersections more likely. But enforcing vocabulary control adds complexity to the description process, so a balance must be struck between maximizing potential intersections and making description as simple as practical.[445]

A set is a type or class of structure. We can refine the definition of different kinds of sets by introducing **constraints**. For example, we might introduce the constraint that a given set has a maximum number of items. Or we might constrain a set to always have the same number of items, giving us a fixed-size set. We can also remove constraints. Sets do not contain duplicate items (think of a tagging system in which it does not make sense to assign the same tag more than once to the same resource). If we remove this *uniqueness* constraint, we have a different structure known as a "bag" or "multiset."

8.2.1.3 Lists

Constraints are what distinguish lists from sets. A **list**, like a *set*, is a collection of items with an additional constraint: their items are *ordered*. If we were designing a tagging system in which it was important that the order of the tags be maintained, we would want to use lists, not sets. Unlike sets, lists may contain duplicate items. In a list, two items that are otherwise the same can be distinguished by their position in the ordering, but in a set this is not possible. For example, we might want to organize the tags assigned to a resource, listing the most used tag first, the least frequently used last, and the rest ordered according their according to their frequency of use.

Again, we can introduce constraints to refine the definition of different kinds of lists such as fixed-length lists. If we constrain a list to contain only items that are themselves lists, and further specify that these contained lists do not themselves contains lists, then we have a *table* (a list of lists of items). A spreadsheet is a list of lists.

8.2.1.4 Dictionaries

One major limitation of lists and sets is that, although items can be individually addressed, there is no way to distinguish the items except by comparing their values (or, in a list, their positions in the ordering). In a set of tags like *Sebald, novel, East Anglia, walking, history*, for example, one cannot easily tell that *Sebald* refers to the author of the book while *East Anglia* and *walking* refer to what it is about. One-way of addressing this problem is to break each item in a set into two parts: a **property** and a **value**. So, for example, our simple set of tags might become *author: Sebald, type: novel, subject: East Anglia, subject: walking, subject: history*. Now we can say that *author*, *type*, and *subject* are the properties, and the original items in the set are the values.

This kind of structure is called a **dictionary**, also known as a *map* or an *associative array*. A dictionary is a set of property-value pairs or *entries*. It is a set of entries, not a list of entries, because the pairs are not ordered and because each entry must have a unique key.[446] Note that this specialized meaning of "dictionary" is different from the more common meaning of "dictionary" as an alphabetized list of terms accompanied by sentences that define them. The two meanings are related, however. Like a "real" dictionary, a dictionary structure allows us to easily find the value (such as a definition) associated with a particular property or *key* (such as a word). But unlike a real dictionary, which orders its keys alphabetically, a dictionary structure does not specify an order for its keys.[447]

Dictionaries are found everywhere in resource descriptions. Structured descriptions entered using a form are easily represented as dictionaries, where the labels of the form items are the properties and the data entered are the values.

Tabular data with a "header row" can be thought of as a set of dictionaries, where the column headers are the properties for each dictionary, and each row is a set of corresponding values. Dictionaries are also a basic type of data structure found in nearly all programming languages (where they usually are referred to as associative arrays).

Again, we can introduce or remove constraints to define specialized types of dictionaries. A sorted dictionary adds an ordering over entries; in other words, it is a list of entries rather than a set. A *multimap* is a dictionary in which multiple entries may have the same key.

8.2.1.5 Trees

In dictionaries as they are commonly understood, properties are terms and values are their corresponding definitions. The terms and values are usually words, phrases, or other expressions that can be ordered alphabetically. But if generalize the notion of a dictionary as abstract sets of property-value pairs, the values can be anything at all. In particular, the values can themselves be dictionaries. When a dictionary structure has values that are themselves dictionaries, we say that the dictionaries are *nested*. Nesting is very useful for resource descriptions that need more structure than what a (non-nested) dictionary can provide.

Figure 8.2, "Four Nested Dictionaries." presents an example of nested dictionaries. At the top level there is one dictionary with a single entry having the property *a*. The value associated with *a* is a dictionary consisting of two entries, the first having property *b* and the second having property *c*. The values associated with *b* and with *c* are also dictionaries.

If we nest dictionaries like this, and our "top" dictionary (the one that contains all the others) has only one entry, then we have a kind of **tree** structure. Figure 8.3, "A Tree of Properties and Values." shows the same properties and values as Figure 8.2, this time arranged to make the tree structure more visible. Trees consist of **nodes** (the letters and numbers in Figure 8.3) joined by **edges** (the arrows). Each node in the tree with a circle around it is a property, and the value of each property consists of the nodes below (to the right of) it in the tree. A node is referred to as the *parent* of the nodes below it, which in turn are referred to as the *children* of that node. The edges show these "parent of" relationships between the nodes. The node with no parent is called the *root* of the tree. Nodes with no children are called *leaf* nodes.

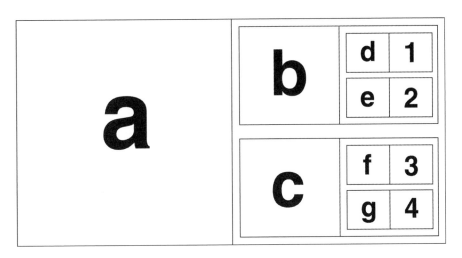

Figure 8.2. Four Nested Dictionaries.

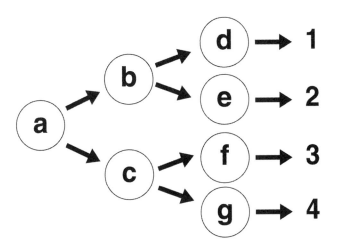

Figure 8.3. A Tree of Properties and Values.

As with the other types of structures we have considered, we can define different kinds of trees by introducing different types of constraints. For example, the predominant metamodel for XML is documents is a kind of tree called the **XML Information Set** or Infoset. [448]

The *XML Information Set* defines a specific kind of tree structure by adding very specific constraints, including ordering of child nodes, to the basic definition of a tree. The addition of an ordering constraint distinguishes XML trees from nested dictionaries, in which child nodes do not have any order (because dictionary entries do not have an ordering). Ordering is an important constraint for resource descriptions, since without ordering it is impossible to (for example) list multiple authors while guaranteeing that the order of authors will be maintained. Figure 8.3 depicts a kind of tree with a different set of constraints: all non-leaf nodes are properties, and all leafs are values. We could also define a tree in which every node has both a property and a value. Trees exist in a large variety of flavors, but they all share a common topology: the edges between nodes are directed (one node is the parent and the other is the child), and every node except the root has exactly one parent.

Trees provide a way to group statements describing different but related resources. For example, consider the description structured as a dictionary here:

Example 8.1. Description structured as a dictionary

> **author given names → Winfried Georg**
> **author surname → Sebald**
> **title → Die Ringe des Saturn**
> **pages → 371**

The dictionary groups together four property-value pairs describing a particular book. (The arrows are simply a schematic way to indicate property-value relations. Later in the chapter we look at ways to "write" these relations using some specific syntax.)

But really the first two entries are not describing the book; they are describing the book's author. So, it would be better to group those two statements somehow. We can do this by nesting the entries describing the author within the book description, creating a tree structure:

Example 8.2. Nesting an author description within a book description

> **author →**
> > **given names → Winfried Georg**
> > **surname → Sebald**
> **title → Die Ringe des Saturn**
> **pages → 371**

Using a tree works well in this case because we can treat the book as the primary resource being described, making it the root of our tree, and adding on the author description as a "branch."

We also could have chosen to make the author the primary resource, giving us a tree like the one in Example 8.3.

Example 8.3. Nesting book descriptions within an author description

given names → Winfried Georg
surname → Sebald
books authored →
    1. title → Die Ringe des Saturn
       pages → 371
    2. title → Austerlitz
       pages → 416

Note that in this dictionary, the value of the *books authored* property is a *list* of dictionaries. Making the author the primary or root resource allows us to include multiple book descriptions in the tree (but makes it more difficult to describe books having multiple authors). A tree is a good choice for structuring descriptions as long as we can clearly identify a primary resource. In some cases, however, we want to connect descriptions of related resources without having to designate one as primary. In these cases, we need a more flexible data structure.

8.2.1.6 Graphs

Suppose we were describing two books, where the author of one book is the subject of the other (Example 8.4, "Two related descriptions").

Example 8.4. Two related descriptions

1. author → Mark Richard McCulloch
   title → Understanding W. G. Sebald
   subject → Winfried Georg Sebald
2. author → Winfried Georg Sebald
   title → Die Ringe des Saturn

By looking at these descriptions, we can guess the relationship between the two books, but that relationship is not explicitly represented in the structure: we just have two separate dictionaries and have inferred the relationship by matching property values. It is possible that this inference could be wrong: there might be two people named *Winfried Georg Sebald*. How can we structure these descriptions to explicitly represent the fact that the *Winfried Georg Sebald* that is the subject of the first book is the same *Winfried Georg Sebald* who authored the second?

One possibility would be to make *Winfried Georg Sebald* the root of a tree, similar to the approach taken in Example 8.3, "Nesting book descriptions within an author description", adding a *book about* property alongside the *books authored* one. This solution would work fine if we felt that people were our primary resources, and it thus made sense to structure our descriptions around them. But suppose that we had decided that our descriptions should be structured around books, and that we were using a vocabulary that took this perspective (with properties such as *author* and *subject* rather than *books authored* and *books about*). We should not let a particular structure limit the organizational perspective we can take, as Batten's cards did. Instead, we should consciously choose structures to suit our organizational perspective. How can we do this?

If we treat our two book descriptions as trees, we can join the two branches (subject and author) that share a value. When we do this, we no longer have a tree, because we now have a node with more than one parent (Figure 8.4, "Descriptions Linked into a Graph."). The structure in Figure 8.4, "Descriptions Linked into a Graph." is a **graph**. Like a *tree*, a *graph* consists of a set of nodes connected by edges. These edges may or may not have a direction (§5.6.3, "Directionality" (page 219)). If they do, the graph is referred to as a "directed graph." If a graph is directed, it may be possible to start at a node and follow edges in a path that leads back to the starting node. Such a path is called a "cycle." If a directed graph has no cycles, it is referred to as an "acyclic graph."

A tree is just a more constrained kind of graph. Trees are *directed* graphs because the "parent of" relationship between nodes is asymmetric: the edges are arrows that point in a certain direction (see §5.3.2.1, "Symmetry" (page 199)). Furthermore, trees are *acyclic* graphs, because if you follow the directed edges from one node to another, you can never encounter the same node twice. Finally, trees have the constraint that every node (except the root) must have exactly one parent.[449]

In Figure 8.4, "Descriptions Linked into a Graph." we have violated this constraint by joining our two book trees. The graph that results is still directed and acyclic, but because the *Winfried George Sebald* node now has two parents, it is no longer a tree.

Graphs are very general and flexible structures. Many kinds of systems can be conceived of as nodes connected by edges: stations connected by subway lines, people connected by friendships, decisions connected by dependencies, and so on. Relationships can be modeled in different ways using different kinds of graphs. For example, if we assume that friendship is symmetric (see §5.3.2.1, "Symmetry" (page 199)), we would use an undirected graph to model the relationship. However, in web-based social networks friendship is often asymmetric (you might "friend" someone who does not reciprocate), so a directed graph is more appropriate.

Often it is useful to treat a graph as a set of pairs of nodes, where each pair may or may not be directly connected by an edge. Many approaches to characterizing structural relationships among resources (see §5.5.3, "Structural Relationships between Resources" (page 213)) are based on modeling the related resources as a set of pairs of nodes, and then analyzing patterns of connectedness

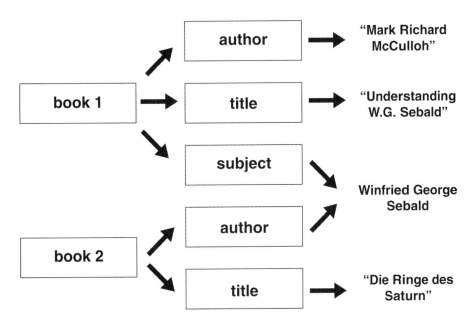

Figure 8.4. Descriptions Linked into a Graph.

among them. As we will see, being able to break down a graph into pairs is also useful when we structure resource descriptions as graphs.

In §8.4.1 we will use XML to model the graph shown in Figure 8.4, "Descriptions Linked into a Graph." by using "references" to connect a book to its title, authors and subject. This will allow us to develop sophisticated graphs of knowledge within a single XML document instance. (See also the Sidebar, "Inclusions and References" (page 332)).[450]

8.2.2 Comparing Metamodels: JSON, XML and RDF

Now that we are familiar with the various *kinds* of metamodels used to structure resource descriptions, we can take a closer look at some *specific* metamodels. A detailed comparison of the affordances of different metamodels is beyond the scope of this chapter. Here we will simply take a brief look at three popular metamodels—JSON, XML, and RDF—in order to see how they further specify and constrain the more general kinds of metamodels introduced above.

8.2.2.1 JSON

JavaScript Object Notation (JSON)

> **JavaScript Object Notation (JSON)** is a textual format for exchanging data that borrows its metamodel from the JavaScript programming language. Specifically, the JSON metamodel consists of two kinds of structures found in JavaScript: lists (called *arrays* in JavaScript) and dictionaries (called *objects* in JavaScript). Lists and dictionaries contain values, which may be strings of text, numbers, Booleans (true or false), or the null (empty) value. Again, these types of values are taken directly from JavaScript. Lists and dictionaries can be values too, meaning lists and dictionaries can be nested within one another to produce more complex structures such as tables and trees.

Lists, dictionaries, and a basic set of value types constitute the JSON metamodel. Because this metamodel is a subset of JavaScript, the JSON metamodel is very easy to work with in JavaScript. Since JavaScript is the only programming language that is available in all web browsers, JSON has become a popular choice for developers who need to work with data and resource descriptions on the web (see §8.3.2, "Writing Systems" (page 342) later in this chapter). Furthermore, many modern programming languages provide data structures and value types equivalent to those provided by JavaScript. So, data represented as JSON is easy to work with in many programming languages, not just JavaScript.

8.2.2.2 XML Information Set

The *XML Information Set* metamodel is derived from data structures used for document markup (see §4.2.2.2). These markup structures—**elements** and **attributes**—are well suited for programmatically manipulating the structure of documents and data together.[451]

XML Infoset

> The **XML Infoset** is a tree structure, where each node of the tree is defined to be an *information item* of a particular type. Each information item has a set of type-specific properties associated with it. At the root of the tree is a document item, which has exactly one element item as its child. An element item has a set of attribute items, and a list of child nodes. These child nodes may include other element items, or they may be character items. (See §8.2.1, "Kinds of Structures" (page 321) below for more on characters.) Attribute items may contain character items, or they may contain typed data, such as name tokens, identifiers and references. Element identifiers and references (ID/IDREF) may be used to connect nodes, transforming a tree into a graph. (See the Sidebar, "Inclusions and References" (page 332)).[452]

Figure 8.5, "A Description Structure." is a graphical representation of how an XML document might be used to structure part of a description of an author and his works. This example demonstrates how we might use element items to model the domain of the description, by giving them names such as author and title. The character items that are the children of these elements hold the content of the description: author names, book titles, and so on. Attribute items are used to hold auxiliary information about this content, such as its language.

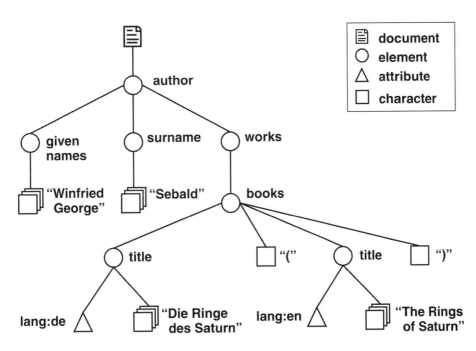

Figure 8.5. A Description Structure.

This example also demonstrates how the XML Infoset supports "mixed content" by allowing element items and character items to be "siblings" of the same parent element. In this case, the Infoset structure allows us to specify that the book description can be displayed as a line of text consisting of the original title and the translated title in parentheses. The elements and attributes are used to indicate that this line of text consists of two titles written in different languages, not a single title containing parentheses.

If not for mixed content, we could not write narrative text with *hypertext links* embedded in the middle of a sentence. It gives us the ability to identify the sub-components of a sentence, so that we could distinguish the terms "Sebald," "walking" and "East Anglia" as an author and two subjects.

Inclusions and References

An XML Infoset is typically the result of processing a well-formed XML document instance.[453] Schemas associated with XML document instances "inform" the corresponding XML Infoset. Thus, the "truth value" of any XML Infoset is dependent upon its related schemas.[454] Traditionally, any documentation that is related to the schema is considered to be part of the schema definition and, at least notionally, informs human understanding and interpretation of corresponding documents.[455]

The XML family offers several mechanisms to create inclusion relationships: by employing element references; by way of entity definition and reference; by using XInclude or XLink. These inclusions and references can also inform the XML Infoset, if they are processed.

Any XML node may refer to another node simply by referencing it by its assigned ID. Assuming attributes are declared, the Infoset exposes this information as a references property as an ordered list of element information items. That is to say that an element may contain other element nodes by subordination, or by reference.[456]

XInclude "specifies a processing model and syntax for general purpose inclusion. Inclusion is accomplished by merging a number of XML information sets into a single composite infoset." XInclude offers the most versatile mechanism for addressing whole documents, specific information items, ranges of information items, and even parts of information items, which has led to its widespread adoption in document processing.[457]

XLink "allows elements to be inserted into XML documents in order to create and describe links between resources. It uses XML syntax to create structures that can describe links similar to the simple unidirectional hyperlinks of today's HTML, as well as more sophisticated links."[458]

Entities are similar to macros found in many programming languages; a value is assigned to a token, the token is referenced wherever the value is needed, and macro expansion happens when the XML document instance is read into the Infoset.[459] Entities are a handy feature, but since they are expanded on their way in, entities do not survive as information items in the XML Infoset. The ID/IDREF feature is more popular than the use of entities because it carries more information into the XML Infoset.

Using schemas to define data representation formats is a good practice that facilitates shared understanding and contributes to long-term maintainability in institutional or business contexts. An XML schema represents a contract among the parties subscribing to its definitions, whereas JSON depends on out-of-band communication among programmers. The notion that "the code is the documentation" may be fashionable among programmers, but modelers prefer to design at a higher level of abstraction and then implement.

The XML Infoset presents a strong contrast to JSON and does not always map in a straightforward way to the data structures used in popular web scripting languages. Whereas JSON's structures make it easier for object-oriented programmers to readily exchange data, they lack any formal schema language and cannot easily handle mixed content.

8.2.2.3 RDF

In Figure 8.4, "Descriptions Linked into a Graph.", we structured our resource description as a graph by treating resources, properties and values as nodes, with edges reflecting their combination into descriptive statements. However, a more common approach is to treat resources and values as nodes, and properties as the edges that connect them. Figure 8.6, "Treating Properties as Edges Rather Than Nodes." shows the same description as Figure 8.4, "Descriptions Linked into a Graph.", this time with properties treated as edges. This roughly corresponds to the particular kind of graph metamodel defined by **RDF**. (§4.2.2.3, "Tagging of Web-Based Resources" (page 144) introduces RDF.)

We have noted that we can treat a graph as a set of pairs of nodes, where each pair may be connected by an edge. Similarly, we can treat each component of the description in Figure 8.6, "Treating Properties as Edges Rather Than Nodes." as a pair of nodes (a resource and a value) with an edge (the property) linking them. In the RDF metamodel, a pair of nodes and its edge is called a ***triple***, because it consists of three parts (two nodes and one edge). The RDF metamodel is a directed graph, so it identifies one node (the one from which the edge is pointing) as the ***subject*** of the triple, and the other node (the one to which the edge is pointing) as its ***object***. The edge is referred to as the ***predicate*** or (as we have been saying) *property* of the triple.

Figure 8.7, "Listing Triples Individually." lists separately all the triples in Figure 8.6 However, there is something missing in Figure 8.7. Figure 8.6 clearly indicates that the *Winfried George Sebald* who is the subject of book 1 is the same *Winfried George Sebald* who is the author of book 2. In Figure 8.7, "Listing Triples Individually." this relationship is not clear. How can we tell if the *Winfried George Sebald* of the third triple is the same as the *Winfried George Sebald* of the triple statement? For that matter, how can we tell if the first three triples all involve the same book 1? This is easy to show in a diagram of the entire description graph, where we can have multiple edges attached to a node. But when we disaggregate that graph into triples, we need some way of uniquely referring to

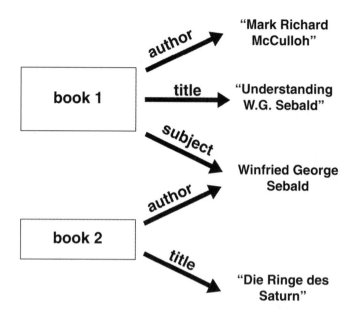

Figure 8.6. Treating Properties as Edges Rather Than Nodes.

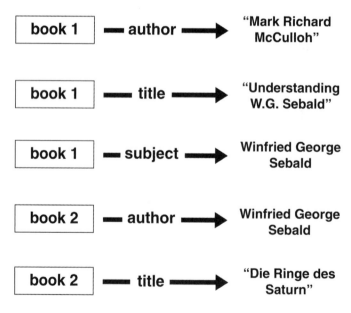

Figure 8.7. Listing Triples Individually.

nodes. We need identifiers (§3.4.3, "Choosing Good Names and Identifiers" (page 119)). When two triples have nodes with the same identifier, we can know that it is the same node. RDF achieves this by associating URIs with nodes (§4.2.2.3, "Tagging of Web-Based Resources" (page 144)).

The need to identify nodes when we break down an RDF graph into triples becomes important when we want to "write" RDF graphs—create textual representations of them instead of depicting them—so that they can be exchanged as data. Tree structures do not necessarily have this problem, because it is possible to textually represent a tree structure without having to mention any node more than once. Thus, one price paid for the generality and flexibility of graph structures is the added complexity of recording, representing or writing those structures.

8.2.2.4 Choosing Your Constraints

This tradeoff between flexibility and complexity illustrates a more general point about constraints. In the context of managing and interacting with resource descriptions, constraints are a good thing. As discussed above, a tree is a graph with very specific constraints. These constraints allow you to do things with trees that are not possible with graphs in general, such as representing them textually without repeating yourself, or uniquely identifying nodes by the path from the root of the tree to that node. This can make managing descriptions and the resources they describe easier and more efficient—*if* a tree structure is a good fit to the requirements of the organizing system. For example, an ordered tree structure is a good fit for the hierarchical structure of the content of a book or book-like document, such as an aircraft service manual or an SEC filing. On the other hand, the network of relationships among the people and organizations that collaborated to produce a book might be better represented using a graph structure. XML is most often used to represent hierarchies, but is also capable of representing network structures.

8.2.3 Modeling within Constraints

A metamodel imposes certain constraints on the structure of our resource descriptions. But in organizing systems, we usually need to further specify the content and composition of descriptions of the specific types of resources being organized. For example, when designing a system for organizing books, it is not sufficient to say that a book's description is structured using XML, because the XML metamodel constrains structure and not the content of descriptions. We need also to specify that a book description includes a list of contributors, each entry of which provides a name and indicates the role of that contributor. This kind of specification is a *model* to which our descriptions of books are expected to conform (§4.3.1.2, "Abstraction in Resource Description" (page 152)).

When designing an organizing system we may choose to reuse a standard model. For example, ONIX for Books is a standard model (conforming to the XML metamodel) developed by the publishing industry for describing books.[460]

If no such standard exists, or existing standards do not suit our needs, we may create a new model for our specific domain. But we will not usually create a new metamodel: instead we will make choices from among the metamodels, such as JSON, XML, or RDF, that have been formally recognized and incorporated into existing standards. Once we have selected a metamodel, we know the constraints we have to work with when modeling the resources and collections in our specific domain.[461]

8.2.3.1 Specifying Vocabularies and Schemas

Creating a model for descriptions of resources in a particular domain involves specifying the common elements of those descriptions, and giving those elements standard names (see §4.3, "The Process of Describing Resources" (page 148)). The model may also specify how these elements are arranged into larger structures, for example how they are ordered into lists nested into trees. Metamodels vary in the tools they provide for specifying the structure and composition of domain-specific models, and in the maturity and robustness of the methods for designing them.[462] RDF and XML each provide different, metamodel-specific tools to define a model for a specific domain. But not every metamodel provides such tools.

In XML, models are defined in separate documents known as *schemas*. An XML schema defining a domain model provides a vocabulary of terms that can be used as element and attribute names in XML documents that adhere to that model. For example, the Onix for Books schema specifies that an author of a book should be called a Contributor, and that the page count should be called an Extent. An XML schema also defines rules for how those elements, attributes, and their content can be arranged into higher-level structures. For example, the Onix for Books specifies that the description of a book must include a list of Contributor elements, that this list must have at least one element in it, and that each Contributor element must have a ContributorRole child element.

If an XML schema is given an identifier, XML documents can use that identifier to indicate that they use terms and rules from that schema. An XML document may use vocabularies from more than one XML schema.[463] Associating a schema with an XML instance enables *validation*: automatically checking that vocabulary terms are being used correctly.[464]

If two descriptions share the same XML schema and use only that schema, then combining them is straightforward. If not, it can be problematic, unless someone has figured out exactly how the two schemas should "map" to one another.

Finding such a mapping is not a trivial problem, as XML schemas may differ semantically, lexically, structurally, or architecturally despite sharing a common implementation form (see Chapter 5, *"Describing Relationships and Structures"*).

Tree structures can vary considerably while still conforming to the XML Infoset metamodel. Users of XML often specify rules for checking whether certain patterns appear in an XML document (document-level validation). This is less often done with RDF, because graphs that conform to the RDF metamodel all have the same structure: they are all sets of triples. This shared structure makes it simple to combine different RDF descriptions without worrying about checking structure at the document level. However, sometimes it is desirable to check descriptions at the document level, as when part of a description is required. As with XML, if consumers of those descriptions want to assert that they expect those descriptions to have a certain structure (such as a required property), they must check them at the document level.

Because the RDF metamodel already defines structure, defining a domain-specific model in RDF mainly involves specifying URIs and names for predicates. A set of RDF predicate names and URIs is known as an ***RDF vocabulary***. Publication of vocabularies on the web and the use of URIs to identify and refer to predicate definitions are key principles of Linked Data and the *Semantic Web* (see §5.8.1, as well as later in this chapter).[465]

For example, the Resource Description and Access (RDA) standard for cataloging library resources includes a set of RDF vocabularies defining predicates usable in cataloging descriptions. One such predicate is:

<http://rdvocab.info/Elements/extentOfText>

which is defined as "the number and type of units and/or subunits making up a resource consisting of text, with or without accompanying illustrations." The vocabulary further specifies that this predicate is a refinement of a more general predicate:

<http://rdvocab.info/Elements/extent>

which can be used to indicate, "the number and type of units and/or subunits making up a resource" regardless of whether it is textual or not.

JSON lacks any standardized way to define which terms can be used. That does not mean that one cannot use a standard vocabulary when creating descriptions using JSON, only that there is no agreed-upon way to use JSON to communicate which vocabulary is being used, and no way to automatically check that it is being used correctly.

8.2.3.2 Controlling Values

So far, we have focused on how models specify vocabularies of terms and how those terms can be used in descriptions. But models may also constrain the values or content of descriptions. Sometimes, a single model will define both the terms that can be used for property names and the terms that can be used for property values. For example, an XML schema may enumerate a list of valid terms for an attribute value.[466]

Often, however, there are separate, specialized vocabularies of terms intended for use as property values in resource descriptions. Typically these vocabularies provide values for use within statements that describe what a resource is about. Examples of such subject vocabularies include the Library of Congress Subject Headings (LOC-SH) and the *Medical Subject Headings (MeSH)*.[467] Other vocabularies may provide authoritative names for people, corporations, or places. Classification schemes are yet another kind of vocabulary, providing the category names for use as the values in descriptive statements that classify resources.

Because different metamodels such as XML and RDF take different approaches to specifying vocabularies, there will usually be different versions of these vocabularies for use with different metamodels. For example the LCSH are available both as XML conforming to the *Metadata Authority Description Standard (MADS)* schema, and as RDF using the *Simple Knowledge Organization System (SKOS)* vocabulary.

Specifying a vocabulary is just one way models can control what values can be assigned to properties. Another strategy is to specify what "types" of values can be assigned. For example, a model for book descriptions may specify that the value of a *pages* property must be a positive integer. Or it could be more specific; a course catalog might give each course an identifier that contains a two-letter department code followed by a 1-3 digit course number. Specifying a data type like this with a *regular expression* narrows down the set of possible values for the property without having to enumerate every possible value. (See the Sidebar.)

In addition to or in lieu of specifying a type, a model may specify an encoding scheme for values. An **encoding scheme** is a specialized *writing system* or syntax for particular types of values. For example, a model like Atom for describing syndicated web content requires a publication date. But there are many different ways to write dates: 9/2/76, 2 Sept. 1976, September 2nd 1976, etc. So, Atom also specifies an encoding scheme for date values. The encoding scheme is RFC3339, a standard for writing dates. When using RFC3339, one always writes a date using the same form: 1976-09-02.[468]

Regular Expressions

Regular expressions have been used to describe patterns in text documents since the early days of computing and came into widespread use when Ken Thompson incorporated them into early UNIX text processing tools, such as ed and grep. There are too many variations of regular expression syntax for us to detail them here, but it is worthwhile to consider them briefly while we are on the subject of controlling values.[469]

Regular expressions are employed by modern text processing tools for selection and retrieval purposes. In search and replace applications, one might search for the string "`Chapter [1-5]`" to express your intent to select chapters 1 through 5, or "`it[']?s`" to locate every use of "it's" and "its" in a manuscript; this capability is highly valued by anyone who has to had edit a book. Programmers and data modelers use regular expressions to describe expected encoding schemes when they design documents, data elements, databases, and encoding schemes. You experience regular expression processing when you enter a phone number or postal code into a Web-based form. Many data modeling, programming and XML schema languages employ regular expressions to control data entry and validation of values. In the context of controlling values, we can use regular expressions to describe data values as varied as identifiers, names, dates, telephone numbers, and postal codes. We can, likewise, define rules for white space handling and punctuation within a data value.

Encoding schemes are often defined in conjunction with standardized identifiers (see §3.4.3.1, "Make Names Informative" (page 120)). For example, International Standard Book Numbers (ISBN) are not just sequences of Arabic numerals: they are values written using the ISBN encoding scheme. This scheme specifies how to separate the sequence of numerals into parts, and how each of these parts should be interpreted. The ISBN 978-3-8218-4448-0 has five parts, the first three of which indicate that the resource with this identifier is 1) a product of the book publishing industry, 2) published in a German-speaking country, and 3) published by the publishing house Eichborn.

Encoding schemes can be viewed as very specialized models of particular kinds of information, such as dates or book identifiers. But because they specify not only the structure of this information, but also how it should be written, we can also view them as specialized *writing systems*. That is, encoding schemes specify how to *textually represent* information.

In the second half of this chapter, we will focus on the issues involved in textually representing resource descriptions—writing them. Graphs, trees, dictionaries, lists, and sets are general types of structures found in different metamodels. Thinking about these broad types and how they fit or do not fit the ways we want to model our resource descriptions can help us select a specific metamodel. Specific metamodels such as the XML Infoset or RDF are formalized and standardized definitions of the more general types of structures discussed above. Once we have selected a metamodel, we know the constraints we have to work with when modeling the *resources* and collections in our specific domain. But because metamodels are abstract and exist only on a conceptual level, they can only take us so far. If we want to create, store, and exchange individual resource descriptions, we need to make the structures defined by our abstract metamodels concrete. We need to write them.

8.3 Writing Descriptions

Suppose that I am organizing books, and I have decided that it is important for the purposes of this organizing to know the title of each book and how many pages it has. Before me I have a book, which I examine to determine that its title is *Die Ringe des Saturn* and it has 371 pages. Table 8.1, "Basic ways of writing part of a book description." lists a few of the ways to write this description. Let us examine these various forms of writing to see what they have in common and where they differ.

Table 8.1. Basic ways of writing part of a book description.

The title is *Die Ringe des Saturn* and it has 371 pages.

```
{ book {"title":"Die Ringe des Saturn","pages":371} }
```

```
<book pages="371"> <title>Die Ringe des Saturn</title> </book>
```

```
<div class="book">The title is
<span class="title">Die Ringe des Saturn</span>
and it has <span class="pages">371 pages.</span>
```

```
<http://lccn.loc.gov/96103072>
<http://rdvocab.info/Elements/title> "Die Ringe des Saturn"@de ;
<http://rdvocab.info/Elements/extentOfText> "371 p." .
```

We examine the notations, writing systems and syntax of each of the examples in the following sections.

8.3.1 Notations

First, let us look at the actual marks on the page. To write you must make marks or—more likely—select from a menu of marks using a keyboard. In either case, you are using a ***notation***: a set of characters with distinct forms.[470] The Latin alphabet is a notation, as are Arabic numerals. Some more exotic notations include the symbols used for editorial markup and alchemical symbols.[471] The characters in a notation usually have an ordering. Arabic numerals are ordered *1 2 3* and so on. English-speaking children usually learn the ordering of the Latin alphabet in the form of an alphabet song.[472]

A character may belong to more than one notation. The examples in Table 8.1, "Basic ways of writing part of a book description." use characters from a few different notations: the letters of the Latin alphabet, Arabic numerals, and a handful of auxiliary marks: . { } " :< > / $ Collectively, all of these characters—alphabet, numerals, and auxiliary marks—also belong to a notation called the American Standard Code for Information Interchange (ASCII).[473]

ASCII is an example of a notation that has been codified and standardized for use in a digital environment. A traditional notation like the Latin alphabet can withstand a certain degree of variation in the form of a particular mark. Two people might write the letter *A* rather differently, but as long as they can mutually recognize each other's marks as an "A," they can successfully share a notation. Computers, however, cannot easily accommodate such variation. Each character must be strictly defined. In the case of ASCII, each character is given a number from 0 to 127, so that there are 128 ASCII characters.[474] When using a computer to type ASCII characters, each key you press selects a character from this "menu" of 128 characters. A notation that has had numbers assigned to its characters is called a ***character encoding***.

The most ambitious character coding in existence is Unicode, which as of version 6.0 assigns numbers to 109,449 characters.[475] Unicode makes the important distinction between ***characters*** and ***glyphs***. A character is the smallest meaningful unit of a written language. In alphabet-based languages like English, characters are letters; in languages like Chinese, characters are ideographs. Unicode treats all of these characters as abstract ideas (*Latin capital A*) rather than specific marks (A A A **A**). A specific mark that can be used to depict a character is a glyph. A ***font*** is a collection of glyphs used to depict some set of characters. A Unicode font explicitly associates each glyph with a particular number in the Unicode character encoding. The inability of computers to use contextual understanding to bridge the gap between various glyphs and the abstract character depicted by those glyphs turns out to have important consequences for organizing systems.

Different notations may include very similar marks. For example, modern music notation includes marks for indicating the pitch of note, known as accidentals. One of these music notation marks is ♯ ("sharp"). The sharp sign looks very much like the symbol used in English as an abbreviation for the word *number*, as in *We're #1!*[476] If you were to write a sharp sign and a number sign by hand, they would probably look identical. In a non-digital environment, we would rely on context to understand whether the written mark was being used as part of music notation, or mathematical notation, or as an English abbreviation.

Computers, however, have no such intuitive understanding of context. Unicode encodes the number sign and the sharp sign as two different characters. As far as a computer using Unicode is concerned, ♯ and # are completely different, and the fact that they have similar-looking glyphs is irrelevant. That is a problem if, for example, a cataloger has carefully described a piece of music by correctly using the sharp sign, but a person looking for that piece of music searches for descriptions using the number sign (since that is what you get when you press the keyboard button with the symbol that most closely resembles a sharp sign).[477]

8.3.2 Writing Systems

A **writing system** employs one or more notations, and adds a set of rules for using them. Most writing systems assume knowledge of a particular human language. These writing systems are known as *glottic* writing systems. But there are many writing systems, such as mathematical and musical ones, that are not tied to human languages in this way. Many of the writing systems used for describing resources belong to this latter group, meaning that (at least in principle) they can be used with equal facility by speakers of any language.

Glottic writing systems, being grounded in natural human languages, are difficult to describe precisely and comprehensively. Non-glottic writing systems, on the other hand, can be described precisely and comprehensively using an abstract model. That is the connection between the structural perspective taken in the previous section, and the textual perspective taken in this section. A non-glottic writing system is described by a particular metamodel, and structures that fit within the constraints of a given metamodel can be textually represented using one or more writing systems that are described by that metamodel.

Some writing systems are closely identified with specific metamodels. For example, XML and JSON are *both* 1) metamodels for structuring information *and* 2) writing systems for textually representing information. In other words, they specify both the abstract structure of a description and how to write it down. It is possible to conceive of other ways to textually represent the structure of these metamodels, but for each of these metamodels just one writing system has been standardized.[478]

RDF, on the other hand, is *only* a metamodel, not a writing system. RDF only defines an abstract structure, not how to write that structure. So how do we write information that is structured as RDF? It turns out that we have many choices. Unlike XML and JSON, several different writing systems for the RDF metamodel have been standardized, including N-Triples, Turtle, RDFa, and RDF/XML.[479] Each of these is a writing system that is abstractly described by the RDF meta-model.

Writing systems provide rules for arranging characters from a notation into meaningful structures. A character in a notation has no inherent meaning. Characters in a notation only take on meaning in the context of a writing system that uses that notation. For example: what does the letter *I* from the Latin alphabet mean? That question can only be answered by looking at how it is being used in a particular writing system. If the writing system is American English, then whether *I* has a meaning depends on whether it is grouped with other letters or whether it stands alone. Only in the latter case does it have an assignable meaning. However in the arithmetic writing system of Ancient Rome, which also uses as a notation the letters of the Latin alphabet, *I* has a different meaning: *one*.

This example also serves to illustrate how the ordering of a notation can differ from the ordering of a writing system that uses that notation. According to the ordering of the Latin alphabet, the twelfth letter *L* comes before the twenty-second letter *V*. But in the Roman numeric writing system, *V* (the number 5) comes before *L* (the number 50). Unless we know which ordering we are using, we cannot arrange *L* and *V* "in order."[480]

This kind of difference in ordering can arise in more subtle ways as well. When we alphabetically order names, we first compare the first character of each name, and arrange them according to the ordering of the writing system. The first known use of alphabetical ordering was in the Library of Alexandria about two thousand years ago, when Zenodetus arranged the collection according to the first letter of resource names.[481] If the first characters of two names are the same, we compare the second character, and so on. We can also apply this same kind of ordering procedure to sequences of numerals. If we do, then *334* will come before *67*, because *3* (the first character of the first sequence) comes before *6* (the first character of the second sequence) according to the ordering of our notation (Arabic numerals). However, it is more common when ordering sequences of numerals to treat them as decimal numbers, and thus to use the ordering imposed by the decimal system. In the decimal writing system, *67* precedes *334*, since the latter is a greater number.

This difference is important for organizing systems. Computers will sort values differently depending on whether they are treating sequences of numerals as numbers or just as sequences. Some organizing systems mix multiple ways of ordering the same characters. For example, Library of Congress call numbers have four parts, and sequences of Arabic numerals can appear in three of them. In the second part, indicating a narrow subject area, and fourth part, indicating year of publication, sequences of numerals are treated as numbers and ordered according to the decimal system. In the third part, however, sequences of numerals are treated as sequences and ordered "notationally" as in the example above (*334* before *67*).

Differences in ordering demonstrate just one way that multiple writing systems may use the same notation differently. For example, the American English and British English writing systems both use the same Latin alphabet, but impose slightly different spelling rules.[482] The Japanese writing system employs a number of notations, including traditional Chinese characters (*kanji*) as well as the Latin alphabet (*rōmaji*). Often writing systems do not share the same exact notation but have mostly overlapping notations. Many European languages, for example, extend the Latin alphabet with characters such as *Å* and *Ü* that add additional marks, known as diacritics, to the basic characters.[483]

In organizing systems it is often necessary to represent values from one writing system in another writing system that uses a different notation, a process known as **transliteration**. For example, early computer systems only supported the ASCII notation, so text from writing systems that extend the Latin alphabet had to be converted to ASCII, usually by removing (or sometimes transliterating) diacritics. This made the non-ASCII text usable in an ASCII-based computerized organizing system, at the expense of information loss.

Even in modern computer systems that support Unicode, however, transliteration is often needed to support organizing activities by users who cannot read text written using its original system. The Library of Congress and the American Library Association provide standard procedures for transliterating text from over sixty different writing systems into the (extended) Latin alphabet.

8.3.3 Syntax

The examples in Table 8.1, "Basic ways of writing part of a book description." express the same information using different writing systems. The examples use the same notation (ASCII) but differ in their *syntax*: the rules that define how characters can be combined into words and how words can be combined into higher-level structures.[484]

Consider the first example: *The title is* Die Ringe des Saturn *and it has 371 pages*. The leading capital letter and the period ending this sequence of characters indicate to us that this is a sentence. This sentence is one way we might use the English writing system to express two statements about the book we are describing. A *statement* is one distinct fact or piece of information. In glottic writing systems like English, there is usually more than one sentence we could write to express the same statement. For example, instead of *it has 371 pages* we might have written *the number of pages is 371*. English writing also enables us to construct complex sentences that express more than one statement.[485]

In contrast, when we create descriptions of resources in an organizing system, we generally use non-glottic writing systems in which each sentence only expresses a single statement, and there is just one way to write a sentence that expresses a given statement.[486] These restrictions make these writing systems less expressive, but simplify their use. In particular, since there is a one-to-one correspondence between sentences and statements, we can drop the distinction and just talk about the statements of a description.

Now we return to our example and look at the structure of the statement, *The title is* Die Ringe des Saturn *and it has 371 pages.* Spaces are used to separate the text into words, and English syntax defines the functions of those words. The verb **is** in this statement functions to link the word title to the phrase *Die Ringe des Saturn*. This is typical of the kind of statements found in a resource description. Each statement identifies and describes some aspect of the resource. In this case, the statement attributes the value *Die Ringe des Saturn* to the property *title*.

As we saw when we looked at description structures, we can analyze descriptions as involving properties of resources and their corresponding values or content. In a writing system like English, it is not always so straightforward to determine which words refer to properties and which refer to values. (This is why blobs are not ideal description structures.) Writing systems designed for expressing resource descriptions, on the other hand, usually define syntax that makes this determination easier. In our dictionary examples above, we used an arrow character → to indicate the relationship between properties and values.

This ease of distinguishing properties and values comes at a price, however. The syntax of English is forgiving: we can read a sentence with somewhat garbled syntax such as *371 pages it has* and often still make out its meaning.[487] This is usually not the case with writing systems intended for expressing resource descriptions. These systems strictly define their rules for how characters can be combined into higher-level structures. Structures that follow the rules are *well formed* according to that system.

Take for example the second entry in Table 8.1, "Basic ways of writing part of a book description.". This example is written in JSON. As explained earlier in this chapter, JSON is a metamodel for structuring information using lists and dictionaries. But JSON is also a writing system, which borrows its syntax from Java-Script. The JSON syntax uses brackets to textually represent lists `[1,2,3]` and braces to textually represent dictionaries `{title:"Die Ringe des Saturn", "pages":371}`. Within braces, the colon character : is used to link properties with their values, much as is was used in the previous example. So `"pages":371` is a statement assigning the value `371` to the property `pages`.

The third example is written in XML. Like JSON, XML is a metamodel and also a writing system. Here we have XML elements and attributes. XML elements are textually represented as *tags* that are marked using the special characters <, > and /. So, this fragment of XML consists of a book element with a child element, title and a pages attribute each of which has some text content. In this case, pages="371" is a statement assigning the value 371 to the property pages. The difference is syntax is subtle; quotation marks surround the value and equal sign = is used to assign the property to its value.

The fourth example is a fragment of HTML. The writing system that HTML employs is close enough to XML to ignore any differences in syntax. In this example, the CLASS attribute contains the property name and the property value is the element content.

The fifth example is a fragment of Turtle, one of the writing systems for RDF. Turtle provides a syntax for writing down RDF *triples*. Each triple consists of a subject, predicate, and object separated by spaces. Recall that RDF uses URIs to identify subjects, predicates, and some objects; these URIs are written in Turtle by enclosing them in angle brackets < >. Triples are separated by period . characters, but triples that share the same subject can be written more compactly by writing the subject only once, and then writing the predicate and object of each triple, separated by a semicolon ; character. This is what we see in Table 8.1, "Basic ways of writing part of a book description.": two triples that share a subject.

Table 8.2. Writing part of a book description in Semantic XML.

```
<book xmlns:dc="http://purl.org/dc/terms/" dc:extent="371 p.">
<dc:title>Die Ringe des Saturn</title>
...
</book>
```

```
<book xmlns:db="http://www.docbook.org/xml/4.5/docbookx.dtd">
<bookinfo>
<title>Die Ringe des Saturn</title>
<pagenums>371 p.</pagenums>...</bookinfo>
...
</book>
```

The two examples in Table 8.2, "Writing part of a book description in Semantic XML." demonstrate namespaces, terms from the Dublin Core and DocBook namespaces, and the facility with which XML embraces semantic encoding of description resources. The first example extends the third example from Table 8.1, "Basic ways of writing part of a book description."; the xmlns:dc="..." segment is a namespace declaration which is associating dc with the quoted URI, which happens to be the Dublin Core Metadata Initiative (DCMI); the child <dc:title> element and the attached dc:extent="371" tell us that the corresponding values are attributable to the title and extent properties, respectively, from the Dublin Core namespace. The next example employs DocBook DTD namespace; we now have a `<pagenums>` element for which the meaning is contextually obvious; the title is still a title; an extra layer of markup reflects the fact that it could be metadata in the source file of a book that is being edited, is in production or is on your favorite tablet right now.[488]

Table 8.3. Writing part of a book description in RDFa or microdata.

```
<div class="book">The title is
<span property="http://purl.org/dc/terms/title">Die Ringe des Saturn</span>
and it has <span property="http://purl.org/dc/terms/extent">371 p.</span></div>
```

```
<div itemscope itemtype="book">The title is
<span itemprop="http://purl.org/dc/terms/title">Die Ringe des Saturn</span>
and it has <span itemprop="http://purl.org/dc/terms/extent">371 p.</span></div>
```

The two examples in Table 8.3, "Writing part of a book description in RDFa or microdata." demonstrate RDFa and microdata formats, which each rely upon specific attributes to establish the type of the property values contained by the HTML elements. In each example, the book title is contained by a `<span>` element. Whereas RDFa relies upon the `property` attribute, the microdata example employs the `itemprop` attribute to specify that the contents of the element is, effectively a "title" in exactly the same sense as we know that the contents of `<dc:title>` is a "title."

8.4 Worlds of Description

In the previous two sections we have considered descriptions as designed objects with particular structures, and as written documents with particular syntaxes. As we have seen, there are many possible choices of structure and syntax. But these choices are never made in isolation. Just as an architect or designer must work within the constraints of the existing built environment, and just as any author must work with existing writing systems, descriptions are always created as part of a pre-existing "world" over which any one of us has little control.

In the final part of this chapter, we will consider how choices of structure and syntax have converged historically into broad patterns of usage. For lack of a better term, we call these broad patterns "worlds." "World" is not a technical term and should not be taken too literally: the broad areas of application sketched here have considerable overlap, and there are many other ways one might identify patterns of description structure and syntax. That said, the three "worlds" described here do reflect real patterns of description form that influence tool and technology choices. In your own work creating and managing resource descriptions, it is likely that you will need to think about how your descriptions fit into one or more of these worlds.

8.4.1 The Document Processing World

The first world we will consider is concerned primarily with the creation, processing and management of hybrid narrative-transactional documents such as instruction manuals, textbooks, or annotated medieval manuscripts (see "The Document Type Spectrum" (page 101)). These are quite different kinds of documents, but they all contain a mixture of narrative text and structured data, and they all can be usefully modeled as tree structures. Because of these shared qualities, tools as different as publishing software, supply-chain management software, and scholarly editing software have all converged on common XML-based solutions. ("The XML world" would be another appropriate name for the document-processing world.)

This convergence was no accident, because XML was designed specifically to address the problem of how to add structure and data to documents by "marking them up." XML is the descendant of Standard Generalized Markup Language (SGML), which in turn descended from International Business Machines (IBM)'s Generalized Markup Language, which was invented to enable the production and management of large-scale technical documentation. The explicitness of markup makes it well-suited for representing structure and content type distinctions in institutional contexts where the scope, scale, and expected lifetime of organizing systems for information implies reuse by unknown people for unanticipated purposes.

The abstract data model underlying XML is called the XML Information Set or Infoset. The Infoset defines a document as a partially ordered tree of "information items." Every XML document can thus be understood as a specific kind of tree, although not every tree structure is expressible as an XML document.[489]

As we discussed in "Inclusions and References" (page 332), XML has the ability to describe graphs by incorporating the use of ID and IDREF attribute types to create references among element information items within the same document. This modest form of hypertext linking allows us to present the following document fragment that approximates the graph we saw modeled in Figure 8.4, "Descriptions Linked into a Graph."

Example 8.5. XML implementation of a biblio-graph

```
<person id="WG.Sebald">Winfried George Sebald</person>
<person id="MR.McCulloch>Mark Richard McCulloch</person>

<book>
    <title>Understanding W.G. Sebald</title>
    <subject idref="WG.Sebald"/>
    <author idref="WG.Sebald"/>
    <author idref="MR.McCulloch"/>
</book>
```

```
<book pages="371">
    <title lang="de">Die Ringe des Saturne</title>
    <title lang="en">The Rings of Saturn</title>
    <author idref="WG.Sebald"/>
</book>

<book pages="416">
    <title lang="de">Austerlitz</title>
    <author idref="WG.Sebald"/>
</book>
```

As one might expect, tools and technologies in the document-processing world are optimized for manipulating and combining tree structures. A "toolchain" is set of tools intended to be used together to achieve some goal.

The XML Toolchain

The XML toolchain is quite comprehensive. It consists of tools for creating XML documents (XML editors), tools for expressing logical document and data models (DTD, XML Schema, *REgular LAnguage for XML Next Generation (RELAX NG)*, Schematron), tools for transforming XML documents (XSLT), tools for describing document processing "pipelines" (*XProc: An XML Pipeline Language*), and tools for storing and querying collections of XML documents (XML databases, queried using XML Query Language (XQuery)). Used together, these tools provide very powerful means of working with tree-structured documents. XML editors incorporate knowledge of DTDs, schemas, transformations, style sheets, queries, databases and pipelines. Pipelines choreograph the plumbing and inter-dependencies involved in processing a complex dataset and publishing a useful result in one or more output formats.

For programmers who do not to use the XML toolchain, other programming languages also provide libraries for working with XML. This fact has led some to propose, and others to believe, that XML is a kind of "universal" format for exchanging data among systems. However, programmers have observed that a random XML Infoset does not map easily to the data structures commonly found in many programming languages. "Working with XML" frequently means translating from XML tree structures to data structures native to another language, usually meaning lists and dictionaries. This translation can be problematic and often means giving up many of the strengths of XML. By the same token, there are decades more practical experience working with markup languages and institutional publishing than there is with JSON and RDF.

XML is not a universal solution for every possible problem. That does not mean that it is not the best solution for a wide variety of problems, including yours. To gauge whether your resource descriptions are, or ought to be, part of the document-processing world, ask yourself the following questions:

- Do my resource descriptions contain mixtures of narrative text, hypertext, structured data and a variety of media formats?
- Can my descriptions easily be modeled using tree structures, hypertext links and transclusion?
- Are the vocabularies I need or want to use made available using XML technologies?
- Do I need to work with a body of existing descriptions already encoded as XML?
- Do I need to interoperate with processes or partners that utilize the XML toolchain?
- Do I need to publish my resource descriptions in multiple formats from a single source?

If the answer to one or more of these questions is "yes," then chances are good that you are working within the document processing world, and you will need to become familiar with conceptualizing your descriptions as trees and working with them using XML tools.

8.4.2 The Web World

The second "world" emerged in the early 1990s with the creation of the World Wide Web. The web was developed to address a need for simple and rapid sharing of scientific data. Of course, it has grown far beyond that initial use case, and is now a ubiquitous infrastructure for all varieties of information and communication services. ("The browser world" would be another appropriate name for what we are calling the Web World.)

Documents, data, and services on the web are conceptualized as resources, identified using Uniform Resource Identifiers (URI), and accessible through *representations* transferred via Hypertext Transfer Protocol (HTTP). Representations are sequences of bytes, and could be HTML pages, JPEG images, tabular data, or practically anything else transferable via HTTP. No matter what they are, representations transferred over the web include descriptions of themselves. These descriptions take the form of property-value pairs, known as "HTTP headers." The HTTP headers of web representations are structured as dictionaries.

Dictionary structures appear many other places in web infrastructure. URIs may include a *query* component beginning with a ? character. This component is used for purposes such as providing query parameters to search services. The query component is commonly structured as a dictionary, consisting of a series of property-value pairs separated by the & character. For example, the following URI:

```
https://www.google.com/search?q=sebald&tbs=qdr:m
```

includes the query component q=sebald&tbs=qdr:m. This is a dictionary with the properties q and tbs, respectively specifying the search term and temporal constraints on the search.

Microformats, RDFa and Microdata

When Tim Berners-Lee deployed HTML, it contained the basic elements and attributes needed to make statements about the document as a whole by using <LINK/>, or about specific parts of the document by using the <A> element. Each of these elements had four attributes in common: the famous HREF attribute contains a URI that names an object resource; the NAME attribute allowed the element to be the target end of a link, and; the REL and REV attributes contains descriptions of the link relations. Microformats, RDFa and Microdata are the latest generation of metadata extensions to HTML. Each approach is widely used on the web and by search engines. As such, they are potential targets when transforming into HTML from richer semantic formats.

Microformats are the simplest of the three. It uses controlled vocabularies of terms in REL/REV, and in the CLASS attribute, to declare high-level information types.

RDFa is RDF in Attributes. That is, RDFa is a formal specification for writing RDF expressions by using attributes in XML and HTML documents. It uses an ABOUT attribute to name the subject of the relation; the REL and REV attributes; HREF is joined by SRC and RESOURCE to name the object of the link, and; a TYPEOF attribute declares a type; PROPERTY and CONTENT attributes are used to *attribute* a value to an object's property.

Microdata is similar, inasmuch as it uses attributes extensively. The presence of an ITEMSCOPE attribute identifies an item while the ITEMTYPE attribute value identifies its type; ITEMID declares an items name or unique identifier; ITEMPROP is a name value pair, and; ITEMREF relates this item to other elements that are outside of the scope of the container element.

Data entered into an HTML form is also structured as a dictionary. When an HTML form is submitted, the entered data is used either to compose the query component of a URI, or to create a new representation to be transferred to a web server. In either case, the data is structured as a set of properties and their corresponding values.

HTML documents are structured as trees, but descriptions embedded within HTML documents can also be structured as dictionaries. HTML documents may include a dictionary of metadata elements, each of which specifies a property and its value. Recently support for *microdata* was added to HTML, which is another method of adding dictionaries of property-value pairs to documents. Using *microdata*, authors can annotate web content with additional information, making it easier to automatically extract structured descriptions of that content.[490] *Microformats* are another method for doing this by mapping existing HTML attributes and values to (nested) dictionary structures.[491]

Dictionary structures are easy to work with in any programming language, and they pervade various popular frameworks for programming the Web. In the programming languages used to implement web services, HTTP headers and query parameters are easily mapped to dictionary data structures native to those languages. On the client side, there is only one programming language that runs within all web browsers: JavaScript. The dictionary is the fundamental data structure within JavaScript as well.

Thus it is unsurprising that JSON, a dictionary-structured, JavaScript-based syntax, has become the de facto standard for application-to-application interchange of data on the web in contexts that do not involve business transactions. Web services providing structured data intended for programmatic use can make that data available as JSON, which is well-suited for use either by JavaScript programs running within browsers, or by programs written in other languages running outside of browsers (for example, smart phone applications).

It is now commonly accepted that there are useful differences of approach between the document-processing world and the Web World. This does not mean that the two worlds do not have significant overlaps. Some very important web representation types are XML-based, such as the Atom syndication format. Trees will continue to be the structure of choice for web representations that consist primarily of narrative rather than transactional data. But for structured descriptions that are intended to be accessed and manipulated on the Web, dictionary structures currently rule.

To gauge whether your resource descriptions are or ought to be part of the Web world, ask yourself the following questions:

- Is the web the primary platform upon which I will be making my descriptions available?

- Are my resource descriptions primarily structured, transaction-oriented data?

- Can my descriptions easily be modeled as lists of properties and values (dictionaries)?

- Are the vocabularies I need or want to use made available primarily using HTML technologies such as microdata or microformats?

- Do I need to make my descriptions easily usable for use within a wide array of programming languages?

If the answer to one or more of these questions is "yes," then chances are good that you are working within the Web World, and you will need to become familiar with conceptualizing your descriptions as dictionaries and working with them using programming languages such as JavaScript.

8.4.3 The Semantic Web World

The last world we consider is still somewhat of a "possible world," at least in comparison with the previous two. While the document processing world and the web world are well-established, the Semantic Web world is only starting to emerge, despite having been envisioned over a decade ago.

The vision of a *Semantic Web* world builds upon the web world, but adds some further prescriptions and constraints for how to structure descriptions. The Semantic Web world unifies the concept of a resource as it has been developed in this book, with the web notion of a resource as anything with a URI. On the Semantic Web, anything being described must have a URI. Furthermore, the descriptions must be structured as graphs, adhering to the RDF metamodel and relating resources to one another via their URIs. Advocates of Linked Data further prescribe that those descriptions must be made available as representations transferred over HTTP.[492]

This is a departure from the web world. The web world is also structured around URIs, but it does not require that every resource being described have a URI. For example, in the web world a list of bibliographic descriptions of books by W. G. Sebald might be published at a specific URI, but the individual books themselves might not have URIs. In the Semantic Web world, in addition to the list having a URIs, each book would have a URI too, in addition to whatever other identifiers it might have.[493]

Making an HTTP request to an individual book URI may return a graph-structured description of that book, if best practices for Linked Data are being followed. This, too, is a departure from the web world, which is agnostic about the form representations or descriptions of resources should take (although as we have seen, dictionary structures are often favored on the web when the clients consuming those descriptions are computer programs). On the Semantic Web, all descriptions are structured as RDF graphs. Each description graph links to other description graphs by referring to these related resources using their URIs. Thus, at least in theory, all description graphs on the Semantic Web are linked into a single massive graph structure. In practice, however, it is far from clear that this is an achievable, or even a desirable, goal.

Although the Semantic Web is in its infancy, a significant number of resource descriptions have already been made available in accordance with the principles outlined above. Descriptions published according to these principles are often referred to as "Linked Data." Prominent examples include: DBpedia, a graph of descriptions of subjects of Wikipedia articles; the Virtual International Authority File (VIAF), a graph of descriptions of names collected from various national libraries' name authority files; GeoNames, a graph of descriptions of places; and Data.gov.uk, a graph of descriptions of public data made available by the UK government.[494]

Despite the growing amount of Linked Data, tools for working with graph-structured data are still immature in comparison to the XML toolchain and Web programming languages. Although there is an XML syntax for RDF, using the XML toolchain to work with graph-structured data is generally a bad idea. And just as most programming languages do not support natively working with tree structures, most do not support natively working with graph structures either. Storing and querying graph-structured data efficiently requires a graph database or *triple store*.

Still, the Semantic Web world has much to recommend it. Having a common way of identifying resources (the URI) and a single shared metamodel (RDF) for all resource descriptions makes it much easier to combine descriptions from different sources. To gauge whether your resource descriptions are or ought to be part of the Semantic Web world, ask yourself the following questions:

- Is the web the primary platform upon which I will be making my descriptions available?
- Is it important that I be able to easily and freely aggregate the elements of my descriptions in different ways and to combine them with descriptions created by others?
- Are my descriptions best modeled as graph structures?
- Have the vocabularies I need or want to use been created using RDF?
- Do I need to work with a body of existing descriptions that have been published as Linked Data?

If the answer to one or more of these questions is "yes," then chances are good that you should be working within the Semantic Web world, and you ought to become familiar with conceptualizing your descriptions as graphs and working with them using Semantic Web tools.

8.5 Key Points in Chapter Eight

- We can approach the problem of how to form resource descriptions from two perspectives: structuring and writing.
- Metamodels describe structures commonly found in resource descriptions and other information resources, regardless of the specific domain.
- Blobs, sets, lists, dictionaries, trees, and graphs are kinds of structures that can be used to form resource descriptions.
- A **list**, like a set, is a collection of items with an additional constraint: their items are *ordered*.
- A ***dictionary***, also known as a *map* or an *associative array*, is a set of property-value pairs or *entries*.
- Nested dictionaries form a ***tree***.
- Trees consist of ***nodes*** joined by ***edges***.
- JSON consists of two kinds of structures: lists (called *arrays* in JavaScript) and dictionaries (called *objects* in JavaScript).
- The XML Infoset is a tree structure, where each node of the tree is defined to be an *information item* of a particular type.
- Using schemas to define data representation formats is a good practice that facilitates shared understanding and contributes to long-term maintainability.
- The RDF metamodel is a directed graph, so it identifies one node (the one from which the edge is pointing) as the ***subject*** of the triple, and the other node (the one to which the edge is pointing) as its ***object***. The edge is referred to as the ***predicate*** or (as we have been saying) *property* of the triple.
- An "encoding scheme" is a specialized writing system or syntax for particular types of values. Encoding schemes specify how to *textually represent* information.
- A ***writing system*** employs notations, and adds a set of rules for using them.
- Differences in ordering demonstrate just one way that multiple writing systems may use the same notation differently.
- Syntax is the rules that define how characters can be combined into words and how words can be combined into higher-level structures.

- The document processing world is concerned primarily with the creation, processing and management of hybrid narrative-transactional documents.

- In the web world, documents, data, and services are conceptualized as resources, identified using Uniform Resource Identifiers (URI), and accessible through *representations* transferred via the Hypertext Transfer Protocol (HTTP).

- The Semantic Web world unifies the concept of a resource as it has been developed in this book, with the web notion of a resource as anything with a URI. Descriptions must be structured as graphs, adhering to the RDF metamodel and relating *resources* to one another via their URIs.

Notes

439. [Computing] This discussion of Batten's cards is based on (Lancaster 1968, pages 28-32). Batten's own explanation is in (Batten 1951).

440. [Linguistics] (Silman 1998).

441. [Linguistics] The technique of diagramming sentences was invented in the mid-19th century by Stephen W. Clark, a New York schoolmaster; (Clark 2010) is an exact reprinting of a nearly 100 year old edition of his book *A Practical Grammar*. A recent tribute to Clark is (Florey 2012).

442. [CogSci] It is easy to underestimate the incredible power of the human perceptual and cognitive systems to apply neural computation and knowledge to enable vision and hearing to seem automatic. Computers are getting better at extracting features from visual and auditory signals to identify and classify inputs, but our point here is that none of these features are explicitly represented in the input "blob" or "stream."

443. [Computing] As we commented earlier, an oral description of a resource may not be especially useful in an organizing system because computers cannot easily understand it. On the other hand, there are many contexts in which an oral description would be especially useful, such as in a guided tour of a museum where visitors can use audio headsets.

444. [LIS] What was lost was the previously invisible structure provided by the grammar, which made us assign roles to each of these terms to create a semantic interpretation.

445. [Computing] It is rarely practical to make things as simple as possible. According to Einstein, we should endeavor to "Make everything as simple as possible, but not simpler."

446. [Computing] This structural metamodel only allows one value for each property, which means it would not work for books with multiple authors or that discuss multiple subjects.

447. [LIS] Going the other direction is not so easy, however: just as real dictionaries do not support finding a word given a definition, neither do dictionary structures support finding a key given a value.

448. [Computing] RDF/XML is one example where meta models meet. In *Document Design Matters*, (Wilde and Glushko 2008b) point out that "If the designer of an exchange format uses a non-XML conceptual metamodel because it seems to be a better fit for the data model, XML is only used as the physical layer for the exchange model. The logical layer in this case defines the mapping between the non-XML conceptual model, and any reconstruction of the exchange model data requires the consumer to be fully aware of this mapping. In such a case, it is good practice to make users of the API aware of the fact that it is using a non-XML metamodel. Otherwise they might be tempted to base their implementation on a too small set of examples, creating implementations which are brittle and will fail at some point in time."

449. [Computing] Technically, what is described here is referred to as "rooted tree" by mathematicians, who define trees more generally. Since trees used as data structures are always rooted trees, we do not make the distinction here.

450. [Computing] This feature relies upon the existence of an XML schema. An XML schema can declare that certain attributes are of type ID, IDREF or IDREFS. Whether an XML DTD or one of the many schema languages that have been developed under the auspices of the W3C or ISO.

451. [Computing] *http://www.w3.org/TR/xml-infoset/*.

452. [Computing] The *XML Infoset* is one of many metamodels for XML, including the DOM and XPath. Typically, an XML Infoset is created as a by-product of parsing a well-formed XML document instance. An XML document may also be informed by its DTD or schema with information about the types of attribute values, and their default values. Attributes of type ID, IDREF and IDREFs provide a mechanism for intra-document hypertext linking and transclusion. An XML document instance may contain entity definitions and references that get expanded when the document is parsed, thereby offering another form of transclusion.

453. [Computing] A well-formed XML document instance, when processed, will yield an XML Information Set, as described here. Information sets may also be constructed by other means, such as transforming from another information set. See the section on *Synthetic Infosets* at *http://www.w3.org/TR/xml-infoset/#intro.synthetic* for details.

454. [Computing] The Infoset contains knowledge of whether all related declarations have been read and processed, the base URI of the document instance, information about attribute types, comments, processing instructions, unparsed entities and notations, and more.

A well-formed XML document instance for which there are associated schemas, such as a DTD, may contribute information to the Infoset. Notably, schemas may associate data types with element and attribute information items, and it may also specify default or fixed values for attributes. A DTD may define entities that are referenced in the document instance and are expanded in-place when processed. These contributions can affect the truth value of the document.

455. [Computing] The SGML standard explicitly stated that documentation describing or explaining a DTD is part of the document type definition. The implication being that a schema is not just about defining syntax, but also semantics. Moreover, since DTDs do not make possible to describe all possible constraints, such as co-occurrence constraints, the documentation could serve as human-consumable guidance for implementers as well as content creators and consumers.

456. [Computing] Attribute types may be declared in an XML DTD or schema. Attributes whose type is ID must have a valid XML name value that is unique within that XML document; an attribute of type IDREF whose value corresponds to a unique ID has a "references" property whose value is the element node that corresponds to the element with that ID. An attribute of type IDREFS whose value corresponds to a list of unique ID has a "references" property whose value is a list of element node(s) that corresponds to the element(s) with matching IDs.

457. [Computing] XML Linking Language (XLink) is (Marsh, Orchard, and Veillard 2006).

458. [Computing] XML Linking Language (XLink) is (DeRose, Maler, Orchard, and Walsh 2010).

459. [Computing] Within the document's DTD, one simply declares the entity and its corresponding value, which could be anything from an entire document to a phrase and then it may be referenced in place within the XML document instance. The entity reference is replaced by the entity value in the XML Infoset. Entities, as nameable wrappers, effectively disappear on their way into the XML Infoset.

460. [Business] ONIX is the international standard for representing and communicating book industry product information in electronic form: *http://www.editeur.org/11/Books/*.

461. [Computing] Do not take on the task of creating a new XML model lightly. Literally thousands of XML vocabularies have been created, and some represent

hundreds or thousands of hours of effort. See (Bray 2005) for advice on how to reduce the risk of vocabulary design if you cannot find an existing one that satisfies your requirements.

462. [Computing] See (Glushko and McGrath 2005) for a synthesis of best practices for creating domain-specific languages in technical publishing and business-to-business document exchange contexts. You need best practices for big problems, while small ones can be attacked with *ad hoc* methods.

463. [Computing] Unless an XML instance is associated with a schema, it is fair to say that it does not have any model at all because there is no way to understand the content and structure of the information it contains. The assignment of a schema to an XML instance requires a "Document Type Declaration." If some of the same vocabulary terms occur in more than one XML schema, with different meanings in each, using elements from more than one schema in the same instance requires that they be distinguished using *namespaces.* For example, if an element named "title" means the "title of the book" in one schema and "the honorific associated with a person" in another, instances might have elements with namespace prefixes like <book:title>The Discipline of Organizing</book:title> and <hon:title>Professor</hon:title>. Namespaces are a common source of frustration in XML, because they seem like an overly complicated solution to a simple problem. But in addition to avoiding naming collisions, they are important in schema composition and organization.

464. [Computing] What "correctly" means depends on the schema language used to encode the conceptual model of the document type. The XML family of standards includes several schema languages that differ in how completely they can encode a document type's conceptual model. The Document Type Definition (DTD) has its origins in publishing and enforces structural constraints well; it expresses strong data typing through associated documentation resources. XML Schemas (XSD) are better for representing transactional document types but their added expressive power tends to make them more complex.

465. [Web] For example, see Linked Open Vocabularies at *http://lov.okfn.org/dataset/lov/index.html.*

466. [Computing] Attribute values can be constrained in a schema by specifying a data type, a default value, and a list of potential values. Data types allow us to specify whether a value is supposed to be a name, a number, a date, a token or a string of text. Having established the data type, we can further constrain the value of an attribute by specifying a range of values, for a number or a date, for example. We can also use *regular expression* patterns to describe a data type such as a postal code, telephone number or ISBN number. Specifying default values and lists of legal values for attributes simplifies content creation and quality assurance processes. In Schematron, a rule-based XML schema language for making test assertions about XML documents, we can express con-

straints between elements and attributes in ways that other XML schema languages cannot. For example, we can express the constraint that if two `<title>` elements are provided, then each must contain a unique string value and different language attribute values.

467. [LIS] See LOC-SH as *http://id.loc.gov/authorities/subjects.html*; MeSH at *http://www.nlm.nih.gov/mesh/*.

468. [Computing] The Atom Publishing Protocol is IETF RFC 5023, (*https://tools.ietf.org/html/rfc5023*); a good introduction is (Sayre 2005). IETF RFC is *http://www.ietf.org/rfc/rfc3339.txt*.

469. [Computing] There is no single authority on the subject of regular expressions or their syntax. A good starting point is the Wikipedia article on the subject: *http://en.wikipedia.org/wiki/Regular_expression*.

470. [Computing] The terminology here and in the following sections comes from (Harris 1996).

471. [Computing] See *http://unicode.org/charts/PDF/U1F700.pdf*.

472. [CogSci] Entitled "The ABC," the song was copyrighted in 1835 by Boston Music publisher Charles Bradlee. It is sung to a tune that was originally developed by Wolfgang Amadeus Mozart, and is commonly recognizable as *Twinkle, Twinkle, Little Star*.

473. [Computing] *http://tools.ietf.org/html/rfc20*.

474. [Computing] Only 95 of these characters are actually "marks" in the sense of being visible and printable. The other 33 ASCII characters are "control codes" that indicate things like horizontal and vertical tabs, the ends of printed lines, form feeds, and transmission control. We can think of many of these as special auxiliary marks, similar to the kind of symbols editors and proofreaders use to annotate texts.

475. [Computing] The Unicode standard is maintained by a global non-profit organization. Everything you need to know is at *http://www.unicode.org/*.

476. [Linguistics] The Chinese character 井 (water well) looks like the # character too. The # symbol was historically used to denote pounds, the Imperial unit of weight, as in 10# of potatoes. In the United Kingdom, the # character is called"hash." We could go on, but we will leave it to you to discover more.

477. [Computing] To add to the confusion, while the American standard (ASCII) places the # character at position 23, the British equivalent (BS 4730) places the currency symbol £ at the same position. As a result, improperly configured computers sometimes display # in place of £ and vice versa.

478. [Computing] Recently, an alternative writing system for XML-structured data has been standardized: Efficient XML Interchange (EXI). However it is not yet widely used.

479. [Computing] RDF/XML is a bit confusing; it is a writing system that uses XML syntax to textually represent RDF structure. This means that while XML tools can read and write RDF/XML, they cannot manipulate the graph structures it represents, because they were designed to work with XML's tree structures.

480. [Linguistics] Although we use the Roman alphabetic characters today to represent Roman numerals, originally they were represented by unique symbols.

481. [Linguistics]It took a few hundred years before alphabetization became recursive and applied to letters other than the first (Casson 2002, p. 37). Alphabetization relies on the ordering of the writing system, not the notation. For example, Swedish and German are two writing systems that assign different orderings to the same notation.

482. [Linguistics] For example, the American spelling of the words "center" and "color" contrasts slightly with the English spelling of "centre" and "colour." There are too many examples to include here. Wikipedia has a comprehensive analysis of American and British spelling differences at *http://en.wikipe dia.org/wiki/American_and_British_English_spelling_differences*.

483. [Computing] ASCII's 128 characters are insufficient to represent these more complex character sets, so a new family of character encodings was created, ISO-8859, in which each encoding enumerates 256 characters. Each encoding thus has more space to accommodate the additional characters of regionally-specific notations. ISO 8859-5, for example, has extensions to support the Cyrillic alphabet.

484. [Computing] In discussions of glottic writing systems, "syntax" usually refers only to the rules for combining words into sentences. In discussions of programming languages, "syntax" has the broader sense we use here.

485. [Linguistics] Compund sentences contain two independent clauses joined by a conjunction, such as "and," "or," "nor," "but." For example: I went to the store and I bought a book." Complex sentences contain an independent clause joined by one or more dependent clauses. For example: "I read the book that I bought at the store."

486. [Computing] In truth, even non-glottic writing systems designed to encode resource descriptions unambiguously can have variant forms of the same statement. For example, XML permits some variation in the way the same Infoset may be textually represented. Often these variations involve the treatment of

content that may under some circumstances be treated as optional, such as white space. The difference is that in writing systems designed for resource description, these variations can be precisely enumerated and rules developed to reconcile them, while this is not generally true for glottic writing systems.

487. [Linguistics] Fortunately for Yoda. There are many web services for converting English to Yoda-speak; an example is *http://www.yodaspeak.co.uk/*.

488. [Computing] DocBook (Walsh 2010) is widely used to publish academic, commercial, industrial book, scientific, and computing book, papers and articles. The book that you are reading is encoded with DocBook markup; complete bibliographic information for the book is contained within the source files, ready to be extracted on the way into one of the latest eBook formats.

489. [Computing] It should be noted that the content of the Infoset for a given document may be affected by knowledge of any related DTDs or schemas. That is to say that, upon examination of a given XML document instance, its Infoset may be augmented with some useful information, such as default attribute values and attribute types. (See "Inclusions and References" (page 332).)

490. [Web] Microdata, an invention of WHATWG and exists and part of what they call a "living standard" It is supported by Google, so it is widely used and there exist numerous controlled vocabularies, including those for creative works, persons, events and organizations.

491. [Web] Microformats is a non-standard that emerged from the community and has been sponsored by CommerceNet and Microformats.org.

492. [Web] (Bizer, Heath, and Berners-Lee 2009).

493. [Web] It is worth noting that URIs are not required to have anything at their endpoints. Resolvability of URIs is evangelized as a best practice for Linked Data but not a requirement within the broader Semantic Web paradigm. Merely asserting that a URI is associated with a book is enough. If the URI can return a description or a resource, so much the better, but if not, at least you can talk about the book by referring to the same URI.

494. [Web] Many more available datasets are listed at *http://linkedda ta.org/*.

Chapter 9

Interactions with Resources

Vivien Petras
Robert J. Glushko
Karen Joy Nomorosa
J.J.M. Ekaterin
Hyunwoo Park
Sean Marimpietri

9.1 Introduction

Once our resources have been described and are suitably organized, we can focus our attention on the third main activity we outlined in Chapter 2, *"Activities in Organizing Systems"*: designing resource-based interactions. What kinds of interactions do we encounter and what interactions are needed in *Organizing Systems*?

The interactions necessary to select, describe, and organize resources were discussed in Chapter 2, Chapter 4, and Chapter 6 and we do not need to consider them again in this chapter. Furthermore, while it is crucial to understand all interactions that are possible within an organizing system context, this chapter will concentrate on interactions that are purposefully designed into them rather than those that arise naturally from the affordances of the resources (§2.4.1, "Affordance and Capability" (page 61)).

Implementing designed interactions depends on a careful analysis of requirements and resource properties. More interactions might make a system more capable, but not always, and they might make it more complicated to maintain. For example, if a library provides an access interaction for users by giving them direct access to the stacks, it is not necessary to provide personnel to retrieve the books for users, but books might get lost or misplaced. In other words, it is important to consider the tradeoffs that arise from any interaction you might implement.

Initially, we will look at several organizing system environments and some of their main designed interactions. Although resources and their descriptions might be different, it turns out that similar interactions occur in every organizing system—just in different implementations.

9.1.1 Interactions in Libraries

The main interaction supported by most libraries is borrowing. Library resources are checked out by their users; i.e., books are accessed and taken from the library by patrons. Libraries buy and describe books so that they can be found by patrons and borrowed. When you need to find a book on a certain topic, by a certain author, or with a certain title, you access the resource descriptions in the library catalog to search for resources that satisfy your requirement. You then access the resource directly, or ask a librarian to retrieve the resource for you. A check-out interaction leaves a record of the resource identifier, the borrower identifier, and the *effectivity* dates of the loan.

Library catalogs offer a search interaction to enable queries about particular fields in resource descriptions like "author" or "title." Finding a description record for a book in a library catalog usually means that the book is owned by the library and that it can be borrowed.

A much more powerful search interaction is enabled by a union catalog (e.g., OCLC's Worldcat), where resource descriptions from multiple libraries are merged before they are offered for search. Union catalogs allow patrons to find out with a single search whether a resource is available from any library that is accessible to them.[495]

9.1.2 Interactions in Museums

In contrast to libraries, visitors to museums interact with resources mostly *to look* at them rather than by borrowing them. Museums enable people to discover or experience resources by *exhibiting* artifacts in creative contexts. When museums implement this interaction in a website, visitors are not only able to discover what is presented to them by the museum curators; they can also interact with resources in new ways. Virtual collections enable patrons who are unable to visit remote museums to search and view their resources. Patrons who intend to visit museums can direct their searches to locate resources that are not currently on view.

The digitization of museum resources also allows visitors to experience them from a perspective that might not be possible in a physical museum. For example, in Google's Art Project users can zoom in to view fine details of digitized paintings.[496] Museums are starting to leverage technology and the popularity of Web 2.0 features such as tagging and social networking in order to attract new audiences.[497] Implemented in 2004, the MuseumFinland project aims to provide a portal for publishing heterogeneous museum collections on the semantic web.[498] Institutions such as the Getty Information Institute and the International Committee for Documentation of the International Council of Museums have worked on standards that ensure worldwide consistency in how museums manage information about their collections.[499]

9.1.3 Interactions in Retail Supply Chains

Walmart is the largest retailer in the US. It works to streamline its operations and maximize business intelligence in order to have a supply chain that brings products that customers want to the store when it is needed. The most important interactions in the Walmart organizing system are those that manage the access and movement of physical goods efficiently and effectively. This lowers costs in terms of distribution and inventory management and serves to meet customer expectations at the same time. Walmart pushed for the use of technology such as the bar code and RFID and required suppliers to comply with company-set standards, which allows them to keep track of the products that they sell, regardless of which manufacturer or supplier the product comes from. All information exchanges use an *Electronic Data Interchange (EDI)* format employing a data model that Walmart specifies and requires, which then enables the company to push information from individual stores to warehouses and suppliers, enabling efficient stocking and ordering processes.[500]

9.1.4 Interactions in Online Retail Stores

Buying a coat from the online retail store Shopstyle.com requires the shopper to choose the appropriate shopping category from the homepage ("clothing," subcategory "outerwear") and then select a coat from hundreds of choices that are offered in the category. Once a desired coat is selected, Shopstyle redirects the shopper to another online shopping site—Nordstrom, Neiman Marcus, Lord & Taylor, and so on—where the actual sale happens. Shopstyle.com aggregates different catalogs from over 250 online stores providing a seamless access interaction for shoppers, as if they were searching only one organizing system. So rather than moving physical resources like Walmart, Shopstyle's most important interactions involve moving and combining digital resource descriptions.

As we have seen in these four examples (and others), accessing and merging resources or resource descriptions—whether physically or digitally—are fundamental interactions that occur in almost every organizing system. Combining resources or resource descriptions poses numerous strategy, design and implementation challenges as producers often use different identifiers, descriptions or cataloging formats and practices for similar resources. Different service providers use different technologies, have different information policies, and follow different processes developed in their organizing systems. Some partners can exert power and determine description standards (e.g. Walmart), others have to adapt to whatever their counterparts develop (e.g. Shopstyle), and still others choose to abide by what a standard-setting body decides.[501] Elsewhere, a laborious democratic process has to be started in order to align organizing practices and interactions (e.g. museums and libraries).

How can these differences be handled in order to provide seamless interactions within and across organizing systems? Which requirements have to be met in order to provide the interactions that are desired? How are different interaction types implemented? Finally, how can the quality of interactions be evaluated with respect to their requirements? These are the main questions for interactions that we will try to answer.

This chapter concentrates on the processes that develop interactions based on leveraging the resources of organizing systems in order to provide valuable services to their users (human or computational agents). It will discuss the determination of the appropriate interactions, the organization of resources for interactions, the implementation of interactions, and their evaluation and adaptation. Although the fundamental questions pertain to all types of organizing systems, this chapter focuses on systems that use computers to satisfy their goals.

9.2 Determining Interactions

Creating a strategy for successfully implementing interactions involves an intricate balance between the resources, the organizing system that arranges and manages them, its producers, and its intended users or consumers. The design of interactions is driven by user requirements and their impact on the choices made in the implementation process. It is constrained by resource and technical system properties and by social and legal requirements. Determining the scope and scale of interactions needs a careful analysis of these individual factors, their combination, and the consequences thereof. It is useful to distinguish decisions that involve choices, where multiple feasible alternatives exist, from decisions that involve constraints, where design choices have been eliminated or rendered infeasible by previous ones. The goal when creating an organizing system is to make design decisions that preserve subsequent choices or that create constraints that impose design decisions that would have been preferred anyway.

FRBR and Svenonius define five universal purposes for organizing systems: find, navigate, identify, select, and obtain (§4.3, "The Process of Describing Resources" (page 148)). The associated interactions for these purposes *retrieve* resources according to various criteria (e.g., a stated information need in a query, predetermined categories, a distinguishing criterion or other formal criteria such as licensing). To increase the scope or precision of access, a frequent prerequisite interaction step is the integration, joining, clustering or merging of resources to provide a wider range of resources and more homogeneous descriptions to search.

Interactions can be distinguished by user requirements, which layer of resource properties is used, and the legal, social, and organizational environment. All impose constraints on the type of interactions that can be offered by an organizing system.

9.2.1 User Requirements

Users (human or computational agents) search or navigate resources in organizing systems not just to identify them, but also to obtain and further use the selected resources (e.g. read, cluster, annotate, buy, copy, distribute, adapt, etc.). How resources are used and by whom affects how much of the resource or its description is exposed, across which channels it is offered, and the *precision* and *accuracy* of the interaction.

An organizing system should enable interactions that allow users to achieve their goals. User requirements can be stated or implied, depending on the sophistication and functional capabilities of the system.

In a closet, which is a personal organizing system for physical resources, the person searching with an intent to find a particular shirt might think, "Where's my yellow Hawaiian shirt?" but does not need to communicate the search criteria to anyone else in an explicit way. In a business or institutional organizing system, however, the user needs to describe the desired resource and interact with the system to select from candidate resources. This interaction might involve a human intermediary like a sales person or a reference librarian, or a computational one like a search engine.

The more abstract and intermediated the interaction between a user and an organizing system becomes—from a person accessing their self-described organizing system to human users interacting with human or machine intermediaries to computational agents interacting with other computational agents—the more precisely the requirements must be expressed.

A user's information need usually determines the kind and content of resources required. User information needs are most often expressed in search queries (whatever is typed into a search box) or manifest themselves in the selection of one or more of the system categories that are offered for browsing. Queries can be as simple as a few keywords or very complex and specialized, employing different search fields or operators; they may even be expressed in a query language by expert users. Techniques like spelling correction, query expansion and suggestion assist users in formulating queries. Techniques like breadcrumb navigation and faceted filtering assist users in browsing an organizing system's category system. Some systems allow the query to be expressed in natural language and then transform it into a description that is easier for the system to process. Queries for non-textual information like photos or videos are typically expressed as text, but some systems compute descriptions from non-textual queries such as images or audio files. For example, a user can hum a tune and the system will transform it to locate the desired audio recording.[502]

While search queries are explicitly stated user information needs, organizing systems increasingly attempt to solicit the user's context or larger work task in order to provide more suitable or precise interactions. Factors such as level of education, physical disabilities, location, time, or deadline pressure often specify and constrain the types of resources needed as well as the types of interactions the user is willing or able to engage in. Using mostly implicit information collected from user behavior—for example, search or buying history, current user location or language, and social or collaborative behavior (other people with the same context) —interactions are targeted toward individual user situations. Information needs of computational agents are determined by rules and criteria set by the creators of the agents, i.e., the function or goal of the agent.

Organizing systems should plan for interactions based on non-purposeful user behavior. A user who does not have a particular resource need in mind might interact with an organizing system to see what it contains or to be entertained or educated. Imagine a user going to a museum to avoid the heat outside. Their requirement is to be out of the heat and—possibly—to see interesting things. A visitor to a zoo might go there to view a specific animal, but most of the time, visitors follow a more or less random path along the zoo's resources. Similarly, "web surfing" is random, non-information-need-driven behavior. This type of requirement cannot be satisfied by providing search capabilities alone; other interaction types (e.g. browsing, suggestions) must be provided as well.

Lastly, not all users are human beings, typing in search queries or browsing through catalogs. An organizing system should plan for interaction scenarios where computational agents access the system via APIs (application programming interfaces), which require heavily standardized access procedures and resource descriptions in order to enable interactions.

9.2.2 Resource Property Layers

Chapter 2, *"Activities in Organizing Systems"*, introduced the concept of *affordance* or behavioral repertoire—the inherent actionable properties that determine what can be done with resources. We will now look at affordances (and constraints) that resource properties pose for interaction design. The interactions that an individual resource can support depend on the nature and extent of its inherent and described properties and internal structure. However, the interactions that can be designed into an organizing system can be extended by utilizing collection properties, derived properties, and any combination thereof. These three types of resource properties can be thought of as creating layers because they build on each other.

The further an organizing system moves up the layers, the more functional capabilities are enabled and more interactions can be designed. The degree of possible interactions is determined by the extent of the properties that are organized, described and created in an organizing system. This marks a correlation between the extent of organization and the range of possible interactions: *the more extensive the organization and the number of identifiable resource properties, the larger the universe of "affordable" interactions.*

Resource properties can be distinguished by three layers:

Organization based on properties of individual resources
> Resource properties have been described extensively in Chapter 3 and Chapter 4. Any information or property that describes the resource itself can be used to design an interaction. If a property is not described in an organizing system or does not pertain to certain resources, an interaction that needs this information cannot be implemented. For example, a retail site like Shopstyle cannot offer to reliably search by color of clothing if this property is not contained in the resource description.

Organization based on collection properties
> Collection-based properties are created when resources are aggregated (see Chapter 1). An interaction that compares individual resources to a collection average (e.g., average age of publications in a library or average price of goods in a retail store) can only be implemented if the collection average is calculated.

Organization based on derived or computed properties
> Derived or computed properties are not inherent in the resources or collections but need to be computed with the help of external information or tools. The popularity of a digital resource can be computed based on the frequency

of its use, for example. This computed property could then be used to design an access interaction that searches resources based on their popularity. An important use case for derived properties is the analysis of non-textual resources like images or audio files. For these content-based interactions, intrinsic properties of the resources like color distributions are computationally derived and stored as resource properties. A search can then be performed on color distributions (e.g. a search for outdoor nature images could return resources that have a high concentration of blue in the upper half and a high concentration of green on the bottom: a meadow on a sunny day).

9.2.3 Socio-Political and Organizational Constraints

An important constraint for interaction design choices is the access policies imposed by the producers of organizing systems, as already described in §2.4.3, "Access Policies" (page 66). If resources or their descriptions are restricted, interactions may not be able to use certain properties and therefore cannot be supported.

Socio-political constraints are imposed when certain parties in an interaction or even producers of an organizing system can exert power over other parties and therefore control the nature of the interaction (or even the nature of the resource descriptions). We can distinguish different socio-political aspects:

Information and Economic Power Asymmetry
Some modern organizations are able to impose their requirements for interactions and their resource description formats upon their clients. For example, in 2012, Google and Apple each have the power to control the extent of interoperability attainable in products, services, or applications that utilize their numerous platforms through mandated APIs and the process by which third-party applications are approved. The asymmetry between these dominant players and the myriad of smaller entities providing peripheral support, services, or components can result in de facto standards that may pose significant burden for small businesses and reduce overall competition.

Standards
To enable interoperability between systems, applications, and devices, the establishment and publication of industry and user-community standards are essential. A standard interface describes the data formats and protocols to which systems should conform such that they can achieve interoperability through adherence to generic requirements.[503] Not adhering to standards complicates the merging of resources from different organizing systems. Challenges to standardization include organizational inertia, closed policies, processes, or development groups, intellectual property, credentialing, lack of specifications, competing standards, high implementation costs, lack of

conformance metrics, lack of clarity or awareness, and abuse of standards as trade barriers.

Public Policy

Beyond businesses and standards-setting organizations, the government sector wields substantial influence over the implementation and success of possible interactions in organizing systems. As institutions with large and inalienable constituents, governments and governmental entities have similar influences as large businesses due to their size and substantial impact over society at large. Different forms of government around the world, ranging from centrally planned autocracy to loosely organized nation states, can have far-reaching consequences in terms of how resource description policies are designed. Laws and regulations regarding data privacy prevent organizing systems from recording certain user data, therefore prohibiting interactions based on this information.[504]

Organizational constraints may manifest in multiple contradictory policies for organizing systems or even cause the implementation of separate, disjoint systems that cannot be integrated without additional investment. Siloed business functions may be resistant to the merging of resources or resource descriptions in order to gain competitive advantage or command resources over other business functions.

Often characterized by different kinds of value contribution, different policies, processes, and practices, organizational units must clearly define and prioritize different interaction goals, align and coordinate processes, and build collaboration capabilities to achieve a high level of interoperability within the organizing system or between different organizing systems in the organization.

In addition to information exchange, organizational interoperability also aims to provide services that are widely available, easily identifiable, and accessible across the enterprise.

Nevertheless, organizational constraints are less deterministic than socio-political constraints, because they can be changed internally once it is decided that an interaction is important enough to warrant the change of institutional policies or formats or even category systems (see §6.2.3, "Institutional Categories" (page 241)).

Once the scope and range of interactions is defined according to requirements and constraints, the resources and the technology of the organizing system have to be arranged to enable the implementation of the desired interactions.

9.3 Organizing Resources for Interactions

Commonly, resource descriptions (which properties of a resource are documented in an organizing system) are determined at the beginning of a development process of the organizing system. It follows that most required interactions need to be clarified at the beginning of the development process as well; that is, resource descriptions are determined based on the desired interactions that an organizing system should support. Most of these processes have been described in detail in Chapter 4, Chapter 5 and Chapter 8.

Resources from different organizing systems are often aggregated to be accessed within one larger organizing system (warehouses, portals, search engines, union catalogs, cross-brand retailers), which requires resources and resource descriptions to be transformed in order to adapt to the new organizing system with its extended interaction requirements.[505] Elsewhere, legacy systems often need to be updated to accommodate new standards, technologies and interactions (e.g, mobile interfaces for digital libraries). That means that the necessary resources and resource descriptions for an interaction need to be identified, and, if necessary, changes have to be made in the description of the resources. Sometimes, resources get merged or transformed in order to perform new interactions.

9.3.1 Identifying and Describing Resources for Interactions

Determining which resources or resource descriptions will be used in an interaction is simple when all resources are included (for example, in a simple search interaction). However, sometimes resources need to be identified according to more selective criteria: for example, all resources belonging to a collection or all resources exhibiting a certain property.

Individual and collection resource descriptions need to be carefully considered in order to record the necessary information for the designed interactions (see Chapter 8). The type of interaction determines whether new properties need to be derived or computed with the help of external factors and whether these properties will be represented permanently in the organizing system (e.g., an extended topical description added due to a user comment) or created on the fly whenever a transaction is transformed (e.g., a frequency count).

9.3.2 Transforming Resources for Interactions

Sometimes it becomes necessary to transform resources to enable the desired interactions. The processing and transformation steps required to produce the expected modification can be applied at different resource property layers:

Infrastructure or notation transformation
When resources are aggregated, the organizing systems must have a common basic infrastructure to communicate with one another and speak the same language. This means that participating systems must have a common set of communication protocols and an agreed upon way of representing information in digital formats, i.e., a notation (§8.3.1), for example, the Unicode encoding scheme.[506]

Writing system transformation
During a writing system transformation (Chapter 8), the syntax or vocabulary—also called the data exchange format—of the resource description will be changed to conform to another model, e.g., when library records are mapped from the MARC21 standard to the Dublin Core format in order to be aggregated, or when information in a business information system is transformed into an EDI or XML format so that it can be sent to another firm.[507] There are instances when customized vocabularies are used to represent certain types of properties. These vocabularies were probably introduced to reduce errors or ambiguity or abbreviate common organizational resource properties. These customized vocabularies need to be explained and agreed upon by organizations combining resources to prevent interoperability problems.

Semantic transformation
Agreeing on a category or classification system (Chapter 6 & Chapter 7) is crucial so that organizing systems agree semantically—that is. so that resource properties and descriptions not only share technology but also meaning. For example, because the US Census has often changed its system of race categories, it is difficult to compare data from different censuses without some semantic transformation to align the categories.[508]

Resource or resource description transformation
Resources or resource descriptions are often directly transformed, as when they are converted to another file format. In computer-based interactions like search engines, text resources are often pre-processed to remove some of the ambiguity inherent in natural language. These steps, collectively called text processing, include decoding, filtering, normalization, stopword elimination, and stemming. (See the Sidebar, "Text Processing" (page 374)).

Text Processing

Decoding
> A digital resource is first a sequence of bits. Decoding transforms those bits into characters according to the encoding scheme used, extracting the text from its stored form (see §8.3.1, "Notations" (page 340)).

Filtering
> If a text is encapsulated by formatting or non-semantic mark-up, these characters are removed because this information is rarely used as the basis of further interactions.

Tokenization
> Segments the stream of characters (in an encoding scheme, a space is also a character) into textual components, usually words. In English, a simple rule-based system can separate words using spaces. However, punctuation makes things more complicated. For example, periods at the end of sentences should be removed, but periods in numbers should not. Other languages introduce other problems for tokenization; in Chinese, a space does not mark the divisions between individual concepts.

Normalization
> Normalization removes superficial differences in character sequences, for example, by transforming all capitalized characters into lower-case. More complicated normalization operations include the removal of accents, hyphens or diacritics and merging different forms of acronyms (e.g., U.N. and UN are both normalized to UN).

Stopword elimination
> Stopwords are those words in a language that occur very frequently and are not very semantically expressive. Stopwords are usually articles, pronouns, prepositions or conjunctions. Since they occur in every text, they can be removed because they cannot distinguish them. Of course, in some cases, removing stopwords might remove semantically important phrases (e.g., "To be or not to be").

Stemming
> These processing steps normalize inflectional and derivational variations in terms, e.g., by removing the "-ed" from verbs in the past tense. This homogenization can be done by following rules (stemming) or by using dictionaries (lemmatization). Rule-based stemming algorithms are easy to implement, but can result in wrongly normalized word groups, for example when "university" and "universe" are both stemmed to "univers."

9.3.2.1 Granularity and Abstraction

Within writing system and semantic transformations, issues of granularity and level of abstraction (§4.3.1, "Determining the Scope and Focus" (page 151) and §6.4.1, "Category Abstraction and Granularity" (page 255)) pose the most challenges to cross-organizing system interoperability.[509] **Granularity** refers to the level of detail or precision for a specific information resource property. For instance, the postal address of a particular location might be represented as several different data items, including the number, street name, city, state, country and postal code (a high granularity model). It might also be represented in one single line including all of the information above (a low granularity model). While it is easy to create the complete address by aggregating the different information components from the high granularity model, it is not as easy to decompose the low granularity model into more specific information components.

This does not mean, however, that a high granularity model is always the best choice, especially if the context of use does not require it, as there are corresponding tradeoffs in terms of efficiency and speed in assembling and processing the resource information. For example, requests for AccuWeather data have exploded in the last years, due to automated requests from mobile devices to keep weather apps updated. The company has dealt with this challenge by truncating the GPS coordinates sent by the mobile device when it requests weather data (a transformation to lower granularity). If the request with the truncated coordinates is identical to one recently made, a cached version of the content is served, resulting in 300 million to 500 million fewer requests a day.[510]

The level of abstraction is the degree to which a resource description is abstracted from the concrete use case in order to fit a wider range of resources. For example, many countries have an address field called state, but in some countries, a similar regional division is called province. In order to accommodate both concepts, we can abstract from the original concrete concepts and establish a more abstract description of administrative region. Granularity and abstraction differences can occur at every resource property layer when resources need to be transformed; therefore, they need to be recognized and analyzed at every layer.

9.3.2.2 Transforming Resources from Multiple Organizing Systems

The traditional approach to enabling heterogeneous organizing systems to be accessed together has been to fully integrate them, which has allowed the "unrestricted sharing of data and business processes among any connected applications and data sources" in the organization.[511] This can be a strategic approach to improving the management of resources, resource descriptions and organizing systems as a whole, especially when organizations have disparate systems and redundant information spread across different groups and departments. However, it can also be a costly approach as integration points may be numerous, with vastly different technologies needed to get one system to integrate with another. Maintenance also becomes an issue, as changes in one system may entail changes in all systems integrating with it.[512]

Planning the transformation of resources from different organizing systems to be merged in an aggregation is called *data mapping* or alignment. In this process, aspects of the description layers (most often writing system or semantics) are compared and matched between two or more organizing systems. The relationship between each component may be unidirectional or bidirectional.[513] In addition, resource properties and values that are semantically equivalent might have different names (the *vocabulary problem* of §3.4.2.1). The purpose of mapping may vary from allowing simple exchanges of resource descriptions, to enabling access to longitudinal data, to facilitating standardized reporting.[514] The preservation of version histories of resource description elements and relations in both systems is vital for verifying the validity of the data map.

Similar to mapping, a straightforward approach to transformation is the use of **crosswalks**, which are equivalence tables that relate resource description elements, semantics, and writing systems from one organizing system to those of another.[515] Crosswalks not only enable systems with different resource descriptions to interchange information in real-time but are also used by third-party systems such as harvesters and search engines to generate union catalogs and perform queries on multiple systems as if they were one consolidated system.[516]

In the digital library space, WorldCat allows users to access many library databases to locate items in their community libraries and, depending on patron privileges, to request items through their local libraries from libraries all over the world. For this powerful tool to accurately locate holdings in each library, two resource description standards are involved. At the book publisher, wholesaler, and retailer end, the international standard Online Information Exchange (ONIX) is used to standardize books and serials metadata throughout the supply chain.[517] ONIX is implemented in book suppliers' internal and customer-facing information systems to track products and to facilitate the generation of advance information sheets and supplier catalogs.[518] At the library end, the Machine-Readable Cataloging (MARC) formats manage and communicate bibliographic and related information.[519] When a member library acquires a title, information in ONIX format is sent from the supplier to the Online Computer Library Center (OCLC) where it is matched with a corresponding MARC record in the WorldCat database by using an ONIX to MARC *crosswalk*.[520] This enables WorldCat to provide accurate real-time holdings information of its member libraries.

9.3.2.3 Modes of Transformation

As the number of organizing systems increases, crosswalks and mappings become increasingly impractical if each pair of organizing systems requires a separate crosswalk. A more efficient approach would be the use of one vocabulary or format as a switching mechanism (also called a pivot or *hub language*) for all other vocabularies to map towards.[521] Another possibility, which is often used in asymmetric power relationships between organizing systems, is to force all systems to adhere to the format that is used by the most powerful party.

The conceptual relationships between different descriptions can be mapped out manually when creating simple maps. This, however, becomes more difficult as maps become more complex, due to the number of properties being mapped or when there are more structural or granularity issues to consider. The use of automatic tools to create these alignments become vital in ensuring their accuracy and robustness. Graphical mapping tools provide users with a graphical user interface to connect description elements from source to target by drawing a line from one to the other.[522] Other tools perform automatic mappings based on predetermined rules and criteria.[523]

The time of the transformation—at design time when organizing system resources are merged or at run time when a certain interaction is performed—can have a profound impact on the structure of the new system.

We often perform manual run-time transformations for decisions that require consulting more than one organizing system in our daily lives. For example, when planning a vacation, we use a variety of systems to negotiate a wide set of *ad hoc* requirements such as our resources and time, our fellow travelers and their availability, and the bookings for hotel and transportation, as well as desirable destinations and their various offerings. We somehow reconcile the different descriptions used in each of the systems and match these against each other so that the relevant information can be combined and compared. Even though the systems use different formats, vocabularies and structures, they are targeted toward human users and are relatively easy to interpret. For automatic run-time transformations, which need to be handled computationally, designers face the challenge of creating more structured processes for merging information from different systems.[524]

Design-time transformations depend on highly cooperative environments where specific design requirements (like mapping rules and criteria) can be negotiated ahead of the system implementation. In cases where high-flexibility, *ad hoc* or real-time transformations would not be possible due to a lack of cooperation (such as the ShopStyle.com), run-time transformation processes may provide appropriate alternatives. Some low-level incompatibilities between organizing systems, such as the presence of syntactical, encoding, and particular structural and content issues, can also be rectified by implementing run-time transformation techniques, creating more loosely-coupled interoperating systems.

9.3.2.4 Accuracy of Transformations

Automatic mapping tools can only be as accurate as the specifications and criteria that are included in the mapping guidelines. Intellectual checks and tests performed by humans are almost always necessary to validate the *accuracy* of the transformation. Because description systems vary in expressive power and complexity, challenges to transformations may arise from differences in semantic definitions, in rules regarding whether an element is required or requires multiple values, in hierarchical or value constraints, and in controlled vocabularies.[525] As a result of these complexities, absolute transformations that ensure exact mappings will result in a loss of precision if the source description system is substantially richer than the target system.

In practice, relative crosswalks where all elements in a source description are mapped to at least one target regardless of semantic equivalence are often implemented. This lowers the quality and *accuracy* of the mapping and can result in "down translation" or "dumbing down" of the system for resource description. As a result of mapping compromises due to different granularity or abstraction levels, transformations from different organizing systems usually result in less granular or specific resource descriptions. Consequently, whereas some interactions are now enabled (e.g. cross-organizing system search), others that were once possible can no longer be supported.

9.4 Implementing Interactions

Whether a desired interaction can be implemented depends on the layers of resource properties that have been incorporated into the organizing system. How an interaction is implemented (especially in digital organizing systems) depends also on the algorithms and technologies available to access the resources or resource descriptions. Most implementations of resource-based interactions depend on three basic actions:

Comparing resources
>A core step in any interaction is to compare a user requirement (usually a stated or implied information need) or a given resource with the descriptions of other available resources, resulting in exact matches or some measurable similarity. Resources whose descriptions are similar to the description of an information need can be the output of a search interaction; similar resources to a given resource can be the output of a clustering or a classification interaction.

Ranking or sorting resources

Determining the similarity of resources is often not enough to satisfy the goal of an interaction. Another important step is therefore to rank or sort the selected resources according to particular criteria determined in the interaction. Ranking resources according to their relevance for a query is a typical interaction step in a ranking-based search system. Sorting resources by update frequency is a typical step for a push-based recommender system.

Locating resources

Sometimes only resource descriptions are compared or ranked, so another step is then required to locate or retrieve the resource from its storage location. This could mean retrieving the Hawaiian shirt that you want to wear from your closet or locating the address of a retailer that sells a resource. In a digital library context, the full text of a textual resource or the complete digital representation of an image might be located in a local or remote repository.

Understanding resource-based interactions as combinations of comparing, ranking and locating steps provides us with a unifying framework, in which we can easily see what different interactions have in common, while also making it easier to see how they differ.

Some might find it useful to distinguish primary interactions from ancillary interactions, that is, interactions that follow another interaction. For example, one can only annotate a resource after it has been retrieved (searched and located) from an organizing system. However, in the context of this book, we will consider all interactions similarly as a combination of actions. Ancillary interactions can then be interpreted as interactions based on a series of grouped actions that by themselves represent more basic interactions.

The next sections describe some common interactions in digital organizing systems. One way to distinguish among them is to consider the source of the algorithms that are used in order to perform them. We can mostly distinguish information retrieval interactions (e.g., search and browse), *machine learning* interactions (e.g., cluster, classify, extract) or natural language processing interactions (e.g., named entity recognition, summarization, sentiment analysis, anaphoric resolution). Another way to distinguish among interactions is to note whether resources are changed during the interaction (e.g., annotate, tag, rate, comment) or unchanged (search, cluster). Yet another way would be to distinguish interactions based on their absolute and relative complexity, i.e., on the progression of actions or steps that are needed to complete the interaction. Here, we will distinguish interactions based on the different resource description layers they act upon.

Retrieval interactions can be found in any organizing system. Search is probably the most common form of access in an organizing system. When looking through your closet to find a particular Hawaiian shirt, you perform a retrieval interaction, albeit without computational tools to support the interaction. Information retrieval interactions perform a combination of comparing, ranking and locating steps (often in this order, but not always). Any information retrieval interaction must contain a compare interaction to enable the selection of resources that will match a requirement in the interaction.[526] Information retrieval algorithms and systems can be compared using an abstraction called the Information Retrieval Model (See Sidebar).

Information Retrieval Models

In information retrieval interactions, we distinguish several models that determine how a search operation is performed. Information retrieval interactions assume that every interaction starts with an information need that is formulated as a query and submitted to search a collection of resources, of which some may satisfy the information need.[527]

Different information retrieval models can be distinguished by:

- the way queries and resources are represented,
- the way the comparison between resources and queries are performed, and
- the type of calculations performed or features used to rank resources according to their relevance with respect to the information need.

In our examples, we write primarily about textual resources or resource descriptions. Information retrieval of physical goods (e.g. finding a favorite cookie brand in the supermarket) or non-textual multimedia digital resources (e.g. finding images of the UC Berkeley logo) also involves the same actions of comparing, ranking and locating, but with different algorithms and different resource properties that are used for comparisons.

9.4.1 Interactions Based on Instance Properties

Interactions in this category depend only on the properties of individual resource instances. Often, using resource properties on this lower layer coincides with basic action combinations in the interaction.

9.4.1.1 Boolean Search / Retrieval Model

In a Boolean search, a query is specified by stating the information need and using operators from Boolean logic (AND, OR, NOT) to combine the components. The query is compared to individual resource properties (most often terms), where the result of the comparison is either TRUE or FALSE. The TRUE results are returned as a result of the query, and all other results are ignored. A Boolean search does not compare or rank resources so every returned resource is considered equally relevant. The advantage of the Boolean search is that the results are predictable and easy to explain. However, because the results of the Boolean model are not ranked by relevance, users have to sift through all the returned resource descriptions in order to find the most useful results.[528]

9.4.1.2 Tag / Annotate

A tagging or annotation interaction allows a user (either a human or a computational agent) to add information to the resource itself or the resource descriptions. A typical tagging or annotation interaction locates a resource or resource description and lets the user add, edit, change or substitute their chosen resource property. The resulting changes are stored in the organizing system and can be made available for other interactions, for example, when additional tags are used to improve the search.

A change in the resource properties might result in a change of an organizing system's vocabulary or semantics when all layers of the properties are made available for changes. That is one of the reasons why some changes in resource properties are typically made only by professionals (see §4.3.6, "Creating Resource Descriptions" (page 168)). On the other hand, an interaction that adds information from users can also enhance the quality of the system and improve its usability.[529]

9.4.2 Interactions Based on Collection Properties

Interactions in this category utilize collection-level properties in order to improve the interaction, for example to improve the ranking in a search or to enable comparison to collection averages.

9.4.2.1 Vector Space Retrieval

The simplicity of the Boolean model makes it easy to understand and implement, but its binary notion of relevance does not fit our intuition that terms differ in how much they suggest what a document is about. Gerard Salton invented the vector space model of information retrieval to enable a continuous measure of relevance.[530] In the vector space model, each resource and query in an organizing system is represented as a vector of terms (see Figure 9.1, "Three Resources and a Query in a Three-Dimensional Vector Space."). Resources and queries are compared by comparing the directions of vectors in an n-dimensional space (as many dimensions as terms in the collection), with the assumption is that "closeness in space" means "closeness in meaning." A vector space ranking utilizes an intrinsic resource property called the **term frequency (tf)**. For each term, term frequency (tf) measures how many times the term appears in a resource.

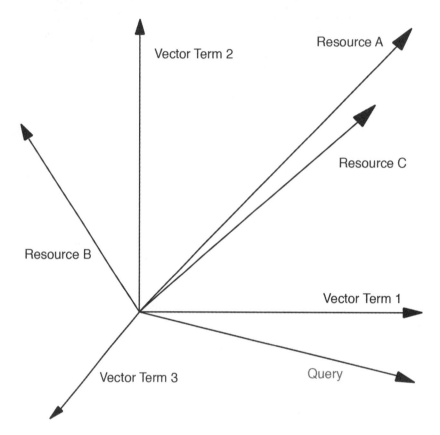

Figure 9.1. Three Resources and a Query in a Three-Dimensional Vector Space.

It is intuitive that term frequency itself has an ability to summarize a resource. If a term such as "apple" appears frequently in a resource, we can assume that one of the content topics of the resource is apples and that a query for "apple" should retrieve this resource. However, only relying on term frequency to determine the relevance of a resource for a query has a drawback: if the term occurs in every resource in the repository, it has no distinguishing power between resources. For example, if an organizing system contains only resources about apples, all resources are potentially relevant for an "apple" query. Hence, there should be an additional mechanism to penalize the term appearing in too many resources. This is done with inverse document frequency, which signals how often a term or property occurs in a collection.

Inverse document frequency (idf) is a collection-level property. The ***document frequency*** (df) is the number of resources containing a particular term. The inverse document frequency (idf) for a term is defined as $idf_t = \log(N/df_t)$, where N is the total number of documents. The inverse document frequency of a term decreases the more documents contain the term, providing a discriminating factor for the importance of terms in a query. For example, in an apple resource collection, an information retrieval interaction can handle a query for "apples oranges" by lowering the importance of "apples" and increasing the importance of "oranges" in the resources that are selected as result set.

Another problem with the term frequency measure occurs when resource descriptions have different lengths (a very common occurrence in organizing systems). Let's say a resource description contains 20 terms and apple appears 4 times. Another resource description contains 200 terms and apple occurs 10 times. According to the term-frequency-based relevance, the second resource is more relevant because it contains apple more often. However, the first resource has a much higher concentration of apple: 20% of its content is apple, whereas apple occurs only in a 5% concentration in the second resource. In order to compensate for different resource description lengths that would bias the term frequency count and the calculated relevance towards longer documents, the length of the term vectors are normalized.

In a first step of a vector space search, resource descriptions are compared with the terms in the query. Then, a metric combining the term frequency and the inverse document frequency is used to rank resources according to their relevance with respect to the query.[531]

9.4.2.2 Latent Semantic Indexing

Latent semantic indexing is a variation of the vector space model where a mathematical technique known as singular value decomposition is used to group similar term vectors into larger vectors.[532] This method is based mostly on collection-level properties like co-occurrence of terms in a collection. Based on the terms that occur in all resources in a collection, the method calculates which terms might be synonyms of each other or otherwise related. Put another way, latent semantic indexing groups terms into topics. Let's say the terms "roses" and "flowers" often occur together in the resources of a particular collection. The latent semantic indexing methodology recognizes statistically that these terms are related. Now queries for "flower" will also retrieve resources that mention "roses." This increases the chance of a resource being found relevant to a query even if the query terms do not match the resource description terms exactly; the technique can therefore improve the quality of search.

Latent semantic indexing has been shown to be a practical technique for estimating the substitutability or semantic equivalence of words in larger text segments, which makes it effective in information retrieval, text categorization, and other NLP applications like question answering. In addition, some people view it as a model of the computational processes and representations underlying substantial portions of how knowledge is acquired and used, because latent semantic analysis techniques produces measures of word-word, word-passage, and passage-passage relations that correlate well with human cognitive judgments and phenomena involving association or semantic similarity. These situations include vocabulary tests, rate of vocabulary learning, essay tests, prose recall, and analogical reasoning.[533]

Another approach for increasing the quality of search is to add similar terms or properties to a query from a controlled vocabulary or classification system. When a query can be mapped to terms in the controlled vocabulary or classes in the classification, the inherent semantic structure of the vocabulary or classification can suggest additional terms (broader, narrower, synonymous) whose occurrence in resources can signal their relevance for a query.

9.4.2.3 Probabilistic Retrieval

In contrast to the vector space model, the underlying idea of the probabilistic model is that given a query and a resource or resource description (most often a text), probability theory is used to estimate how likely it is that a resource is relevant to an information need. A probabilistic mode returns a list of resources that are ranked by their estimated *probability of relevance* with respect to the information need: P(R=1 | d, q) where R is relevance, d is the document and q is the query so that the resource with the highest probability to be relevant is ranked highest. In the vector space model, by comparison, the resource, whose term vector is most similar to a query term vector (based on frequency counts) is ranked highest.[534]

The probability ranking principle is mathematically and theoretically better motivated than the vector space ranking principle. However, multiple methods have been proposed to estimate the probability of relevance. Well-known probabilistic retrieval methods are Okapi BM25, language models (LM) and divergence from randomness models (DFR).[535] Although these models vary in their estimations of the probability of relevance for a given resource and differ in their mathematical complexity, intrinsic properties of resources like term frequency and collection-level properties like inverse document frequency and others are used for these calculations.

9.4.2.4 Structure-Based Retrieval

When the internal structure of a resource is represented in its resource description a search interaction can use the structure to retrieve more specific parts of a resource. This enables parametric or zone searching,[536] where a particular component or resource property can be searched while all other properties are disregarded. For example, a search for Shakespeare in the title field in a bibliographic organizing system will only retrieve books with Shakespeare in the title, not as an author.

A common structure-based retrieval technique is the search in relational databases with Structured Query Language (SQL). With the help of tools to facilitate selection and transformation, particular tables and fields in tables and in many combination or with various constraints can be applied to yield highly precise results.

A format like XML enables structured resource descriptions and is therefore very suitable for search and for structured navigation and retrieval. XPath (see §5.5.2) describes how individual parts of XML documents can be reached within the internal structure. *XML Query Language (XQuery)*, a structure-based retrieval language for XML, executes queries that can fulfill both topical and structural constraints in XML documents. For example, a query can be expressed for documents containing the word "apple" in text, and where "apple" is also mentioned in a title or subtitle, or in a glossary of terms.

9.4.2.5 Clustering / Classification

Clustering (§6.5.2) and computational classification (§7.7) are both interactions that use intrinsic and collection-level resource properties to execute their operation. During clustering (unsupervised learning), all resources are compared and ranked with respect to their similarity to each other. During computational classification (supervised learning), an individual resource or a group of resources is compared to a given classification or *controlled vocabulary* in an organizing system and the resource is assigned to the most similar class or descriptor. Another example for a classification interaction is spam detection (see §7.7). Author identification or characterization algorithms attempt to determine the author of a given work (a classification interaction) or to characterize the type of author that has or should write a work (a clustering interaction).

9.4.3 Interactions Based on Derived Properties

Interactions in this category derive or compute properties or features that are not inherent to the resources themselves or the collection. External data sources, services and tools are employed to support these interactions. Building interactions with conditionality based on externally derived properties usually increases the quality of the interactions by increasing the system's context-awareness.

9.4.3.1 Popularity-Based Ranking

Google's PageRank (see section 5.5.4) is the most well-known popularity measure for websites.[537] The basic idea of PageRank is that a website is as popular as the number of links referencing the website. The actual calculation of a website's PageRank involves more sophisticated mathematics than counting the number of in-links, because the source of links is also important. Links that come from quality websites contribute more to a website's PageRank than other links and links to qualitatively low websites will hurt a website's PageRank.

An information retrieval model for web pages can now use PageRank to determine the value of a web page with respect to a query. Google and other web search engines use many different ranking features to determine the final rank of a web page for any search, PageRank as a popularity measure is only one of them.

Other popularity measures, for example the frequency of use, buying frequency for retail goods, the number of laundry cycles a particular piece of clothing has gone through, and even whether it is due for a laundry cycle right now—all of these can be used to rank resources.

9.4.3.2 Citation-Based Search

Citation-based search is a sophisticated and highly effective information retrieval technique employed within bibliographic information systems. Bibliographic resources are linked to each other by citations, that is, when one publication cites another. When a bibliographic resource is referenced by another resource, those two resources are probably thematically related. The idea of citation-based search is to use a known resource as the information need and retrieve other resources that are related by citation.

Citation-based search can be implemented by directly following citations from the original resource or to find resources that cite the original resource. Another comparison technique is the principle of bibliographic coupling, where the information retrieval system looks for other resources that cite the same resources as the original resource. Citation-based search results can also be ranked, for example by the number of in-citations a publication has received (the PageRank popularity measure actually derives from this principle).

9.4.3.3 Translation

During translation, resources are transformed into another language with varying degrees of success. In contrast to the transformations that are performed in order to merge resources from different organizing systems to prepare them for further interactions, a translation transforms the resource after it has been retrieved or located. Dictionaries or parallel corpora are external resources that drive a translation.

During a dictionary-based translation, every individual term (sometimes phrases) in a resource description is looked up in a dictionary and replaced with the most likely translation. This is a simple translation, as it cannot take grammatical sentence structures or context into account. Context can have an important impact on the most likely translation: the French word *avocat* should be translated into lawyer in most organizing systems, but probably not in a cookbook collection, in which it is the avocado fruit.

Parallel corpora are a way to overcome many of these challenges. Parallel corpora are the same or similar texts in different languages. The Bible or the protocols of United Nations (UN) meetings are popular examples because they exist in parallel in many different languages. A machine learning algorithm can learn from these corpora to determine in which contexts which phrases and other grammatical structures can be translated. This knowledge that then be applied to further resource translation interactions.

9.4.4 Interactions Based on Combining Resources

Interactions in this category combine resources mostly from different organizing systems to provide services that a single organizing system could not enable. Sometimes different organizing systems with related resources are created on purpose in order to protect the privacy of personal information or to protect business interests. Releasing organizing systems to the public can have unwanted consequences when clever developers detect the potential of connecting previously unrelated data sources.

9.4.4.1 Mash-Ups

A mash-up combines data from several resources, which enables an interaction to present new information that arises from the combination.[538] For example, housing advertisements have been combined with crime statistics on maps to graphically identify rentals that are available in relatively safe neighborhoods.

Mash-ups are usually *ad-hoc* combinations at the resource level and therefore do not impact the "mashed-up" organizing systems' internal structures or vocabularies; they can be an efficient instrument for rapid prototyping on the web. On the other hand, that makes them not very reliable or robust because a mash-up can fail in its operation as soon as the underlying organizing systems change.

9.4.4.2 Linked Data Retrieval and Resource Discovery

In §8.4.3, "The Semantic Web World" (page 353), linked data relates resources among different organizing system technologies via standardized and unique identifiers (URIs). This simple approach connects resources from different systems with each other so that a cross-system search is possible.[539] For example, two different online retailers selling a Martha Stewart bedspread can link to a website describing the bedspread on the Martha Stewart website. Both retailers use the same unique identifier for the bedspread, which leads back to the Martha Stewart site.

Resource discovery or linked data retrieval are search interactions that traverse the network (or semantic web graph) via connecting links in order to discover semantically related resources. A search interaction could therefore use the link from one retailer to the Martha Stewart website to discover the other retailer, which might have a cheaper or more convenient offer.

9.5 Evaluating Interactions

Managing the quality of an interaction with respect to its intent or goal is a crucial part of every step from design through implementation and especially during operation. Evaluating the quality of interactions at different times in the design process (design concept, prototype, implementation, and operation) reveals both strengths and weaknesses to the designers or operators of the organizing system.

During the design and implementation stages, interactions need to be tested against the original goals of the interaction and the constraints that are imposed by the organizing system, its resources and external conditions. It is very common for processes in interactions to be tweaked or tuned to better comply with the original goals and intentions for the interaction. Evaluation during these stages often attempts to provide a calculable way to measure this compliance and supports the fine-tuning process. It should be an integral part of an iterative design process.

During the later implementation and operation stages, interactions are evaluated with respect to the dynamically changing conditions of the organizing system and its environment. User expectations as well as environmental conditions or constraints can change and need to be checked periodically. A systematic evaluation of interactions ensures that changes that affect an interaction are observed early and can be integrated in order to adjust and even improve the interaction. At these stages, more subjective evaluation aspects like satisfaction, experience, reputation or "feel" also play a role in fine-tuning the interactions. This subjective part of the evaluation process is as important as the quantitative, objective part. Many factors during the design and implementation processes need to be considered and made to work together. Ongoing quality evaluation and feedback ensures that interactions work as intended.

Let's assume that Shopstyle.com develops a new interaction that lets you compare coat lengths from the offerings of their various retailers. Once the interaction is designed, an evaluation takes place in order to determine whether all coats and their lengths are integrated in the interaction and whether the coat lengths are measured and compared correctly. The designers would not only want to know whether the coat lengths are represented correctly but also whether the interaction performs efficiently. When the interaction is ready to be released (usually first in beta or test status), users and retailers will be asked whether the interaction improves their shopping experience, whether the comparison performs as they expected, and what they would change. These evaluation styles work hand in hand in order to improve the interaction.

9.5.1 Interaction Aspects for Evaluation

Evaluation aspects can be distinguished in numerous ways: by the effort and time to perform them (both data collection and analysis); by how quantifiable they are or how comparable they are with measures in other organization systems; by what component of the interaction or organizing system they focus on; or by the discipline, expertise or methodologies that are used for the evaluation.

A common and important distinction is the difference between efficiency, effectiveness and satisfaction. An interaction is efficient when it performs its actions in a timely and economical manner. An interaction is effective when it performs its actions correctly and completely. An interaction is satisfactory when it performs as expected. Satisfaction is the least quantifiable of the evaluation aspects because it is highly dependent on individual tastes and experiences.

Efficiency measures are usually related to engineering aspects such as the time to perform an action, number of steps to perform an interaction, or amount of computing resources used. Effectiveness measures are often developed in the fields that developed the algorithm for the interaction, information retrieval or machine learning. Satisfaction measures arise out of the user's experience with the interaction—they are mostly aspects of user interfaces, usability, or subjective and aesthetic impressions.

Although efficiency, effectiveness and satisfaction are measured differently and affect different components of the interaction, they are equally important for the success of an interaction. Even if an interaction is fast, it is not very useful if it arrives at incorrect results. Even if an interaction works correctly, user satisfaction is not guaranteed. One of the challenges in designing interactions is that these factors invariably involve tradeoffs. A fast system cannot be as precise as one prioritizes the use of contextual information. An effective interaction might require a lot of effort from the user, which does not make it very easy to use, so the user satisfaction might decrease. The priorities of the organizing system and its designers will determine which properties to optimize.

Let's continue our Shopstyle coat-length comparison interaction example. When the coat length calculation is performed in an acceptable amount of time and does not consume a lot of the organizing systems resources, the interaction is efficient. When all coat lengths are correctly measured and compared, the interaction is effective. When the interaction is seamlessly integrated into the shopping process, is visually supported in the interface and is not cognitively exhausting, is it probably satisfactory for a user as it provides a useful service (especially for someone with irregular body dimensions). What aspect should Shopstyle prioritize? It will probably weigh the consequences of effectiveness versus efficiency and satisfaction. For a retail- and consumer-oriented organizing system, satisfaction is probably one of the more important aspects, so it's highly likely that efficiency and effectiveness might be sacrificed (in moderation) in favor of satisfaction.

For a lot of organizing system interactions, however, effectiveness is the more important aspect, particularly for those interactions that we have looked at so far. If search results are not correct, then users will not be satisfied by even the most usable interface. Many interactions are evaluated with respect to their ability to return relevant resources. Why and how this is evaluated is the focus of the remainder of this section.

9.5.2 Relevance

The concept of **relevance** is pivotal in information retrieval and machine learning interactions. Relevance is widely regarded as the fundamental concept of information retrieval, and by extension, all of information science. Despite being one of the more intuitive concepts in human communication, relevance is notoriously difficult to define and has been the subject of much debate over the past century.

Historically, relevance has been addressed in logic and philosophy since the notion of inference was codified (to infer B from A, A must be relevant to B). Other fields have attempted to deal with relevance as well: sociology, linguistics, and psychology in particular. The subject knowledge view, subject literature view, logical view, system's view, destination's view, pertinence view, pragmatic view and the utility-theoretic interpretation are different perspectives on the question of when something is relevant.[540] In 1997, Mizzaro surveyed 160 research articles on the topic of relevance and arrived at this definition: "relevance can be seen as a point in a four-dimensional space, the values of each of the four dimensions being: (*i*) Surrogate, document, information; (*ii*) query, request, information need, problem; (*iii*) topic, context, and each combination of them; and (*iv*) the various time instants from the arising of problem until its solution."[541] This rather abstract definition points to the terminological ambiguity surrounding the concept.

For the purpose of organizing systems, relevance is a concept for evaluating effectiveness that describes whether a stated or implicit information need is satisfied in a particular user context and at a particular time. One of the challenges for the evaluation of relevance in organizing systems is the gap between a user's information need (often not directly stated), and an expression of that information need (a query). This gap might result in ambiguous results in the interaction. For example, suppose somebody speaks the word "Paris" (query) into a smart phone application seeking advice on how to travel to Paris, France. The response includes offers for the Paris Hotel in Las Vegas. Does the result satisfy the information need? What if the searcher receives advice on Paris but has already seen every one of the resources the organizing system offers? What is the correct decision on relevance here?

The key to calculating effectiveness is to be aware of what is being measured. If the information need as expressed in the query is measured, the topical relevance or topicality—a system-side perspective is analyzed. If the information need as in a person's mind is measured, the pertinence, utility or situational relevance—a subjective personal perspective is analyzed. This juxtaposition is the point of much research and contention in the field of information retrieval, because topical relevance is objectively measurable, but subjective relevance is the real goal. In order to evaluate relevance in any interaction, an essential prerequisite is deciding which of these notions of relevance to consider.

9.5.3 The Recall / Precision Trade-Off

Another decision is whether recall or precision are preferred in an interaction.

Precision and *recall* are the fundamental measures of *relevance* or effectiveness in information retrieval or machine learning interactions. **Precision** measures the *accuracy* of a result set, that is, how many of the retrieved resources for a query are relevant. **Recall** measures the completeness of the result set, that is, how many of the relevant resources in a collection were retrieved. Let's assume that a collection contains 20 relevant resources for a query. A retrieval interaction retrieves 10 resources in a result set, 5 of the retrieved resources are relevant. The precision of this interaction is 50% (5 out of 10 retrieved resources are relevant); the recall is 25% (5 out of 20 relevant resources were retrieved).[542]

It is in the nature of information retrieval interactions that recall and precision trade off with each other. To find all relevant resources in a collection, the interaction has to cast a wide net and will not be very precise. In order to be very precise and return only relevant resources to the searcher, an interaction has to be very discriminating and will probably not find all relevant resources. When a collection is very large and contains many relevant resources for any given query, the priority is usually to increase precision. However, when a collection is small or the information need also requires finding all relevant documents (e.g., in case law, patent searches, or medical diagnosis support), then the priority is put on increasing recall.

The completeness and granularity of the organizing principles in an organizing system have a large impact on the trade-off between recall and precision (Chapter 3). When resources are organized in fine-grained category systems and many different resource properties are described, high-precision searches are possible because a desired resource can be searched as precisely as the description or organization of the system allows. However, very specialized description and organization may preclude certain resources from being found; consequently, recall might be sacrificed. If the organization is superficial—like your sock drawer, for example—you can find all the socks you want (high recall) but you have to sort through a lot of socks to find the right pair (low precision). The trade-off between recall and precision is closely associated with the extent of the organization.

9.6 Key Points in Chapter Nine

- Interactions arise naturally from the affordances of resources or are purposefully designed into organizing systems.

- Accessing and merging resources are fundamental interactions that occur in almost every organizing system.

- The design of interactions is driven by choices and constraints that expand and limit the design space.

- User requirements, which layer of resource properties is used, and the legal, social and organizational environment can distinguish interactions.

- Resource property layers build on each other: interactions based on individual resource properties, interactions based on collection-level properties, and interactions based on externally derived or computed properties.

- In order to enable interactions, it is necessary to identify, describe, and sometimes transform the resources in an organizing system.

- Resource transformations happen within the infrastructure or notation, the writing system, the organizing system's semantics or the resources themselves.

- Merging transformations can be distinguished by type (mapping or crosswalk), time (design time or run time) and mode (manual or automatic).

- Most implementations of resource-based interactions depend on three basic actions: comparing, ranking and locating resources.

- Implementations can be distinguished by the source of the algorithm (information retrieval, machine learning, natural language processing), by their complexity (number of actions needed), by whether resources are changed, or by the resource description layers they are based on.

- An information retrieval model describes the components of an information retrieval interaction: the way queries and resources are represented, the way the comparison between resources and queries is performed, and the type of calculations performed or features used to rank resources according to their relevance.

- Important aspects for the evaluation of interactions are efficiency (timeliness and cost-effectiveness), effectiveness (accuracy and relevance) and satisfaction (positive attitude of the user).

- The trade-off between recall and precision decides whether a search finds all relevant documents (high recall) or only relevant documents (high precision).

- The extent of the organization principles also impacts recall and precision: more fine-grained organization allows for more precise interactions.

Notes

495. [LIS] *http://www.worldcat.org/*.

496. [Museums] (Proctor 2011).

497. [Museums] (Srinivasan, Boast, Furner, Becvar 2009).

498. [Museums] (Hyvönen et al. 2004). Museum visitors are presented with intelligent, content-based search and browsing services that offer a consolidated view across Finnish museums from the National Museum to the Lahti City Museum. To enable these goals, MuseumFinland mapped the variety of existing terms used by different museums onto shared ontologies, which now enable aggregated searching and browsing.

499. [Museums] (Bower and Roberts 2001).

500. [Business] Walmart uses its market power to impose technology and process decisions on its suppliers and partners. See (Fishman 2003), (Grean and Shaw 2005), (Wilbert 2006). Walmart's website for suppliers is *http://walmart stores.com/Suppliers/248.aspx/*.

501. [Business] In order to more easily use and reuse content, as well as have the ability to integrate different learning tools into a single learning management system, the LMS, Global Learning Consortium, an organization composed of 140 members from leading educational institutions and education-related companies, has released specifications to make this possible. Called *Common Cartridge and Learning Tools Interoperability* (*http://www.imsglobal.org/commoncartridge.html*), the specifications provide a common format and guidelines to construct tools and create content that can be easily imported into learning management systems. Common Cartridge (CC) specifications give detailed descriptions of the directory structure, metadata and information models associated with a particular learning object. For example, a learning package from a provider from McGraw-Hill may contain content from a book, some interactive quizzes, and some multimedia to support the text. CC specifies how files would be organized within a directory, how links would be represented, how the package would communicate with a backend server, how to describe each of the components, and the like. This would enable a professor or a student using any capable learning management system to import a "cartridge" or learning material and have it appear in a consistent manner with all other learning materials within the LMS. This means that content providers need not maintain multiple versions of the same content just to conform to the formats of different systems, allowing them to focus their resources on creating more content as opposed to maintaining the ones they already have. Looking at this in the context of the interoperability framework, we see that while information from providers are in a structured digital form, the main problem was that users were consuming the content using competing systems that had their own data formats by which to accept content. Huge publishers, wanting to increase distribution of their product, offered their content in all these different formats. While the specifications that the LMS created refer to the technical considerations in creating content and tools, the process of getting to that point involved a lot of organizational and political discussions. Internally, content and LMS providers needed to set aside the necessary resources to refactor their products to conform to the standards. Externally, competing providers had to collaborate with one another to create the specifications.

502. [Computing] (Fidel 2012).

503. [Computing] (von Riegen 2006).

504. [Business] A good example for the importance of standards and interoperability rules is E-government. E-government refers to the ability to deliver government services through electronic means. These services can range from government-to-citizen, government-to-business, government-to-employees, government-to-government, and vice-versa (Guijarro 2007, Scholl 2007). This could range from a government unit providing a portal where citizens can apply for a driver's license or file their taxes, to more complex implementations such

as allowing different government agencies to share certain pertinent information with one another, such as providing information on driver's license holders to the police. Because the government interacts with heterogeneous entities and their various systems, e-government planners must consider how to integrate and interoperate with different systems and data models. Countries belonging to the *Organization for Economic Cooperation and Development (OECD)* have continuously refined their strategies for e-government.

An example of a highly successful implementation of a business-to-government implementation is the use of the Universal Business Language (UBL) by the Government of Denmark. UBL is a "royalty-free library of standard electronic XML business documents such as purchase orders and invoices" [oasis-open.org]. The Government of Denmark localized these standards, and mandated all organizations wanting to do business with the government to use these formats for invoicing. By automating the matching process between an electronic order and an electronic invoice, the government expects total potential savings of about 160 million Euros per year [UBL case study], thus highlighting the need for a standard format by which businesses can send in orders and invoices electronically.

Recognizing that its position as government entails that all types of suppliers, big or small, must have equal opportunity to sell its products and services, the Government of Denmark not only set data format standards, it also gave several options by which information can be exchanged. Paper-based invoices would be sent to scanning agencies that would scan and create electronic versions to be submitted to the government. This highlights the different organizational and consumption issues that the government of Denmark had to consider when designing the system.

505. [LIS] Major library system vendors now market so-called discovery portals to their customers, which allow libraries to integrate their local catalogs with central indexes of journal and other full-text databases. The advantages of discovery portals are the seamless access for patrons to all the library's electronic materials (including externally licensed databases) while maintaining a local and customized look and feel. By providing out-of-the-box solutions, vendors on the other hand bind libraries more closely to their products.

See for an example Exlibris Primo (*http://www.exlibrisgroup.com/category/ PrimoOverview/*) or OCLC WorldCat Local (*http://www.oclc.org/worldcatlo cal/default.htm*).

506. [Computing] While data encoding describes how information is represented, and data exchange formats describe how information is structured, communication protocols refer to how information is exchanged between systems. These protocols dictate how these documents are enclosed within messages, and how these messages are transmitted across the network. Things such as

message format, error detection and reporting, security and encryption are described and considered. Nowadays, there are a number of communication protocols that are used over networks, including *File Transfer Protocol (FTP)*, Hypertext Transfer Protocol (HTTP) commonly used in the Internet, *Post Office Protocol (POP)* commonly used for e-mail, and other protocols under the *Transmission Control Protocol/Internet Protocol (TCP/IP)* suite. Different product manufacturers normally also have more proprietary protocols that they employ, including Apple Computer Protocols Suite and Cisco Protocols. In addition, different types of networks would also have corresponding protocols, including Mobile Wireless Protocols and such.

507. [Business] Electronic Data Interchange (EDI), is used to exchange formatted messages between computers or systems. Organizations use this format to conduct business transactions electronically without human intervention, such as in sending and receiving purchase orders or exchange invoice information and such. There are four main standards that have been developed for EDI, including the *UN/EDIFACT* standard recommended by the *United Nations (UN)*, *ANSI ASC X12* standard widely used in the US, TRADACOMS standard that is widely used in the UK, and the ODETTE standard used in the European automotive industry. These standards include formats for a wide range of business activities, such as shipping notices, fund transfers, and the like. EDI messages are highly formatted, with the meaning of the information being transmitted being highly dependent on its position in the document. For instance, a line in an EDI document with BEG*00*NE*MOG009364501**950910*CSW11096^ corresponds to a line in the X12 standard for Purchase Orders (standard 850). "BEG" specifies the start of a Purchase Order Transaction Set. The asterisk (*) symbol delineates between items in the line, with each value corresponding to a particular field or information component described in the standard. "NE," for example, corresponds to the Purchase Order Type Code, which in this instance is "New Order." As can be seen in the example, the description of the information being transmitted is not readily available within the document. Instead, parties exchanging the information must agree on these formats beforehand, and need to ensure that the information instance is at the right position within the document so that the receiving party can correctly interpret it.

*EDI samples come from *http://miscouncil.org*.

American National Standards Association (ANSI) can be found at *http://www.ansi.org*.

508. [Computing] This and more examples for difficult categorizations can be found in: (Bowker and Star 2000).

509. [Computing] For an in-depth discussion of interoperability challenges, see Chapter 6 of (Glushko and McGrath 2005).

510. [Computing] (AT&T 2011).

511. [Business] (Linthicum 1999).

512. [Business] Allowing unrestricted access to data and business processes also becomes a problem when working across organizations. Fully integrating systems between two companies, for instance, may entail the exposure of business intelligence and information that should be kept private. This type of exposure is too much for most businesses, regardless of whether the relationship with the other business is collaborative rather than competitive. There are security issues to be considered, as collaborating organizations would need to access private networks and secure servers. The heterogeneity in supporting organizing systems along with the need to quickly evolve with the rapid changes in an organization's competitive and collaborative environment has pushed organizations to shift from more vertical, isolated structures to a more loosely coupled, ecosystem paradigm This has led to more componentized and modularized systems that need only to exchange information or transform resources when an interaction requires it.

The emerging paradigm then is to enable independent systems to interoperate, or to have "the ability of two or more systems or components to exchange information and to use the information that has been exchanged." Because the focus is in the exchange of resources or resource descriptions, independent systems need not necessarily know other systems' underlying logic or implementation, for example, how they store resources. What is important is knowing what kind of resource is expected and in what format (notation, writing system, semantics), and what kind of information is returned for a particular. This is a strategic approach to exchanging resources, as systems can remain highly independent of each other. Changes in one system need not necessarily affect how other systems work as long as the information that is sent and received through an interface stays the same. This allows greater adaptability, as changes to system logic or business processes can be done in self-contained modules without necessarily affecting others. The transformation then happens in an intermediate space where the agreements on resource descriptions are fixed.

513. [LIS] To illustrate the difference between a unidirectional and bidirectional map, consider two systems, the *Systematized Nomenclature of Medicine — Clinical Terms (SNOMED-CT)* and the *International Classification of Diseases, Tenth Revision, Clinical Modification* (ICD-10-CM).

SNOMED-CT is a medical language system for clinical terminology maintained by the International Health Terminology Standards Development Organization (IHTSDO) and a designated electronic exchange standard for clinical health information for US Federal Government systems (*http://www.nlm.nih.gov/research/umls/Snomed/snomed_main.html*).

The ICD-10-CM, on the other hand, is an international diagnostic classification system for general epidemiological, health management, and clinical use maintained by the *World Health Organization (WHO)* and used for coding and classifying morbidity data from inpatient/outpatient records, physicians offices, and most National Center for Health Statistics (NCHS) surveys (*http:// www.who.int/classifications/icd/en/*).

Because many different SNOMED-CT concepts can be mapped to a single ICD-9-CM code, a map in this direction cannot be used in reverse without introducing confusion and ambiguity.

514. [Computing] (McBride et al. 2006).

515. [Computing] (NISO 2004).

516. [Computing] *http://journal.code4lib.org/articles/54* (Section 1.), *http://www.dlib.org/dlib/june06/chan/06chan.html*.

517. [Business] (EDItEUR 2009a).

518. [Business] (EDiTEUR 2009b).

519. [LIS] *http://www.loc.gov/marc/*.

520. [Computing] (Godby, Smith, and Childress 2008), Sections 1 and 2.

521. [Museums] "Toward element-level interoperability in bibliographic metadata" (Godby, Smith, and Childress 2008), Sec. 4.4, "Switching-Across." Consider how the Getty has created a crosswalk called *Categories for the Description of Works of Art* (CDWA) to switch between eleven metadata standards, including *Machine-Readable Cataloging/Anglo-American Cataloging Rules* (MARC) and *Dublin Core* (DC). In this instance, the "Creation Date" element in CDWA is mapped to "260c Imprint — Date of Publication, Distribution, etc." in MARC/ AACR and to "Date.Created" in DC. Although this creates a two-step look-up in real-time, a direct mapping of this element from MARC/AACR to DC is no longer necessary for systems to interoperate.

522. [Computing] More commonly, graphical data mapping tools are included in an extract, transform, and load (ETL) database suite that provides additional powerful data transformation capabilities. Whereas data mapping is the first step in capturing the relationships between different systems, data transformation entails code generation that uses the resulting maps to produce an executable transformational program that converts the source data into target format. ETL databases *extract* the information needed from the outside sources, *transform* these into information that can be used by the target system using the necessary data mappings, and then *loads* it into the end system.

523. [Computing] Languages such as XSLT and TXL facilitate the ease of data transformation while various commercial data warehousing tools provide vary-

ing functionalities such as single/multiple source acquisition, data cleansing, and statistical and analytical capabilities. Based on XML, XSLT is a declarative language designed for transforming XML documents into other documents. For example, XSLT can be used to convert XML data into HTML documents for web display or PDF for print or screen display. XSLT processing entails taking an input document in XML format and one or more XSLT style sheets through a template-processing engine to produce a new document.

524. [Computing] (Carney et al. 2005).

525. [LIS] (Chan and Zeng 2006). Section 4.3.

526. [Computing] Each of the four information retrieval models discussed in the chapter has different combinations of the comparing, ranking, and location activities. Boolean and vector space models compare the description of the information need with the description of the information resource. Vector space and probabilistic models rank the information resource in the order that the resource can satisfy the user's query. Structure-based search locates information using internal or external structure of the information resource.

527. [Computing] Our discussion of information retrieval models in this chapter does not attempt to address information retrieval at the level of theoretical and technical detail that informs work and research in this field (See Manning et al. 2008), (Croft et al. 2009). Instead, our goal is to introduce IR from a more conceptual perspective, highlighting its core topics and problems using the vocabulary and principles of IO as much as possible.

528. [Computing] (Manning et al. 2008), Ch. 1.

529. [LIS] A good discussion of the advantages and disadvantages of tagging in the library field can be found in (Furner 2007).

530. [Computing] Salton was generally viewed as the leading researcher in information retrieval for the last part of the 20th century until he died in 1995. The vector model was first described in (Salton, Wong, and Yang 1975).

531. [Computing] See (Manning et al. 2008), Ch. 6 for more explanations and references on the vector space model.

532. [Computing] (Deerwester, Dumais et al. 1990).

533. [CogSci] See (Dumais 2003).

534. [Computing] (Manning et al. 2008), p.221.

535. [Computing] See (Robertson 2005), (Manning et al. 2008), Ch. 12 for more explanations and references.

536. [Computing] (Manning et al. 2008), Section 6.1.

537. [Web] (Page et al. 1999).

538. [Web] (Yee 2008).

539. [Web] (Bizer, Heath, and Berners-Lee 2009).

540. [LIS] Space does not permit significant discussion of these views here, see (Saracevic 1975), and (Schamber et al. 1990).

541. [LIS] (Mizzaro 1997).

542. [Computing] Recall and precision are only the foundation of measures that have been developed in information retrieval to evaluate the effectiveness of search algorithms. See (Baeza-Yates and Ribeiro 2011), (Manning et al. 2008) Ch. 8; (Demartini and Mizzaro 2006).

Chapter 10
The Organizing System Roadmap

Robert J. Glushko

10.1 Introduction

Chapter 1 defined an organizing system as "an intentionally arranged collection of resources and the interactions they support." An organizing system emerges as the result of decisions about **what** is organized, **why** it is organized, **how much** it is organized, **when** it is organized, and **how or by whom** it is organized. These decisions and the tradeoffs they embody are manifested in the four common activities of organizing systems—selecting resources, organizing them, designing and supporting interactions with them, and maintaining them—which we described in Chapter 2. Chapters 3-9 progressively explained each of the parts of the organizing system: resources, resource descriptions, resource categories and collections, and interactions with resources—introducing additional concepts and methods associated with each of these parts.

Along the way we described many types of organizing systems. Sometimes we discussed broad categories of organizing systems like those for libraries, museums, business information systems, and compositions of web-based services. At other times we described specific instances of organizing systems like those in the Seed Library, the Flickr photo sharing site, Amazon.com's drop shipment store, and your home kitchen or closet.

We can now build on the foundation created by Chapters 1-9 to create a "roadmap" that organizes and summarizes the design issues and choices that emerge during an organizing system's lifecycle. These design choices follow patterns that help us understand existing organizing systems better while also suggesting how to invent new ones by making a different set of design choices.

The roadmap is extensively annotated with references to the preceding chapters where the issues and choices mentioned in the roadmap were introduced and discussed in detail. We use this roadmap to analyze a variety of case study examples and to explore the "design neighborhood" around each of them. The five design questions from Chapter 1 serve as a template to give each case study the same structure, which we hope enables instructors, students, and others who read this book to add to this collection of case studies by contributing their own at `DisciplineOfOrganizing.org`.

10.2 The Organizing System Lifecycle

System lifecycle models exhibit great variety; for our purposes it suffices to use a generic four-phase model that distinguishes a domain definition and scoping phase, a requirements phase, a design and implementation phase, and an operational and maintenance phase. These phases are brief and mostly inseparable for some simple organizing systems, more sequential for others, and more systematic and iterative for complex organizing systems.

Most of the specific decisions that must be made for an organizing system are strongly shaped by the initial decisions about its domain, scope (the breadth or variety of the resources), and scale (the number of resource instances). In organizing systems with limited scope and scale most of these decisions are made in an informal, unanalyzed, and holistic manner. For example, when we arrange our bookshelves or closets it is not necessary to think explicitly about scoping, requirements, design, implementation and operational phases. For complex organizing systems, however, especially those in information-intensive domains, it is important to follow a more systematic methodology. More careful attention to scope and requirements during the design and implementation phases is essential because the initial decisions can create lasting technology and process legacies that impact operational efficiency and flexibility.

The technical, social, business, and legal contexts in which the organizing system must operate (§9.2.3) also shape these decisions, as does the context created by other organizing systems in the same or related domains.

10.3 Defining and Scoping the Organizing System Domain

The most fundamental decision for an organizing system is defining its domain, the set or type of resources that are being organized. This is why "What is Being Organized?" (§1.3.2) was the first of the five design decisions we introduced in Chapter 1.

We refine how we think about an organizing system domain by breaking it down into five interrelated aspects: (1) the scope and scale of the collection, (2) the number and nature of users, (3) the time span or lifetime over which the organizing system will operate, (4) the physical or technological environment in which the organizing system is situated, and (5) the relationship of the organizing system to other ones that overlap with it in domain or scope. Answering these questions is a prerequisite for prioritizing requirements for the organizing system, proposing the principles of its design, and implementing the organizing system.

10.3.1 Scope and Scale of the Collection

The scope of a collection is the dominant factor in the design of an organizing system because it largely determines the extent and complexity of the resource descriptions needed by organizing principles and interactions (§4.3.1.3). The impact of broad scope arises more from the heterogeneity of the resources in a collection rather than from its absolute scale. It takes more effort to manage a broad and large collection than a narrow and small one. However, it takes less effort to manage a large collection if it has a narrow scope.

Consider a business information system being designed to contain millions of highly structured and similar instances of a small number of related resource types, like orders and their corresponding invoices.[543] The analysis to determine the appropriate properties and principles for resource description and organization is straightforward, and any order or invoice is an equally good instance to study.[544]

Contrast this large but very narrow collection with a small but very broad one that contains a thousand highly variable instances of dozens of different resource types. This heterogeneity makes it difficult to determine if an instance is representative of its resource type, and every resource might need to be analyzed. This variability implies a large and diverse set of resource descriptions where individual resource instances might not be described with much precision because it costs too much to do it manually (§4.3.6.1). We can extrapolate to understand why organizing systems whose resource collections are both broad and deep, like those of Amazon.com or eBay, have come to rely on machine learning techniques to identify description properties and construct resource taxonomies (§4.3.6.4, §6.5.2).[545]

A partial remedy or compromise when the resource instances are highly dissimilar is to define resource types more broadly or abstractly, reducing the overall number of types. We illustrated this approach in §7.2.2.1 when we contrasted how kitchen goods might be categorized broadly in a department store but much more precisely in a wholesale kitchen supply store. The broader categories in the department store blur many of the differences between instances but in doing so yield a small set of common properties that can be used to describe them. Because these common properties will be at a higher level of abstraction, using them to describe resources will require less expertise and probably less effort (§4.3.1.3, §6.4.1). However, this comes at a cost: Poets, painters, composers, sculptors, technical writers, and programmers all create resources, but describing all of them with a "creator" property as the Dublin Core requires loses a great deal of precision.

Challenges caused by the scale of a collection are often related to constraints imposed by the physical or technological environment in which the collection exists that limit how large the collection can be or how it can be organized (§2.3.1). Only a few dozen books can fit on a small bookshelf but thousands of books can fit in your two-car garage, which is a typical size because most people and families don't have more than two cars. On the other hand, if you are a Hollywood mogul, superstar athlete, or sultan with a collection of hundreds of cars, a two-car garage is orders of magnitudes too small to store your collection.[546] Even collections of digital things can be limited in size by their technological environment, which you might have discovered when you ran out of space for your songs and photos on your portable media player.

Estimating the ultimate size of a collection at the beginning of an organizing system's lifecycle can reduce scaling issues related to storage space for the resources or for their descriptions. Other problems of scale are more fundamental. Larger collections need more people to organize and maintain them, creating communication and coordination problems that grow much faster than the collection, especially when the collection is distributed in different locations.

The best way to prevent problems of scope and scale is through standardization. Standardization of resources can take place if they are created by automated means so that every instance conforms to a schema or model (§6.5.1).[547] Standards for describing bibliographic resources enable libraries to centralize and share much resource description, and using the same standards for resources of diverse types helps address the challenge of broad scope by reducing the need for close monitoring and coordination. Analogous standards for describing information resources, services, or economic activities business, governmental, or scientific information systems to systematically manage hundreds of millions or even billions of transactional records or pieces of data (§4.3.1.3).

10.3.2 Number and Nature of Users

An organizing system might have only one user, as when an individual creates and operates an organizing system for a clothes closet, a home bookcase or file cabinet, or for digital files and applications on a personal computer or smart phone. Collections of personal resources are often organized for highly individualized interactions using *ad hoc* categories that are hard to understand for any other user (§6.2.2). Personal collections or collections used by only a small number of people typically contain resources that they themselves selected, which makes the most typical interaction with the organizing system searching for a familiar known resource (§9.2.1).

At the other extreme, an organizing system can have national or even global scope and have millions or more users like the Library of Congress classification system, the United Nations Standard Products and Services Code, or the Internet Domain Name System. These organizing systems employ systems of institutional categories (§6.2.3) that are designed to support systematically specified and purposeful interactions, often to search for previously unknown resources. In between these extremes are the many kinds of organizing systems created by informal and formal groups, by firms of every size, and by sets of cooperating enterprises like those that carry out supply chains and other information-intensive business processes.

The nature and number of users strongly shapes the contents of an organizing system and the interactions it must be designed to support (§9.2.1). Some generic categories of users that apply in many domains are customers, clients, visitors, operators, and managers. We can adapt the generic interactions supported by most organizing systems (§4.3.2) to satisfy these generic user types. For example, while most organizing systems allow any type of user to browse or search the collection to discover its content, only operators or managers are likely to have access to information about the browsing and searching activities of customers, clients, or visitors.

Once we have identified the organizing system's domain more precisely we can refine these generic user categories, classifying users and interactions with more precision. For example, the customers of university libraries are mostly professors and students, while the customers of online stores are mostly shoppers seeking to find something to purchase.

Just as it is with collection scope, the heterogeneity of the user base is more critical than its absolute size. An airport bookstore typically has a narrowly focused collection and treats its customers as generic travelers browsing imprecisely for something to fill their time in the terminal or on the airplane. In contrast, the local public library will have a much broader collection because it has to meet the needs of a more diverse user base than the airport bookstore, and it will support a range of interactions and services targeted to children learning to read, school students, local businesses, retirees, and other categories of users. A company library will focus its collection on its industry segment, making it narrower in coverage than a local or university research library, but it might provide specialized services for marketing, engineering, research, legal, or other departments of the firm.

Each category of users, and indeed each individual user, brings different experiences, goals, and biases into interactions with the organizing system. As a result, organizing systems in the same domain and with nominally the same scope can differ substantially in the resources they contain and the interactions they support if they have different categories of users. The library for the Centers for Disease Control and the WebMD website both contain information about diseases and symptoms, but the former is primarily organized to support research in public health and the latter is organized for consumers trying to figure out why they are sick and how to get well. These contrasting purposes and targeted users are manifested in different classification systems and descriptive vocabularies.[548]

10.3.3 Expected Lifetime of the Resources and of the Organizing System

The scope and scale of a collection and the size of its user population are often correlated with the expected lifetime of its organizing system. Because small personal organizing systems are often created in response to a specific situation or to accomplish a specific task, they generally have short lifetimes (§6.2.2).

The expected lifetime of the organizing system is not the same as the expected lifetime of the resources it contains because motivations for maintaining resources differ a great deal (§2.5.1). As we have just noted, some organizing systems created by individuals are tied to specific short-term tasks, and when the task is completed or changes, the organizing system is no longer needed or must be superseded by a new one. At the other extreme are libraries, museums, archives, and other memory institutions designed to last indefinitely because they exist to preserve valuable and often irreplaceable resources.

However, most business organizing systems contain relatively short-lived resources that arise from and support day-to-day operations, in which case the organizing system has a long expected lifetime with impermanent resources. Finally, just to complete our 2 x 2 matrix, the auction catalog that organizes valuable paintings or other collectibles is a short-lived single-purpose organizing system whose contents are descriptions of resources with long expected lifetimes.

10.3.4 Physical or Technological Environment

An organizing system is often tied to a particular physical or technological environment. A kitchen, closet, card cabinet, airplane cockpit, handheld computer or smartphone, and any other physical environment in which resources are organized provides affordances to be taken advantage of and constraints that must be accommodated by an organizing system (§2.4.1).[549]

The extent of these physical and technological constraints affects the lifetime of an organizing system because they make it more difficult to adapt to changes in the set of resources being organized or the reasons for their organization. A desk or cabinet with fixed "pigeon holes" or drawers affords less flexible organization than a file cabinet or open shelves. A building with hard-walled offices constrains how people interact and collaborate more than an open floor plan with modular cubicles does. Business processes implemented in a monolithic enterprise software application are tightly coupled; those implemented as a choreography of loosely-coupled web services can often transparently substitute one service provider for another.

10.3.5 Relationship to Other Organizing Systems

The same domain or set of resources can have more than one organizing system, and one organizing system can contain multiple others. The organizing system for books in a library arranges books about cooking according to the Library of Congress or Dewey Decimal classifications and bookstores use the BISAC ones, mostly using cuisine as the primary factor (§7.3). In turn, cookbooks employ an organizing system for their recipes that arranges them by type of dish, main ingredient, or method of preparation. Within a cookbook, recipes might follow an organizing system that standardizes the order of their component parts like the description, ingredients, and preparation steps.

Sometimes these multiple organizing systems can be designed in coordination so they can function as a single hierarchical, or nested, organizing system in which it is possible to emphasize different levels depending on the user's task or application. Most books and many documents have an internal structure with chapters and hierarchical headings that enable readers to understand smaller units of content in the context of larger ones (§5.5.2). Similarly, a collection of songs can be treated as an album and organized using that level of abstraction for the item, but each of those songs can also be treated as the unit of organization, especially when they are embodied in separate digital files.

Organizing systems overlap and intersect. People and enterprises routinely interact with many different organizing systems because what they do requires them to use resources in ways that cut across context, device, or application boundaries. Just consider how many different organizing systems we use as individuals for managing personal information like contacts, appointments, and messages. As company employees we create and organize information in email, document repositories, spreadsheets, and CRM and ERP systems. Now consider this at an institutional scale in the inter-enterprise interactions among the organizing systems of physicians, hospitals, medical labs, insurance companies, government agencies, and other parties involved in healthcare. Finally, think about web "mash-ups" and composite services.

We have come to expect that the boundaries between organizing systems are often arbitrary and that we should be able to merge or combine them when that would create additional value. It is surely impossible to anticipate all of these *ad hoc* or dynamic intersections of organizing systems, but it is surely necessary to recognize their inevitability, especially when the organizing systems contain digital information and are implemented using web architectures.

10.4 Identifying Requirements for an Organizing System

The two parts of the definition of an organizing system explicitly suggest two categories of requirements, those that specify the intentional arrangement of the resources and those that specify the interactions with the resources. These categories of requirements both depend on resource descriptions, which are implied by but not explicitly called out in the definition of an organizing system.

Because description, arrangement, and interaction are interrelated it is impossible to describe them separately without some redundancy. Nevertheless, in this book we have done that on purpose because taking different perspectives on organizing systems in Chapters 2-9 has enabled us to introduce a broad range of concepts, issues, and methods:

- Every organizing system must enable users to interact with its collection of resources (Chapters 2 and 9);
- The possible interactions depend primarily on the nature and extent of the descriptions associated with the resources (Chapters 3, 4 and 5);
- Intentional arrangement emerges when one or more resource descriptions are used by organizing principles (Chapters 6 and 7);
- Different implementations of the same organizing principle can determine the efficiency or effectiveness of the interactions it enables (Chapter 9).

If you are creating a personal organizing system or otherwise small-scale one with only a small number of users, you might think there is little reason to think explicitly about requirements. However, any project benefits from the discipline of being more systematic about its purposes and their priorities. In addition, being explicit about requirements enables traceability and impact analysis. Traceability means being able to relate an interaction or feature of a system to the requirement it satisfies; impact analysis runs the causal link between requirements and features in the opposite direction to assess what or who will be affected if requirements change.[550]

10.4.1 Requirements for Interactions in Organizing Systems

When we describe interactions in a generic or broad way as we did in Chapter 2, *"Activities in Organizing Systems"* we see that all organizing systems have some common interactions, but most of the time we want to pay attention to the more specific interactions that are designed to create value in a particular organizing system because of the kind of resources it contains (§2.4.2). The domain, scope, and scale of the organizing system determines which interactions are possible and which ones must be explicitly supported, but the priorities of different interactions are more often determined by decisions about intended users (§10.3.2).

For most organizing systems other than personal ones, the set of interactions that are implemented in an organizing system is strongly determined by business model considerations, funding levels, or other economic factors. For-profit firms often differentiate themselves by the number and quality of the interactions they support with their resources, some by supporting many of them and some by supporting a minimal number. This differentiation is strongly shaped by and also shapes user preferences; some people prefer self-service or unmediated interactions, while others prefer full service and mediated interactions.[551] Non-profit institutions like public libraries and museums are also subject to these constraints, but unfortunately they have fewer options for adjusting service levels or changing their targeted user populations when their funding is reduced.[552]

Some requirements for interactions come along with technology requirements, to have resources in a particular format, to conform to a particular specification or standard in order to operate in some technology environment, or to interoperate with other parties or their organizing systems.

An essential requirement in every organizing system is ensuring that the supported interactions can be discovered and invoked by their intended users. In organizing systems with physical resources, good designers enhance the inherent affordances of resources with navigation and orientation aids that direct users to points of interactions (§2.4.1). With digital resources and information-intensive organizing systems, interactions are not immediately perceivable, and poor design can create overly complicated user interfaces in which many interactions are never discovered and thus never used.

It is tricky to compare the overall capabilities of organizing systems in terms of the number of variety of their interactions because what matters more is how much value they create. Organizing systems with active resources can create value on their own without an explicit user interaction (§3.2.3.2). Other organizing systems exploit stored, computed, or contextual information to create value by eliminating the need for user interactions (§2.4.1).[553]

10.4.2 Requirements about the Nature and Extent of Resource Description

Interactions with resources within an organizing system often depend on descriptions of individual resources or descriptions of the collections that contain them. In the bibliographic domain, generic or common interactions make use of descriptions that can be associated with almost any type of resource, such as the name, creator, and creation date.[554] For example, any resource with a sortable name or identifier can be arranged alphabetically to enable it to be easily found, and any resource with a creation date can be discovered by a "what's new" query to a resource collection.

Different types of resources must have differentiating properties, otherwise there would be no reason to distinguish them as different types. These resource properties can be recorded in the terms of a description language to support one or more interactions or to answer one or more questions. Simply put, choices about the nature and extent of resource description depend on which interactions or questions are most frequent or important (§4.3.1.1). If a particular property of a resource has no interactions that depend on it, there is no need to describe it. However, if an interaction depends on a description of a particular resource property, a missing description or one of inadequate precision and granularity means that the interaction will be impossible or inefficient to carry out because the resource will need to be further analyzed to create or extract the required description. An ISBN is a sufficient description to find a book in a directory, but if the ISBN is the only description associated with the book you will not be able to tell who wrote it. The tradeoffs imposed by the extent and timing of resource description have been a recurring theme in this book, with the tradeoff between recall and precision being the most salient (§1.3.5, §2.4.1, §6.4.1, §6.4.3).

The properties of resources that are easiest to describe are not always the most useful ones, especially for information resources where the property of aboutness is critical but challenging to describe. For non-text information resources this problem is magnified because the content is often in a semantically opaque format that cannot usefully be analyzed by people.

Business strategy and economics strongly influence the extent of resource description. In many museums and archives there are not enough trained people and time to describe every pottery fragment or document, and many resources are described only at an aggregate level. In contrast, some people argue that the explosion of content in physical and digital form mandates significant investment in descriptions that facilitate resource discovery in a crowded marketplace.[555]

Automated and computerized processes can create the resource descriptions in an organizing system and their use is primarily driven by scale (§4.3.6.4). Search engines index web pages and analyze their link structures because it would be impossible to treat the web as a traditional library and organize it by human effort. The benefits of digital cameras, video recorders, and similar devices would be far fewer if people had to manually identify and describe each resource when creating it. Instead, these devices can automatically assign some contextual metadata. Similarly, competitive pressures on vendors to provide real-time and context-sensitive information services mandate automated collection of contextual information like location from mobile phones, portable book readers and tablet computers.

We might seek some optimal degree of description given some set of requirements or purposes for an organizing system and some estimate of the organizing effort that could be applied; in practice this is elusive for two reasons, both relating to scope and scale. First, as the number of users of an organizing system increases, it becomes more difficult to identify and anticipate all its possible purposes and constraints it must satisfy. Even if most users share the goals for the organizing system, any particular user might have some additional specialized use for some attributes or relationships that would require more description to satisfy.[556]

Second, even if it were possible to implement some optimal degree of description in a particular organizing system, we would still encounter problems when multiple organizing systems exist in the same domain or in domains that intersect across context, device, or application boundaries. Since organizing systems are designed and evolve to satisfy the specific requirements of their particular context, companies will often describe the same resources differently, which creates integration and interoperability problems when companies need to exchange and combine information resources(§9.3.2).

10.4.3 Requirements about Intentional Arrangement

Organizing principles depend on resource descriptions, so requirements for the former are always intertwined with those for the latter. Specifying requirements for the intentional arrangement of resources is analogous to specifying why and how resource categories can be created (§6.3). In turn, the creation of resource categories often becomes a question about the number and kind of resource properties that might be analyzed and exploited by organizing principles.

We noted that there is a continuum of category formation that ranges from minimal use of resource properties to more rigorous use of multiple properties, and finally to statistical or composite use of multiple properties, some of which are induced or inferred rather than explicit. The simplest principle for defining a category is by enumeration, just putting the resources into a set without any specification of any properties they might share. The enumerated resources might very well have common properties, but the principle of enumeration ignores them; the only property that matters for that principle is that the resources are in the same set. This corresponds to the simplest principle of intentional arrangement, that of collocation, just putting the resources in the same location without any additional organization.

Collocated resources often acquire some additional arrangement as a result of their use; consider how the books, papers, or other resources gathered for some writing project often end up in piles in your office or on your desk close to your work area. For a small collection, this proximity-to-use organizing principle is the easiest way to satisfy a requirement to minimize the time to find frequently used resources.

As we've often seen, the scope and scale of the organizing system is a dominant design consideration and it applies to principles of resource arrangement too. The collocation principle of arrangement is sufficient for small resource collections because it is not necessary to define the optimal organization if the time to find any particular resource is short even for an inefficient search method of scanning the entire collection. Using the extrinsic property of frequency of use makes search slightly more efficient, but only in organizing systems where the user population is small or interacts with the resources in similar ways. Otherwise, arranging resources to facilitate their frequent access for some users would hinder other users who never use them. Imagine if you shared your office desk with someone who works all night on other writing projects and leaves his frequently used resources in piles close to his work area – which becomes your work area in the morning.

Larger resource collections usually require multiple organizing principles to manage the complexity that emerges when more users and more varied interactions must be supported. It is essential to establish the priority of users and interactions because these requirements determine the order in which the principles are applied to arrange the resources. This ordering creates a logical resource hierarchy that affects the efficiency of interactions and the maintenance of the organizing system over time.

Information resources are invariably challenging to arrange because their aboutness is not an easily perceived property and because of the open-ended purposes they can serve. Information collections with broad scope most often use a standard system of bibliographic classification (§7.3). In contrast, special libraries have narrower collections that need to support domain-specific interactions for a relatively small set of users, and as a result they require more specialized organizational schemes.[557] The principles for resource arrangement in large firms of every type are often required to conform with laws and regulations for accounting, taxes, human resources, data retention and non retention, access control, and other functions (§2.5.4.1, §7.1.5.4).

10.4.4 Dealing with Conflicting Requirements

Any individual, group, or enterprise can create an organizing system that meets their specific requirements, but once this organizing system involves two or more parties with different requirements, there is a potential for conflict. Roommates or spouses sometimes argue about how to organize items in the kitchen, in the refrigerator, or in some other shared space. To a person who arranges spices alphabetically and condiment jars by size, arranging them according to cuisine or frequency of use makes no sense. Similarly, if you are the sole user of a Dropbox or other cloud storage account, you can organize it any way you want. You can use any number of folders that need only make sense to you, or you can leave everything unorganized in a single folder. However, if you share the Dropbox account with another person, they are likely to have different organizational needs or preferences. Perhaps you tend to organize resources by file type, while they prefer to organize resources by topic or project.

A small number of people can often agree on an organizing system that meets the needs of each participant through informal negotiations. The potential for conflict increases when more people are involved, and "bottom-up" *ad hoc* negotiations to resolve every disagreement between every pair of participants just aren't feasible. In many domains conflicts are avoided or suppressed because the parties have developed or agreed to conform to standards (§7.1.5). Nevertheless, conflicts in organizing principles for large-scale organizing systems are often resolved by parties with the legal authority or economic power to impose a solution on all the participants in a "top-down" manner.[558]

10.5 Designing and Implementing an Organizing System

Requirements define what must be done but NOT how to do it; that's the role of the design and implementation phases. Being explicit about requirements and the intended scope and scale of an organizing system before moving onto these phases in an organizing system's lifecycle avoids two problems. The first is taking a narrow and short-term focus on the initial resources in a collection, which might not be representative of the collection when it reaches its planned scope and scale. This can result in overly customized and inflexible resource descriptions or arrangements that cannot easily accommodate the future growth of the collection. A second problem, often a corollary of the first, is not separating design principles from their implementation in some specific environment or technology.

10.5.1 Choosing Scope- and Scale-Appropriate Technology

A simple organizing system to satisfy personal record keeping or some short-lived information management requirements can be implemented using folders and files on a personal computer or by using "off the shelf" generic software such as web forms, spreadsheets, databases, and wikis. Other simple organizing systems run as applications on smart phones. Some small amount of configuration, scripting, structuring or programming might be involved, but in many cases this work can be done in an *ad hoc* manner. The low initial cost to get started with these kinds of applications must be weighed against the possible cost of having to redo a lot of the work later because the resources and the resource descriptions might not be easily exported to new ones.

More capable organizing systems that enable the persistent storage and efficient retrieval of large amounts of structured information resources generally require additional design and implementation efforts. Flat word processing files and spreadsheets are not adequate. Instead, XML document models and database schemas often must be developed to ensure more control of and validation of the information content and its descriptions. Software for version and configuration management, security and access control, query and transformation, and for other functions and services must also be developed to implement the organizing system.

Technology for organizing systems will always evolve to enable new capabilities. For example, cloud computing and storage are radically changing the scale of organizing systems and the accessibility of the information they contain. It might be possible to implement these capabilities and services to an organizing system in an incremental fashion with informal design and implementation methods. If information models, processing logic, business rules and other constraints are encoded in the software without explicit traceability to requirements and design decisions the organizing system will be difficult to maintain if the context, scope or requirements change. This is why we have repeatedly emphasized the importance of architectural thinking about organizing systems, beginning in §1.2.3.1 where we proposed that organizing principles should ideally be expressed in a way that did not assume how they would be implemented (See also §2.3.2.2, §7.1.3, and §8.1).

10.5.2 Architectural Thinking

Architectural thinking leads to more modularity and abstraction in design, making it easier to change an implementation to satisfy new requirements or to take advantage of new technologies or procedures. It is also important to think architecturally about the design of the vocabularies and schemas for resource description and of classification systems to leave room for expansion to accommodate new resource types (§6.5 and §7.2.2.3). Doing so is easier if the descriptions are logically and physically distinct from the resources they describe.

Nevertheless, architectural thinking requires more careful analysis of resources and implementation alternatives, and most people don't think this way, especially for personal and informal organizing systems. You can imagine that someone might arrange a collection of paperback books in a small bookcase whose shelf height and width were perfectly suited for the paperbacks they currently own. However, this organizing system would not work at all for large format books, and a paperback could not be added to the collection unless one was purged from the collection. It would be more sensible to start with a bigger bookcase with adjustable shelves so that the organizing system would have a longer lifetime.

You might think that large institutional organizing systems would avoid these problems caused by tying a collection too tightly to the physical environment in which it is initially organized, but sometimes they don't. A famous example involves the art collection of the Barnes Foundation, which had to keep its paintings in the exact same crowded arrangements when the museum made a controversial move from a small building to a larger one because the donor had mandated that the paintings never be moved from their original settings. (See the Sidebar, "The Barnes Collection" (page 416)).

For digital resources, inexpensive storage and high bandwidth have largely eliminated capacity as a constraint for organizing systems, with an exception for *big data*, which is defined as a collection of data that is too big to be managed by typical database software and hardware architectures.[559] Even so, big data collections are often large but homogeneous, so their scale is not their most important challenge from an organizing system perspective (§10.3.1).

> **The Barnes Collection**
>
> Albert Barnes was a chemist who made a fortune inventing a preventive treatment for gonorrhea and who then amassed perhaps the greatest private art collection ever, one that contained over 800 paintings by artists like Picasso, Renoir, Matisse, van Gogh, and Cezanne. In 1922 Barnes built a museum for his collection in his residential neighborhood in Merion, PA, a suburb of Philadelphia. Barnes did not open his collection to the public and in his will mandated that the collection never be moved, loaned, or sold.
>
> In the decades after Barnes died in 1951 the Merion museum needed extensive repairs and security upgrades, and some people suggested that its remote location and access restrictions jeopardized its financial viability. However, a proposal to relocate the collection to Philadelphia seemingly violated the terms of the Barnes will.
>
> A legal fight dragged on for decades. Finally in 2004 a judge ruled that the collection could be moved to Philadelphia, but only if the new museum contained exact copies of the gallery rooms of the original museum and arranged the paintings exactly as they were in Merion. The new museum building, opened in 2012, is ten times larger than thae old one, but the collection takes up the same space as it did in Merion. The other 90% of the building is occupied by an auditorium, offices, classrooms, a gift shop, and other space that contains none of the collection.[560]

10.5.3 Distinguishing Access to Resources from Resource Control

Because large resource collections are often used for multiple purposes by many different people or projects, they illustrate another important architectural issue for collections of digital resources. A requirement for access to resources does not imply a need to directly own or control them, and information-intensive and web-based businesses have increasingly adopted organizing system designs that involve storage of digital resources in the cloud, licensing of globally distributed resources, and outsourcing of information services. Designs that use these architectural concepts can realize functional and quality improvements because the location and identity of the service provider is hidden by an abstraction layer (§2.4.2.1, §3.4.3.5). However, separating access from ownership has been a cultural challenge for some libraries and museums whose institutional identities emphasize the resources they directly control and the physical buildings in which they control them.[561]

10.5.4 Standardization and Legacy Considerations

As we noted with the Barnes Collection, a building becomes old and outdated over time. The technology used in digital organizing systems becomes obsolete faster than physical buildings do. The best way to slow the inevitable transformation of today's cutting edge technology to tomorrow's legacy technology is to design with standard data formats, description vocabularies and schemas, and classification systems unless you have specific requirements that preclude these choices.

Even a requirement to interoperate with an organizing system that uses proprietary or non-standard specifications can usually be satisfied by transforming from a standard format (§7.1.5.2, §9.2.3). Similarly, it is better to design the APIs and data feeds of an organizing system in a generic or standard way that abstracts from their hidden implementation. This design principle makes it easier for external users to understand the supported interactions, and also prevents disclosure of any aspects of resource description or organization that provide competitive advantage. For example, the way in which a business classifies products, suppliers, customers, or employees can be competitively important.

Two important design questions that arise with data transformation or conversion, whether it is required by a technology upgrade or an interoperability requirement, are when to do it and where to do it. The job of converting all the resources in a collection can typically be outsourced to a firm that specializes in format conversion or resource description, and a batch or pre-emptive conversion of an entire collection enables an upgraded or new organizing system to operate more efficiently when it is not distracted by ongoing conversion activity. On the other hand, if resources vary greatly in their frequency of use, a "do-it-yourself on-demand" method is probably more cost effective as long as the conversion does not impact the interactions that need to be supported.

10.6 Operating and Maintaining an Organizing System

After the organizing system has been designed and implemented it can be put into its operation and maintenance phases. We will look at these from two perspectives, first from the point of view of individual resources, and then from the point of view of the organizing system's design and implementation. These two perspectives are not always clearly distinguished. Curation, for example, is often used to describe actions taken to maintain individual resources as well as those that result in new arrangements of them.

10.6.1 Maintaining an Organizing System: Resource Perspective

Sometimes an organizing system is implemented with its organizing structures and relationships waiting to be populated by resources as they are acquired and described. The scope and scale of the organizing system shapes how the descriptions are created and how the descriptions are then used to assign resources to the logical or physical containers of the organizing system. The most important decisions to be made at this point involve determining an appropriate mix of methods for creating the resource descriptions, because their cost, quality, consistency, completeness, and semantic richness depends on which human or computational agents do the work (§4.3.6).

For web-based and consumer-focused organizing systems, it is tempting to rely on users to assign descriptions, tags, or ratings to resources (§4.2.2.3). Some of these systems attempt to improve the quality and precision of these descriptions by providing forms, controlled vocabularies, or suggestions. Finding a balance is tricky; too much direction and control is demotivating to uncompensated volunteer describers, and too little of it results in the proverbial "tag soup."

An essential operational and maintenance activity is evaluation of resource descriptions, first with respect to the time and process by which they are created, and second with respect to how when they support the designed interactions (§4.3.7).

Some organizing systems are initiated with a fixed set of resources that will not change in any way. For example, in an archive as most narrowly defined, neither the individual resources nor the organization of the collection as a whole will change. If an archive of Abraham Lincoln letters is established, we know that Lincoln will never revise any letters or write any new ones, and any new classifications or descriptions devised by people studying the archive will not be used to rearrange the letters.

Most organizing systems, however, need to support ongoing interactions with a collection that changes over time as new resources enter the collection and old ones leave. These selection and collection management processes are explicit in libraries, museums and similar institutions that maintain collections to satisfy the changing needs and preferences of their user communities (§2.2.2).

10.6.2 Maintaining an Organizing System: Properties, Principles and Technology Perspective

It is useful to consider how an organizing system as a whole is operated and maintained over time. We can analyze how the system's organizing properties, principles and technology might change, and we can roughly order different types of change according to their overall impact.

The most predictable maintenance activities for an organizing system with an expected long lifetime (§10.3.3) are incremental changes in description vocabularies and classification schemes (§7.2.2.3). These need to evolve when new instances or contexts require additional properties to maintain the distinctions between types of resources, but the basic principles embodied in the organizing systems are not affected.

Incremental category maintenance takes place even in personal organizing systems where the categories are not always explicit. The collection of clothes in a college student's closet and the categories and properties for arranging them will change somewhat when he graduates and takes a job in a downtown office building where he needs to dress more formally than he did as a student. He will learn that despite the common term in the category name, "student casual" and "business casual" do not contain the same sets of resources.

Category maintenance is an ongoing activity in institutional organizing systems. The most commonly used bibliographic classification systems all have numbering and naming schemes that allow for subdivision and extension to create new subcategories to accommodate resources about new fields of knowledge and technology.

As another example, the Association for Computing Machinery (ACM) professional society created a keyword classification in 1964 to organize articles in its many publications, but relentless change in the computing field driven by Moore's Law has required the ACM to significantly revise the system almost every decade.[562]

In contrast, changes in business organizing systems are more likely to be driven by economic factors. Resource properties for managing collections of resource and the information that describes them often change over time as a result of new products and services, mergers and acquisitions, or refined customer segmentation. More substantial changes in business organizing systems reflect the need to comply with laws and regulations that impose new requirements for tracing money flows or transactions. These mandated classifications and processes might require new organizing principles, not just incremental properties (§7.1.5.4).

The choice of implementation technology influences how easy it is to handle these types of changes in organizing systems. In databases this problem is known as "schema migration." With XML implementations, schemas can be designed with "extension" or "codelist" elements to enable changes that will not invalidate existing information. Business processes that are driven by "executable specifications" like the Business Process Execution Language (BPEL) can be easily modified because the BPEL XML instance is used to configure the software that carries out the process it describes.[563]

Another very predictable type of activity over time with organizing systems is a technology upgrade that improves its quality or capabilities without affecting the organizing principles. A student might replace his handwritten lecture notes with typed notes on a laptop or tablet computer but not significantly change the way the notes are organized.

Institutional organizing systems are adopting tiered storage systems that automatically move resources between different types of storage media to meet performance, availability and recovery requirements. For example, firms with high financial impact of downtime like banks run critical organizing systems with copies in "failsafe" or "hot" modes that are synchronized with the production environments to prevent any interruptions in information access if the latter are disrupted. All the relevant resources are immediately available. On the other hand, resources needed for regulatory compliance can be kept on lower cost disk storage.

The most challenging kinds of maintenance activities for organizing systems involve changes to the principles for arranging resources along with changes in the implementing technology. An example is the ambitious effort to introduce semantic web and linked data concepts in bibliographic organizing systems (§5.8.2, §8.4.3). And change comes faster to businesses than to libraries and museums. New technologies can have a disruptive impact on business organizing system, forcing major changes to enable strategy changes that involve faster finding, retrieval, or delivery of informational or physical goods.[564]

Sometimes these major changes to organizing principles and technologies can be introduced incrementally, with changes "rolled out" to different sets of resources or user groups during a transition period. However, sometimes the changes are inherently '"all or none" because it is impossible to have two conflicting organizing systems operating in the same context. An easy to understand example of an organizing system that changed radically is the system governing which side of the road you drive on, which was changed in Samoa in 2009. (See the Sidebar, "Driving in Samoa" (page 421)).

Driving in Samoa

Whether you travel by bus, car, or bicycle, you always keep to one side of the road. The convention of driving on either the right side or the left side is a legal standard that you, and others who share the road, take for granted. However, you must follow it to ensure safe driving and avoid running into other vehicles and pedestrians.

This standard of which side of the road you drive on, simple as it seems, was not decided arbitrarily, but rather, it was adopted as a result of history, convention, and the need for organization. If you were the only person in your country to use the road, you could choose to travel on any side you wanted, even travel right down the middle. As soon as more than one person needs to use the same road, the risk of collisions compels the creation of a coordinating standard.

In 2009, the government of Samoa took the rare step of changing the side of the road standard from driving on the right to driving on the left. The original standard reflected the influence of German colonization in the early 1900s. However, Samoa is both geographically close to and economically intertwined with Australia and New Zealand, former British colonies that follow the British convention of driving on the left side. This proximity gives Samoa access to a nearby source of used cars that would be attractive to Samoa's relatively poor population. So, the Samoan government decided to use its authority to change the driving standard so that more of its people could afford to buy cars.

As one could imagine, this decision was not implemented without controversy and opposition. While the decision benefited people currently without cars, it negatively affected those who already owned them. After a switch like this, what happens to the current market value of the thousands of cars designed to drive on the right? Opponents also claimed that the switch would cause unprecedented safety hazards. If even a small fraction of drivers were not able to immediately get the hang of driving on the other side, the accident rate could increase tremendously. Imagine the current pool of buses designed with doors that open on the right hand side—would they now let passengers out in the middle of the street? Who would pay to have the buses modified to put doors on the left hand side?[565]

10.7 Applying the Roadmap: Organizing Systems Case Studies

We now fulfill the promise of this chapter, and this book, with a set of case study examples that apply the concepts and phases of the roadmap. The five design questions from Chapter 1, *"Foundations for Organizing Systems"* serve as a template to ensure consistency.

10.7.1 A Multigenerational Photo Collection

OVERVIEW. Your grandfather has died, at age 91, and under his bed is a suitcase containing several photo albums with a few hundred photos. Some of them have captions, but many don't. What do you do with them?

Your first thought was to create a digital photo archive of Grandpa's collection so that you and all your relatives could see them, and you would also want to generate accurate captions where none exist. Since you have an extensive digital photo collection of your own in a web-based application perhaps you can combine the two collections to create a multigenerational photo organizing system.

This project involves digitization, archiving, social media issues, and negotiations with and collecting information from other family members who might have different views about what to do.

WHAT RESOURCES ARE BEING ORGANIZED? It is easy to find advice about how to digitize old photos, but there are more choices than you might think. What resolution and format should you use? Should you do the work yourself or send Grandpa's precious photos to a service and take the risk that they might get lost? Should you do any restoration or enhancement of the photos as part of the digitization process?[566]

More fundamental design questions concern the scope and scale of the organizing system. If you're digitizing Grandpa's photos and combining them with yours, you're skipping a generation. Shouldn't you also include photos from your parents and the rest of Grandpa's children? That generation has both printed photos and digital ones, but it is not as comfortable with computers as you are, and their digital photos are stored less systematically on a variety of CD-ROM, DVDs, flash memory sticks, and SD photo cards, making the digitizing and organizing work more complicated. Do these differences in storage media reflect an intentional arrangement that needs to be preserved? And what about that box full of Super 8 cartridges and VHS tapes with family videos on them, and the audio cassettes with recordings made at long-ago family gatherings?

A family history management system that includes many different resource types is a much bigger project than the one you contemplated when you first opened Grandpa's suitcase. It is easier to consider using separate but related organizing systems for each media type, because there are many web-based applications you could use. In fact, there are far too many choices of web applications for you to consider. You might compare some for their functionality and usability, but given that the long expected lifetime of your organizing system there are more critical considerations: whether the site is likely to last as long as your collection and if it doesn't, how easily you can export your resources and resource descriptions.[567]

WHY ARE THE RESOURCES ORGANIZED? The overall goal of preserving Grandpa's photos needs no justification, but is preservation the primary goal? Or is to enable access to the images for far-flung family members? Or is it to create a repository for family photos as they continue to be produced? Alternatively, is it less about the images themselves and perhaps more about collecting family-history information contained in the photos, thus making the collection of metadata (accurate information about when and where the photo was taken, who is in it, etc.) most important?

These decisions determine requirements for the interactions that the photo organizing system must support, but the repertoire of interactions is mostly determined by the choice of photo storage and sharing application. Some applications combine photo storage in a cloud-based repository tied to a very powerful set of digital photography tools, but this functionality comes with complexity that would overwhelm your less technology-savvy relatives. They would be happy just to be able to browse and search for photos.

HOW MUCH ARE THE RESOURCES ORGANIZED? Because you realize that a carefully designed set of categories and a controlled tagging vocabulary will enable precise browsing and search, you chose an application that supports grouping and tagging. But not everyone should be allowed to group or tag photos, and maybe some of the more distant relatives can view photos but not add any.

Will your categories and tags include all of those that Grandpa used when he arranged pictures in albums and made notes on the back of many of them? Do you want to allow annotations? Maybe this is a picture from a vacation; if you go back to the same place, do you want to create an association between the pictures?

Don't forget to keep Grandpa's original albums in a safe place, not under a bed somewhere.

WHEN ARE THE RESOURCES ORGANIZED? Once you create your categories and tags, you can require people to use them when they add new photos to the collection. Perhaps the existing resource descriptions can be completed or enhanced as a collective activity at a family reunion. Don't put this off too long—the people who can identify Grandpa's sister Gladys, her second husband, and his sister in an uncaptioned photo are getting on in years.

WHO DOES THE ORGANIZING? You have taken on the role of the editor and curator, but you can't do everything and having a group of people involved will probably result in more robust organizing. A group can also better handle sticky situations like what to do if people get divorced or have a falling out with other family members; do pictures taken of or by them get deleted?

OTHER CONSIDERATIONS. Maintenance of this collection for an indefinite time raises the important issue or a succession plan for the curator. If only one name is on the account and only that person knows the password, you run the risk of losing access to the photos if that person dies. One of Grandpa's mistakes was dying without clearly specifying his intentions for his photo collection, so whatever you decide you should document carefully and include a continuity plan when you are no longer the curator.[568]

10.7.2 Knowledge Management for a Small Consulting Firm

OVERVIEW. A senior professor who has done part-time consulting for many years is very pleased when his latest book becomes a best-seller and he is inundated with new consulting opportunities. He decides to take a two-year leave of absence from his university to start a small consulting firm with several of his current and former graduate students as his junior consulting partners.

An organizing system for knowledge management is required, but what gets designed will depend on the scoping decision. Is the goal of the system to support the consulting business, or also to support ongoing and future research projects that sooner or later will generate the consulting opportunities?

WHAT RESOURCES ARE BEING ORGANIZED? The professor concludes that since his consulting is based on his research, he needs to include in the new knowledge management system his research articles and the raw and analyzed data that is discussed in the articles. These resources are already organized to a great extent according to the research project that led to their creation. These have been kept in the professor's university office.

The professor also has a separate collection of consulting proposals, client reports, and presentations that he has made at client firms. Because of restrictive university rules about faculty consulting, the professor has always kept these resources in his home office rather than on campus.[569]

In addition to these existing resource types, it will be necessary to create new ones that make systematic and explicit information that the professor has managed in an informal and largely tacit manner. This includes consulting inquiries, information about prospects, and information about specific people in client firms.

WHY ARE THE RESOURCES ORGANIZED? The professor has usually just done one consulting project at a time, very opportunistically. He has often turned down projects that involved more work than he could do himself. He now sees the opportunity to do much more consulting and to take on more significant projects if he can leverage his expertise in a more efficient way.

The professor can take on the "rainmaker" role to secure new consulting engagements and make the important decisions, and he is confident that he can train and support his new staff of current and former students to do much of the actual consulting work.

The knowledge management system must enable everyone in the firm to access and contribute to project repositories that contain proposals, plans, work in progress, and project deliverables. Much of this work can be reused from one project to another, increasing the productivity of the firm and the quality of its deliverables.[570]

Just as it is essential that the professor's knowledge is systematized and made available via a knowledge management system, so must the knowledge created by the new staff of consultants. The professor cannot expect that all of the students will work for him forever, so any knowledge that they acquire and create in the course of their work will be lost to the firm unless it is captured along with the professor's.

The consulting firm probably won't have an indefinite lifetime. After his leave of absence, the professor might return to his university duties, perhaps on a part-time basis. The knowledge management system will enable him to leave the firm in someone else's hands while enabling him to keep tabs on and possibly contribute to ongoing projects. Alternatively, if the firm is doing very well, perhaps the professor will resign his university position and take on the role of growing the firm. A larger consultancy might want to acquire the professor's firm, and the firm's valuation will in part be determined be the extent to which the firm's capabilities and resources are documented in the knowledge management system.

HOW MUCH ARE THE RESOURCES ORGANIZED? A small firm has neither the money nor the people to invest in complex technology and a rigorous process for knowledge management, but appropriate technology is readily available and affordable. Decisions about organizing principles must be made that reflect the mix of consulting projects; resources might be organized in a shared file system by customer type, project type, by the lead consultant – or in all of these ways using a faceted classification approach.

Standard document templates and style sheets for the resource types created by consultants can be integrated into word processors and spreadsheets. Contact and customer management functionality can be licensed as a hosted application.

Many small teams make good use of wikis for knowledge management because they are very flexible in the amount of structure they impose.[571]

WHEN ARE THE RESOURCES ORGANIZED? The professor's decision to take a leave of absence reflects his belief that getting the firm started quickly is essential if he is to capitalize on his recent bestselling book to generate consulting business. This makes managing the prospect pipeline and the proposal-writing process the highest priority targets for knowledge management.

Much of the other organizing work can emerge as adjuncts to consulting projects if some effort is made to coordinate the organizing across projects.

WHO DOES THE ORGANIZING? Because many of the early organizing decisions have implications for the types of customers and projects that the firm can take on, only the professor is capable of making most of them. The principal goal of the knowledge management system is to enable the professor to delegate work to his consulting staff, so he needs to enlist them in the design of the organizing system to ensure it is effective.

OTHER CONSIDERATIONS. As the consulting firm grows, it is inevitable that some consultants will be better than others at creating and using knowledge to create customer value, and they will expect to be compensated accordingly. It is essential for the ongoing success of the firm not to let this create disincentives for knowledge capture and sharing between consultants. The solution is to develop a company culture that promotes and rewards them.[572]

10.7.3 Japanese Farms Look to the Cloud

OVERVIEW. Unlike the first two case studies, this is an actual case rather than a hypothetical or composite one. It shares with the first two cases a focus on preserving valuable resources but in the radically different domain of farming.

This case concerns an initiative by Fujitsu, a Japanese technology firm, to apply "smart computing" and lean manufacturing techniques to the agricultural sector, which lags in technology use. Fujitsu is testing a "farm work management system" at six Japanese farms. In this case study we will focus on the farm highlighted in a 2011 *Wall Street Journal* story.[573]

This test farm is located in southern Japan. It has 60 different crops spread over 100 hectares (about 250 acres), an area slightly larger than the central campus of the University of California at Berkeley.

WHAT RESOURCES ARE BEING ORGANIZED? Sensors are deployed in each of 300 different farm plots to collect readings on temperature, soil and moisture levels. Video cameras also monitor each plot.

The 72 relatively unskilled workers on the farm are also managed resources. Each of them carries a mobile phone for communication, for transmission of pictures, and for GPS tracking of their location.

WHY ARE THE RESOURCES ORGANIZED? The highest level goal for Fujitsu is to expand its reach as a technology firm by applying the concepts of lean manufacturing, statistical process control, and continual improvement to new domains. Farming is an obvious choice in Japan because it is a relatively unproductive sector where the average age is over 60. It is essential that farms use more computing capability to increase efficiency and to capture and reuse the scarce knowledge possessed by aging workers.

The Fujitsu farm work management system supports numerous types of interactions to achieve these goals. For example, workers can send pictures of infected crops for diagnosis by an expert farmer in the farm's office, who can then investigate further by studying recorded video from the affected plot.

As more farms deploy the Fujitsu system, the aggregated knowledge and sensor information can be analyzed to enable economies of scale that will allow separate and widely distributed farms to function as if they were all part of a single large firm with centralized management.[574]

HOW MUCH ARE THE RESOURCES ORGANIZED? The current design of the system treats farm workers as relatively passive resources that are managed very closely. The system generates a daily schedule of planting, maintenance, harvesting, and other activities for each worker. At a daily wrap-up meeting the farm manager reviews each worker's performance based on GPS and sensor readings.

The sensor data is analyzed and organized extensively by Fujitsu computers to make recommendations, both agricultural ones (such as what crop grows best in each plot and the work schedule that optimizes quality and yield), and business ones (what is the profitability of growing this crop on this plot of land).

WHEN ARE THE RESOURCES ORGANIZED? The farm work management system is continually organizing and reorganizing what it knows about the farm as it analyzes sensor and production information. In contrast, the information created by the workers is captured but its analysis is deferred to an expert.

It is conceivable that as the farm workers become more expert as a result of the guidance and instruction they receive from the system that they can be more autonomous and do more analysis and interpretation on their own. It is also likely that the inexorable forces of Moore's Law will enable more data collection and more processing of the sensor data at its time of collection, which might result in increased real-time information exchange with the workers.

WHO DOES THE ORGANIZING? The physical organization of the farm, with 300 small plots of land with 60 different fruits and vegetables is the legacy arrangement of the farm before the Fujitsu trial began. Because of the sizable investment that Fujitsu has made in the farm to deploy the system, it is likely that the farm manager defers to recommendations made by the system to change crop arrangements. So it is reasonable to conclude that most of the decisions about the organizing system are made by computational processes rather than by people.

OTHER CONSIDERATIONS. Fujitsu built this system for managing farms, but there are several other resource domains with similar challenges about capturing and reusing operational knowledge: vineyards, forests, and fish farms come to mind.[575] It will be interesting to see if the farm work management system can be made more abstract and configurable so that the same system can be used in all of these domains.

Farm crops, vineyards, trees, and fish pens don't move around, so a more challenging application of sensor technologies arises with cattle herd management. Nevertheless, sensors inserted in the genitals of a female dairy cow can trigger a text message to a herd manager's cell phone when the cow is in heat, preventing the economic loss of missing a reproductive cycle.[576]

Somewhat more remote domains for potential application of systems that combine sensor networks with workforce management include sales, field support, and logistics.

10.7.4 Single-Source Textbook Publishing

OVERVIEW. The fourth case is also an actual case – a self-referential one. It is a case study about the organizing system involved in the creation, production, and distribution of *The Discipline of Organizing*.

We have known since the beginning of this project that this book should not just be a conventional text. A printed book is an intellectual snapshot that is already dated in many respects the day it is published. In addition, the pedagogical goal of *TDO* as a textbook for information schools and similar programs is made more difficult by the relentless growth of computing capability and the resulting technology innovation in our information-intensive economy and culture. We think that the emergence of ebook publishing opens up innovative possibilities as long as we can use a single set of source files to produce and update the print and digital versions of this book.

WHAT RESOURCES ARE BEING ORGANIZED? The content of this book began in early 2010 as more than 1000 slides and associated instructor notes for a graduate course on "Information Organizing and Retrieval" that Robert J. Glushko, the primary author and editor of *TDO*, was teaching at the University of California at Berkeley. These slides and notes were created in XML and transformed to HTML for presentation in a web browser.[577]

The first decision to be made about resource organization led to the iterative sorting of the slides from 26 lectures into the 10 chapters in the initial outline for the book. The second decision concerned the granularity of the new content resources being created for the book. The team of authors was organized by chapters, which made chapters the natural granularity for file management and version control. Because authors were widely dispersed we relied on the Dropbox cloud storage service to synchronize work. Nevertheless, the broad and deep topical coverage of the book meant that chapters had substantial internal structure (four levels of headings in some places), and many of these subsections became separately identified resources that moved from chapter to chapter until they found their natural home.

In addition to the text content and illustrations that make up the printed text, we needed to organize short videos, interactive examples, and other applications to incorporate in digital versions of the book.

Finally, it has been essential to view the software that transforms, assembles, formats, and assigns styles when turning source files into deliverable artifacts as resources that must be managed. We have been fortunate to get much of the required software from O'Reilly and Associates, an innovative technology publisher that has been developing an XML-based single-source publishing system called Atlas.

WHY ARE THE RESOURCES ORGANIZED? Publishing print and ebook versions of a text from the same source files is the only way to produce both in a cost-effective and maintainable fashion. Approaches that require any "handcrafting" would make it impossible to revise the book on a timely schedule. Furthermore, a survey of Berkeley students in the summer of 2012 revealed a great diversity of preferred platforms for reading digital books that included laptop computers, Apple and Android tablets, and seven different dedicated ebook readers. Only an automated single-source publishing strategy could produce all these outputs.

The highly granular structure for the content resources that comprise this book makes cross-referencing vastly more precise, making it easier to use the book as a textbook and job aid. It will also make it easier to maintain and adapt the text for use in online courses. (The emerging best practice for online courses is to break up lectures and study content into smaller units than used in traditional classroom lectures.)

HOW MUCH ARE THE RESOURCES ORGANIZED? The nature and extent of resource organization for this book reflects its purpose of bringing together multiple disciplines that recognize organizing as a fundamental issue but from different perspectives. The book contains many specialized topics and domain-specific examples that might overwhelm the shared concepts. Our solution was to write a lean core text and to move much of the disciplinary and domain-specific content into tagged endnotes. These categories of endnotes are somewhat arbitrary, but the authoring task of identifying content to go into endnotes is a non-trivial one.

The extent of resource organization is also affected by the choice of XML vocabulary, and we carefully considered whether to choose DITA or DocBook. DITA has the benefit of having more native support for modular authoring and transparent customization and updating, but DocBook is much older and hence has better tool kits. We eventually chose DocBook.[578]

WHEN ARE THE RESOURCES ORGANIZED? Despite the fact that the lecture notes with which the book began were in XML, we decided to author the book using Microsoft Word. Many of the authors had little experience with XML editors, and the highly-developed commenting and revision management facilities in Word proved very useful. This tradeoff imposed the burden of converting files to XML during the production process but only two of the authors were still working on the book at that stage, and both have decades of experience with XML.

WHO DOES THE ORGANIZING? The chapter authors used Word style sheets in a careful manner, tagging text with styles rather than using formatting overrides. This enabled a conversion vendor to convert most of the book from Word to XML semi-automatically. Some cleanup of the markup is inevitable because of the ambiguity created when the source markup with Word styles is less granular than the target markup in XML. We do not know whether the amount of work left for us was atypical.

Nevertheless, waiting until the book was substantially finished to convert to XML meant that we were also deferring the effort to mark up the text with cross references, glossary terms, and index entries, because these types of content were not included in the Word authoring templates and style sheets. As a result, a substantial amount of effort has been required of our copy and markup editor that could have been done by chapter editors if they had authored natively in XML. However, having a single markup editor has given this book a more consistent and complete glossary and index than would be have possible with multiple authors.

OTHER CONSIDERATIONS. Our ambitious effort to use tagged endnotes to create a book that could meet the needs of different courses and academic programs is a bit ahead of its time, because the current generation of ebook readers cannot do it justice. We are working on a next-generation ebook application that can create a vastly more engaging and integrated reader experience with the tagged endnotes. Instead of requiring the reader to follow a hypertext link, our ebook application will present selectable icons that dynamically transclude the endnote text into the core text. Furthermore, we are making the set of endnote types completely extensible. In addition to the six types that occur in the book as first published, any instructor or institution will be able to can create other endnote types to meet new requirements for customization.

This design for a book challenges conventional definitions of book editions and forces us to imagine new ways to acknowledge collaborative authorship. But asking "What is *The Discipline of Organizing* given these new authoring and publishing models is a similar question to the one asked in Chapter 3, "What is *Macbeth*?"

10.7.5 Your Own Case Study Goes Here

We have reached the end of this book, but we are just at the beginning of *The Discipline Of Organizing*. We hope that we have demonstrated why thinking of the art and science of organizing in a more abstract way can enable communication and cooperation across the numerous disciplines that are concerned with organizing, especially library and information science, computer science, informatics, law, economics, and business. Instead of just appropriating concepts and methods from these fields, we have tried to unify them, filling in the gaps between their complementary perspectives to yield a more comprehensive and generative understanding of how they fit together.

Now it is your turn. Perhaps you have a job in one of the fields we have brought together that involves organizing resources of one type or another. After reading this book, you surely won't approach that work the same way you did before. You will be able to apply the design patterns and principles of *The Discipline of Organizing* to make your existing organizing systems more capable, and will be able to create entirely new ones that fill the white space between the traditional categories.

If you're reading this book in its printed edition, this is §10.7.5, "Your Own Case Study Goes Here" (page 431), which follows four case studies that were in the book when it was first published. If you're reading this as an ebook, it might be section 10.7.7 or even 10.7.70. We encourage people who read this book to contribute their own case studies at DisciplineOfOrganizing.org, and we expect to incorporate the most interesting and entertaining ones into this collection.

10.8 Key Points in Chapter Ten

- Most of the specific decisions that must be made for an organizing system are strongly shaped by the initial decisions about its domain, scope, and scale.

- The impact of broad scope arises more from the heterogeneity of the resources and users in a collection rather than from their absolute number.

- Larger collections need more people to organize and maintain them, creating communication and coordination problems that grow much faster than the collection.

- The best way to prevent problems of scope and scale is through standardization.

- Organizing systems in the same domain and with nominally the same scope can differ substantially in the resources they contain and the interactions they support if they have different categories of users.

- For most organizing systems other than personal ones, the set of interactions that are implemented in an organizing system is strongly determined by economic factors.

- An essential requirement in every organizing system is ensuring that the supported interactions can be discovered and invoked by their intended users.

- Automated and computerized processes can create the resource descriptions in an organizing system and their use is primarily driven by scale.

- Organizing principles depend on resource descriptions, so requirements for the former are always intertwined with those for the latter.

- Larger resource collections usually require multiple organizing principles to manage the complexity that emerges when more users and more varied interactions must be supported.

- Overly customized and inflexible resource descriptions or arrangements cannot easily accommodate the future growth of the collection.

- Architectural thinking leads to more modularity and abstraction in design, making it easier to change an implementation to satisfy new requirements or to take advantage of new technologies or procedures.

- The cost, quality, consistency, completeness, and semantic richness of resource descriptions depends on the mix of human or computational agents that create them.

- The most predictable maintenance activities for an organizing system with an expected long lifetime are incremental changes in description vocabularies and classification schemes.

- Another very predictable type of activity over time with organizing systems is a technology upgrade that improves its quality or capabilities without affecting the organizing principles.

- The most challenging kinds of maintenance activities for organizing systems involve changes to the principles for arranging resources along with changes in the implementing technology.

- Now it is your turn to put *The Discipline of Organizing* into practice; maybe develop your own case study.

- There is much more... at `DisciplineOfOrganizing.org`.

Notes

543. [Computing] For some kinds of resources with highly regular structure, the distinction between the resource and its description is a bit arbitrary. A transactional document like a payment contains at its core a specification of the amount paid, which we could consider the payment resource. Information about the payer, the payee, the reason for the payment, and other essential information might be viewed as descriptions of the payment resource. In a payment or financial management system, the entire document might be treated as the resource.

544. [Computing] The results of this analysis can be represented in a conceptual model or document /database schema that can guide the automated creation of the resource instances and their descriptions (§4.3.1.2). Furthermore, these models or schemas can also be used in "model-based" or "model-driven" architectures to generate much of the software that implements the functionality to store the instances and interchange them with other information systems; "imagine if the construction worker could take his blueprint, crank it through a machine, and have the foundation for the building simply appear." Quote comes from (Miller and Mukerji 2003). See also (Kleppe, Warmer, and Bast 2003).

545. [Computing] See (Chen, Li, Liang, and Zhang 2010), (Pohs 2013).

546. [Business] See *http://autos.ca.msn.com/editors-picks/the-worlds-biggest-car-collectors*.

547. [Computing] Model-driven software generation can be simple – an XFORM specification that creates an input form on a web page. Or it can be complex, a detailed architectural specification in UML sufficient to generate a complete application.

548. [LIS] Compare www.cdc.gov/philc and www.webmd.com.

549. [Business] Service design, architecture, and user interaction design are the primary disciplines that care about the influence of layout and spatial arrangement on user interaction behavior and satisfaction. One type of physical framework is the "Servicescape" (Bitner 1992), defined as the description of the manmade physical context in which services are delivered. For example, the arrangement of waiting lines in banks, supermarkets, and post offices or the use of centrally-visible "take a number" systems strongly influence the encounters in service systems (Zhou and Soman 2003). Related concepts for describing the use of features and orienting mechanisms in "the built environment" come from the "Wayfinding" (Arthur and Passini 1992) literature in urban planning and architecture.

550. [Business] An easy to remember framework for prioritizing requirements is MoSCoW, which classifies them as Must, Should, Could, and Won't (Desoky 2010). (Winkler and Pilgrim 2010) is a comprehensive review of academic research and best practices for requirements traceability.

551. [Business] "Customer segments" or "customer models" are well-established constructs in product and service marketing and operations (Batt 2000) (Zeithami, Rust, and Lemon 2001). They are key parts of strategies for acquiring customers, increasing market share, and retaining customers. Customer segments can be identified using numerous overlapping criteria, including demographic variables, product or behavior choices, and preferred interaction locations or channels. For example, an airline might segment its customers according to their age, gender, home airport, ticketing class, and travel frequency.

552. [LIS] Funding cuts for public libraries lead to reduced staffing, reduced hours, and reduced acquisitions and many of them serve populations facing economic challenges of their own. (Johnson 2010).

553. [Business] Organizing systems differ in the extent they can initiate interactions or use information to make them unnecessary. In libraries the organizing systems are typically designed not to preserve user activity records longer than absolutely necessary; in commercial organizing systems, user activity records are the basis of business processes that create highly detailed user models (called "microsegments" or "microcategories") that enable personalized catalogs and ad placement with targeted product and service offerings. See (Taylor and Raden 2007), (Rosen 2012).

554. [LIS] The Dublin Core was proposed in 1995 as a small vocabulary with 15 common elements that could be broadly applied. The emergence of many specialized derivatives of the Dublin Core since then illustrates the inherent tension between the simplicity of using a small set of common descriptive elements and the precision enabled by a large or more domain specific vocabulary.

555. [LIS] (Register and McIlroy 2012) *http://themetadatahandbook.com/*.

556. [Business] For example, we have often used a home kitchen as a setting for organizing systems. Suppose the home kitchen is to be used as the set for a cooking show and the designers want to arrange cookbooks to make the background visually pleasing. It seems unreasonable to expect that they could search a catalog of cookbooks on the basis of size and spine color because these additional descriptive elements are of little value to users who are not designers of sets for cooking shows.

557. [LIS] The category of special libraries includes law libraries, corporate libraries – both those that support the head office and the research organization, medical libraries, military libraries, museum libraries, prison libraries, and might even be stretched to include libraries of software components.

558. [Business] Some people call this the "Walmart" approach to standardization. A firm with dominant market power does not need to negotiate standards because it can impose whatever standards it chooses on its partners as a condition of doing business with them. When there are conflicting requirements, different relationships within the set of participants trying to reach agreement, and different extents to which they are subject to the authority behind the desired agreement, it is not surprising that approaches "that require perfect coordination and altruism are of no practical interest" (Rosenthal et al. 2004, p 47).

559. [Computing] Note that this definition doesn't include any specific size threshold, such as some number of terabytes (thousands of gigabytes). This allows the threshold size that makes a collection a big data one to increase as storage technology advances. It also recognizes that different industries or domains have different thresholds (Manyika et al 2011).

560. [Museums] The history of the collection and the legal battle are described in (Anderson 2003). A documentary film with a conspiracy perspective is (Argott 2009). See also BarnesFoundation.org.

561. [LIS] See (Sandler 2006), (Freeman et al. 2005).

562. [Computing] No classification scheme ever devised is as unstable as the ACM's because new computing concepts, technologies, and application areas are constantly emerging. Even the society's name seems outdated.

563. [Computing] For a formal computer science treatment of BPEL see (Fu, Bultan, and Su 2004); for a commercial perspective see *http://www.oracle.com/technetwork/middleware/bpel/overview/index.html*.

564. [Computing] This means that the organizing systems used by business applications more often employ configuration management, version control, model-based code generation, and other computing techniques that robustly support the need for qualitative changes in the organizing systems.

565. [Business] (Barta 2009).

566. [CogSci] (Ctein 2010) and (Taylor 2010) are popular guides for photo digitization and restoration.

567. [Web] For example, *http://web.appstorm.net/roundups/media-roundups/top-20-photo-storage-and-sharing-sites/* reviews 20 photo storage and sharing sites and *http://photo-book-review.toptenreviews.com/* compares 10 sites for creating printed albums from digital photos in case you want to "round trip" from Grandpa's photos and print photo books for family members.

568. [Law] (Herbst 2009) is a thoughtful legal primer on the novel property, jurisdiction, and terms of service complexities in gaining access to accounts of deceased people. A popular treatment about what has come to be called the "digital afterlife" is (Carroll and Romano 2011).

569. [Law] *http://www.spo.berkeley.edu/guide/consultquick.html* is an example of such a policy. Indeed, it is because of rules like these that the professor determined he needed to take a leave of absence from the university.

570. [Business] For a high-level theoretical framework about capturing value from knowledge assets see (Teece 1998); for a detailed case study see (Goodwin et al. 2012).

571. [Business] (Poole and Grudin 2010).

572. [Business] (Hansen 2009).

573. [Business] (Wakabayashi 2011).

574. [Business] (Hori, Kawashima, and Yamazaki 2010). Fujitsu expects that the system will eventually integrate business management functions, production history, and operational support for best practices.

575. [Computing] See (Burrell, Brooke, and Beckwith 2004) for a study of the use of sensor networks in Oregon vineyards.

576. [Linguistics] (Tagliabue 2012). We cannot resist describing this as "sexting" by cows.

577. [Computing]] (Wilde and Catin 2007). Looking back it seems ironic to start with a single-source XML publishing system, abandon it to author the book in Word, and then convert the files Word back to XML to enable single-source publishing.

578. [Computing]] (Kimber 2012) seems destined to become the definitive resource for DITA-based publishing. The definitive source for DocBook has long been (Walsh 2010).

Acknowledgments

Philosophers, scientists, designers, and many others have sought to make sense of how we organize our physical and intellectual worlds for over two thousand years. We owe a great general obligation to all of them, so we dedicated this book to them. However, it is more important to acknowledge more specifically the people who made this *Discipline of Organizing* book happen. I think it is befitting of a book about organizing to be organized in making these acknowledgments, as follows in three categories:

The Motivators

Annalee Saxenian, the Dean of the UC Berkeley School of Information, challenged me in 2005 to teach the "Information Organization and Retrieval" course required of all entering graduate students and provided me with a supportive environment in which to do it. The lecture notes of my predecessors, Berkeley colleagues Marti Hearst, Ray Larson, and Mark Davis, provided important intellectual scaffolding as I developed my own syllabus and lectures.

When I discovered the little red book by Elaine Svenonius, *The Intellectual Foundation of Information Organization*, my mind opened up to library and information science. I aspired to write a book that could build on and broaden those foundations to connect with my own background in cognitive and computer science. A few months later when I met Elaine I was very pleased when she endorsed this ambitious effort.

I have been continually encouraged by faculty members and deans whenever I talked about this project at Schools of Information or similar academic units. These include the U.S. universities of Indiana, Kentucky, Michigan, and North Carolina, Canadian universities of Toronto and Western Ontario, and European universities in Vienna and Berlin. In particular, I would like to thank Colin Allen, Ron Day, Miles Efron, Thomas Finholt, Dan O'Hair, Margaret Hedstrom, Michael Jones, John King, Kathryn LaBarre, Kelly Lyons, Gary Marchionini, Jerry McDonough, Allen Renear, Seamus Ross, Victoria Rubin, Michael Seadle, and Linda Smith. I especially appreciate the encouragement that Deans Marchionini and Seadle gave to Ryan Shaw and Vivien Petras, two of the principal authors of this book. I apologize to those of you that I've forgotten to list here.

Margy Avery of The MIT Press has pushed hard when she needed to and has been very receptive when I needed her to be.

The Contributors

It took me four years of teaching the IO & IR course at Berkeley before I knew enough (or too little) to think I could put together a book that might replace the diverse set of textbooks that course was using. I did not realize at the time how much I was learning from these teaching assistants, and I thank them for not making it obvious to me. Later on, after the book project was underway, my teaching assistants were invaluable in pointing out problems with the book, often proposing their solutions as well.

Almost exactly three years ago the project to write this book began in a graduate seminar whose goals were to define the topical coverage and structure of the book, and then to write chapters starting with my course lecture notes. Among the courageous students in that seminar were many authors of the book being published here: Rachelle Annechino, J.J.M. Ekaterin, Ryan Greenberg, Jess Hemerly, Michael Manoochehri, Sean Marimpietri, Kimra McPherson, Karen Nomorosa, Hyunwoo Park, Dan Turner, and Longhao Wang. Nick Doty, Mohit Gupta, Erin Knight, and Joyce Tsai also contributed during this start-up period.

In Spring 2011 Erik Wilde and I conducted a seminar titled "Principles and Patterns of Organizing Systems" to refine the key concepts of the evolving book. This seminar added Brendan Curran, Krishna Janakiraman, Julian Limon, Rowyn McDonald, Elisa Oreglia, Monica Rosenberg, Karen Rustad, Bailey Smith, Leslie Tom, and Anne Wootton to the growing set of student contributors. Leslie gets credit for the book's title.

In Spring 2012 Andrea Angquist, Jacob Portnoff, and Brian Rea, supervised capably by Anne Wootton, were essential editorial assistants in my end-to-end effort to rewrite the drafts of Chapters 1-7 to improve their conceptual integration and continuity.

I used draft chapters of the book in my IO & IR course three times, beginning in Fall 2010. The final version of the book in 2013 barely resembles those early drafts, which means that many students suffered to improve the book. But they didn't suffer passively. Many students submitted problems with the Twitter hashtag #tdofix, and submitted examples using #tdoexample, which benefited the book greatly but which surely confused their regular Twitter followers.

Many other Berkeley students did important work on the book. Jen Wang designed the cover; Divya Anand, Ajeeta Dhole, Christina Pham, and Raymon Sutedjo-The did the illustrations; Lisa Jervis, Shohei Narron, and Anne Wootton worked on the extensive bibliography. A group of students whose work does not appear in the printed book but whose efforts will be revealed in future ebooks include Luis Aguilar, Fred Chasen, Philip Foeckler, Jake Hartnell, Eliot Nahman, and AJ Renold.

Eliot Kimber showed me that it was possible to write a book that could be published simultaneously in print and in ebooks. It hasn't turned out to be as simple as someone as talented as Kimber can make it seem, but I am grateful to Eliot for convincing me that I should try to do it. With help from Bob Stayton, Adam Witwer (and O'Reilly Media) we will get there.

I must also thank Christine Borgman of UCLA for bringing a group of energetic and thoughtful UCLA graduate students into the project. Two of them, Matt Mayernik and Alberto Pepe, are contributing authors. Amelia Acker, Jillian Wallis, and Laura Wynholds taught me a great deal about libraries and archives, and I am certain they tried to teach me much more than I was able to learn.

Many people read draft chapters and were thankfully unsparing in their criticism because they wanted to make this book as good as it could be. Thank you Scott Abel, Larry Barsalou, Marcia Bates, Christine Borgman, Michael Cohen, David Kirsh, Jeff Elman, Rob Goldstone, Jonathan Grudin, Ben Hill, Mano Marks, Patrick Schmitz, Elaine Svenonius, Jeff Zych, and everyone else whom I have carelessly forgotten.

Few books have been as battle tested before they went to print as this one. Let me thank those who have been willing to teach from a book that did not entirely exist: Jane Greenberg, Irith Hartman, Lauren Plews, Sarah Ramdeen, Christian Sandvig, Emily Seitz, Isabelle Sperano, Konstantin Tovstiadi, Hong Zhang, and especially Vivien Petras and Ryan Shaw who went to battle with (and for) this book multiple times.

The Essentials

The third and final category of acknowledgments is for people who were essential, without whom this project would never have been finished.

Jess Hemerly and Kimra McPherson joined the project in the "first crusade" of Spring 2010, worked tirelessly through that summer to make chapter drafts course-worthy, and served as teaching assistants in Fall 2010 when the book was first tested with students. They helped me believe that there might be a book in there somewhere when it took a lot of faith to see that.

Erik Wilde taught me much through our multi-year collaboration and dialectic when he was on the Berkeley faculty from 2006-2011. Erik made me understand the elegance and great scope of the word "resource," which became the central concept in this book. His meticulously annotated reviews of many chapters from a computer science perspective helped inspire the idea of discipline-tagged end-notes.

Ryan Shaw and Vivien Petras, both young professors at schools a long distance from Berkeley, found courage in themselves and had confidence in the draft book coming out of Berkeley in 2011—first to teach with it, and then to help write it, becoming the primary reviewers of my chapters and the first authors of Chapters 8 and 9.

Murray Maloney joined the project in April 2012 as copy editor, but we together soon recognized that his nearly three decades of SGML, XML, and publishing experience were too valuable not to exploit further for the benefit of this book. Without Murray's work as the markup and production editor, indexer and glossary-maker, there would be too much work left to do and no one capable of doing it as well as Murray has. Somehow along the way he also found time to make important intellectual contributions as a co-author to Chapters 5 and 8.

Finally, I want to thank Pam Samuelson. She has been far too patient with me as I talked with her, to her, and at her for three years while this book was being written, who turned many quarter-baked ideas into half-baked ones, and who turned many half-baked ones into cornerstones of this book. Most importantly, she has helped me focus on this book and get it finished when it would have been easy to give up on it. I promise not to take on another book project any-time soon because Pam has suffered enough for this one.

Robert J. Glushko, 31 December 2012

Bibliography

[Aalbersberg2011] AALBERSBERG, Ijsbrand Jan. *"Supporting Science through the Interoperability of Data and Articles": D-Lib Magazine.* 2011. `http://www.dlib.org/dlib/january11/aalbersberg/01aalbersberg.html` .

[Agrawal1989] AGRAWAL, Rakesh, BORGIDA, Alexander, and JAGADISH, H. V. *"Efficient Management of Transitive Relationships in Large Data and Knowledge Bases": SIGMOD '89: Proceedings of the 1989 ACM SIGMOD international conference on management of data.* 1989. pp. 253-262.

[Allmendinger2005] ALLMENDINGER, Glen and LOMBREGLIA, Ralph. *"Four Strategies for the Age of Smart Services": Harvard Business Review.* 2005. `http://hbr.org/2005/10/four-strategies-for-the-age-of-smart-services/ar/1` .

[Anderson2001a] ANDERSON, James D. and PÉREZ-CARBALLO, José. *"The nature of indexing: how humans and machines analyze messages and texts for retrieval. Part I: Research, and the nature of human indexing": Information Processing and Management.* 2001. pp. 231-254. `http://www.sciencedirect.com/science/article/pii/S0306457300000261` .

[Anderson2001b] ANDERSON, James D. and PEREZ-CARBALLO, Jose. *"The nature of indexing: how humans and machines analyze messages and texts for retrieval. Part II: Machine indexing, and the allocation of human versus machine effort": Information Processing and Management.* 2001. pp. 255-277. `http://www.sciencedirect.com/science/article/pii/S0306457300000467` .

[Anderson2001c] ANDERSON, Stephen R. *"Morpholology": In The MIT Encyclopedia of the Cognitive Sciences.* A Bradford Book, 2001. 562-563.

[Anderson2003] ANDERSON, John. *Art Held Hostage: The Battle over the Barnes Collection*. W. W. Norton & Company, 2003.

[Anderson2006] ANDERSON, James and HOFFMAN, Melissa. *"A Fully Faceted Syntax for Library of Congress Subject Headings": Cataloging & Classification Quarterly*. 2006. pp. 7-38.

[Apte1995] APTE, Uday M. and MASON, Richard O. *"Global Disaggregation of Information-Intensive Services": Management Science*. 1995. pp. 1250-1262. *http://www.jstor.org/stable/2632780* .

[Arasu2001] ARASU, Arvind, et al. *"Searching the Web": ACM Transactions on Internet Technology*. 2001. pp. 2-43.

[Argott2009] ARGOTT, Don. *The Art of the Steal*. New York: IFC Films, 2009.

[Arthur1992] ARTHUR, Paul and PASSINI, Romedi. *Wayfinding: People, Signs and Architecture*. McGraw-Hill, 1992.

[Atkins2000] ATKINS, Helen Barsky and CRONIN, Blaise. *The Web of Knowledge: A Festschrift in Honor of Eugene Garfield*. Information Today Inc., 2000.

[Atran1987] ATRAN, Scott. *"Ordinary Constraints on the Semantics of Living Kinds: A Commonsense Alternative to Recent Treatments of Natural-Object Terms": Mind & Language*. 1987. pp. 27-63. *http://onlineli brary.wiley.com/doi/10.1111/j.1468-0017.1987.tb00107.x/abstract* .

[ATT2011] AT&T. *"An AccuWeather Cloudlet Answers a Hail of Data Requests"*. 2011. *http://www.business.att.com/content/customertestimonial/ Case_Study-_AccuWeather_4.7.11.pdf* .

[Atzori2010] ATZORI, Luigi, IERA, Antonio, and MORABITO, Giacomo. *"The Internet of Things: A survey": Computer Networks*. 2010. pp. 2787-2805. *http://www.sciencedirect.com/science/article/pii/ S1389128610001568* .

[Aufderheide2011] AUFDERHEIDE, Patricia and JASZI, Peter. *Reclaiming Fair Use: How to Put Balance Back in Copyright*. University of Chicago Press, 2011.

[Baeza-Yates2011] BAEZA-YATES, Ricardo and RIBEIRO-NETO, Berthier. *Modern Information Retrieval: The Concepts and Technology behind Search*. Addison Wesley, 2011.

[Bailey2007] BAILEY, Charles W. *"Open Access and Libraries": Collection Management*. 2007. pp. 351-383.

[Baker1962] BAKER, Keith M. *"An unpublished essay of Condorcet on technical methods of classification": Annals of Science*. 1962. pp. 99-123.

[Banzhaf2009] BANZHAF, Wolfgang. *"Self-organizing Systems": Proceedings of Encyclopedia of Complexity and Systems Science*. 2009. pp. 8040-8050.

[BarIlan2008] BAR-ILAN, Judit. *"Informetrics at the beginning of the 21st century—A review": Journal of Informetrics*. 2008. pp. 1-52. `http://www.science direct.com/science/article/pii/S1751157707000740` .

[Barsalou1983] BARSALOU, Lawrence W. *"Ad hoc categories": Memory & Cognition*. 1983. pp. 211-227. `http://www.ncbi.nlm.nih.gov/pubmed/6621337` .

[Barta2009] BARTA, Patrick. *"Shifting the Right of Way to the Left Leaves Some Samoans Feeling Wronged": The Wall Street Journal*. 2009. `http://online.wsj.com/article/SB125086852452149513.html` .

[Bates2005] BATES, Marcia J. *"Information and knowledge: an evolutionary framework for information science": Information Research*. 2005.

[Batley2005] BATLEY, Sue. *Classification in Theory and Practice*. Chandos Publishing, 2005.

[Batt2000] BATT, Rosemary. *"Strategic Segmentation in Frontline Services: Matching Customers, Employees, and Human Resource Systems": International Journal of Human Resource Management*. 2000. pp. 540-561.

[Batten1951] BATTEN, W. E. *"Specialized Files for Patent Searching": In Punched Cards: Their Applications to Science and Industry*. Reinhold Publishing Corporation, 1951. 169-181.

[Battistella1996] BATTISTELLA, Edwin. *The Logic of Markedness*. Oxford University Press, 1996.

[Battles2003] BATTLES, Matthew. *Library: An Unquiet History*. W. W. Norton & Company, 2003.

[Bean2001] BEAN, Carol A. and GREEN, Rebecca. *Relationships in the Organization of Knowledge*. Kluwer, 2001.

[Bentivogli2000] BENTIVOGLI, Luisa and PIANTA, Emanuele. *"Looking for lexical gaps": Proceedings of Euralex-2000 International Congress*. 2000.

[Bergmark2002] BERGMARK, Donna, LAGOZE, Carl, and SBITYAKOV, Alex. *"Focused Crawls, Tunneling, and Digital Libraries": Proceedings of the 6th European Conference on Research and Advanced Technology for Digital Libraries.* 2002. pp. 91-106.

[Berners-Lee1998] BERNERS-LEE, Tim. *Cool URIs don't change: World Wide Web Consortium (W3C).* 1998. `http://www.w3.org/Provider/Style/URI.html` .

[Berners-Lee2001] BERNERS-LEE, Tim, HENDLER, James, and LASSILA, Ora. *"The Semantic Web": Scientific American.* 2001.

[Biasiotti2008] BIASIOTTI, Mariangela, et al. *"Legal informatics and management of legislative documents".* Global Centre for ICT in Parliament, 2008.

[Bitner1992] BITNER, Mary Jo. *"Servicescapes: The impact of physical surroundings on customers and employees": Journal of Marketing.* 1992. pp. 57-71.

[Bizer2009a] BIZER, Christian. *"The Emerging Web of Linked Data": IEEE Intelligent Systems.* 2009. pp. 87-92. `http://ieeexplore.ieee.org/xpls/abs_all.jsp?arnumber=5286174` .

[Bizer2009b] BIZER, Christian, HEATH, Tom, and BERNERS-LEE, Tim. *"Linked Data—The Story So Far": International Journal on Semantic Web and Information Systems.* 2009. pp. 1-22.

[Blanzieri2009] BLANZIERI, Enrico and BRYL, Anton. *"A survey of learning-based techniques of email spam filtering": Artificial Intelligence Review.* 2009. pp. 63-92.

[Bleecker2006] BLEECKER, Julian. *A Manifesto for Networked Objects — Cohabiting with Pigeons, Arphids and Aibos in the Internet of Things: Near Future Laboratory.* 2006. `http://nearfuturelaboratory.com/2006/02/26/a-manifesto-for-networked-objects/` .

[Board2002] BOARD ON ENERGY AND ENVIRONMENTAL SYSTEMS, DIVISION ON ENGINEERING AND PHYSICAL SCIENCES, and TRANSPORTATION RESEARCH BOARD. *Effectiveness and Impact of Corporate Average Fuel Economy (CAFE) Standards.* The National Academies Press, 2002. `http://www.nap.edu/openbook.php?isbn=0309076013` .

[Bolshakov2004] BOLSHAKOV, Igor A. and GELBUKH, Alexander. *"Synonymous Paraphrasing Using WordNet and Internet": Proceedings of NLDB: International Conference on Applications of Natural Language to Information Systems.* 2004. pp. 312-323.

[Borgman2000] BORGMAN, Christine L. *From Gutenberg to the Global Information Infrastructure: Access to Information in the Networked World.* The MIT Press, 2000.

[Borgman2011] BORGMAN, Christine L. *"The Conundrum of Sharing Research Data": Journal of the American Society for Information Science and Technology.* 2011. pp. 1-40. *http://papers.ssrn.com/abstract=1869155* .

[Boroditsky2003] BORODITSKY, Lera. *"Linguistic Relativity": In Encyclopedia of Cognitive Science.* Wiley, 2003.

[Boroditsky2010] BORODITSKY, Lera. *"Lost in Translation": The Wall Street Journal.* 2010. *http://online.wsj.com/article/ SB10001424052748703467304575383131592767868.html* .

[Boroditsky2011] BORODITSKY, Lera. *"How Language Shapes Thought": Scientific American.* 2011. *http://www.sciamdigital.com/index.cfm?fa=Prod ucts.ViewIssuePreview&ARTICLEID_CHAR=94C85092-237D-9F22- E874366AD6B49809* .

[Bower2001] BOWER, Jim and ROBERTS, Andrew. *"Developments in International Museum and Cultural Heritage Information Standards".* International Committee for Documentation (CIDOC) of the International Council of Museums (ICOM), 2001.

[Bowker2000] BOWKER, Geoffrey C. and STAR, Susan Leigh. *Sorting Things Out: Classification and Its Consequences.* The MIT Press, 2000.

[Brailsford1999] BRAILSFORD, David F. *"Separable Hyperstructure and Delayed Link Binding": ACM Computing Surveys.* 1999.

[Bray2005] BRAY, Tim. *"On Language Creation": XML 2005.* 2005.

[Brin2009] BRIN, Sergey. *"A Library to Last Forever": The New York Times.* 2009. *http://www.nytimes.com/2009/10/09/opinion/09brin.html* .

[Brown2002] BROWN, John Seely and DUGUID, Paul. *The Social Life of Information.* Harvard Business Press, 2002.

[Brown2009] BROWN, Bruce C. *How to Stop E-Mail Spam, Spyware, Malware, Computer Viruses, and Hackers from Ruining Your Computer or Network: The Complete Guide for Your Home and Work.* Atlantic Publishing Group Inc., 2009.

[Bruner1957] BRUNER, Jerome S. *"Going beyond the information given"*: In *Contemporary approaches to cognition*. Harvard University Press, 1957. 41-69. *http://www.jimdavies.org/summaries/bruner1957.html* .

[Buckland1991] BUCKLAND, Michael K. *"Information as thing"*: *Journal of the American Society for Information Science*. 1991. pp. 351-360. *http://onlinelibrary.wiley.com/doi/10.1002/%28SICI %291097-4571%28199106%2942:5%3C351::AID-ASI5%3E3.0.CO;2-3/ abstract* .

[Buckland1997] BUCKLAND, Michael K. *"What Is a 'Document'?"*: *Journal of the American Society for Information Science*. 1997. pp. 804-809.

[Budanitsky2006] BUDANITSKY, Alexander and HIRST, Graeme. *"Evaluating WordNet-based Measures of Lexical Semantic Relatedness"*: *Computational Linguistics*. 2006. pp. 13-47.

[Buettcher2010] BUETTCHER, Stefan, CLARKE, Charles L. A., and CORMACK, Gordon V. *Information Retrieval: Implementing and Evaluating Search Engines*. The MIT Press, 2010.

[Buhrmester2007] BUHRMESTER, Jason. *"NFL Films' Exhaustive Archive Is Rushing Into the Digital Age"*: *Wired*. 2007. *http://www.wired.com/ culture/lifestyle/magazine/15-10/ps_nfl* .

[Bulmer1970] BULMER, R. N. H. *"Which came first, the chicken or the egg-head?"*: In *Échanges et communications: mélanges offerts à Claude Lévi-Strauss à l'occasion de son 60ème anniversaire*. Mouton & Co., 1970. pp. 1069-1091.

[Burrell2004] BURRELL, Jenna, BROOKE, Tim, and BECKWITH, Richard. *"Vineyard Computing: Sensor Networks in Agricultural Production"*: *Pervasive Computing, IEEE*. 2004. pp. 38-45.

[Bush1945] BUSH, Vannevar. *"As We May Think"*: *The Atlantic*. 1945.

[Buttcher2010] BÜTTCHER, Stefan, CLARKE, Charles, and CORMACK, Gordon V. *Information retrieval: Implementing and evaluating search engines*. The MIT Press, 2010.

[Byrne2010] BYRNE, Gillian. *"The Strongest Link: Libraries and Linked Data"*: *D-Lib Magazine*. 2010. *http://www.dlib.org/dlib/november10/byrne/ 11byrne.html* .

[Byya2008] BYYA, Rajkumar, PATHAN, Mukaddim, and VAKALI, Athena. *Content Delivery Networks*. Springer, 2008.

[Campbell2011] CAMPBELL, Joseph Keim, O'ROURKE, Michael, and SLATER, Matthew H. *Carving Nature at Its Joints: Natural Kinds in Metaphysics and Science*. A Bradford Book, 2011.

[Cano2005] CANO, Pedro, et al. *"Audio Fingerprinting: Concepts And Applications": In Computational Intelligence for Modelling and Prediction*. Springer, 2005.

[Carey1991] CAREY, Susan and GELMAN, Rochel. *The Epigenesis of Mind: Essays on Biology and Cognition*. Psychology Press, 1991. `http://www.amazon.co.uk/The-Epigenesis-Mind-Cognition-Symposia/dp/toc/0805804382` .

[Carney2005] CARNEY, David, et al. *Some Current Approaches to Interoperability: Carnegie Mellon Software Engineering Institute*. 2005.

[Carr2010] CARR, Patrick. *"Forcing the moment to its crisis: Thoughts on pay-per-view and the perpetual access ideal": Against the Grain*. 2010. pp. 16-18. `http://hdl.handle.net/10342/2181` .

[Carroll2010] CARROLL, Evan and ROMANO, John. *Your Digital Afterlife: When Facebook, Flickr, and Twitter Are Your Estate, What's Your Legacy?*. New Riders, 2010.

[Casson2002] CASSON, Lionel. *Libraries in the Ancient World*. Yale University Press, 2002.

[Cerf1969] CERF, Vint. *ASCII Format for Network Interchange*. 1969. `http://tools.ietf.org/html/rfc20` .

[Chaffin1984] CHAFFIN, Roger and HERRMANN, Douglas J. *"The similarity and diversity of semantic relations": Memory & Cognition*. 1984. pp. 134-41.

[Chan2006] CHAN, Lois Mai and ZENG, Marcia Lei. *"Metadata Interoperability and Standardization: A Study of Methodology Part I": D-Lib Magazine*. 2006. `http://www.dlib.org/dlib/june06/chan/06chan.html` .

[Chandler1977] CHANDLER JR., Alfred Dupont. *The Visible Hand: The Managerial Revolution in American Business*. Belknap Press, 1977.

[Chapman2009] CHAPMAN, Nigel and CHAPMAN, Jenny. *Digital Multimedia*. Wiley, 2009.

[Chen2010] CHEN, Donglin, et al. *"Research on the Theory of Customer-Oriented E-Catalog Ontology Automatic Construction"*: *2010 International Conference on E-Business and E-Government*. 2010. pp. 2961-2964. *http://ieeex plore.ieee.org/xpl/articleDetails.jsp?arnumber=5590430* .

[Cherbakov2005] CHERBAKOV, Luba, et al. *"Impact of service orientation at the business level"*: *IBM Systems Journal*. 2005. pp. 653-668. *http://ieeex plore.ieee.org/xpl/articleDetails.jsp?arnumber=5386696* .

[Cho2000] CHO, Junghoo and GARCIA-MOLINA, Hector. *"The Evolution of the Web and Implications for an Incremental Crawler"*: *Proceedings of the 26th International Conference on Very Large Data Bases*. 2000. pp. 200-209.

[Chomsky1957] CHOMSKY, Noam. *Syntactic Structures*. Mouton & Co., 1957.

[Chomsky1965] CHOMSKY, Noam. *Aspects of the Theory of Syntax*. The MIT Press, 1965. *http://www.worldcat.org/title/aspects-of-the-theory-of-syntax/oclc/309976* .

[Christen2006] CHRISTEN, Peter. *A Comparison of Personal Name Matching: Techniques and Practical Issues: The Australian National University*. 2006. p. 14.

[Clark1868] CLARK, Stephen Watkins. *A Practical Grammar: In Which Words, Phrases, and Sentences Are Classified According to Their Offices and Their Various Relations to One Another*. A.S. Barnes & Co., 1868. *http://archive.org/details/practicalgrammar00clar* .

[Clark2010] CLARK, Stephen Watkins. *A Practical Grammar: In Which Words, Phrases, and Sentences Are Classified According to Their Offices and Their Various Relations to One Another*. Nabu Press. Originally published in 1847 by A.S. Barnes & Co., 2010. *http://archive.org/details/practicalgram mar00clar* .

[Coase1937] COASE, Ronald H. *"The Nature of the Firm"*: *Economica, New Series*. 1937. pp. 386-405.

[Codd1970] CODD, E. F. *"A relational model of data for large shared data banks"*: *Communications*. 1970. pp. 377-387. *http://www.ncbi.nlm.nih.gov/pubmed/9617087* .

[Conklin1987] CONKLIN, Jeff. *"Hypertext : An Introduction and Survey"*: *IEEE Computer*. 1987. pp. 17-41.

[Conklin1988] CONKLIN, Jeff and BEGEMAN, Michael L. *"gIBIS : A Hypertext Tool for Exploratory Policy Discussion": ACM Transactions on Information Systems.* 1988. pp. 303-331.

[Constantin1994] CONSTANTIN, James A. and LUSCH, Robert F. *Understanding Resource Management: How to deploy your people, products, and processes for maximum productivity.* Irwin Professional, 1994.

[Cormen2009] CORMEN, Thomas H., et al. *Introduction to Algorithms.* The MIT Press, 2009.

[Cowan2004] COWAN, John and TOBIN, Richard. *XML Information Set: Recommendation of the World Wide Web Consortium (W3C).* 2004. `http:// www.w3.org/TR/xml-infoset/` .

[Cox2007] COX, Ingemar, et al. *Digital Watermarking and Steganography.* Morgan Kaufmann, 2007.

[Coyle2006] COYLE, Karen. *"Identifiers: Unique, Persistent, Global": The Journal of Academic Librarianship.* 2006. pp. 428-431.

[Coyle2010a] COYLE, Karen. *"Library Data in a Modern Context": Library Technology Reports.* 2010. pp. 5-13.

[Coyle2010b] COYLE, Karen. *"RDA in RDF": Library Technology Reports.* 2010. pp. 26-36.

[Croft2009] CROFT, Bruce W., METZLER, Donald, and STROHMAN, Trevor. *Search Engines: Information Retrieval in Practice.* Addison Wesley, 2009.

[Crow2010] CROW, David. *Visible Signs: An Introduction to Semiotics in the Visual Arts.* AVA Publishing, 2010.

[Ctein2010] CTEIN. *Digital Restoration from Start to Finish: How to Repair Old and Damaged Photographs.* Focal Press, 2010.

[Cutter1876] CUTTER, Charles. *Rules for a printed dictionary catalogue: Issued as part 2 of Special report on public libraries, by the United States Education Bureau.* Government Printing Office, 1876. `http://www.openli brary.org/books/OL24156277M` .

[Darnton2011] DARNTON, Robert. *"Google's Loss: The Public's Gain": The New York Review of Books.* 2011. `http://www.nybooks.com/articles/ archives/2011/apr/28/googles-loss-publics-gain` .

[Das2002] DAS, Sajal K., et al. *"The role of prediction algorithms in the Mav-Home smart home architecture": IEEE Wireless Communications.* 2002. pp. 77-84.

[Date2003] DATE, C.J. *An Introduction to Database Systems.* Addison Wesley, 2003.

[Datta2008] DATTA, Ritendra, et al. *"Image retrieval: ideas, influences, and trends of the new age": ACM Computing Surveys.* 2008.

[Deerwester1990] DEERWESTER, Scott, et al. *"Indexing by Latent Semantic Analysis": Journal of the American Society for Information Science.* 1990. pp. 391-407.

[deLeon2003] DE LÉON, David. *"Actions, Artefacts, and Cognition: An Enthnography of Cooking": Lund University Cognitive Studies.* 2003.

[Demartini2006] DEMARTINI, Gianluca and MIZZARO, Stefano. *"A Classification of IR Effectiveness Metrics IR Metrics: A Survey and a Classification": In Advances in Information Retrieval: 28th European Conference on IR Research, ECIR 2006.* Springer Berlin Heidelberg, 2006. 488-491.

[Denton2007] DENTON, William. *"FRBR and the History of Cataloging": In Understanding FRBR: What It Is and How It Will Affect Our Retrieval Tools.* Libraries Unlimited, 2007. 35-57.

[DeRose1989] DEROSE, Steven J. *"Expanding the Notion of Links": Proceedings of the second annual ACM conference on Hypertext (HYPERTEXT '89).* 1989. pp. 249-257.

[DeRose2010] DEROSE, Steven J., et al. *XML Linking Language (XLink): Recommendation of the World Wide Web Consortium (W3C).* 2010. `http://www.w3.org/TR/xlink11/` .

[Desoky2010] DESOKY, Ashraf. *MoSCoW Prioritisation.* 2010. `http://certifications.groupsite.com/beta/discussion/topics/310632/messages` .

[Deutscher2011] DEUTSCHER, Guy. *Through the Language Glass: Why the World Looks Different in Other Languages.* Arrow Books, 2011.

[Dey2001] DEY, Anind K. *"Understanding and Using Context": Personal and Ubiquitous Computing.* 2001. pp. 4-7.

[Diaz2005] DIAZ, Alejandro M. *Through the Google Goggles: Sociopolitical Bias in Search Engine Design: Stanford University Program in Science, Technology and Society.* 2005.

[Ding2004] DING, Li, et al. *"Swoogle: a search and metadata engine for the semantic web"*: *Proceedings of the 2004 Conference on Information and Knowledge Management*. 2004. pp. 652-659.

[Doctorow2001] DOCTOROW, Cory. *Metacrap*. 2001. *http://www.well.com/ ~doctorow/metacrap.htm* .

[Donnellan1966] DONNELLAN, Keith S. *"Reference and Definite Descriptions"*: *The Philosophical Review*. 1966. pp. 281-304.

[Dorai2002] DORAI, Chitra and VENKATESH, Svetha. *"Bridging the Semantic Gap in Content Management Systems: Computational Media Aesthetics"*: *Media Computing*. 2002. pp. 1-9.

[Dougherty1985] DOUGHERTY, Janet W. D. and KELLER, Charles M. *"Taskonomy: A practical approach to knowledge structures"*: *In Directions in cognitive anthropology*. University of Illinois Press, 1985. pp. 161-174.

[Drapeau2010] DRAPEAU, Mark. *"The Three Phases of Government 2.0"*: *O'Reilly Radar*. 2010. *http://radar.oreilly.com/2010/05/the-three-pha ses-of-government.html* .

[Dumais2003] DUMAIS, Susan. *"Data-driven approaches to information access"*: *Cognitive Science*. 2003. pp. 491-524. *http:// onlinelibrary.wiley.com/doi/10.1207/s15516709cog2703_7/abstract* .

[Efron2011] EFRON, Miles. *"Information Search and Retrieval in Microblogs"*: *Journal of the American Society for Information Science and Technology*. 2011. pp. 996-1008. *http://onlinelibrary.wiley.com/doi/10.1002/asi. 21512/abstract* .

[Efthyvoulou2008] EFTHYVOULOU, George. *"Alphabet Economics: The link between names and reputation"*: *The Journal of Socio-Economics*. 2008. pp. 1266-1285. *http://sheffield.academia.edu/GeorgiosEfthyvoulou/ Papers/330894/Efthyvoulou_G._2008_._Alphabet_Econom ics_The_link_between_names_and_reputation._The_Journal_of_Socio- _Economics_37_3_1266-1285* .

[Elman2009] ELMAN, Jeffrey L. *"On the meaning of words and dinosaur bones: Lexical knowledge without a lexicon"*: *Cognitive Science*. 2009. pp. 547-582. *http://onlinelibrary.wiley.com/doi/10.1111/j. 1551-6709.2009.01023.x/abstract* .

[Engelbart1963] ENGELBART, Douglas. *"A Conceptual Framework for the Augmentation of Man's Intellect"*: *In Vistas in Information Handling*. Spartan Books, 1963. 1-29.

[Erl2005a] ERL, Thomas. *Service-Oriented Architecture (SOA): Concepts, Technology, and Design.* Prentice Hall, 2005.

[Erl2005b] ERL, Thomas. *Service-Oriented Architecture: A Field Guide to Integrating XML and Web Services.* Prentice Hall, 2005.

[Evans2000] EVANS, G. Edward and ZARNOSKY, Margaret R. *Developing Library and Information Center Collections.* Libraries Unlimited, 2000.

[Farish2002] FARISH, J. Brian. *What's in a Name?: Vertaasis.* 2002. *http://www.vertaasis.com/articles/whats_in_a_name.htm* .

[Feinberg2012] FEINBERG, Melanie. *"Synthetic Ethos: The Believability of Collections at the Intersection of Classification and Curation": The Information Society.* 2012. pp. 329-339. *http://www.tandfonline.com/doi/abs/10.1080/01972243.2012.708709* .

[Fetterly2003] FETTERLY, Dennis, et al. *"A Large-Scale Study of the Evolution of Web Pages": Proceedings of the Twelfth International World Wide Web Conference.* 2003.

[Few2012] FEW, Stephen. *Show Me the Numbers: Designing Tables and Graphs to Enlighten.* 2nd edition. 2012.

[Fidel2012] FIDEL, Raya. *Human Information Interaction: An Ecological Approach to Information Behavior.* The MIT Press, 2012.

[Fillmore2000] FILLMORE, Charles J. and ATKINS, B. T. S. *"Describing polysemy: The case of 'crawl'": In Polysemy: Theoretical and computational approaches.* Oxford University Press, 2000. 91-110.

[Fishman2003] FISHMAN, Charles. *"The Wal-Mart You Don't Know": Fast Company.* 2003. *http://www.fastcompany.com/47593/wal-mart-you-dont-know* .

[Fister2009] FISTER, Barbara. *"The Dewey Dilemma": Library Journal.* 2009.

[Florey2012] FLOREY, Kitty Burns. *"A Picture of Language": The New York Times.* 2012.

[Freeman2005] FREEMAN, Geoffrey T., et al. *Library as Place: Rethinking Roles, Rethinking Space.* Council on Library and Information Resources, 2005.

[Frege1892] FREGE, Gottlob. *"Uber Sinn und Bedeutung": In Zeitschrift fur Philosophie und philosophische Kritik 100.* Translated as "On sense and reference." In Translations from the Philosophical Writings of Gottlob Frege, edited by P.T. Geach and M. Black, 1952, pp. 56-78. Oxford: Basil Blackwell, 1892. pp. 25-50.

[Fu2004] FU, Xiang, BULTAN, Tevfik, and SU, Jianwen. *"Analysis of interacting BPEL web services": Proceedings of the 13th conference on World Wide Web—WWW '04.* 2004.

[Furnas1987] FURNAS, G W, et al. *"The Vocabulary Problem in Human-System Communication: an Analysis and a Solution": Communications of the ACM.* 1987. pp. 964-971.

[Furner2007] FURNER, Jonathan. *"User tagging of library resources: Toward a framework for system evaluation": International Cataloguing and Bibliographic Control.* 2007. pp. 47-51. `http://archive.ifla.org/IV/ifla73/papers/157-Furner-en.pdf` .

[Furner2008] FURNER, Jonathan. *"Interrogating 'identity': A philosophical approach to an enduring issue in knowledge organization": Knowledge Organization.* 2008. pp. 3-16.

[Garfield2000] GARFIELD, Eugene, ATKINS, Helen Barsky, and CRONIN, Blaise. *The Web of Knowledge: A Festschrift in Honor of Eugene Garfield.* Information Today Inc., 2000.

[Gaukroger2001] GAUKROGER, Stephen. *Francis Bacon and the Transformation of Early-Modern Philosophy.* Cambridge University Press, 2001.

[Geller1999] GELLER, Jacklyn. *"The Contemporary Wedding Invitation: A Social Document in Crisis": Salmagundi.* 1999. pp. 175-187.

[Gentner1983] GENTNER, Dedre. *"Structure-mapping: A theoretical framework for analogy": Cognitive Science.* 1983. pp. 155-170. `http://onlinelibrary.wiley.com/doi/10.1207/s15516709cog0702_3/abstract` .

[Gershenfeld2004] GERSHENFELD, Neil, KRIKORIAN, Raffi, and COHEN, Danny. *"The Internet of Things": Scientific American.* 2004. `http://www.scientificamerican.com/article.cfm?id=the-internet-of-things` .

[Getty2006] J. PAUL GETTY TRUST. *CDWA Lite: Specification for an XML Schema for Contributing Records via the OAI Harvesting Protocol.* 2006. `http://getty.edu/research/publications/electronic_publications/cdwa/cdwalite.pdf` .

[Gibson1977] GIBSON, James J. *"The Theory of Affordances"*: In *Perceiving, Acting, and Knowing: Toward an Ecological Psychology*. Lawrence Erlbaum Associates, 1977.

[Gill2008] GILL, Tony, et al. *Introduction to Metadata*. Getty Publications, 2008. *http://www.getty.edu/research/publications/electronic_publica tions/intrometadata/index.html* .

[Gillies2000] GILLIES, James and CAILLIAU, Robert. *How the Web Was Born: The story of the World Wide Web*. Oxford University Press, USA, 2000.

[Gilliland-Swetland2000] GILLILAND-SWETLAND, AJ. *"Enduring paradigm, new opportunities: the value of the archival perspective in the digital environment"*: *Communications*. 2000.

[Gladwell1996] GLADWELL, Malcolm. *"The Science of Shopping"*: *The New Yorker*. 1996.

[Glushko1988] GLUSHKO, Robert J., et al. *"Hypertext engineering: practical methods for creating a compact disk encyclopedia"*: *Proceedings of the ACM Conference on Document Processing Systems—DOCPROCS '88*. 1988. pp. 11-19.

[Glushko2005] GLUSHKO, Robert J. and MCGRATH, Tim. *Document Engineering: Analyzing and Designing Documents for Business Informatics and Web Services*. The MIT Press, 2005. *http://mitpress.mit.edu/catalog/item/ default.asp?ttype=2&tid=10476* .

[Glushko2008] GLUSHKO, Robert J., et al. *"Categorization in the wild"*: *Trends in cognitive sciences*. 2008. pp. 129-35. *http://www.ncbi.nlm.nih.gov/ pubmed/18343710* .

[Glushko2013] GLUSHKO, Robert J. and NOMOROSA, Karen J. *"Substituting Information for Interaction: A Framework for Personalization in Service Encounters and Service Systems"*: *Journal of Service Research*. 2013. pp. 21-38.

[Godby2008] GODBY, Carol Jean, SMITH, Devon, and CHILDRESS, Eric. *"Toward element-level interoperability in bibliographic metadata"*: *Code{4}lib*. 2008.

[Goldberg2008] GOLDBERG, Kevin Howard. *XML: Visual QuickStart Guide*. Peachpit Press, 2008.

[Golder2006] GOLDER, Scott A. and HUBERMAN, Bernardo A. *"Usage patterns of collaborative tagging systems.": Journal of Information Science*. 2006. 198-208.

[Goldstone1994] GOLDSTONE, R L. *"The role of similarity in categorization: providing a groundwork": Cognition*. 1994. pp. 125-57. `http://www.ncbi.nlm.nih.gov/pubmed/7924201` .

[Goodwin2012] GOODWIN, Richard, et al. *"Effective Content Reuse for Business Consulting Practices": 2012 Annual SRII Global Conference*. 2012. pp. 682-690. `http://ieeexplore.ieee.org/lpdocs/epic03/wrapper.htm?arnumber=6311054` .

[Gorman2004] GORMAN, Michael. *The Concise AACR2*. American Library Association Editions, 2004.

[Grappone2011] GRAPPONE, Jennifer and COUZIN, Gravida. *Search Engine Optimization (SEO): An Hour a Day*. Sybex, 2011.

[Grean2005] GREAN, Michael and SHAW, Michael J. *"Supply-Chain Integration through Information Sharing: Channel Partnership between Wal-Mart and Procter & Gamble": Center for IT and e-Business Management, University of Illinois at Urbana-Champaign*. 2005.

[Grimmelmann2009] GRIMMELMANN, James. *"How to Fix the Google Book Search Settlement": Journal of Internet Law*. 2009. `http://works.bepress.com/james_grimmelmann/23/` .

[Gross1990] GROSS, Derek and MILLER, Katherine J. *"Adjectives in WordNet": International Journal of Lexicography*. 1990. pp. 265-277.

[Gruber1993] GRUBER, Thomas R. *"A Translation Approach to Portable Ontology Specifications": Knowledge Acquisition*. 1993. pp. 199-220.

[Grudin1994] GRUDIN, Jonathan. *"Groupware and social dynamics: eight challenges for developers": Communications of the ACM*. 1994. pp. 92-105.

[Guarino1998] GUARINO, Nicola. *"Formal Ontology and Information Systems": Formal ontology in information systems: proceedings of FOIS '98*. 1998. pp. 3-15.

[Guenther2009] GUENTHER, Rebecca and WOLFE, Robert. *"Integrating Metadata Standards to Support Long-Term Preservation of Digital Assets: Developing Best Practices for Expressing Preservation Metadata in a Container Format": iPRES 2009: the Sixth International Conference on the Preservation of Digital Objects, California Digital Library, UC Office of the President.* 2009.

[Guijarro2007] GUIJARRO, Luis. *"Interoperability frameworks and enterprise architectures in e-government initiatives in Europe and the United States": Government Information Quarterly.* 2007. pp. 89-101. *http://linking hub.elsevier.com/retrieve/pii/S0740624X06000864* .

[Halasz1994] HALASZ, Frank and SCHWARTZ, Mayer. *"The Dexter Hypertext Reference Model": Communications of the ACM.* 1994. pp. 30-39.

[Halvey2007] HALVEY, Martin and KEANE, Mark T. *"An Assessment of Tag Presentation Techniques": Proceedings of the 16th international conference on World Wide Web (WWW '07).* 2007. pp. 1313-1314.

[Hamilton2012] HAMILTON, Kate and WOOD, Lauren. *"Schematron in the Context of the Clinical Document Architecture (CDA)": Proceedings of Balisage: The Markup Conference 2012.* 2012.

[Hammond2004] HAMMOND, Tony, et al. *"Social Bookmarking Tools (I): A General Review": D-Lib Magazine.* 2004. *http://www.dlib.org/dlib/april05/ hammond/04hammond.html* .

[Hansen2009] HANSEN, Morten. *Collaboration: How leaders avoid the traps, build common ground, and reap big results.* Harvard Business Press, 2009.

[Harinarayana2010] HARINARAYANA, N.S. and RAJU, N. Vasantha. *"Web 2.0 features in university library web sites": The Electronic Library.* 2010. pp. 69-88.

[Harpring2009] HARPRING, Patricia. *Categories for the Description of Works of Art: Getty Research Institute.* 2009. *http://getty.edu/research/publica tions/electronic_publications/cdwa/* .

[Harris1996] HARRIS, Roy. *Signs of Writing.* Routledge, 1996.

[Haspelmath2010] HASPELMATH, Martin and SIMS, Andrea. *Understanding Morphology.* Routledge, 2010.

[Haviland1998] HAVILAND, John B. *"Guugu Yimithirr Cardinal Directions": Ethos.* 1998. pp. 25-47.

[He2007] HE, Bin, et al. *"Accessing the Deep Web: A Survey": Communications of the ACM*. 2007. pp. 94-101.

[Hearst2009] HEARST, Marti A. and STOICA, Emilia. *"NLP Support for Faceted Navigation in Scholarly Collections": Proceedings of the 2009 Workshop on Text and Citation Analysis for Scholarly Digital Libraries*. 2009. pp. 62-70.

[Heath2011] HEATH, Tom and BIZER, Christian. *Linked Data: Evolving the Web into a Global Data Space*. Morgan & Claypool Publishers, 2011.

[Heller2012] HELLER, Daphna, GORMAN, Kristen S., and TANENHAUS, Michael K. *"To name or to describe: shared knowledge affects referential form": Topics in cognitive science*. 2012. pp. 290-305. `http://www.ncbi.nlm.nih.gov/pubmed/22389094` .

[Helper2003] HELPER, Susan and MACDUFFIE, John Paul. *B2B and modes of exchange: evolutionary and transformative effects: The Global Internet Economy*. 2003. 331-380.

[Hemerly2011] HEMERLY, Jess. *"Making Metadata: The Case of MusicBrainz": SSRN Electronic Journal*. 2011. `http://papers.ssrn.com/abstract=1982823` .

[Hensen2009] HANSEN, Morten T. *Collaboration: How leaders avoid the traps, build common ground, and reap big results*. Harvard Business Press, 2009.

[Herbst2009] HERBST, Charles. *"Death in cyberspace": Res Gestae*. 2009. pp. 16-25.

[Hillmann2005] HILLMANN, Diane. *Using Dublin Core—The Elements: Dublin Core Metadata Initiative*. 2005. `http://dublincore.org/documents/usage guide/elements.shtml` .

[Hjørland1992] HJØRLAND, Birger. *"The Concept of 'Subject' in Information Science": Journal of Documentation*. 1992. pp. 172-200. `http://www.emeral dinsight.com/journals.htm?issn=0022-0418&volume=48&issue=2&arti cleid=1650137&show=html` .

[Hjørland2001] HJØRLAND, Birger. *"Why is meta analysis neglected by information scientists?": Journal of the American Society for Information Science and Technology*. 2001. pp. 1193-1194.

[Hoffman2008] HOFFMAN, Michael. *"Details emerging on how fuses got to Taiwan": Air Force Times*. 2008. `http://www.airforcetimes.com/news/2008/03/airforce_loose_fuses3_032708w/` .

[Hofweber2009] HOFWEBER, Thomas. *"Logic and Ontology": In The Stanford Encyclopedia of Philosophy.* 2009. `http://plato.stanford.edu/archives/spr2009/entries/logic-ontology/` .

[Holman2001] HOLMAN, G. Ken. *Definitive XSLT and XPath.* Prentice Hall, 2001.

[Hori2010] HORI, Mitsuyoshi, KAWASHIMA, Eiji, and YAMAZAKI, Tomihoro. *"Application of Cloud Computing to Agriculture and Prospects in Other Fields": Fujitsu Scientific and Technical Journal.* 2010. pp. 446-454.

[Howard2011] HOWARD, Jennifer. *"Librarians Puzzle Over E-Books They May Buy but Not Truly Own": The Chronicle of Higher Education.* 2011. `http://chronicle.com/article/Hot-Type-Librarians-Puzzle/127538/` .

[Howe2006] HOWE, Jeff. *"The Rise of Crowdsourcing": Wired.* 2006. `http://www.wired.com/wired/archive/14.06/crowds.html` .

[Howe2008] HOWE, Jeff. *Crowdsourcing: Why the Power of the Crowd Is Driving the Future of Business.* Random House, 2008.

[Hu2004] HU, Minqing and LIU, Bing. *"Mining and summarizing customer reviews": Proceedings of the 2004 ACM SIGKDD International Conference on Knowledge Discovery and Data Mining.* 2004. pp. 168.

[Hutchins2010] HUTCHINS, Edwin. *"Cognitive Ecology": Topics in cognitive science.* 2010. pp. 705-715. `http://philpapers.org/rec/EDWCE` .

[Hutchins1977] HUTCHINS, W. John. *"On the problem of 'aboutness' in document analysis.": Journal of Informatics.* no. 1. 1977. 17-35.

[Hyvönen2004] HYVÖNEN, Eero, et al. *"Finnish Museums on the Semantic Web: The User's Perspective on MuseumFinland": Museums and the Web 2004: International Conference for Culture and Heritage On-line.* 2004. `http://www.museumsandtheweb.com/mw2004/papers/hyvonen/hyvonen.html` .

[Jackendoff1996] JACKENDOFF, Ray S. *The Architecture of the Language Faculty.* The MIT Press, 1996.

[John2006] JOHN, Ajita and SELIGMANN, Dorée. *"Collaborative Tagging and Expertise in the Enterprise": Proceedings of the Fifteenth International World Wide Web Conference.* 2006.

[Johnson2010] JOHNSON, Marilyn. *"U.S. public libraries: We lose them at our peril": The Los Angeles Times.* 2010. `http://articles.latimes.com/2010/jul/06/opinion/la-oe-johnson-libraries-20100706` .

[Jones2007] JONES, William. *Keeping Things Found: The Study and Practice of Personal Information Management.* Morgan Kaufmann, 2007.

[Kaser2007] KASER, Owen and LEMIRE, Daniel. *"Tag-Cloud Drawing : Algorithms for Cloud Visualization": WWW'07 Workshop on Taggings and Metadata for Social Information Organization.* 2007.

[Kaynak1997] KAYNAK, Erdener and HERBIG, Paul. *Handbook of Cross-Cultural Marketing.* Routledge, 1997.

[Kent2012] KENT, William and HOBERMAN, Steve. *Data and Reality: A Timeless Perspective on Perceiving and Managing Information in Our Imprecise World.* Technics Publications, LLC, 2012.

[Kilgour1998] KILGOUR, Frederick G. *The Evolution of the Book.* Oxford University Press, 1998.

[Kim2009] KIM, Kenneth, NOFSINGER, John R., and MOHR, Derek J. *Corporate Governance.* Prentice Hall, 2009.

[Kimber2012] KIMBER, Eliot. *DITA for Practitioners Volume 1: Architecture and Technology.* XML Press, 2012.

[Kirschenbaum2008] KIRSCHENBAUM, Matthew G. *Mechanisms: New Media and the Forensic Imagination.* The MIT Press, 2008.

[Kirschenbaum2009] KIRSCHENBAUM, Matthew G., et al. *"Digital Materiality: Preserving Access to Computers as Complete Environments": iPRES 2009: The Sixth International Conference on the Preservation of Digital Objects, California Digital Library, UC Office of the President.* 2009. `http://escholarship.org/uc/item/7d3465vg` .

[Kirsh1995] KIRSH, David. *"The Intelligent Use of Space": Artificial Intelligence.* 1995. pp. 31-36.

[Kirsh2000] KIRSH, David. *"A Few Thoughts on Cognitive Overload": Intellectica.* 2000. pp. 19-51.

[Kleppe2003] KLEPPE, Anneke, WARMER, Jos, and BAST, Wim. *MDA Explained: The Model Driven Architecture: Practice and Promise.* Addison Wesley, 2003.

[Knapp2011] KNAPP, Alex. *"Pro Lacrosse Team Replaces Names With Twitter Handles On Jerseys": Forbes.* 2011. `http://www.forbes.com/sites/alex knapp/2011/12/30/pro-lacrosse-team-replaces-names-with-twitter-handles-on-jerseys/` .

[Knut2001] *"Knut, the $140 Million Polar Bear": Businessweek.com.* 2011. `http://www.businessweek.com/magazine/content/11_23/b4231085935993.htm` .

[Kogut2003] KOGUT, Bruce. *The Global Internet Economy.* The MIT Press, 2003.

[Kulish2009] KULISH, Nicholas. *"High Court in Germany Pops Names That Balloon": The New York Times.* 2009. `http://www.nytimes.com/2009/05/06/world/europe/06germany.html` .

[Kuniavsky2010] KUNIAVSKY, Mike. *Smart Things: Ubiquitous Computing User Experience Design.* Morgan Kaufmann, 2010.

[Lackey1999] LACKEY, Douglas P. *"What are the modern classics? The Baruch poll of great philosophy in the twentieth century": Philosophical Forum.* 1999. pp. 329-346. `http://philpapers.org/rec/LACWAT` .

[Lakoff1990] LAKOFF, George. *Women, Fire, and Dangerous Things.* University of Chicago Press, 1990.

[Lancaster1968] LANCASTER, Frederick Wilfrid. *Information Retrieval Systems: Characteristics, Testing, and Evaluation.* John Wiley & Sons, 1968.

[Langevoort2006] LANGEVOORT, Donald. *"Internal Controls After Sarbanes-Oxley: Revisiting Corporate Law's 'Duty of Care as Responsibility for Systems'": Georgetown Law Faculty Publications and Other Works.* 2006. `http://scholarship.law.georgetown.edu/facpub/144` .

[Langville2012] LANGVILLE, Amy and MEYER, Carl. *Google's Page Rank and Beyond: The Science of Search Engine Rankings.* Princeton University Press, 2012.

[Laskey2005] LASKEY, Kenneth J. *"Metadata Concepts to Support a Net-Centric Data Environment": In Net-Centric Approaches to Intelligence and National Security.* Springer, 2005. 29-54.

[Lee1993] LEE, Sharon M. *"Racial classifications in the US census: 1890-1990": Ethnic and Racial Studies.* 1993. pp. 75-94.

[Lee2007] LEE, John A. and VERLEYSEN, Michel. *Nonlinear Dimensionality Reduction*. Springer, 2007.

[Leonardi2010] LEONARDI, Paul M. *"Digital materiality? How artifacts without matter, matter": First Monday*. 2010. `http://www.uic.edu/htbin/cgiwrap/bin/ojs/index.php/fm/article/view/3036/2567` .

[Levitin2002] LEVITIN, Daniel J. *Foundations of Cognitive Psychology: Core Readings*. A Bradford Book, 2002.

[Levy2006] LEVY, Robert L. and CASEY, Patricia L. *Electronic Evidence and the Large Document Case: Common Evidence Problems: Haynes and Boone, LLP*. 2006.

[Levy2010] LEVY, Steven. *"How Google's Algorithm Rules the Web": Wired*. 2010. `http://www.wired.com/magazine/2010/02/ff_google_algorithm/` .

[Lewis2003] LEWIS, Michael. *Moneyball: The art of winning an unfair game*. WW Norton, 2003.

[Linnaeus1735] LINNAEUS, C. von. *Systema Naturae 1*. Editio Decima, Reformata. (Holmiae, fasc reprint 1939) (1758), 1735.

[Linthicum1999] LINTHICUM, David S. *Enterprise Application Integration*. Addison Wesley, 1999.

[Lorch1989] LORCH, Robert F. *"Text-signaling devices and their effects on reading and memory processes": Educational Psychology Review*. 1989. pp. 209-234.

[Loshin2008] LOSHIN, David. *Master Data Management*. Morgan Kaufmann, 2008.

[Lovink2011] LOVINK, Geert and TKACZ, Nathaniel. *Critical Point of View: A Wikipedia Reader*. Institute of Network Cultures, 2011. `http://www.amazon.co.uk/CRITICAL-POINT-OF-VIEW-WIKIPEDIA/dp/9078146133` .

[Lubetzky2001] LUBETZKY, Seymour. *Seymour Lubetzky: Writings on the Classical Art of Cataloging*. Libraries Unlimited, 2001.

[Lusch2007] LUSCH, Robert F. *"Reframing Supply Chain Management: A Service-Dominant Logic Perspective": Journal of Supply Chain Management*. 2007. pp. 14-18.

[Mach2003] MACH, Michelle. *Real Job Titles for Library and Information Science Professionals*. 2003. `http://www.michellemach.com/jobtitles/realjobs.html` .

[Macmanus2009] MACMANUS, Richard. *The Tweeting House: Twitter + Internet of Things: Readwrite.com*. 2009. `http://www.readwriteweb.com/ archives/the_tweeting_house_twitter_internet_of_things.php` .

[Madrigal2009] MADRIGAL, Alexis. *"Autonomous Robots Invade Retail Warehouses": Wired*. 2009. `http://www.wired.com/wiredscience/2009/01/ retailrobots/` .

[Maglio2009] MAGLIO, Paul P., et al. *"The service system is the basic abstraction of service science.": Information Systems and e-business Management*. 2009. 395-406.

[Malaga2008] MALAGA, Ross A. *"Worst Practices in Search Engine Optimization": Communications of the ACM*. 2008. pp. 147-150.

[Malone1983] MALONE, Thomas W. *"How do people organize their desks?: Implications for the design of office information systems": ACM Transactions on Information Systems*. 1983. pp. 99-112.

[Malt1995] MALT, Barbara C. *"Category Coherence in Cross-Cultural Perspective": Cognitive Psychology*. 1995. pp. 85-148. `http://www.eric.ed.gov/ ERICWebPortal/detail?accno=EJ514283` .

[Maness2006] MANESS, Jack M. *"Library 2.0 Theory: Web 2.0 and its Implications for Libraries": Webology*. 2006. `http://www.webology.org/2006/ v3n2/a25.html` .

[Mann1988] MANN, William C. and THOMPSON, Sandra A. *"Rhetorical Structure Theory: A Theory of Text Organization": Text*. 1988. pp. 243-281.

[Manning2008] MANNING, Christopher D., RAGHAVAN, Prabhakar, and SCHÜTZE, Hinrich. *Introduction to Information Retrieval*. Cambridge University Press, 2008.

[Manyika2011] MANYIKA, James, et al. *"Big data: The next frontier for innovation, competition, and productivity": Kinsey Global Institute*. 2011. `http:// www.mckinsey.com/insights/mgi/research/technology_and_innova tion/big_data_the_next_frontier_for_innovation` .

[Mardia1980] MARDIA, Kanti V., KENT, J. T., and BIBBY, J. M. *Multivariate Analysis*. Academic Press, 1980.

[Margolis1999] MARGOLIS, Eric and LAURENCE, Stephen. *Concepts: Core Readings*. A Bradford Book, 1999.

[Markoff2011] MARKOFF, John and SENGUPTA, Somini. *"Separating you and me? 4.74 degrees": The New York Times.* 2011.

[Marlow2006] MARLOW, Cameron, et al. *"HT06, tagging paper, taxonomy, Flickr, academic article, to read.": In Proceedings of the Seventeenth Conference on Hypertext and Hypermedia.* ACM, 2006. 31-40.

[Maron1977] MARON, M. E. *"On indexing, retrieval and the meaning of about": Journal of the American Society for Information Science.* 1977. pp. 38-43.

[Marsh2006] MARSH, Jonathan, ORCHARD, David, and VEILLARD, Daniel. *XML Inclusions (XInclude): Recommendation of the World Wide Web Consortium (W3C).* 2006. *http://www.w3.org/TR/xinclude/* .

[Marshall2007] MARSHALL, Catherine C., MCCOWN, Frank, and NELSON, ML. *"Evaluating personal archiving strategies for Internet-based information": Proceedings of IS&T Archiving 2007.* 2007. *http://arxiv.org/abs/0704.3647* .

[Marshall2008] MARSHALL, Catherine C. *"Rethinking Personal Digital Archiving Part 1: Four Challenges from the Field": D-Lib Magazine.* 2008. *http://www.dlib.org/dlib/march08/marshall/03marshall-pt1.html* .

[McBride2006] MCBRIDE, S., et al. *"Data Mapping": Journal of the American Health Information Management Association.* 2006. pp. 44-52.

[McCartney2006] MCCARTNEY, Scott. *"When Pilots Pass the BRBON, They Must Be in Kentucky": The Wall Street Journal.* 2006. *http://online.wsj.com/article/SB114291174429403797.html* .

[Medin1993] MEDIN, Douglas L., GOLDSTONE, Robert L., and GENTNER, Dedre. *"Respects for Similarity": Psychological Review.* 1993. pp. 254-278.

[Medin1997] MEDIN, Douglas L., et al. *"Categorization and reasoning among tree experts: do all roads lead to Rome?": Cognitive psychology.* 1997. pp. 49-96. *http://www.ncbi.nlm.nih.gov/pubmed/9038245* .

[Merryman2006] MERRYMAN, John Henry. *Imperialism, Art and Restitution.* Cambridge University Press, 2006.

[Mervis1981] MERVIS, Carolyn B. and ROSCH, Eleanor. *"Categorization of natural objects": The Annual Review of Psychology.* 1981. pp. 89-115.

[Miksa1984] MIKSA, Francis. *The development of classification at the Library of Congress: University of Illinois Graduate School of Library and Information Science.* 1984.

[Millen2005] MILLEN, David, FEINBERG, Jonathan, and KERR, Bernard. *"Social bookmarking in the enterprise": Queue.* 2005. pp. 28.

[Millen2006] MILLEN, David R., FEINBERG, Jonathan, and KERR, Bernard. *"Dogear: Social Bookmarking in the Enterprise": Proceedings of the SIGCHI Conference on Human Factors in Computing Systems (CHI '06).* 2006. pp. 111-120.

[Miller1956] MILLER, George. *"The Magical Number Seven, Plus or Minus Two: Some Limits on our Capacity for Processing Information": Psychological Review.* 1956. pp. 81-97.

[Miller1976] MILLER, George A. and JOHNSON-LAIRD, Philip. *Language and Perception.* Belknap Press, 1976.

[Miller1998] MILLER, George A. *"Nouns in WordNet": In WordNet: An Electronic Lexical Database.* The MIT Press, 1998.

[Miller2003] MILLER, Joaquin and MUKERJI, Jishnu. *MDA Guide Version 1.0.1: Object Management Group.* 2003. `http://www.omg.org/cgi-bin/doc?omg/03-06-01` .

[Mizzaro1997] MIZZARO, Stefano. *"Relevance: The Whole History": Journal of the American Society for Information Science.* 1997. pp. 810-832.

[Mockapetris1987] MOCKAPETRIS, Paul. *RFC 1035: Domain Name System (DNS).* 1987. `http://tools.ietf.org/html/rfc1035`.

[Montague2010] MONTAGUE, James. *The rise and fall of fantasy sports.* 2010. `http://www.cnn.com/2010/SPORT/football/01/06/fantasy.football.moneyball.sabermetrics/index.html`.

[Morgan1871] MORGAN, Lewis Henry. *Systems of Consanguinity and Affinity of the Human Family.* University of Nebraska Press, 1871.

[Morgan1997] MORGAN, Lewis Henry. *Systems of consanguinity and affinity of the human family.: Reprint of Morgan(1871).* Smithsonian Institution, 1997.

[Morville2006] MORVILLE, Peter and ROSENFELD, Louis. *Information Architecture for the World Wide Web.* O'Reilly, 2006.

[Munk2004] MUNK, Nina. *Fools Rush In: Steve Case, Jerry Levin, and the Unmaking of AOL Time Warner.* HarperCollins, 2004.

[Nelson1974] NELSON, Theodor Holm. *Computer Lib.* Microsoft Press, 1974.

[Nelson1981] NELSON, Theodor H. *Literary Machines: The Report On, and Of, Project Xanadu Concerning Word Processing, Electronic Publishing, Hypertext, Thinkertoys, Tomorrow's Intellectual Revolution, and Certain Other Topics Including Knowledge, Education and Freedom.* 3rd edition. T. Nelson, 1981.

[Neuhaus2008] NEUHAUS, Christoph and DANIEL, Hans-dieter. *"Data sources for performing citation analysis: An overview": Journal of Documentation.* 2008. pp. 193-210.

[Newell1972] NEWELL, Allen and SIMON, Herbert Alexander. *Human Problem Solving.* Prentice Hall, 1972.

[NISO2004] NATIONAL INFORMATION STANDARDS ORGANIZATION. *Understanding Metadata.* NISO Press, 2004. *http://www.niso.org/standards/resources/UnderstandingMetadata.pdf* .

[Norman1988] NORMAN, Donald A. *The psychology of everyday things.* Basic Books, 1988.

[Norman1999] NORMAN, Donald A. *"Affordance, conventions, and design": interactions.* 1999. pp. 38-43.

[Norman2006] NORMAN, Donald A. *"Logic Versus Usage: The Case for Activity-Centered Design": interactions.* 2006. pp. 45-ff.

[Nova2011] TYSON, Neil deGrasse and RANDALL, Terri. *The Pluto Files.* Boston, MA: WGBH, 2011.

[Nunberg1996] NUNBERG, Geoffrey. *"Farewell to the Information Age": In The Future of the Book.* University of California Press, 1996.

[Nunberg2009] NUNBERG, Geoffrey. *"Google's Book Search: A Disaster for Scholars": The Chronicle of Higher Education.* 2009. *http://chronicle.com/article/Googles-Book-Search-A/48245/* .

[Nunberg2011] NUNBERG, Geoffrey. *"James Gleick's History of Information": The New York Times.* 2011. *http://www.nytimes.com/2011/03/20/books/review/book-review-the-information-by-james-gleick.html* .

[OASIS2003] OASIS. *XML Common Biometric Format.* 2003. *http://www.oasis-open.org/committees/download.php/3353/oasis-200305-xcbf-specification-1.1.doc* .

[OASIS2006] OASIS. *Universal Business Language (UBL).* 2006. *http://docs.oasis-open.org/ubl/os-UBL-2.0/UBL-2.0.html* .

[OReilly2005] O'REILLY, Tim. *What Is Web 2.0: Design Patterns and Business Models for the Next Generation of Software: O'Reilly Media.* 2005. `http://oreilly.com/web2/archive/what-is-web-20.html` .

[Page1999] PAGE, Lawrence, et al. *"The PageRank Citation Ranking: Bringing Order to the Web": Stanford InfoLab.* 1999. `http://ilpubs.stanford.edu:8090/422/` .

[Pandey2010] PANDEY, Upasana and CHAKRAVARTY, Shampa. *"A Survey on Text Classification Techniques for E-mail Filtering": 2010 Second International Conference on Machine Learning and Computing.* 2010. pp. 32-36.

[Panizzi1841] PANIZZI, Anthony. *Rules for the Compilation of the Catalogue.* 1841.

[Panofsky1972] PANOFSKY, Erwin and PANOFSKY, Gerda S. *Studies in Iconology: Humanistic Themes in the Art of the Renaissance.* Westview Press, 1972.

[Park2009] PARK, Jung-Ran. *"Metadata Quality in Digital Repositories: A Survey of the Current State of the Art": Cataloging & Classification Quarterly.* 2009. pp. 213-228. `http://dx.doi.org/10.1080/01639370902737240` .

[Pathan2008] PATHAN, Mukaddim, BUYYA, Rajkumar, and VAKALI, Athena. *"Content Delivery Networks: State of the Art , Insights, and Imperatives": In Content Delivery Networks.* Springer, 2008. pp. 3-32.

[Pirolli2007] PIROLLI, Peter L. T. *Information Foraging Theory: Adaptive Interaction with Information.* Oxford University Press, 2007.

[Pogue2009] POGUE, David. *"Should You Worry About Data Rot?": The New York Times.* 2009. `http://pogue.blogs.nytimes.com/2009/03/26/should-you-worry-about-data-rot/` .

[Pohs2013] POHS, Wendi. *"Building a taxonomy for auto-classification": Bulletin of the American Soceity for Information Science and Technology.* 2013. pp. 34-38.

[Poole2010] POOLE, Erika Shehan and GRUDIN, Jonathan. *"A taxonomy of Wiki genres in enterprise settings": Proceedings of the 6th International Symposium on Wikis and Open Collaboration - WikiSym '10.* 2010. `http://portal.acm.org/citation.cfm?doid=1832772.1832792` .

[Pope2011] POPE, Julia T. and HOLLEY, Robert P. *"Google Book Search and Metadata": Cataloging & Classification Quarterly.* 2011. pp. 1-13.

[Pouillon1970] POUILLON, Jean. *Échanges et communications: mélanges offerts à Claude Lévi-Strauss à l'occasion de son 60ème anniversaire*. Mouton & Co., 1970. `http://www.worldcat.org/title/echanges-et-communications-melanges-offerts-a-claude-levi-strauss-a-loccasion-de-son-60eme-anniversaire/oclc/645325210` .

[Pralahad1990] PRALAHAD, C. K. and HAMEL, Gary. *"The Core Competence of the Corporation": Harvard Business Review*. 1990. `http://hbr.org/1990/05/the-core-competence-of-the-corporation/ar/1` .

[Prats2008] PRATS, Mario, et al. *"The UJI librarian robot": Intelligent Service Robotics*. 2008. pp. 321-335. `http://www.springerlink.com/content/15164724vxp07704/` .

[PREMIS2011] PREMIS EDITORIAL COMMITTEE. *Data Dictionary for Preservation Metadata: PREMIS version 2.0*. Library of Congress, 2008. `http://www.loc.gov/standards/premis/` .

[Proctor2011] PROCTOR, Nancy. *"The Google Art Project: A New Generation of Museums on the Web?": Curator: The Museum Journal*. 2011. pp. 215-221.

[Queenan2011] QUEENAN, Joe. *"Wotan, Your Double-Skim Latte Is Ready": The Wall Street Journal*. 2011. `http://online.wsj.com/article/SB10001424053111904106704576582834147448392.html` .

[Rahm2006] RAHM, Erhard and BERNSTEIN, Philip A. *"An Online Bibliography on Schema Evolution": ACM SIGMOD Record*. 2006. pp. 30-31.

[Ranganathan1967] RANGANATHAN, Shiyali Ramamrita. *Prologmena to Library Classification*. Asia Publishing House, 1967.

[RDFWorkingGroup2004] RDF WORKING GROUP. *Resource Description Framework: Recommendation of the World Wide Web Consortium (W3C)*. 2004. `http://www.w3.org/RDF/` .

[Reaney1997] REANEY, P. H. and WILSON, R. M. *A Dictionary of English Surnames*. Oxford University Press, 1997.

[Regazzoni2010] REGAZZONI, Carlo S., et al. *"Video Analytics for Surveillance: Theory and Practice": IEEE Signal Processing*. 2010. pp. 16-17.

[Register2012] REGISTER, Renée and MCILROY, Thad. *The Metadata Handbook: A Book Publisher's Guide to Creating and Distributing Metadata for Print and Ebooks*. DataCurate, 2012.

[Rehder2004] REHDER, Bob and HASTIE, Reid. *"Category coherence and category-based property induction": Cognition.* 2004. pp. 113-153. *http://link inghub.elsevier.com/retrieve/pii/S0010027703001677* .

[Renear2003] RENEAR, Allen and DUBIN, David. *"Towards Identity Conditions for Digital Documents": International Conference on Dublin Core and Metadata Applications.* 2003. pp. 181-189. *http://dcpapers.dublincore.org/ index.php/pubs/article/view/746* .

[Resnick2001] RESNICK, P. *"Internet Message Format": The Internet Society.* 2001.

[Rips2012] RIPS, Lance J., SMITH, Edward E., and MEDIN, Douglas L. *"Concepts and Categories: Memory, Meaning, and Metaphysics": In The Oxford Handbook of Thinking and Reasoning.* Oxford University Press, USA, 2012. pp. 177-209.

[Robertson2005] ROBERTSON, Stephen. *"How Okapi came to TREC": In TREC: Experiment and Evaluation in Information Retrieval.* The MIT Press, 2005. 287-299.

[Robinson2008] ROBINSON, David, et al. *"Government Data and the Invisible Hand": Yale Journal of Law and Technology.* 2008. pp. 160-176. *http:// papers.ssrn.com/abstract=1138083* .

[Rogers2008] ROGERS, Timothy T. and MCCLELLAND, James L. *"Précis of Semantic Cognition: A Parallel Distributed Processing Approach": Behavioral and Brain Sciences.* 2008. pp. 689-749.

[Rosch1975] ROSCH, Eleanor. *"Cognitive representations of semantic categories": Journal of Experimental Psychology: General.* 1975. pp. 192-233. *http://psycnet.apa.org/journals/xge/104/3/192/* .

[Rosch1999] ROSCH, Eleanor. *"Principles of Categorization": In Concepts: Core Readings.* The MIT Press, 1999. pp. 189-206.

[Rosen2012] ROSEN, Jeffrey. *"Who Do Online Advertisers Think You Are?": The New York Times Magazine.* 2012. *http://www.nytimes.com/2012/12/02/ magazine/who-do-online-advertisers-think-you-are.html* .

[Rosenthal2004] ROSENTHAL, Arnon, SELIGMAN, Len, and RENNER, Scott. *"From semantic integration to semantics management: case studies and a way forward": ACM SIGMOD Record.* 2004. pp. 44-50.

[Rothenberg1999] ROTHENBERG, Jeff. *"Ensuring the Longevity of Digital Information": RAND.* 1999.

[Rothfarb2007] ROTHFARB, Robert J. and DOHERTY, Paul. *"Creating Museum Content and Community in Second Life": Museums and the Web 2007: International Conference for Culture and Heritage On-line.* 2007. `http://www.museumsandtheweb.com/mw2007/papers/rothfarb/rothfarb.html` .

[Rubinsky1997] RUBINSKY, Yuri and MALONEY, Murray. *SGML on the Web: Small Steps Beyond HTML.* Prentice Hall, 1997.

[Sag2012] SAG, Matthew. *"Orphan Works as Grist for the Data Mill": SSRN Electronic Journal.* 2012. `http://papers.ssrn.com/abstract=2038889` .

[Salton1975] SALTON, Gerard, WONG, Anita, and YANG, Chung-Shu. *"A Vector Space Model for Automatic Indexing": Communications of the ACM.* 1975. pp. 613-320.

[Samuelson2009] SAMUELSON, Pamela. *Google Books Is Not a Library: Huffington Post.* 2009. `http://www.huffingtonpost.com/pamela-samuelson/google-books-is-not-a-lib_b_317518.html` .

[Samuelson2010] SAMUELSON, Pamela. *"Google Book Search and the Future of Books in Cyberspace": Miinnesota Law Review.* 2010. pp. 1308-1374.

[Samuelson2011] SAMUELSON, Pamela. *"The Google Book Settlement as Copyright Reform": Wisconsin Law Review.* 2011. pp. 479-562. `http://papers.ssrn.com/abstract=1683589` .

[Sandler2006] SANDLER, Mark. *"Collection Development in the Age Day of Google": Library Resources & Technical Services.* 2006. pp. 239. `http://connection.ebscohost.com/c/articles/22421812/collection-development-age-day-google` .

[Saracevic1975] SARACEVIC, Tefko. *"Relevance: A Review of the Literature and a Framework for Thinking on the Notion in Information Science": Journal of the American Society for Information Science.* 1975. pp. 321-343.

[Satija2001] SATIJA, Mohinder P. *"Relationships in Raganathan's Colon Classification": In Relationships in the Organization of Knowledge.* Kluwer, 2001. 199-210.

[Savodnik2011] SAVODNIK, Peter. *"Knut, the $140 Million Polar Bear": Bloomberg BusinessWeek.* 2011. `http://www.petersavodnik.com/articles/knut-the-140-million-polar-bear/` .

[Sayre2005] SAYRE, Robert. *"Atom: The Standard in Syndication": IEEE Internet Computing.* 2005. pp. 71-78.

[Schamber1990] SCHAMBER, Linda, EISENBERG, Michael B., and NILAN, Michael S. *"A re-examination of relevance: toward a dynamic, situational definition": Information Processing & Management*. 1990. pp. 755-776. *http:// linkinghub.elsevier.com/retrieve/pii/030645739090050C* .

[Schatz1994] SCHATZ, Bruce R. and HARDIN, Joseph B. *"NCSA Mosaic and the World Wide Web: Global Hypermedia Protocols for the Internet": Science*. 1994. pp. 895-901.

[Schmandt-Besserat1997] SCHMANDT-BESSERAT, Denise. *How Writing Came About*. University of Texas Press, 1997.

[Schmidt2009] SCHMIDT, Desmond. *"Merging Multi-Version Texts: A General Solution to the Overlap Problem": Proceedings of Balisage: The Markup Conference 2009*. 2009. *http://www.balisage.net/Proceedings/vol3/ print/Schmidt01/BalisageVol3-Schmidt01.html* .

[Schmitz2008] SCHMITZ, Patrick L. and BLACK, Michael T. *"The Delphi Toolkit: Enabling Semantic Search for Museum Collections": Museums and the Web 2008: International Conference for Culture and Heritage On-line*. 2008.

[Scholl2007] SCHOLL, Hans Jochen and KLISCHEWSKI, Ralf. *"International Journal of Public E-Government Integration and Interoperability: Framing the Research Agenda": International Journal of Public Administration*. 2007. pp. 889-920.

[Schreibman2005] SCHREIBMAN, Susan, SIEMENS, Ray, and UNSWORTH, John. *A Companion to Digital Humanities*. Wiley-Blackwell, 2005.

[Schwartz2005] SCHWARTZ, Barry. *The Paradox of Choice: Why More Is Less*. Harper Perennial, 2005.

[Sebald1995] SEBALD, W.G. *The Rings of Saturn. (English Ed.). (Die Ringe des Saturn. Eine englische Wallfahrt.)*. Harvill, 1998.

[Sen2004] SEN, Arun. *"Metadata management: past, present and future": Decision Support Systems*. 2004. pp. 151-173. *http://dx.doi.org/10.1016/ S0167-9236(02)00208-7* .

[Sen2006] SEN, Shilad, et al. *"tagging, communities, vocabulary, evolution": CSCW '06: Proceedings of the 2006 20th Anniversary Conference on Computer Supported Cooperative Work*. 2006. pp. 181-190.

[Shadbolt2006] SHADBOLT, Nigel, BERNERS-LEE, Tim, and HALL, Wendy. *"The Semantic Web Revisited": IEEE Intelligent Systems*. 2006. pp. 96-101.

[Shah2006] SHAH, Rajiv C. and KESAN, Jay P. *"Open Standards and the Role of Politics": The Proceedings of the 8th Annual International Digital Government Research Conference*. 2006.

[Shapiro1998] SHAPIRO, Carl and VARIAN, Hal R. *Information rules: a strategic guide to the network economy*. Harvard Business Review Press, 1998.

[Shirky2005] SHIRKY, Clay. *Ontology Is Overrated: Categories, Links, and Tags*. 2005. *http://www.shirky.com/writings/ontology_overrated.html* .

[Shneiderman2008] SHNEIDERMAN, Ben. *"Science 2.0": Science*. 2008. pp. 1349-50. *http://www.sciencemag.org/content/319/5868/1349.short* .

[Silman1998] SILMAN, Roberta. *"In the Company of Ghosts": The New York Times*. 1998. *http://www.nytimes.com/books/98/07/26/reviews/980726.26silmant.html* .

[Silverston2000] SILVERSTON, Len. *The Data Model Resource Book, Vol. 2: A Library of Data Models for Specific Industries*. John Wiley & Sons, 2000.

[Simon1996] SIMON, Herbert Alexander. *The Sciences of the Artificial*. The MIT Press, 1996.

[Simon1997] SIMON, Herbert Alexander. *Administrative Behavior*. Free Press, 1997.

[Simon2010] SIMON, Nina. *The Participatory Museum*. Museum 2.0, 2010. *http://www.participatorymuseum.org/read/* .

[Simpson1989] SIMPSON, John and WEINER, Edmund. *The Oxford English Dictionary*. Oxford University Press, 1989.

[Sinclair2007] SINCLAIR, James and CARDEW-HALL, Michael. *"The folksonomy tag cloud: when is it useful?": Journal of Information Science*. 2007. pp. 15-29.

[Smiraglia1994] SMIRAGLIA, Richard P. *"Derivative Bibliographic Relationships: Linkages in the Bibliographic Universe": Navigating the Networks: Proceedings of the ASIS Mid-Year Meeting, Portland, Oregon, May 21-25, 1994*. 1994. pp. 115-135.

[Smiraglia1999] SMIRAGLIA, Richard P. and LEAZER, Gregory H. *"Derivative Bibliographic Relationships: The Work Relationship in a Global Bibliographic Database": Journal of the American Society for Information Science*. 1999. pp. 493-504.

[Smith1981] SMITH, Edward E. and MEDIN, Douglas L. *Categories and Concepts*. Harvard University Press, 1981.

[Smith2003] SMITH, Linda B. and THELEN, Esther. *"Development as a dynamic system": Trends in Cognitive Sciences*. 2003. pp. 343-348. *http://linking hub.elsevier.com/retrieve/pii/S1364661303001566* .

[Spiteri1998] SPITERI, Louis. *"A simplified model of facet analysis": Canadian Journal of Information and Library Science*. 1998. pp. 1-30.

[Srinivasan2009] SRINIVASAN, Ramesh, et al. *"Digital museums and diverse cultural knowledges: Moving past the traditional catalog": The Information Society*. 2009. pp. 265-278.

[Stewart1997] STEWART, Thomas A. *Intellectual Capital: The New Wealth of Organizations*. Crown Business, 1997.

[Storey1993] STOREY, Veda C. *"Understanding Semantic Relationships": VDLB Journal*. 1993. pp. 455-488.

[Strout1956] STROUT, Ruth French. *"The development of the catalog and cataloging codes": The Library Quarterly*. 1956. pp. 254-275.

[Suehle2012] SUEHLE, Ruth. *"The Periodic Tables of Everything but Elements": Wired*. 2012. *http://www.wired.com/geekmom/2012/03/the-periodic-tables-of-everything-but-elements/* .

[Svenonius2000] SVENONIUS, Elaine. *The Intellectual Foundation of Information Organization*. The MIT Press, 2000.

[Tagliabue2012] TAGLIABUE, John. *"Swiss Cows Send Texts to Announce They're in Heat": The New York Times*. 2012. *http://www.nytimes.com/2012/10/02/world/europe/device-sends-message-to-swiss-farmer-when-cow-is-in-heat.html* .

[Taylor2009] TAYLOR, Arlene G. and JOUDREY, Daniel N. *The Organization of Information*. Libraries Unlimited, 2009.

[Taylor2006] TAYLOR, Hugh. *The Joy of SOX: Why Sarbanes-Oxley and Service-Oriented Architecture May Be the Best Thing That Ever Happened to You*. Wiley, 2006.

[Taylor2007] TAYLOR, James and RADEN, Neil. *Smart (Enough) Systems: How to Deliver Competitive Advantage by Automating Hidden Decisions*. Prentice Hall, 2007.

[Taylor2010] TAYLOR, Maureen A. *Preserving Your Family Photographs*. Picture Perfect Press, 2010.

[Teece1998] TEECE, David J. *"Capturing Value from Knowledge Assets: The New Economy, Markets for Know-how, and Intangible Assets": California Management Review*. 1998. pp. 55-79.

[Teper2005] TEPER, Thomas H. *"Current and emerging challenges for the future of library and archival preservation": Library Resources & Technical Services*. 2005. pp. 32-39.

[Tidwell2008] TIDWELL, Doug. *XSLT: Mastering XML Transformations*. O'Reilly, 2008.

[Tillett1991] TILLETT, Barbara B. *"A Taxonomy of Bibliographic Relationships": Library Resources & Technical Services*. 1991. pp. 150-158.

[Tillett1992] TILLETT, Barbara B. *"Bibliographic relationships: An empirical study of the LC machine-readable records": Library Resources & Technical Services*. 1992. pp. 162-188.

[Tillett2001] TILLETT, Barbara B. *"Bibliographic Relationships": In Relationships in the Organization of Knowledge*. Kluwer, 2001. 19-36.

[Tillett2003] TILLETT, Barbara. *"What is FRBR? A Conceptual Model for the Bibliographic Universe": Technicalities*. 2003.

[Tillett2005] TILLETT, Barbara B. *"FRBR and Cataloging for the Future": Cataloging & Classification Quarterly*. 2005. pp. 197-205.

[Trant2009a] TRANT, Jennifer. *"Studying Social Tagging and Folksonomy: A Review and Framework": Journal of Digital Information*. 2009. pp. 1-42.

[Trant2009b] TRANT, Jennifer. *"Emerging convergence? Thoughts on museums, archives, libraries, and professional training": Museum Management and Curatorship*. 2009. pp. 1-24.

[Travers1969] TRAVERS, Jeffrey and MILGRAM, Stanley. *"An experimental study of the small world problem": Sociometry*. 1969. pp. 425-443.

[Turban2010] TURBAN, Efraim, SHARDA, Ramesh, and DELEN, Dursun. *Decision Support and Business Intelligence Systems*. Prentice Hall, 2010.

[Tufte1983] TUFTE, Edward R. *The Visual Display of Quantitative Information*. Graphics Press, 1983.

[Turnbull2009] TURNBULL, Giles. *"A Common Nomenclature for Lego Families": The Morning News.* 2009. `http://www.themorningnews.org/article/a-common-nomenclature-for-lego-families` .

[Tyson2011] TYSON, Neil deGrasse and RANDALL, Terri. *The Pluto Files.* Boston, MA: WGBH, 2011.

[Underhill2008] UNDERHILL, Paco. *Why We Buy: The Science of Shopping – Updated and Revised for the Internet, the Global Consumer, and Beyond.* Simon & Schuster, 2008.

[Upsana2010] UPSANA and CHAKRAVARTY, S. *A survey of text classification techniques for e-mail filtering.: Second International Conference on Machine Learning and Computing.* 2010. 32-36.

[vanderVlist2007] VAN DER VLIST, Eric. *Schematron.* O'Reilly, 2007.

[VanderWal2007] VANDER WAL, Thomas. *Folksonomy: vanderwal.net.* 2007. `http://vanderwal.net/folksonomy.html` .

[VandeSompel2010] VANDESOMPEL, Herbert, NELSON, Michael, and SANDERSON, Robert. *HTTP framework for time-based access to resource states —Memento: IETF Tools.* 2010. `http://tools.ietf.org/html/draft-vandesompel-memento-00` .

[Vargo2004] VARGO, Stephen and LUSCH, Robert F. *"Evolving to a new dominant logic for marketing.": Journal of marketing.* 2004. 1-17.

[Viswanadham2002] VISWANADHAM, N. *"The past, present, and future of supply-chain automation": IEEE Robotics & Automation Magazine.* 2002. pp. 48-56. `http://ieeexplore.ieee.org/articleDetails.jsp?arnumber=1019490&contentType=Journals+&+Magazines` .

[vonAhn2004] VON AHN, Luis and DABBISH, Laura. *"Labeling images with a computer game": Proceedings of the 2004 Conference on Human Factors in Computing Systems.* 2004. pp. 319-326.

[vonAhn2008] VON AHN, Luis and DABBISH, Laura. *"Designing games with a purpose": Communications of the ACM.* 2008. pp. 57-67.

[vonRiegen2006] VON RIEGEN, Claus. *How Standards Address Interoperability Needs: An Industry View: OASIS Symposium, May 10, 2006, San Francisco.* 2006.

[Wakabayashi2011] WAKABAYASHI, Daisuke. *“Japanese Farms Look to the ‘Cloud’”: The Wall Street Journal.* 2011. `http://online.wsj.com/article/SB10001424052748704029704576087910899748444.html` .

[Walker2009] WALKER, Rob. *“The Song Decoders at Pandora”: The New York Times.* 2009. `http://www.nytimes.com/2009/10/18/magazine/18Pandora-t.html` .

[Wallach1998] WALLACH, Alan. *Exhibiting Contradiction.* University of Massachusetts Press, 1998.

[Walsh2010] WALSH, Norman. *DocBook 5: The Definitive Guide.* O’Reilly, 2010.

[Want2006] WANT, Roy. *“An Introduction to RFID Technology”: Pervasive Computing.* 2006. pp. 25-33.

[Watson2007] WATSON, Hugh J. and WIXOM, Barbara H. *“The Current State of Business Intelligence”: Computer.* 2007. pp. 96-99.

[Watts2004] WATTS, Duncan J. *“The ‘New’ Science of Networks”: Annual Review of Sociology.* 2004. pp. 243-270.

[Weill2004] WEILL, Peter and ROSS, Jeanne. *IT Governance: How Top Performers Manage IT Decision Rights for Superior Results.* Harvard Business Review Press, 2004.

[Weinberger1985] WEINBERGER, Jerry. *Science, Faith, and Politics: Francis Bacon and the Utopian Roots of the Modern Age; A Commentary on Bacon’s Advancement of Learning.* Cornell University Press, 1985.

[Weinberger2007] WEINBERGER, David. *Everything Is Miscellaneous: The Power of the New Digital Disorder.* Times Books, 2007.

[Weinreich2001] WEINREICH, Harald, OBENDORF, Hartmut, and LAMERS-DORF, Winfried. *“The Look of the Link—Concepts for the User Interface of Extended Hyperlinks”: Proceedings of the 12th ACM Conference on Hypertext and Hypermedia (HYPERTEXT ’01).* 2001. pp. 19-28.

[Wheatley2004] WHEATLEY, Malcolm. *“Operation Clean Data”: CIO.* 2004. `http://www.cio.com.au/article/166533/operation_clean_data/` .

[Wilbert2006] WILBERT, Caroline. *How Wal-Mart Works: HowStuffWorks.com.* 2006. `http://money.howstuffworks.com/wal-mart.htm` .

[Wilde2002] WILDE, Erik and LOWE, David. *XPath, XLink, XPointer, and XML: A Practical Guide to Web Hyperlinking and Transclusion.* Addison Wesley, 2002.

[Wilde2007] WILDE, Erik and CATTIN, Philippe. *"Presenting in HTML": DocEng '07: Proceedings of the 2007 ACM Symposium on Document Engineering.* 2007.

[Wilde2008a] WILDE, Erik. *The Plain Web.* 2008. `http://dret.net/netdret/docs/wilde-wsw2008/` .

[Wilde2008b] WILDE, Erik and GLUSHKO, Robert J. *"Document design matters": Communications of the ACM.* 2008. pp. 43-49. `http://portal.acm.org/citation.cfm?doid=1400181.1400195` .

[Wilde2011] WILDE, Erik and PAUTASSO, Cesare. *REST: From Research to Practice.* Springer, 2011.

[Williams2012] WILLIAMS, Robin. *The Non-Designer's Design Book.* Peachpit Press, 2012.

[Williamson1975] WILLIAMSON, Oliver E. *"Markets and hierarchies: analysis and antitrust implications: a study in the economics of internal organization": University of Illinois at Urbana-Champaign's Academy for Entrepreneurial Leadership Historical Research Reference in Entrepreneurship.* 1975. `http://ssrn.com/abstract=1496220` .

[Williamson1998] WILLIAMSON, Oliver E. *The Economic Institutions of Capitalism.* Free Press, 1998.

[Wilson1968] WILSON, Patrick. *Two Kinds of Power: An Essay on Bibliographical Control.* University of California Press, 1968.

[Winkler2010] WINKLER, Stefan and VON PILGRIM, Jens. *"A survey of traceability in requirements engineering and model-driven development": Software and Systems Modeling.* 2010. pp. 529-565.

[Witten2011] WITTEN, Ian H., FRANK, Eibe, and HALL, Mark A. *Data Mining: Practical Machine Learning Tools and Techniques.* Morgan Kaufmann, 2011.

[Wittgenstein2002] WITTGENSTEIN, Ludwig. *"Philosophical Investigations, Sections 65-78": In Foundations of Cognitive Psychology: Core Readings.* The MIT Press, 2002. pp. 271-276.

[Winston1987] WINSTON, Morton E., CHAFFIN, Roger, and HERRMANN, Douglas. *"A taxonomy of part-whole relations": Cognitive science.* 1987. 417-444.

[Wright2010] WRIGHT, Alex. *"Managing Scientific Inquiry in a Laboratory the Size of the Web": The New York Times.* 2010. `http://www.nytimes.com/2010/12/28/science/28citizen.html` .

[Wu2012] WU, Michael. *The Science of Social: Beyond Hype, Likes, and Followers.* Lithium Technologies, 2012.

[Wynholds2011] WYNHOLDS, Laura. *"Linking to Scientific Data: Identity Problems of Unruly and Poorly Bounded Digital Objects": The International Journal of Digital Curation.* 2011. pp. 214-225.

[Xu2009] XU, Chen, OUYANG, Fenfei, and CHU, Heting. *"The Academic Library Meets Web 2.0: Applications and Implications": The Journal of Academic Librarianship.* 2009. pp. 324-331.

[Yau2011] YAU, Nathan. *Visualize This: The FlowingData Guide to Design, Visualization, and Statistics.* Wiley, 2011.

[Yee2008] YEE, Raymond. *Pro Web 2.0 Mashups: Remixing Data and Web Services.* Apress, 2008.

[Yee2009] YEE, Martha M. *"Can Bibliographic Data Be Put Directly Onto the Semantic Web?": UC Los Angeles, California Digital Library eScholarship.* 2009. `http://escholarship.org/uc/item/91b1830k` .

[Zeithami2001] ZEITHAMI, Valarie A., RUST, Roland T., and LEMON, Katherine N. *"Customer Pyramid: Creating and Serving Profitable Customers": California Management Review.* 2001. pp. 118-142.

[Zhou2003] ZHOU, Rongron and SOMAN, Dilip. *"Looking Back : Exploring the Psychology of Queuing and the Effect of the Number of People Behind": Journal of Consumer Research.* 2003. pp. 517-530.

Glossary

AACR2

Anglo-American Cataloguing Rules

(*http://www.aacr2.org/*)

AAP

Association of American Publishers

(*http://www.publishers.org/*)

AAT

Art and Architecture Thesaurus

(*http://www.getty.edu/research/
tools/vocabularies/aat/*)

aboutness

"Subject matter" organization involves the use of a classification system that provides categories and descriptive terms for indicating what a resource is about. Because they use properties like *aboutness* that are not directly perceived, methods for assigning subject classifications are intellectually-intensive and require rigorous training to be performed consistently and appropriately for the intended users.

absolute synonyms

The strictest definition is that *synonyms* "are words that can replace each other in some class of contexts with insignificant changes of the whole text's meaning."

See also synonym

abstract models

Abstract models describe structures commonly found in resource descriptions and other information resources, regardless of the specific domain.

accessioning

Adding a resource to a library collection is called *acquisition*, but adding to a museum collection is called *accessioning*.

See also acquisition, collection development

accuracy

See precision.

ACM

Association for Computing Machinery

(*http://www.acm.org/*)

acquisition

Adding a resource to a library collection is called *acquisition*, but adding to a museum collection is called *accessioning*.

See also accessioning, collection development

active resources

Active resources create effects or value on their own, sometimes when they initiate interactions with passive resources. Active resources can be people, other living resources, computational agents, active information sources, or web-based services

activities

There are four activities that occur naturally in every *organizing system*; how explicit they are depend on the scope, the breadth or variety of the resources, and the scale, the number of resources that the organizing system encompasses.

See also selecting, organizing, designing resource-based interactions, maintaining

ad hoc category

An **ad hoc category** or goal-derived category is a collection of resources that happen to go together to satisfy a goal. The resources might not have any discernible properties in common.

affordance

The concept of ***affordance***, introduced by J. J. Gibson and then extended and popularized by Donald Norman, captures the idea that physical resources and their environments have inherent actionable properties that determine, in conjunction with an actor's capabilities and cognition, what can be done with the resource.

See also capability

agency

Agency, the extent to which a resource can initiate actions on its own is the third distinction we make about a resource. Another way to express this contrast is between passive resources that are acted upon and active resources that can initiate actions.

agent

We use the more general word, ***agent***, for any entity capable of autonomous and intentional organizing effort, because it treats organizing work done

by people and organizing work done by computers as having common goals, despite obvious differences in methods.

agents

Basically, people and the various groups and organizations with which they identify, whether based on physical, mental, socio-economic, or political characteristics—e.g., "stonemasons" or "socialists."

alias

See synonym.

alphabetical ordering

Alphabetical ordering is arranging resources according to their names.

See also chronological ordering

analytico-synthetic classification

In library science a classification system that builds categories by combination of facets is sometimes also called ***analytico-synthetic***. The most common types of facets are enumerative (mutually exclusive); Boolean (yes or no); hierarchical or taxonomic (logical containment); and spectrum (a range of numerical values).

anchor

See also hypertext

anchor text

In web contexts, the words in which a structural link is embedded are called the *anchor text*.

See also hypertext

ANSI

American National Standards Association

(*http://www.ansi.org/*)

antonymy

Antonymy is the lexical relationship between two words that have opposite meanings. Antonymy is a very salient lexical relationship, and for adjectives it is even more powerful than synonymy.

APA
American Psychiatric Association

(*http://www.psych.org*)

API
Application Programming Interface

appraisal
What is the value of this resource? What is its cost? At what rate does it depreciate? Does it have a shelf life? Does it have any associated ratings, rankings, or quality measures? Moreover, what is the quality of those ratings, rankings and measures?

architectural perspective
The architectural perspective emphasizes the number and abstraction level of the components of a relationship, which together characterize its complexity.

arity
The *degree* or *arity* of a relationship is the number of entity types or categories of resources in the relationship. This is usually, though not always, the same as the number of arguments in the relationship expression.

See also degree

ARPA
Advanced Research Projects Agency

(*http://www.darpa.mil/*)

artifact
See resource.

ASCII
American Standard Code for Information Interchange

American National Standard for Information Systems—Coded Character Sets—7-Bit American National Standard Code for Information Interchange (7-Bit ASCII), ANSI X3.4-1986, American National Standards Institute, Inc., March 26, 1986

asset
See resource.

associated resource
See description resources.

associative array
dictionary

asymmetric relationships
Asymmetric relationships express a one-way relationship from the subject to the object. For example, "is-parent-of."

See also hypertext, directionality one-way link

attribute
Attribute is a synonym for "*property*."

An **attribute** is a syntactic component of XML elements and a conceptual component of the XML Infoset, consisting of a potentially qualified name and a value, whose type may influence its interpretation. The value of an attribute in an XML document is a Unicode string. The value of that attribute in the XML Infoset could be a simple string of text, a precisely-typed numeric or temporal value, a list of references to document nodes, a hypertext link, or a reference to a formal notation.

To **attribute** is to assert or assign a value to a property. See attribution relationship

See also element item

attribution relationship
Asserting or assigning values to properties; the predicate depends on the property: "is-the-author-of," "is-married-to," "is-employed-by," etc.

authentication

Is the resource what it claims to be? (§3.5.3, "Authenticity"). Resource descriptions that can support authentication include technological ones like time stamps, watermarking, encryption, checksums, and digital signatures.

authenticity

In ordinary use we say that something is **authentic** if it can be shown to be, or has come to be accepted as what it claims to be. The importance and nuance of questions about authenticity can be seen in the many words we have to describe the relationship between "the real thing" (the "original") and something else: copy, reproduction, replica, fake, phony, forgery, counterfeit, pretender, imposter, ringer, and so on.

See also provenance

authority control

For bibliographic resources important aspects of vocabulary control include determining the authoritative forms for author names, uniform titles of works, and the set of terms by which a particular subject will be known. In library science, the process of creating and maintaining these standard names and terms is known as **authority control**.

BI

Business Intelligence

bi-directional

See symmetric relationships.

bi-directional links

When a bi-directional link is created between an anchor and a destination, it is as though a one-way link that can be followed in the opposite direction is automatically created. Two one-way links serve the same purpose, but the return link is not automatically established when the first one is created.

See also hypertext, directionality, one-way link

bibliographic description

Bibliographic descriptions characterize information resources and the entities that populate the bibliographic universe, which include works, editions, authors, and subjects. Despite the "biblio-" root, bibliographic descriptions are applied to all of the resource types contained in libraries, not just books. Note also that this definition includes not just the information resources being described as distinct instances, but also as sets of related instances and the nature of those relationships.

bibliography

A **bibliography** is a description resource in the domain of library science.

bibliometrics

Information scientists began studying the structure of scientific citation, now called *bibliometrics*, nearly a century ago to identify influential scientists and publications.

big data

For digital resources, inexpensive storage and high bandwidth have largely eliminated capacity as a constraint for organizing systems, with an exception for *big data*, which is defined as a collection of data that is too big to be managed by typical database software and hardware architectures.

binary antonyms

Contrasting or **binary antonyms** are used in mutually exclusive contexts where one or the other word can be used, but never both. For example, "alive" and "dead" can never be used at the same time to describe the state of some entity, because the meaning of one excludes or contradicts the meaning of the other.

binary link
A **binary link** connects one anchor to one destination.

See also hypertext

BISAC
Book Industry Standards Advisory Committee Classification

BISG
Book Industry Study Group

(*http://www.bisg.org/*)

blob
A **blob** is any resource whose internal structure is functionally opaque for the purpose at hand.

Boolean facet
Take on one of two values, yes (true) or no (false) along some dimension or property.

See also faceted classification

born digital
Resources in organizing systems that are created in digital format are **born digital**. These include resources created by word processors and digital cameras, or by audio and video recorders. Other resources are produced in digital form by "smart things" and by the systems that create digital resources when they interact with barcodes, QR ("quick response") codes, RFID tags, or other mechanisms for tracking identity and location.

BPEL
Business Process Execution Language

(*https://www.oasis-open.org/ committees/tc_home.php?wg_ab brev=wsbpel*)

CAFE
Corporate Average Fuel Economy

http://www.nhtsa.gov/stati cfiles/rulemaking/pdf/cafe/CAFE-GHG_MY_2012-2016_Final_Rule_FR.pdf

capability
Capability is a function of the affordances offered by an *organizing system* and the possible interactions they imply.

See also affordance

capability and compatibility
Will the resource meet functional or interoperability requirements? Technology-intensive resources often have numerous specialized types of descriptions that specify their functions, performance, reliability, and other "-ilities" that determine if they fit in with other resources in an organizing system.

cardinality
The *cardinality* of a relationship is the number of instances that can be associated with each entity type in a relationship.

cataloging
Documenting the contents of library and museum collections to organize them is called *cataloging*

See also collection development

categories
Categories are *equivalence classes*, sets or groups of things or abstract entities that we treat the same.

See also equivalence class

CBS
CBS Corporation and CBS Broadcasting Inc.

(*http://www.cbs.com/*)

CC

Common Cartridge and Learning Tools Interoperability

(*http://www.imsglobal.org/common cartridge.html*)

CDWA

Categories for the Description of Works of Art

(*http://www.getty.edu/research/ publications/electronic_publica tions/cdwa/*)

centrality

The centrality of a resource instance as a member of a category is a measure of how close it is to a mathematical average on some measures or property values that apply to all the members.

CERN

European Organization for Nuclear Research (*Centre Européen de Research Nuclear*)

(*http://public.web.cern.ch/ public/*)

character

Unicode makes the important distinction between *characters* and *glyphs*. A character is the smallest meaningful unit of a written language. In alphabet-based languages like English, characters are letters; in languages like Chinese, characters are ideographs.

character encoding

A notation that has had numbers assigned to its characters is called a *character encoding*.

The most ambitious character coding in existence is Unicode, which as of version 6.0 assigns numbers to 109,449 characters. Unicode makes the important distinction between characters and glyphs.

chronological ordering

Chronological ordering is arranging resources according to the date of their creation or other important event in the lifetime of the resource.

See also alphabetical ordering

CIDR

Classless Inter-Domain Routing

circulation

We might treat **circulation,** borrowing and returning the same item, as one of the interactions with resources that defines a library.

See also collection development

classes

In object-oriented programming languages, *classes* are schemas that serve as templates for the creation of objects. A class in a programming language is analogous to a database schema that specifies the structure of its member instances, in that the class definition specifies how instances of the class are constructed in terms of data types and possible values. Programming classes may also specify whether data in a member object can be accessed, and if so, how.

classical categories

Categories defined by necessary and sufficient properties are also called *monothetic*. They are also sometimes called *classical categories* because they conform to Aristotle's theory of how categories are used in logical deduction using syllogisms.

classification

The systematic assignment of resources to a system of intentional categories, often institutional ones

Classification is applied categorization – the assignment of resources to a system of categories, called classes, using a predetermined set of principles.

See also inclusion

classification scheme
See classifications

classifications
A system of categories and its attendant rules or access methods are typically called a **classification scheme** or just the **classifications**. A system of categories captures the distinctions and relationships among its resources that are most important in a domain and for a particular context of use, creating a reference model or conceptual roadmap for its users.

classifying
When we make an assertion that a particular instance is a member of class, we are **classifying** the instance.

class inclusion
is the fundamental and familiar "**is-a,**" "**is-a-type-of,**" or "**subset**" relationship between two entity types or classes where one is contained in and thus more specific than the other more generic one.

See also inclusion

clustering
Clustering techniques share the goal of creating meaningful categories from a collection of items whose properties are hard to directly perceive and evaluate; this is especially true with large collections of heterogeneous documents, where goals might be to find categories of documents with the same topics, genre, sentiment, or other characteristic that cannot easily be reduced to specific property tests.

The end result of clustering is a statistically optimal set of categories in which the similarity of all the items within a category is larger than the similarity of items that belong to different categories.

collection
A **collection** is a group of resources that have been selected for some purpose. Similar terms are set (mathematics), aggregation (data modeling), dataset (science and business), and corpus (linguistics and literary analysis).

collection development
Libraries and museums usually make their *selection* principles explicit in **collection development** policies. Adding a resource to a library collection is called **acquisition**, but adding to a museum collection is called **accessioning**. Documenting the contents of library and museum collections to organize them is called **cataloging**. **Circulation** is a central interaction in libraries, but because museum resources don't circulate the primary interactions for museum users are **viewing** or **visiting** the collection. *Maintenance* activities are usually described as **preservation** or *curation*.

collocation
The Organizing System for a small collection can sometimes use only the minimal or default organizing principle of **collocation**—putting all the resources in the same container, on the same shelf, or in the same email inbox.

compliance
Compliance is a maintenance activity.

component-object inclusion
Component-Object is the relationship type when the part is a separate component that is arranged or assembled with other components to create a larger resource.

See also inclusion

compounding
> **Compounding** is putting two "free" morphemes together.

constraint
> A constraint is a limit or bound on a data type or structure, most usefully expressed in a schema or regular expression. Constraints on data types and structures can be expressed in a variety of natural, programming and schema languages with varying degrees of efficacy.

content rules
> *Content rules* are similar to controlled vocabularies because they also limit the possible values that can be used in descriptions. Instead of specifying a fixed set of values, content rules typically restrict descriptions by requiring them to be of a particular data type (integer, Boolean, Date, and so on).

contextual properties
> *Contextual properties* are those related to the situation or context in which a resource is described. Dey defines context as "any information that characterizes a situation related to the interactions between users, applications, and the surrounding environment."

controlled vocabulary
> One way to encourage good names for a given resource domain or task is to establish a **controlled vocabulary**. A *controlled vocabulary* can be thought of as a fixed or closed dictionary that includes all the terms that can be used in a particular domain. A controlled vocabulary shrinks the number of words used, reducing synonymy and homonymy and eliminating undesirable associations, leaving behind a set of words with precisely defined meanings and rules governing their use.

coverage
> The values of a facet should be able of classifying all instances within the intended scope.

CRM
> Customer Relationship Management

crosswalk
> Similar to mapping, a straightforward approach to transformation is the use of *crosswalks*, which are equivalence tables that relate resource description elements, semantics, and writing systems from one organizing system to those of another.

cultural categories
> *Cultural categories* are the archetypical form of categories upon which individual and institutional categories are usually based. Cultural categories tend to describe our everyday experiences of the world and our accumulated cultural knowledge.

cultural properties
> **Cultural properties** derive from conventional language or culture, often by analogy, because they can be highly evocative and memorable.

curation
> **Curation** is a maintenance activity.

> *Curation* usually refers to the methods or systems that add value to and preserve resources, while the concept of *governance* more often emphasizes the institutions or organizations that carry out those activities. The former is most often used for libraries, museums, or archives and the latter for enterprise or inter-enterprise contexts.

> See also collection development

data activities
> **Data** capture, extraction and generation are resource selection activities.

Data cleaning and cleansing are maintenance activities.

Data insertion and integration add resources to a collection.

data rot

Data rot is a colloquial term intended to convey the fact that the physical medium of a digital resource deteriorates over time.

data schema

Data schemas that specify data entities, elements, identifiers, attributes, and relationships in databases and XML document types on the transactional end of the Document Type Spectrum (§3.2.1) are implementations of the categories needed for the design, development and maintenance of information organization systems. Like the classical model of categorization, data schemas tend to rigidly define resources.

DC

Dublin Core

(*http://dublincore.org/documents/dcmi-terms/*)

DCMI

Dublin Core Metadata Initiative

(*http://dublincore.org/*)

DDC

Dewey Decimal Classification

(*http://www.oclc.org/dewey/*)

decision tree

The most direct way to implement classical categories is as a *decision tree*. A simple decision tree is an algorithm for determining a decision by making a sequence of logical or property tests.

decoding

A digital resource is first a sequence of bits. Decoding transforms those bits into characters according to the encoding scheme used, extracting the text from its stored form (see §8.3.1, "Notations").

degree

The *degree* or *arity* of a relationship is the number of entity types or categories of resources in the relationship. This is usually, though not always, the same as the number of arguments in the relationship expression.

derivational morphology

Derivational morphology deals with how words are created by combining morphemes.

description resources

Any primary resource can have one or more description resources associated with it to facilitate finding, interacting with, or interpreting the primary one. Description resources are essential in organizing systems where the primary resources are not under its control and can only be accessed or interacted with through the description. Description resources are often called **metadata**.

Description resources, such as physical or online catalog records, describe the *primary resources* that comprise the collection.

descriptor

In the library science context of "bibliographic description," a *descriptor* is one of the terms in a carefully designed language that can be assigned to a resource to designate its properties, characteristics, or meaning, or its relationships with other resources.

designed resource access policies

Designed resource access policies are established by the designer or operator of an organizing system to satisfy internally generated requirements.

designing resource-based interactions
Designing and implementing the actions, functions or services that make use of the resources.

DFR
Divergence From Randomness

dictionary
A dictionary is a set of property-value pairs or *entries*. It is a set of entries, not a list of entries, because the pairs are not ordered and because each entry must have a unique key.

Note that this specialized meaning of "dictionary" is different from the more common meaning of "dictionary" as an alphabetized list of terms accompanied by sentences that define them.

digitization
Because tangible things can only be in one place at a time, many Organizing Systems—like that in the modern library with online catalogs and physical collections—resolve this constraint by creating digital proxies or surrogates to organize their tangible resources, or create parallel digital resources like digitized books.

directionality
The *directionality* of a relationship defines the order in which the arguments of the relationship are connected. A *one-way* or *uni-directional* relationship can be followed in only one direction, whereas a *bi-directional* one can be followed in both directions.

See also hypertext, directionality, one-way link, bi-directional

discipline
A **discipline** is an integrated field of study in which there is some level of agreement about the issues and problems that deserve study, how they are interrelated, how they should be studied, and how findings or theories about the issues and problems should be evaluated.

discovery
What resources are available that might be added to a collection? New resources are often listed in directories, registries, or catalogs. Some types of resources are selected and acquired automatically through subscriptions or, contracts.

DNA
Deoxyribonucleic Acid

DNS
Domain Name System

(*http://tools.ietf.org/html/rfc1035*)

document
See resource.

document frequency
Inverse document frequency (idf) is a collection-level property. The ***document frequency*** (df) is the number of resources containing a particular term. The inverse document frequency (idf) for a term is defined as $idf_t = \log(N/df_t)$, where N is the total number of documents. The inverse document frequency of a term decreases the more documents contain the term, providing a discriminating factor for the importance of terms in a query.

DOI
Digital Object Identifier

(*http://www.doi.org*)

domain
Every resource has some essence or type that distinguishes it from other resources, which we call the resource ***domain***. Domain is an intuitive notion that we can help define by contrasting it with the alternative of *ad hoc* or arbitrary groupings of resources that just happen to be in the same place at

some moment, rather than being based on natural or intrinsic characteristics.

DPLA

Digital Public Library of America

`http//dp.la/`

DRM

Digital Rights Management

DSM

Diagnostic and Statistical Manual of Mental Disorders

(`http://www.dsm5.org/`)

DTD

Document Type Definition

ECM

Enterprise Content Management

edge

See tree.

EDI

Electronic Data Interchange

Typically refers to one or all of the UN/EDIFACT, ANSI ASC X12, TRAD-COMS and ODETTE standards.

EDM

Enterprise Data Management

effectivity

Many resources, or their properties, also have ***effectivity***, meaning that they come into effect at a particular time and will almost certainly cease to be effective at some future date. Effectivity is sometimes known as time-to-live and it is generally expressed as a range of two dates. It consists of a date on which the resource is effective, and optionally a date on which the resource ceases to be effective, or becomes stale.

element item

An element item has a set of attribute items, and a list of child nodes. These child nodes may include other element items, or they may be character items.

encoding scheme

An ***encoding scheme*** is a specialized *writing system* or syntax for particular types of values.

energy facet

The action or activity of the thing. One of Ranganathan's universal facets in colon classification.

entity

See resource.

entity type

See classes

enumeration

The simplest principle for creating a category is ***enumeration***; any resource in a finite or countable set can be deemed a category member by that fact alone.

See also extensional definition.

enumerative classification

Classification schemes in which all possible categories to which resources can be assigned are defined explicitly are **enumerative**.

enumerative facets

Have mutually exclusive possible values.

equivalence class

See categories

equivalence relationship

Any relationship that is both symmetric and transitive is an *equivalence* relationship; "is-equal-to" is obviously an equivalence relationship because if A=B then B=A and if A=B and B=C, then A=C. Other relationships can be equivalent without meaning "exactly equal," as is the relationship of "is-congruent-to" for all triangles.

ERP
Enterprise Resource Planning

ETL
Extract, Transform, and Load

EXIF
Exchangeable Image File Format

(*http://www.exif.org/*)

expression
The distinctions put forth by Lubetzky, Svenonius and other library science theorists have evolved today into a four-step abstraction hierarchy (illustrated in Figure 3.5, "The Abstraction Hierarchy for Identifying Resources.") between the abstract *work*, an *expression* in multiple formats or genres, a particular *manifestation* in one of those formats or genres, and a specific physical *item*.

extensibility of classification
See flexibility

extension
See extensional definition

extensional definition
The simplest principle for creating a category is *enumeration*; any resource in a finite or countable set can be deemed a category member by that fact alone. This principle is also known as *extensional definition*, and the members of the set are called the *extension*.

faceted classification
In a faceted classification system, each resource is described using properties from multiple facets, but an agent searching for resources does not need to consider all of the properties (and consequently the facets) and does not need to consider them in a fixed order, which an enumerative hierarchical classification requires.

family resemblance
Sharing some but not all properties is akin to **family resemblances** among the category members.

FCC
Federal Communications Commission

(*http://www.fcc.gov/*)

FDA
Food and Drug Administration

(*http://www.fda.gov/*)

feature-activity inclusion
Feature-Activity is a relationship type in which the components are stages, phases, or sub activities that take place over time. This relationship is similar to component-object in that the components in the whole are arranged according to a structure or pattern.

See also inclusion

FERPA
Family Educational Rights and Privacy Act

(*http://www2.ed.gov/policy/gen/guid/fpco/ferpa/*)

finding
What resources are available that "correspond to the user's stated search criteria" and thus can satisfy an information need? Before there were online catalogs and digital libraries, we found resources by referencing catalogs of printed resource descriptions incorporating the title, author, and subject terms as access points into the collection; the subject descriptions were the most important finding aids when the user had no particular resource in mind. Modern users accept that computerized indexing makes search possible over not only the entire description resource, but often over the entire content of the primary resource.

flexibility of classification

A related principle about maintaining classifications over time is **flexibility**, the degree to which the classification can accommodate new categories. Computer scientists typically describe this principle as **extensibility**, and library scientists sometimes describe it as **hospitality**.

FOAF

Friend of a Friend

(*http://www.foaf-project.org/*)

focus

The contrast between primary resources and description resources is very useful in many contexts, but when we look more broadly at organizing systems, it is often difficult to distinguish them, and determining which resources are primary and which are metadata is often just a decision about which resource is currently the **focus** of our attention.

fonds

The "original order" of the resources in an archive embodies the implicit or explicit Organizing System of the person or entity that created the documents and it is treated as an essential part of the meaning of the collection. As a result, the unit of organization for archival collections is the *fonds*—the original arrangement or grouping, preserving any hierarchy of boxes, folders, envelopes, and individual documents—and thus they are not reorganized according to other (perhaps more systematic) classifications.

font

A *font* is a collection of glyphs used to depict some set of characters. A Unicode font explicitly associates each glyph with a particular number in the Unicode character encoding.

form

We treat the set of implementation decisions about character notations, syntax, and structure as the *form* of resource description

format

Information resources can exist in numerous **formats** with the most basic format distinction being whether the resource is physical or digital.

FRAD

Functional Requirements for Authority Data

(*http://www.ifla.org/publica tions/functional-requirements- for-authority-data*)

framework

A *framework* is a set of concepts that provide the basic structure for understanding a domain, enabling a common vocabulary for different explanatory theories.

FRBR

Functional Requirements for Bibliographic Records

(*http://www.ifla.org/publica tions/functional-requirements- for-bibliographic-records*)

frequency of use principle

Some organization emerges implicitly through a *frequency of use* principle. In your kitchen or clothes closet, the resources you use most often migrate to the front because that is the easiest place to return them after using them.

FRSAD

Functional Requirements for Subject Authority Data

(*http://www.ifla.org/files/ assets/classification-and- indexing/functional- requirements-for-subject-*

authority-data/frsad-final-report.pdf)

FTC

Federal Trade Commission

(*http://www.ftc.gov/*)

FTP

File Transfer Protocol

(*http://tools.ietf.org/html/rfc959*)

globally unique identifier (GUID)

A **globally unique identifier** (or GUID), is an identifier that will never be the same as another identifier in any organizing system anywhere else.

glyph

A specific mark that can be used to depict a character is a glyph.

See also character, font

governance

Curation usually refers to the methods or systems that add value to and preserve resources, while the concept of **governance** more often emphasizes the institutions or organizations that carry out those activities. The former is most often used for libraries, museums, or archives and the latter for enterprise or inter-enterprise contexts.

GPS

Global Positioning System

(*http://www.schriever.af.mil/GPS/*)

grammar

The **syntax** and **grammar** of a language consists of the rules that determine which combinations of its words are allowed and are thus grammatical or **well-formed.** Natural languages differ immensely in how they arrange nouns, verbs, adjectives, and other parts of speech to create sentences.

granularity

Granularity refers to the level of detail or precision for a specific information resource property. For instance, the postal address of a particular location might be represented as several different data items, including the number, street name, city, state, country and postal code (a high granularity model). It might also be represented in one single line including all of the information above (a low granularity model).

graph

Like a *tree*, a *graph* consists of a set of nodes connected by edges. These edges may or may not have a direction (§5.6.3, "Directionality"). If they do, the graph is referred to as a "directed graph." If a graph is directed, it may be possible to start at a node and follow edges in a path that leads back to the starting node. Such a path is called a "cycle." If a directed graph has no cycles, it is referred to as an "acyclic graph."

GUID

Globally Unique Identifier

HHS

US Department of Health and Human Services

(*http://www.hhs.gov/*)

hierarchical classification

When multiple resource properties are considered in a fixed sequence, each property creates another level in the system of categories and the classification scheme is **hierarchical** or **taxonomic**.

hierarchical facet

Organize resources by logical inclusion (§5.3.1.1).

See also inclusion

HIPAA
Health Insurance Portability and Accountability Act

(*http://www.hhs.gov/ocr/privacy/ hipaa/understanding/*

homographs
When two words are spelled the same but have different meanings they are **homographs**; if they are also pronounced the same they are ***homonyms***. If the different meanings of the homographs are related, they are called ***polysemes***.

homonyms
Homonyms are homographs that are pronounced the same.

hospitality of classification
See flexibility

HR
Human Resources

HTML
HyperText Markup Language

(*http://www.w3.org/community/ webed/wiki/HTML/Specifications*)

HTTP
Hypertext Transfer Protocol

(*http://www.w3.org/Protocols/*)

hypernym
When words encode the semantic distinctions expressed by class inclusion, the word for the more specific class in this relationship is called the *hyponym*, while the word for the more general class to which it belongs is called the *hypernym*.

hypertext
Hypertext expresses relationships among resources. Hypertext is "a provision whereby any item may be caused at will to select immediately and automatically another." It can be used to create non-sequential narratives that gives choices to readers.

The field is vast and we would perform a disservice by attempting to summarize here. Instead, we can advise you that, within this text, we discuss hypertext as it has been practically applied by contemporary practitioners, using SGML, HTML, XML and RDF surface syntaxes to host a wide variety of link types.

hypertext link
The concept of read-only or follow-only structures that connect one document to another is usually attributed to Vannevar Bush in his seminal 1945 essay titled "As We May Think." Bush called it "associative indexing," defined as "a provision whereby any item may be caused at will to select immediately and automatically another."

hyponym
When words encode the semantic distinctions expressed by class inclusion, the word for the more specific class in this relationship is called the *hyponym*, while the word for the more general class to which it belongs is called the *hypernym*.

IAU
International Astronomical Union

(*http://www.iau.org/*)

IBM
International Business Machines

(*http://www.ibm.com*)

ICANN
Internet Corporation for Assigned Names and Numbers

(*http://www.icann.org/*)

ICD-10-CM
International Classification of Diseases, Tenth Revision, Clinical Modification

(*http://www.cdc.gov/nchs/icd/
icd10cm.htm*)

identifier

An ***identifier*** is a special kind of name assigned in a controlled manner and governed by rules that define possible values and naming conventions.

identifying

Another purpose of resource description is to enable a user to confirm the identity of a specific resource or to distinguish among several that have some overlapping descriptions. In bibliographic contexts this might mean finding the resource that is identified by its citation. Computer processable resource descriptions like bar codes, QR codes, or RFID tags are also used to identify resources. In Semantic Web contexts, URIs serve this purpose.

identity

When some thing or things are treated as a single resource this establishes an identity.

IEEE

Institute of Electrical and Electronics Engineers

(*http://www.ieee.org/index.html*)

IETF

Internet Engineering Task Force

(*http://ietf.org*)

IFLA

International Federation of Library Associations and Institutions

(*http://www.ifla.org/*)

IHTSDO

International Health Terminology Standards Development Organization

(*http://www.ihtsdo.org/*)

implementation perspective

The implementation perspective considers how the relationship is implemented in a particular notation and syntax and the manner in which relationships are arranged and stored in some technology environment.

implicit classification

Because names and dates can take on a great many values, an organizing principle like *alphabetical* or *chronological* ordering is unlikely to enumerate in advance an explicit category for each possible value. Instead, we can consider these organizing principles as creating an **implicit or latent** classification system in which the categories are generated only as needed. For example, the Q category only exists in an alphabetical scheme if there is a resource whose name starts with Q.

imposed policies

Imposed Policies are mandated by an external entity and the organizing system must comply with them.

inclusion relationship

One entity type contains or is comprised of other entity types; often expressed using "is-a," "is-a-type-of," "is-part-of," or "is-in" predicates.

See also component-object, feature-activity inclusion, locative, member-collection, meronymic, part-whole, phase-activity, place-area, portion-mass, stuff-object, temporal, topological, taxonomy and classification

See Also component-object inclusion.

index

An ***index*** is a *description resource* that contains information about the locations and frequencies of terms in a document *collection* to enable it to be searched efficiently.

individual categorization

Individual categories are created in an organizing system to satisfy the *ad hoc* requirements that arise from a person's unique experiences, preferences, and resource collections. Unlike cultural categories, which usually develop slowly and last a long time, individual categories are created by intentional activity, in response to a specific situation, or to solve an emerging organizational challenge.

inflectional morphology
Inflectional mechanisms change the form of a word to represent tense, aspect, agreement, or other grammatical information. Unlike derivation, inflection never changes the part-of-speech of the base morpheme. The **inflectional morphology** of English is relatively simple compared with other languages.

information architecture
Abstract patterns of information content or organization are sometimes called architectures, so it is straightforward from the perspective of the discipline of organizing to define the activity of **Information Architecture** as **designing an abstract and effective organization of information and then exposing that organization to facilitate navigation and information use**.

instance
See resource.

institutional semantics
Systems of **institutional semantics** offer precisely defined abstractions or information components (§3.3.3, "Identity and Information Components") needed to ensure that information can be efficiently exchanged and used.

institutional taxonomies
Institutional taxonomies are classifications designed to make it more likely that people or computational

agents will organize and interact with resources in the same way. Among the thousands of standards published by the *International Organization for Standardization (ISO)* are many institutional taxonomies that govern the classification of resources and products in agriculture, aviation, construction, energy, healthcare, information technology, transportation, and almost every other industry sector.

integration
Integration is the controlled sharing of information between two (or more) business systems, applications, or services within or between firms. Integration means that one party can extract or obtain information from another one, it does not imply that the recipient can make use of the information.

integrity of classification
Changes in the meaning of the categories in a classification threaten its **integrity**, the principle that categories should not move within the structure of the classification system.

intension
Categories whose members are determined by one or more properties or rules follow the principle of **intensional definition**, and the defining properties are called the **intension**.

intensional definition
Categories whose members are determined by one or more properties or rules follow the principle of **intensional definition**, and the defining properties are called the **intension**.

intentional arrangement
Intentional arrangement emphasizes explicit or implicit acts of organization by people, or by computational processes acting as proxies for, or as implementations of, human intention-

ality. Intentional arrangement excludes naturally-occurring patterns created by physical, geological, biological or genetic processes.

interaction

An **interaction** is an action, function, service, or capability that makes use of the resources in a collection or the collection as a whole. The interaction of **access** is fundamental in any collection of resources, but many Organizing Systems provide additional functions to make access more efficient and to support additional interactions with the accessed resources. For example, libraries and similar Organizing Systems implement catalogs to enable interactions for **finding** a known resource, **identifying** any resource in the collection, and discriminating or **selecting** among similar resources.

interoperability

Interoperability goes beyond integration to mean that systems, applications, or services that exchange information can make sense of what they receive. Interoperability can involve identifying corresponding components and relationships in each system, transforming them syntactically to the same format, structurally to the same granularity, and semantically to the same meaning.

intrinsic meaning interpretation

One of Panofsky's three levels of description for artistic resources. At this level, context and deeper understanding come into play—including what the creator of the description knows about the situation in which the work was created. Why, for example, did this particular artist create this particular depiction of *The Last Supper* in this way? Panofsky posited that professional art historians are needed here, because they are the ones with the education and background necessary to draw meaning from a work.

inverse document frequency

Inverse document frequency (idf) is a collection-level property. The ***document frequency*** (df) is the number of resources containing a particular term. The inverse document frequency (idf) for a term is defined as $idf_t = \log(N/df_t)$, where N is the total number of documents. The inverse document frequency of a term decreases the more documents contain the term, providing a discriminating factor for the importance of terms in a query.

inverse relationship

For asymmetric relationships, it is often useful to be explicit about the meaning of the relationship when the order of the arguments in the relationship is reversed. The resulting relationship is called the ***inverse*** or the converse of the first relationship.

IRB

Institutional Review Board

(*http://www.thehastingscenter.org/Publications/IRB/*)

ISBN

International Standard Book Number

(*http://www.isbn.org/*)

ISO

International Organization for Standardization

(*http://www.iso.org/iso/*)

item

The distinctions put forth by Lubetzky, Svenonius and other library science theorists have evolved today into a four-step abstraction hierarchy (illustrated in Figure 3.5, "The Abstraction Hierarchy for Identifying Resources.") between the abstract ***work***, an ***expression*** in multiple formats or genres, a particular *manifestation* in one of those formats or genres, and a specific physical *item*.

See also resource

ITIL
Information Technology Infrastructure Library

(*http://www.itil-officialsite.com/*)

JavaScript Object Notation (JSON)
JavaScript Object Notation (JSON) is a textual format for exchanging data that borrows its metamodel from the JavaScript programming language. Specifically, the JSON metamodel consists of two kinds of structures found in JavaScript: lists (called *arrays* in JavaScript) and dictionaries (called *objects* in JavaScript). Lists and dictionaries contain values, which may be strings of text, numbers, Booleans (true or false), or the null (empty) value. Again, these types of values are taken directly from JavaScript. Lists and dictionaries can be values too, meaning lists and dictionaries can be nested within one another to produce more complex structures such as tables and trees.

JPEG
Joint Photographic Experts Group

(*http://www.jpeg.org/*)

JSON
JavaScript Object Notation

(*http://www.json.org/*)

KFC
Kentucky Fried Chicken

(*http://www.kfc.com/*)

KM
Knowledge Management

KMS
Knowledge Management System

knowledge management systems (KMS)
Knowledge management systems (KMS) are a type of business organizing system whose goal is to capture and systematize these information resources.

LCC
Library of Congress Classification

(*http://www.loc.gov/catdir/cpso/lcc.html*)

learns
See machine learning.

lexical gap
A lexical gap in a language exists when it lacks a word for a concept that is expressed as a word in another language.

lexical perspective
The lexical perspective focuses on how the conceptual description of a relationship is expressed using words in a specific language.

linguistic relativity
Languages differ a great deal in the words they contain and also in more fundamental ways that they require speakers or writers to attend to details about the world or aspects of experience that another language allows them to ignore. This idea is often described as *linguistic relativity*.

link
See hypertext link

link base
A **link base** is a collection of links stored separately from the resources that they link.

link type
When it is evident, this semantic property of the link is called the *link type.*

list

A *list*, like a *set*, is a collection of items with an additional constraint: their items are *ordered*.

literary warrant

The principle of **literary warrant** holds that a classification must be based only on the specific resources that are being classified.

LM

Language Model

LMS

Learning Management System

loading

Adding resources to a collection.

LOC

Library of Congress

(*http://www.loc.gov*)

LOC-CN

Library of Congress Call Number

LOC-SH

Library of Congress Subject Headings

locative inclusion

Locative inclusion is a type of inclusion relationship between an area and what it surrounds or contains. It is most often expressed using "is-in" as the relationship. However, the entity that is contained or surrounded is not a part of the including one, so this is not a part-whole relationship.

See also inclusion

logical hierarchy

If multiple resource properties are considered in a fixed order, the resulting arrangement forms a *logical hierarchy*.

machine learning

Machine learning is a subfield of computer science that develops and applies algorithms that accomplish tasks that are not explicitly programmed; creating categories and assigning items to them is an important subset of machine learning. Two subfields of machine learning that are particularly relevant to organizing systems are **supervised** and **unsupervised** learning.

MADS

Metadata Authority Description Standard

(*http://www.loc.gov/standards/ mads/*)

maintaining

Managing and adapting the resources and the organization imposed on them as needed to support the interactions.

manifestation

The distinctions put forth by Lubetzky, Svenonius and other library science theorists have evolved today into a four-step abstraction hierarchy (illustrated in Figure 3.5, "The Abstraction Hierarchy for Identifying Resources.") between the abstract **work**, an **expression** in multiple formats or genres, a particular **manifestation** in one of those formats or genres, and a specific physical **item**.

MARC

Machine-Readable Cataloging

(*http://www.loc.gov/marc/*)

map

See dictionary

markup

Markup is an encoding of character content with a layer of intentional coding, typically by surrounding the character text with "pointy brackets" or tags whose name suggests a content type, structural role, or formatting.

materiality

It is the requirement to recognize the **materiality** of the environment that enables people to create and interact with digital resources

materials facet
Concerned with the actual substance of which a work is made, like "metal" or "bleach." "Materials" differ from "Physical Attributes" in that the latter is more abstract than the former.

matter facet
The constituent material of the thing. One of Ranganathan's universal facets in colon classification.

member-collection inclusion
Member-Collection is the part-whole relationship type where "is-part-of" means "belongs-to," a weaker kind of association than component-object because there is no assumption that the component has a specific role or function in the whole.

See also inclusion

meronymic inclusion
See part-whole

See also inclusion

MeSH
Medical Subject Headings

(*http://www.nlm.nih.gov/mesh/*)

metadata
Metadata is often defined as "data about data," a definition that is nearly as ubiquitous as it is unhelpful. A more content-full definition of metadata is that it is structured description for information resources of any kind, which makes it a superset of *bibliographic description*.

See also description resources

metamodels
When common sets of design decisions can be identified that are not specific to any one domain, they often become systematized in textbooks and in design practices, and may eventually be designed into standard formats and architectures for creating organizing systems. These formally recognized sets of design decisions are known as ***abstract models*** or ***metamodels***. Metamodels describe structures commonly found in resource descriptions and other information resources, regardless of the specific domain.

metonymy
Part-whole or meronymic semantic relationships have lexical analogues in *metonomy*, when an entity is described by something that is contained in or otherwise part of it.

mixed content
Mixed content distinguishes XML from other data representation languages. It is this structural feature, combined with the fact that child nodes in the XML Infoset (§8.2.2.2) are ordered, that makes it possible for XML documents to function both as human reader-oriented, textual documents and as structured data formats. It allows us to use natural language in writing descriptions while still enabling us to identify content by type by embedding markup to enclose "semantic nuggets" in otherwise undifferentiated text.

monothetic categories
Monothetic categories are defined by necessary and sufficient properties.

See classical categories

morphemes
See morphology

morphology
The basic building blocks for words are called *morphemes* and can express semantic concepts (when they are called *root words*) or abstract concepts like "pastness" or "plural"). The

analysis of the ways by which languages combine *morphemes* is called *morphology*.

MPAA

Motion Picture Association of America

(*http://www.mpaa.org/*)

n-ary links

n-ary links connect one anchor to multiple types of destinations.

NAICS

North American Industry Classification System

(*http://www.census.gov/eos/www/naics/*)

name

A **name** is a label for a resource that is used to distinguish one from another.

name matching

In organizing systems that contain data, there are numerous tools for "name matching," the task of determining when two different text strings denote the same person, object, or other named entity.

namespace

We can prevent or reduce identifier collisions by adding information about the **namespace**, the domain from which the names or identifiers are selected, thus creating what are often called **qualified names**.

NAPO

National Association of Professional Organizers

(*http://www.napo.net/*)

navigation

If users are not able to specify their information needs in a way that the "finding" functionality requires, they should be able to use relational and structural descriptions among the resources to navigate from any resource to other ones that might be better. Svenonius emphasizes generalization, aggregation, and derivational relationships.

NCHS

National Center for Health Statistics

(*http://www.cdc.gov/nchs/*)

NCSA

National Center for Supercomputing Applications

(*http://www.ncsa.illinois.edu/*)

NFL

National Football League

(*http://www.nfl.com/*)

NIH

National Institute of Health

(*http://www.nih.gov/*)

NIST

National Institute of Standards and Technology

(*http://www.nist.gov/*)

NLP

Natural Language Processing

node

Nodes are objects in an entity-relationship system.

In the RDF metamodel, a pair of nodes and its edge is called a **triple**, because it consists of three parts (two nodes and one edge). The RDF metamodel is a directed graph, so it identifies one node (the one from which the edge is pointing) as the **subject** of the triple, and the other node (the one to which the edge is pointing) as its **object**. The edge is referred to as the **predicate** or (as we have been saying) *property* of the triple.

notation

> A **notation** a set of characters with distinct forms.
>
> The Latin alphabet is a notation, as are Arabic numerals. Some more exotic notations include alchemical symbols and the symbols used for editorial markup.

NSF

> National Science Foundation
>
> (*http://www.nsf.gov/*)

OASIS

> Organization for the Advancement of Structured Information Standards
>
> (*https://www.oasis-open.org/*)

object

> In the RDF metamodel, a pair of nodes and its edge is called a ***triple***, because it consists of three parts (two nodes and one edge). The RDF metamodel is a directed graph, so it identifies one node (the one from which the edge is pointing) as the ***subject*** of the triple, and the other node (the one to which the edge is pointing) as its ***object***. The edge is referred to as the ***predicate*** or (as we have been saying) *property* of the triple.
>
> See also: resource

object warrant

> The principle of **literary warrant** holds that a classification must be based only on the specific resources that are being classified.

objectivity

> Although every classification has an explicit or implicit bias (§7.2.3, "Classification Is Biased"), facets and facet values should be as unambiguous and concrete as possible to enable reliable classification of instances.

objects facet

> The largest facet, "Objects" contains the actual works, like "sandcastles" and "screen prints."

obtaining

> Physical resources often require significant effort to obtain after they have been selected. Catching a bus or plane involves coordinating your current location and time with the time and location the resource is available. With information resources in physical form, obtaining a selected resource usually meant a walk through the library stacks. With digital information resources, a search engine returns a list of the identifiers of resources that can be accessed with just another click, so it takes little effort to go from selecting among the query results to obtaining the corresponding primary resource.

OCAD

> Ontario College of Art and Design
>
> (*http://www.ocadu.ca/*)

OCLC

> Online Computer Library Center
>
> (*http://www.oclc.org/*)

OECD

> Organization for Economic Cooperation and Development
>
> (*http://www.oecd.org/*)

OMG

> Object Management Group
>
> (*http://www.omg.org/*)

one-way

> Allowing physical or conceptual movement in one direction only.

one-way link

> A **one-way link** asserts a link from a resource to one or more resources. A one-way link does not imply a link in

the return direction, or among the target resources.

See also hypertext

See also directionality

ONIX
ONline Information eXchange

(*http://www.editeur.org/8/ONIX*)

ontology
Ontology is a branch of philosophy concerned with what exists in reality and the general features and relations of whatever that might be. Computer science has adopted ontology to refer to any computer-processable resource that represents the relationships among words and meanings in some knowledge domain.

organize
To *organize* is **to create capabilities by intentionally imposing order and structure.**

organizing
Specifying the principles or rules that will be followed to arrange the resources.

organizing principles
Organizing principles are directives for the design or arrangement of a *collection* of resources that are ideally expressed in a way that does not assume any particular implementation or realization.

organizing system
Organizing System: **an intentionally arranged collection of resources and the interactions they support.**

orthogonality
Facets should be independent dimensions, so a resource can have values of all of them while only having one value on each of them.

OWL
Web Ontology Language

(*http://www.w3.org/TR/owl2-overview/*)

part-whole inclusion
Part-whole inclusion or *meronymic inclusion* is a second type of inclusion relationship. It is usually expressed using "is-part-of," "is-partly," or with other similar predicate expressions.

See also inclusion

passive resources
Passive resources are usually tangible and static and thus they become valuable only as a result of some action or interaction with them.

PDF
Portable Document Format

(*http://www.adobe.com/products/acrobat/adobepdf.html*)

persistence
Persistence is the quality of resisting change over time.

personality facet
The type of thing. One of Ranganathan's universal facets in colon classification.

phase-activity inclusion
Phase-Activity is similar to *feature-activity* except that the phases do not make sense as standalone activities without the context provided by the activity as a whole.

See also inclusion

physical attributes facet
Material characteristics that can be measured and perceived, like "height" and "flexibility."

PIM
Personal Information Management

place-area inclusion

Place-Area relationships exist between areas and specific places or locations within them. Like members of collections, places have no particular functional contribution to the whole.

See also inclusion

polysemes

If the different meanings of the homographs are related, they are called **polysemes**.

polysemy

Polysemy is the linguistic term for words with multiple meanings or senses.

polythetic

Categories defined by family resemblance or multiple and shifting property sets are termed **polythetic**.

POP

Post Office Protocol

(*https://tools.ietf.org/html/ rfc1939*)

portion-mass inclusion

Portion-Mass is the relationship type when all the parts are similar to each other and to the whole.

See also inclusion

possession relationship

Asserting ownership or control of a resource; often expressed using a "has" predicate, such as "has-serial-number-plate."

precision

Precision measures the *accuracy* of a result set, that is, how many of the retrieved resources for a query are relevant.

predicate

A *predicate* is a verb phrase template for specifying properties of objects or a relationship among objects.

PREMIS

Preservation Metadata Implementation Strategies

(*http://www.loc.gov/standards/ premis/*)

preservation

Preservation is a maintenance activity.

See also curation, collection development

preservation metadata

Preservation metadata is technical information about resource formats and technology needed to ensure resource and collection integrity in a maintenance context.

primary resource

Treating as a ***primary resource*** anything that can be identified is an important generalization of the concept because it enables web-based services, data feeds, objects with RFID tags, sensors or other "smart devices" or computational agents to be part of Organizing Systems.

primary subject matter

One of Panofsky's three levels of description for artistic resources. At this level, we describe the most basic elements of a work in a generic way that would be recognizable by anyone regardless of expertise or training. The painting *The Last Supper*, for example, might be described as "13 people having dinner."

property

In this book we use "property" in a generic and ordinary sense as a synonym for "feature" or "characteristic." Many cognitive and computer scientists are more precise in defining these terms and reserve "property" for binary predicates (e.g., something is red or not, round or not, and so on).

If multiple values are possible, the "property" is called an "attribute," "dimension," or "variable."

property-based categorization

Property-based categorization works tautologically well for categories like "prime number" where the category is defined by necessary and sufficient properties. Property-based categorization also works well when properties are conceptually distinct and the value of a property is easy to perceive and examine, as they are with man-made physical resources like shirts.

propositional synonyms

Propositional synonyms are not identical in meaning, they are equivalent enough in most contexts in that substituting one for the other will not change the truth value of the sentence that uses them.

provenance

Provenance is the history of the ownership of a collection or the resources in it, where they have been and who has possessed them. In organizing systems like museums and archives that preserve rare or culturally important objects or documents, **provenance** describes a record of who has authenticated a resource over time.

QR

Quick Response

(*http://www.iso.org/iso/iso_cata logue/catalogue_tc/cata logue_detail.htm?csnumber=43655*)

qualified names

Qualified names are identifiers which explicitly identify the domain, or namespace, from which they are drawn, thereby reducing identifier collision.

quality

A **quality** is an attribute or property of a resource. A quality is logically ascribable by a subject.

Quality is a measure of the fitness of purpose of a resource or service. It is the difference between what was planned or expected versus what was realized or manifest; it is as an assessment of the suitability of a resource or interaction.

querying

A common interaction with an organizing system.

RDA

Resource Description and Access

(*http://www.loc.gov/aba/rda/*)

RDF

Resource Description Framework

(*http://www.w3.org/RDF/*)

RDF vocabulary

A set of RDF predicate names and URIs is known as an **RDF vocabulary**.

reachability

Reachability is the "can you get there from here" property between two resources in a directed graph.

recall

Recall measures the completeness of the result set, that is, how many of the relevant resources in a collection were retrieved.

regular expressions

Regular expressions are used in computing for matching text patterns. A regular expression is written in a formal language, which may vary among implementations. Regular expressions are supported by many text editors and search engines. Schema languages employ regular expressions to specify the format of element and attribute values. For example, a regular expression for a North American telephone number might be: `^\(?([2-9][0-9]{2})\)?[-. ]?([0-9]{3})[-. ]?([0-9]{4})$`

relationship

A **relationship** is "an association among several things, with that association having a particular significance."

RELAX-NG

REgular LAnguage for XML Next Generation

(*http://relaxng.org/*)

relevance

The concept of **relevance** is pivotal in information retrieval and machine learning interactions. Relevance is widely regarded as the fundamental concept of information retrieval, and by extension, all of information science. Despite being one of the more intuitive concepts in human communication, relevance is notoriously difficult to define and has been the subject of much debate over the past century.

reporting

A common interaction with an organizing system.

representation

A principle of good descriptions: Use descriptions that reflect the how the resources describe themselves; assume that self-descriptions are accurate.

resolution

For a digital resource, its identifier serves as the input to the system or function that determines its location so it can be retrieved, a process called **resolving** the identifier or **resolution**.

resource

Resource has an ordinary sense of "anything of value that can support goal-oriented activity." This definition means that a resource can be a physical thing, a non-physical thing, information about physical things, information about non-physical things, or anything you want to organize. Other words that aim for this broad scope are **entity**, **object**, **item**, and **instance**. **Document** is often used for an information resource in either digital or physical format; **artifact** refers to resources created by people, and **asset** for resources with economic value.

Resource has specialized meaning in Internet architecture. It is conventional to describe web pages, images, videos, product catalogs, and so on as resources and the protocol for accessing them, *Hypertext Transfer Protocol (HTTP)*, uses the *Uniform Resource Identifier (URI)*.

Resource Description Framework (RDF)

The Resource Description Framework (RDF) *metamodel* is a directed graph, so it identifies one node (the one from which the edge is pointing) as the subject of the triple, and the other node (the one to which the edge is pointing) as its object. The edge is referred to as the predicate of the triple.

REST

Representational State Transfer

RFID

Radio-frequency Identification

See US Patent 4,384,288

rich descriptions

Rich descriptions are created by trained and disciplined professionals, often in institutional contexts.

See §4.3.6, "Creating Resource Descriptions" (page 168)

root word
> The form of a word after all affixes are removed.

scalability
> Facet values must accommodate potential additions to the set of instances. Including an "Other" value is an easy way to ensure that a facet is flexible and hospitable to new instances, but it not desirable if all new instances will be assigned that value.

scale
> The number of resources and interactions that the collection entails.

schema
> A *schema* (or model, or metadata standard) specifies the set of descriptions that apply to an entire resource type.

scientific warrant
> The principle of **scientific warrant** argues that only the categories recognized by the scientists or experts in a domain should be used in a classification system, and it is often opposed by the principle of **user** or **use warrant**, which chooses categories and descriptive terms according to their frequency of use by everyone, not just experts.

scope
> The resource **domain** and **scope** circumscribe the describable properties and the possible purposes that descriptions might serve.

secondary subject matter
> One of Panofsky's three levels of description for artistic resources. Here, we introduce a level of basic cultural understanding into a description. Someone familiar with a common interpretation of the Bible, for example, could now see *The Last Supper* as representing Jesus surrounded by his disciples.

selecting
> Determining the scope of the organizing system by specifying which resources should be included.

> The user activity of using resource descriptions to support a choice of resource from a collection, not the institutional activity of selecting resources for the collection in the first place. Search engines typically use a short "text snippet" with the query terms highlighted as resource descriptions to support selection. People often select resources with the least restrictions on uses as described in a Creative Commons license.

self-organizing systems
> **Self-organizing systems** can change their internal structure or their function in response to feedback or changed circumstances.

semantic balance
> Top-level facets should be the properties that best differentiate the resources in the classification domain. The values should be of equal semantic scope so that resources are distributed among the subcategories. Subfacets of "Cookware" like "Sauciers and Saucepans" and "Roasters and Brasiers" are semantically balanced as they are both named and grouped by cooking activity.

semantic gap
> The *semantic gap* is the difference in perspective in naming and description when resources are described by automated processes rather than by people.

semantic perspective
> The **semantic perspective** characterizes the meaning of the association between resources.

semantic web

The vision of a *Semantic Web* world builds upon the web world, but adds some further prescriptions and constraints for how to structure descriptions. The Semantic Web world unifies the concept of a resource as it has been developed in this book, with the web notion of a resource as anything with a URI. On the Semantic Web, anything being described must have a URI. Furthermore, the descriptions must be structured as graphs, adhering to the RDF metamodel and relating resources to one another via their URIs. Advocates of Linked Data further prescribe that those descriptions must be made available as representations transferred over HTTP.

SEO

Search Engine Optimization

set

The simplest way to structure a description is to give it parts and treat them as a *set*.

SGML

Standard Generalized Markup Language

(*http://www.w3.org/TR/html4/ intro/sgmltut.html*)

Shepardizing

The analysis of legal citations to determine whether a cited case is still good law is called **Shepardizing** because lists of cases annotated in this way were first published in the late 1800s by Frank Shepard, a salesman for a legal publishing company.

SKOS

Simple Knowledge Organization System

(*http://www.w3.org/2004/02/skos/*)

SKU

Stock Keeping Unit

similarity

Similarity is a very flexible notion whose meaning depends on the domain within which we apply it, thereby requiring specification of how the similarity measure is determined. There are four major psychological approaches that propose different functions for frameworks: feature- or property-based, geometry-based, alignment-based, and transformational.

simple description

Automated processes create **simple description**s by extracting data from the resource itself.

smart things

See active resources.

social classification

Using any property of a resource to create a description is an uncontrolled and often unprincipled principle for creating categories is called **social classification** or **tagging**.

SNOMED-CT

Systematized Nomenclature of Medicine—Clinical Terms

(*http://www.ihtsdo.org/snomed-ct/*)

SOA

Service Oriented Architecture

space facet

Where the thing occurs. One of Ranganathan's universal facets in colon classification.

spectrum facets

Assume a range of numerical values with a defined minimum and maximum. Price and date are common spectrum facets. The ranges are often modeled as mutually exclusive regions (potential price facet values might include "$0 - $49," "$50 - $99," and "$100 - $149").

SQL
  Structured Query Language

  ISO/IEC 9075:2011 "Information technology – Database languages – SQL"

standardization
  A principle of good description: Standardize descriptions to the extent practical, but also use aliasing to allow for commonly used terms.

statistical pattern recognition
  In unsupervised learning, the program gets the samples but has to come up with the categories on its own by discovering the underlying correlations between the items; that is why unsupervised learning is sometimes called **statistical pattern recognition**.

stemming
  These processing steps normalize inflectional and derivational variations in terms, e.g., by removing the "-ed" from verbs in the past tense. This homogenization can be done by following rules (stemming) or by using dictionaries (lemmatization). Rule-based stemming algorithms are easy to implement, but can result in wrongly normalized word groups, for example when "university" and "universe" are both stemmed to "univers."

stopword elimination
  Stopwords are those words in a language that occur very frequently and are not very semantically expressive. Stopwords are usually articles, pronouns, prepositions or conjunctions. Since they occur in every text, they can be removed because they cannot distinguish them. Of course, in some cases, removing stopwords might remove semantically important phrases (e.g., "To be or not to be").

storage
  Storage is a maintenance activity.

See also preservation, curation

structural perspective
  The **structural perspective** analyzes the patterns of association, arrangement, proximity, or connection between resources without primary concern for their meaning or the origin of these relationships.

structured descriptions
  See §4.3.6, "Creating Resource Descriptions" (page 168)

stuff-object inclusion
  Stuff-Object relationships are most often expressed using "is-partly" or "is-made-of" and are distinguishable from component-object ones because the stuff cannot be separated from the object without altering its identity. The stuff is not a separate ingredient that is used to make the object; it is a constituent of it once it is made.

See also inclusion

styles and periods facet
  Artistic and architectural eras and stylistic groupings, such as "Renaissance" and "Dada."

subject
  In the RDF metamodel, a pair of nodes and its edge is called a *triple*, because it consists of three parts (two nodes and one edge). The RDF metamodel is a directed graph, so it identifies one node (the one from which the edge is pointing) as the **subject** of the triple, and the other node (the one to which the edge is pointing) as its **object**. The edge is referred to as the **predicate** or (as we have been saying) *property* of the triple.

sufficiency and necessity
  Descriptions should have enough information to serve their purposes and not contain information that is not necessary for some purpose; this

might imply excluding some aspects of self-descriptions that are insignificant.

supervised learning

In **supervised learning**, a machine learning program is trained by giving it sample items or documents that are labeled by category, and the program learns to assign new items to the correct categories.

surrogate resource

See description resources.

SUV

Sport Utility Vehicle

SVM

Support Vector Machine

symmetric relationships

Symmetric relationships are bidirectional; they express the same relationship from the subject to object as they do from the object to the subject. For example, "is-married-to."

synonym

When something has more than one name, each of the multiple names is a **synonym** or **alias**.

synonymy

Synonymy is the relationship between words that express the same semantic concept.

synset

An unordered set of synonyms is often called a **synset**. Synsets are interconnected by both semantic relationships and lexical ones, enabling navigation in either space.

syntax

The *syntax* and *grammar* of a language consists of the rules that determine which combinations of its words are allowed and are thus grammatical or *well-formed.* Natural languages differ immensely in how they arrange nouns, verbs, adjectives, and other parts of speech to create sentences.

tag cloud

Folksonomies are often displayed in the form of a **tag cloud**, where the frequency with which the tag is used throughout the site determines the size of the text in the tag cloud. The tag cloud emerges through the bottom-up aggregation of user tags and is a statistical construct, rather than a semantic one.

tagging

Using any property of a resource to create a description is an uncontrolled and often unprincipled principle for creating categories is called **social classification** or **tagging**.

tagsonomy

When users or communities establish sets of principles to govern their tagging practices, tagging is even more like classification. Such a tagging system can be called a **tagsonomy**, a neologism we have invented to describe more systematic tagging.

taskonomy

A task or activity-based classification system is called a **taskonomy**.

taxonomic classification

When multiple resource properties are considered in a fixed sequence, each property creates another level in the system of categories and the classification scheme is **hierarchical** or **taxonomic**.

taxonomic facets

Taxonomic facets, also known as hierarchical facets are based on logical containment.

taxonomy

A **taxonomy** is a hierarchy that is created by a set of interconnected class inclusion relationships.

See also inclusion

TCP/IP

Transmission Control Protocol/Internet Protocol

(*https://tools.ietf.org/html/rfc1180*)

TEI

Text Encoding Initiative

(*http://www.tei-c.org/index.xml*)

temporal inclusion

Temporal inclusion is a type of inclusion relationship between a temporal duration and what it surrounds or contains. It is most often expressed using "is-in" as the relationship. However, the entity that is contained or surrounded is not a part of the including one, so this is not a part-whole relationship.

See also inclusion

term frequency

A vector space ranking utilizes an intrinsic resource property, the number of individual terms in a resource, called the **term frequency**. For each term, term frequency measures how many times the term appears in a resource.

theory-based category

Another principle for creating categories is organizing things in ways that fit a theory or story that makes a particular categorization sensible. A **theory-based category** can win out even if "family resemblance" or "similarity" with respect to visible properties would lead to a different category assignment.

thesaurus

A **thesaurus** is a reference work that organizes words according to their semantic and lexical relationships. Thesauri are often used by professionals when they describe resources.

time facet

When the thing occurs. One of Ranganathan's universal facets in colon classification.

tokenization

Segments the stream of characters (in an encoding scheme, a space is also a character) into textual components, usually words. In English, a simple rule-based system can separate words using spaces. However, punctuation makes things more complicated. For example, periods at the end of sentences should be removed, but periods in numbers should not. Other languages introduce other problems for tokenization; in Chinese, a space does not mark the divisions between individual concepts.

topological inclusion

Topological inclusion is a type of inclusion relationship between a container and what it surrounds or contains. It is most often expressed using "is-in" as the relationship. However, the entity that is contained or surrounded is not a part of the including one, so this is not a part-whole relationship.

See also inclusion

training set

A **training set** for supervised learning is taken from the labeled instances. The remaining instances are used for validation.

transclusion

The inclusion, by hypertext reference, of a resource or part of a resource into another resource is called *transclusion*. Transclusion is normally performed automatically, without user intervention. The inclusion of images in web documents is an example of transclusion. Transclusion is a frequently used technique in business and legal document processing, where re-use of consistent and up-to-date content is essential to achieve efficiency and consistency.

transformation

Transformation is a very broad concept but in the context of organizing systems it typically means a change in a resource representation or description. The transformation can involve the selection, restructuring, or rearrangement of resources or parts of them.

transitivity

Transitivity is a property of some semantic relationships. When a relationship is transitive, if X and Y have a relationship, and Y and Z have the same relationship, then X also has the relationship with Z. Any relationship based on ordering is transitive, which includes numerical, alphabetic, and chronological ones as well as those that imply qualitative or quantitative measurement.

tree

Trees consist of nodes joined by edges, recursively nested. When a single, root dictionary is connected to child nodes that are themselves dictionaries, we say that the dictionaries are nested into a kind of **tree** structure.

A tree is a constrained graph. Trees are directed graphs because the "parent of" relationship between nodes is asymmetric: the edges are arrows that point in a certain direction. Trees are acyclic graphs, because if you follow the directed edges from one node to another, you can never encounter the same node twice. Finally, trees have the constraint that every node (except

the root) must have exactly one parent.

triple

In the RDF metamodel, a pair of nodes and its edge is called a **triple**, because it consists of three parts (two nodes and one edge). The RDF metamodel is a directed graph, so it identifies one node (the one from which the edge is pointing) as the **subject** of the triple, and the other node (the one to which the edge is pointing) as its **object**. The edge is referred to as the **predicate** or (as we have been saying) *property* of the triple.

TXL

Turing eXtender Language

(*http://www.txl.ca/*)

typicality

Typicality or **centrality** considers some members of the category better examples than others, even if they share most properties.

UBL

Universal Business Language

(*https://www.oasis-open.org/committees/tc_home.php?wg_abbrev=ubl*)

UDC

Universal Decimal Classification

(*http://www.udcc.org/*)

UK

United Kingdom

(*https://www.gov.uk/*)

UN

United Nations

(*http://www.un.org/en/*)

uniqueness principle

The **uniqueness principle** means the categories in a classification scheme are mutually exclusive. Thus, when a logical concept is assigned to a particular category, it cannot simultaneously be assigned to another category.

UNSPC

United Nations Standard Products and Services Code

(*http://www.unspsc.org/*)

unsupervised learning

In unsupervised learning, the program gets the samples but has to come up with the categories on its own by discovering the underlying correlations between the items; that is why unsupervised learning is sometimes called **statistical pattern recognition**.

See also: machine learning and supervised learning

URI

Uniform Resource Identifier

(*http://www.w3.org/Addressing/*)

URL

Uniform Resource Locator

(*http://www.w3.org/TR/url/*)

URN

Uniform Resource Name

(*http://www.w3.org/TR/uri-clarification/*)

user convenience

Choose description terms with the user in mind; these are likely to be terms in common usage among the target audience.

user warrant

The principle of **scientific warrant** argues that only the categories recognized by the scientists or experts in a domain should be used in a classification system, and it is often opposed by the principle of **user** or **use warrant**, which chooses categories and descriptive terms according to their frequency of use by everyone, not just experts.

UUID

Universally Unique Identifier

(*http://www.ietf.org/rfc/rfc4122.txt*)

validation

Validation is the process of verifying that a document or data structure conforms with its schema or schemas. Markup validation confirms the structure of the document. Type validation confirms that the content of leaf nodes conforms with the specification of data types. Content validation confirms that the values of the leaf nodes are appropriate. Link validation confirms the integrity of the links between nodes and between documents. Cross validation is the method commonly used for model selection. Business rule validation confirms compliance with business rules.

value

We distinguish between the type of the *attribute* and the *value* that it has. For example, the color of any object is an *attribute* of the object, and the value of that attribute might be "green."

VIAF

Virtual International Authority File

(*http://viaf.org/*)

viewing

Viewing is a central interaction in museums and zoos.

See also collection development

VIN

Vehicle Identification Number (ISO 3779:2009)

visiting

Visiting is a central interaction in museums and zoos.

See also collection development

visualization
A common interaction with an organizing system.

vocabulary problem
Every natural language offers more than one way to express any thought, and in particular there are usually many words that can be used to refer to the same thing or concept. The words people choose to name or describe things are embodied in their experiences and context, so people will often disagree in the words they use. Moreover, people are often a bit surprised when it happens, because what seems like the natural or obvious name to one person isn't natural or obvious to another.

VPN
Virtual Private Network

W3C
World Wide Web Consortium

(*http://www.w3.org/*)

warrant principle
The **warrant** principle concerns the justification for the choice of categories and the names given to them.

See also: literary warrant, scientific warrant, user warrant and object warrant

WHO
World Health Organization

(*http://www.who.int/en/*)

work
An abstract idea of an author's intellectual or artistic creation.

The distinctions put forth by Lubetzky, Svenonius and other library science theorists have evolved today into a four-step abstraction hierarchy (illustrated in Figure 3.5, "The Abstraction

Hierarchy for Identifying Resources.") between the abstract **work**, an **expression** in multiple formats or genres, a particular **manifestation** in one of those formats or genres, and a specific physical **item**.

writing system
A **writing system** employs one or more notations, and adds a set of rules for using them. Most writing systems assume knowledge of a particular human language. These writing systems are known as *glottic* writing systems. But there are many writing systems, such as mathematical and musical ones, that are not tied to human languages in this way. Many of the writing systems used for describing resources belong to this latter group, meaning that (at least in principle) they can be used with equal facility by speakers of any language.

Some writing systems, such as XML and JSON, are closely identified with specific metamodels.

WSDL
Web Services Description Language

(*http://www.w3.org/TR/wsdl*)

XCBF
XML Common Biometric Format

(*https://www.oasis-open.org/committees/tc_home.php?wg_abbrev=xcbf*)

XInclude
XML Inclusions

(*http://www.w3.org/TR/xinclude/*)

XML
Extensible Markup Language

(*http://www.w3.org/XML/*)

XML Information Set
The **XML Infoset** is a tree structure, where each node of the tree is defined

to be an *information item* of a particular type. Each information item has a set of type-specific properties associated with it. At the root of the tree is a document item, which has exactly one element item as its child. An element item has a set of attribute items, and a list of child nodes. These child nodes may include other element items, or they may be character items. (See §8.2.1, "Kinds of Structures" below for more on characters.) Attribute items may contain character items, or they may contain typed data, such as name tokens, identifiers and references. Element identifiers and references (ID/IDREF) may be used to connect nodes, transforming a tree into a graph. (See the Sidebar, "Inclusions and References").

XSD

XML Schema Definition Language

(*http://www.w3.org/XML/Schema.html*)

XSLT

Extensible Stylesheet Language Transformations

(*http://www.w3.org/TR/xslt*)

ZOO

A zoo is an organizing system for living animals that arranges them according to principles of biological taxonomy or common habitat.

Index

dictionary, 323, 488
graph, 328, 492
    reachability, 504
list, 323, 498
logical hierarchy, 60, 498
map, 498
node, 500
object, 501
self-organizing system, 10, 506
set, 507
sets, 322
tree, 511
dataset, 10
datetime negotiation, 89
DBpedia, 354
DC, 346, 398, 487
    creator, 182
DCMI, 182, 346, 487
DDC, 278, 279, 280, 290, 407, 487
decision support, 88
decision tree, 260, 271, 315, 487
Declaration of Independence, 88
decoding, 374
default attribute values, 362
definition
    extensional, 490
definition of marriage, 227
degree, 217, 487
    architectural perspective, 217
    arity, 481
    of organizing systems, 28
delivery service, 64
Delphi, 86
Deoxyribonucleic Acid (see DNA)
derivational morphology, 207,
    208, 487
derivative relationships, 223
    Smiraglia, 223
    Tillett, 223
DeRose, Steve, 358
describing
    images, 175
    museum and artistic resour-
        ces, 173
    music, 176
    non-text resources, 173
    relationships, 190
    resource context, 177
    resource description, 140

video, 177
description
    bibliographic, 142
    inclusive term, 141
    kinship relationship, 141
    vocabulary, 164
descriptive control, 180
descriptive metadata, 148
descriptive relationship, 223
design
    patterns, 84
    space, 19
design decisions, 18
designed resource access policies,
    67
designing
    description vocabulary, 164
    faceted classification system,
        302
    resource description
        form and implementation,
            167
    resource-based interactions,
        47, 48, 61
determining
    interactions, 366
        access policies, 370
        resource property layers,
            369
        user requirements, 367
Dewey Decimal Classification (see
    DDC)
Dewey Dilemma, 313
Dewey, Melvil, 290
DFR, 384, 488
Diagnostic and Statistical Manual
    of Mental Disorders (see DSM)
diagramming sentences, 356
dictionary, 323, 488
    defined, 323
    reverse lookup, 357
Die Ringes des Saturn, 340
digital library, 3, 12, 42, 64, 71,
    109
Digital Object Identifier (see DOI)
digital resources
    organizing, 57
    rights management, 82
    selecting, 53

Digital Rights Management (see
    DRM)
digital signatures, 126
digital things, 1
digitization, 14, 53, 488
dimensionality reduction, 184
    with vocabulary control, 167
directionality, 488
    architectural perspective, 219
disambiguating homonymy, 228
discipline, 6, 488
    information architecture, 59
    of organizing, 6
discovery, 156
DITA, 436
Divergence From Randomness
    (see DFR)
DNA, 137, 488
DNS, 58, 84, 122, 185, 488
DocBook, 212, 362, 436
Doctorow, Cory, 186
document engineering, 132
document frequency (df), 383, 488
document processing, 348
document semantics, 359
Document Type Definition (see
    DTD)
document type model, 90
Document Type Spectrum, 101,
    114, 211, 260
DOI, 124, 138, 488
domain, 99, 100, 488
    resource, 100
Domain Name System (see DNS)
domain ontologies, 132
Dougherty, Dale, 35
driving in Samoa, 421
DRM, 41, 160, 489
DSM, 279, 308, 489
DTD, 143, 349, 489
Dublin Core (see DC)
Dublin Core Metadata Initiative
    (see DCMI)
Duguid, Paul, 72
Dumais, Susan, v, 99, 383

properties
    conceptual versus physical,
        180
    contextual, 164, 486
    cultural, 486
    extrinsic dynamic, 163
    extrinsic static, 163
    identifying
        for resource description,
            160
    intrinsic dynamic static, 163
    intrinsic static, 161
    of semantic relationships, 199
property, 82, 503
    attribute, 481
    essence, 163
    gradience, 252
    inherited, 247
    intension, 245, 495
    persistence, 163
    value, 512
property-based interactions
    implementing, 378
propositional synonyms, 504
provenance, 126, 504
providing access, 86
purpose
    category, 258
    classification, 282
    resource description, 155

Q

Q
    SCIENCE
        in LCC, 292
QR, 102, 109, 158, 504
qualified names, 504
quality, 504
    criteria, 171
quality movement, 186
querying, 504
Quick Response (see QR)

R

R
    MEDICINE
        in LCC, 292
Radio-frequency Identification
    (see RFID)

Ranganathan, S. R., v, 298
ranking
    and relevance, 76
    descriptions, 39
    false descriptions, 172
    manipulating, 92
    quality of, 156
    search results, 32
    SEO, 282
rating manipulation, 91
RDA, 182, 223, 224, 337, 504
RDF, 144, 222, 224, 505
    metamodel, 329
        defined, 330
    obstacles to adoption, 181
    property, 503
    subject, 508
    triple, 333, 511
    vocabulary, 504
reachability, 232, 504
real estate ads, 182
recall, 391, 504
    precision tradeoff, 257
recall and precision
    tradeoffs
        interactions, 391
regular expressions, 504
REgular LAnguage for XML Next
    Generation (see RELAX-NG)
relation, 230
relationship, 505
    among word meaning, 204
    asymmetric, 481
    attribution, 481
    cardinality, 218, 483
    class inclusion, 194, 485
    describing, 190
    directionality, 219, 488
    edge, 511
    equivalence, 200, 489
    in organizing systems, 222
    in surnames, 180
    inclusion, 193, 494
    introduction, 189
    inverse, 200, 496
    kinship, 190
    one-way, 501
    ontology, 502
    possession, 194, 503

semantic, 192
    semantic perspective, 506
    symmetric, 509
    taxonomy, 509
    to other organizing systems,
        407
    traditional marriage, 193
    transitive, 200
    transitivity, 511
relationships
    among organizing systems, 51
RELAX-NG, 349, 505
relevance
    of interactions, 390
reporting, 505
representation, 164
Representational State Transfer
    (see REST)
requirements
    conflicting, 413
    for implementation syntax, 221
    intentional arrangement, 411
    traceability, 408, 414
research libraries, 435
resolution, 505
resolvability of URIs, 362
resolving names, 505
resource, 8, 505
    aboutness, 55, 479
    access policies, 370
    access vs control, 416
    active, 105
    ad hoc category, 480
    affordance, 61, 480
    agency, 105
    appraisal, 155
    authentication, 155
    authenticity, 126
    bibliography, 482
    born digital, 483
    capability and compatibility,
        155
    collection, 10, 485
    collection development, 48,
        485
    creating, 50
    curation, 74
    describing
        for interaction, 372

About the Authors

Robert J. Glushko is an Adjunct Full Professor in the School of Information at the University of California, Berkeley. After receiving his PhD in Cognitive Psychology at the University of California, San Diego in 1979, he spent about ten years working in corporate R&D, mostly at Bell Laboratories. After earning an MS in Software Enginering at the Wang Institute, he then spent about ten years as a Silicon Valley entrepreneur as the founder or co-founder of four companies in the areas of electronic publishing and e-business. He now has worked more than ten years as a professor. He is the author (with Tim McGrath) of *Document Engineering: Analyzing and Designing Documents for Business Informatics and Web Services*, published by The MIT Press in 2005. (*http://people.ischool.berkeley.edu/~glushko/*)

Jess Hemerly is a Senior Public Policy and Government Relations Analyst at Google. Jess earned her Master's in Information Management and Systems from UC Berkeley's School of Information in 2011, and received the James R. Chen Award for Outstanding Master's Project in Information Research. As a freelance blogger and journalist, Jess's writing has appeared in MAKE, The Onion, and AlterNet and on Boing Boing. In 2009, Jess was nominated as co-founder for a Webby Award in the "Weird" category for "Sad Guys on Trading Floors," blog that satirized the financial crisis.

Murray Maloney is a technical writer by trade, an electronic technician by training, a markup expert by circumstance and an inventor by necessity. He attended Santa Barbara City College and Seneca College in Toronto. He has over thirty years of experience in technical communication and publishing. He has written, edited and published on topics such as computer operating systems, typesetting and print publishing, markup and schema languages, hypertext and electronic commerce. (*http://www.linkedin.com/in/murraymaloney*)

Kimra McPherson is a user experience researcher in the San Francisco Bay Area. She previously worked as a newspaper and online journalist and holds a Bachelor's of Science in Journalism from Northwestern University in Evanston, Ill. She received her Master's of Information Management and Systems from the School of Information at the University of California, Berkeley in 2011. (*http://www.aboutkimra.com*)

Vivien Petras is a professor at the Berlin School of Library and Information Science at Humboldt-Universität zu Berlin, Germany. She received her PhD in Information Management & Systems at the University of California, Berkeley in 2006 and worked in the information systems R&D department of the GESIS Leibniz Institute for Social Sciences, Cologne, Germany before joining the faculty in Berlin. (*http://www.ibi.hu-berlin.de/institut/personen/petras*)

Ryan Shaw is an Assistant Professor in the School of Information and Library Science at the University of North Carolina at Chapel Hill, where he teaches courses on information organization, Web architecture, and digital humanities. In his research he studies how people use information systems to conceptualize and model their worlds and pasts. Before getting his Ph.D. from the School of Information at the University of California, Berkeley, he worked as a web software engineer in Tokyo, Japan for several years. (*http://aeshin.org/*)

Erik Wilde is an Architect at EMC's Information Intelligence Group in Pleasanton, California. After receiving his PhD in Computer Science from ETH Zürich, he worked as researcher at ETH Zürich, and then worked for five years as Associate Professor at the School of Information at the University of California, Berkeley. He is the author, co-author, or co-editor of five books on web technologies and architectures. In 2011, he started working for EMC, where his focus is on service-orientation, web technologies and architecture, and standardization. (*http://dret.net/netdret/*)

Rachelle Annechino is an Associate Research Scientist at the Pacific Institute for Research and Evaluation, where she studies substance use in different cultural contexts, and develops systems for collecting research data. She writes about culture and technology for Ethnography Matters (*http://ethnography matters.net*), a group blog that she co-founded.

J.J.M. Ekaterin is a project/program manager with over ten years of experience in consulting and implementing software solutions for the financial services industry. With a BS in computer science, MBA in finance, and Master in Information Management, Ekaterin has consistently led multi-disciplinary teams to tackle complex enterprise issues.

Ryan Greenberg is a senior software engineer at Twitter in San Francisco. He received his B.A. in philosophy from the University of Notre Dame and spent two years working as a volunteer in Santiago, Chile. In 2010, he earned a masters degree at UC Berkeley's School of Information.

Michael Manoochehri is a Developer Programs Engineer at Google, focusing on making large scale data analysis more accessible and affordable. He has many years of experience working for research and non-profit organizations, has written for tech blog ProgrammableWeb.com, and has a Masters degree from UC Berkeley's School of Information. (*http://gplus.to/manoochehri*)

Sean Marimpietri is a master's graduate of the School of Information at the University of California, Berkeley. After receiving his bachelor's degree in linguistics and anthropology from the University of North Carolina at Chapel Hill, he worked in the translation industry in quality assurance. From 2004 to 2010 he worked with a research group at the National Library of Medicine as a linguistic analyst.

Matthew Mayernik is a Research Data Services Specialist in the library of the National Center for Atmospheric Research (NCAR)/University Corporation for Atmospheric Research (UCAR). He has a MLIS and Ph.D. from the UCLA Department of Information Studies. His work within the NCAR/UCAR library focuses on developing research data services, and includes research projects related to data publication and citation, metadata practices and standards, data curation education, and social aspects of research data.

Karen Joy Nomorosa is a Senior Semantic Analyst for Rearden Commerce, Inc., developing ontologies and using different semantic technologies to create smarter products. Before finishing her Masters in Information Management and Systems at UC Berkeley, she worked for several years designing and implementing systems for multinational corporations as well as government organizations.

Hyunwoo Park is a doctoral student in industrial and systems engineering and a fellow of the Tennenbaum Institute at the Georgia Institute of Technology. His research interest encompasses service science, social network analysis, and platform competition. He holds a master's in information management and systems from the University of California, Berkeley.

Alberto Pepe is a postdoctoral researcher at Harvard University and co-founder of Authorea. At Harvard, he is the in-house information scientist at the Center for Astrophysics, a fellow of the Berkman Center for Internet & Society and an affiliate of the Institute for Quantitative Social Science. He recently obtained a Ph.D. in Information Science from the University of California, Los Angeles with a dissertation on scientific collaboration networks. Prior to starting his Ph.D., Pepe worked at CERN, in Geneva, Switzerland. Pepe holds a M.Sc. in Computer Science and a B.Sc. in Astrophysics, both from University College London, U.K. He was born and raised in the wine-making town of Manduria, in Puglia, Southern Italy. (*http://albertopepe.com/*)

Daniel D. Turner is a co-founder of the Journalist Lab for Apps and Technology and blogs at www.twoangstroms.com. After over a decade as a journalist and editor, he attended the School of Information at the University of California, Berkeley, to study user experience research and interaction design. Turner is active in the hackathon and mentoring community.

Longhao Wang is currently a law student at Georgetown University. He previously studied information systems at the University of California, Berkeley and computer science at Renmin University of China. He is interested in intellectual property and technology law.